I0816868

Applied Research and Design Publishing
Publishers of Academic Theory in the Built Environment
An Imprint of ORO Editions, Gordon Goff: Publisher
Supported by the University of Houston

USA, ASIA, EUROPE, MIDDLE EAST
www.appliedresearchanddesign.com
info@appliedresearchanddesign.com

ISBN: 978-1-940743-00-4

Authors: Ila Berman and Andrew Kudless

Graphic Design: Bob Aufuldish, Aufuldish & Warinner
Publication Assistants: Clayton Williams, Anesta Kothari, Juan Barron

Color Separations and Printing: ORO Editions Inc.
Printed in China.

Text printed using offset sheet-fed printing process in 4 color on 157gsm premium matte art paper.

AR+D Publishing has made every effort to minimize the overall carbon footprint of this project. As part of this goal, AR+D, in association with Global ReLeaf, have arranged to plant two trees for each and every tree used in the manufacturing of the paper produced for this book. Global ReLeaf is an international campaign run by American Forests, the nation's oldest nonprofit conservation organization. Global ReLeaf is American Forests' education and action program that helps individuals, organizations, agencies, and corporations improve the local and global environment by planting and caring for trees.

North American Distribution:
Actar Distribution
151 Grand Street, 5th Fl.
New York, New York 10013 USA

International Distribution:
www.appliedresearchanddesign.com/distribution

FLUX
ILA BERMAN & ANDREW KUDLESS
ARCHITECTURE IN A PARAMETRIC LANDSCAPE
APPLIED RESEARCH +DESIGN PUBLISHING

Contents

Computational technologies have evolved from being representational tools invested in the depiction of pre-existing models of architectural space to become performative machines that have transformed the ways in which we both conceive and configure space and material.

With dynamic forms of intelligence and generative capacities that not only emulate, but also instigate genetic evolutionary processes, these toolsets have radically altered the ways in which we integrate disparate types of information into the design process, while significantly altering the methodological strategies that we use to encode and configure an already intricate matter.

In Flux: From Encoded Matter to Computational Craft

Since the mid-1990s computational technologies have catalyzed one of the most creative and prolific periods in architecture since the early twentieth century. During what has been a relatively short history, these have evolved from being representational tools invested in the depiction of pre-existing models of architectural space to become performative machines that have transformed the ways in which we both conceive and configure space and material. These tools for design, simulation, and fabrication, which have proliferated in the background as well as in parallel to their experimental application within architecture, are understood as entities, with their own logics and hidden forms of agency, that are as potent as they are diverse and, whose computational logics are very different from our own ways of processing information. Akin to powerful, and sometimes "out of control" prostheses that amplify and transform the animating capacity of their users (which, as the intelligence of these machines increases, we might in the future consider as true collaborators), these have allowed for unanticipated possibilities that have dramatically changed the ways we design, model, and build. With dynamic forms of intelligence and generative capacities that not only emulate, but also instigate genetic evolutionary processes, these toolsets have radically altered the ways in which we integrate disparate types of information into the design process, while significantly altering the methodological strategies that we use to encode and configure an already intricate matter.

Contemporary models of architectural space are necessarily linked, albeit in a nonlinear and complex way, to the formal, spatial, and numerical logics of the tools used to produce them. These models are inevitable byproducts of the ever-expanding capacities of computation and its impact on a wide range of traditional and contemporary tools for making as these intersect with new materials, processes, and conceptual trajectories that long ago dismantled the social, functional, and technological truths of modern architecture. No longer simply importing and (mis)using tools and theoretical models borrowed from other disciplines, architects have engendered and developed their own diverse suite of sophisticated concepts, tools, techniques, and ever-evolving processes. These are complex, layered, and hybridized methodologies that operate across vastly disparate scales and that engage a wide range of objects and materials from the highly refined and synthetic to the salvaged, indigenous, terrestrial, and biotic.

After the nascent digital explosion that occurred just before the turn of the millennium, and where the majority of what was produced remained embedded in media, that is, on the computer screen or in graphic form, the adoption and integration of computational tools and methods into material and fabrication systems—referred to as a form of "digital tectonics"—permeated both the discipline and the profession. This first became apparent not only in smaller experimental practices such as Matsys, Gramazio & Kohler, Aranda/Lasch, Höweler + Yoon, MOS, Emerging Objects, and theverymany, but was also evident in the growth of architectural research labs at academic institutions and their replication in leading design firms around the world. Academic research groups such as those led by Gramazio Kohler Research (DFAB) and the Block Research Group (BRG) at the ETH in Zurich, the ICD/ITKE Group led by Achim Menges and Jan Knippers at the University of Stuttgart, the Self-Assembly Group led by Skylar Tibbits, and the Mediated Matter Group led by Neri Oxman, more recent outgrowth's of MIT's Media Lab in Cambridge co-founded by Nicholas Negroponte and the Center for Information Technology (CITA) at the Royal Danish Academy of Arts in Copenhagen, for example, exponentially extended the terrain of computational practices primarily through advanced architectural research and smaller-scale architectural prototypes and projects. This work was promoted by a burgeoning group of affiliated organizations such as ACADIA, eCAADe, and Smart Geometry that held annual conferences to advance the exchange of new knowledge in this area and was also complemented by the efforts of large international architecture and engineering firms that integrated internal research groups, such as the Specialist Modeling Group at Foster and Partners and the Advanced Geometry Unit at Arup, into the composition of their practices. These embedded research units along with the firms that supported them were responsible for implementing and realizing, at a much increased scale, some of the world's most geometrically complex and architecturally sophisticated projects using computational techniques as evidenced in the Swiss Re Tower in London by Foster and Partners, the

Beijing Olympic Stadium by Herzog & de Meuron and Arup, and the Taichung Metropolitan Opera House by Toyo Ito and Associates among many others. These works, tied to the global expansion of both computational and architectural practices, varied widely in scope and program, and were located in many distinct cities and regions around the world.

This widespread uptake of computational tools, however, did not necessarily yield a singular architectural or urban typology. Despite statements to the contrary,[1] and the sharing of what we might refer to as genetic traits derived from the use of common tools and methods, there never emerged such a thing as a singular parametric, algorithmic, or computational style. Such an outcome would seem to be entirely antithetical to ways in which information technologies have evolved over the last quarter century. Rather, as is reflected in the relatively small sampling of seminal projects included in this volume (intended to exemplify a period of intensive transformation within the discipline rather than be a comprehensive overview of work), the diversity of heterogeneous products emerging at the intersection of computation and design is both a reflection of the rejection of the drive toward universality indicative of modernism and its desires to promote an international style, as well as a reflection of the complexity of the advancing tools, logics, and systems whose evolution continuously breeds new provisional types. Thus, even against the backdrop of the initial proliferation of continuous splines, surfaces, and volumes that characterized the architectural works of early digital adopters such as Greg Lynn who elaborated this work in his book *Animate Form* (that was radical in its inclusion of a CD at the back), the rapid and continuous evolution of the technologies themselves and the wide range of materials that they encountered, generated endless possibilities for experimentation and, over time, an unlimited diversity of architectural species. Experimentation, which is at the root of much of the work in this book, is also a force contributing to this diversity. To borrow a term from Deleuze, true to the "nomadology" that characterizes experimental practices,[2] relentless invention (happening simultaneously in both the realms of technology and architecture) demands that the works resulting from such practices never reify into a repeatable and singular set of attributes despite how these might be disseminated and later implemented within architectural practice.

This variability of computationally designed architectural works is not only intrinsic to the potential of associative and algorithmic software to generate innumerable outputs from an infinite range of parameters and variable inputs (made explicit in the analytical segments of this book), but also to the extrinsic environmental complexity resulting from the evolution of these technologies and their relationship to experimental architectural models. Such variability is also consistent with the displacement of modernism's ideology of homogeneity and sameness with post-modernism's call for heterogeneity and diversity—a hallmark of the last half-century. This heterogeneity was evident in all strands of post-modern theory, whether expressed as the complexity of the text and its infinitely bifurcating and deferred referents within the context of post-structural approaches to meaning, or as the advancement of the multiple over the one that characterized the works of material philosophers such as Gilles Deleuze. If the capacity for variation—held under the banner of mass-customization—was one of the key traits of the digital revolution, in opposition to the repetitive sameness and standardization of industrial production, then it is precisely this variation that is also a key characteristic of the flurry of creative products that have emerged within architecture spawned by its link t o information-based technologies. Mario Carpo has stated that this variability and its ties to the idea of customization and the bespoke is also a deep-rooted ambition of architects and designers in general.[3] We would certainly agree in the sense that uniqueness is an essential characteristic of creativity and innovation (always intent on finding and expressing a new transformative "line of flight' in relation to a pre-existing reality),[4] to authorship in the sense that it reflects the particularity of individuals, and to users whose diversity results from the complexity of a networked global culture. Further, we might also argue that the act of making is inherently tied to matter and material culture whose emergence is always specific to a history and an environmental context.

This project therefore has its own specific material history and context. It began many years ago at California College of the Arts (CCA) with an installation and exhibition that we launched in concert with the 2009 Smart Geometries Conference in San Francisco. The initial Flux exhibition ran down the central "nave" space of CCA. The installation armature, which was to be an exemplification and embodiment of the ideas expressed in the exhibition and therefore a part of its content, was supported by an undulating and segmented white, twisted, and tubular serial structure defined by a changing hexagonal cross-section that had three elongated sides. The changing dimensions of the hexagonal section were parametrically controlled through a set of relationships defined by its formal, performative, and fabrication constraints so that the piece incrementally rotated as its dimensions increased or decreased in length. The four tubes of the installation armature were each constituted by a series of approximately 30 vertical ribs that held planar segments canted for viewing that supported the exhibition content. This content was curated through eight thematic categories each of which explored a set of formal and spatial logics that have been transformed through advanced computational practices.

Although more than a decade has passed and the works included in this book extend far beyond those that were part of this early inaugural exhibition, the eight thematic categories—Stacked Aggregates, Modular Assemblages, Pixelated Fields, Cellular Clusters, Serial Iterations, Woven Meshes, Emergent Surfaces, and Multi-Agent Networks—have been retained as a way of tracing the evolution of this taxonomy over time. Each of the eight sections of this book explores a dominant logic or morphological trait evident in the development of digitally influenced or computationally generated works and investigates its evolution through a range of projects. This evolution has seen a dramatic shift from an emphasis on form- to matter-based systems, and from highly synthetic to biotic, primitive, and salvaged materials, indicating a convergent interest in biomimetic and ecological systems as the emergence of more complex tools for making enabled computation to be more directly applied to the matrix of real material systems. We also argue that although digital tools can certainly be used to make any type of object or architecture (and that, as these tools become pervasive, their application becomes less evident especially within the context of the computerization of the profession), there are specific logics that have been drawn from the expanded capabilities of computation that have generated new, and often, inherently complex material formations that would not have been possible to generate otherwise.

We begin in the first section with Stacked Aggregates because of its reference to archaic forms of building where the making of walls and enclosures happens through a process of additively accumulating matter into larger stereometric assemblies. With the introduction of computation, three fundamental changes occurred in our understanding and making of these aggregated assemblies. First, was the re-conception of the wall as a digital surface, an array of incremental units that, like the pixelated field of a computer screen, could now be coordinated and described by numeric information. The second change occurred through the encoding of the wall, which began to operate, no matter what the formal or material attributes of the base elements that constituted it, as an abstract medium that could be reconfigured by procedural, programmatic, and environmental forces. This process enabled any form of data to be transcoded in the making of the wall's surface, whether this was the information that transformed the wall from a solid boundary into a permeable screen to register the emergence of an outdoor courtyard in Casa La Roca, that pictorially revealed a basket filled with grapes to signify the process and products of the Gantenbein Winery, or that reinterpreted the parameters of a building code meant to enable the making of classical masonry ornamentation now rethought as the corbelled-brick, triangulated pattern of the façade of 290 Mulberry Street. In each of these projects homogeneous ready-made elements, the residue of industrial production, were converted into continuously variable, heterogeneous surfaces and volumes that depended on the changing value of variables, the degrees of freedom of the aggregated units, and the quantity and complexity of information encoded in the system. Thirdly, the introduction of robotics and other computationally controlled processes for fabrication and assembly enabled the high-speed precise placement and bonding of elements within this aggregative system without any additional time, cost, or energy due to the system's complexity. This re-emergence of artisanal craft and the possibility of the unique artifact that had been all but eliminated within the first waves of industrialization, were enabled through direct engagement with building materials amplified by sophisticated digitally controlled tools and the high speeds and extreme forms of precision made possible by computation.

In the evolution and transformation of these stacked aggregates, the shift from frame to fill, which marks a departure from cartesian gridded logics and is emblematized in the digitized wall, finds its companion in Rock Print, a thickened mass of gravel that emulates a low-resolution 3D printed form. The analog here is no longer the digital surface but its material counterpart, the 3D printer, that distributes layered micro-increments of matter in a numerically controlled space. Within the context of computation, the differentiation between continuous and discrete systems is not simply an issue of the displacement of continuous spatial and material logics with a discretized numeric code as in the way scanning devices replace the continuity of color with discrete, numerically codified pixels. It is also a question of resolution, that is, the high degrees of resolution made possible by computation that exceed the limits of our own perceptual apparatuses. This is what makes it impossible for us to distinguish (except at extremely low resolutions) the discretized pixels on a computer screen, the colored dots distributed by an inkjet printer, or the infinitesimal layers of a 3D print of what appears to be a continuous volume. The high resolution continuous differentiation made possible by computation thus enabled us to connect the discrete with the continuous, calling attention to the fact that, even within the context of the material world, how we perceive this difference is often a question of scale, akin to the way in which a sand dune is perceived as continuous despite its actual composition of distinct granules of sand. It is no wonder that this topic has received so much attention within the realm of architecture[5] and whose limits have been explored in projects such as the Digital Grotesque II, an extremely intricate and complex 3D printed synthetic grotto by Michael Hansmeyer and Benjamin Dillenburger that is made up of 260 million surfaces and occupies a space at a resolution of 30 billion voxels.

In Modular Assemblages, the emphasis is on part-to-whole relationships, since the module potentially always operates as a fractional or relational part of a larger system while simultaneously acting as an independent entity that can occupy a wide range of positions within a closed organizational system. Modularity has a deep history within modern architecture given that the Cartesian spatial system was intrinsically relational, based on a three-dimensional projective system. This was expressed in Le Corbusier's modular—a continuum of fractional relations—that aligned abstracted increments with the dimensions of the human body that would then be formally and spatially applied to architectural works such as his design for the Unité d'habitation in Marseille. The Berlin Free University, completed two decades later by Candilis, Josic, and Woods, however, exhibits new potentials for this modularity in its planning and the development of its façade, the latter of which highlights not only the fractional relationship of components, but also the generative logics of their distribution and attribution. This work acts a precursor to the Porter House façade by SHoP, and computational projects such as the Resolution Wall that explores these logics in an aggregated concrete block wall through scaling and resolution.

In principle, modular systems are constituted by a family of genetically related elements with a limited number of types, that produce larger "wholes," and whose bottom-up patterns of assembly or growth, as evident in the Ivy coat hook system, the Bloom Game, and Wireflies, are controlled through a set of generative rules and operations. These projects, in addition to the modular experimental works of Gilles Retsin and the AUAR group, call attention to the relationship between modularity and the discretization of what are referred to as "digital materials." George Popescu and Neil Gershenfeld from the MIT Center for Bits and Atoms make the argument that a digital material is a discrete set of related components, made from any material and of any size and shape, which can fit together in various ways.[6] Yet, it is the specific configuration of each component that determines precise limits on the ways in which two elements within the system can conjoin, establishing a limit on the methods of assembly and the aggregation of the whole, while also ensuring that these systems are entirely reversible in that they can be disassembled. They compare such structures to the ways in which atoms assemble to form a crystalline lattice, and that, depending on the scale of resolution, there is not necessarily a relationship between the forms of the micro-element and the macro-structures that they can produce when, as discussed previously, such micro-elements exist below the threshold of our perceptual capability so that they appear to create continuous structures. Their interest, however, is less in the modular relationship between parts and wholes than in the application of such modular digital materials to next-generation reversible forms of 3D printing with space-filling voxels. Although Retsin's more recent work operates at the architectural scale using very large, rather than microscopically-scaled, components, the relationship of this work to digitalization is highlighted. This is evident not only through the clear modularity of discrete parts and the generative possibilities of their larger configurations, but also through the projected potential automation of their computationally driven robotic assembly.

Pixelated Fields, already discussed in their influence over stacked aggregates, transform the ways in which we think about space by shifting our perception from the framing device and the boundaries it might produce to the populations of elements that are scattered in space and that territorialize it through their occupation, akin to the changing distribution and density of columns in the KAIT workshop by Junya Ishigama. The digitization of the field or bit-mapped surface influenced many architectural projects and has been instrumentalized and expressed in numerous ways. This was exhibited early on in the de Young Museum façade that, in its design process, used digitally filtered images from its environs in Golden Gate Park to generate its perforated skin. Certainly one of the best examples of the influence of the bit-mapped surface on architecture is the Agbar Tower that employed the digital diagram as a mediating device to conflate multiple influences from the polychromatic façades of Catalan architecture to the pixelated field of Barcelona's surrounding urbanization. The pixelated surface, which also generates a new relationship between a spatial increment and the data that defines and informs it, finds its three dimensional equivalent in voxelated space (a reference to "volume-elements") as elaborated in the two very different scales of the Why Factory's PoroCity exhibition and EZCT's Computational Chair Design project. In the former, the voxelization of space allows for its occupation to be read as a datascape of the programmatic and environmental parameters responsible for the project's development. Whereas in the latter case, the voxel stands in for a "bit" of matter needed to withstand the load of a sitting body that is progressively eroded through an automated computational process intended to find the lightest chair constituted by the smallest number of voxels. Here, the design authorship of the artifact is replaced by the design of the system—setting parameters so that a form of artificial intelligence can be used to simulate the automated evolution of a population of chairs whose low resolution expression of the voxelated field, still evident in the final object, is a continual reminder of the digitized spatial model upon which it depends.

The section entitled Cellular Clusters marks a clear departure from the insistent orthogonality of modern models, while exposing the relationship between, and subtle overlay of biological, chemical, geological, and geometric spatial models. An extension of the patterned spatial explorations of Buckminster Fuller's geodesic domes and the cellular architectural experiments of the 1960s and 70s that followed, which, like the Metabolists, looked to biotic systems and their structures and processes for architectural inspiration, more recent computationally-generated cellular architectures moved closer to these naturally evolving systems through their abandonment of regularity indicative of their predecessors. The re-emergence of cellular architectures was influenced by the introduction of digital tools such as Voronoi generators and automated processes of tessellation that divide and pattern surfaces and volumes according to the opportunistic occupation of space, as well as by the intricately patterned yet differentiated micro-morphology of cells, bubbles, and crystalline structures found in natural systems that simultaneously respond to internal coding for their patterned structuration and external pressures that influence the particularity of their cellular form and distribution.

Although highly pervasive in the serial splines of computer models and the tool paths and print layers evident in objects fabricated with CNC milling machines and 3D printers, the section on Serial Iteration explores both the continuation of one of the most central ideas of modern industrialization and its radical transformation within the computational paradigm. This evolution of serial models resulted from three related phenomena: the ability to model complex curvilinear volumes with a high degree of precision; the introduction of algorithmic differentiation into the repetition of serial elements to produce variation while maintaining continuity—a dominant strategy used within digitally generated projects across a range of morphological types and materials; and the shift from strategies of framing to filling space made possible by the ever-increasing reduction of the size of the spatial interval and the ability to compute enormous quantities of data and prototype at extremely high speeds. While all these transformations have been exemplified by numerous projects such as One Main by dECOi and the Inventioneering Architecture installation by DesigntoProduction that each illustrate the progressive differentiation of the serial section, the ability to increase precision and the quantity of data computed while simultaneously decreasing the size of the serial interval in both space and time is made most explicit in Michael Hansmeyer's Subdivided Columns project where the 6 million faces of an intricate 3D model are serially intersected with planes that are translated into 1 mm-thick CNC-milled ABS sheets.

Just as the striated Cartesian system that structures the bit-mapped digital field of the computer screen is hidden below the fluid intensity of its images, so too are the composite horizontal layers generated by rapid prototyping technologies rendered visually undetectable when embedded within the inflected topographical surfaces they produce. Yet while the first generation of serial projects animated architecture through formal variation, the next generation shifted toward the inherent variability of material (already anticipated in these earlier projects) by exploiting the increasing complexity of evolving tools in conjunction with an already intricately encoded matter. Adjusting the path, rhythm, and speed of material extrusion to exploit the micro-looping of bioplastic in the printing of the Strand Table, for example, or the natural slumping of concrete in the making of the columns of Concrete Choreography, thus exposes and augments the serial layering of 3D printing once hidden behind the smoothness of the intricate volumetric forms it was able to produce, while enabling the expressiveness of matter to exceed the striated limits of its serial form.

The increasing emphasis on animate, material, and biotic models, and their link to the capacities of computation, although evidenced throughout this book, are rendered most apparent in its last three sections. The rise of complex woven systems, for example, that displaced the striated gridded frames of modern architecture with complex meshworks, find their analogs both in the stranded connectivity of nature's rhizomatic systems and in our technologically amplified network culture. Thus, while architectures such as the Beijing National Stadium by Herzog & de Meuron known as the "Bird's Nest" or the Sendai Mediatheque by Toyo Ito attempted to misalign the true functioning of these assemblies in relation to their perceptual effects to undermine our expectations of an ordered tectonic as a nod to the true complexity of material systems, the work of Neri Oxman with the Mediated Matter Group and Achim Menges with the Institute for Computational Design begin their research on woven systems with the fibrous composites of the biological world. They therefore initiated their work through studying the cellulose in plants, collagen in animals, chitin in insects and crustaceans, and silk in the woven webs of spiders and silkworms, recognizing that the heterogeneity of stranded systems in nature is critical to the specificity of their adaptation and functioning. Each of these research groups and the architectural prototypes that they developed, however, draws from the capacity of computation in different ways. The Aguahoja projects, for example, experiment with the development of 3D printed woven structures using biocompatible polymers extracted from natural substances, while the Silk Pavilions use both biomimetic algorithms for weaving in addition to 6500 live silkworms employed as biological printers to establish a computationally directed, bio-informed material ecology. As a complement to this research, the 2012 ICD/ITKE Pavilion applies the chitinous fiber morphology adapted from the endoskeleton of a lobster to the robotic winding of carbon and glass-fiber reinforced polymer filaments in the making of the pavilion's structural surface. These stranded filaments are layered in different directions to generate a material surface with anisotropic qualities that, like the arthropod it emulates, is highly efficient and locally adaptable. Notwithstanding this project's dependency on the precision and agility of computationally controlled robotic fabrication, it's design would not have been possible without the power of digital simulation and computational form-finding methods that are biomimetic not in form, but perhaps in their evolutionary logics. These digital methods can process enormous volumes of data, radically compress time, and quickly evaluate an architectural species' fitness for survival by iteratively testing hundreds, and often thousands of virtual models in the absence of physical precedents.

The use of computational form-finding in concert with material experimentation is highlighted in the section Emergent Surfaces, which investigates complex emergent behavior evolving at the nexus of matter and computation. Digital design tools such as CADenary created by Axel Killian that simulate the physics of membrane systems and analog experiments such as the catenary structures by Ball-Nogues and the P_Wall series by Matsys exhibit, through their very capacity to self-organize, what has been referred to as a form of "material computation."[7] Following the evolutionary trajectory of Gaudi, Isler, and Otto, these more contemporary works extend the explorations of their predecessors using the augmented capacity of digital tools to compute material complexity. They also move beyond earlier digital expressions of dynamic form generation that, akin to the abstract planes of modern architecture, had entirely discounted the complexity of the materials out of which they were made. The evolution of computationally enhanced material form-finding at the architectural scale has been best exemplified both in the digital tool development and full scale experimental projects by the Block Research Group (BRG) at the ETH, where, for example, Otto's cable net tensile structures and Candela's shells find their progeny in Knit Candela and the HiLo roof, freeform concrete shells constructed using a suspended cable net falsework system and fabric formwork to support and mold the shell. Philippe Block's PhD research on Thrust Network Analysis (TNA) over time evolved into the development of many new software tools including RhinoVAULT—an interactive and intuitive form-finding tool for the design of funicular shell structures. This tool was then used for the creation of multiple projects which included the Armadillo Vault constructed for the *Beyond Bending* exhibition at the 2016 Venice Biennale, one of the most spectacular contributions to this oeuvre. This structure, a freeform doubly-curved vault made of mortar free, dry-assembled discrete pieces of stone with a thickness proportional to less than one-half that of an eggshell, is an explicit material manifestation of the potential of geometry when linked with the intrinsic capacity of matter to self-organize through the alignment of form and force. It exposes what a truly endogeneous, expressive, and encoded matter-based architecture might become when design is supported by computational form-finding strategies and tools.

Finally, the last section on Multi-Agent Networks operates as a cursory introduction to the enormous territory of smart systems and artificial forms of intelligence beginning with multi-agent, self-organizing systems whose local rules governing the interactions of individual elements lead to complex forms of global behavior. Such emergent systems, which are found in the biological, social, and computational realms, have been used as models to rethink both the processes of architectural and urban design, and its operative and adaptive performative capacities. Although such systems are relevant to a wide range of applications, within the context of this book, the works included are classified according to three broader types. The first, multi-agent matters, applies swarm logic to the formation and making of continuous material artifacts. This is exemplified in the methods used by Alisa Andrasek to induce meteorologically inspired mobile vectors to create the whirling mathematized cloud in the making of Cloud Pergola. It is also descriptive of the generative process employed by Francois Roche in I've Heard About, which, akin to the making of a termite mound, is a communal habitat that evolves over time while indexing the desires, needs, and material depositions of its mobile agents. The second type of application has been found in multi-agent urbanisms focused on the collective emergence and behaviors of urban populations, networked vehicular structures, the cellular distribution of buildings, and other territorial elements whose interactions are defined by local rules responding to programmatic, environmental, economic, and other influences. These have been used to model potential settlement scenarios or develop optimized systems of territorial distribution based on influences and attractors, gaining traction in urban planning and design given their pertinence to the evolution and ongoing occupation of cities that are necessarily constituted by self-organizing populations and their highly dynamic localized activities. The third type of multi-agent network, exemplified in projects such as White Noise White Light, Cirriform, and Urban Syncopation, are systems constituted by fields of components that locally respond to the changing dynamics of the populations with which they interact (or as in the case of HygroScope and Oculus, the atmospheric conditions that activate them), and are programmed to operate continuously in real time.

When applied to the design or performance of architectural artifacts, the intelligence of these models is not simply a result of computational calisthenics or the sheer quantity of numerical data pulsing through the system. Rather it is dependent on the intelligence of the design of the system itself—that is, the ways in which architectural intentions, values, and influences might be encoded in the definition of agents and the rules governing their local interactions as these are propagated through the system. This includes the point at which procedures might be halted within the evolution of a form or organization and is distinct from other generative design processes that might establish criteria for the search and selection of results considered to be successful manifestations of the objects, architectures, or urban environments produced. Against the backdrop of a design process meant to incorporate the expertise of numerous contributors or participation models designed to engage multiple users one would think that self-organizing, agent-based systems might have far greater import than their limited applications to date and will no doubt expand the ways in which we think about the promise of higher-order forms of evolving collective intelligence and the somewhat paradoxical concept of "bottom-up" design.

Notwithstanding the clear differentiation of the sections of this book, many of the projects traverse two or more taxonomies given the complex interweaving of their influences and procedures. The Cloud Pergola, for example, was initially designed using a multi-agent system, which was then voxelized and later 3D printed as an extruded lattice. This project has been located within the section on woven meshes highlighting its lattice structure, yet it could have as easily been put into dialog with EZCT's computational chair design exemplifying the voxelization of space, or in relation to Roland Snook's swarm influenced urbanism. Similarly, a few of the projects located under Emergent Surfaces such as the LaVoute de LeFevre, Shellstar, and the Confluence Park Pavilion, were all created using cellular geometries in addition to the tessellated modular façade of the Ravensbourne College and the stacked polygonal blocks that aggregate to form the Round Room. This internal complexity of each project reveals another aspect of the way in which hybrid procedures within a computational environment allow for internal encoded differentiation and diversity while still facilitating synthetic wholes, like the emergence of an organism with distinct genetic parents, which remains a multiplicity despite its apparent coherence.

The analytical segments at the end of each section expose the generative logics and processes, as well as a virtual matrix of the generative potential of a selection of projects included in the book. These are not necessarily the processes used to design each work. Rather, they make explicit their formal and organizational logics when conceived as computationally-driven, parametrically derived artifacts. Drawings and models are familiar tools that we use to probe and analyze architectural works. Here, the analysis occurs through the creation of parametrically encoded models, that reveal a set of procedures used to produce each project, and that extend it by revealing how a change in its potential inputs—the values of its variables—translates into an incremental change in its customized output or design. The purpose of this analysis is to expose the hidden virtual envelope that surrounds every parametrically generated project which, akin to a game, might include not just the rules of interaction but also the plurality of all possible plays that these rules enable. This intrinsic mutability built into the designed machine that produces the artifact ensures that the architectural work is, at its root, a multiplicity. That is, a unique artifact that contains within it a genetically coded framework able to generate multiple related siblings, thereby transforming our ideas of what might constitute a "proto-type" within computational design. The variability of computationally designed works as discussed earlier in this introduction is therefore also intrinsic to the virtual field of every parametric model that contains an unlimited range of potential objects. These are reduced, over time, as one arrives at a final solution through a selection process that itself is based on multiple evaluative parameters. It is also expanded as the making of that object is analyzed and disseminated to influence the next generation of architects and designers, which ultimately is one of the purposes of this book.

Within *Flux*, the architectures presented are considered as a population of objects responsible for the evolution of something that far exceeds the trajectory of a single project. They are thus explored less as autonomous projects than as a collection of interrelated and interacting cultural artifacts in flux, whose formation, methods, and tools, as well as their experience, perception, and meaning are necessarily tied to a broader field of cultural production. Notwithstanding the theoretical links between computational logics and the architectures that they may have engendered, the latter always operate within a broad set of cultural parameters and material possibilities and are therefore not predetermined in advance by technological inventions but rather creatively inspired by them, since architectural and material products are also inevitably engaged with aesthetic and other considerations. Thus, despite that it has been argued that computational systems exist outside of, and are indifferent to aesthetic judgements, architecture certainly is not, and as a result, the effects of computation on the discipline are necessarily also entangled with aesthetic and cultural parameters that exist outside of the digital realm. Our investigation is therefore not presented to underscore a positivist approach to technological progress (characterized more broadly by those that eschew aesthetics and design, human-based authorship, and analog methods to name a few) but rather to highlight the capacities of computational technologies as they have been drawn into relationship with the design and making of things with formal, spatial, and material attributes, and the ability of these technologies to contribute to the dynamic generation of new architectural and urban models. It is for this reason that the eight themes that define the structure of this book have morphological attributes and operate as a larger taxonomy of computational logics and their relationship to architectural craft. Throughout this book these themes are elaborated through the presentation of over 140 built works and experimental architectural projects, expanded through theoretical essays and analytical and generative models that further the design potential of the logics used to create them.

Notes:

1. See, for example, Patrik Schumacher's many writings on parametricism as a style, including his *Parametricist Manifesto* presented at the 2008 Venice Architecture Biennale, and his publications "Parametricism: A New Global Style for Architecture and Urban Design" *Architectural Design* 79, No. 4 (July/August, 2009): 14–23, and *The Autopoiesis of Architecture, Volume II* (Hoboken: Wiley, 2012).
2. "It seems that nomad science is more immediately in tune with the connection between content and expression in themselves, each of these two terms encompassing both form and matter. Thus matter, in nomad science, is never prepared and therefore homogenized matter, but is essentially laden with singularities. . . [in Royal Science] The search for laws consists in extracting constants, even if those constants are only relations between variables (equations). An invariable form for variables, a variable matter of the invariant: such is the foundation of the hylomorphic schema. But for the dispars as an element of nomad science the relevant distinction is material-forces rather than matter-form. Here, it is not exactly a question of extracting constants from variables but of placing the variables themselves in a state of continuous variation. . . . They seize or determine singularities in the matter instead of constituting a general form." See Deleuze and Guattari's discussion of Nomad vs. Royal Science in Gilles Deleuze and Félix Guattari, *A Thousand Plateaus: Capitalism and Schizophrenia*, trans. Brian Massumi (Minneapolis: University of Minnesota Press, 1987), 369.
3. "When the digital turn came in the 1990s, architects—not all of them, but the best—adopted digital tools and embraced digital change sooner than any other trade, industry, or creative profession. For this was a technology meant to produce variations, not identical copies; customized, not standardized products: far more than a postmodern dream come true, variability is a deep-rooted ambition of architects and designers, craftsmen and engineers of all times and places." See Mario Carpo, *The Second Digital Turn: Design Beyond Intelligence* (Cambridge: MIT Press, 2017), loc. 201.
4. The expression "line of flight" as an act of deterritorialization and becoming is drawn from Deleuze and Guattari, *A Thousand Plateaus*. 88–89.
5. See Gilles Retsin, "Discrete Architecture in the Age of Automation," *Architectural Design* 89, No. 2 (March/April, 2019), 6–13.
6. See the paper by George A. Popescu, Neil Gershenfeld, and Tushar Mahale, "Digital materials for digital printing," presented at DF 2006 International Conference on Digital Fabrication Technologies (Denver, Colorado, 2006). Accessed from the MIT Center for Bits and Atoms site: https://www.cba.mit.edu/docs/papers/index.html.
7. That computation is entirely indifferent to aesthetics and should operate outside of human involvement has been championed by many technophiles and is discussed by Nick Pisca in his paper: "Forget Parametricism" in *Computational Design*, ed. Neil Leach and Philip F. Yuan (Shanghai: Tongji University Press), 43–45.

STACKED AGGREGATES

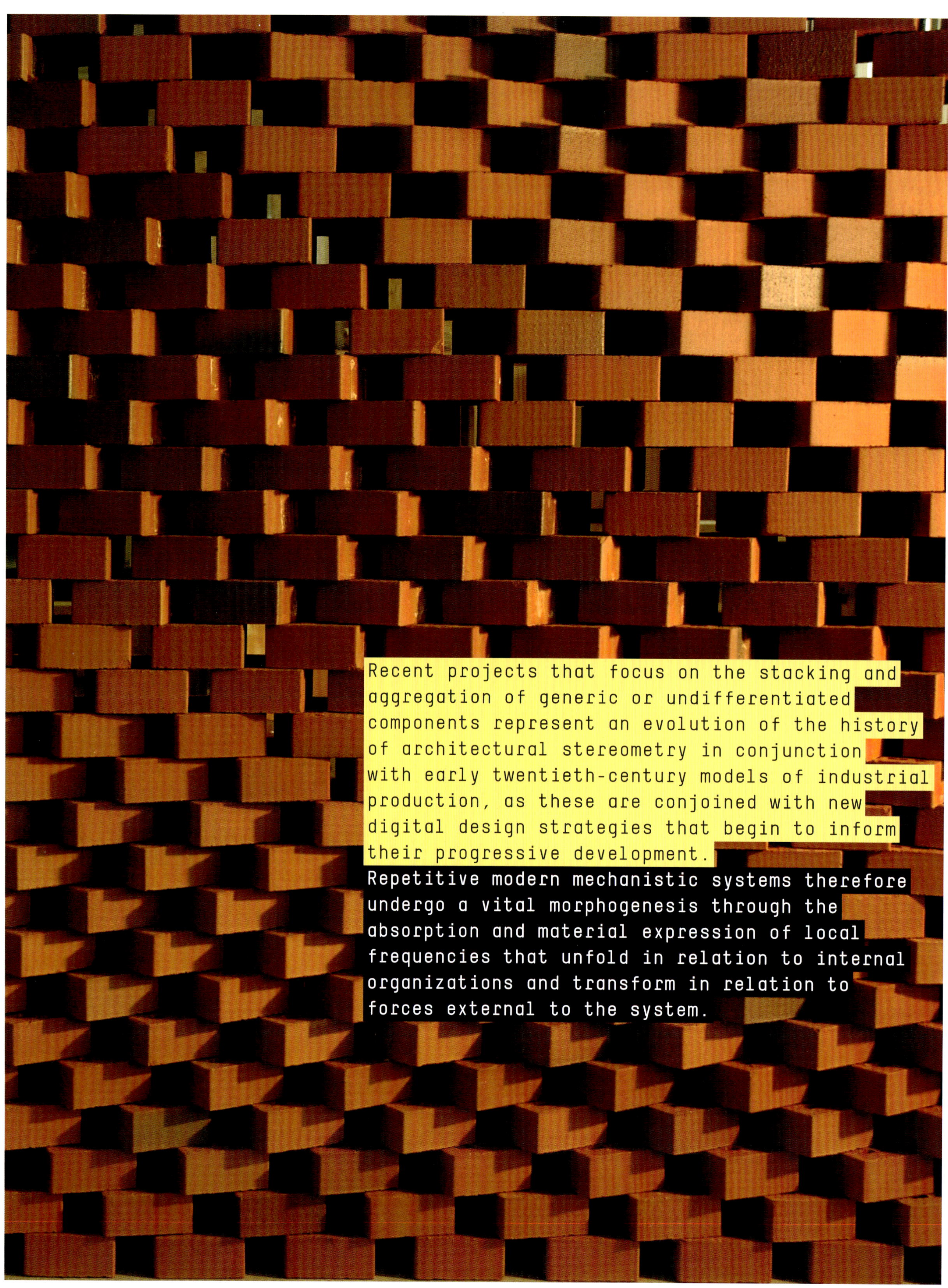

Recent projects that focus on the stacking and aggregation of generic or undifferentiated components represent an evolution of the history of architectural stereometry in conjunction with early twentieth-century models of industrial production, as these are conjoined with new digital design strategies that begin to inform their progressive development.

Repetitive modern mechanistic systems therefore undergo a vital morphogenesis through the absorption and material expression of local frequencies that unfold in relation to internal organizations and transform in relation to forces external to the system.

Stacked Aggregates

Encoded Stereometry

Architecture is largely made up of the addition of incremental parts that aggregate into larger assemblies. Beginning with the simple addition of mass-produced elements, contemporary stacked aggregates refer to some of the most archaic forms of building that are dependent upon the simple accumulation of material and transform these into complex iterative systems. Recent projects that focus on the stacking and aggregation of generic or undifferentiated components represent an evolution of the history of architectural stereometry in conjunction with early twentieth-century models of industrial production, as these are conjoined with digital design and fabrication strategies that begin to inform their progressive development. Locally varied iterative processes, digital modeling, parametric algorithmic methods, and programmed robotic fabrication techniques are employed to expand the potential of these aggregative systems, while reconnecting the technologically produced, discrete cultural artifact with the programmatic complexity of the environments in which they are embedded. Repetitive modern mechanistic systems therefore undergo a vital morphogenesis through the absorption and material expression of local frequencies that unfold in relation to internal organizations and transform in relation to forces external to the system.

In principle, the aggregative system begins with the repetition of the ready-made unit, where, most often, each unit is essentially the same form, material, and scale as its neighbor, and is dependent on the proximity, friction, and load-bearing capacity of adjacent elements to ensure the structural stability of the whole. In contemporary stacked systems, however, the highly striated method of fabrication responsible for the generation of individual components is no longer repeated in the making of a wall, surface, or space as it once was. The modern tendency to signify industry and its repetitive modes of production through the homogeneity of its architectural assemblies is thereby countered in recent projects by a more complex and intricate form of differential aggregation that smoothly distributes frequencies locally and statistically. In this process, the performative application of the ready-made becomes other to the initial trajectory of its production, transformed into a matter-vector as it is absorbed into the evolution of a larger affective whole. Here, quality directly relies on the strategic deployment of quantity, and "difference" within the system is the result of changes in the mode of assembly rather than the changing form of individual elements. These modifications engender transformations in the series of repeated units, resulting in a heterogeneous system comprised of homogeneous elements, whose complexity is dependent on the variability and increased quantity of information injected into, and continuously modulated across the assemblage.

In the architectural surfaces of the Casa La Roca by Office dA ❶, a precursor to the programmed walls of Gramazio & Kohler and the prefabricated undulating masonry panels of SHoP, the repetitive industrial production of ready-made terracotta bricks is countered by a complex form of assembly that locally animates the wall in response to internal programmatic demands and the changing external conditions of the surrounding site. In its multiplication and destabilization, the "type" of the masonry unit is de-figured and transformed into a consistent abstract medium in order to receive, and be deformed by, procedural, programmatic and environmental forces. These are fluid material events that are external to the artifact that animate the masonry surface while introducing a dynamic flow space into the work. Along one edge, for example, the hollow blocks are translated in space and then progressively rotated to enable the boundary condition of the wall to be locally disrupted. The wall is thus aerated to admit light and enable views that vary in relation to the position of both the sun and the observer relative to the wall, while still retaining its characterization as a consistent and continuous mono-material skin. After having wrapped the corner, along the adjacent wall the bricks are again incrementally and laterally shifted to generate a smooth gradient that transitions from closed to open, the subtle conversion of which refers to the changing relationship between functions on either side of the wall. The increasing porosity of this stacked aggregate system, as it transforms from solid boundary to permeable screen, acts to register the emergence of an outdoor courtyard veiled behind the wall, whose gradual dematerialization is further augmented by the larger segments of this screen that appear to fold and undulate in space. Through these local transformations, a strategy repeated in Archi Union's Silk Wall ❷, the wall is converted from a stacked aggregate to a woven curtain, pushing its stereometric nature to a new tectonic

❶

❷

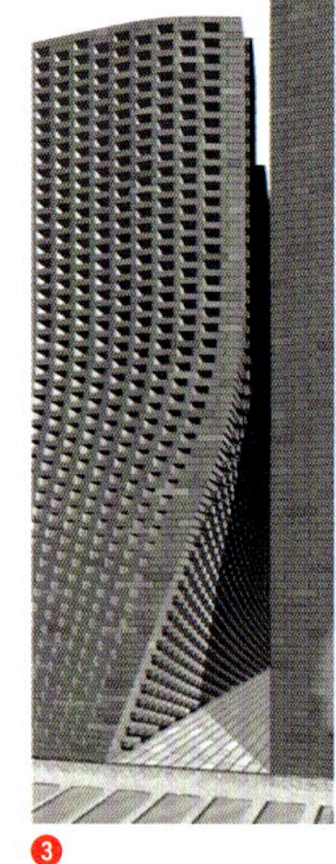

❸

❹

❺

limit while undermining the wall's apparent weight and solidity.

Although both consistent and continuous in its materiality, this aggregative whole is undermined by the heterogeneity of local movements that constitute its fill, its references to an additive process of accumulation, and its insistence that space is determined by material occupation rather than formal delimitation. Akin to "a line that fills a plane without ceasing to be a line," here there is no geometric supplementary dimension to the units that occupy the surface, that is, no "dimension higher than that which moves through it or is inscribed in it."[1] A product of accumulation and proximity that is continuously undergoing morphological transformation, this aggregative form not only contains space by its capacity to enclose, but also fills space through local adjustments that refer back to its individuated aggregative nature, whereby the space referenced, and the elements that occupy it, tend to become identified.[2]

Rather than linking the changing function of the wall to either the specificity of a material, component, or constructive logic, the innovation in this project is in its exploitation of a single material system to support multiple performative parameters. New information is integrated into the aggregative logic of the masonry skin leading to the local adjustment of the position and relationship of units within the system. In the Tongxian Cultural Center ❸, for example, another stacked aggregate project by Office dA, a programmatic force is responsible for phenomenally pushing back the wall to create an opening to allow the flow of bodies into the building and signify entry, whereas an environmental force is referenced in the apparent stretching of another segment of that same wall to render it porous and allow the transmission of light. The initial striated material system thus imparts a smooth space by movements that are different to, yet that superpose themselves upon, a relatively homogeneous field. The serial reiteration of the masonry unit then registers these movements as highly specific, yet graduated differentials that induce continuous modulations of the architectural structure or cladding, whereby the progressive complexity of the whole is directly proportional to the density of information and degrees of difference absorbed by the system. These generate a rhythmic and continuous multiplicity, a plastic yet complex whole, that displaces the simple repetition of discrete units. Unlike the repetitive module that divides the whole in advance and therefore regulates its spatial intervals, "that counts in order to occupy," these aggregative units locally "occupy [space] without counting."[3] The system is internally integrated yet externally open, allowing for infinite modes of exchange with its environment. These are provisionally limited only by the local positional variability of the unit, its local structural capacity, and the rules by which external information is assimilated.

In the Gantenbien Winery project by Gramazio & Kohler ❹, the specific information that is parametrically incorporated into the intelligence of the masonry surface allows for a fine-grained response to the desire for permeability and surface articulation. The specificity of this response is dependent on the relative weighting of influences within a given interval, such as the degree of rotation of a brick that determines the amount of light that is allowed to penetrate a space, and where the potential variability both within the interval and across the surface is essentially unlimited. The precision that enables the differentiation of micro-intervals as these masonry units shift position or rotate, favors tonality, that is, gradients of light and dark that are deployed across the surface. The semiotic distinction between a window and wall is thereby undone by a locally responsive and syntactically defined permeable hybrid that substitutes molar architectural objects with the variable distribution of micro-matters.

In the winery and the programmed wall projects of Gramazio & Kohler, such as Structural Oscillations developed for the 2008 Venice Architecture Biennale and the interior walls of the Max Planck Institute ArtLab, the precision needed to assure this continuum of local adjustments within the stacked aggregate is guaranteed by a robotic fabrication process that imbues the material tectonic with digital characteristics ❺. The robotically generated wall is a literal form of digital fabrication operating according to algorithms—programmed sequences—that provide mathematical instructions for its fabrication. Industrial processes dependent on, and limited by the fixed parameters of physical machines, those that are responsible for producing the homogeneity of the masonry units themselves, for example, are thereby replaced

6

7

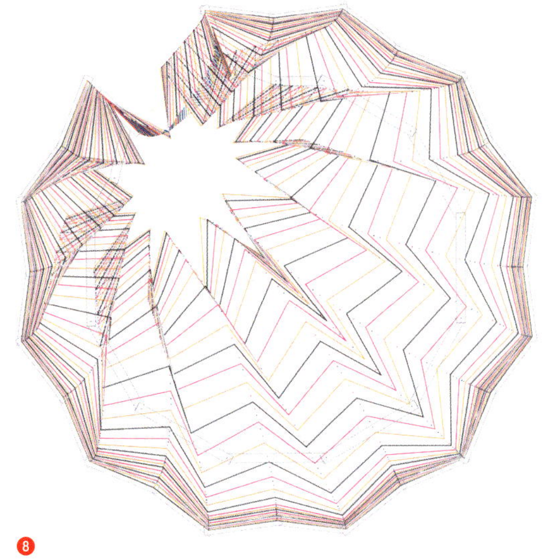

8

by a variable mode of assembly that is controlled by a set of transformational rules programmed into the movement paths of a 7-axis robot. These arithmetically determine the relative positioning of masonry units as they are rotated or shifted laterally in accordance with a governing algorithm, a process that is further complexified in the Flight Assembled Architecture project, where the wall is constructed by deploying a programmed swarm of flying robots. The making of the wall is therefore no longer controlled by the limits of a preexistent set of fixed parameters defined either by the individual masonry unit or its preconceived mode of construction, but instead is allowed to morphologically transform according to new information that is incorporated into the aggregative process and that instructs its animate and evolutionary behavior.

As the stacked aggregate is reconceived as a "digital" surface, the wall is divided into an array of incremental units each of which is coordinated and described by numeric information, just as the pixelated field of a computer image that is varied in tone corresponds to a precise matrix of discrete levels of gray. In the walls of the winery, for example, the digital platform is what enables the transcoding of information between two distinct material environments, whereby an image, in this case, the result produced by simulating the animation of a randomly packed basket of grapes—a symbolic referent for the winery—is numerically translated into the permeable brick screen walls that wrap the building. These screen walls are modulated to emit and distribute light yet protect the fermentation process, while simultaneously allowing air to be filtered into the building. In the recoding or transcoding of information, each pixel within the image is numerically translated into a precise interval and angle of deflection for each brick, such that the shadows and depth perceived within the image are transformed into the actual shadows generated by the rotating and spacing of aggregated masonry units. The local distribution of light through and across the surface gives the wall a plasticity and thickness that exceeds both the two dimensionality of the original image and the regularity of the bricks from which the walls were generated.

This determination by Gramazio & Kohler to strategically link new modes of formal and spatial representation with the programming of material and structural techniques, allows us to understand how virtual spatial models might be actualized, not only by furnishing a direct relationship between digital and tectonic logics, but also by operating on, and transforming an already given set of traditional building technologies and typological architectural artifacts. This is a tactical strategy in that it draws upon our invested belief in a dominant and already familiar (and therefore naturalized) set of objects, techniques, and typologies that represent the "real," and then incrementally modifies these realities in order to generate new materials for architectural expression.

In 290 Mullberry Street, SHoP expands upon this tactical approach through their reinterpretation of the parameters of a building code by exposing the spatial limits of its implicit structure. Originally written to allow a limited percentage of a façade to project over the property line to enable the expression of classical masonry ornamentation, the existing building code provided the spatial flexibility to engender a new form of folded and triangulated masonry surface as the numeric parameters of the legal rule set were computationally transcoded. Although initially written in relation to a specific form of architecture, the abstraction of the rule set of the code lends itself to creative parametric reinterpretation to move beyond the specific cultural and formal limitations of the artifacts from which it was originally derived. These parameters, which set the outer and inner limits of the ridgelines of the triangular facets used to model the exterior building envelope, were then used to digitally model and fabricate a rubber mold system that was blocked out to create the L-shaped corbelled-brick precast panels that comprise the different components of the façade 6. This system was employed not only to maximize the allowable cantilever of each brick in relation to its neighbor to produce the progressive stepped inclinations and diagonal sloping pattern of the surface and to ensure that these were compliant with the parameters of the building code, but also to maximize the efficiency of the process of prefabricating the panels by ensuring that the multiple typological conditions of the aggregated surface could be embedded within, and therefore generated by, the geometry of a single mold. The result is a compelling aesthetic articulation of the entire skin that

9

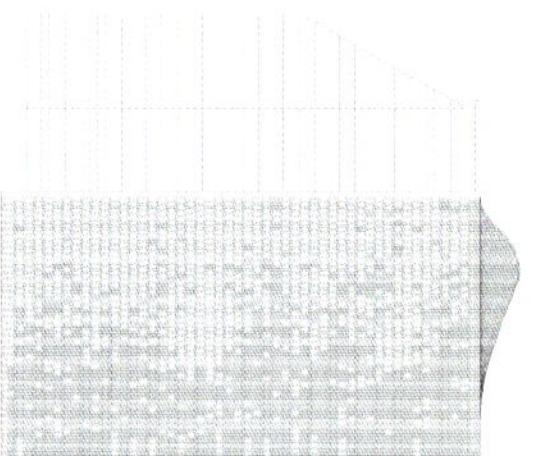

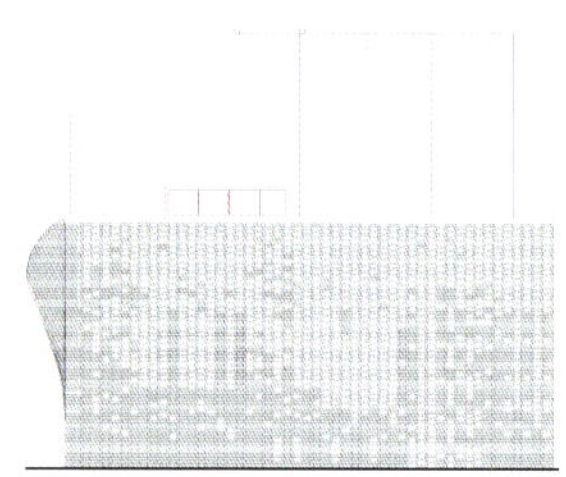

10

11

transforms the ways in which we think about masonry detailing.

In the Sequential Wall projects 7 and the Mantra Hookah Den 8, the shift from the aggregation of masonry units to the stacking of timber lengths allows the expanded constructive logic of one architectural material to be applied to another. This migration not only enables a radicalization of the medium, but also exponentially augments the potential expressiveness of the woven structures generated by integrating additional degrees of variation, such as the changing lengths of the wood battens, into the parametric system. Just as a curved line can be atomized into its coordinate points, the intricate digitization of curvature evident along these surfaces index the overlapping intersections or endpoints of stacked alternating elements that aggregate to form the complex wooden structures of each project. These points of overlap and intersection, which in the hookah den mark the interlocking endpoints of the pleats that thicken the wall and provide it with structural stability, are local registrations that foreground the distinction between the discrete repetitive modules of the system and the continuous and unique curvatures that are inscribed as waves along its surface. Quantity and scale become critical concepts to be exploited within these aggregative systems, not only because repetition is the necessary prerequisite to register differentiation and variation within the system, but also because the repetitive elements approach the behavioral continuity of matter through the sheer number of parts present in the system, in combination with their intensification, that is, the size of incremental units relative to the size of the whole. The difference between the perception of formal pattern and material surface texture within stacked aggregates is often dependent on the intersection of these two values where the intense deployment of quantity generates a distinct appreciable quality of its own.

In the Chi She Gallery project by Archi-Union 9 an emphasis on the salvage and reuse of existing materials—a response to the local regional context as well as to larger ecological imperatives—exposes the difficulty of applying older mechanistic models to post-industrial materials, whose degenerative form has already begun to literally take on a life of its own. This challenge also points to the problematic limits of these models when confronted with the full life cycle of material objects. As exposed in the weathered articulation of the full façade 10, the salvaged brick, like the clay matter from which it was derived, exceeds, due to its material transformation over time, the abstract form that once enabled its easy integration into a highly constrained geometric wall system. The new form of this old brick is far more geometrically complex than its antecedent and therefore contains more information to be processed in its use. Advanced computation enabled this information, reflected in the subtle differentiations in the form and edges of the salvaged bricks, to be registered and incorporated as local data used for the robotic selection and precise placement of individual bricks in the making of the highly animated wall. This form of artificial intelligence points to an important area of computational development that might enable us to better integrate the transformative matters of a wider range of materials, as they evolve throughout their lifecycles, into the design process.

The shift from the variable aggregation of highly regular, industrially produced elements such as bricks, to the masonry walls of the Round Room 11 by Matter Design and the Sean Collier Memorial by Höweler + Yoon, returns us to pre-industrial historical precedents such as the complex configurations of Inca stonework in the former, and the stereotomy of unreinforced massive stone vaults in the latter. These projects both draw upon archaic yet highly sophisticated artisanal practices—the construction of compression-only shell structures assembled from the careful selection, carving and placement of unique masonry units—now advanced by the intelligence, precision, and capacity of digital design tools and computationally driven fabrication techniques. Each is therefore dependent on the shaping of space through the sculpting of mass that calls upon subtractive and divisive logics as much as the addition of predefined components, the complex geometries and increased size of the individuated and unique masonry units that comprise the work, and their subservience to a larger plastic whole. Yet, whereas for the Incas the process was as dependent on the selection and placement of found stones and boulders as on the precise and refined hand carving of their irregular edges to enable an exact fit—a highly labor-intensive and tedious process, the Round Room walls are generated by digitally modeling and

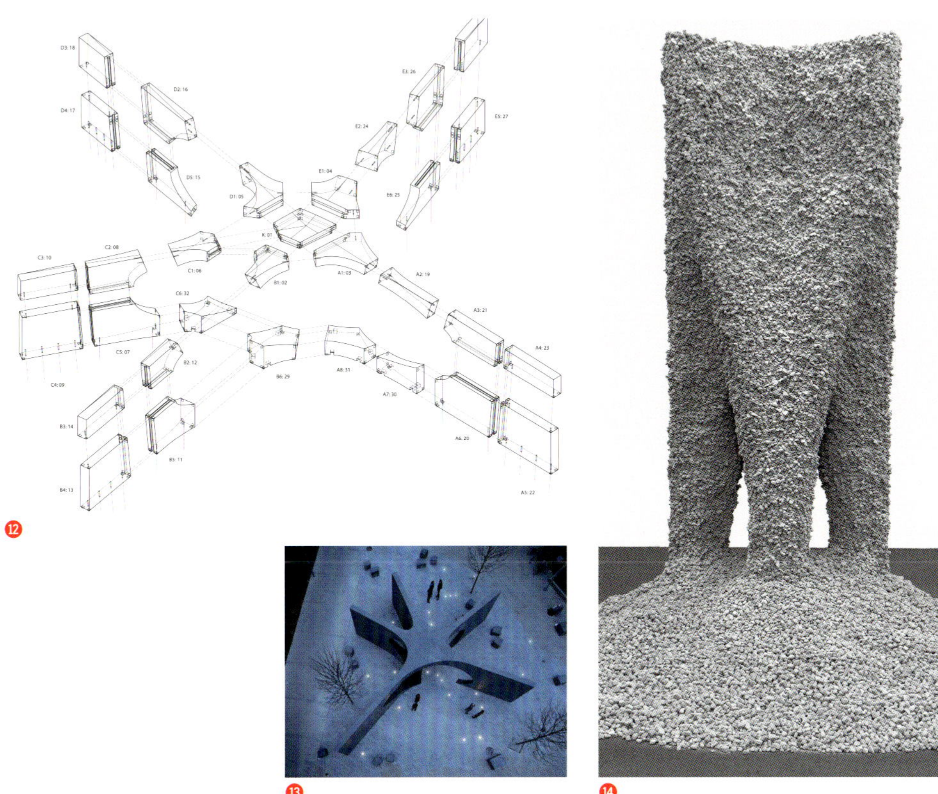

12

13

14

15

tessellating a continuous thickened volumetric surface into hexagonally shaped, discrete polygonal units. Since these are derived using a three-dimensional Voronoi calculation to geometrically subdivide the initial surface, the precise alignment of these units and their tight packing along their front surface is guaranteed in advance and ensured during their fabrication by the exactitude of the water-fed robotic arm used to cut them.

While the Collier Memorial 12 similarly takes on the challenge of intelligently carving volumetric material into unique geometric components that precisely align with each other and aggregate to form a stable, funicular, stereometric structure 13, it does so without any reinforcing or hidden bonding agents, and with far fewer stone units. An extension of older analog techniques, such as Gaudi's hanging chain models used to materially compute the geometry of a vaulted surface by allowing gravitational forces to be directly translated into form, the memorial uses advanced form-finding methods based on computational graphic statics to ensure the stability of its overall form and the voussoir geometry of its individuated massive stone blocks. The project defines in absentia, an interior volume defined by a five-way flat stone vault that is buttressed by five thin radial walls. The absence of surface material along the implied sides of the volume renders the structure perceptually weightless, despite the true enormity of the weight of the six stones miraculously floating above, while almost concealing its aggregative nature behind the refined continuity of its overall form.

The shift from frame to fill that marks a departure from cartesian gridded logics and that was previously emblematized in the digitized stacked aggregate of the pixelated wall, finds its companion and counterpoint in Rock Print 14, an unrecognizable, seemingly primitive, large-scale volumetric aggregate that emulates a low-resolution 3D printed form. Akin to the Round Room and Collier Memorial that look to history to inspire architectural innovation, Rock Print, a collaboration between Gramazio Kohler Research and MIT's Self Assembly Lab, immerses itself in a far deeper geological past, bringing the simplicity and crudeness of an undifferentiated pile of loose rocks, the first form of stackable aggregates, into relation with the most sophisticated computational and robotic processes. The structure is comprised of alternating compacted layers of rock and string, exploiting the compressive strength of the gravel and the tensile strength of string, using a method of jamming to remove the space between rocks and increase their surface friction. The robotically laid string is used as a binding agent whose precise geometrical patterning interlaced with the gravel is responsible for maintaining the solidity of the jammed structure while determining the filled volume's overall configuration 15. The return to ordinary raw materials enables the structure to be fully reversible, displacing the highly processed materials typical of normative construction with a far more sustainable and terrestrially based alternative.

If within the industrial paradigm the intent of the automated process was to capture and functionalize time and space through repetition, the intensive variability that characterizes the complexity of these stacked aggregates becomes a reaffirmation of life in their capacity for improvisation and the seemingly limitless range through which their plasticity is expressed. Here, incarnated form serves as potential matter for a new operation that foregrounds animate rather than mechanistic qualities. Modern industrialism had ensured the instrumentalization of material and activity, by subjecting life to the laws of the mechanical, governed by the principle that every movement of a machine is geometric and measurable, and that every mechanism must follow a precisely determined sequence of discrete operations toward performing a particular task.[4] Through repetition and purposive action, force was striated, so that increases in efficiency and speed would be achieved but only at the expense of a loss of complexity. Thus, if utilitarian efficiency necessitated the elimination of the aleatory, the animate and the affective, its return in these works in some way signifies a profound politics of the living as it links up with a new machinic complexity.

Notes:
1. Gilles Deleuze and Félix Guattari, *A Thousand Plateaus: Capitalism and Schizophrenia*, trans. Brian Massumi (Minneapolis: University of Minnesota Press, 1987), 488.
2. Ibid.
3. Ibid., 477.
4. Georges Canguilhem, "Machine and Organism," trans. Mark Cohen and Randall Cherry, ed. Jonathan Crary and Sanford Kwinter, *Incorporations, Zone* 6 (New York: Urzone, 1992), 45–69.

Church of Christ the Worker

Eladio Dieste

Built 1958-1960
Atlantida, Uruguay

1.1a

1.1b

1.1c

The hyperbolic brick and concrete structure of the Church of Christ the Worker, by Uruguayan architect and engineer Eladio Dieste, exemplifies the relationship between stacked ready-made masonry units and the complex configurations of unitary shell constructions typical of architects such as Luigi Nervi. A renovation and reconstruction of an existing church, the building is rectangular at its base referring back to the orthogonal plan of the large nave space of the original structure, whose side walls have been transformed by Dieste from planar edges into undulating waves as they move from the ground up 19 meters to the roof. Although collectively operating as continuous curvilinear surfaces, these walls are constituted by discrete orthogonal masonry units, their smooth curvature resulting from the aggregation, and incremental, sequential rotation of successive bricks, as well as the extreme difference in scale between the component parts of the assembly and the monumental plastic whole. Despite their thinness, the curved geometry of the walls renders them structurally stable and enables them to act as a framework to support the doubly-curved, vaulted roof—a thin-shell structure of composite reinforced masonry units that functions as a continuous series of catenary arches. The complex geometry and fluid transformations that enable the straight linear sections of both the walls and roof to ripple into sine waves of increasing amplitude is also what allows the serial undulations of the roof to conversely decrease in amplitude so that these curvilinear surfaces can be stitched together at the eaves where these meet in a flattened plane. The project is seminal in its creation of a new expressive form for masonry construction that foregrounds the interdependence of material, structure, and geometry and that integrates parametric thinking into its evolution and development.

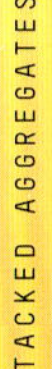

1.1d

1.1e

1.1f

Casa la Roca

Office Da

Unbuilt 1995
Caracas, Venezuela

1.2a

Casa La Roca owes its name to what has emerged as the project's main protagonist: a colossal rock that occupies the rear of the property. The rock sits atop of one of the many hills that define the southern edge of Caracas, and its peak affords a spectacular view of the city. Given the excessive exposure of the site to public views and the limitation of space resulting from the presence of the rock, the aim of the design is to intimate a sense of openness while maintaining adequate privacy and closure for a domestic space. Aggregated terracotta block, brick, and tile are pushed to their material and tectonic limits to achieve this two-fold objective, expanding the functional capabilities of the wall while amplifying its perceptual effects. The house is enveloped by a continuously animated masonry surface that appears to be stretched and folded as it wraps the space. This is achieved through the differential stacking, spacing, and rotating of bricks that enables the wall to locally respond to changing programmatic demands while retaining its mono-material characterization and consistency. Through its gradual dematerialization, the aggregated terracotta wall transforms from solid surface to permeable screen, signifying the emergence of a monumental outdoor space that is carved out of the northwest corner of the site in alignment with the adjacent rock. This outdoor room simultaneously functions as a living space and backyard that is shielded from public view and the elements. Contained within the larger volume of the house, the interior façades of this outdoor space are clad in continuous bands of sliding glass doors and windows, making its relationship with the building's interior as seamless as possible.

1.2b

1.2c

1.2d

1.2e

Gantenbien Winery

Gramazio & Kohler + ETH DFAB Group

Built 2006-2008

Zürich & Fläsch, Switzerland

1.3a

The fermentation room of the Gantenbien Winery consists of a concrete skeleton with a masonry infill that acts as a thermal buffer and screen to filter the sunlight entering the space. The aggregated bricks are offset to enable daylight to penetrate the hall through the gaps between the bricks, while simultaneously shielding the space from direct sunlight, which would have a detrimental effect on the fermentation process. From a distance, the masonry of the vineyard's façade looks like an enormous basket filled with grapes. In contrast to this smooth pictorial effect that is perceived at a distance, at close range the sensual, textile softness of the walls transforms into a low-resolution material aggregate—a solidified yet dynamic skin composed of shifting masonry units whose differential aggregation and subsequent pixelated gradations of tone and shadow are both derived from, and responsible for, the image in the landscape. A robotic production method was developed to lay each one of the 20,000 bricks according to precisely programmed parameters—at the prescribed angles and spaced intervals to generate the larger complex pattern of aggregated bricks. The individual bricks reflect light differently according to the angle at which each is set, and thus take on different tonal gradations and degrees of lightness, which collectively, similar to pixels on a computer screen, add up to a distinctive image. The production of the wall thus requires the transcoding of information whereby each pixel within the initial two-dimensional image is numerically translated into a position and angle of deflection for each brick, so that the shadows perceived within the image are transformed into the actual tonal variations generated by the depth and plasticity of the wall and the dramatic play between color, tone, and shadow that is dependent on the viewer's position and the angle of the sun. This modulation of the stacked aggregative system is what allows the wall panels to possess the desired permeability for light and air and the changing luminous atmosphere on the interior, while simultaneously creating an overall visual pattern mimetic of the initial image that both symbolizes and communicates the identity of the vineyard.

1.3b

1.3c

1.3d

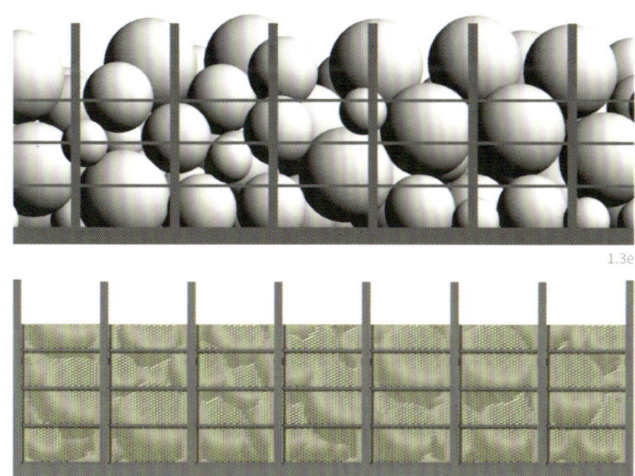

1.3e

1.3f

1.3g

290 Mulberry Street

SHoP

Built 2007-2009

New York, United States

1.4a

290 Mulberry is a 13-story, 27,000-square-foot residential and commercial development that is defined by its context through a direct response to zoning and building code regulations. Located in Nolita, New York, this building is bound on the north by Houston Street and on the west by the historic Puck Building on Mulberry Street. A zoning district requirement specifying a masonry enclosure for the two street walls created an opportunity to respond directly to the Puck Building, one of New York's most recognizable masonry buildings. Through the reinterpretation of local laws and regulations, the project generates a contemporary response to masonry construction and detailing that doesn't attempt to imitate the past. A literal interpretation of the building code written for classical ornamentation allowed the enclosure of the building to project over the property line at 10 percent intervals for every 100 square feet. Maximizing the amount of projected area, while minimizing the overall depth of the enclosure became key criteria for the design. When coupled with material properties and fabrication constraints, these criteria began to define an approach to aggregating and stacking masonry units that enabled a contemporary reinterpretation of brick detailing. The modulated masonry system generated—a result of transcoding the numeric parameters of the building code—produced a folded, triangulated surface pattern that undulates across the façade, the abstraction of the rule set determining the inner and outer limits of the faceted masonry skin. The textured wrapper was produced using a rubber mold system to customize a set of L-shaped, precast corbelled-brick panels that aggregate to form the envelope of the building. This system maximized the efficiency of the process of prefabricating the panels by ensuring that multiple components of the surface could be embedded within, and therefore generated by, the geometry of a single mold, thereby maximizing the intended architectural effect while minimizing the cost of its production.

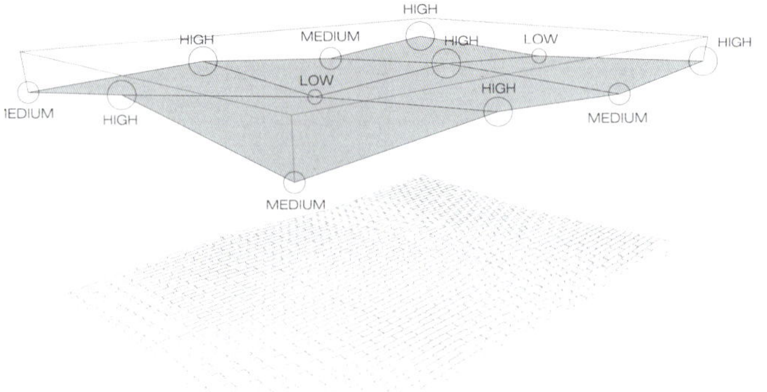

1.4b

1.4c

1.4d

Structural Oscillations

Gramazio & Kohler + ETH DFAB Group

Built 2008

Venice, Italy

1.5a

1.5b

Conceived for the 11th Venice Architecture Biennale, Structural Oscillations is a 100-meter-long undulating brick wall that runs as a continuous ribbon through the Swiss Pavilion. The design of the wall follows algorithmic rules and was built on site by the R-O-B mobile robotic fabrication unit. The wall consists of 14,961 individually rotated bricks that aggregate to produce a looped form, defining an involuted central space and an interstitial space beyond, situated between the brick wall and the existing structure of the pavilion. Through its materiality and spatial configuration the wall enters into a direct dialogue with the modernist brick structure from 1951 by Swiss architect Bruno Giacometti. The wall's design was conceived as an open parametric system where each continuous curve functions as a generative, modifiable interface. The curvature in the lower layers of the wall is balanced by a counter-curvature in the upper layers to ensure the wall's stability. Individual bricks are rotated according to the degree of concavity of the curve, further emphasizing the plastic malleability of the wall, which acquires a textile-like character in contrast to the firm structure and materiality of the bricks.

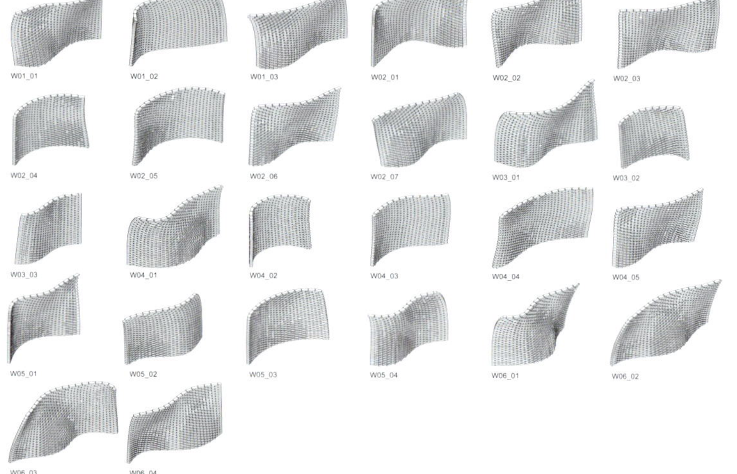

1.5c

1.5d

The Sequential Wall Series
Gramazio & Kohler + ETH DFAB Group

Built 2008
Zürich, Switzerland

1.6a

1.6b

1.6c

The Sequential Wall series investigates the architectonic and constructive potential of additive digital fabrication in timber construction. In this process, a seven-axis robotic arm was programmed to cut commercially available wooden framing members to length and then to stack them according to specific parameters that would morphologically challenge the modularity of the pre-cut units. A reinterpretation of the layering of shingled systems, this wall series combines the logics of serial stacking and weaving in its development. Akin to industrialized masonry wall systems, one of the limitations of this series of structures is that the primary timber battens used to produce the front surface of the wall be of the same length. In one of these structures, these straight timber battens are tilted downward and protrude horizontally from the back of the cavity wall. As the angle of each of these wooden units is incrementally and progressively altered relative to its neighbor, continuous shifting curvatures are generated that appear as "waves" intersecting along the wall's front façade. The intersection of waves is made possible, not only by the pivoting of protruding elements, but also by the initial rhythm of the structure of wooden members, which weaves together two systems that alternate in both plan and section. Even- and odd-numbered members are therefore each responding to different sets of parameters, and each series is essentially producing two distinct sets of curves that define the undulations moving across the surface. The programming of the wall allows the subtle movements and incremental transitions of distinct members to be designed to a high degree of resolution, generating continuities that run counter to the modular expression, repetition, and individuation of the stacked aggregates. Straight lines flow seamlessly into curved ones, and on the wall's surface, an interplay is created between the rhythmic repetition of the protruding wooden slats as well as the fine gradation of their shifting positions and the changing lengths of the vertical cavity wall structure that acts as their support.

The West Fest Stacked Pavilion

Gramazio & Kohler + ETH DFAB Group

Built 2009

Wettswil am Albis, Switzerland

1.7a

1.7b

1.7c

The West Fest Stacked Pavilion was conceived as a temporary spatial structure with an integrated bar for a major public event hosted by the Canton Zurich. The wooden structure, which operates simultaneously as the structure, roof, and skin of the building and defines its spatial organization, consists of sixteen hollow, twisting columns that progressively widen and meet as they move upward to form the roof. Each of the tubular columns is constructed by serially stacking 372 horizontally oriented, standard timber battens whose alternating layers enable the weaving and interlocking of elements at the corners and along the curving façades of each of these supports. The joining surfaces of aggregated wooden members allow the transfer of vertical loads directly through the surface of the assembly. These timber slats are densely packed at the base of each column where support is needed the most, whereas at the top of the columns the density of material is dispersed. This not only aerates and lightens the self-weight of the structure as the splayed columns are transformed into a roof, but also allows each column to be lit from within to perceptually amplify the effects of the gradient distribution of material while simultaneously revealing the intricacies of its geometry and logic of its assembly. Each column was fabricated by a digitally controlled robotic arm that cut and precisely placed the wooden slats according to an algorithmic pattern that defined the length and position of each member, as well as the incremental stacking and progressive rotation of the whole. The logics of construction are readily expressed in the final work though such things as the negotiation between the minimum required overlap and maximum length of elements that, through their distribution, reveal the shifting geometry and curvature of the columns as well as the pattern of their aggregated tectonic. The digital prefabrication process enables the potential integration of structure, form, and material as these are synthetically transcoded into parameters for design and construction while simultaneously bestowing a new expressive form and geometry upon a traditional architectural material.

Mantra Hookah Den

Office dA

Built 2001
Boston, United States

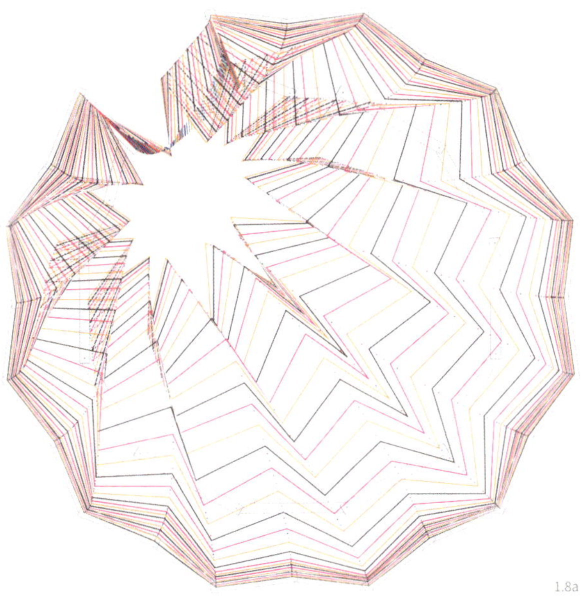

1.8a

The Mantra Hookah Den is located in a French-Indian restaurant in a space formerly occupied by the Old Colony Trust Bank in downtown Boston. The Mantra Den is a free-standing, inhabitable, woven wooden structure—a pleated monumental figure—that, together with the reflective folded ribbon of steel behind the bar, act as the elements of a still life, providing a backdrop for the activities of the restaurant. Conceptually influenced by Indian silks, tents, and Jali screens, the Mantra Den reinterprets textile construction and the spatial billowing, draping, and folding attributed to fabric and apparel through the differential aggregation of stacked linear plywood elements. The project explores the possibility of simultaneously addressing geometry and patterning as connubial ingredients in the generation of space by creating a direct relationship between the tectonic unit and geometric logic. The tectonic units of the structure are stacked plywood "bricks" whose individual lengths are determined by the banquettes set against them in the interior, and whose rotation in plan determines the spatial shape of the volumetric enclosure. Similar to typical ready-made masonry units, the plywood segments are equal in length, their incrementally shifting spatial positions both determining, and determined by the geometry and pleated morphology of the whole. The stacking of elements is articulated at the joints through the overlap of the orthogonally shaped units that express the difference between the local geometry of the repetitive plywood units and the global geometry of the continuous fluid volume. These stacked units are woven together with simple vertical fasteners at the joints where they intersect without the aid of any additional structural members or reinforcement. Instead, the structural rigidity of the whole is produced through its folding geometry. The dimension of the "brick" is used as a measure for the layout, and for ease of manufacturing this size is maintained throughout. The pleats never compromise the dimension of this tectonic unit. In turn, these pleats are also derived in direct relationship to the quoined plywood overlaps at the juncture of the geometry. Thus the plywood "brick" joint both precedes and follows the layout of the geometry in a precise one-to-one correspondence, expressing the project's symbiotic integration of part and whole.

1.8b

1.8c

Olzweg
New Territories/R&Sie(n)
Unbuilt 2006
Orleans, France

Olzweg is a conceptual narrative architectural project designed for the courtyard of the FRAC Museum, whose mission is to bring together contemporary art with experimental architecture. The project involves coating the interior courtyard of the museum with a thickened layer of horizontally aggregated sticks of green glass. These protrude from the walls of the courtyard to form a newly inhabitable zone—a dense poché into which a labyrinth of tunnels are embedded. Operating as figured voids carved out of the impenetrable, yet orthogonally organized bramble of glass, these tunnels link up with the entrances of the surrounding building and form a contiguous maze-like circulatory network that wraps the courtyard. By eliminating the long distance vision necessary to establish navigational coordinates for orientation, this labyrinth demands that visitors to the installation reorient themselves according to the sensory and technological specificities of the exhibition itself, which incorporates RIFD-PDA devices to establish local coordinate positioning based on sound, video, and GPS. The linear glass sticks, imagined to be derived from a "citizen glass bottle recycling process" that re-circuits the discarded byproducts of consumption by transforming them into raw materials for construction, form a furry, amorphous interior skin to the courtyard, an artificially overgrown nature that, as the antithesis to the architectonic, adheres to and envelopes the building. Defying the assumed rationality of the mechanistic construction process, this thickened skin of glass sticks is designed to be fabricated by a robot programmed to aggregate these elements based on a scattering script to introduce uncertainty into the project's development, whose indeterminacy is further amplified by a construction phase anticipated to be protracted over a ten-year period to progressively adapt to the evolution of desires of its occupants. The robot, simultaneously conceived as an efficient, precise, and productive tool, as well as a subjectivized "desiring machine" that embodies the anthropomorphic sentience projected upon it, is a stochastic device used to create a real and imaginary landscape that operates according to local generative rules without the finality of a completed form.

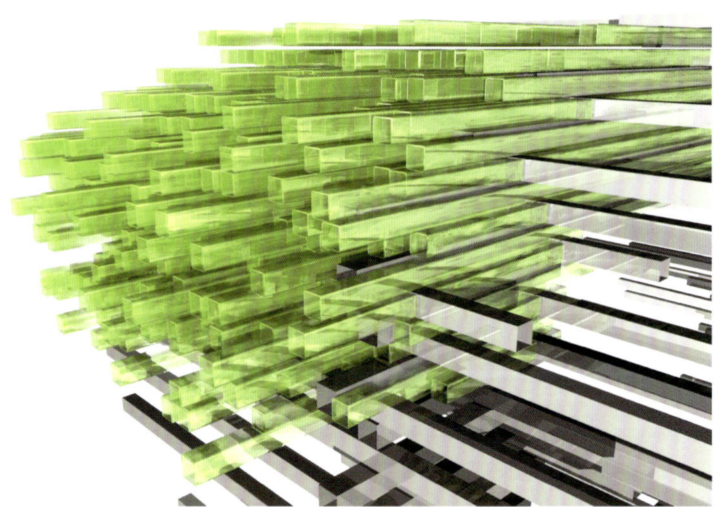
1.9a

1.9b

1.9c

1.9d

1.9e

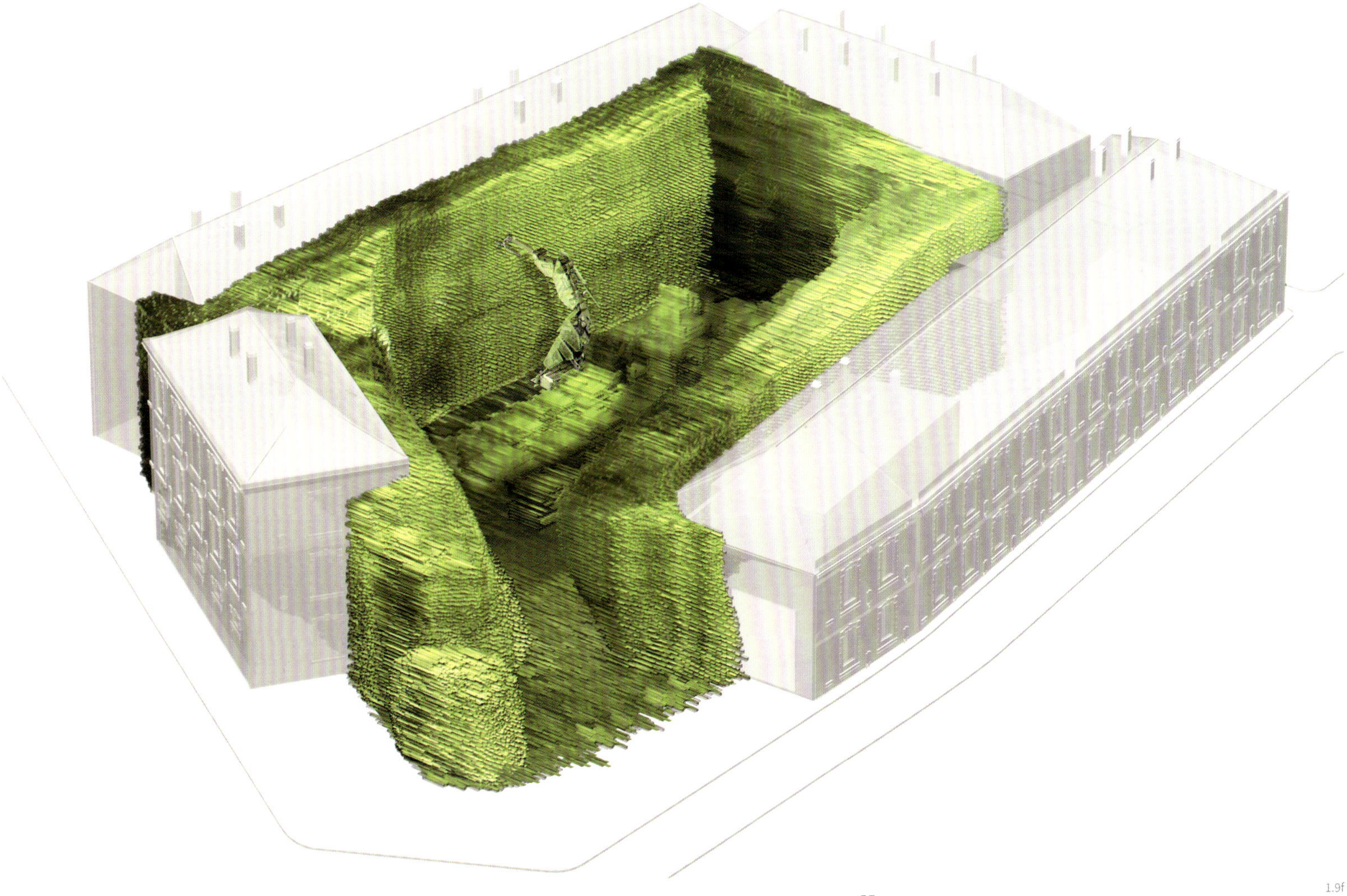

1.9f

Max Planck Institute ArtLab
Gramazio & Kohler

Built 2014-2015
Frankfurt, Germany

1.10a

The MPI ArtLab is a multipurpose event space dedicated to behavioral and psychological studies in the field of the aesthetic evaluation of music, literature, performing arts, and media. The geometric deformation of the interior brick walls and ceiling surfaces that envelope the event space function as an acoustic diffuser by scattering and diffusing the reflected sound, thereby decontouring the sound image. The need to create a balanced sonorous environment by homogenizing the sound field across a wide range of listening positions determined the apparently random, protruding pattern of the wall's interior surface. This was designed using a simulation process to adjust both the angle and degree of recession or projection of each brick in the wall until the tone and volume of reverberating sound was equalized across all seats in the space. This process defined the parameters for the positioning of individual bricks relative to each other within the walls which were then precisely constructed in prefabricated panels by robotically stacking the bricks according to the computationally programmed results of the simulation process. The intricate texture of the brick not only diffuses the sound, but also produces a highly articulate and perceptually soft surface—a haptic environment that enables the listener to be enveloped in a cloud of materialized space and sound.

1.10d

1.10b

Chi She Gallery
Archi-Union

Built 2016
Shanghai, China

1.11a

Located in Shanghai's West Bund Art Exhibition Area, the Chi-She Gallery by Archi-Union Architects seeks to evoke an enigmatic spatial appeal through the desire to both harmonize and integrate the building with its surroundings, while at the same time offering a formal expression of the artistic mission of the works contained inside. The project is sensitive to deep traditional cultural building practices, materials, and environments in China while simultaneously integrating computational and robotic technologies into its design and construction. The existing exterior walls were retained, shored up, and structurally reinforced as necessary to maximize the interior space. The roof structure was replaced by a more efficient, lightweight, tensioned timber structure, a section of which was lifted, to bring in light and connect those inside to the exterior, while enabling an unobstructed view of the sky. Gray-green salvaged bricks were used to blend in with and complement the existing structure, merging the traditional craftsmanship of the recycled bricks with advanced digital fabrication technologies. The subtle differentiations of the form of the individuated found bricks were registered and incorporated as local data that impacted their selection and placement in the global form of the new undulating façade, which animates the entry to the gallery while expressing the vitality of the Chi-She community. The brick pattern is then further articulated along its surface, producing a diffuse, pixelated, patterned field of light and shadow as the wall moves from the ground to the sky. The complexity of the masonry skin would not have been possible using typical construction methods. Instead, robotic fabrication technologies were employed on site, promoting a new tectonic of post-industrial digital craft that combines local existing materials and traditional, artisanal methods with computational techniques.

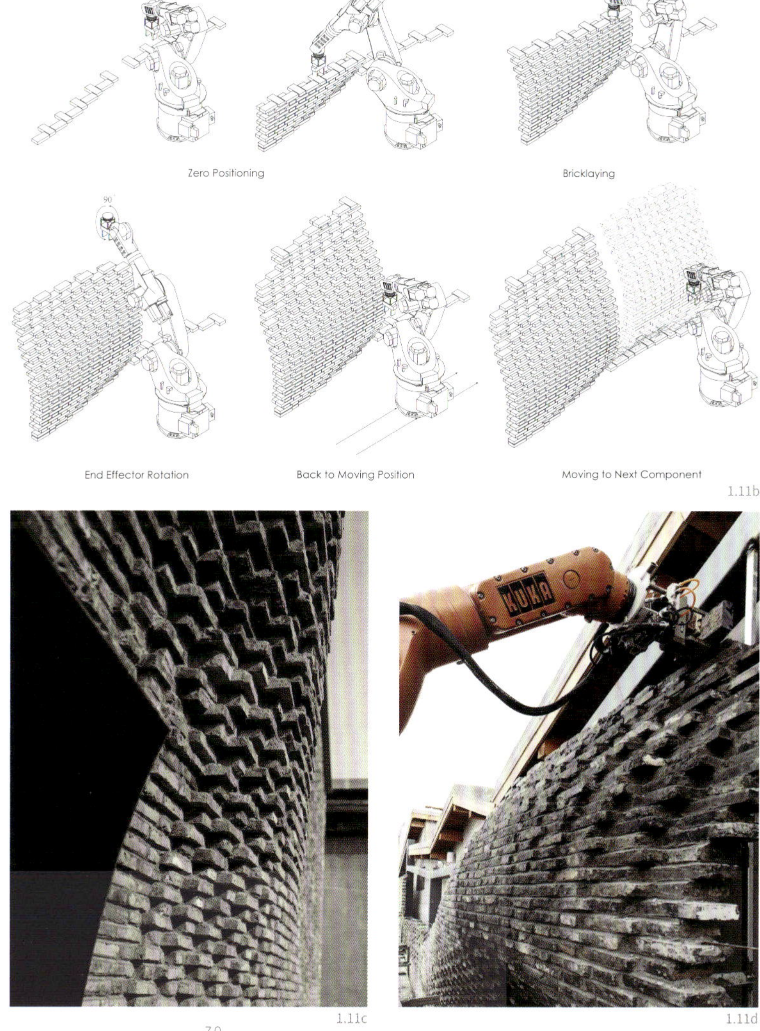

1.11b

1.11c

1.11d

Flight Assembled Architecture

Gramazio & Kohler + Raffaello D'Andrea

Built 2011-2012
Orléans, France

1.12b

Flight Assembled Architecture is one of the first architectural installations assembled by flying robots. The project was designed by Gramazio & Kohler in collaboration with Raffaello D'Andrea who led the design of the robotic system. The installation is comprised of 1,500 prefabricated polystyrene foam modules that culminate in a 6-meter-tall tower, 3.5 meters in diameter. It is a 1:100 scale model of what was originally conceived as a 600-meter-high "vertical village"—a megastructure for 30,000 inhabitants to be located in the rural area of Meuse outside of Paris. The project addresses radical new ways of thinking and materializing architecture as a physical process of dynamic formation. An exploration of aerial fabrication in architecture, the installation was constructed in eighteen hours during a four day-long live exhibition at the FRAC Centre (Fonds Regional d'Art Contemporain) in Orleans, France. It was assembled by four quadrocopters, collaborating according to mathematical algorithms that translate digital design data into the behavior of communicating mobile agents. These hovering robotic vehicles operate as a swarm of living architectural machines that are interactively programmed and synchronized to dynamically lift, transport, and assemble the aggregate building units through their choreographed movements. Distinct from the fixity of robotic arms and computer numerical control (CNC) machines that are limited by predefined working areas, thus constraining the size of the object that they can act upon, the aerial robotic vehicles are not confined by such limits. The space that flying machines can act upon is substantially larger than the size of the machines themselves, making it feasible for them to work on such structures at a 1:1 scale, offering architecture a new framework for realization.

1.12a

1.12c

Helix
Matter Design
Built 2013
Boston, United States

Helix is a half-scale spiral stair. While this reduced size resolves a number of practical concerns—weight, liability, access—the piece celebrates its impracticality. It is both column and stair, yet hangs from the ceiling. The stair expresses a form of "plastic rhetoric." The solid, heavy, and volumetric action of casting concrete transforms a liquid matter into a solid mass that wants to crack. The stair's plastic and curvaceous treads reflect the materials earlier liquid state. Its twisting phenomenally accelerates as it wraps around the support column, appearing to re-plasticize the figure, and thus resisting its perception as a composite made up of stacked, discrete elements. The construct's organic and malleable appearance is counterintuitive in light of the zero-tolerance system of nesting and keying from unit to unit. The stair is produced with precast unreinforced concrete, a material that has minimal tensile capacity thereby rendering this project as a structural prototype to assess some claims as the design team moves closer to stone as a testing material. Each tread is cast in a fully encapsulated custom rubber mold that is embedded in a solid wood mother mold to clamp the assembly together. The molds are vibrated rigorously during the pouring process and then immediately steamed for twelve hours to cure.

The entire stair assembly hangs from a beam two stories tall. This beam then drops down a threaded rod to a base that serves as a pendulum balance. Each tread is designed to hook over this threaded rod and be bolted down to its neighbor below. The geometry of these treads lock into each other with a series of three-dimensional keys that reduce any shear or slipping between units. Typically a stone spiral stair is held from the perimeter. In this case, the stair is compressed in the column to ensure stability.

1.13a

1.13b

1.13c

1.13d

1.13e

Round Room
Matter Design
Built 2014
Cambridge, United States

1.14a

Round Room, located in the Keller Gallery at MIT is a translation of the Inca wedge method into a digital process that manifests in the baroque tradition of sculpting mass and volumetrically shaping space through the use of an interior model. A stacked aggregate defined by the divisive logics of tessellation rather than the addition of repetitive elements, Round Room is composed of unique units carved with a water-fed robotic arm. This method of cutting ensures that each stereometric unit shares its boundaries with its adjacent hexagonal cells and is therefore aligned perfectly and packed tightly with its neighbors along its visible (interior) edges. Following the Inca wedge method, the exterior edges of the aerated concrete blocks (hidden within the poché) are conversely spaced more openly to allow mortar to be packed in from behind. In contrast to typical masonry construction that relies on in-situ adjustment and that employs mortar for tolerance, this method of neighboring alignment relies on precision carving to inform the assembly. In this case, the mortar is fill. Inherent to this process is a direction to the assembly—an interior and an exterior condition—thus re-engaging the rubble-fill wall, a ubiquitous type in the history of volumetric architecture, whereby precision is visible, and fill is utilitarian. This method is anti-isomorphic. The perimeter vermiculated box contrasts with the voluptuous interior, each rendered as mass and volume. While this project samples knowledge from the Incas, it advances this knowledge by translating their method into three-dimensional space. The complex figure of Round Room is assembled without the requirement of alignment jigs or formwork since the precise registration of units is determined by the local figuration of unique masonry units. The purpose of this research is not, however, to revert to a form of antiquated architecture, but rather to re-inform contemporary practice with the knowledge of the past and, by expanding the performance of volumetric methods, to consider alternative spatial opportunities for development.

1.14b

1.14c

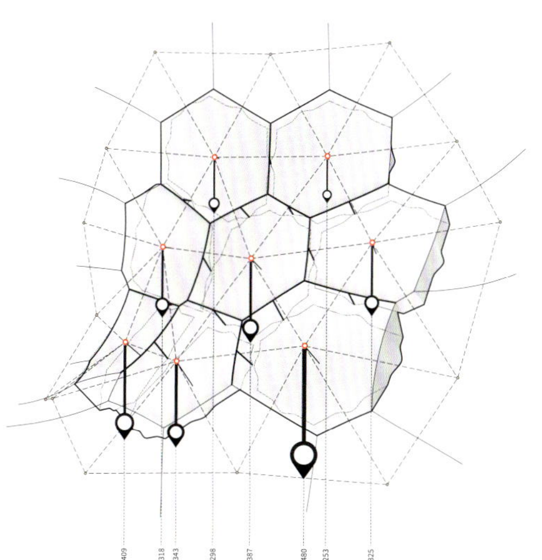

1.14d

1.14e

1.14f

Sean Collier Memorial MIT

Höweler + Yoon

Built 2015

Cambridge, United States

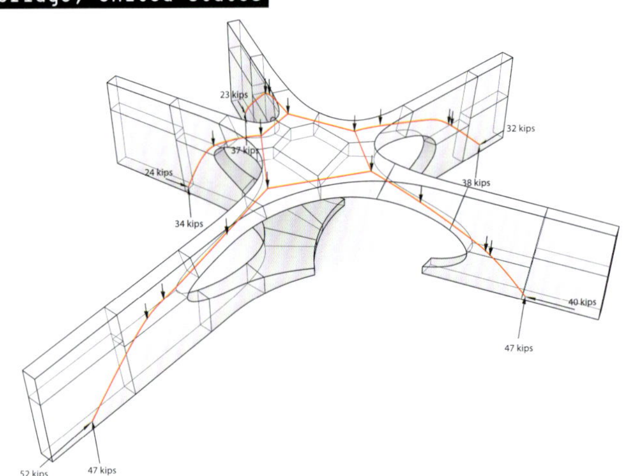

1.15a

1.15b

Situated on the MIT campus, the Collier Memorial—created in honor of Officer Sean Collier—marks the site of tragedy with a timeless structure—translating the resilience of the MIT and Boston community in the wake of the Boston Marathon bombings into a space of remembrance through a form that embodies the concept of strength through unity. The memorial is composed of thirty-two blocks of granite that form a five-way stone vault. Each block supports the other to create a covered space for reflection. The Collier Memorial evokes a star shape as well as an open hand, referencing MIT's motto, *Mens et Manus* (Mind and Hand). The ovoid space at the center of the radial walls creates a passage, a marker, and an aperture that reframes the site. The design combines traditional structural techniques for spanning masonry vaults with digital fabrication and structural computational technologies to create an unprecedented form. Although giving the appearance of operating in suspension, the vaulted structure relies on the exact fit of thirty-two stone blocks to transfer loads in pure compression from stone to stone. The exactitude of the fit required for this project prompted a different approach to its fabrication and the development of interactive design software that enabled feedback between geometry and structure in real time. The didactic visualization of forces evident in the Memorial's structure is consistent with MIT's ethos of openness and transparency, while the idea that all five walls are needed to achieve a stable form is symbolic of a community coalescing to commemorate a loss. The Memorial offers the opportunity to remember Officer Sean Collier and honor his life and service, while representing the shared values of openness in the face of threat, unity through diversity, and strength through community.

1.15c

1.15d

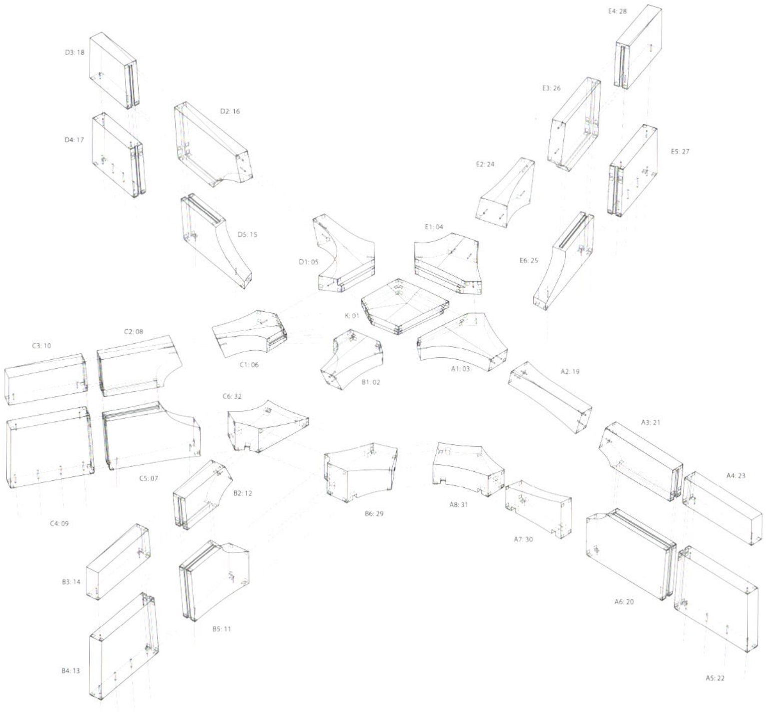

1.15e

1.15f

1.15g

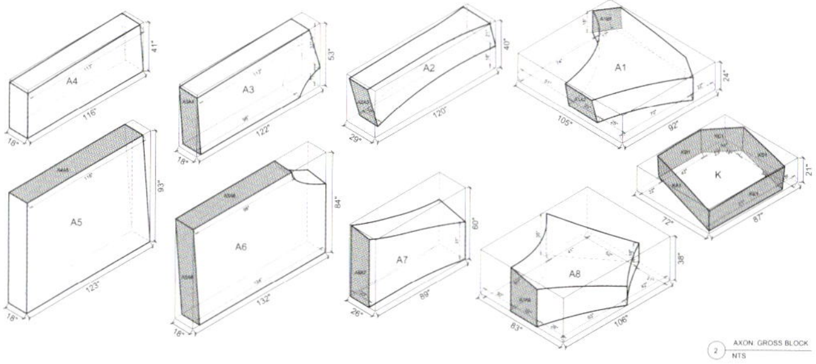

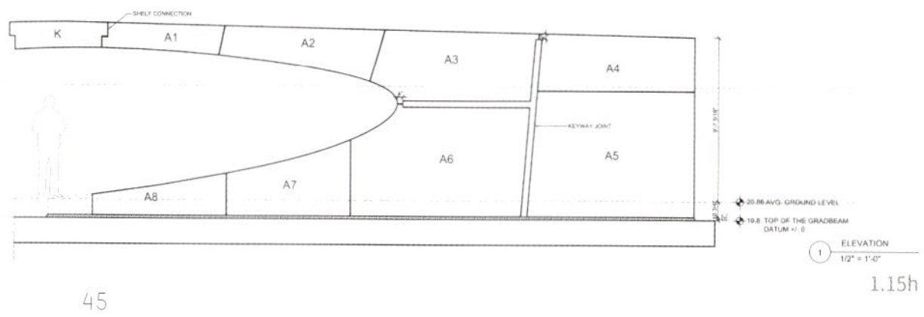

1.15h

Rock Print
Gramazio Kohler Research / Self Assembly Lab MIT
Built 2015
Chicago, United States

1.16a

Rock Print is the first architectural installation to be built from low-grade, granular material and constructed by precision robotics. Exemplifying a full-scale 3D "rock printing process," it was designed to display the potential of jammed structures in architecture at the inaugural 2015 Chicago Architecture Biennial, "The State of the Art of Architecture," where it was exhibited as a four-meter-high centerpiece in one of the Chicago Cultural Center's largest rooms. The installation presents a radically innovative approach, bringing forward a new category of randomly packed, potentially fully reusable, poly-dispersed jammed structures that can be automatically fabricated in nonstandard shapes. The structure, an intriguing vertical object, is a towering mass supported by four tapering legs, that is configured out of rock and string, two ordinary materials with opposite structural behaviors. Combining the compressive strength of the gravel, the tensile strength of the string, and the digital control of the amalgamation process of the materials allows for the creation of solid structures with unique material properties. The base of the structure consists of four slender legs, indicating the structural capacities of the system, which meet and form the massive, star-shaped, and cantilevered upper body of the structure. The legs start with an almost round profile, growing toward their neighbors until they merge and extend to the boundary of the robotic operational range. The upper part accommodates a higher amount of mass than the lower, to increase the compression of the bottom part and thereby assure a stronger surface strength on the parts more exposed near the base. The construction system of Rock Print uses jamming, the physical phenomenon by which granular matter becomes rigid under certain conditions, when the free volume per particle is decreased, thereby increasing the strain between aggregates. The volumetric boundary of the object is defined by the string placement, which interlaces the granular matter and is responsible for the jamming phenomenon, guiding the overall geometry and structural behavior of the material. Removing the string therefore causes the complete collapse of the structure, enabling the full material reversibility and reusability of the aggregated materials. This large-scale architectural artifact exhibits additional distinct features such as structurally active interlocking, differentiated structural performance, while yielding high geometric flexibility and articulation.

1.16e

1.16f

1.16g

1.16h

1.16b

1.16c

1.16d

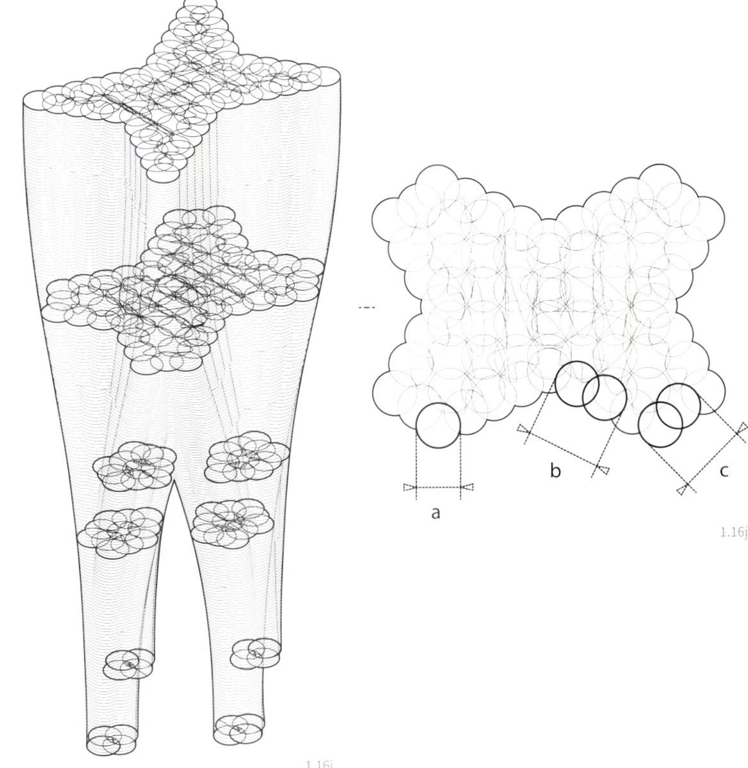

1.16i

1.16j

Generative Logic Curvature Resolution

Curvature can be implied through the use of short, straight segments. The smoothness of the curve or surface is inversely proportional to the size of the segment (i.e. as the segments get smaller, the curve appears smoother although it is still made of discrete straight segments). When designing with curved geometry, the designer can chose to create custom curved components or use more standardized straight elements to approximate a smooth appearance.

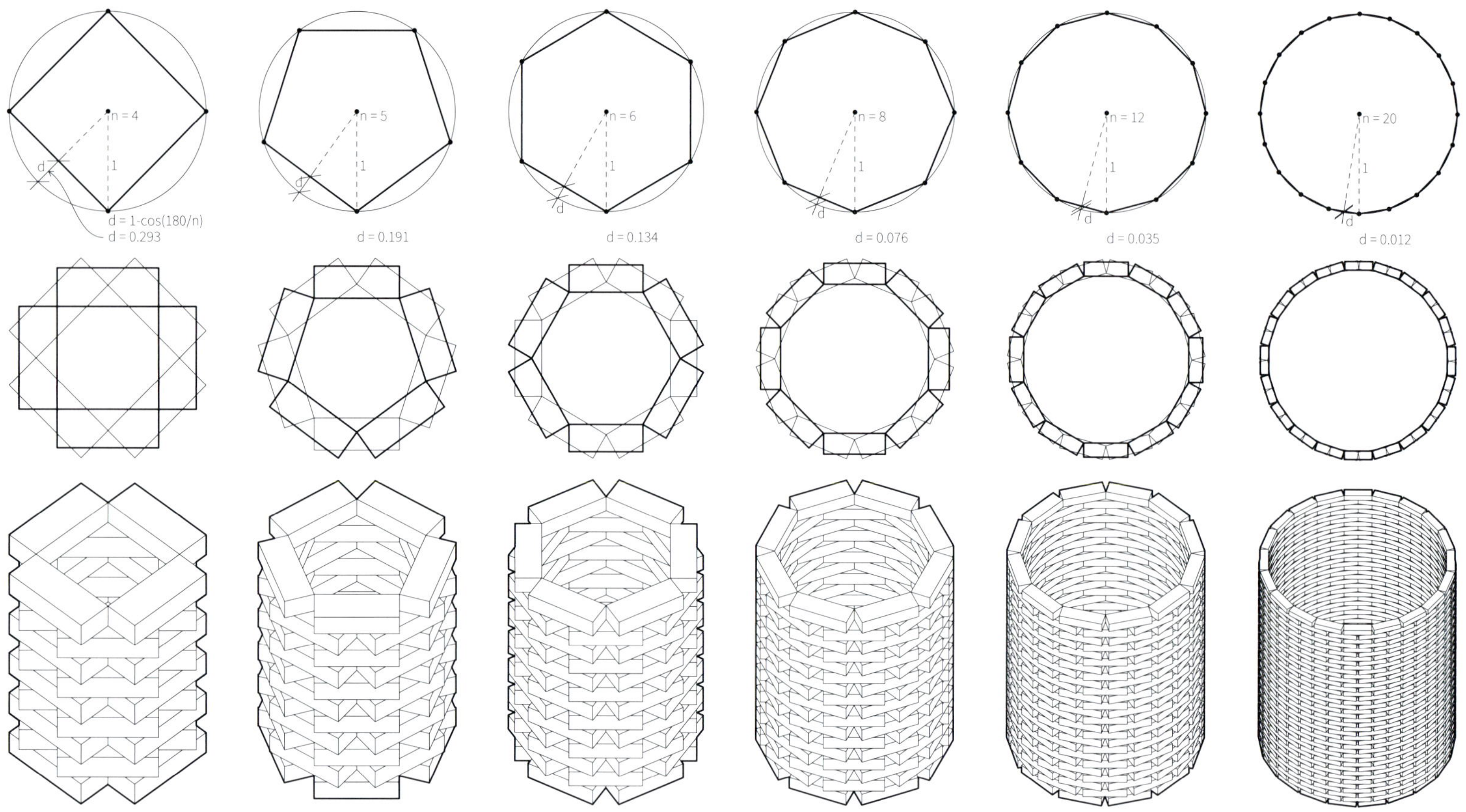

n = 4, d = 1-cos(180/n), d = 0.293

n = 5, d = 0.191

n = 6, d = 0.134

n = 8, d = 0.076

n = 12, d = 0.035

n = 20, d = 0.012

Generative Process Church of Christ the Worker

Eladio Dieste's Church of Christ the Worker uses surface curvature to increase the stiffness of both the walls and roof. The undulating curvature of the walls is achieved through small shifts in the orientation of each brick. Due to the time, labor, and accuracy needed to fabricate brick structures using this method, it has not gained wider use until the early 2000s through the use of automated robotic assembly.

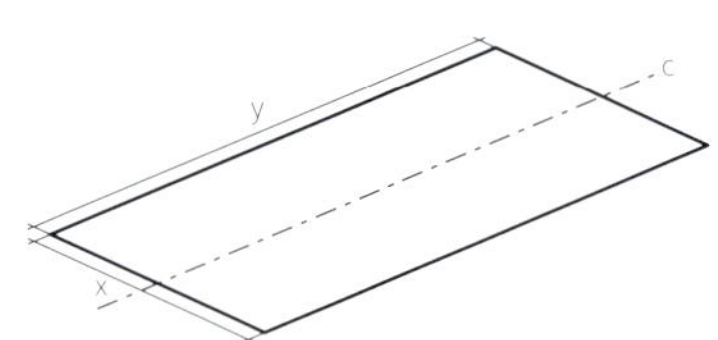

1. Establish Base Length (y) and Width (x) Dimensions about Center Axis (c).

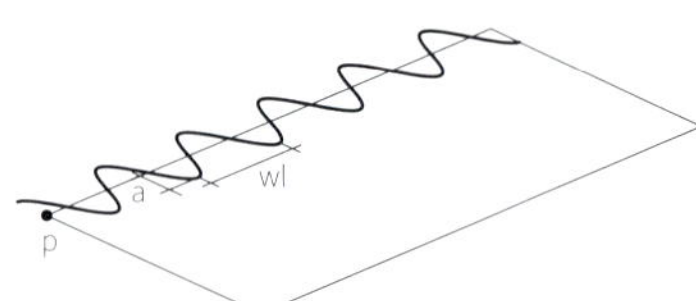

2. Create a Sine Wave Curve with desired Wave Count (wc), defined by Amplitude (a), Wave Length (wl), and Start Point (p).

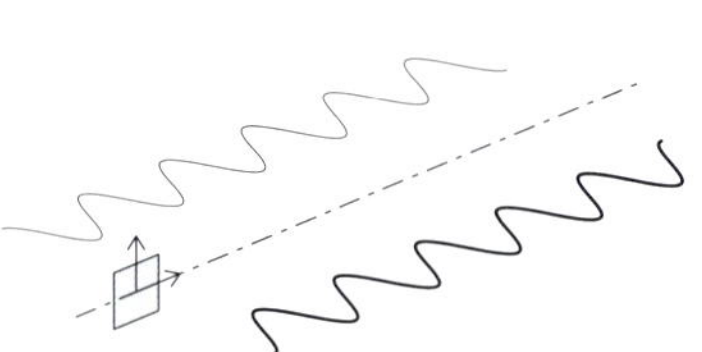

3. Mirror the Sine Wave Curve about Center Axis (c).

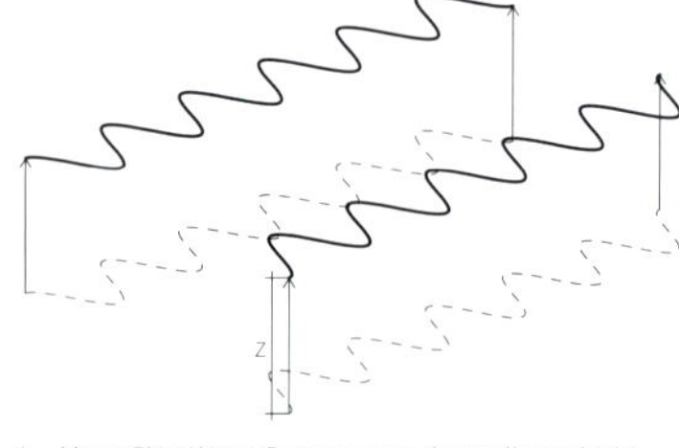

4. Move Sine Wave Curves up to the Wall Height (z).

5. Loft Sine Wave Curves with Wall Base Lines to create Ruled Surfaces.

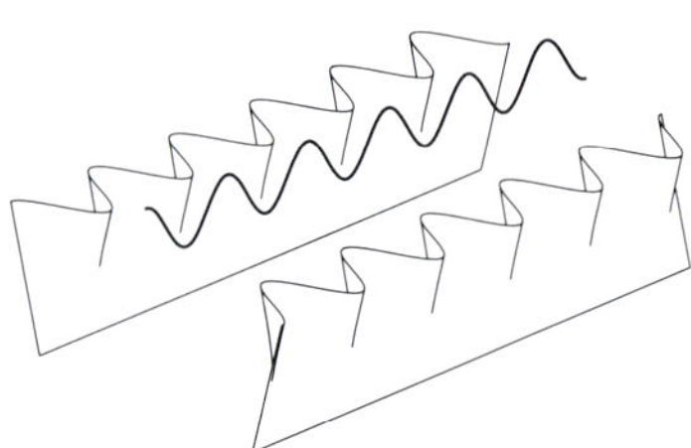

6. Create third Sine Wave Curve along the Central Axis.

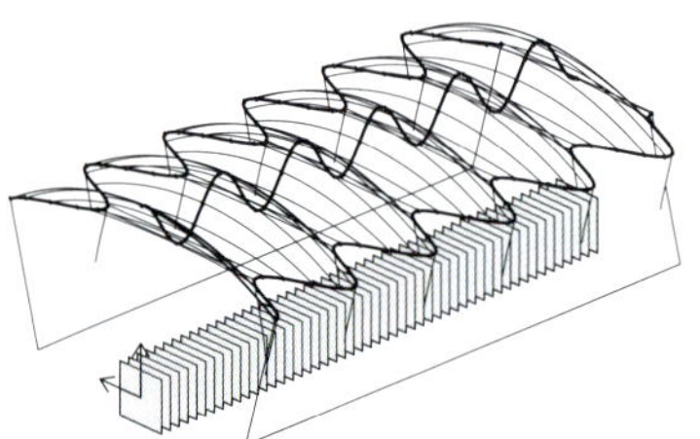

7. Intersect Sine Wave Curves with planes perpendicular to the Central Axis. Create Roof Curves from the resulting intersection points.

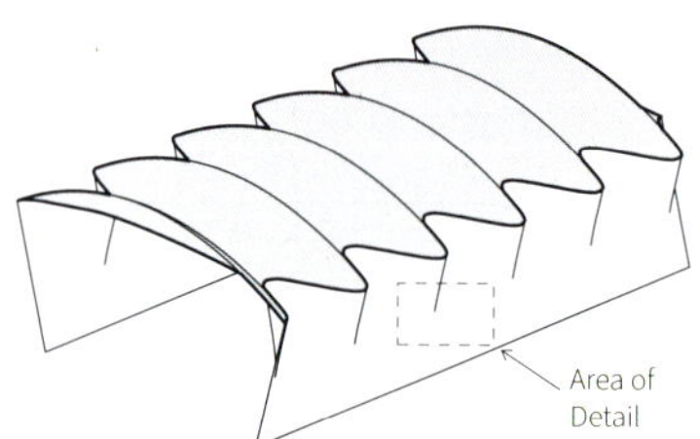

8. Loft Roof Surface from the Roof Curves.

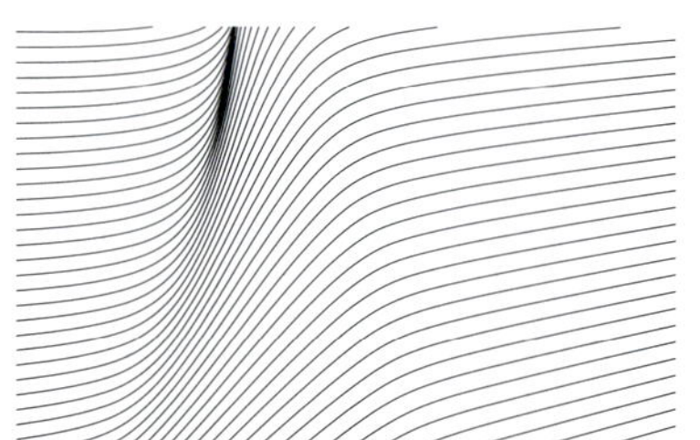

9. Section Walls into the Brick Courses based on Brick Height (bh).

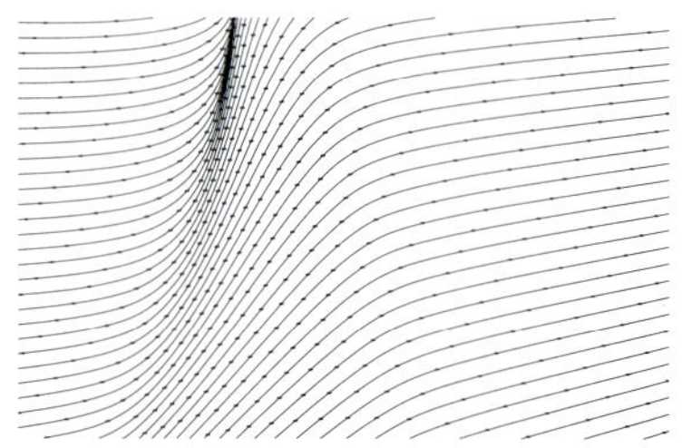

10. Divide Curves based on Brick Length (bl).

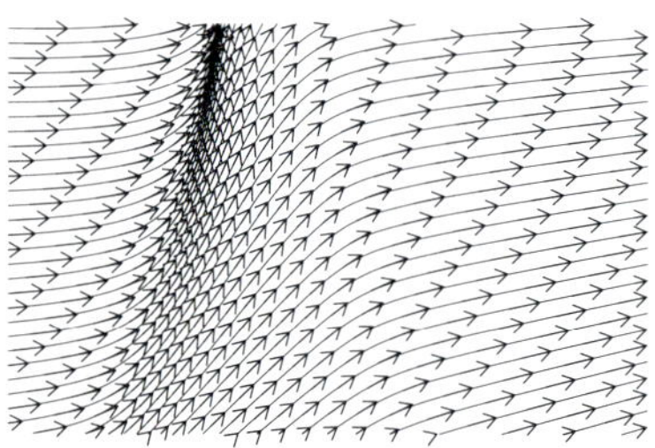

11. Align Planes with Curve Tangents.

12. Construct bricks at each plane.

Generative Matrix

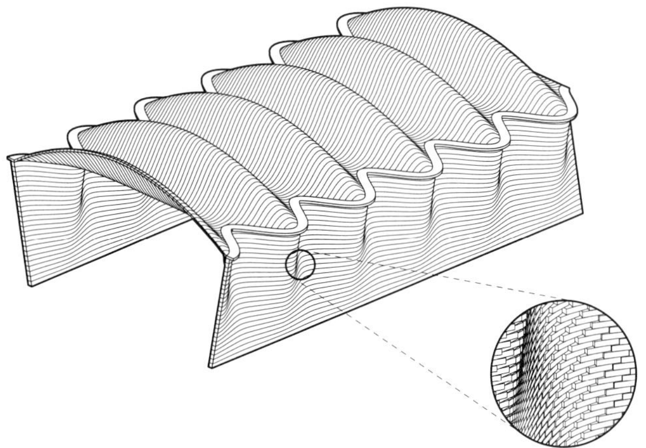

x = 30 m
y = 15 m
z = 7.5 m
c = 0°
bl = 300 mm
bw = 150 mm
bh = 75 mm
wc1 = 0.0
a1 = 0.0 m
p = 0.0
wc2 = 5.5
a2 = 1.5 m
p2 = 0.0
wc3 = 5.5
a3 = 1.5 m
p3 = π/2

Control Model

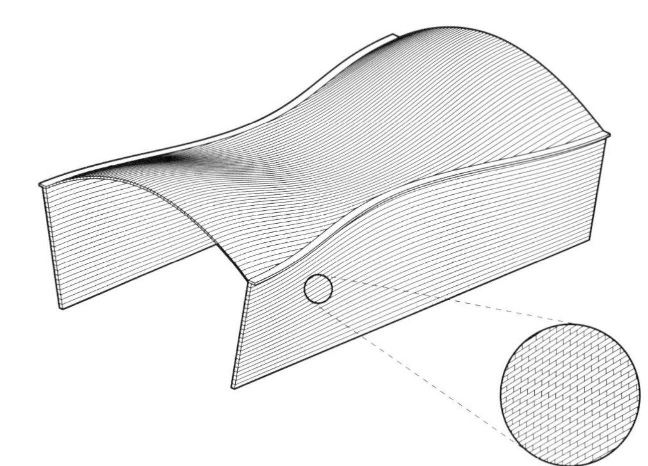

x = 30 m
y = 15 m
z = 7.5 m
c = 0°
bl = 300 mm
bw = 150 mm
bh = 75 mm
wc1 = 0.0
a1 = 0.0 m
p = 0.0
wc2 = 1.0
a2 =1.5 m
p2 = 0.0
wc3 = 1.0
a3 = 1.5 m
p3 = π/2

Single Wave

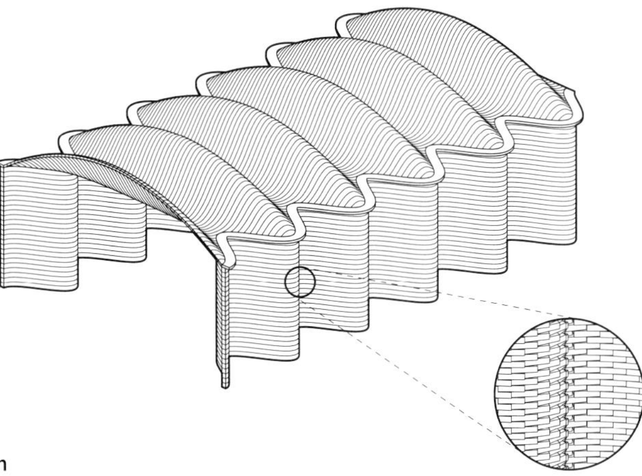

x = 30 m
y = 15 m
z = 7.5 m
c = 0°
bl = 300 mm
bw = 150 mm
bh = 75 mm
wc1 = 5.5
a1 = 1.5 m
p = 0.0
wc2 = 5.5
a2 = 1.5 m
p2 = 0.0
wc3 = 5.5
a3 = 1.5 m
p3 = π/2

Straight Extrusion

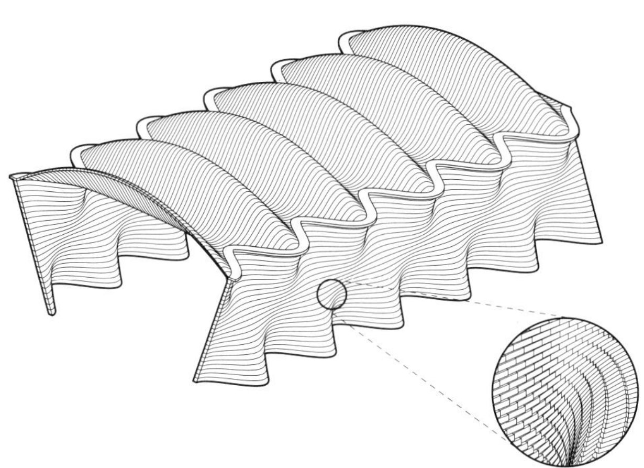

x = 30 m
y = 15 m
z = 7.5 m
c = 0°
bl = 300 mm
bw = 150 mm
bh = 75 mm
wc1 = 5.5
a1 = 5.0
p = π
wc2 = 5.5
a2 = 1.5 m
p2 = 0.0
wc3 = 5.5
a3 = 1.5 m
p3 = π/2

Inverse Waves

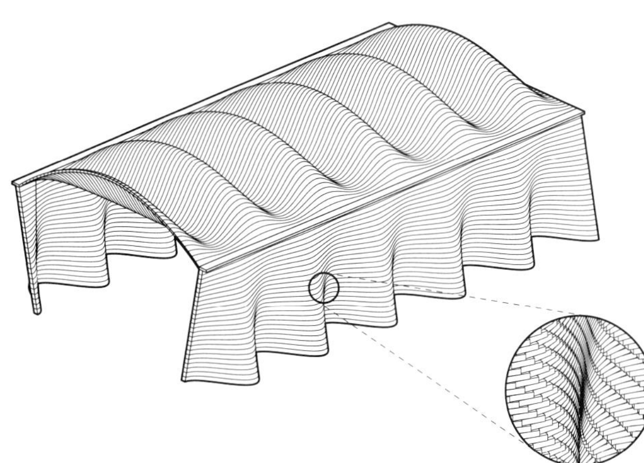

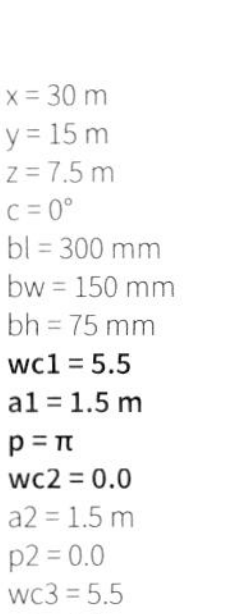

x = 30 m
y = 15 m
z = 7.5 m
c = 0°
bl = 300 mm
bw = 150 mm
bh = 75 mm
wc1 = 5.5
a1 = 1.5 m
p = π
wc2 = 0.0
a2 = 1.5 m
p2 = 0.0
wc3 = 5.5
a3 = 1.5 m
p3 = π/2

Straight Eaves

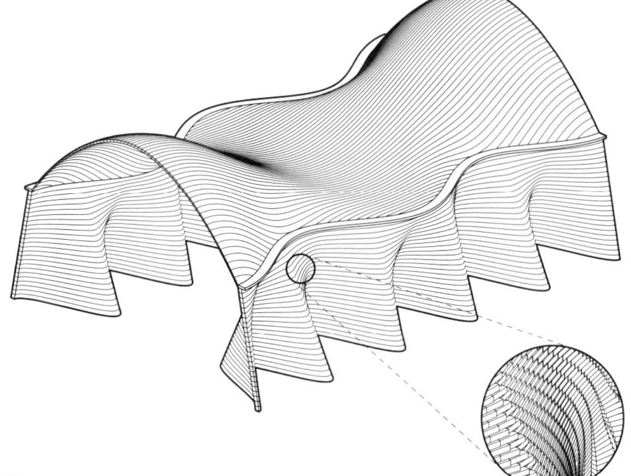

x = 30 m
y = 15 m
z = 7.5 m
c = 0°
bl = 300 mm
bw = 150 mm
bh = 75 mm
wc1 = 5.0
a1 = 3 m
p = 0.0
wc2 = 2.0
a2 = 1.5 m
p2 = 0.0
wc3 = 1.0
a3 = 3 m
p3 = π/2

Misaligned Waves

x = 30 m
y = 15 m
z = 7.5 m
c = 30° - 190°
bl = 300 mm
bw = 150 mm
bh = 75 mm
wc1 = 0.0
a1 = 0.0 m
p = 0.0
wc2 = 5.5
a2 = 1.5 m
p2 = 0.0
wc3 = 5.5
a3 = 1.5 m
p3 = π/2

Curved Centerline

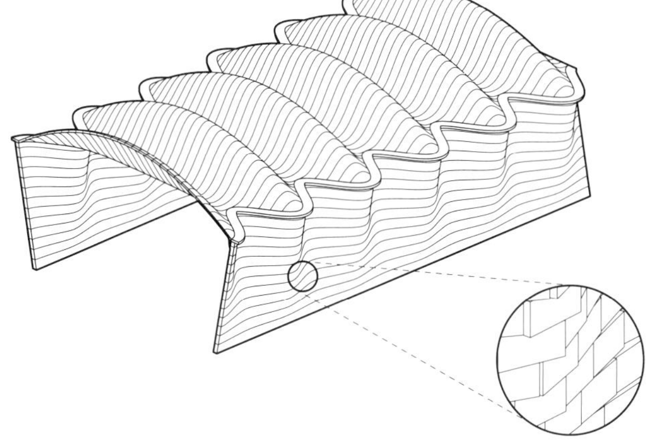

x = 30 m
y = 15 m
z = 7.5 m
c = 0°
bl = 915 mm
bw = 457 mm
bh = 457 mm
wc1 = 0.0
a1 = 0.0 m
p = 0.0
wc2 = 5.5
a2 = 1.5 m
p2 = 0.0
wc3 = 5.5
a3 = 1.5 m
p3 = π/2

Larger Bricks

Generative Logic
Unit Property Variation

Gradients can be achieved by incremental translation and rotation of a modular unit or through incremental profile variation within custom units across a set domain. The visual effect of gradation is directly related to the unit's dimensions, domain of variation, and pattern of change across the surface. In addition to gradations of translation, rotation, and form, other properties of the unit such as color, texture, or reflectivity could be used to produce a gradient effect.

Translation

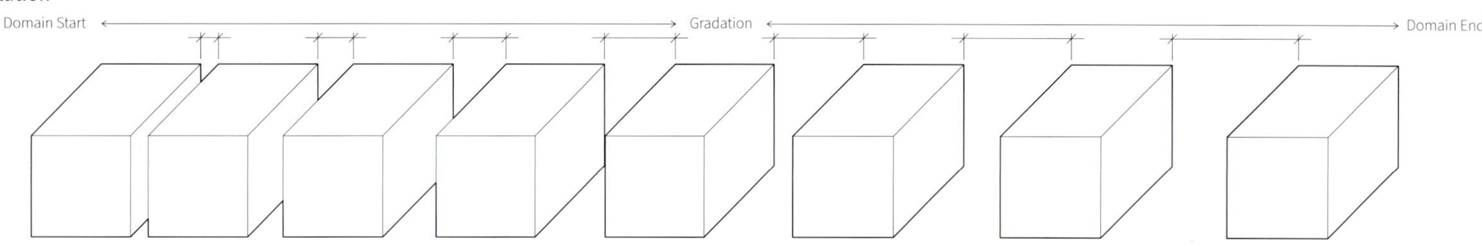

Rotation

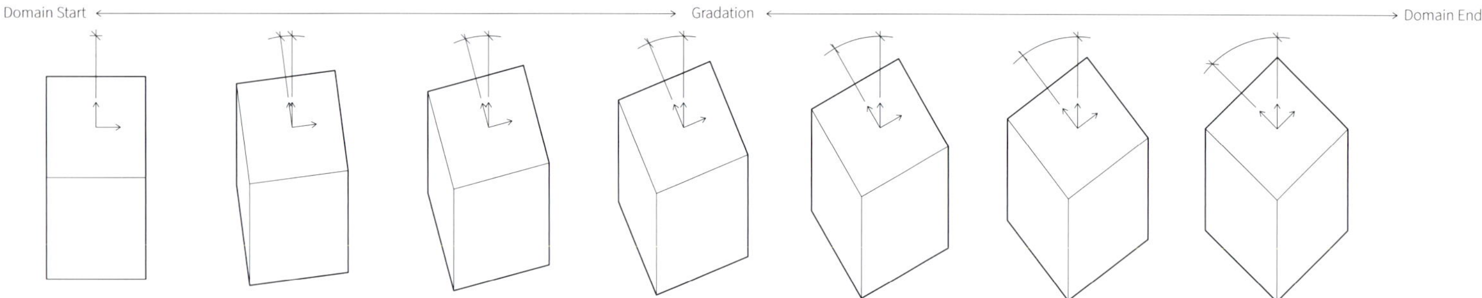

Form

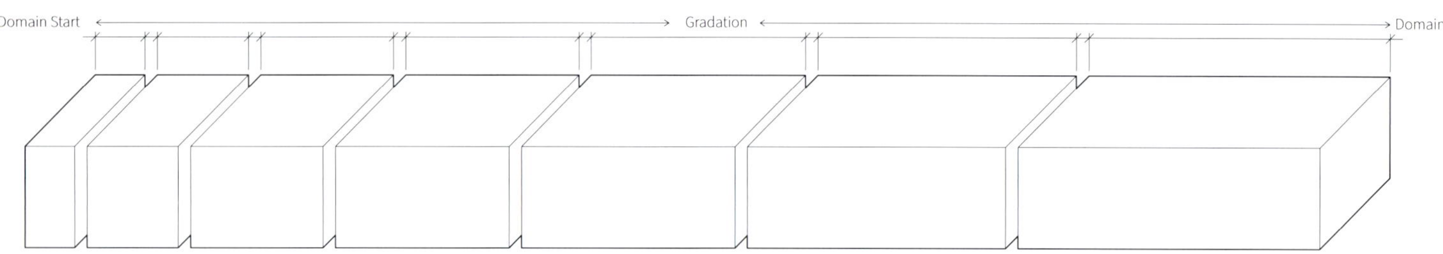

Generative Process
Casa la Roca

Casa la Roca uses at least four methods of variation in relation to modular units: translation of unit (1) on the second floor of the front façade to modulate privacy in the bedroom, rotation of unit (2) at the living room to modulate view from the living room, rotation of groups of units (3) to produce a twisting chimney, and a combination of translation and rotation (4) to produce a folded brick curtain enclosing an outdoor room.

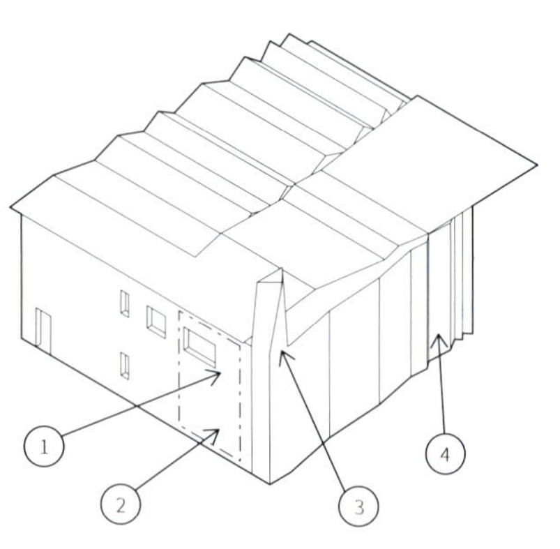

1. Of the four areas that modular variation is deployed, the following diagrams focus on areas 1 and 2.

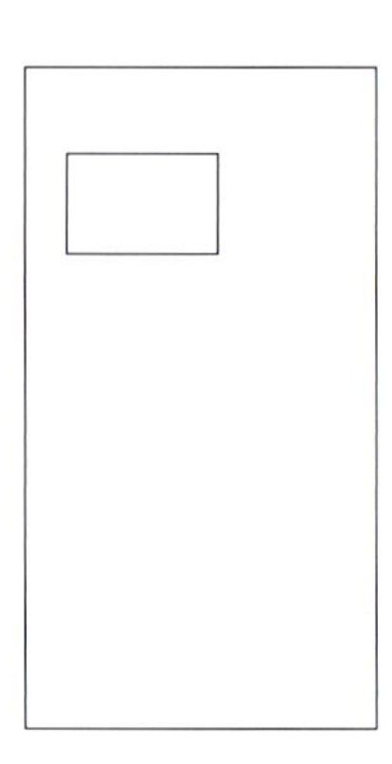

2. Establish Base Wall Surface

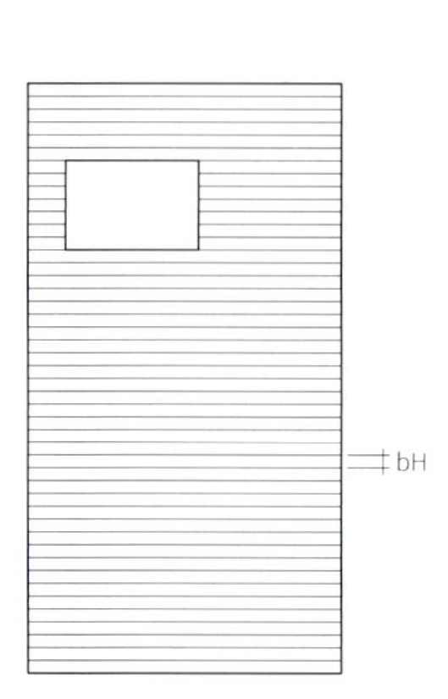

3. Section Wall into Brick Courses by Height (bH)

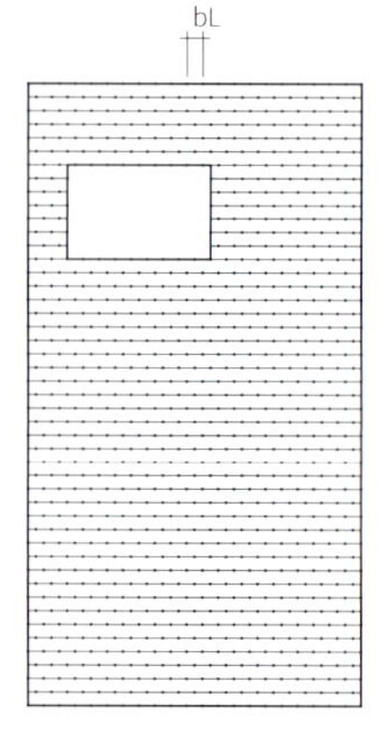

4. Divide Curves based on Brick Length (bL)

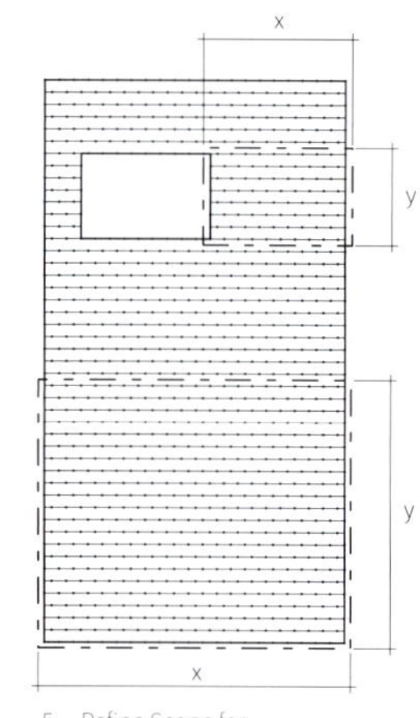

5. Refine Scope for Operations

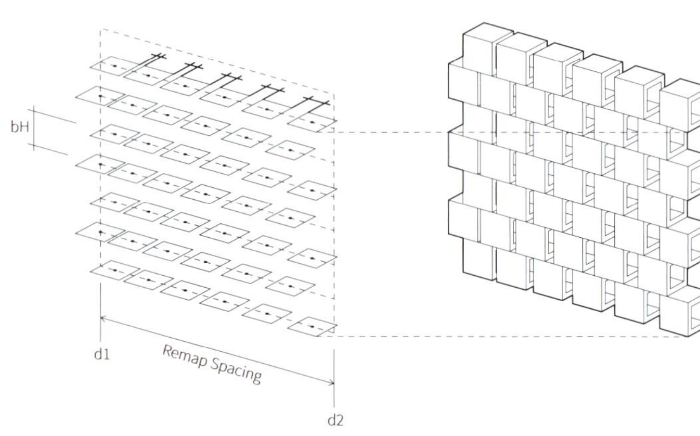

6. Define Domain Start (d1) and End (d2) for Brick Spacing and Remap Horizontal Locations

7. Place Bricks on Planes

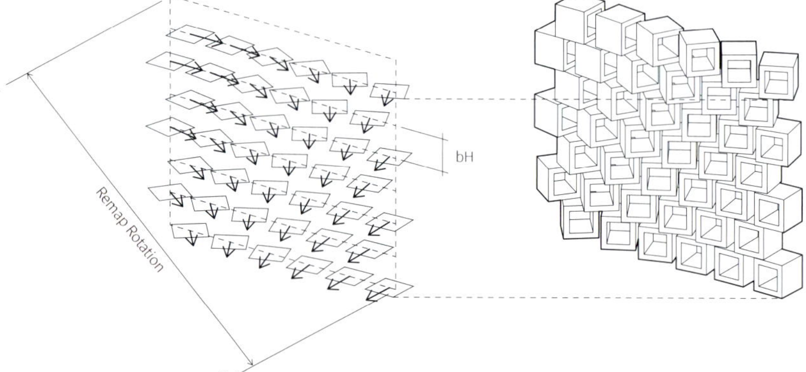

8. Define Domain Start (d1) and End (d2) for Brick Rotation and Remap Plane Orientations

9. Place Bricks on Planes

Generative Matrix

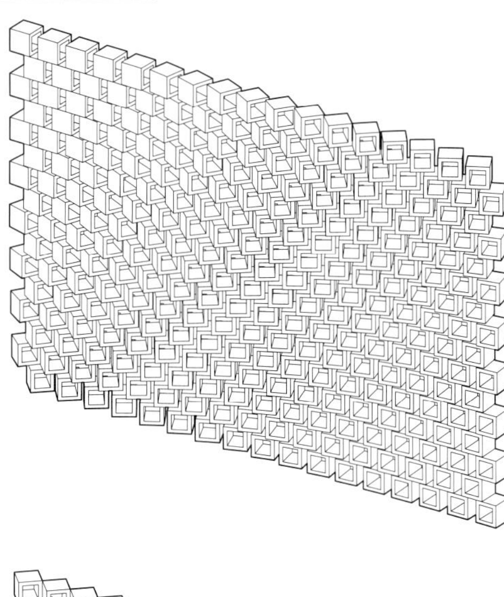

bL = 152 mm
bW = 152 mm
bH = 152 mm
x = 3660 mm
y = 2400 mm
d1 = 0°
d2 = 90°
Pattern = 45° Linear

Rotation Control Model

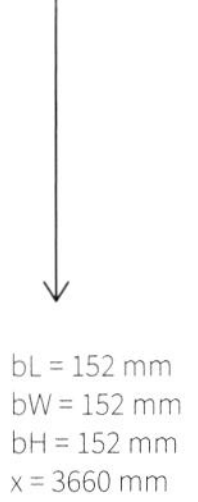

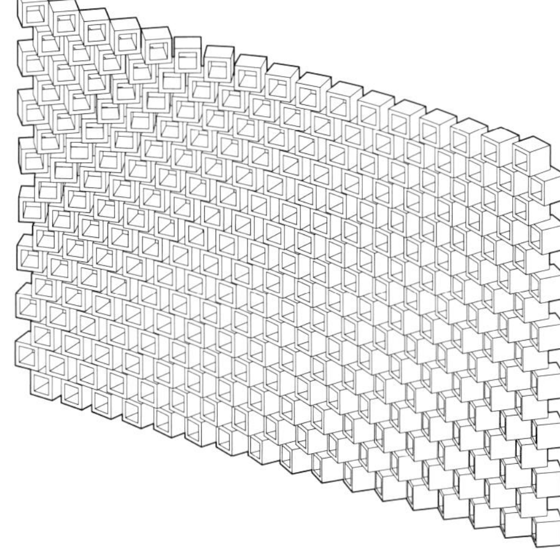

bL = 152 mm
bW = 152 mm
bH = 152 mm
x = 3660 mm
y = 2400 mm
d1 = -45°
d2 = 45°
Pattern = 45° Linear

Domain Change

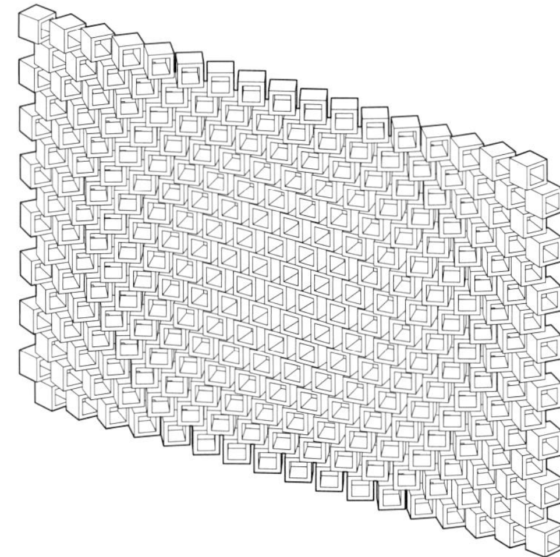

bL = 152 mm
bW = 152 mm
bH = 152 mm
x = 3660 mm
y = 2400 mm
d1 = 0°
d2 = 90°
Pattern = Radial

Radial Variation

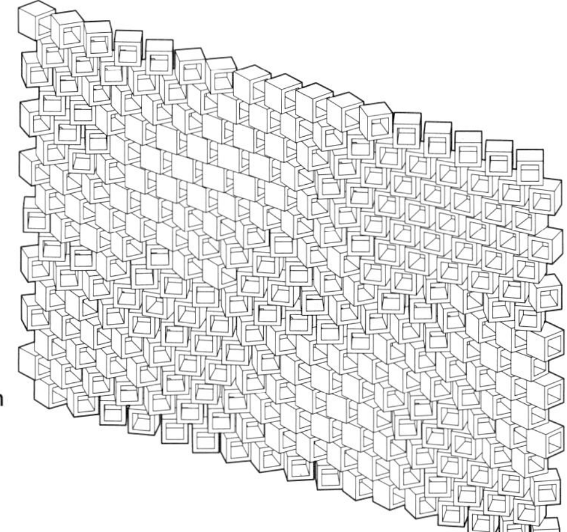

bL = 152 mm
bW = 152 mm
bH = 152 mm
x = 3660 mm
y = 2400 mm
d1= 0°
d2 = 90°
Pattern = Image Map

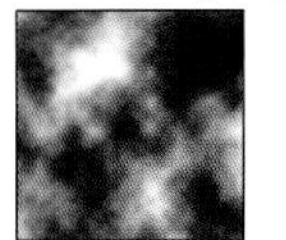

Image Map Variation

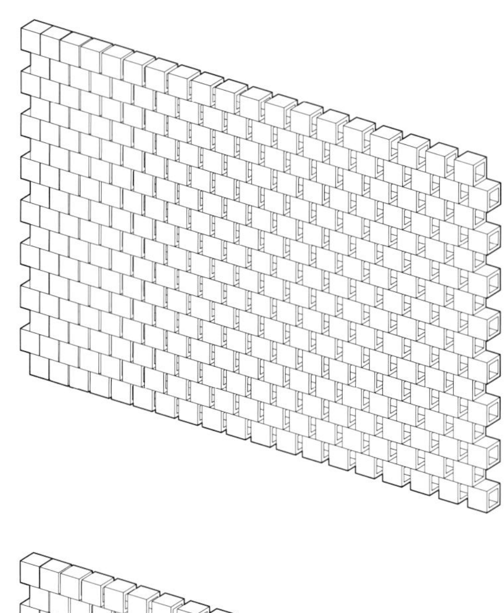

bL = 152 mm
bW = 152 mm
bH = 152 mm
x = 3660 mm
y = 2400 mm
d1 = 0 mm
d2 = bL*0.5 mm
Pattern = Linear

Translation Control Model

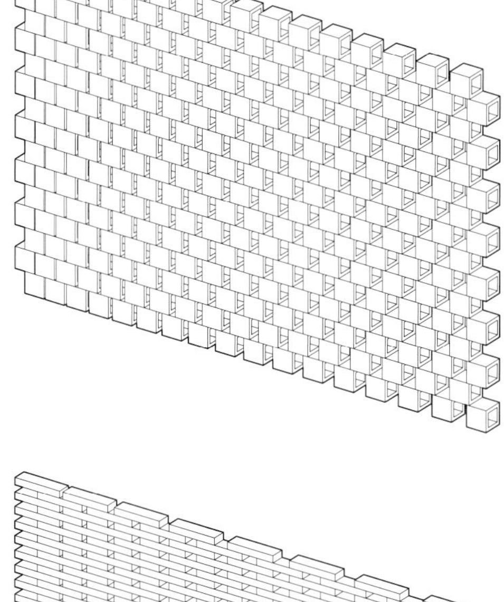

bL = 152 mm
bW = 152 mm
bH = 152 mm
x = 3660 mm
y = 2400 mm
d1 = 0 mm
d2 = bL*0.75 mm
Pattern = Linear

Domain Change

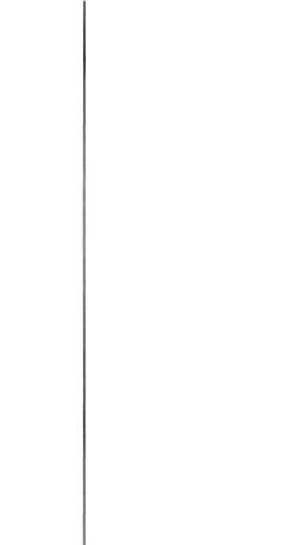

bL = 356 mm
bW = 102 mm
bH = 152 mm
x = 3660 mm
y = 2400 mm
d1 = 0 mm
d2 = bL*0.5 mm
Pattern = Linear

Unit Dimension

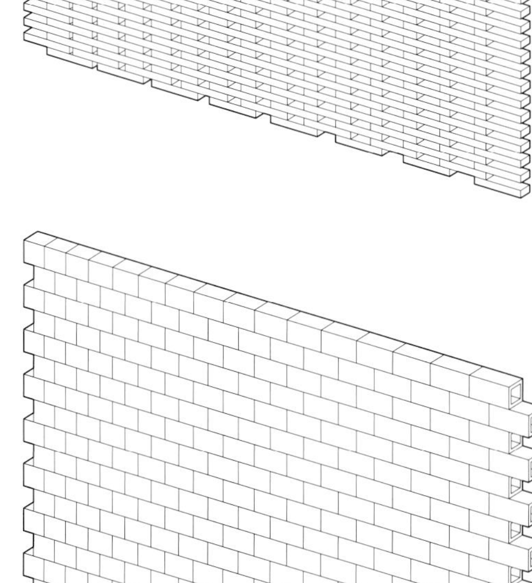

bL = Range 152 - 304 mm
bW = 152 mm
bH = 152 mm
x = 3660 mm
y = 2400 mm
d1 = bL mm
d2 = bL*2 mm
Pattern = Linear

Unit Length Variation

Generative Logic Fixed Length Chains

A fixed-length chain is a collection of modules that have a fixed length, but each module is free to rotate at each joint. Like a chain on a bicycle, the chain is flexible and can adapt to many forms while still being composed of repetitive elements. As the angle between modules decreases, the overall length of the chain remains constant but its perceived length (or area for closed loops) decreases.

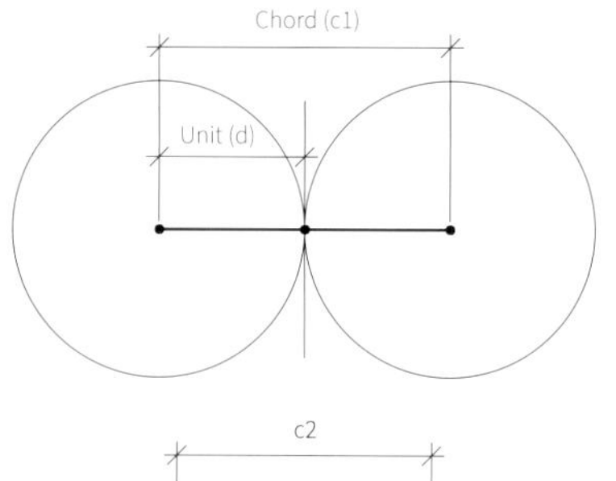

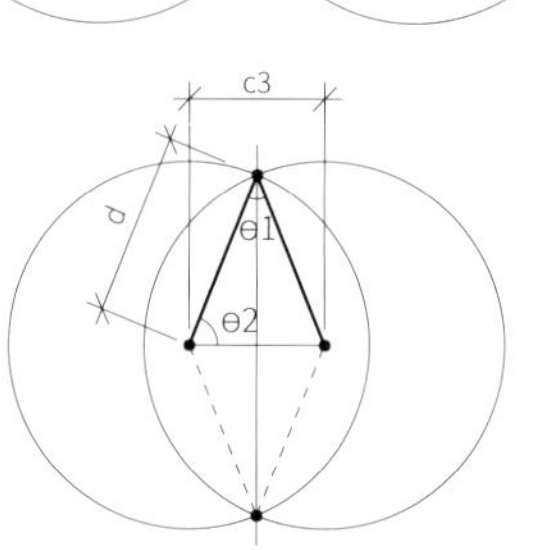

Linear Chain

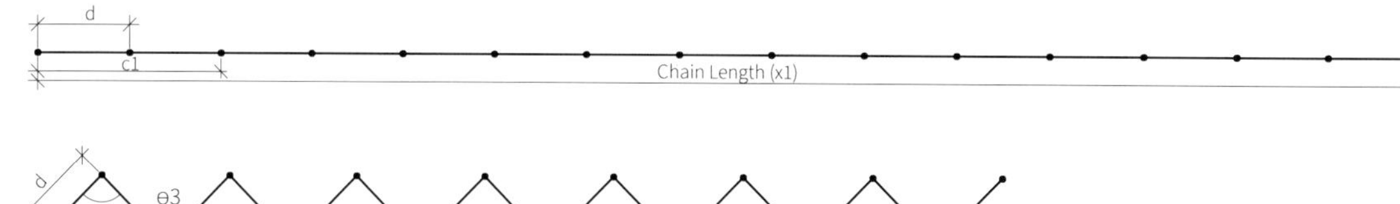

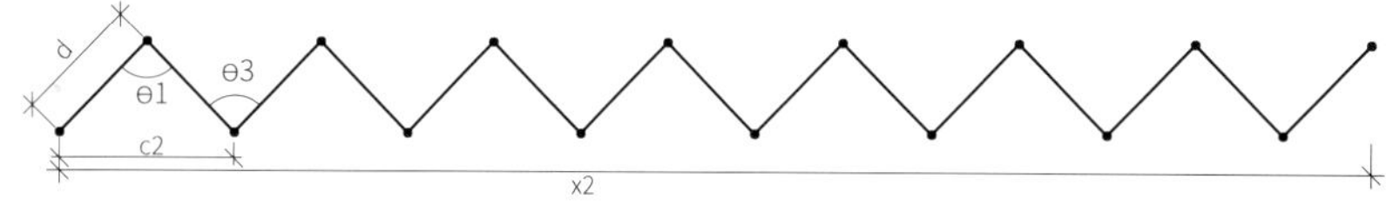

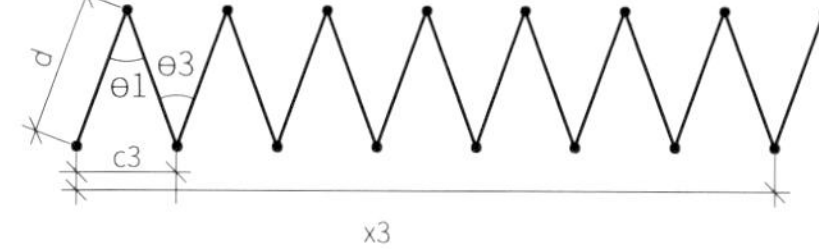

Continuous Chain

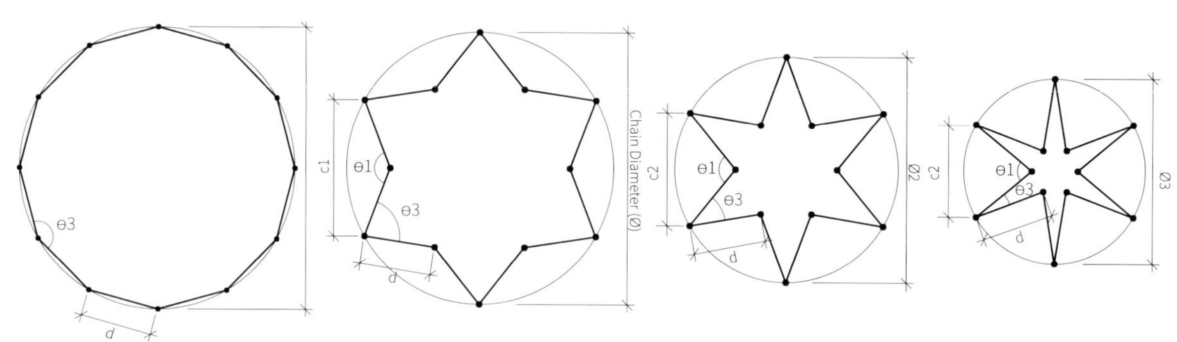

Generative Process Mantra Hookah Den

The Mantra Hookah Den uses a circular fixed-length chain composed of identical, stacked wooden units. As the diameter of the control geometry changes with its height, the units rotate in toward the circle's center.

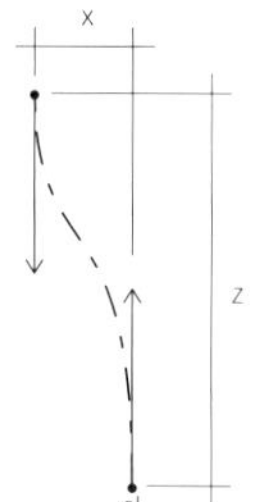

1. Establish centerline curve by height (z) and shift (x)

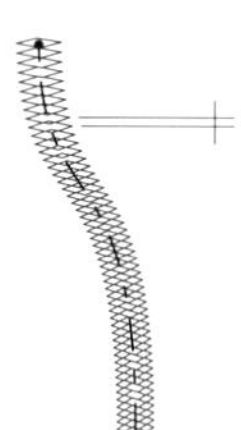

2. Divide centerline by unit height (h)

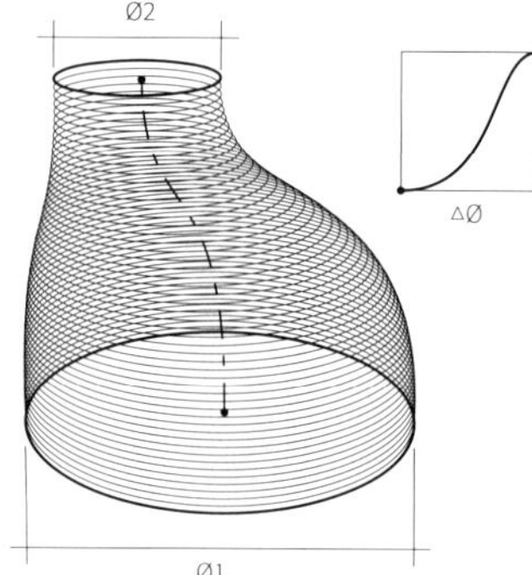

3. Define diameter domain start (Ø1) and end (Ø2) and pattern of change within domain (ΔØ)

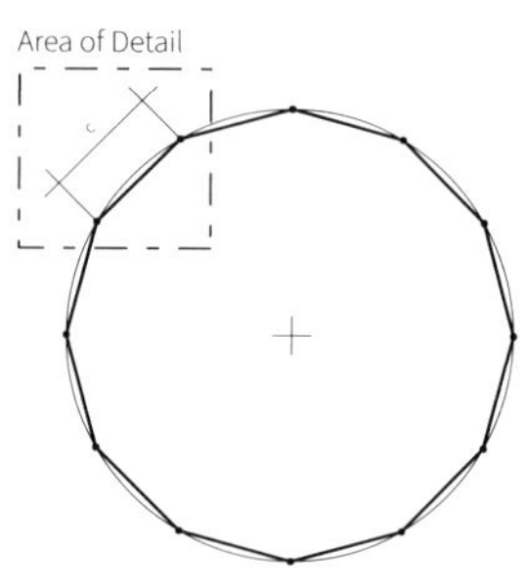

4. Divide circles by number of chords (cNum)

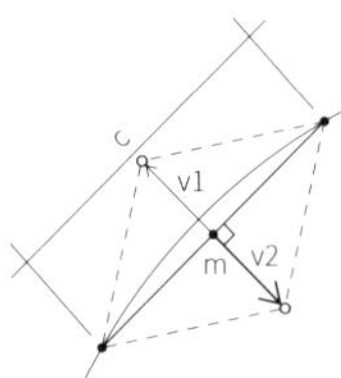

5. Find midpoint (m) of chord (c) and determine hinge direction (v1 or v2)

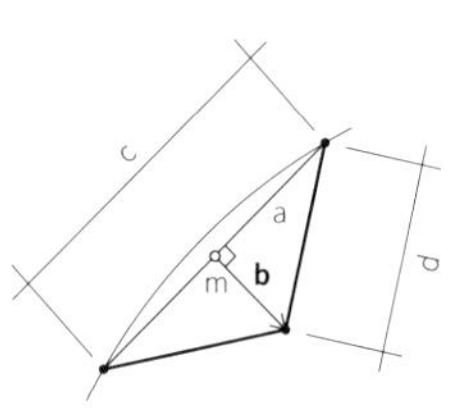

6. Solve for "b" to locate inner pivot between units, given unit length (d), a=d*0.5, b=√(d2+a2)

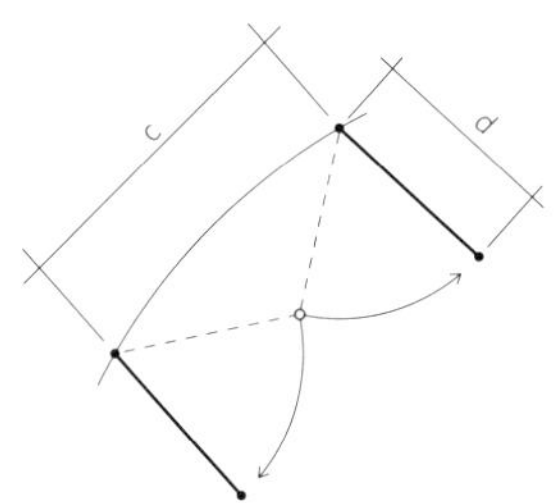

7. Rotate around outer pivots to define opening

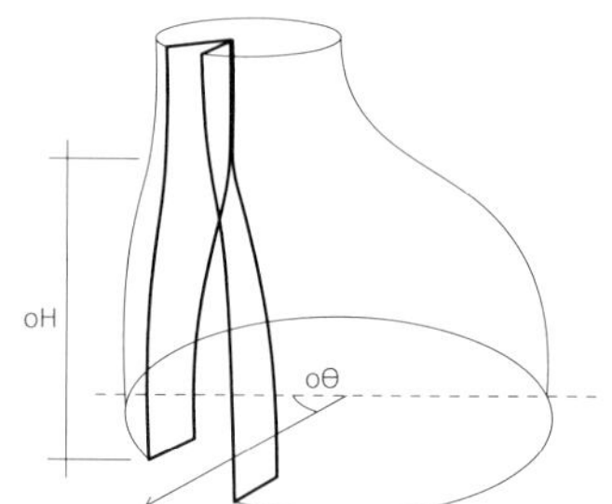

8. Define the opening height (oH) and the opening orientation (oθ)

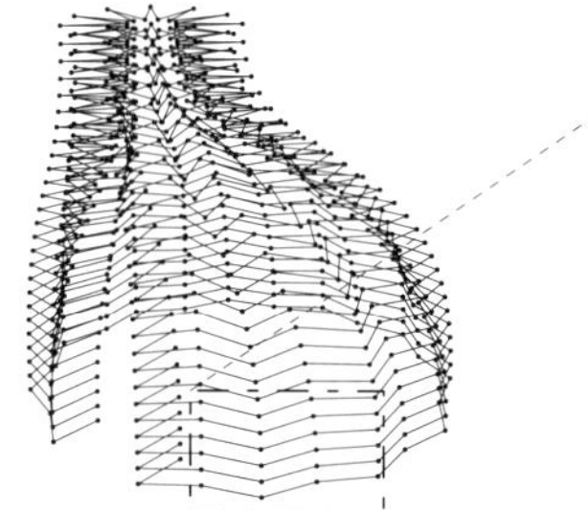

9. Connect outer and inner pivot point

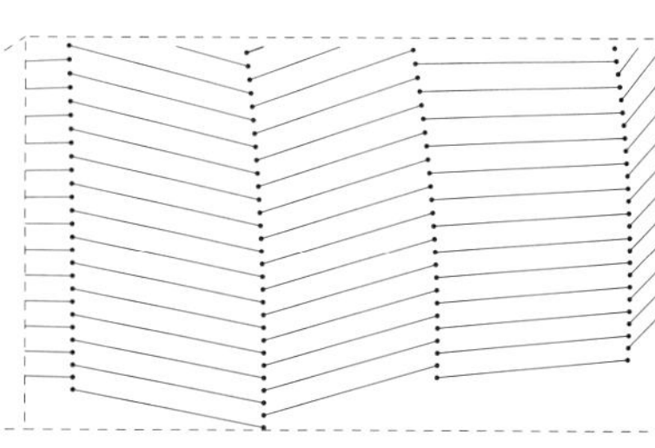

10. Remove members in alternating pattern

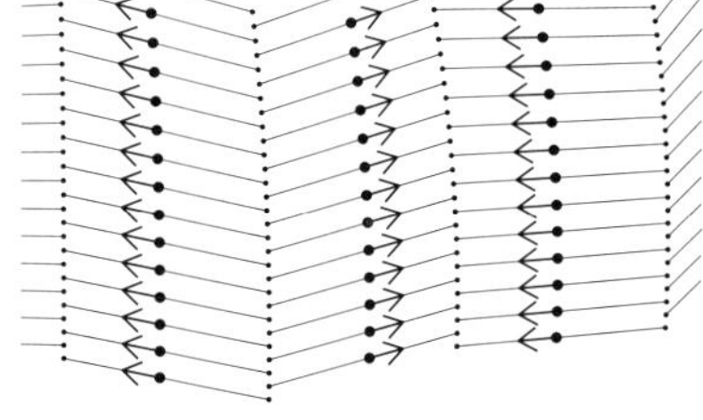

11. Align planes with members

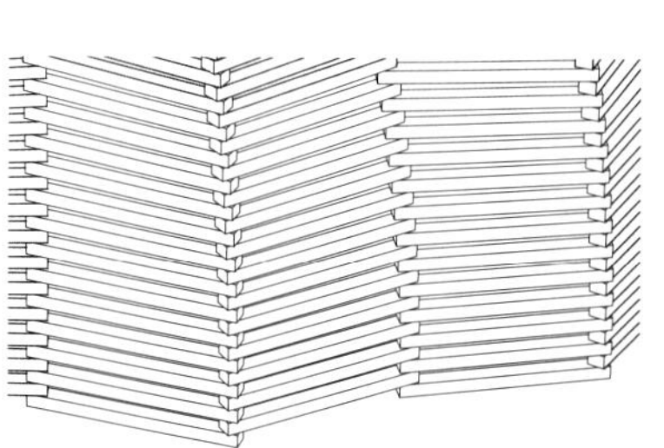

12. Place units on planes

Generative Matrix

d = 610 mm
w = 76 mm
h = 76 mm
x = 1.3 m
z = 4.1 m
Ø1 = 4.3m
Ø2 = 1.5 m
ΔØ = curve A

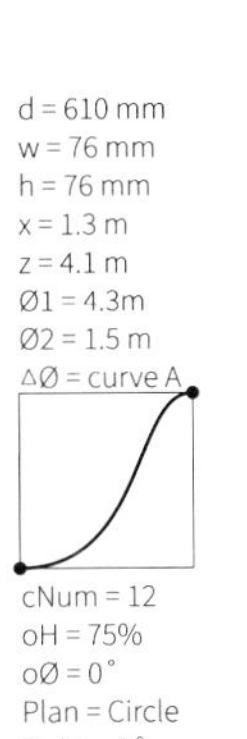

cNum = 12
oH = 75%
oØ = 0°
Plan = Circle
Twist = 0°

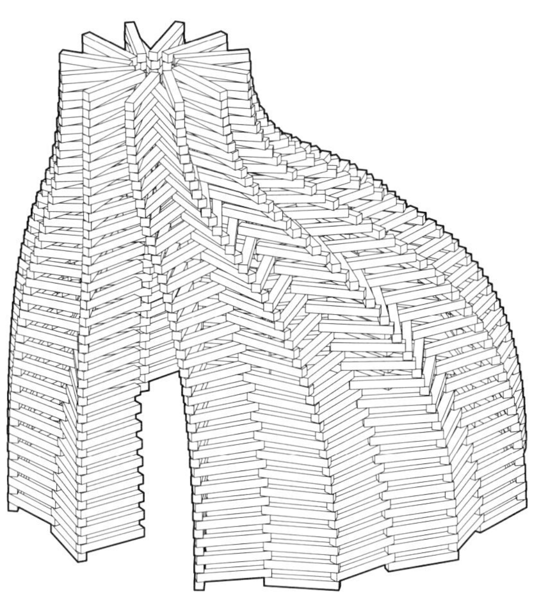

Control Model

d = 762 mm
w = 152 mm
h = 152 mm
x = 1.3 m
z = 4.1 m
Ø1 = 4.3m
Ø2 = 1.5 m
ΔØ = curve A
cNum = 12
oH = 75%
oØ = 0°
Plan = Circle
Twist = 0°

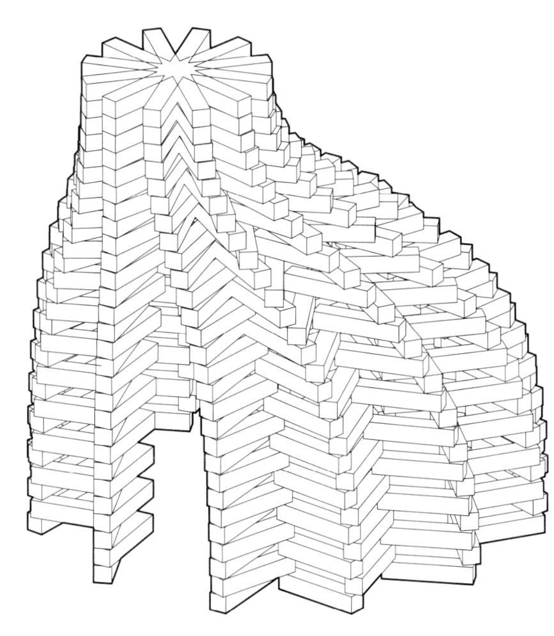

Unit Dimensions

d = 610 mm
w = 76 mm
h = 76 mm
x = 2.5 m
z = 5.1 m
Ø1 = 4.3m
Ø2 = 1.5 m
ΔØ = curve A
cNum = 12
oH = 75%
oØ = 0°
Plan = Circle
Twist = 0°

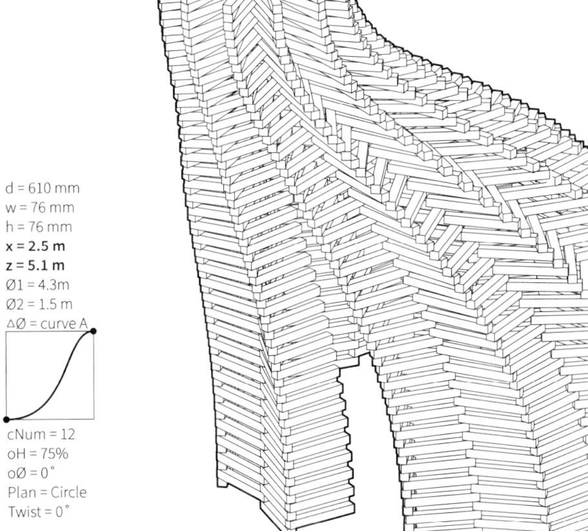

Centerline

d = 610 mm
w = 76 mm
h = 76 mm
x = 1.3 m
z = 4.1 m
Ø1 = 4.3m
Ø2 = 1.5 m
ΔØ = curve A
cNum = 12
oH = 75%
oØ = 0°
Plan = Circle
Twist = 0°

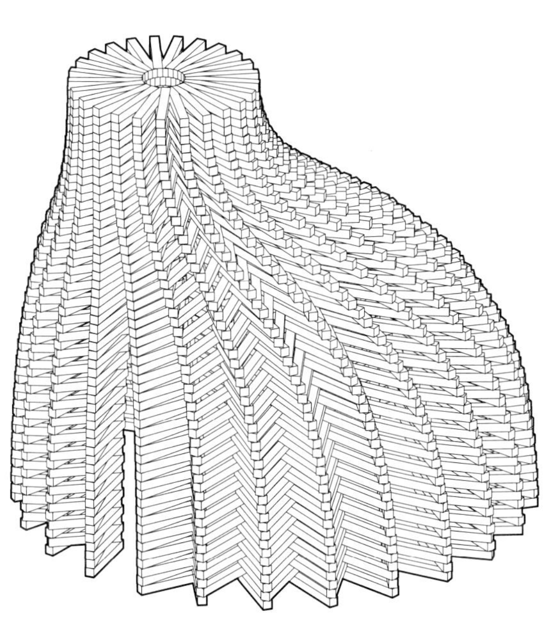

Fold Count

d = 305 mm
w = 76 mm
h = 76 mm
x = 1.3 m
z = 4.1 m
Ø1 = 5.1 m
Ø2 = 2.0 m
ΔØ = curve A
cNum = 24
oH = 75%
oØ = 0°
Plan = Square
Twist = 0°

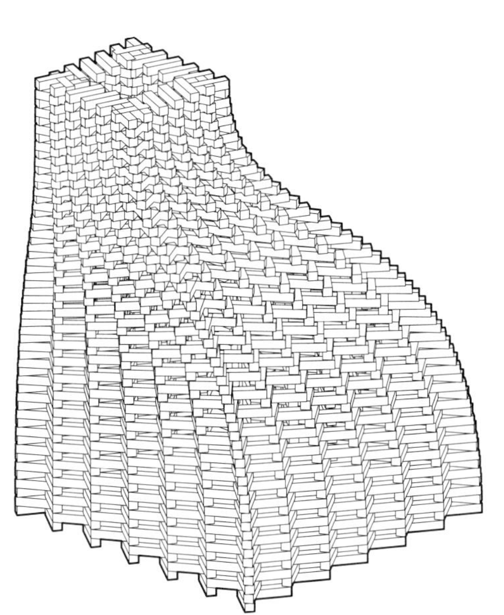

Plan Geometry

d = 610 mm
w = 76 mm
h = 76 mm
x = 0 m
z = 4.1 m
Ø1 = 5.1 m
Ø2 = 1.5 m
ΔØ = curve B
cNum = 10
oH = 50%
oØ = 0°
Plan = Circle
Twist = 90°

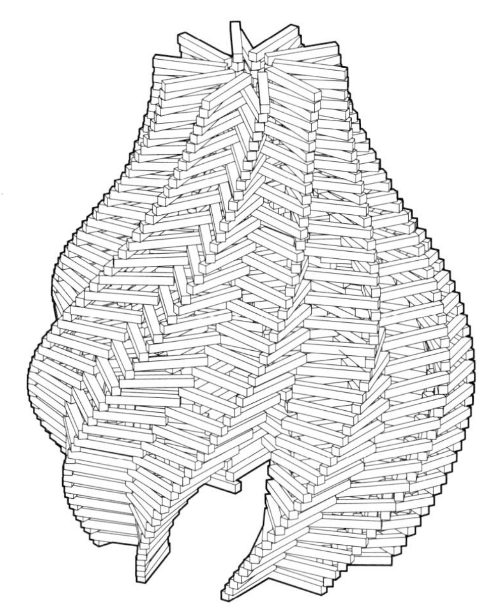

Twist

MODULAR ASSEMBLAGES
MODULAR ASSEMBLAGES

Modulation adjusts the dimensional or spatial properties of an object along a spectrum of values, yet expresses the transformative potential of the architectural component in clearly defined increments, discrete wholes, in order to exploit the distributive and combinatorial possibilities of the module as it assembles into different organizational patterns.

Components are designed to adhere to a set of standardized attributes or interfaces that enable them to connect or interact in multiple ways. This allows elements to be exchanged within the system and therefore provides a range of potential options for adjacency and interconnection.

Modular Assemblages

Part-to-Whole Relations and Genetic Families

Modular assemblages are aggregative multiplicities composed of a family of individuated yet interrelated similar elements. The module is simultaneously part and whole. It is a fractional unit or partial component that is intrinsically connected to the larger whole (the "parent") from which it was derived, as well as an independent self-contained entity, a subsystem or element, that can be interchanged or rearranged within a closed organizational system. First divide, then recombine. The "modular," Le Corbusier's attempt to realign abstract forms of measurement with the dimensional spectrum of the body, expresses the desire of the modulus to establish a seemingly organic continuum of relations across a range a variable elements, each of which exhibits a particular degree of difference with respect to the other elements within the system. Modulation adjusts the dimensional or spatial properties of an object along a spectrum of values yet expresses the transformative potential of the architectural component in clearly defined increments, discrete wholes, in order to exploit the distributive and combinatorial possibilities of the module as it assembles into different organizational patterns.

That modular elements evolve as a transformational series ensures that the typological and uniquely identifiable qualities of the object, those that contribute to its autonomy, are suppressed in order to foreground its relational or familial characteristics, those that link it to the other components of the genetic system and ensure a high degree of internal integration within the assemblage. Notwithstanding their ability to integrate internally, modular systems also often exhibit a great deal of internal flexibility. Components are designed to adhere to a set of standardized attributes or interfaces that enable them to connect or interact in multiple ways. This allows elements to be exchanged within the system and therefore provides a range of potential options for adjacency and interconnection. Whereas a tightly integrated design product is dependent on the customization of its individual parts whose specificity is also tied to its position and orientation within the configuration, thus restricting its flexibility, modular systems often "substitute loosely coupled forms for tightly integrated, hierarchical structures."[1]

Modular assemblages adhere to the five principles of new media proposed by Lev Manovich: numerical representation, modularity, automation, variability, and transcoding.[2] They are also inherently statistical in that they are constituted by a closed set of arrayed components that externally refer to a larger informational set. As such, in many cases (depending on the complexity of variables within the system) they can be understood as visually legible manifestations of the data required to produce them—materialized datascapes—whose elements have been rarified along a reduced spectrum of values so that their differentiation within the assembly is readily apparent. The patterning of this data, which is algorithmically dependent, is generated from a web of need-based requirements and their interrelationships. These are statistically represented by the number of each different type of module (the kind and number of variables), and the programmatic, material, or aesthetic parameters that can be digitally encoded and assigned arithmetic weights or values to guide their selection and distribution within the whole. The legibility of the materially encoded data is thus dependent on the formal complexity of the encoding process and the patterning of the range of elements within the field. Each assemblage therefore emerges out of the different types of information embedded in the system such as the various types of modular dwelling units and the demographics of urban populations to which these refer as in the MVRDV Delft Housing project ❶, or the rhythm of modular constructive systems, interior partitions, and cladding elements, and the tectonic, environmental or programmatic requirements that each of these fulfill, within the Berlin Free University project by Candilis-Josic-Woods and Prouvé.

Early and mid-twentieth century modular assemblages, which range from Moisei Ginzberg's prefabricated housing units for Green City to the Eames's case study houses and modular furniture systems, were intended to be simultaneously aesthetic signifiers and material indexes for the capacity of industry to displace traditional construction methods with prefabricated components that would be mass-manufactured and assembled according to the logics of industrial production. The significant change, however, in the development of more contemporary modular models that exploit digital processes, is in the range of mass-customizable components available

❶

❷

❸

❹

(those considered to be equally functionally efficient in that they potentially require no additional time or machinery to produce despite their formal diversity), and the complexity by which different variations of these prefabricated industrial components are patterned and assembled so that the continuous variation of parts is given as an intrinsic property of the whole.

When these two distinct forms of difference are added to the homogeneous repetition of the products of modernism, new temporal and spatial rhythms are generated. These reflect the complex algorithmic potential of tectonic systems when computational procedures dependent on automated forms of numerical representation, transcoding, and information-based production, as well as digital fabrication methods are incorporated into the design and construction process. Industrial parameters had instrumentalized time and capitalized on the economies of the "many" by exploiting industrial machinery's capacity for incessant repetition. The addition of computation to this system has enabled the integration of differentiation into this process. This has produced variation at the level of the development of the part through mass-customization, on the one hand, and the whole through endlessly adjustable transformational and combinatorial logics, on the other. This process is further complexified as the development of parts takes on modular attributes. This is evident in the Modular Variations project led by Adam Marcus of Variable Projects ❷, which employs molds assembled from reconfiguring a finite set of stackable, planar subcomponents into different sequences, such that combinatorial permutability becomes an essential trait of both part and whole.

The adaptability of the patterned logics of modulation is evident in the skin of the Porter House project by SHoP ❸, which employs a zinc panel system to clad a vertically extended, six-story volume that appears to intersect and cantilever over a historic brick warehouse building in Manhattan. The system, which cross-pollinates the dimensions of three different module widths and heights with three differentiated panel types—glazed, translucent (back-lit) and solid—is used to generate a variegated, rhythmic surface pattern that transforms the façade into a series of stacked bar codes that change its appearance from day to night ❹ as a reference to the dynamic culture and nightlife of the city in which it is situated. The dimensional relations of the panels themselves not only contribute to the perceived horizontal movements—the phenomenal stretching, compressing and stochastic lateral shifting—of the elements within each band that support the aesthetic reading of the work, but also enable the fabrication of the project to be optimized by calibrating the size and number of each of the modules to ensure that they could be efficiently laid out on, and cut from, standard sheets of zinc. Here, the evolution of the modular system, and the specificity of the seemingly random patterns produced, emerged not from the arbitrary placement of components, but rather from an optimization of the intersection of programmatic, tectonic, and aesthetic parameters.

In the Resolution Wall by Gramazio & Kohler ❺, the modular relationship of differently sized, aerated concrete cubes is established by the dimensions of their edges (5, 10, 20 and 40 cm), each of which is a fraction of the length of one of the sides of the largest cube. Although these dimensions are essentially fractional in nature, the logic of the additive system is dependent on the ability of cubes to recombine without remainder, that is, to ensure that the smaller units divide evenly into the larger ones without excess. In this sense, as with many modular systems, the smallest module acts as a standardized unit of measure and proportion against which all other elements in the system can be defined, and therefore forms a scaling device for the whole (1:2, 1:4 or 1:8). The modular scaling of units produces a higher degree of potential "resolution" as the concrete cubes decrease in size, enabling information to be expressed through patterned surface detail generated by localizing areas of finer grain (in the same way, for example, that smaller brush strokes or tiles are used to highlight intricate details) rather than either changing or adding materials or assuming, as within the optical pixelated space of the computer screen, that such detail is dependent on the consistent resolution of the entire surface. In the wall assembly, resolution varies with dimension producing a heterogeneous pattern of differentially sized elements, each of which adhere to the same formal, procedural, and material parameters ❻. This concept of differentiating areas of scalar resolution in relation to function is found

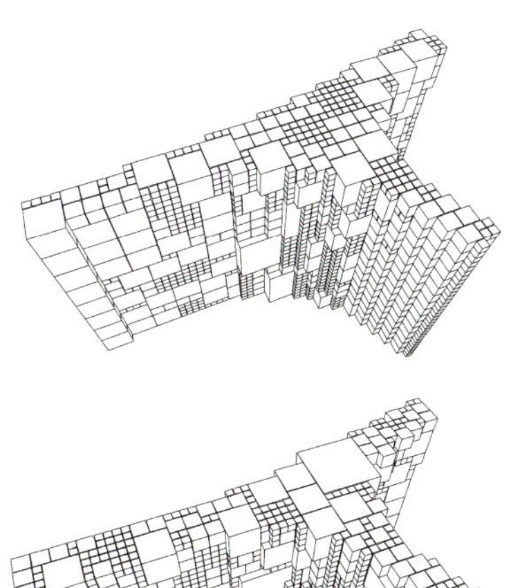
5

6

7

to be similar to biological models that often efficiently focus resolution where it is needed. This is exemplified in the ways in which nerve endings are densely clustered in the fingertips as compared to the rest of the body to enable higher resolution tactile discrimination, or the ways in which the smaller bones and muscles of the hands allow for more subtle and precise movements directed toward intricate operations.

Given that the robotic speed of the stacking of elements is not dependent on size, a wall generated using larger units would require fewer movement paths and therefore accelerate the building sequence while conversely reducing the potential for higher resolution detailing within the surface and interior patterning of the wall itself. Functional efficiency, the rate at which time is captured in the fabrication of the wall, in addition to stability—two factors that favor the employment of the larger modules—are thus evaluated in relation to aesthetic and programmatic demands that might conversely preference the perceptual variation and flexibility given by the smaller modules. The resolution of competing demands is thus played out by assessing the results of an enormous number of combinatorial permutations intrinsic to the modular system. Although such forms of evaluation would never be possible without physically realizing all possible products of the system, digital strategies displace design conjecture and reductive reasoning with graphic simulation in concert with a form of intensified arithmetic brute force: the capacity of the computer to generate and assess vast quantities of information, which might include all possible combinations of a specifically defined modular assembly, at incomprehensible speeds.[3] Given that an extremely large number of realizable solutions can be derived from a single system (dependent on the number of units, types, operational variables, and permutational possibilities), the resolution of competing demands is thus optimized by genetic algorithms that are used to generate a variety of wall types according to specific parameters and then test and evaluate their fitness according to a set of desired results. As with biological evolutionary behavior, the selection process is integrated into the system as a feedback loop ensuring that successive generations of assemblies are developed as positive mutations of what are considered to be the results of successful coding.

The reference of modularity to biological or organic systems is often attributed to the fact that modular systems exhibit intrinsic sets of relations among their component parts due to the ways in which they were mutually derived. In projects such as the Ravensbourne College by Foreign Office Architects 7, which incorporates a non-periodic tessellated tiling system of anodized aluminum tiles used to clad the building envelope, the modular interaction of three differently colored and shaped tiles is therefore determined in advance by the singular dimension shared by all sides of the distinct pentagonal and triangular tiles and the relationship of their interior angles that enable composites produced by their aggregation to fill the plane. The different vortical patterns generated permit the size of openings in the façade to grow and shrink allowing for seven distinctly sized apertures to be collectively and differentially diffused across the surface. These are distributed and modulated based on programmatic need (and are thus intrinsically linked to function) yet remain visually and logically self-referential as a consistent yet variegated form of automated ornament that is seemingly scale-less in relation to both the bodies and spaces veiled behind the skin.

The component parts within these systems are considered to be homologous in that they share a form of genetic ancestry yet have been modified in order to be adapted to different purposes. Thus, despite their relative independence and compartmentalization, modules are also co-evolutionary and therefore necessarily interdependent when operating within a larger system. Perhaps more critical, however, is the idea that every object or architectural artifact produced using a modular system is in principle provisional, temporary, or incomplete in that the value of the system is in its ability to be reconfigured to produce a range of different morphological types. In this sense, modular systems find a correspondence with living systems in their capacity for continual adaptation to different environmental conditions or scales, changing programmatic parameters or transformations over time. Their incompleteness within time, which references their protean natures, is complemented by the fact that, as a locally determined system from which endless variation is possible, they are also intrinsically spatially incomplete.

This is exemplified in MOS's Ivy coat hook system 8 (applicable to any wall or site) whose patterns of growth are controlled through a simple set of rules and operations—an organic growth algorithm—that simulates the programmatic potential of the artifact as it grows over time. This simulation uses weighted probabilities to determine from which connectors the device will grow, a condition that in its real application might be dependent on the proportions and scale of the wall to which it attaches (the dimensions of the site as "host"), the number of pieces of clothing it is intended to support, and the size and aesthetic preferences of the "colony" with which it interacts. Parametric computation is intended to test the potential of these programmatic variables and constraints as part of the design process, yet embedded within the system is the idea that as a global form, the structure is indeterminate and therefore intrinsically incomplete. Whether applicable at the scale of the interior artifact as in the Ivy project or the urban terrain as in MOS's variations for a pavilion for the Shenzhen Architecture Biennale and Alisa Andrasek and Jose Sanchez's project Bloom Game 9, the indeterminacy of the structure is given by the fact that the modules may be assembled without definitive limits on their quantity or placement similar to botanical structures found in nature, such as plants and trees whose branching systems are ultimately dependent on external environmental factors—the presence of water, nutrients, or light, for example—for their expansive development. In architectural models such limits might be set by site constraints, programmatic demands or desires, or the availability of capital, all of which are external to the modular system.

The inversion of bottom-up, extensive modular systems such as the Ivy project or Bloom Game, is found in Emerging Objects' Bloom Pavilion 10 and Seat Slug, 11 where a high degree of customization, both at the level of the configuration of the larger object and of the component part, would make it seem that these works fall outside of a stricter definition of modular systems. Here, what appears to constitute the module is the repeated component, a three-dimensional block supporting a highly particularized surface pattern that is aggregated and assembled. Akin to Jenny Sabin's Polybrick project made of 3D-printed interlocking ceramic bricks, the projects start with a more regular gridded geometry. The module is a basic unit, a single rectilinear cell within this gridded geometry that is then transformed as the initial grid is modified, distorted, and morphed into a mesh that defines the plastic volumes of the serpentine seating element and the undulating walls of the pavilion. Although the module remains, as an elemental component that refers back to the project's origins and its hidden organizational structure, the deformation of the whole, in addition to the complexity and specificity of the pattern inscribed on its surface, ensures that no two parts or modules within the system (except perhaps those determined by the symmetries intrinsic to the Bloom Pavilion) would ever be the same. Each component part, which is relatively similar in size to the other blocks within each project, once manipulated, cannot therefore be exchanged with any other part in the system.

Despite this customization of the whole, the patterning of the surface exposes the shared gene pool of the modules, disguised behind the complexity of their highly articulated surface. The Seat Slug was designed using the Japanese *karakusa* method which, like the logic of Truchet Tiles, ensures that the surface pattern of each tile connects to the pattern of every adjacent tile by sharing specific boundary conditions. Truchet tiles, first described by Sébastien Truchet in 1704 and elaborated by Cyril Smith and many others, are square tiles with rotationally asymmetric patterns imprinted on their surfaces that when rotated and aggregated to tile a plane produce variable patterns. Smith inscribed two diagonally symmetrical, quarter-circle arcs on the tile with radii equal to half the dimension of the tile's edge. These paired arcs could occupy one of two positions by any 90-degree rotation of the tile, and their curved lines, which always ended at the midpoint of a tile, ensured that any aggregation would generate a continuous and uninterrupted curvilinear pattern. Although appearing far more complex and labyrinthine in its surface patterning because of the biomorphic irregularity of its design, the Seat Slug operates in a similar way with two different scales of modulation. One defines the repetitive pattern of meandering lines and amoeba-shaped perforations on the surface, a logic determined by the tiling 12, and the other defines the scale of the actual 3D-printed cement blocks, each of which includes multiple "tiles" per block for ease of assembly. Like the Bloom Game, the high degree of customization

13

14

16

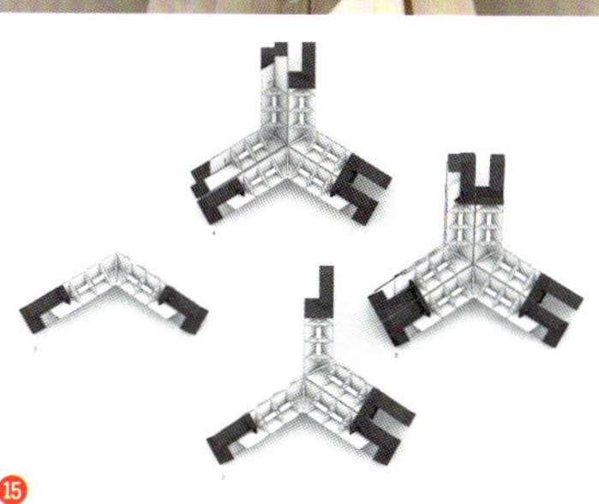

15

of the module diminishes its legibility. In one case, however, this is due to the complexity of the module's external configuration and the degrees of freedom allowable for its aggregation and growth, while in the other case this is due to the module's internal intricacy in combination with the larger deformation of the whole.

Modular systems are inevitably a study in mereology, that is, the relationship between larger-scaled objects and the smaller-scaled objects out of which they are constructed, eliminating the assumed hierarchical bias that might subordinate the latter to the former or vice versa and diminish the autonomy of each as an object. As discussed by Levi Bryant "an object can simultaneously construct its environment and be constrained by its environment, leading local manifestations to take particular forms." In the works of Gilles Retsin, this relationship across scales is pushed to its limit, where the autonomy of smaller-scale modular parts, unlike the continuities of the Seat Slug's embedded modules, threatens to dismantle the large-scale molar object. An architectural expression of Bryant's thesis, Retsin's efforts toward an equalizing autonomy of differently scaled objects, challenge both bottom up and top down systems, that is, those that might privilege the part as evident in the modular system of Bloom Game versus those, like the Bloom Pavilion, that might privilege the whole. The discretization of modules that assures the reading of part as object, evident in the Diamonds House 13, is thus emphasized in several ways, from the rotation of extruded timber components (their diamond and L-shaped sections) and their blackened ends, to the extension of these bundled linear modular logs, and their differential protruding lengths, beyond the exterior surface of the building. These tactics, along with the reduction of the number of different modular types and their large size relative to the scale of the wholes that they construct, a condition that is furthered in the Royal Academy of Arts project 14 15, calls attention to the discreteness of the part, and its relationship to other parts in the system and to the whole that it assembles. In the Royal Academy and House Block 16 projects this mode of equalizing objects in a system, a form of architectural democracy perhaps, is amplified when the differential scale of part to whole is further reduced, and where the coarseness of the grain of the assemblage conspires with the open-endedness of the whole. The emphasis on the "L-shaped" or corner-shaped component that is rendered three dimensional in the House Block, further ensures that the stability of the entire work is subtly challenged by its perception as a fragment of a larger unseen system.

The global parameters of each molar object produced by these systems often have a seemingly tenuous or arbitrary relationship to the modular components—their form, number, and spatial disposition—that comprise the "fill" of the assemblage. Modular systems are determined by local relations established by the geometry of their parts and the rules of their distribution and assembly whether these are used to produce an ornamental surface pattern, a constructive material logic, or a spatial distribution of programmatic components. As such, these systems are essentially incremental phenomena operating step by step whose degree of internal figuration is ultimately dependent on the scalar relationship of part to whole, yet whose external figuration (depending on the coarseness or fineness of the grain of modulation) can be seemingly indifferent to the form of the subcomponents and their mode of assembly. Although flexible, with a large potential range of internal variation, the assemblage is governed by local absolutes, whose global parameters remain relative and open. Despite this, the success of the molar object, its overall coherence, is not simply a result of overdetermination at the level of the whole (an external figure swooping down to contain and capture the unruly activities of the fill), but rather dependent on the capacity of the modular multiplicity to support emergent organizations that constitute the whole whose value may or may not be greater than the sum of its parts.

Notes:

1. M.A. Schilling and K. Steensma, "The use of modular organizational forms: An industry level analysis." *Academy of Management Journal* 44 (2001): 1149–1169.
2. Lev Manovich, *The Language of New Media* (Cambridge: MIT Press, 2002).
3. Kostas Terzidis discusses the difference between what might be considered "intelligent" within the human mind and computational strategies. Whereas in the first case, checking all possible combinations "would be considered overwhelming, pointless or naïve by a human investigator . . . the computational power of a computer [ensures] that such a strategy may only take a few seconds to check millions of possibilities, something inconceivable to the human mind. . . .The power of computation, which involves vast quantities of calculations, combinatorial analysis, randomness, or recursion, point to new thought processes that may have not ever occurred to the human mind." See Kostas Terzidis, *Algorithmic Architecture* (Oxford: Architectural Press, 2006), 17.
4. Levi R. Bryant, *The Democracy of Objects* (Ann Arbor: Open Humanities Press, 2011), 33.

Berlin Free University
Candilis-Josic-Woods

Built 1963–1973
Berlin, Germany

2.1a

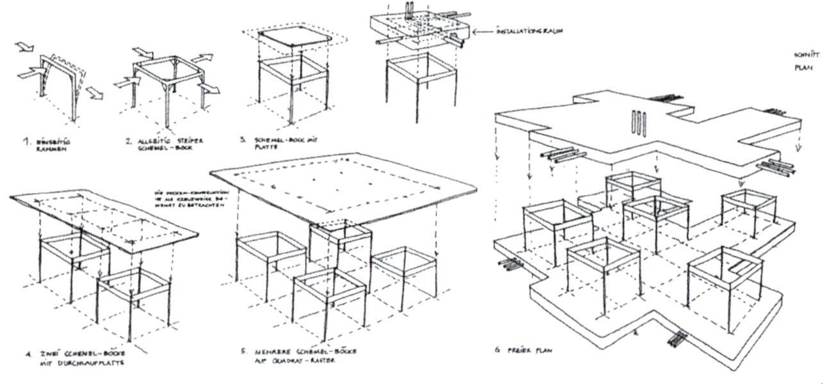

2.1b

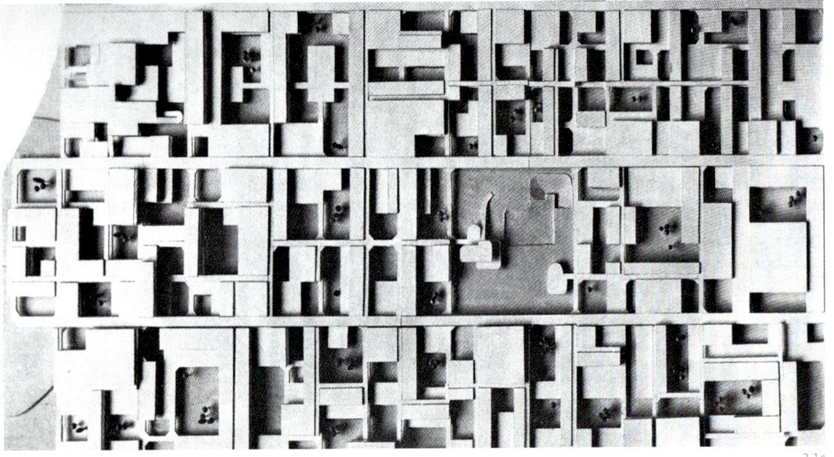

2.1c

The Berlin Free University was designed to incorporate the logics of an interactive urbanism into a single building structure to counter, through its density, connectedness, and modularity, the sprawl resulting from a collection of individuated buildings typical of suburban campus planning models. The intention of the building was to operate like a city—a complex environment that accommodates growth, intensifies exchange, and has the capacity to be altered as the needs of its inhabitants change over time. The building is spatially organized through an infrastructure of "main streets" positioned at 100 meter intervals, that divide and allocate space and set up a hierarchical circulation grid that connects and organizes the main public elements of the program such as the lecture theaters and cafe. Connected to these "streets" are "alleys" that form a secondary circulation network providing access to the more semi-public areas such as classrooms. The most private spaces, such as offices, are placed on the second floor. The distribution of the program was determined based on functional and spatial typologies rather than the clustering of individual departments, to encourage the mixing of students from all disciplinary areas akin to the types of interactions that one would find on a busy street. The modularity of the building is evident not only in the distribution of programmatic spaces, but also in the structural, mechanical, and cladding systems of the building, which share a repetitive dimensional and formal structure, and therefore have the capacity for substitution, variation, and transformation. The steel frame is a repetitive gridded system based on a standard set of increments that determine the units of measurement for the concrete floor slabs, while simultaneously providing the larger framework that is subdivided into a family of interchangeable interior wall panels and external cladding elements that collectively form the façade. These repeatable elements of the envelope operate as windows, walls, or bookcases on the interior, and glazed openings and spandrel panels of different depths on the exterior. The elements within this system share a proportional series of modular dimensions—divisible into halves or thirds in elevation, for example—so that they can be combined and rearranged according to changing programmatic, organizational, and aesthetic requirements that generate distinct rhythms on the surface and expose the permutability of the larger system.

Delft Housing Study

MVRDV

Unbuilt 1995

Delft, Netherlands

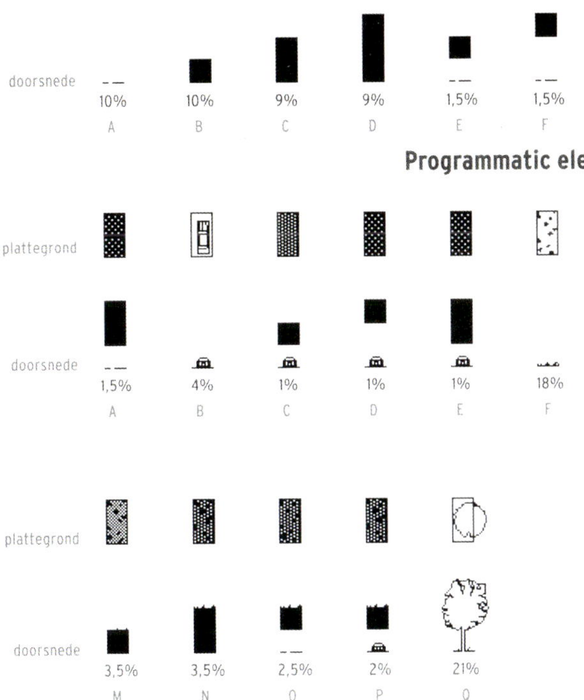

2.2a

2.2b

Given the tight budgets allotted to housing in the Netherlands, the program for residential areas has been rendered as an "urbanism of percentages," that is, a combination of economy and social obligations that determine strict maximum sizes and percentages for all elements of housing projects, including: dwelling types (100 m² and 3 stories maximum), gardens (40 m² per house), parking spaces (1.2 per house), pavement (30 m² per parking space), and greenery (5 m² per house). In response to these limitations and in order to address the demand for individuality and variety—seemingly the only architectural tools for mass housing—this study for the development of 750 houses in Delft generates a modular system promoting differentiation that evolves from the initial spatial parameters and dimensional restrictions governing housing development. The project starts with a diagram of a gridded field based on the incremental dimensions of a parking lot given that the parking space is the one programmatic element that has strict measurement requirements. This parking field operates as the underlying dimensional and organizational datum for the housing project. Variation within this system is achieved by expanding the parking grid to a three-band system for the occupation of housing units and establishing a spectrum of types based on a range of housing sizes (one, two or three stories, for example), in addition to changing the spatial positions, orientations, and juxtapositions that modify the initial set of programmatic elements—living space, garden, parking, greenspace, and pavement—each of which was initially defined based on the dimensional parameters of a parking space. These are then differentially aggregated so that their combinatorial possibilities are expanded to generate a greater diversity within the whole. By composing each band of the parking field differently according to the "percentages" of program, the confrontation between all these bands—from intelligent to absurd—turns the built area into a kasbah-like labyrinth. The neighborhood takes on adventurous qualities in which the unexpected features prominently. To escape the claustrophobic aspect of this complex tapestry, every dwelling sports a tower-like room or a patio, and the shared public spaces, which sit on top of the supermarket and sports hall, have a public view over this "housing carpet" towards the sea.

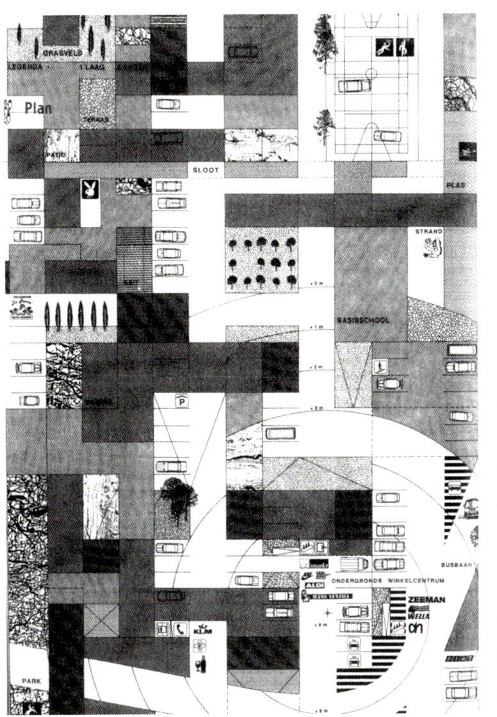

2.2c

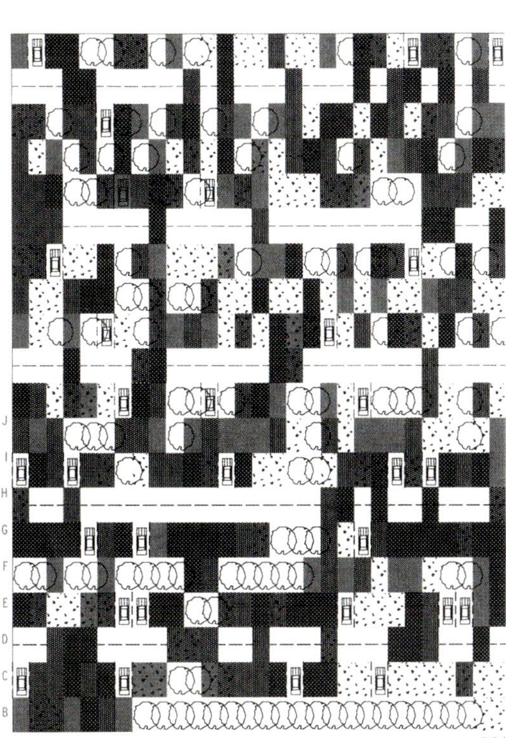

2.2d

2.2e

Porter House

SHoP

Built 2003

New York, United States

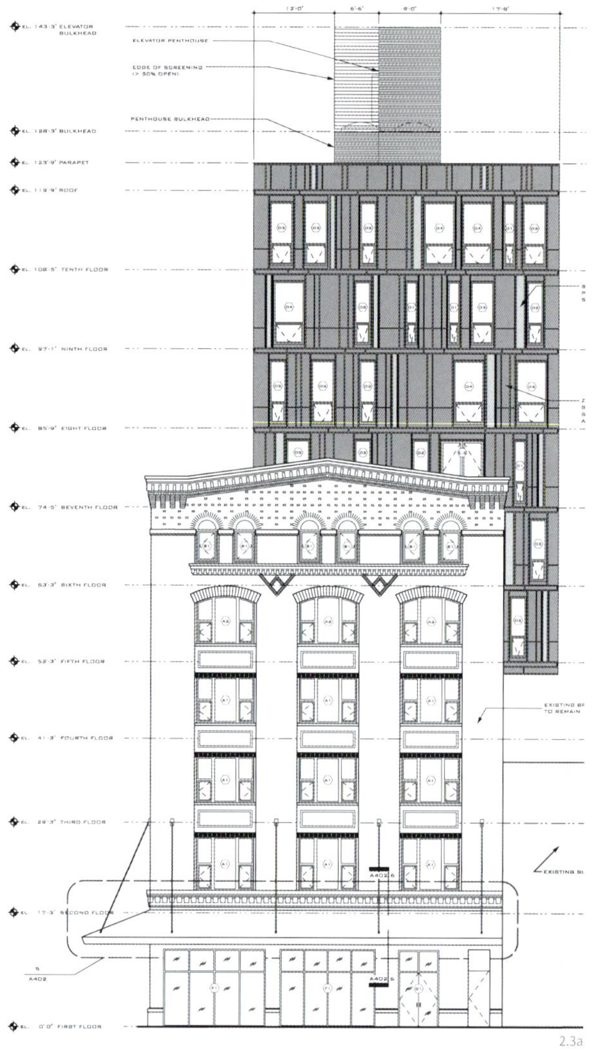

2.3a

Located in the Meatpacking District of Manhattan, the Porter House is a conversion of a six-story, 30,000 square foot, Romanesque brick warehouse into residential condominiums. The transfer of neighboring air rights from an adjacent low-rise building allowed the renovation to include a new 20,000-square-foot addition perched on top of the existing building that added four stories to the historic structure and that incorporates a six-story high, eight-foot cantilever along the building's southern exposure. The new volume created by this cantilever, which appears to intersect the historic structure, is clad in a custom-fabricated, anthracite zinc panel system punctuated by a rhythmic pattern of vertically attenuated floor-to-ceiling windows and translucent lighted strips. The façade system is generated using a set of three different modular dimensions that are applied to three differentiated panel types—glazed, translucent, and solid—to produce a variegated surface pattern that changes its appearance from day to night. The materiality and dynamic rhythm of the new fenestration provide a counterpoint to the solidity of the brick warehouse and symbolize the transformation of the district from industry to arts and nightlife. Minimizing material waste, the modular pattern of the façade was calibrated to optimize the use of standardized sheets of zinc by ensuring that the size and number of panels could be efficiently laid out on, and cut from, standard widths of sheet material, thereby achieving economies in the manufacturing process while maintaining the customization generated by the variable rhythm of the cladding. Each panel was laser-cut directly from the architect's digital files and etched with a reference code that was keyed to the installation drawings indicating the location of panels and sequence of installation. Efficiencies were therefore gained not only by working closely with the fabricators to understand the properties of the material and the parameters that defined its manipulation, but also by ensuring that the evolution of the modular system and specificity of its design emerged from the overlay of multiple intersecting material, tectonic, programmatic, and aesthetic constraints.

2.3b

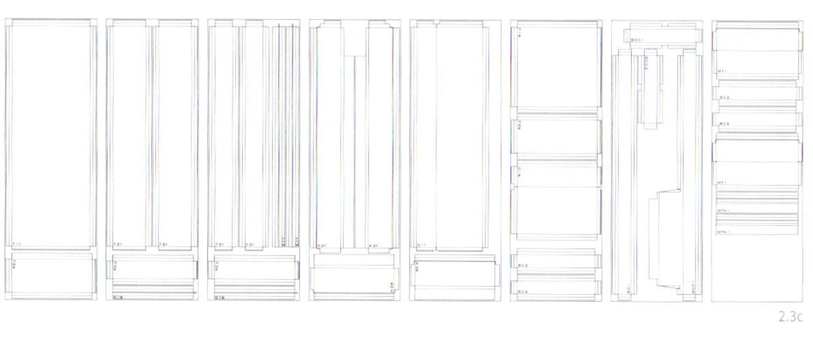

2.3c

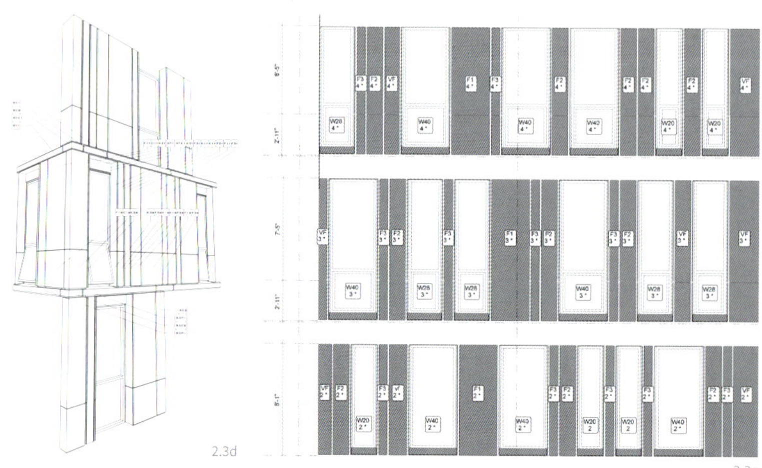

2.3d

2.3e

2.3f

Modular Variations
Variable Projects/Adam Marcus

Built 2013
Minneapolis, United States

2.4a

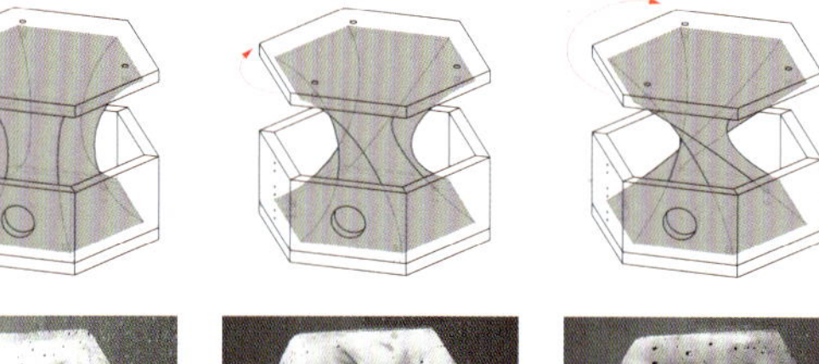
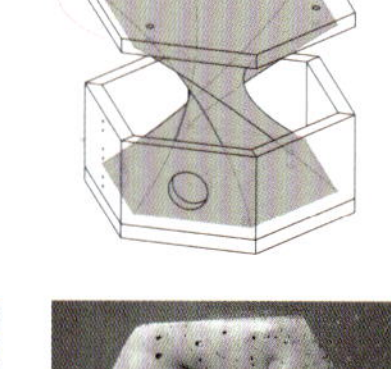
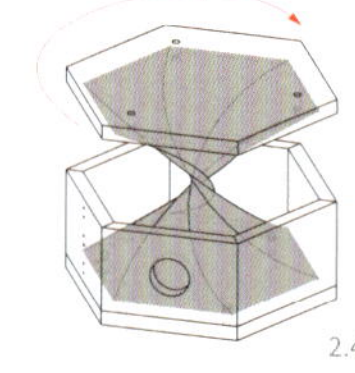

2.4b

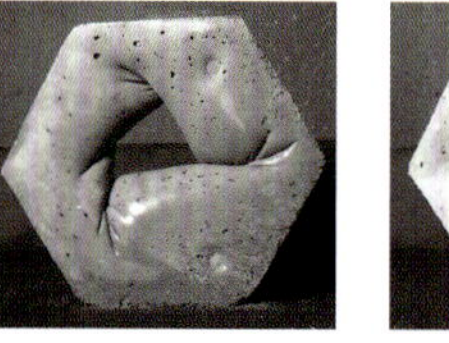

2.4c

2.4d

Modular Variations I and II seek to foreground and problematize the notion of variation as it relates to computational design and digital fabrication using reconfigurable molds and/or flexible formwork. In Modular Variations I, reconfigurable molds are constructed from a set of finite, simple components that are capable of producing a large range of variable cast-plaster modules that can be stacked into a wall assembly. Molds consist of CNC-routed, two-dimensional stackable slides out of which are cut variable openings that operate as a family of parametrically interrelated forms. These wooden slides are then serially assembled according to distinct sequences to produce numerous configurations each of which is perceived as a layered transformational series. The logic of the variation that occurs within each of the cast modules is thus driven by careful calibration of these interstitial apertures, while the logic of the variation of the whole is determined by the sequencing of different modules as they aggregate to form the larger wall assembly. The digital parametric model supported the form-finding process and enabled the visualization of different design iterations—the range of potential sequences both within the module and across the wall assembly—while also continuously updating the fabrication files and assembly instructions for the mold components. In Modular Variations II, flexible formwork is used to cast sixty-six structurally repetitive yet individually unique concrete modules that are aggregated into a full-scale wall prototype. The custom-fabricated molds incorporate a stretchable latex bladder that provides a controlled means for producing variable apertures in the cast modules. Incrementally rotating the mold's hexagonal faces increases the twist of the internal bladder, so that the resulting void in the cast module decreases in size. This adjustability allows for a precise modulation of the aperture's radius, which is then affected by the concrete as it interacts with the mutable formwork during the curing process. The variations produced by the material performance introduce a degree of unpredictability into the process, which amplifies the geometric variation across modules. Throughout the process, parametric design and digital fabrication tools were strategically leveraged to iterate in form finding, generate fabrication instructions, and direct the assembly sequence of the walls providing feedback between analog and digital models.

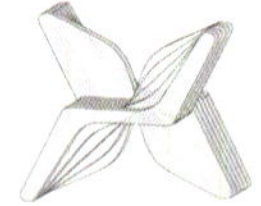

2.4e

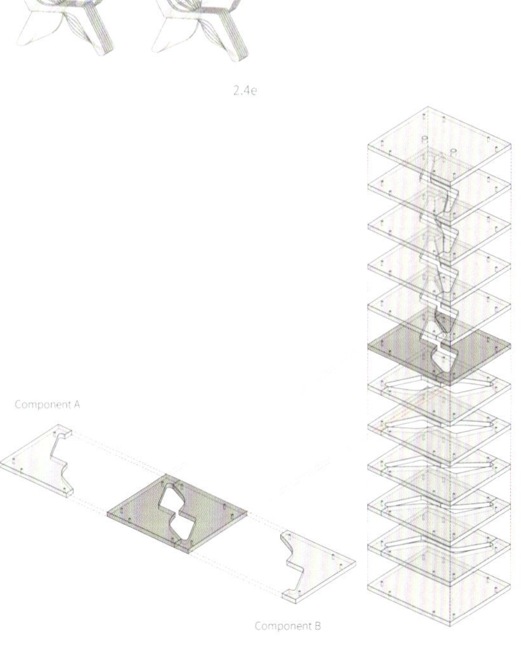

(A) Each mold slide consists of two types of components, each of which has several variations.

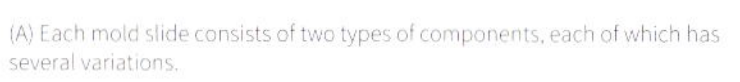

2.4f

(B) Mold slides are stacked together and locked in place with wood dowels.

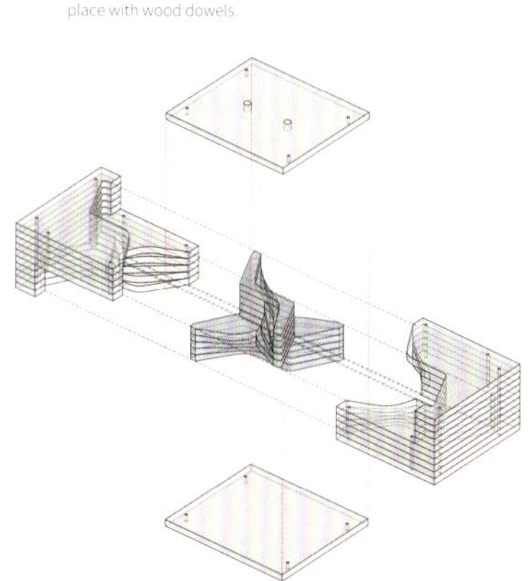

(C) After plaster is poured, mold slide components are removed to reveal the cast module.

2.4g

Resolution Wall

Gramazio & Kohler + ETH DFAB Group

Built 2007

Zurich, Switzerland

This project investigates the additive construction of a wall made of autoclaved aerated concrete cubes of different sizes, their edge lengths varying from 5 to 40 cm where each dimension is derived as a fraction of the length of one of the sides of the largest block. The smallest module therefore acts as a standard unit that defines the size and measure of all of the remaining cubes, each of which is a scaled version of this initial unit, ensuring that the dimensions and volumes of all of the concrete cubes are proportional. Since resolution within a pixelated field is determined by the relationship between a larger image or pattern and the size of the elements that constitute it, in the Resolution Wall, small modules can be placed where a high density of information is desired to express a higher degree of resolution, while areas with low information density can be built quickly and efficiently using large modules. The time needed by the robot to stack and position each of these modules is independent of its size, because the required movement path for each remains the same. The use of large modules can therefore accelerate the building of a wall many times over but reduces its resolution and thus the possible level of detailing on the surface and within the thickness of the wall, whereas smaller units are able to express a higher degree of resolution yet require a longer time for assembly. The time for the construction of the wall is therefore directly proportional to the scaling factors of the modular units and the total number of concrete cubes used in each wall prototype. An intelligent distribution and jointing of different module sizes can resolve the conflict between the aesthetic and functional advantages of the finest resolution and the economic necessity of the most efficient fabrication process.

2.5a

2.5b

2.5c

Federation Square

LAB Architecture Studio + Bates Smart Architects

Built 2002
Melbourne, Australia

2.6a

2.6b

2.6c

Planned in celebration of Australia's centennial, Federation Square is a complex of cultural and commercial buildings surrounding a civic square in Melbourne. It includes new spaces for the National Gallery of Victoria (NGV) and the Australian Centre for the Moving Image (ACMI), facilities for radio and television such as the Special Broadcasting Service (SBS), numerous restaurants and cafes, and an outdoor amphitheater. Despite the complexity of their building geometries and layered surfaces, this assemblage of discrete elements surrounding the plaza finds continuity in the patterned tiling of its façades. This tiling pattern defines not only the intricate geometry of the cladding and glazing system used throughout, but also of its substructural supporting frame. The façades are clad in right-angled triangular tiles composed of sandstone, zinc (solid and perforated), or glass (frosted and transparent), where each triangular tile is a modular element whose side dimensions are based on a ratio of $1{:}2{:}\sqrt{5}$. This specific geometry, based on the nonperiodic tiling patterns of Charles Radin and John Conway, enables each triangle to be subdivided into five isometric copies which, as in all fractal geometries, can be repeated ad infinitum. The continuous division, aggregation, and translation/rotation of this triangle also enables it to infinitely tile a plane with self-similar copies, a process known as pinwheel tiling. In the Federation Square project, five triangular tiles are therefore joined together to produce a larger triangular component, secured to an aluminum frame to form a panel. Five panels are then aggregated and affixed to a galvanized steel frame, which forms the structure for the façade. The same geometric pattern is continued yet complexified in the steel structure that supports the glazing of the Edge Theater and Atrium. Here, not every edge of the triangular pattern is present even if it provides the hidden geometry behind the designed structure.

Ravensbourne College of Design and Communication

Foreign Office Architects

Built 2010

London, United Kingdom

The Ravensbourne College is dominated by the modular tessellated pattern of its skin and the hybridization between distinct types of building envelopes: those that support and refer back to repetitive functions such as classroom spaces and those that are appropriate for more varied types of spaces such as auditoria, libraries, and function rooms that don't necessarily have an optimal depth, height or window type. The fenestration pattern on the exterior emerged from an attempt to diffuse the stratification of windows that is characteristic of school façades in order to turn the building into an abstract container capable of withstanding the nearby presence of the Millennium Dome. The development of the modular patterned skin, which is constituted by three differently colored pentagonal and triangular tiles, renders the building scale ambiguous. The round windows support this reading and enable the surface to be perceived as a punctured pattern that conceals, rather than reveals, the functions occurring within the interior. Rather than prioritizing either the vertical or horizontal dimensions of the building, the fenestration refers back to, and emphasizes, the skin itself. Paradoxically, however, despite the seemingly opaque and disconnected strategy of the fenestration system, within the interior there is a tightly connected dimensional relationship between the fenestration grid, the sectional grid, and the plan grid, thereby binding the envelope pattern and function, even while the surface pattern acts as a device to diffuse the expression of the building's program. Each of the differently shaped, anodized aluminum tiles that populate this ornately patterned surface, share dimensional properties and a set of relations among their interior angles that allow them to aggregate to fill the plane. The tessellation geometries that define the pattern of this skin are unique, yet are based on a nonperiodic tiling system that is complexified with the addition of a triangle in order to make possible the production of linear arrays in addition to polar arrays. This creates a vortical pattern of tiles that changes depending on its relationship to the circular window openings. The tessellation system also enables the diameter of the window openings to increase or decrease by changing the position of certain tiles, creating seven different aperture diameters that are distributed across and punctuate the building's surface.

2.7a

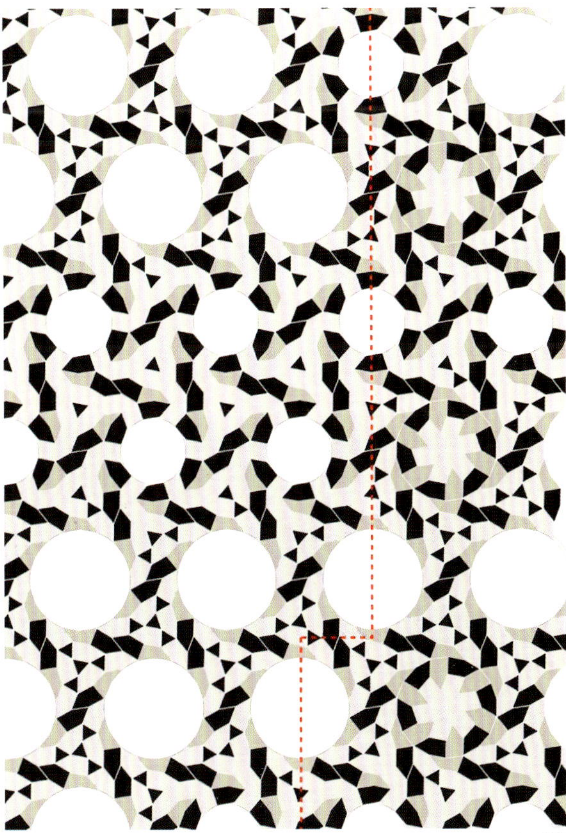

2.7b

2.7c

2.7d

Ivy aka Coathooks

MOS

Built 2005–2006

2.8a

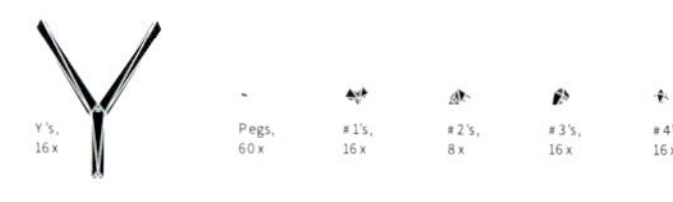

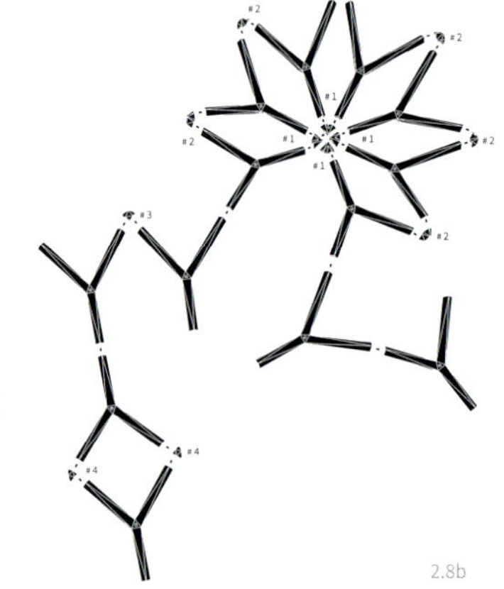

2.8b

The ivy coat hook lattice is a modular system that uses a single plastic "Y" unit and a few connectors to produce a variety of rotational geometric patterns. Akin to a rhizome that forms an infinitely extended network as it grows (and that imbues the complexity of such forms of nature with a geometric and mathematical structure), the organization of IVY is based upon an organic growth algorithm, where, like cellular automata, a set of simple rules and probabilities simulate the growth of ivy. The applet begins by creating a base system which will have the coat hangers as its members. One coat hanger is added to the system as the seed. With each execution of the computer program, the system is asked to grow. It responds by randomly selecting one of its Y units and uses a weighted probability to determine which kind of connector to grow from. The connector chosen determines the geometry of the resulting growth and these decisions, which agglomerate over time, form into a larger and more intricate pattern. The design of the final modular system uses this model to grow IVY and, in so doing, transforms any wall into a support system for a usable lattice. The indeterminacy of the final growth pattern ensures the flexibility of the modular system so that it can respond to the scale, configuration, and dimensions of its planar site and the aesthetic preferences and predilections of its users.

2.8c

2.8d

2.8e

Shenzhen Pavilion
MOS
Built 2011
Shenzhen, China

2.9a

The Shenzhen Variations project was developed as one of the pop-up pavilions of the ultra light village—a series of structures located in front of the Shenzhen Civic Center as part of the 2011 Shenzhen and Hong Kong Bi-City Biennale of Urbanism/Architecture. The pink pavilion is comprised of a series of modular cells made out of bent metal sheets, each of which includes a planar, trapezoidal canopy and a rectangular column that acts as its support. The large trapezoidal "petals" share a common dimension on three of their four sides, enabling them to aggregate as an open series of tiles in rotating and linear clusters. By combining the structure and surface into a singular continuous unit, the modular components of the pavilion remain highly flexible. These can be grouped into any number of elements, allowing for an endless series of aggregate variations to potentially populate the plaza. In the construction of the final pavilion, both canopy and column include bent tabs running the length of their edges that are folded and connected to ensure that the planes comprising each of the modules are stabilized. These units gain further rigidity through their adjacency and interconnection that operate to balance the structural asymmetries intrinsic to the single module. The continuities that govern the work—operating between canopy and column, across conjoined modules, and within the folded details of each component—expose the contradictions evident between the perception of the complex whole (that is dominated by the shape of the aggregate) and the modular logic of its component parts.

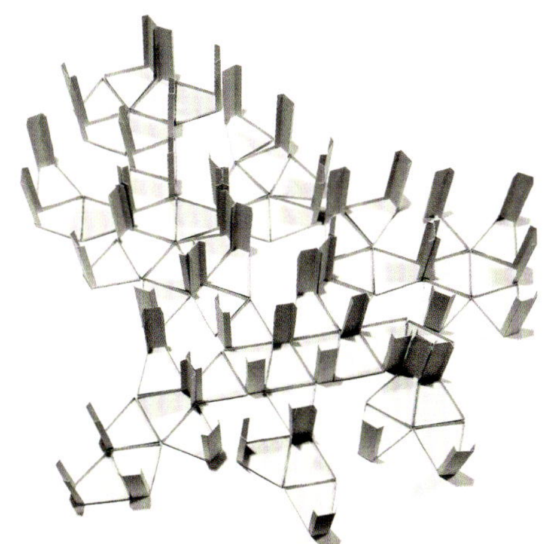

2.9b

2.9c

Bloom Game

Alisa Andrasek + Jose Sanchez

Built 2012

London, United Kingdom

2.10a

2.10b

2.10c

2.10d

2.10e

BLOOM was commissioned by the Greater London Authority as part of its Wonder series celebrating the London Olympics and ParaOlympics in the summer of 2012. Branded in the official Olympics color of neon pink and made of recyclable plastic components, BLOOM is an interactive urban toy, a distributed social game and a collective "gardening" experience that seeks the engagement of people in order to construct fuzzy BLOOM formations. It is a modular system and artificial garden whose capacity for complexity and continuity finds its analog in intricate entanglement of the botanical world. The energy for the garden's creation is sourced from the interaction of people, whereby the collective act of coming to one place and building something becomes a shared memory for all involved. None of the pieces can do anything on its own; only by putting together thousands of them the BLOOM garden begins to emerge. The main components of BLOOM are a series of planar pink plastic modular elements—a massive population of distinct cells that interlock in a variety of sequences to produce larger complex configurations. The complexity of these larger constructions is dependent on the detailed form of the individual modular cell and its capacity for aggregation and continuity. The cell's elongated form and smooth continuous boundary contribute to the continuity of the whole, despite that it is constructed of discrete individuated components. Deep inlets along the boundary of each cell allow for three distinct points of interlock and three different types of connection between modules. The local deviation and shifting orientation of these inlets incorporates differentiation into the system and is what introduces branching and curvature into the larger aggregated whole. Simple combinations of modules in distinct orientations therefore produce different sequences of elements. By recombining these three different forms of connections in each cell, or following rhythms of repeating strings of the same type of linkage, it is possible to build rings, spirals or distributed branching systems that grow as each module locally deviates from the one that preceded it. Despite the simplicity of the individual cell, by recombining modules using different sequences of its three possible connections, just like the genetic coding of life, an infinity of distinct formations can emerge.

2.10f

Polyomino and Wireflies
Plethora Project
Unbuilt 2006
Los Angeles, United States

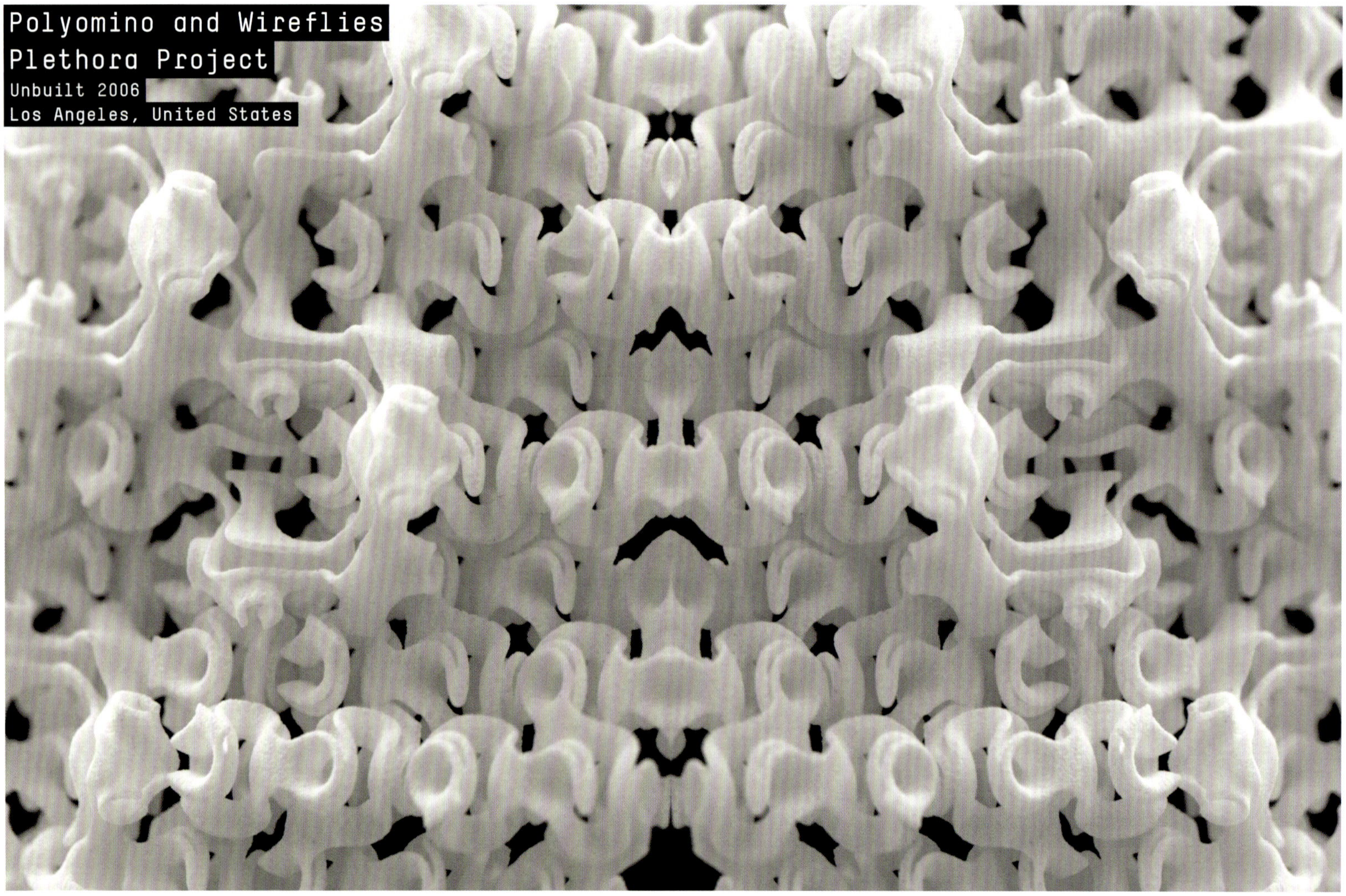

2.11a

Round One Round Two Round Three Round Four Round Five

2.11b

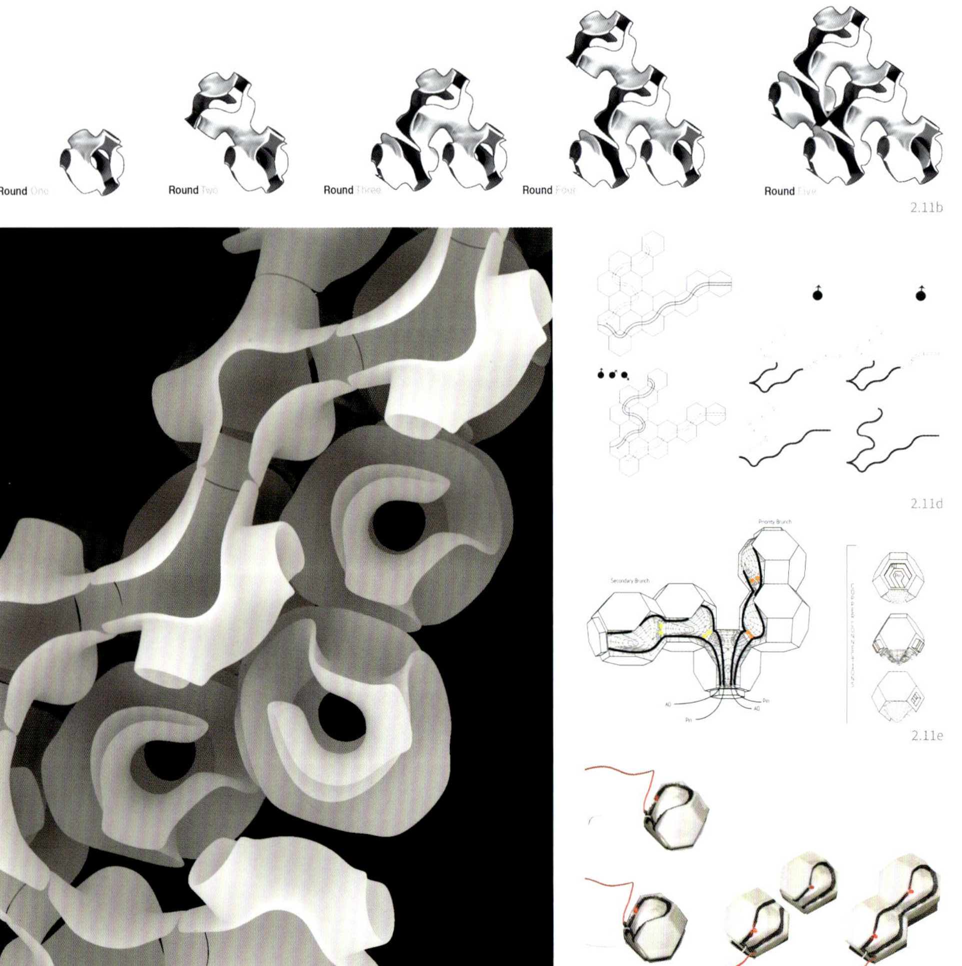

2.11c

2.11d

2.11e

2.11f

Polyomino refers to a series of discrete units and their generative patterns of organization. It is a body of gaming/making research that studies serialization in combinatronics that has the potential to produce a multiplicity of outputs. Each project operates as a discrete kit of polyhedral parts that can be assembled in multiple ways to achieve different ends and that reconsiders pattern languages that stress the combinatory over the parametric. Wireflies, like Polyomino, is based on the space packing of a polyhedral truncated octahedral system whose components have multiple faces and ways of interconnecting with adjacent units. In Wireflies, the aggregate formations create a complex grid structure that collects wind energy and uses this to store and transmit electricity. The individual polyhedral modules are layered with winged surfaces along one face and carved out to enable wiring and other systems to be embedded within them that render each unit asymmetrical and locally specific to allow it to operate. The packing and positioning of juxtaposed components enables or disables connectivity between adjacent modules which are rotated to produce a continuous topological network of circuits running through the aggregate. The generated energy flows through this network, while the light/socket embedded in one of the polyhedral faces indicates the transmission of energy by glowing. In the physical prototype of this system, the components are held together using magnetic connections along the faces of the polyhedron and the LED infrastructure detects the pressure of the system. Polyomino, an extension of Wireflies, allows players to design and 3D print polyhedral combinatory formations that propagate according topological modes of interconnectivity. Like a game of dominoes, each tile or module is rendered locally specific by determining different possibilities for face-to-face connections based on a set of rules, or formally, based on complex geometries carved out of the polyhedral modules that enable different forms of continuity to be expressed across conjoined units. In the latter case, the surface form of the initial polyhedron dissolves in favor of a more complex spatial component, while retaining its capacity for connectivity that is rendered more specific by the manipulation of the volume. Each version operates as a self-organized three-dimensional tileset, that combines digital and nondigital interfaces, and that has embedded possibilities that are elaborated as multiple scenarios as the game unfolds.

2.11g

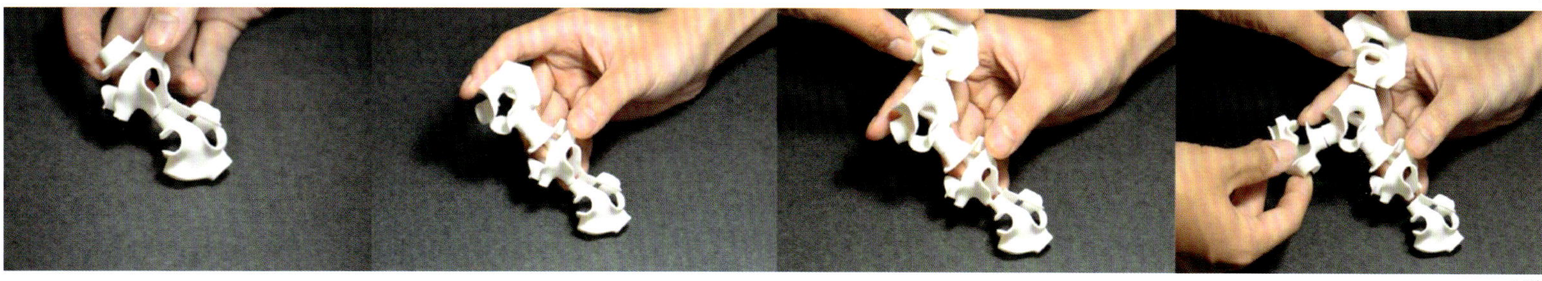

2.11h

2.11i

2.11j

2.11k

Polybrick
Sabin Design Lab
Built 2014
Ithaca, United States

The integration of robust building materials such as ceramics into rapid manufacturing processes have enabled the production of nonstandard modular components, such as PolyBricks, to be used in the development of larger architectural assemblies. PolyBricks are lightweight, 3D-printed ceramic bricks that interlock and therefore require no mortar or adhesives for assembly. The bricks are mass-customized modular components that operate simultaneously as both part and whole. Like typical bricks, they are discrete repetitive elements that aggregate to construct a larger assembly, yet are also fractional units—unique elements—that are derived from, and specifically informed by, the larger whole of which they are a part. Similar to the interlocking pieces of a puzzle or the encoded cells of an organism, every local part is therefore different, yet there is a coherence to the overall form at the global scale. To negotiate between part and whole, a series of algorithms are used to program the shape and placement of the bricks throughout the entire structure. One creates the geometry of the bricks, another labels them, and a third determines how they will morph and orient themselves within the structure. Inspired by living cellular networks, each unit has the same basic geometry, yet its shape is adapted and modified to adjust to its neighbor in support of the design of the larger structure. The boundary condition of each brick features tapered dovetails like those used in woodworking to allow adjacent bricks to be conjoined, yet these modules are also uniquely designed based on their global position and orientation in the wall to ensure that the proper taper angle is implemented to exploit gravity and securely lock the bricks into place. To minimize the overall weight of the structure, the interior of each PolyBrick is aerated using an open web, gridded lattice. This tessellated lattice is structurally optimized within each brick based on its specific location in the wall, in order to maximize the strength, rigidity, and stability of the whole while simultaneously enabling it to respond to the spatial context, geometric orientation, and additional programmatic criteria.

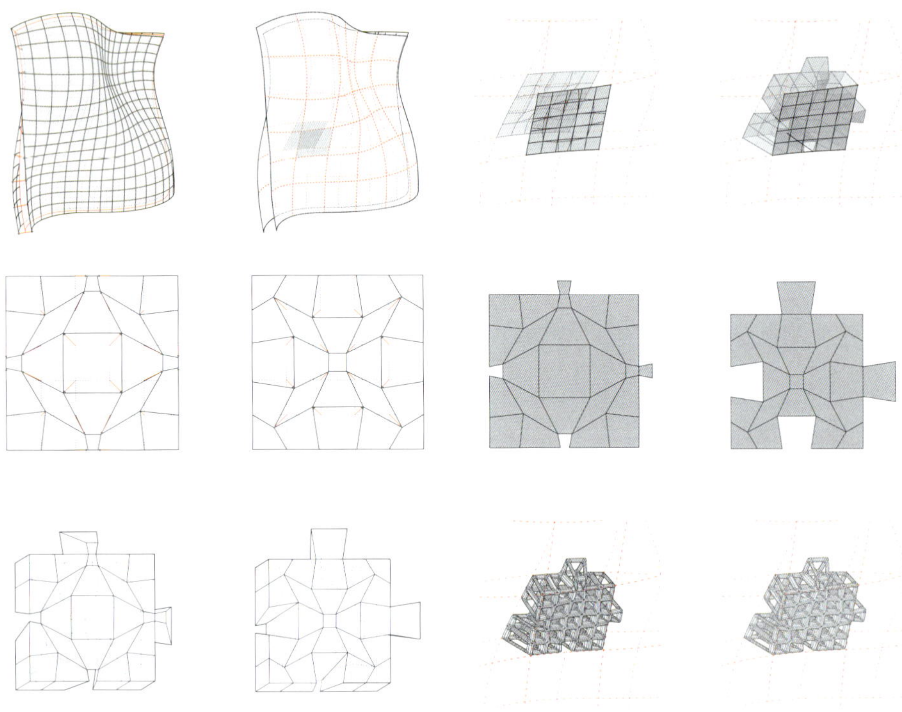
2.12a

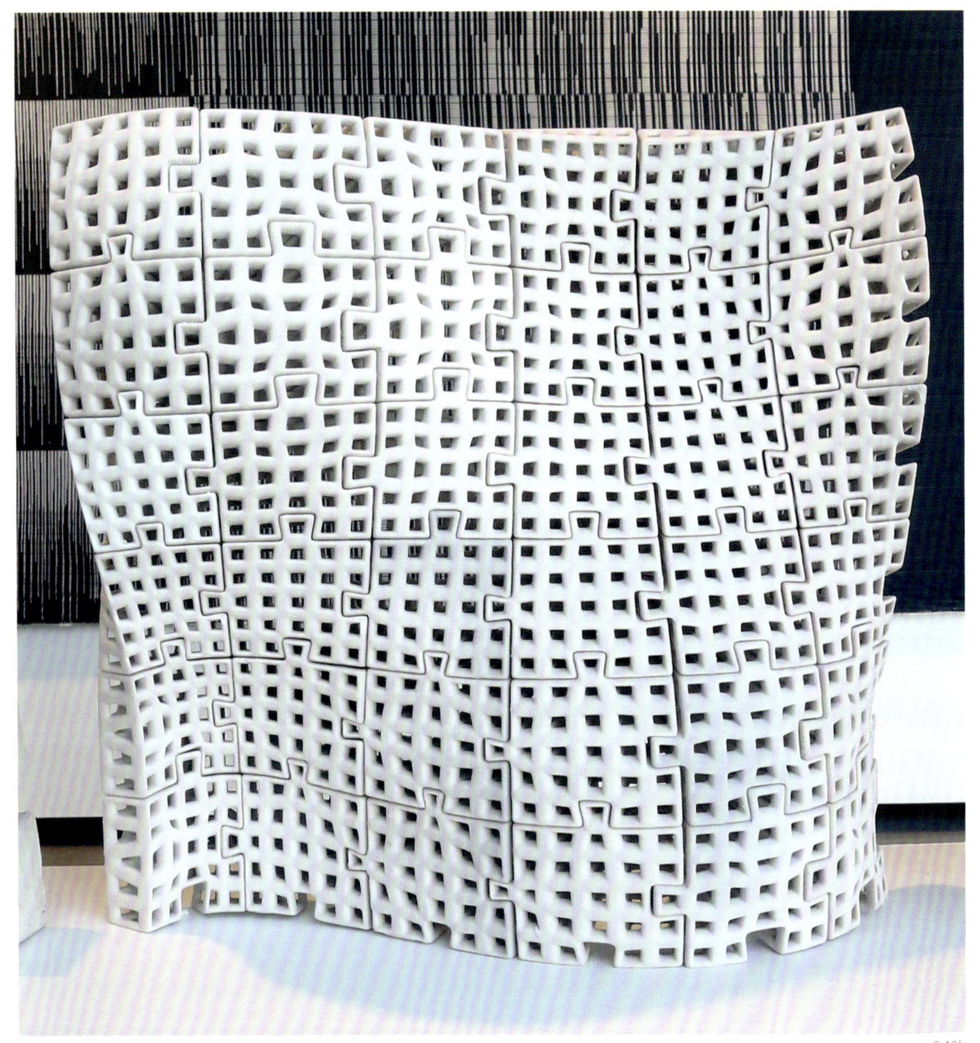
2.12b

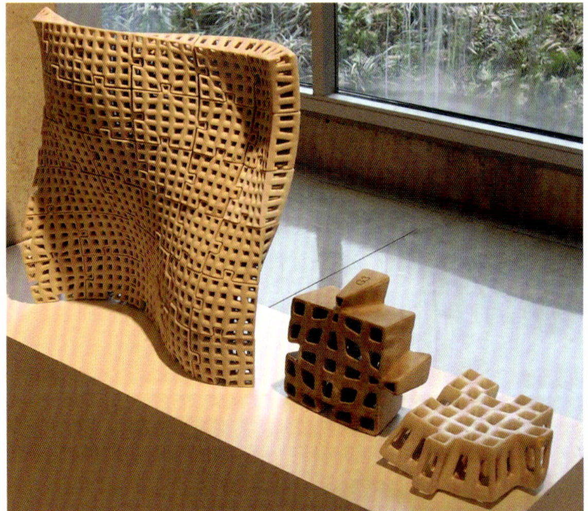
2.12c

2.12d

Seat Slug

Emerging Objects

Built 2011

San Francisco, United States

2.13a

The Seat Slug blurs the lines between biology, technology, and furniture. It is a bio-morphic interpretation of a bench constituted by a family of assembled concrete modules that form a continuous cementitious skin. It is inspired by flabelina goddardi—the newest species of sea slugs discovered in California—and by the infinite tessellations of Japanese karakusa patterns. The Seat Slug is constructed of 230 unique, one-of-a-kind building components that are generated quickly and economically using advanced three-dimensional modeling linked to digital output processes that enable the direct manufacture of structural building components, thereby closing the gaps between design, production, and manufacture. Produced using conventional rapid prototyping hardware, the component tiles of the Seat Slug are individually 3D printed using a translucent, concrete-based fiber-reinforced polymer material that is far more economical than powder printing materials and can reach strengths of up to 4,700 psi in compression. These customized modular tiles, each of which is close to the size of the hand, are then abutted, assembled, and fastened together to form the thickened skin of the bench. The continuity of the surface pattern, with its deep undulating grooves, soft glossy ripples, and serial perforations, conceals, rather than reveals, the joints between component parts, operating in concert with, yet dissimulating the construction system behind the dominant pattern of the skin. Although both the boundary shape and surface pattern of the tiles are dependent on the tessellated division of the surface, while one enables its constructability, the other forms a fluid, continuous cross pattern that emphasizes the haptic contiguity of elements and emulates the sinuous form of the whole.

2.13b

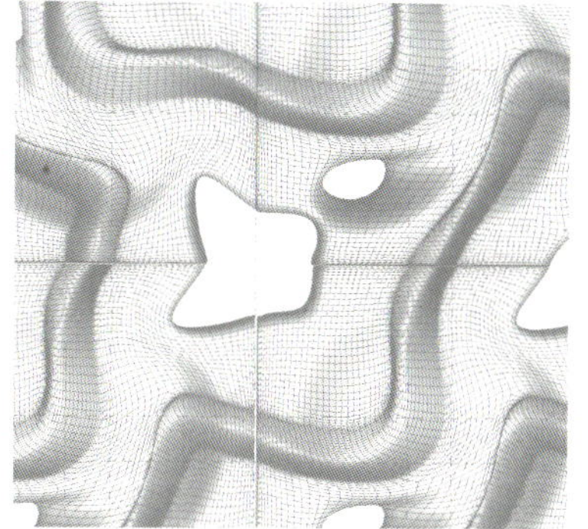

2.13c

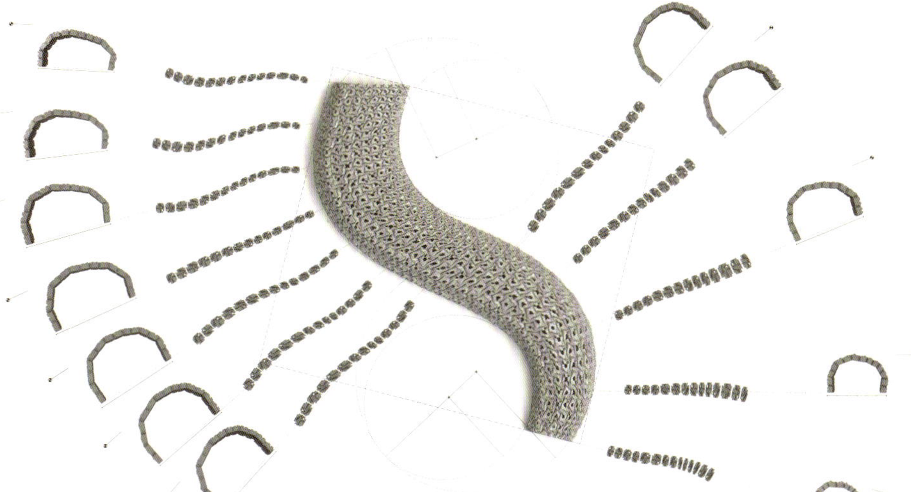

2.13d

Bloom Pavilion
Emerging Objects

Built 2015

Oakland, United States

2.14a

2.14b

2.14c

Bloom is a 9-foot-tall freestanding experimental pavilion comprised of 840 customized 3D-printed blocks, representing a new paradigm in building construction methods. A design derived from traditional Thai flower patterns is mapped onto the surface of the structure, a gridded pattern of sixteen shallow pyramidal pixels per block with variable sized openings, creating stunning visual effects of modulated light, shade, and shadow on the exterior and interior. Each block is printed using a farm of eleven powder 3D printers with a special cement composite formulation comprised chiefly of iron oxide-free Portland cement. Iron oxide imparts a gray color to cement, and its removal makes this print much lighter. Also, 3D-printed cement requires no formwork and produces no waste, and the support material can be reused to produce more blocks. Coupled with Portland cement is an ecologically derived UV resistant polymer that reduces the greenhouse gas emissions from production of resins by 50 percent over conventional petroleum-based epoxies. Each 3D-printed block is enumerated to designate the block's position in the overall structure. Rather than a set of blueprints, a spreadsheet that demonstrated the position of a block was used in constructing Bloom, and each block is assembled and held in place using stainless steel hardware. Each block has a printed structural grid that defines the interior of the tempietto and requires no additional structural support, functioning as a load-bearing 3D-printed enclosure. The curvilinear shape gives added stiffness to the thin, lightweight structure, informed by the thin masonry structures of Uruguayan architect and engineer Eladio Dieste, particularly Iglesia Cristo Obrero, Jefferson's serpentine brick walls at the University of Virginia, and Torqued Ellipse by Richard Serra, which inspire its form.

In plan Bloom is a curved cruciform shape that rises 9 feet to meet the same shape rotated 45 degrees, creating a torqued "x" shape with an entrance 45 degrees from the structure's main axis. The undulated form and spaces recall an elephant's foot or, when coupled with the flower pattern on the surface, the traditional mud houses of the Tiebele people in Ghana—a reference to the earliest inspirations for 3D printing by Emerging Objects.

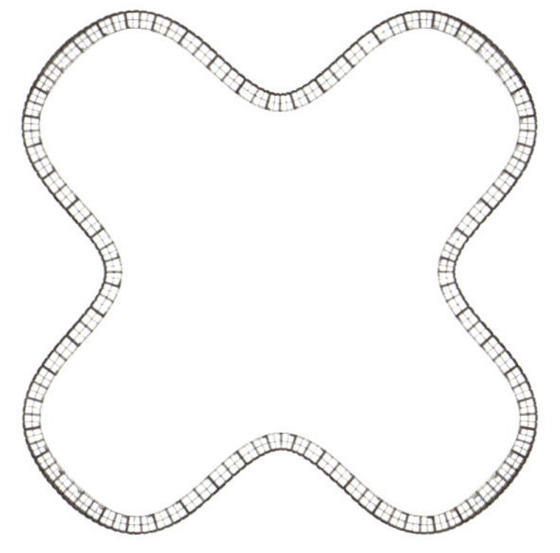

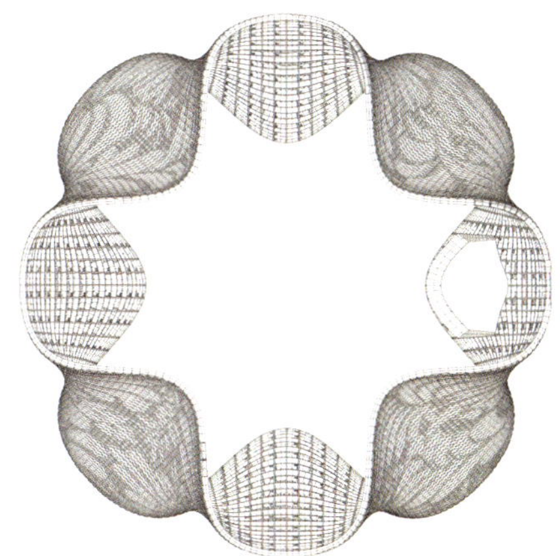

2.14d

2.14e

2.14f

Thinness Pavilion

APTUM / CEMEX

Built 2017

San Francisco, United States

2.15a

2.15b

2.15c

2.15d

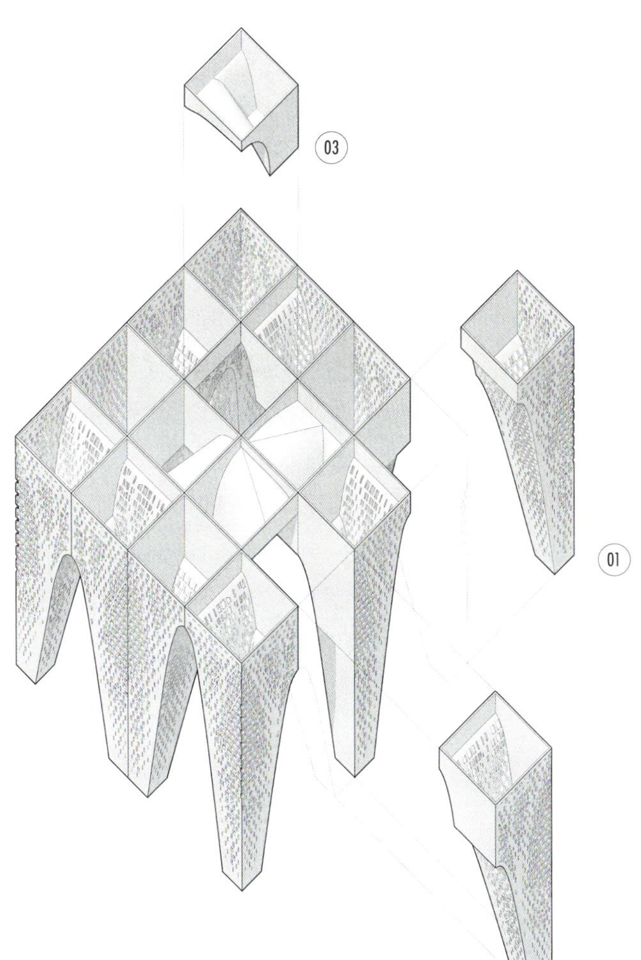

01	02	02	01
02	03	03	02
02	03	03	02
01	02	02	01

2.15f

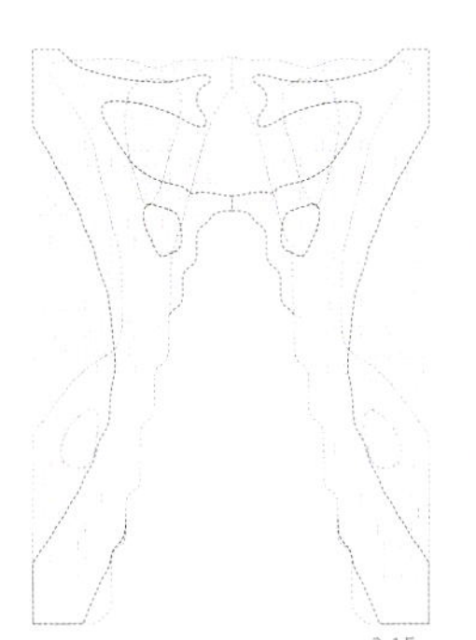

2.15e

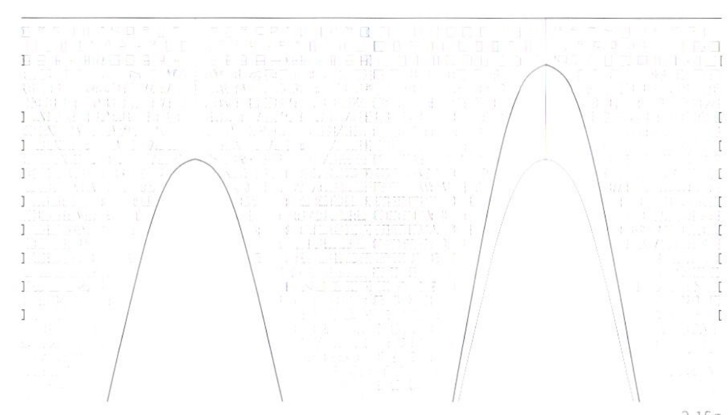

2.15g

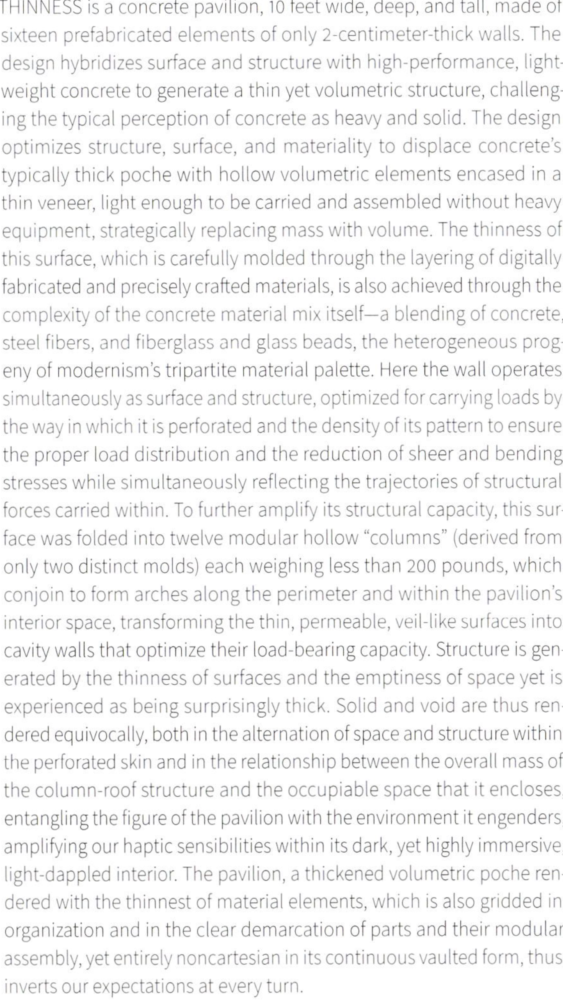

THINNESS is a concrete pavilion, 10 feet wide, deep, and tall, made of sixteen prefabricated elements of only 2-centimeter-thick walls. The design hybridizes surface and structure with high-performance, lightweight concrete to generate a thin yet volumetric structure, challenging the typical perception of concrete as heavy and solid. The design optimizes structure, surface, and materiality to displace concrete's typically thick poche with hollow volumetric elements encased in a thin veneer, light enough to be carried and assembled without heavy equipment, strategically replacing mass with volume. The thinness of this surface, which is carefully molded through the layering of digitally fabricated and precisely crafted materials, is also achieved through the complexity of the concrete material mix itself—a blending of concrete, steel fibers, and fiberglass and glass beads, the heterogeneous progeny of modernism's tripartite material palette. Here the wall operates simultaneously as surface and structure, optimized for carrying loads by the way in which it is perforated and the density of its pattern to ensure the proper load distribution and the reduction of sheer and bending stresses while simultaneously reflecting the trajectories of structural forces carried within. To further amplify its structural capacity, this surface was folded into twelve modular hollow "columns" (derived from only two distinct molds) each weighing less than 200 pounds, which conjoin to form arches along the perimeter and within the pavilion's interior space, transforming the thin, permeable, veil-like surfaces into cavity walls that optimize their load-bearing capacity. Structure is generated by the thinness of surfaces and the emptiness of space yet is experienced as being surprisingly thick. Solid and void are thus rendered equivocally, both in the alternation of space and structure within the perforated skin and in the relationship between the overall mass of the column-roof structure and the occupiable space that it encloses, entangling the figure of the pavilion with the environment it engenders, amplifying our haptic sensibilities within its dark, yet highly immersive, light-dappled interior. The pavilion, a thickened volumetric poche rendered with the thinnest of material elements, which is also gridded in organization and in the clear demarcation of parts and their modular assembly, yet entirely noncartesian in its continuous vaulted form, thus inverts our expectations at every turn.

2.15h

Diamonds House
Gilles Retsin Architecture
Unbuilt 2016
Wemmel, Belgium

2.16a

Diamonds House is a three-story building comprised of a complex stacked assembly of a multitude of discrete, serialized, prefabricated, and interlocking hollow timber components. Although seemingly complex in overall form due to the total number of components and their individuated articulation, the assembly consists of only two different modular linear elements that are repeated on three distinct scales and are designed to be both fabricated and assembled using computational tools. At the scale of the house, these linear, modular components are bundled together, aggregated, and amassed, to read as thickened slabs at each level, such that their ends appear to intersect like Lincoln logs. These timber components, which each have a square section rotated by 45 degrees and are thus perceived to be diamond-shaped, have differing yet complementary "female" and "male" end conditions designed as fractional subcomponents of the original module—either an extruded, three-quarter, L-shaped section, or a smaller quarter-scaled, diamond-shaped section—that enables these discrete pieces to interlock. These ends are painted black to amplify the joints and boundary conditions between elements while intensifying the reading of the modularity of the whole. Discreteness is a characteristic of all architectural works that are necessarily constructed out of many distinct individual smaller elements. The Diamonds House exploits this base architectonic condition while radically reducing the number of key elements, calling attention to this discretization of parts and the relation of parts to wholes through the design of each element and their modes of distribution and assembly. The diamond-shaped section thus differentiates linear elements aggregated along a plane that, if rotated 45 degrees, would seamlessly combine, just as the multitude of stacked elements, each protruding beyond their apparent intersection to differing lengths, calls attention to both their individuation and quantity as well as their genealogy from a single modular type. Here, heterogeneity is produced from a radically limited family of modular parts through syntactical logics that determine the specific ways in which these parts can be assembled, where the assembly is defined by the mass customization of logistics and the syntactical organization of modular parts rather than form.

2.16b

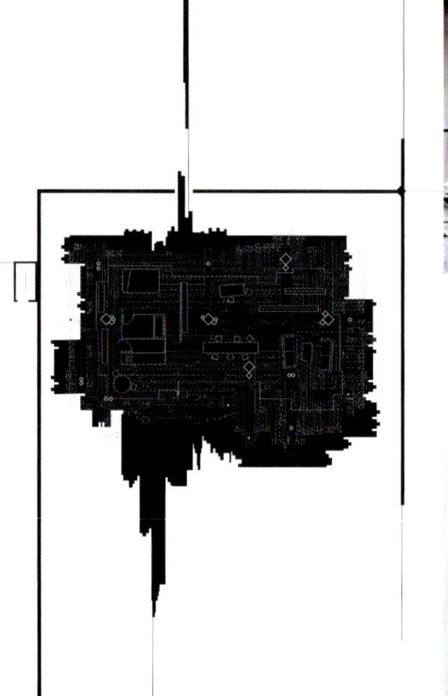

2.16c

2.16d

2.16e

Tallinn Architecture Biennale Pavilion
Gilles Retsin Architecture

Built 2017
Tallinn, Estonia

The Tallinn Architectural Pavilion is one of the first built prototypes of a family of discretized architectures by Gilles Retsin—a smaller abstract fragment that represents the potentials of a new system of modular discrete building blocks using computer-driven automation for their fabrication and assembly. Rather than a single global form comprised of thousands of variant pieces that share a genealogical code, the Tallinn Pavilion is constituted by a series of discrete building blocks, that, akin to LEGO, can be assembled into a variety of structures. These building blocks are based on cheap, locally available, off the shelf, standardized 3.3-by-1.35-meter sheets of 18 mm-thick exterior plywood that were cut by a CNC-machine and then assembled into a stiff, lightweight building blocks capable of bearing structural loads. Operating as a generic part, each building block was based on a simple set of shared parameters for its potential to be placed anywhere within the structure, each block being comprised of a family of straight, 45-degree, 90-degree and 135-degree elements and designed to meet the required structural performance criteria encountered under compression, tension, as a cantilever, or as a column.

2.17a

2.17b

2.17c

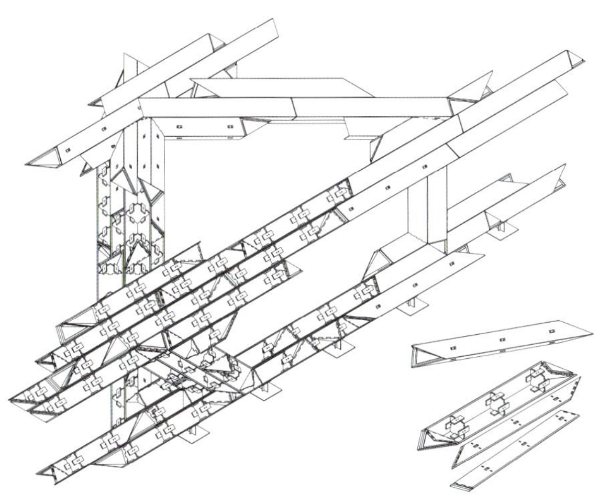

2.17d

2.17e

2.17f

Royal Academy of Arts
Gilles Retsin
Built 2019
London, England

2.18a

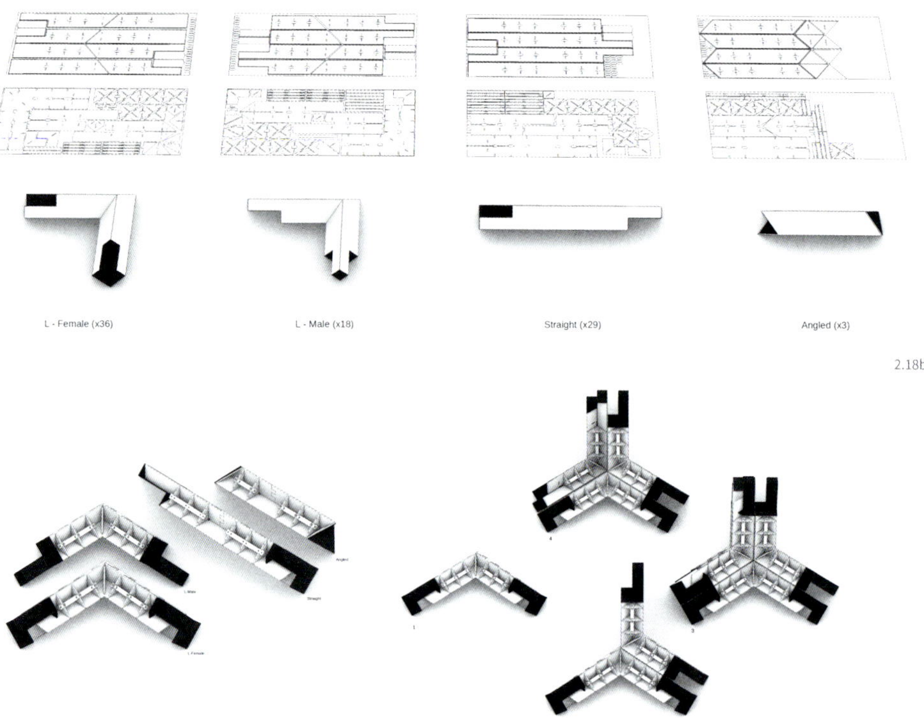

2.18b

2.18c

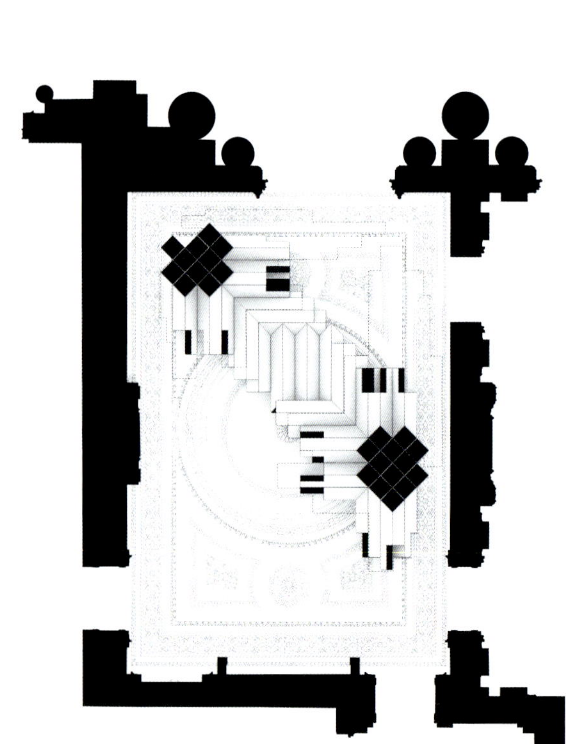
2.18d

2.18e

2.18f

An extension of earlier research on discretized building modules evident in the Diamonds House and Tallinn Architecture Pavilion, the Royal Academy of Arts project is both a unique spatial installation and a testbed for the full-scale construction and assembly of modular building blocks conceived as large scale "digital materials." These digitalized building blocks operate as a kit of parts with embedded syntactical rules, designed into each module, for their local connection and modes of assembly without determining in advance a predefined global form, enabling a range of permutations and the recombination of components. Each of the distinct types of building blocks is assembled from 9 mm-and-12 mm-thick, CNC-milled plywood sheets. These timber modules, which are hollow and lightweight, with interior fins for stability, are engineered to be able to perform in any structural situation within the installation. This allows for their use as generic elements within a range of applications—highly specific in their individuated design but thoroughly flexible in their capacity to be aggregated and assembled as an open system. In aggregate form, the blocks are held together under tension with lateral steel rods placed in specific, repeating connection points between the elements. Each module is therefore relatively weak, but the redundant combination of elements bundled together, such as the clustering of vertical elements to form a loadbearing column, generates a strong structure.

Exploring how Augmented Reality could be used for fabrication, rather than merely visualization, Microsoft's Hololens was used to assemble the modular timber building blocks in real-time. The Hololens overlays a digital model of the envisioned design in the exhibition space, indicating the position of the blocks and their connections. As the blocks are modular and the design is not fixed, adaptations to the design could therefore be done in real-time.

2.18g

2.18h

House Block
AUAR: Automated Architecture Labs
Built 2021
Clapton, East London, United Kingdom

2.19a

House Block is designed and built using a discrete housing system, a modular kit of parts that operates as a full-scale prefabricated automated construction system. The system of prefabricated modules was designed to be used in conjunction with its combinatorial app, which generates, analyzes, and assesses different building assemblies that can be produced using this system. The system is based on the repetition of self-similar parts—a single 120 cm-by-60 cm-by-20 cm timber building block, AUAR Lab's Block Type A, a module comprised of interlocking planar subcomponents CNC-milled, with minimal waste, from a single standardized sheet of plywood that can be assembled by hand. The resulting lightweight building modules can be oriented in any direction, erasing traditional distinctions of floor, wall, and roof, and be conjoined using a simple connector system into different overall configurations that can be adapted or dismantled and reconfigured, to offer a high degree of spatial variation, which responds to the desire for individuation and changing user needs over time. The expansive range of combinatorial permutations demonstrates the enormous flexibility of the system despite the reduced number of different core components, while also supporting participatory approaches to housing, where local communities can take advantage of accessible visualization, fabrication, and assembly tools to upgrade their skillsets, while being provided with a tangible system to build their own housing. Advanced as a new model and platform for decentralized modular housing, House Block was designed for collaborative construction while simultaneously anticipating the full integration of digital design with automated prefabrication and construction methods. As a form of "digital material" these discrete building blocks can be described as an aggregation of voxels, 18 cubic voxels (6-by-3-by-1 voxels) with each voxel having a side dimension of 20 cm. This enables the conflation of physical building modules with a computational voxel grid that collapses material and digital domains, allowing for the direct translation from digital simulation to physical assembly and construction. An equivalence is thus established between the discrete building element and a unit of data that enables it to be "computed," advancing a full-scale experimental project that realizes the potential of "Discrete Automation."

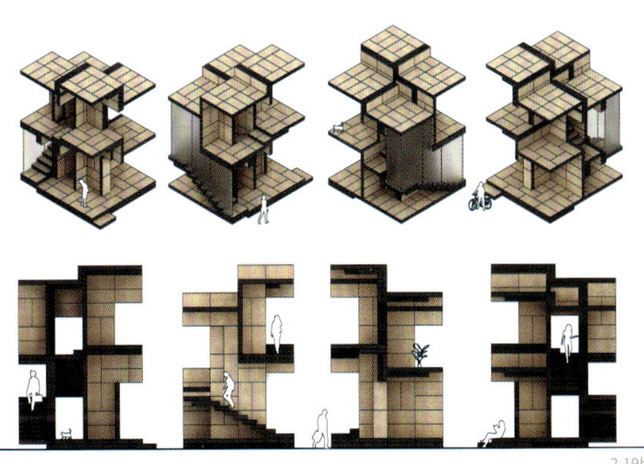

2.19b

2.19c

2.19d

2.19e

2.19f

Generative Logic
Nested Modularity

Nesting multiple levels of modularity in a project is one way to make use of the efficiency of a modular system while having functional and aesthetic flexibility. Each section of a façade or plan can be tuned to its specific needs while adhering to an overall modular system. The appearance of modularity can be further obscured through shuffling of the module types and their attributes.

Generative Process
Berlin Free University

The Berlin Free University uses multiple modular systems to determine both its plan and façade. For the façade, two different module widths are used with several sub-panel heights. Each of these sub-panels are further categorized into different physical attributes such as transparency, operability, and depth. Based on the programmatic requires of the spaces, different combinations are used.

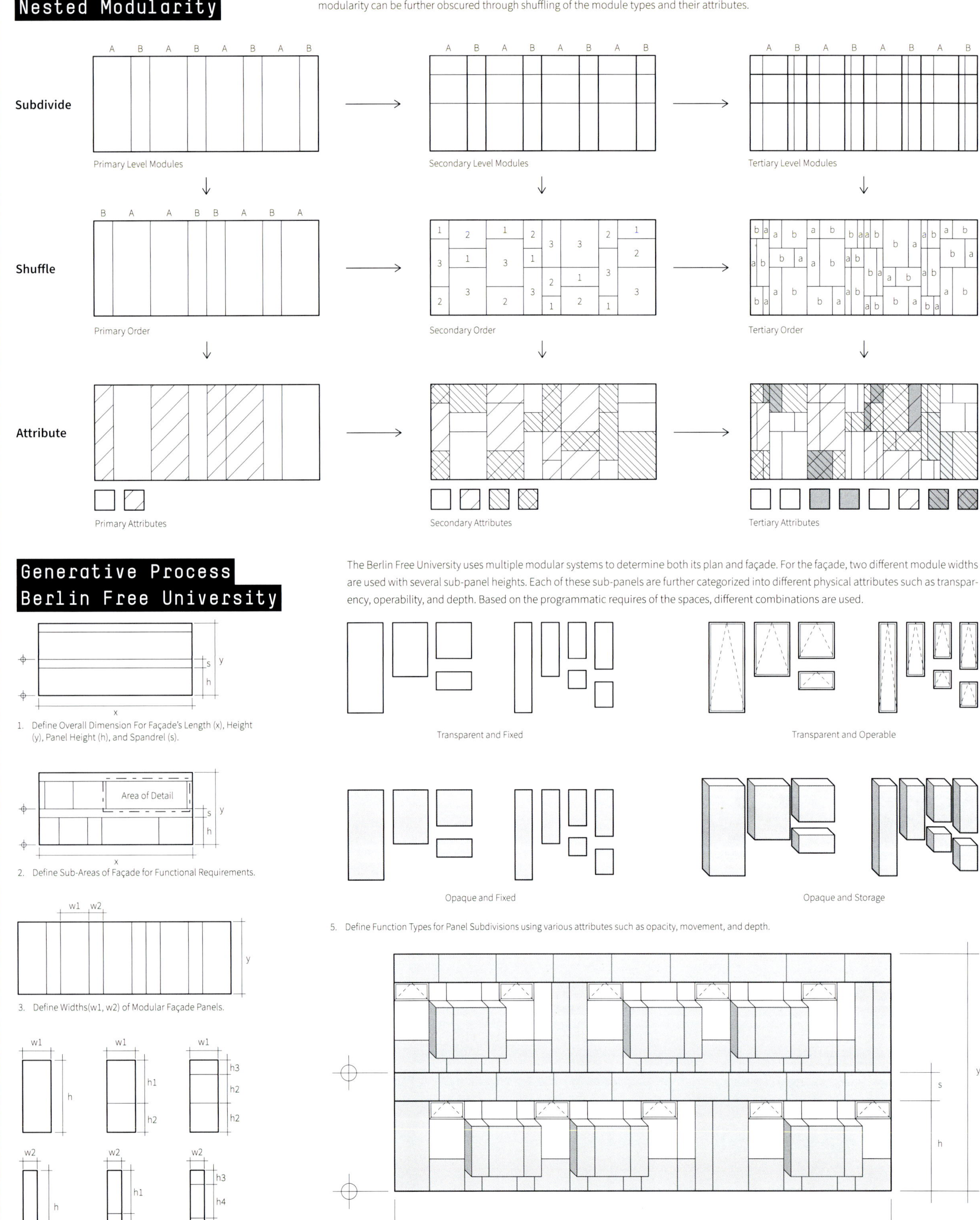

1. Define Overall Dimension For Façade's Length (x), Height (y), Panel Height (h), and Spandrel (s).

2. Define Sub-Areas of Façade for Functional Requirements.

3. Define Widths(w1, w2) of Modular Façade Panels.

4. Define Heights (h1, h2, h3, h4, h5) of Nested Panels.

5. Define Function Types for Panel Subdivisions using various attributes such as opacity, movement, and depth.

6. Apply Hierarchy to Façade for Various Program Requirements. For example, a library might get more storage modules than a meeting space.

Generative Matrix

x = 17069 mm
y = 11887 mm
h = 2048 mm
s = 914 mm
w1 = 610 mm
w2 = 1219 mm
h1 = 610 mm
h2 = 1219 mm
h3 = 1829 mm
h4 = 3048 mm
Performance Types =
100% Opaque
0% Opaque
Function Types =
Storage
Operable Window
Organization =
Room Program

Control Model

x = 17069 mm
y = 11887 mm
h = 2048 mm
s = 914 mm
w1 = 305 mm
w2 = 1676 mm
h1 = 610 mm
h2 = 1219 mm
h3 = 1829 mm
h4 = 3048
Performance Types =
100% Opaque
0% Opaque
Function Types =
Storage
Operable Window
Organization =
Room Program

Module Width

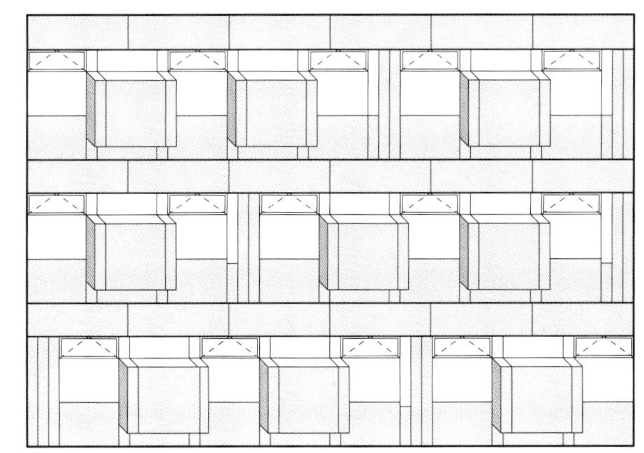

x = 17069 mm
y = 11887 mm
h = 2048 mm
s = 914 mm
w1 = 610 mm
w2 = 1219 mm
h1 = 305 mm
h2 = 914 mm
h3 = 1524 mm
h4 = 3048 mm
Performance Types =
100% Opaque
0% Opaque
Function Types =
Storage
Operable Window
Organization =
Room Program

Nesting Heights

x = 17069 mm
y = 11887 mm
h = 2048 mm
s = 914 mm
w1 = 610 mm
w2 = 1219 mm
h1 = 914 mm
h2 = 2134 mm
h3 = 3048 mm
h4 = 3962 mm
Performance Types =
0% Opaque
Function Types =
Operable Window
Organization =
Room Program

100% Glass

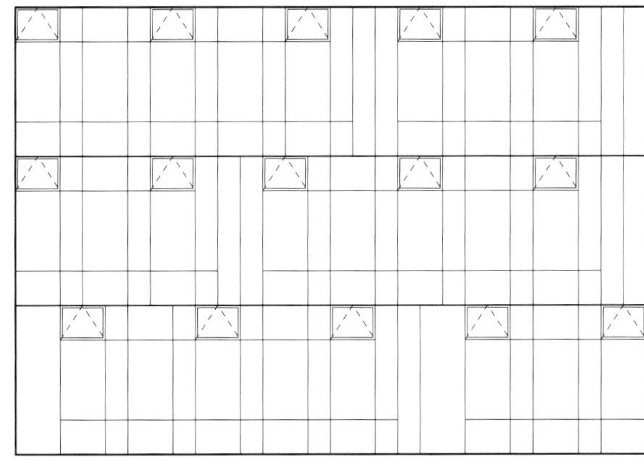

x = 17069 mm
y = 11887 mm
h = 2048 mm
s = 914 mm
w1 = 610 mm
w2 = 1219 mm
h1 = 610 mm
h2 = 1219 mm
h3 = 1829 mm
h4 = 3048 mm
Performance Types =
100% Opaque
0% Opaque
Function Types =
Storage (d=.5, 1, 2)
Swinging Window
Sliding Window
Organization =
Room Program

100% Storage

x = 17069 mm
y = 11887 mm
h = 2048 mm
s = 914 mm
w1 = 610 mm
w2 = 1219 mm
h1 = 610 mm
h2 = 1219 mm
h3 = 1829 mm
h4 = 3048 mm
Performance Types =
100% Opaque
50% Opaque
0% Opaque
Function Types =
Storage
Shading Device
Operable Window
Organization =
Room Program

50% Opaque

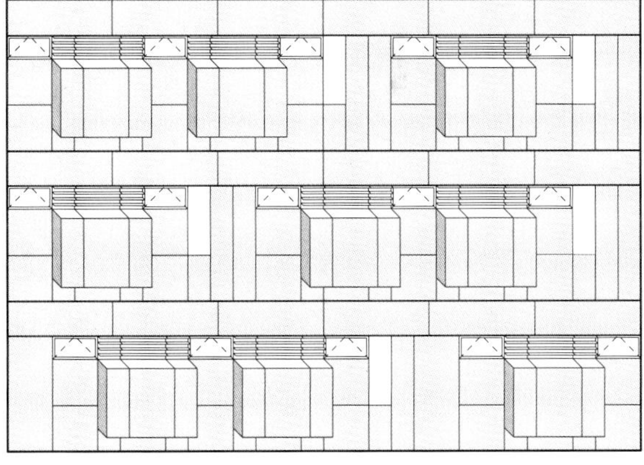

x = 17069 mm
y = 11887 mm
h = 2048 mm
s = 0 mm
w1 = 610 mm
w2 = 1219 mm
h1 = 305mm
h2 = 914 mm
h3 = 1524 mm
h4 = 2134 mm
h5 = 3048 mm
h6 = 3962 mm
Opacity Types =
100% Opaque
0% Opaque
Function Types =
Storage
Operable Window
Organization =
Gradient

Gradient

x = 17069 mm
y = 11887 mm
h = 2048 mm
s = 0 mm
w1 = 610 mm
w2 = 1219 mm
h1 = 914 mm
h2 = 3048 mm
h3 = 3962 mm
Opacity Types =
100% Opaque
0% Opaque
Function Types =
Storage
Operable Window
Organization =
Staggered

Staggered

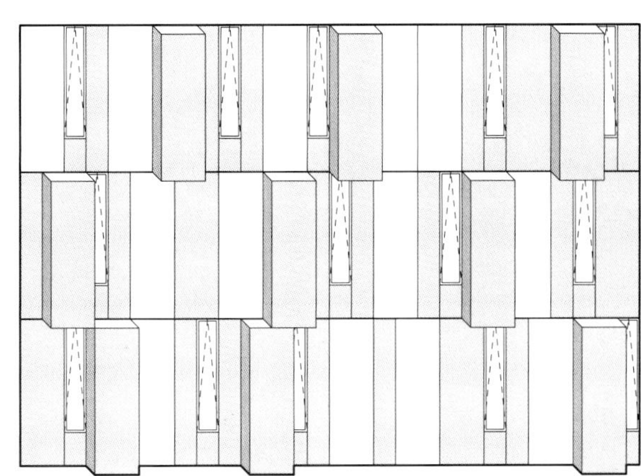

Generative Logic Modular Tessellation

The history of architecture offers thousands of examples of tiled surfaces. Many of these use one of the three regular periodic tilings made by equilateral triangles, squares, or hexagons. However, there are many less common tiling patterns that employ irregular polygons or use more than one tile module in period or aperiodic patterns. These tessellations of the plane can also use inscribed patterns that obscure the base tile edges thereby increasing the appearance of continuity between them.

Regular Periodic

Triangle

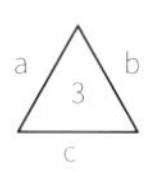

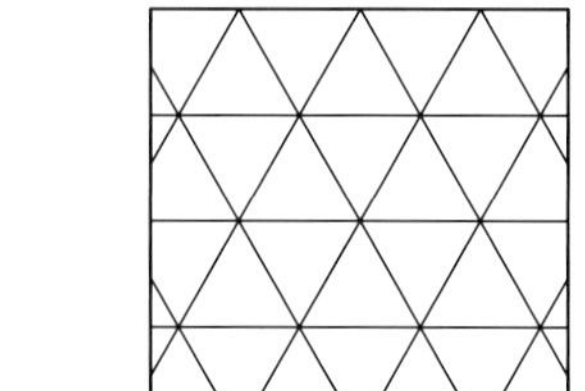

all sides = 1
all angles = 60°

The equilateral triangular tile is one of three regular tilings of the plane.

Square

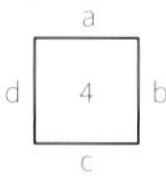

all sides = 1
all angles = 90°

The square tile is the second of three regular tilings of the plane.

Hexagon

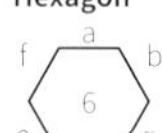

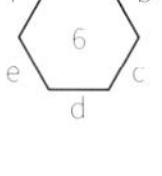

all sides = 1
all angles = 120°

The hexagon tile is the third of three regular tilings of the plane and is also the result of dense circle packing.

Irregular Periodic

Rectangle

a = c, b = d
all angles = 90°

Rectangular, rhombic, kite, and other quadrilateral tilings are topologically identical to square tiling.

Cairo Pentagon

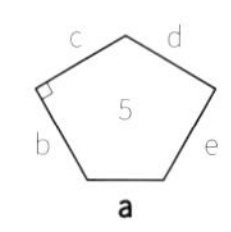

b = c = d = e = 1
a = √3 - 1
<bc = <de = 90°
<ab, <cd, <ea = 120°

One of 15 irregular pentagonal tilings, the Cairo tile was named after its use as a street paving tile in Cairo.

Irregular Hexagon

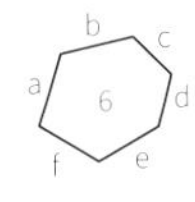

a = b, c = d, e = f
<ab = <cd = < ef = 120°

This is one of three types of irregular hexagonal tilings that can tile the plane without gaps.

Semi-Regular Periodic

Pythagorean Tiling

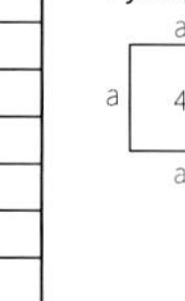

b = a/2
all angles = 90°

Although commonly made from two squares with a 1:2 edge length ratio, other ratios can also be used.

Hexagon / Triangle

all sides = 1
hexagon angles = 120°
triangle angles = 60°

Also known as a triaxial weave, this pattern is used on the façade of the Dome of the Rock in Jerusalem.

Truncated Square

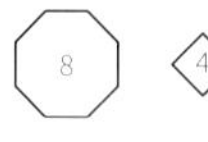

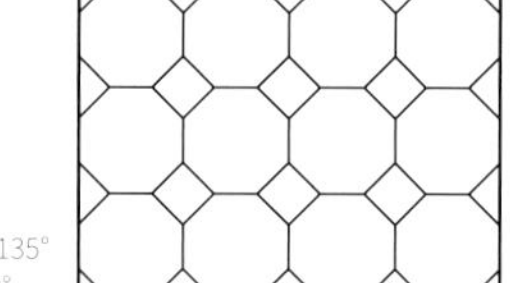

all sides = 1
octagon angles = 135°
square angles = 90°

Also known as Mediterranean tiling, this pattern is commonly used on floors with contrasting tile colors.

Semi-Regular Aperiodic

Pinwheel

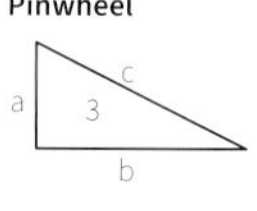

a = 1, b = 2, c = √5
<ab = 90°
<bc = 26.565°
<ca = 63.435°

The Pinwheel tile is a recursive tile that was famously used for Federation Square in 2002 in Melbourne.

Penrose (P2)

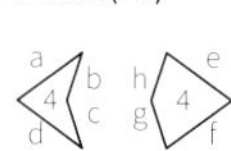

a, d, e, f = (1+√5)/2
b, c, h, g = 1
<ab, <cd = 36°
<ad, <ef , <eh, <fg = 72°
<bc = 144°
<hg = 216°

Developed by Rogar Penrose in the 1970s, the tiles fill a plane without rotational or translational symmetry.

Girih

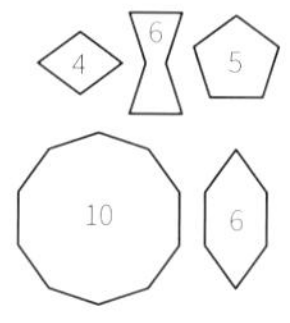

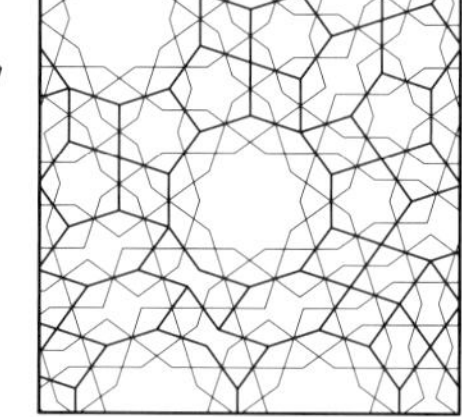

all sides = 1

Girih tiles with inscribed patterns were common within Persian architecture between the 11th-14th centuries.

Generative Process Ravensborne College

The Ravensborne College façade uses four unique tiles with three colors. The arrangement of tiles is aperiodic and can be modified to produce varying scales of rotationally symmetric clusters. When removed from the pattern, these clusters serve as three scales of openings on the façade.

1. Generate tile 1 by defining edge length (X) of an equilateral triangle.

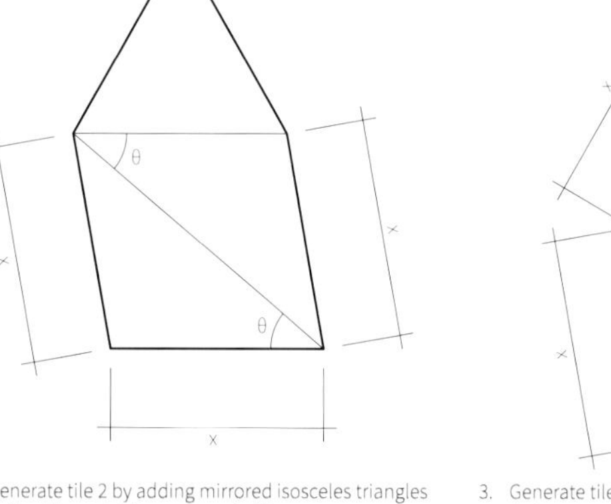

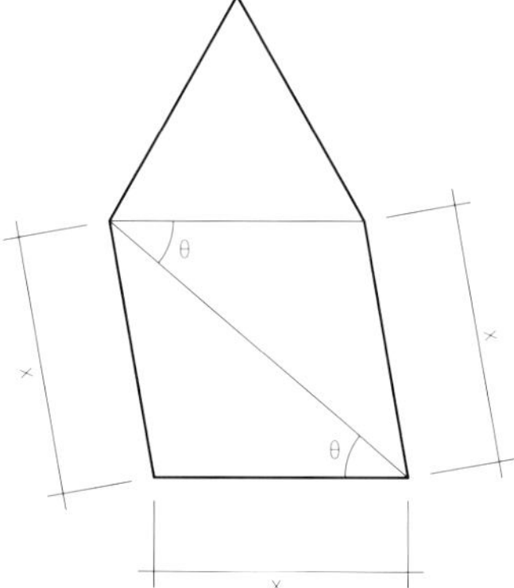

2. Generate tile 2 by adding mirrored isosceles triangles defined by variable acute angle (θ).

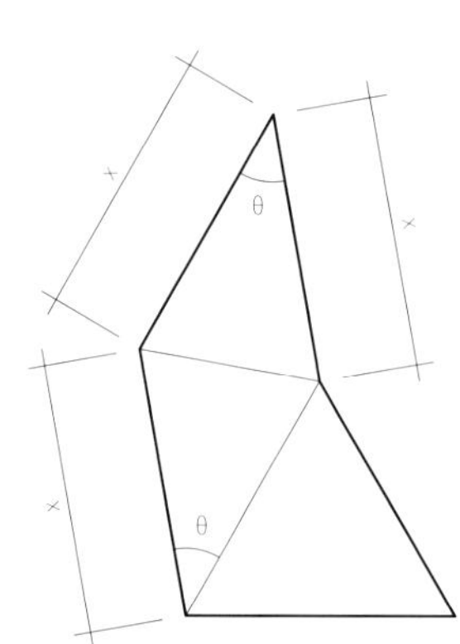

3. Generate tile 3 by adding nirrored isosceles triangles defined by variable acute angle (θ).

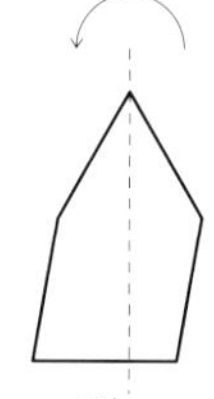

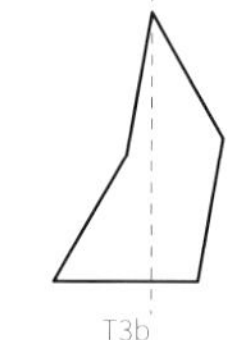

4. Mirror tiles to complete the catalog all tile options.

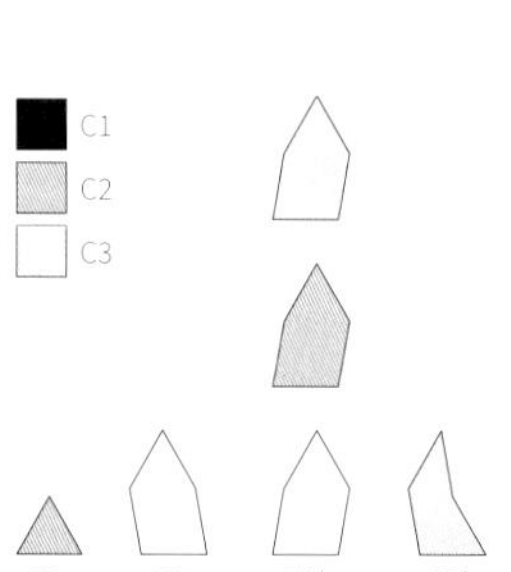

5. Define color/infill scheme.

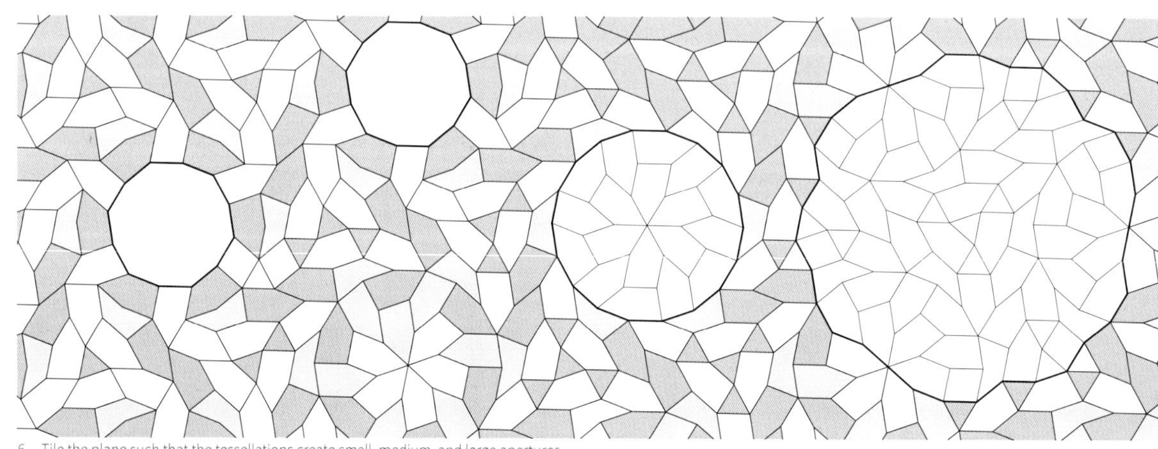

6. Tile the plane such that the tessellations create small, medium, and large apertures.

Generative Matrix

x = 325 mm
θ = 40°
Tiles = set A

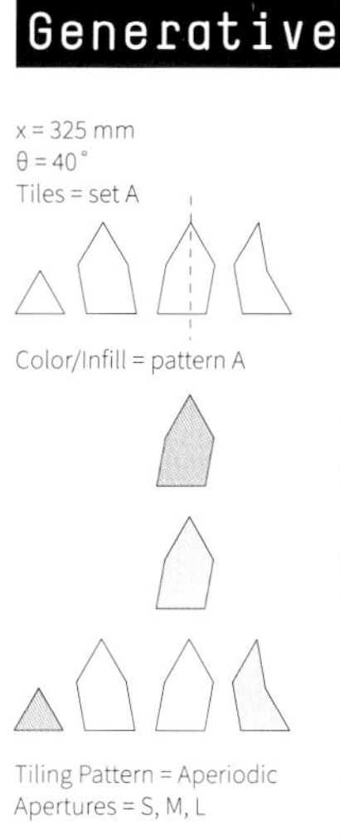

Color/Infill = pattern A

Tiling Pattern = Aperiodic
Apertures = S, M, L

Control Model

x = 325 mm
θ = 40°
Tiles = set A

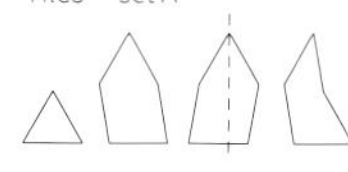

Color/Infill = pattern B

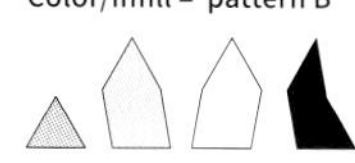

Tiling Pattern = Aperiodic
Apertures = S, M, L

Color Scheme

x = 325 mm
θ = 20°
Tiles = set B

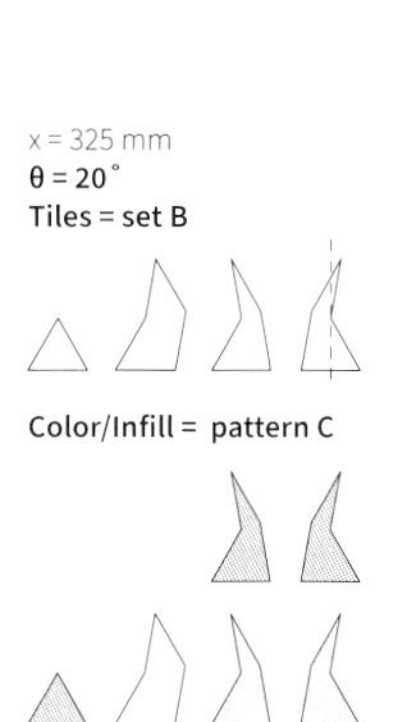

Color/Infill = pattern C

Tiling Pattern = Aperiodic
Apertures = S, M, L

Acute Angle

x = 325 mm
θ = 40°
Tiles = set A

Color/Infill = pattern D

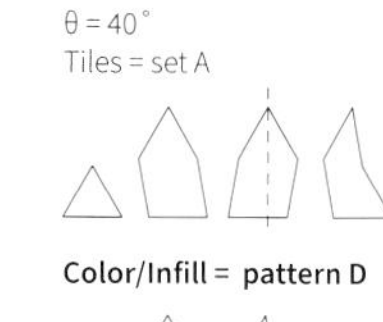

Tiling Pattern = Aperiodic
Apertures = S, M, L

Arc Infill

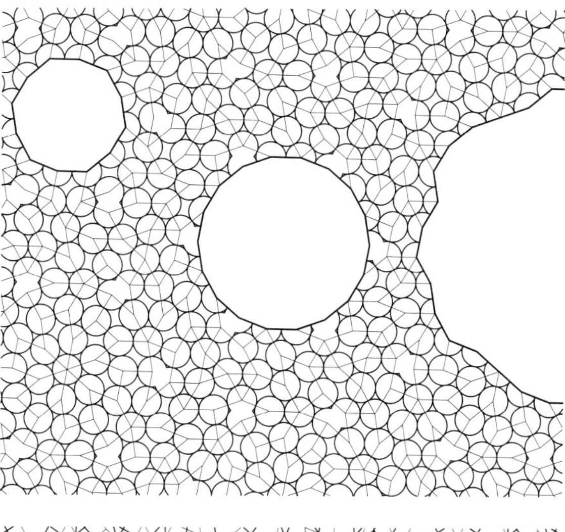

x = 325 mm
θ = 40°
Tiles = set C

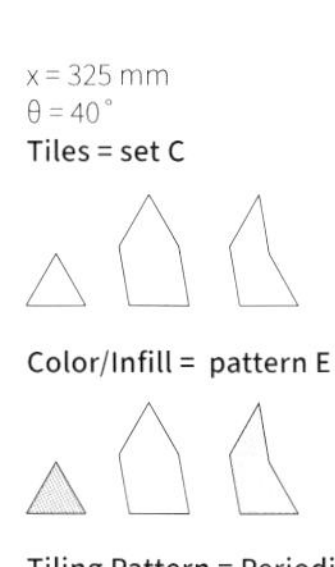

Color/Infill = pattern E

Tiling Pattern = Periodic
Apertures = S, M, L

Periodic

x = 325 mm
θ = 40°
Tiles = set A

Color/Infill = pattern F

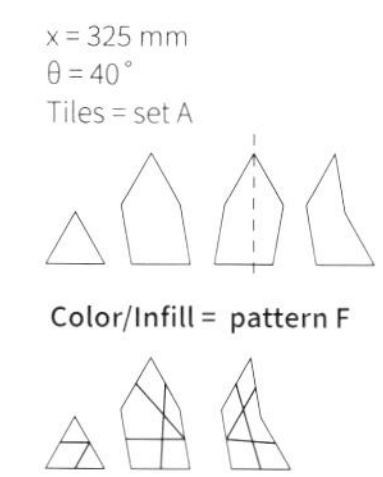

Tiling Pattern = Aperiodic
Apertures = S, M, L

Line Infill

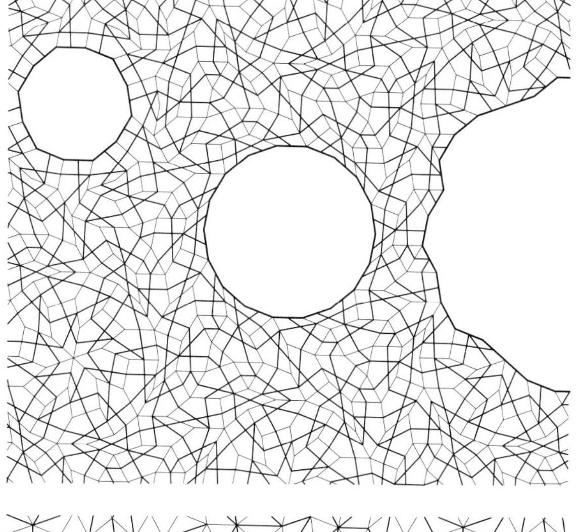

x = 325 mm
θ = 45°
Tiles = set D

Color/Infill = pattern G

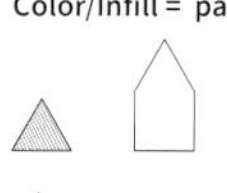

Tiling Pattern = Aperiodic
Apertures = S, M, L

Two Tiles

x = 325 mm
θ = 40°
Tiles = set A

Color/Infill = pattern H

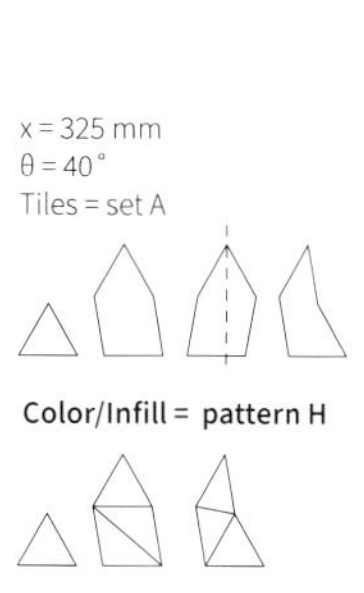

Tiling Pattern = Aperiodic
Apertures = S, M, L

Triangle Infill

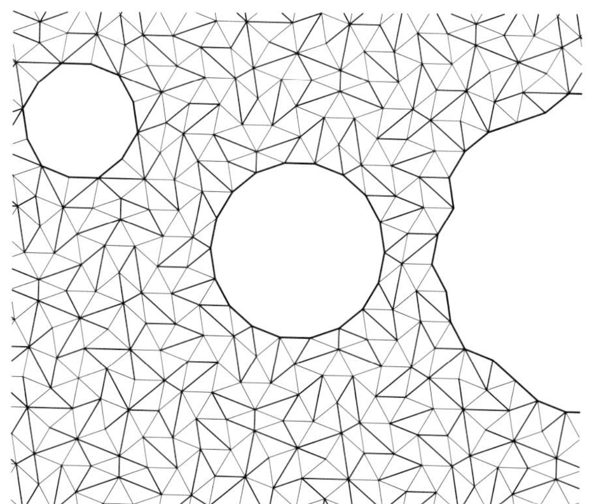

Generative Logic
Modular Growth

There are several procedural systems for the generation of modular systems. Many of these rely on an underlying modular tessellation and then replace the tile with one or more modular components. Tile connectivity can either be assured through careful design of the component pattern or through more complex rule sets (e.g. Wang Tiles), constraint solvers (e.g. Wave Function Collapse), or collision detection.

Truchet Tiles: Sébastien Truchet, a French priest and early typographer, first described this pattern in 1704.

Diagonal Truchet Tiles: A maze-like pattern is the result of only drawing the pattern's diagonals.

Arced Truchet Tiles: Sol Lewitt used this technique in his 1974 project Arcs and Lines.

Truchet-Smith Tiles: This meandering curve version was developed by Cyril Smith in 1987.

Eight Tile Truchet: The tile system can use an unlimited number of tiles and rotations.

Hexagonal Truchet Tiles: A hexagonal grid can be used instead of a square grid.

Cairo Tile Truchet: This modular tile system was used on Confluence Park for the pavers. (Matsys 2018)

Warped Truchet Tiles: A parametric tile can be used that adapts to the constraints of a warped grid.

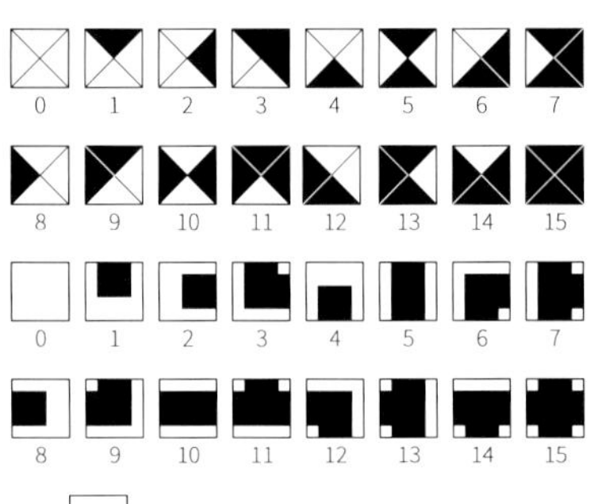

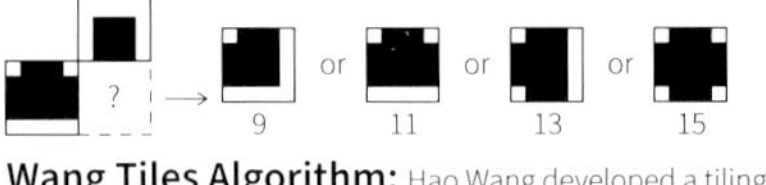

Wang Tiles Algorithm: Hao Wang developed a tiling system in 1961 that allows for greater complexity in the procedural generation of tiled patterns. Rather than rely on a tile set where every side matches, only certain combinations of tiles are possible with Wang Tiles. Using bitwise math, the matching tile can be found for any cell.

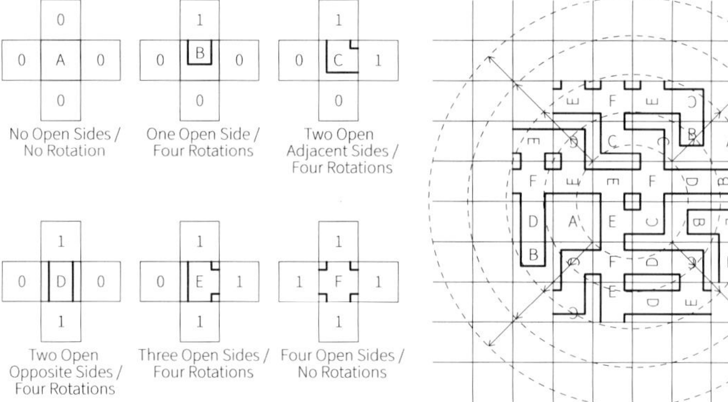

Wave Function Collapse Algorithm: Only tacitly related to the concept of the same name from quantum mechanics, the Wave Function Collapse (WFC) algorithm is similar to Wang tiles but connects it to a constrain solver such that if one tile is changed, it causes a chain-reaction of updates to the pattern to assure the proper connectivity of each cell.

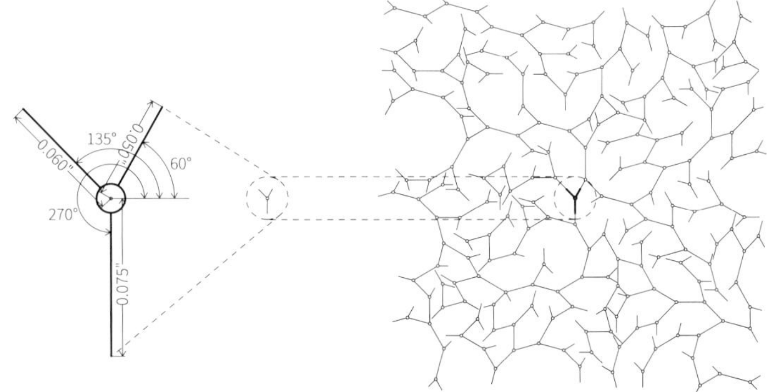

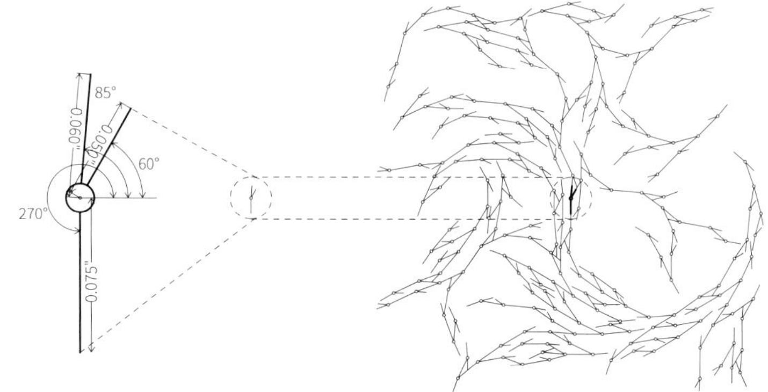

Modular Growth through Collision Detection: Radically different than the modular tile systems above, a different approach can be used that dispenses with the need for a grid of any kind. In this system, a module has connectivity points from which new modules can attach as long as they do not intersect any other existing modules in the network. Small changes in the design of the component can lead to large macro-behaviors in the larger network as seen in the two examples above. The only difference between the two modules in the angle of one arm from 135 to 85 degrees. This modular growth system is related to what are called L-Systems developed by the biologist and botanist Aristid Lindenmayer in 1968. L-Systems can be used to describe the growth properties and morphology of plants.

Generative Process
Bloom Game

The Bloom Game uses one modular component with three slots. Through the rules of combinatorics and collision detection, the game can be digitally simulated prior to construction in reality. By rerunning the simulation and weighting different combination patterns or selecting different module parameters, the designer is able to predict possible game outcomes.

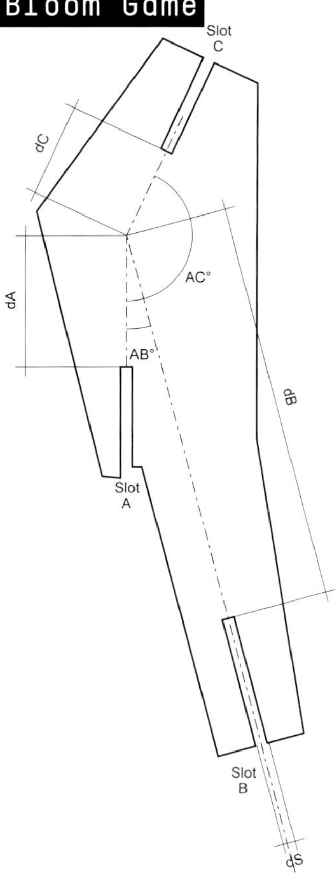

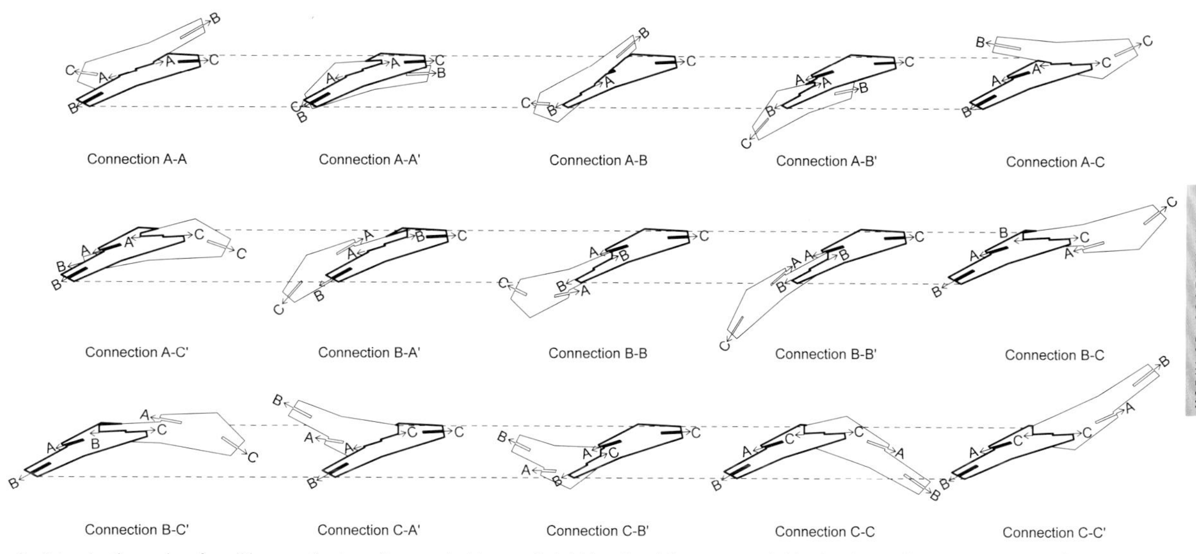

1. Create a component with a number of slot connections at various distances and angles from the component's center.

2. Determine the number of possible connection types. For example, A-A means that slot A on the existing component is joined to slot A on the new component. A-A' flips the second component around the slot's central axis. For this particular component with 3 slots, there are 15 possible connection types. The number of combinations can be found by using the equation C = n!/(n-k)!k! where n is the number of possible slots between two components (6) and k is the number of slots that connect (2): (6 · 5 · 4 · 3 · 2 · 1)/((4 · 3 · 2 · 1) · (2 · 1)) = 15.

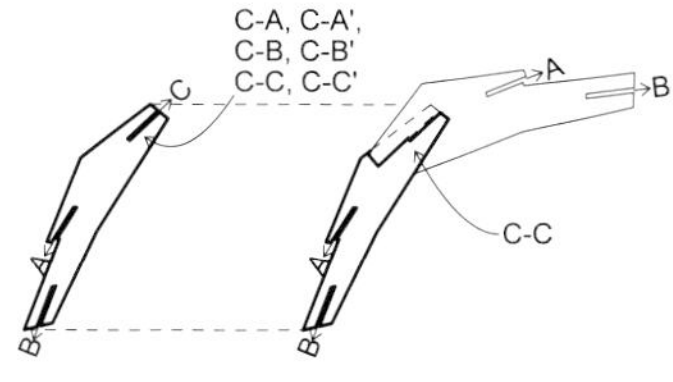

3. For an available slot, select from the available connection types for that slot. Check to see if the new component intersects with any of the existing components. If not, add it to the list of existing components.

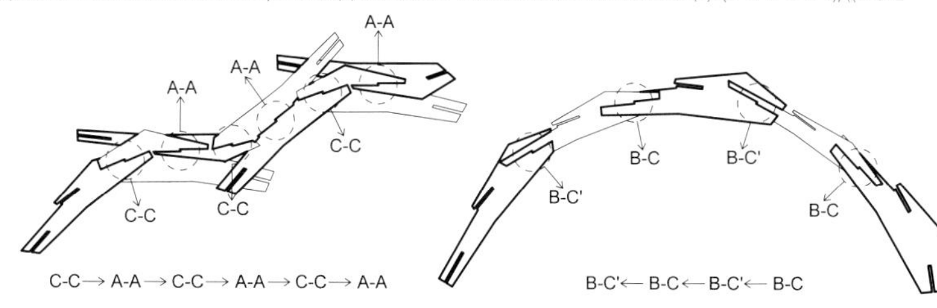

4. Observe patterns of connections and their formal behaviors. Use these patterns when selecting from possible connections to weight the selection process towards desired behaviors.

Generative Matrix

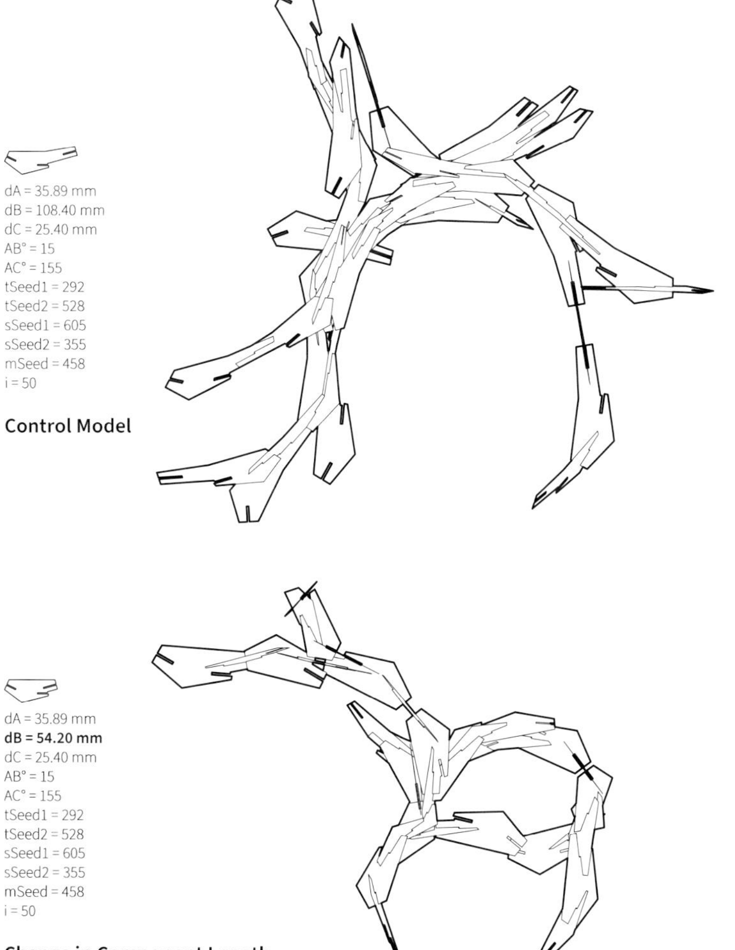

dA = 35.89 mm
dB = 108.40 mm
dC = 25.40 mm
AB° = 15
AC° = 155
tSeed1 = 292
tSeed2 = 528
sSeed1 = 605
sSeed2 = 355
mSeed = 458
i = 50

Control Model

dA = 35.89 mm
dB = 54.20 mm
dC = 25.40 mm
AB° = 15
AC° = 155
tSeed1 = 292
tSeed2 = 528
sSeed1 = 605
sSeed2 = 355
mSeed = 458
i = 50

Change in Component Length

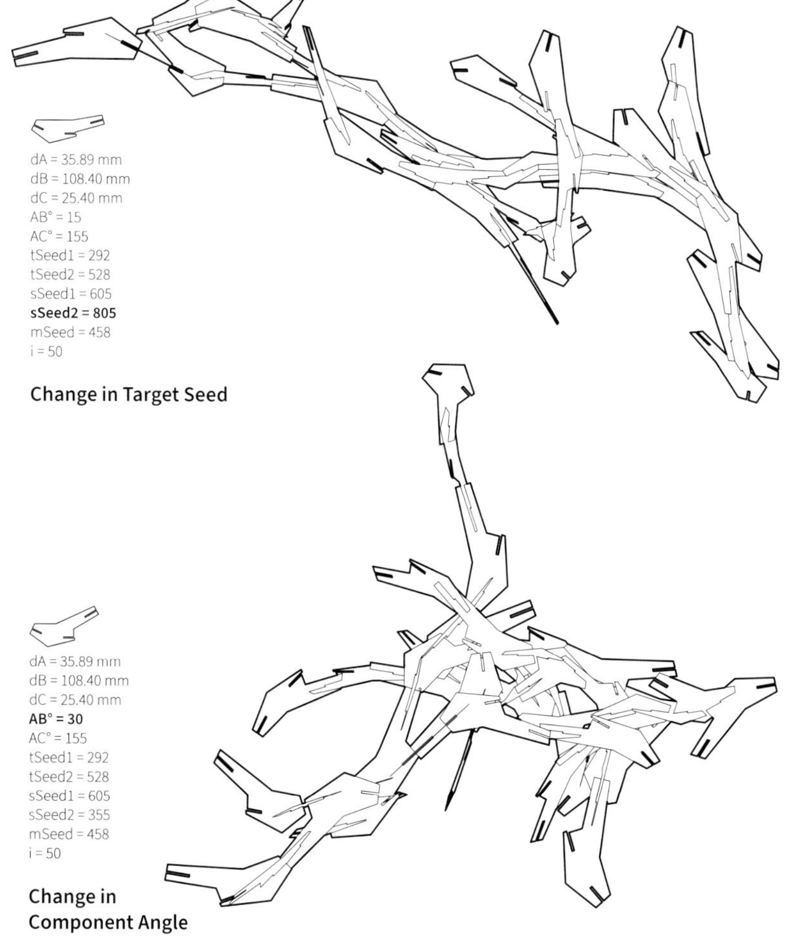

dA = 35.89 mm
dB = 108.40 mm
dC = 25.40 mm
AB° = 15
AC° = 155
tSeed1 = 292
tSeed2 = 528
sSeed1 = 605
sSeed2 = 805
mSeed = 458
i = 50

Change in Target Seed

dA = 35.89 mm
dB = 108.40 mm
dC = 25.40 mm
AB° = 30
AC° = 155
tSeed1 = 292
tSeed2 = 528
sSeed1 = 605
sSeed2 = 355
mSeed = 458
i = 50

Change in Component Angle

PIXELATED FIELDS

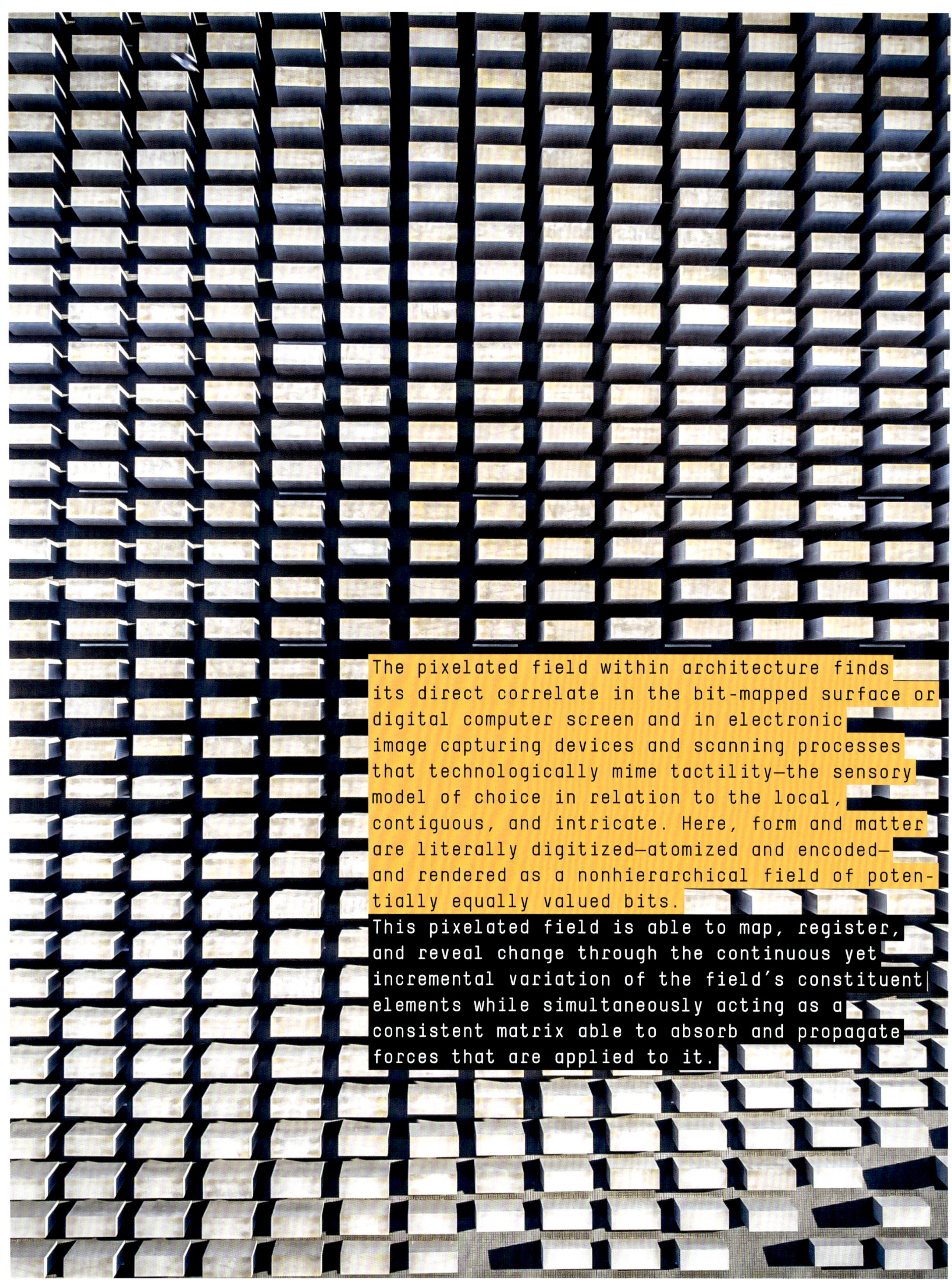

The pixelated field within architecture finds its direct correlate in the bit-mapped surface or digital computer screen and in electronic image capturing devices and scanning processes that technologically mime tactility—the sensory model of choice in relation to the local, contiguous, and intricate. Here, form and matter are literally digitized—atomized and encoded—and rendered as a nonhierarchical field of potentially equally valued bits.

This pixelated field is able to map, register, and reveal change through the continuous yet incremental variation of the field's constituent elements while simultaneously acting as a consistent matrix able to absorb and propagate forces that are applied to it.

Pixelated Fields

Digital Territories to Voxelized Space

The shift from frame to fill, and object to field, moves away from strategies focused on the binding, structuring, and delimitation of space to those that operate through occupation, scattering, and distribution. Although the pixelated field can consist of a collection of any type of punctual element—whether this is the field of lozenge-shaped perforations in the skin of the O-14 Tower or the dispersed forest of columns in Ishigami's Kanagawa Institute of Technology (KAIT) Workshop—the form of individual components is secondary to their necessary repetition. "Field conditions move from the one toward the many, from individuals to collectives, from objects to fields."[1] It is not only that sheer quantity and the multiplication of elements is a precondition of the field, it is also that the repetition of elements, their accumulation, is what initially enables each object within the field to be de-individualized and emptied of semantic meaning, in order to become part of a larger and more abstract collective constellation. Within the field, the part is individuated without being individualized. It is neither a whole in itself nor a fragment of a larger whole, but rather a critical element of a larger matrix whose meaning is dependent on the relationship of its constituent parts—their relative positions, orientations, and scales—and the density, distribution, and differential patterning of the collective field that they create.

The pixelated field within architecture finds its direct correlate in the bit-mapped surface or digital computer screen and in electronic image capturing devices and scanning processes that technologically mime tactility—the sensory model of choice in relation to the local, contiguous, and intricate. In scanning processes, form and matter are literally digitized—atomized and encoded—and rendered as a nonhierarchical field of potentially equally valued bits. These "pix-els," an abbreviation of "picture elements," refer to the smallest single components of a digital image. These are numerically distinct, discrete entities that correspond to different levels and types of measurable information. Hidden below the digital pixelated field is a micro-architecture that operates below the limits of perceptibility. It is a structure that references the grid of Cartesianism, yet also initiates its evolution. In the digitized surface, it is the intensification of the grid, and the specificity and local differentiation of the fill, that displaces the dominance of the grid's frame, while simultaneously translating its static structure into a flexible gradient field. This pixelated field is able to map, register, and reveal change through the continuous yet incremental variation of the field's constituent elements while simultaneously acting as a consistent matrix able to absorb and propagate forces that are applied to it. These systems remain globally coherent because of the repetition, consistency, and sheer quantity of punctual elements, yet support an endless array of locally unique moments—singularities—defined by the specificity of information initially mapped by the system and the rules set up to transcode it, or by the forces introduced into the system that then operate on, and impact the field.

The literal transformation from object to field is thereby the direct result of two conditions generated by digital media. First, a mode of filtering or digital micro-processing that, through the process of digitized intervention, converts real cultural artifacts into mediated bits of quantifiable information that are locally differentiated, yet homogeneous in their immateriality. Despite their use in mapping complex material systems, computers are in fact matter blind and therefore act as a rarefying filter to initially produce smooth consistency and continuity in the new system. What is generated in this process are abstract diagrams extracted from the real that expose and foreground the formal and relational (syntactic) logics of material artifacts. The ability to synthesize disparate types of programmatic, historical, contextual or technological information is therefore facilitated by the operative framework of the digital device, which inevitably ensures that as real molar-forms are transformed into abstract micro-matters, differences in kind, qualitative intrinsic differences, are directly translated into extrinsic differences in degree.[2] The numerical encoding of these diagrams is what allows them to be translated into consistent planes of information—variable datasets that are then able to be manipulated by algorithms employed to transcode and parametrically direct their interaction and transformation.

This is exemplified in projects such as the de Young Museum ❶ and the Agbar Tower, where, in each case, the pixelated envelope of the building is the result of a digital diagram operating as a filter through which contextual material is literally sampled,

❶

❷

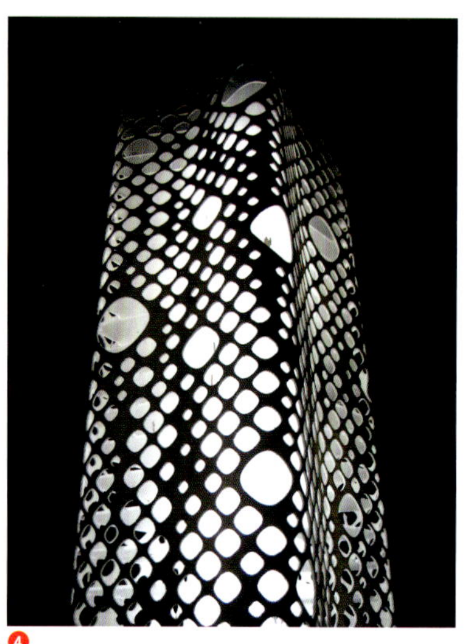

❹

❸

transformed, and redeployed in the making of the exterior skin. In the first case, the tree canopies of Golden Gate Park are photographically indexed and digitally transformed by Herzog & de Meuron as a method to reinterpret context in the making of the permeable copper skin generated for the museum. The pixelated field acts as a rarefying filter through which material is thinned and information eliminated, in order to expose the organizational structures embedded within the original form. Although the figurative specificity, geometry, and materiality of the leaves have been eliminated, the perforated surface acts as an analog for their light-filtering function by retaining the variability of distributed openings evident in the canopy and its characteristic permeability.

In the Agbar Tower ❷❸, the iconic image of a geyser erupting from the volcanic earth that served as an inspiration for the project merges with other contextual information—from the mountain of Monserrat and Gaudi's Sagrada Familia, to the patterning of the surrounding urban fabric and the polychromy of Catalan façades. Here, the pixelated field is the mediating digital device employed to map, selectively interpret and transcode this contextual imagery that is then folded back onto the surface of the tower to become a full-scale architectural materialization of a low-resolution digital display. The mixing of RGB values used to produce the multicolored translucent pixels of the bit-mapped façade are generated by the dynamic interplay of multiple layers of material. These include the three layers of the façade: the modular and heterogeneously perforated interior concrete structure, the colored and corrugated lacquered aluminum panels that range from warmer earth red tones at the bottom to cooler sky blue tones at the top, and the reflective glass-louvered exterior cladding whose responsive system of changing angles blur and modify the perceptual reading of the layers behind. To these material systems is added a fourth component—the complex exterior LED light system, that includes a field of 4,500 separate trichromatic point sources that are integrated into the façade to illuminate the tower at night. The pixelated field is a reference to both the mediating digital diagram employed to parametrically transform the contextual source information for the project as well as the reinvention of the digital surface that is materialized in the making of the building envelope.

In the O-14 Tower by Reiser + Umemoto (RUR) ❹ the layering of different fields of information determine the initial parameters for the development of the perforated concrete shell. Although appearing to be random, the pattern of variable openings that penetrate the surface of the exoskeletal skin is the result of overlaying and parametrically negotiating competing design demands emerging from the optimization of structural requirements, views, ventilation, sun exposure, daylighting, and visual, perceptual effects. Each of these sets of performative requirements was encoded in a patterned field intended to embody the result of a single set of requirements as these would impact and transform an initial field of vertically articulated yet relatively undifferentiated pixels. Although the development of the structure, for example, might demand a capillary branching field that eliminates openings to accommodate the channeling of gravity and lateral loads or a gradient field that reduces the size of openings at the bottom of the envelope to increase its weight-bearing capacity and stability, the gradient field for optimal daylighting preferences a changing porosity that is altered laterally rather than vertically to reflect the differently directed movements of the sun. To these layers that privilege functional and technological optimization is added a turbulent matter field of vortical sworls, perhaps intended to assure that the final pattern of the unrolled façade would be perceived not only as a heterogeneous and random array of variable perforations, but also as a monolithic material whole—a continuous multiplicity—seemingly irreducible to the incremental logics and processes responsible for its evolution. The modulation of this final pixelated field, which operates simultaneously as a diagrid exoskeleton and concrete perforated sunscreen, occurs by locally changing the size, shape, density, and distribution of openings as these respond to competing layers of information. These responses, which include establishing potential lines of repulsion and attraction along capillary networks, for example, that describe the ways in which openings in the field of the façade are programmed to move or shrink when they collide with the location of vectors signifying lines of force or structure, are the result of programming a system that algorithmically defines in advance the possible local moves that can occur given a set of anticipated

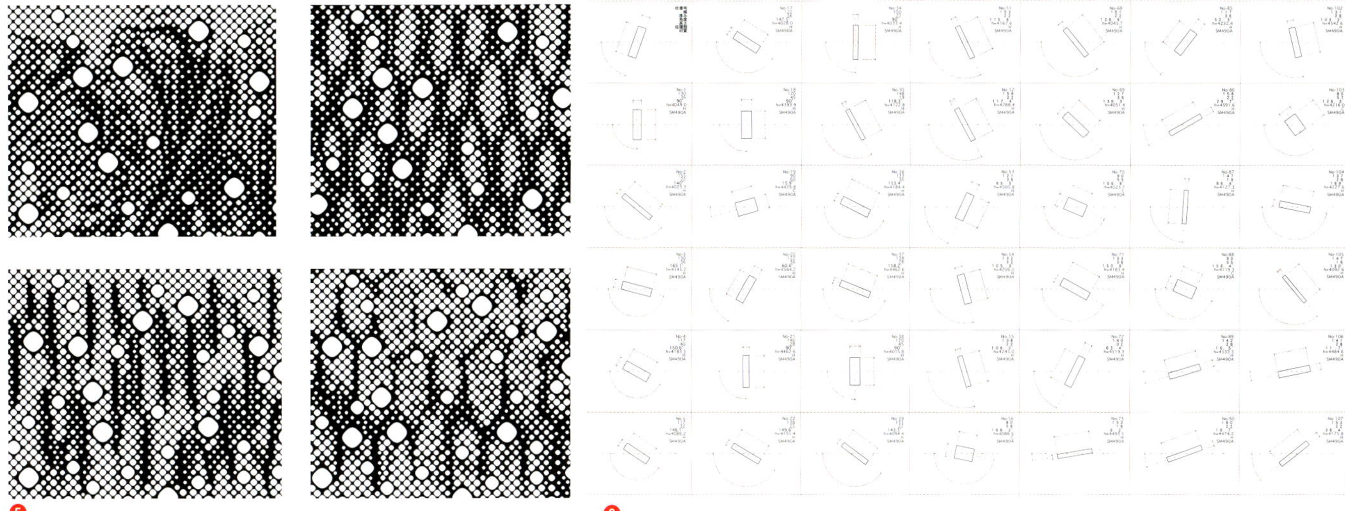

❺ ❻

scenarios ❺. Design is focused less on a predetermined end result, than on the variables introduced into the system and the procedures for their transformation within a changing set of parameters, whereby the design of the generative machine is iteratively tested and refined by repeatedly assessing the results of this process.

As the number of dimensions and degrees of freedom of the pixelated field increase, so does the potential complexity of the field produced. In the KAIT workshop project by Junya Ishigami ❻, the pixels are extruded to create a field of 305 slender white steel columns, each of which is defined by a changing set of parameters. Within the building, space is defined not by boundaries or dimensions, but rather by the changing density of the field where gaseous clouds of points in plan and ethereal lines in elevation accumulate and form fuzzy zones of occupation that reflect and influence the dispersal of program and constellations of activity. Structure is seemingly dissolved by the multiplicity of thin attenuated elements, some operating in compression and others in tension, whose diagrammatic abstraction and heterogeneous placement diffuse their substance into an almost invisible atmospheric field of matter. The shift from a homogeneous grid of pixels to the building's heterogeneous field is achieved by altering four independent parameters of each column. These include its position within the field, its planimetric cross-sectional dimensions, and its degree of rotation within the horizontal plane in relation to the orthogonal axes of the building's enclosure. The minimal approach to the building design in relation to its form, chroma, and materiality, reduces the potential "noise" of the architecture providing a highly rarefied canvas upon which to foreground the spatial complexity of the structural field. This is determined by the vast combinatorial possibilities that are generated by cross-pollinating these four variables and the network of local relations established between the columns that determine their positioning, orientation, and shape. The compression of differentiation into a narrow perceptual range also intensifies the atmospheric experience of the space by focusing awareness on the micro-variations of a gradient field that ultimately dissolves the legibility of architectonic elements.

Our conceptual understanding of the complexity of this field, and its transformation of our thinking of the universal, however, is augmented not only by the expansion of possible permutable column types (which are syntactically rather than semantically defined) but also by the design and specific selection of relational parameters that ensure that the number of different column types appear to be progressively amplified when perceived by a mobile occupant within the space. Just as the extreme vertical elongation of the columns—their thinness in relation to their height—contributes not only to their abstraction but also to their directionality, in plan the generalized "points" of the columns are transformed into a field of dashes—short lines—whose disproportionate cross-sectional dimensions ensure their directionality and mobility. At close range, these are understood as micro-vectors that refer to their process of parametric generation while also subtly alluding to a network of implied connections across the space. When seen in elevation from multiple perspectives, each column also appears to continuously change its width and thickness (almost approaching invisibility when viewed perpendicular to its shortest dimension). This is a perceptual phenomenon given by the variable rotations and highly differentiated cross-sections that together contribute to furthering the complexity and perceptual ambiguity of the field.

The expansion of the pixelated field into three dimensions, augmented by the evolution of spatial modeling and digital fabrication processes, has led to the emergence of "volume elements" known as "voxels" understood as the atomized components of volume that, like the pixel, fill rather than frame space. Ranging in scale from EZCT's computational chair design project to MVRDV's proposals for Rødovre Skyvillage in Copenhagen, the Yongsan Dreamhub in Seoul ❼, and the Why Factory's proposals for a Porous City, the voxelated spatial field is defined not by overarching geometries but rather by changing local relationships whose guiding parameters are responsible for continually modulating the three-dimensional field. It is only perhaps after our experience of the computer's immaterial, weightless, and nongravitational space that we could imagine the suspended pixelated cloud city of the Yongsan Dreamhub in Seoul where humanism's privileging of ground and gravity are foreclosed in favor of the pixelated occupation of space. As a twenty-first-century makeover of Superstudio's

7

8

9

10

ever-extended gridded plane for free occupation, this atomization of space (the underlying hypothesis that precedes design) enacts a three-dimensional digitization of all contextual, programmatic or technological requirements so that these can be algorithmically responded to through the addition, erasure, scaling or redistribution of voxels.

In each case, the voxel field simultaneously acts as a spatial representation of the architectural artifact and a three-dimensional datascape of the changing parameters influencing the design. In the Rødovre Skyvillage project, for example, the cubic pixel is a symbolic mathematical variable that refers to the minimum amount of space required to support a housing unit or office space. As the formulaic relations of the algebraic displace geometry, global forms of organization and the architectural iconographies that they engender are dissolved in favor of a spatial and temporal formlessness generated by changing local parameters. Thus the form of the whole at any moment in time—the shape of the pixelated termite mound or new vertical village mountain—is rendered as a three-dimensional statistical gradient that reflects, through its changing quantities and distribution of pixels, the unstable fluctuations of the Danish real estate economy in relation to its growing and shrinking demographic populations as these are situated in different environmental contexts. The fine-tuning of this field, its density, thickness, or porosity is then governed by increasing the number of parameters that influence the rules for the local distribution and relationship of pixels in the field. The range of possible voxel permutations, a response to potentially shifting parameters, is implied but foreclosed in the selection of a single configuration that, in the end, realizes in built form, the best response to these parameters on a specific site at a single moment in time.

This is distinguished from the range of virtual potentials that are actualized as an extensive series of differentiated skyscrapers in the Why Factory's PoroCity project 8. A twenty-first-century transformation of Kurokawa's Nagakin Capsule Hotel, the skyscraper proposals for a porous city exchange the capsule, a self-contained and removable and exchangeable part of a larger mechanistic whole, for the abstract voxel represented by a piece of white LEGO. Each of these projects defines space based on the individuation of a single unit, a strategy repeated in BIG's residential project for King Street in Toronto. Yet, whereas the capsule in Nagakin had signified the potentials of industrial prefabrication and its capacity to replace worn out parts of a machine over time (likened by the Metabolists' to the regeneration of cells in a living body), the abstract voxels of the PoroCity skyscrapers are a reference to the digitization rather than the mechanization of space where the distinction between solid and void, interior and exterior, or public and private space, is eliminated by the equalizing of all conditions of space given in advance by its division into a voxelated field 9. As a larger effort to inject public space, traditionally relegated to the horizontality of ground plane, into the verticality of the dense skyscraper (a necessity given the increasing populations and densities of our cities and the limited surface area of the earth), the equation of solid and void voxels, akin to white and black pixels distributed on a computer screen, are also an attempt to equalize the private and public domains. The voxel field thus expands the surface area of the planet into a thicker zone of inhabitability and enables the aeration of this zone, that is, access to outdoor space and therefore light and air, by increasing the surface area of the perimeter of the skyscraper without increasing its volume. This strategy of expansion through intension rather than extension, through involution rather than enlargement, is the same condition that enables the highly enfolded surfaces of our lungs, which are exponential in surface area relative to their volume, to oxygenate our bodies. The series of possible outcomes generated by this voxelated space and its defining rule-set—small-grained differentiations that reflect shifting fields of data and are contained within a limited volume—expose the enormous size of the solution space, displacing a reduced set of figured and privileged typologies with an infinite array of potential skyscraper models each defined by a subtle yet specific set of parameters 10.

In the Computational Chair Design (CCD) project 11, the field is the direct result of an automatic computational method intended to displace design authorship with machinic processes that artificially simulate evolutionary development created to "breed" a population of pixelated chairs. Through algorithmic scripting, the genetic

11

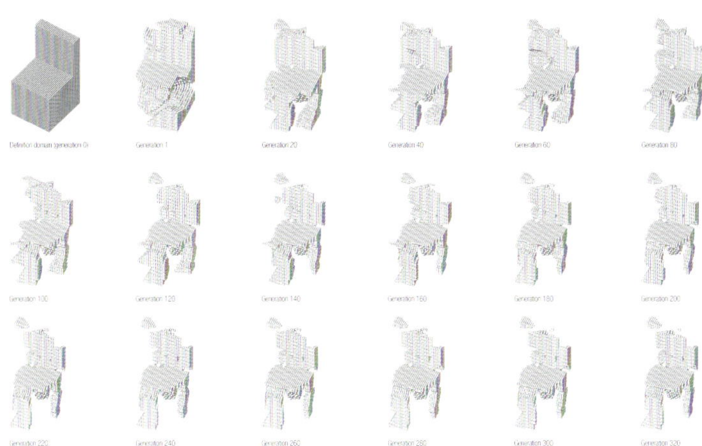

12

PIXELATED FIELDS

transmission of traits from parent to child (that transform over generations of propagation) are synthesized with procedures that simulate the potential for random mutations and natural selection—those that assess the adaptive fitness of the individual chairs generated to their function and environment. Parenting is simulated by the hybridizing of genetic material through the splicing and grafting together of point fields that define the three-dimensional Voronoi cells out of which the chair is constructed. Through computational evolution, the polygonal pixel field that constitutes the chair is then progressively eroded with the intention of breeding the lightest object constructed of the smallest number of voxels that is able to withstand, within a predetermined set of maximal structural deformations, the static load of a sitting body 12. The intention of this experimental process, however, is not to optimize the development of the artifact but rather to create, using artificially intelligent yet unpredictable growth models, a series of objects whose formal definition moves beyond our existing design preconceptions and in so doing, to create a form that is literally unimaginable in advance of its procreation and morphogenetic development. Because of their originary form and incremental structure, these works are seemingly familiar, yet the spatial field that they produce remains, to a certain degree, "unknowable" in the present in relation to current dominant representations of the real.

The movement away from both the clear differentiation of architectural elements, the residue of classical Euclidean geometry, and the homogeneity of modern systems, is evidenced by the disappearance in these works of the intermediary architectural scale and the clearly delimited object. Whether it is through the automated genetic breeding of chairs, the parametric production of an abstract atmospheric forest, or a form of architectural accumulation and exchange that produces village mountains and urban clouds, this new pixelated nature produced is monumental in its consistency (if not also its scale), yet remains unbound and deterritorialized in its collective synthetic form. Just as the grain of sand is linked to both the dune and the mountain, these works establish continuities across scales that exceed our capacity for perceptual and intellectual integration. The monolithic consistency of the whole resonates with intricate micro differentiations at the scale of the detail, yet where the quantitative vastness of the former and the intensive complexity of the latter, conditions which take us to the limits of our intellectual and sensory apparatus, attribute to this work a sublimity that is simultaneously colossal and monstrous, mathematical and dynamic. As the extreme rationalizing effect of computation converges with the dynamic boundlessness of the indeterminate, two opposing historical archetypes and distinct manifestations of the sublime[3] find their synthesis, yielding new forms of architecturalized nature.

Notes

1. Stan Allen, "Field Conditions," in *Points + Lines: Diagrams and Projects for the City* (New York: Princeton Architectural Press, 1999).

2. These terms are drawn from Henri Bergson as interpreted through the writings of Gilles Deleuze in *Bergsonism*, trans. Hugh Tomlinson and Barbara Habberjam (New York: Zone, 1990), 38. Gilles Deleuze and Félix Guattari further elaborate on this concept through a comparison of the games of Chess and Go in *A Thousand Plateaus.* trans. Brian Massumi (Minneapolis: University of Minnesota Press, 1987), 352–353. "Chess pieces are coded; they have an internal nature and intrinsic properties from which their movements, situations, and confrontations derive. They have qualities; a knight remains a knight, a pawn a pawn, a bishop a bishop. . . . Go pieces, in contrast, are pellets, disks, simple arithmetic units, and have only an anonymous, collective, or third-person function: "It" makes a move. . . . Go pieces are elements of a nonsubjectified machine assemblage with no intrinsic properties, only situational ones." For a summary, see also Reiser + Umemoto's *Atlas of Novel Tectonics* (New York: Princeton Architectural Press, 2006), 40–41.

3. Unlike the notion of beauty that attempts the stable integration and unity of reason and sensation, the sublime as defined by Kant in the *Critique of Judgment* emphasizes their discordance by pushing each to its extreme manifestation and producing an immediate juxtaposition between them. According to Kant the tension produces a violent and unstable oscillation between the freedom, chaotic heterogeneity, and boundlessness of the sensible and the totalizing rationality of reason. See Immanuel Kant, "Analytic of the Sublime," in *Critique of Judgement*, trans. J. H. Bernard (New York: MacMillan, 1951), 82–181.

Amsterdam Orphanage
Aldo Van Eyck

Built 1960
Amsterdam, Netherlands

Aldo van Eyck, a member of CIAM and founding member of Team 10, was a supporter of the ideals and language of modernism, yet like many of his contemporaries, was a vocal critic of monumental post-war architecture. He designed the Amsterdam Orphanage to embody his belief that architecture should be anti-monumental and humanizing in character, reflective of the community that it houses, a condition he deemed to be intrinsic to urbanity itself.

The orphanage is thus organized as a small city, a nonhierarchical, unimposing, and decentralized, contiguous field lacking a definitive center or boundary, or the clarity of an overarching figure or form. Extending horizontally along the ground as a system of small-scale interior spaces punctuated by larger shared communal spaces and outdoor courtyards, which group clusters of units and thus establish a mid-scale organization to the whole, the building is primarily ordered by its orthogonal gridded structure and pixelated vaulted roofscape. Despite the linearity of the grid's underlying organization and the zigzagging diagonal along which the primary circulation is organized, the frequent adjacency of indoor and outdoor spaces interspersed within this field encourages an expanded and more free-flowing movement across the whole. Beyond its capacity to provide an ordering device, this pixelated field also anatomizes the architecture into smaller-scale units. These not only appear to transform each room into an individuated spatial element, but also create an analog between the building and the city within which it is situated, while establishing an equivalence between the pixels and the collection of individuals—the community—that they house. This collective is thus rendered evident through the architecture itself, whose scale is modulated to that of its inhabitants, the children occupying the space.

3.1a

3.1b

Nakagin Capsule Hotel
Kisho Kurokawa

Built 1972
Tokyo, Japan

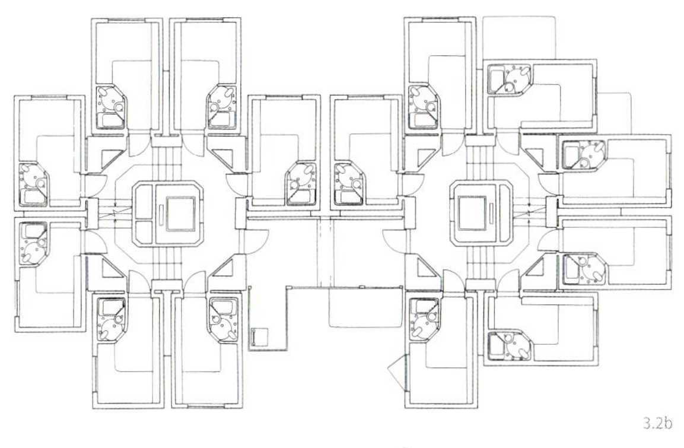

3.2b

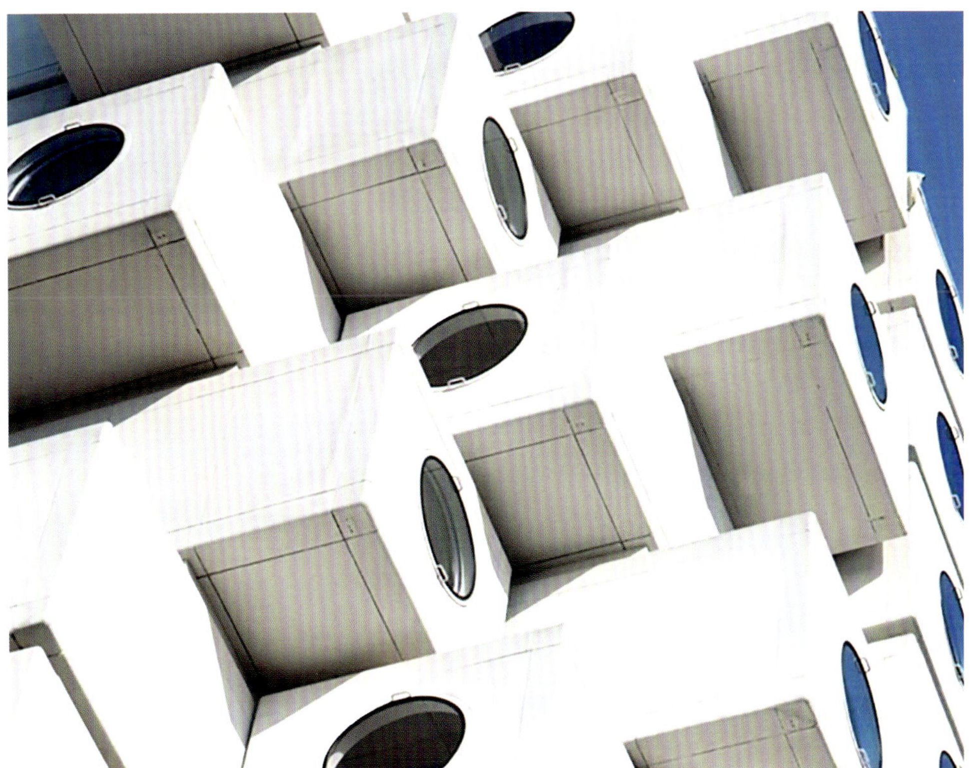

3.2a

3.2e

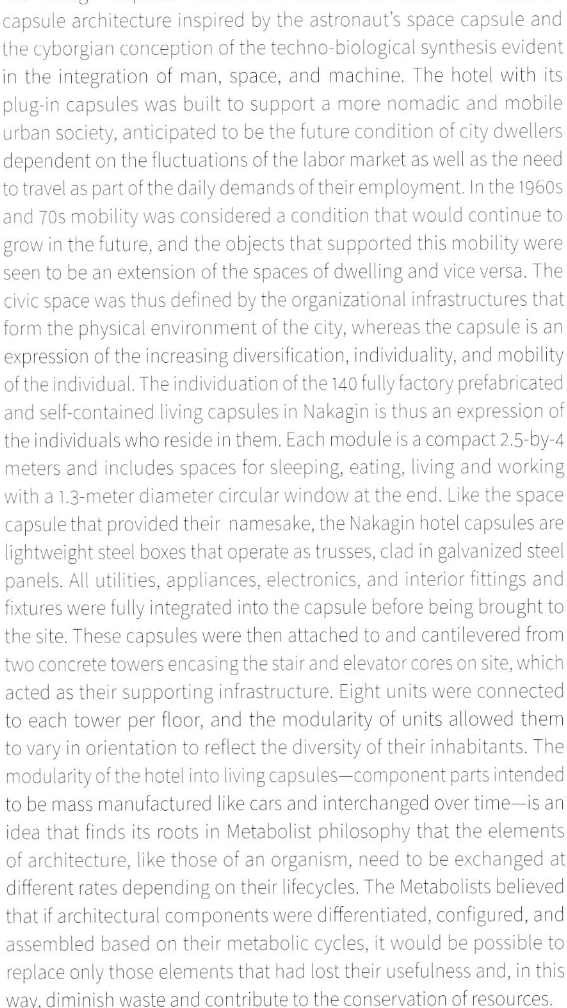

The Nakagin Capsule Hotel is an evolution of Kurokawa's ideas on capsule architecture inspired by the astronaut's space capsule and the cyborgian conception of the techno-biological synthesis evident in the integration of man, space, and machine. The hotel with its plug-in capsules was built to support a more nomadic and mobile urban society, anticipated to be the future condition of city dwellers dependent on the fluctuations of the labor market as well as the need to travel as part of the daily demands of their employment. In the 1960s and 70s mobility was considered a condition that would continue to grow in the future, and the objects that supported this mobility were seen to be an extension of the spaces of dwelling and vice versa. The civic space was thus defined by the organizational infrastructures that form the physical environment of the city, whereas the capsule is an expression of the increasing diversification, individuality, and mobility of the individual. The individuation of the 140 fully factory prefabricated and self-contained living capsules in Nakagin is thus an expression of the individuals who reside in them. Each module is a compact 2.5-by-4 meters and includes spaces for sleeping, eating, living and working with a 1.3-meter diameter circular window at the end. Like the space capsule that provided their namesake, the Nakagin hotel capsules are lightweight steel boxes that operate as trusses, clad in galvanized steel panels. All utilities, appliances, electronics, and interior fittings and fixtures were fully integrated into the capsule before being brought to the site. These capsules were then attached to and cantilevered from two concrete towers encasing the stair and elevator cores on site, which acted as their supporting infrastructure. Eight units were connected to each tower per floor, and the modularity of units allowed them to vary in orientation to reflect the diversity of their inhabitants. The modularity of the hotel into living capsules—component parts intended to be mass manufactured like cars and interchanged over time—is an idea that finds its roots in Metabolist philosophy that the elements of architecture, like those of an organism, need to be exchanged at different rates depending on their lifecycles. The Metabolists believed that if architectural components were differentiated, configured, and assembled based on their metabolic cycles, it would be possible to replace only those elements that had lost their usefulness and, in this way, diminish waste and contribute to the conservation of resources.

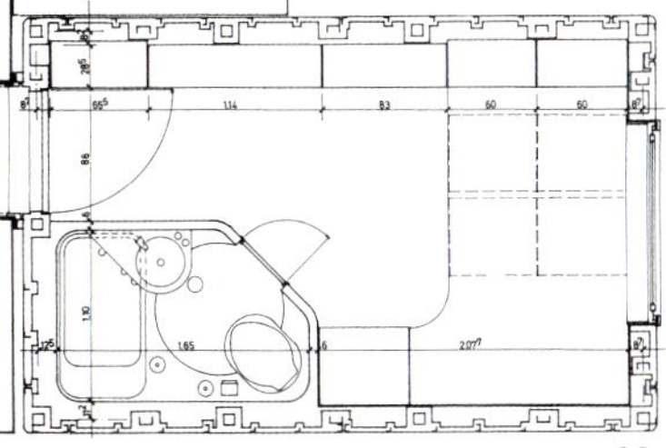

3.2c

3.2d

Memorial to the Murdered Jews of Europe
Peter Eisenman
Built 1998-2005
Berlin, Germany

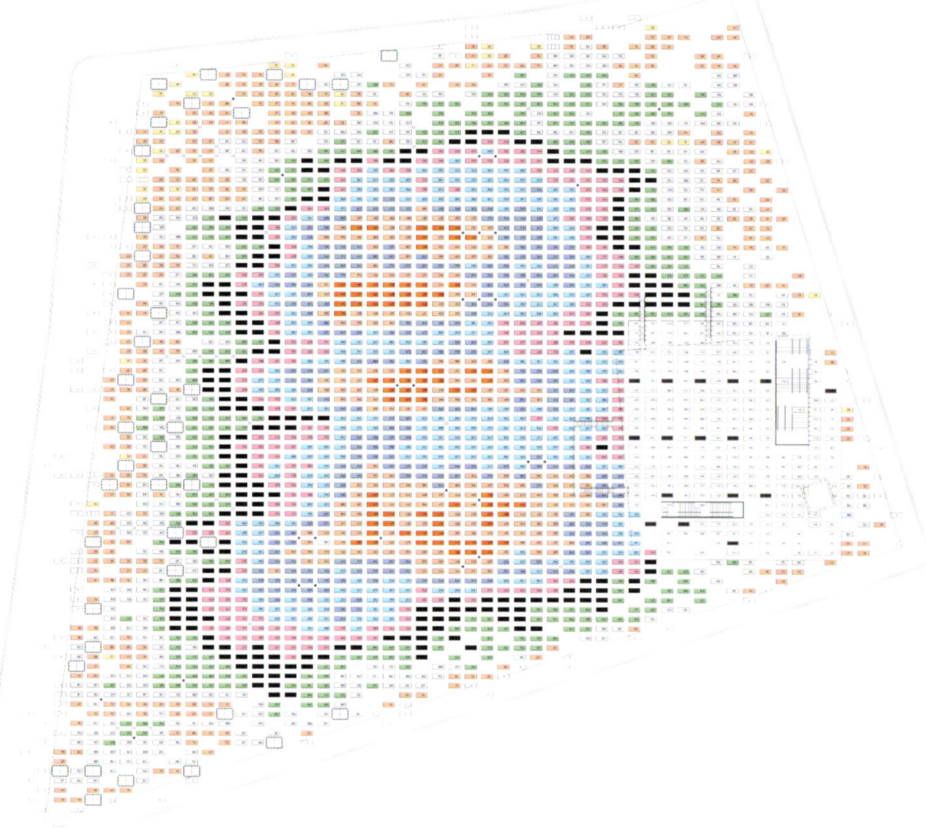

Situated near the Reichstag and adjacent to the Tiergarten in the heart of Berlin, the site of the Memorial to the Murdered Jews of Europe is in an area once occupied by the zone of the Berlin Wall. This public installation project and museum consists of 2,711 solid concrete stelae that are planimetrically organized as a highly regular gridded field. The concrete stelae were formed off site. They are the same dimension in length and width, each 95 cm wide by 2.375 m long with heights that vary from 20 cm at the perimeter to 4.8 m at the center of the site. These abstract and nameless markers materially and dimensionally signify the tombs of the victims that they represent and are spaced apart just wide enough to enable a single body to move between them. The heights of the stelae vary incrementally, so that collectively, the top surfaces of this pixelated field of dark gray slabs form an immense, undulating landscape. The overt repetition of concrete markers is countered by the influence of the changing parameters applied to the field. These adjustments account for the shifting heights and varying vertical positioning of the stelae in relation to the topographies that constitute the ground plane and the implied top surface of the field. They also account for the tilting of the stelae, which rotate up to 2 degrees by a cradle situated at the base of each and that create misalignments and disturbances within the field in addition to subtle vertical undulations that ripple through the site. As the ground plane between the slabs slopes downward, the visitor is compressed within the space between the stelae, which appear to have grown ominously taller as one is drawn into the disorienting underground depths of the site—an experience that foregrounds the overt rationality and brutality of the means by which the victims' lives were extinguished and the magnitude and horror of the Holocaust.

3.3a

3.3b

3.3c

3.3d

3.3e

3.3f

3.4a

3.4b

3.4c

3.4d

Unlike a typical skyscraper, the Agbar Tower was inspired by the iconic image of an erupting geyser and designed to be perceived as a fluid vertical mass bursting forth from the ground and punctuating the horizon of the city. Its form, which also evokes other relationships to its context, such as the towers of Gaudí's Sagrada Familia and the mountain of Monserrat in the distance, is cloaked in a layered pixelated skin that transcodes the geyser into a polychromatic bitmapped image while conflating it with information drawn from the building's surrounding urban and natural environment. The façade is constituted by the interplay of three distinct layers whose superimposition is responsible for the complexity and dynamism of the project. The innermost layer is an internal structural skin of reinforced concrete that is punctuated by 4500 modular rectilinear openings. These produce a semi-random, heterogeneous field of perforations that reflect the gridded patterns of Barcelona's urban fabric and form a changing gradient as one moves from ground to sky. Two distinct layers clad the concrete structure. The middle layer is comprised of lacquered corrugated aluminum panels that are painted in different colors which begin as warmer earth-red tones at the base of the building and become cooler blues and grays as they move toward the sky at its top. The outermost layer is a semi-transparent glass-louvered cladding system, constituted by 59,619 louvers tilted at different angles to deflect direct sunlight and that form a screen that blurs the perception of the inner chromatic envelope. This highly nuanced shimmering surface becomes further articulated by a LED light system, that includes a field of 4,500 separate trichromatic point sources that are integrated into the façade to illuminate the tower at night. The pixelated field becomes an architectural analog to a low resolution RGB image, a reference to both the mediating digital diagram employed to parametrically transform the contextual source information for the project as well as a reinvention of the digital in material and architectural terms.

3.4e

3.4f

3.4g

Kanagawa Institute of Technology Workshop

Junya Ishigami

Built 2010

Kanagawa, Japan

3.5a

The Kanagawa Institute of Technology Workshop is a one-room single story building, approximately 2,000 m² in area, that serves as a flexible studio and workspace for students, and is enveloped in floor-to-ceiling glass and filled with a forest of 305 slender white steel columns. This pixelated field of columns supports a thin, yet expansive white roof plane comprised of a gridded, two-way, steel-framed structure that is banded with parallel linear skylights running the length of the building. Despite the regularity of the building form and the crisscrossed grid of beams that support the roof and delineate the ordering of the ceiling plane, the thin columns appear to be scattered throughout the space, forming a heterogeneous rhythmic field that meets both the floor and ceiling in a random pattern of points. Rather than being positioned in relation to the primary gridded structure, at the ceiling these columns often intersect with a secondary set of beams that are offset from, and bridge, the spaces between this regular patterned structure. The columns filling the space, 42 of which operate in compression for vertical loads and 263 in tension for horizontal loads, are vertically extruded from a planimetric field of rectangular pixels with varying cross-sectional dimensions and axial orientations. Differentiation within this field therefore occurs not only through the global positioning and irregular spacing of columns within the building, but also through the variation of their local parameters—their individual rotations and changing planimetric dimensions—that are defined by shifting structural, programmatic, and aesthetic demands and that complexify the pixelated constellation they produce in plan while subtly transforming their perception in elevation. Within this bright, daylit space, structure is seemingly dissolved by this multiplicity of narrow attenuated elements whose white color, diagrammatic abstraction, and heterogeneous placement diffuse their substance into an almost invisible atmospheric field of matter. Space is defined within the building not by rooms, but rather by the changing density of this pixelated field. Clusters of columns and furniture accumulate and form boundary-less zones of occupation that reflect and influence the patterns of activity dispersed throughout the space.

3.5b

3.5c

3.5d

3.5e

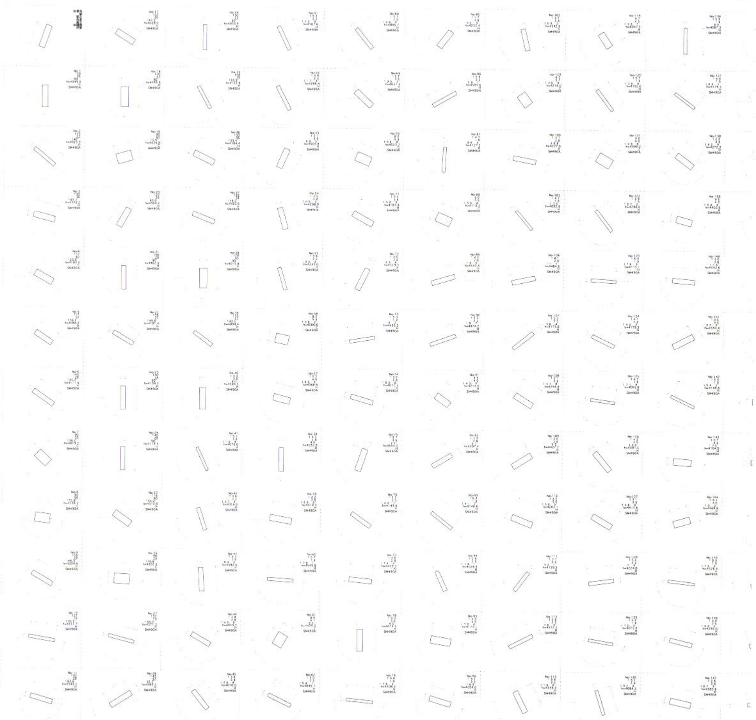

3.5f

O-14 Tower
RUR
Built 2006-2008
Dubai, U.A.E.

3.6a

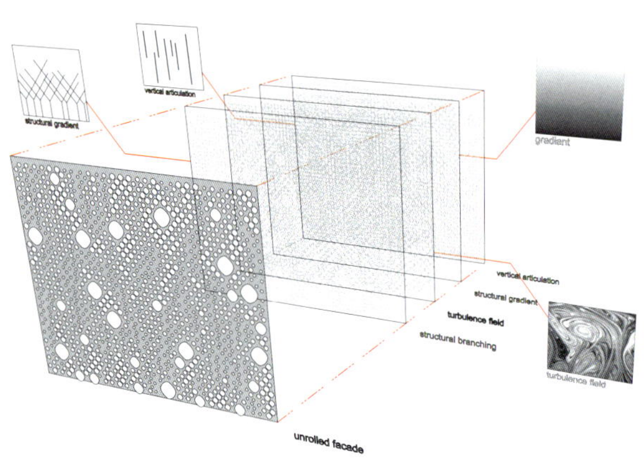

3.6b

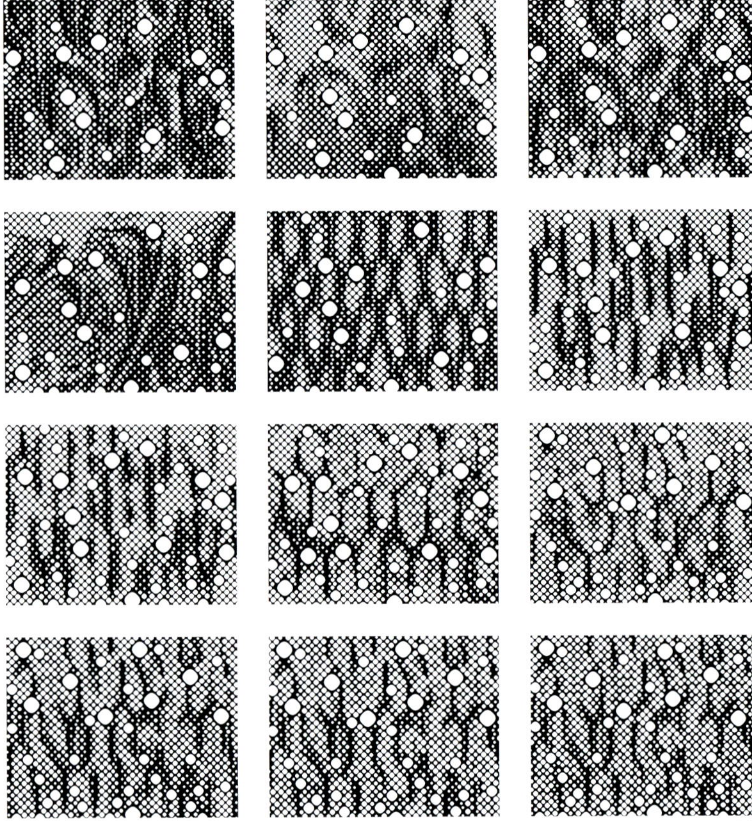

3.6c

3.6d

3.6e

O-14, a 22-story-tall commercial tower perched on a two-story podium, comprises over 300,000 square feet of office space in the heart of Dubai's Business Bay. It is located along the extension of Dubai Creek and occupies a prominent location on the waterfront esplanade. The building is sheathed in a 40-centimeter-thick concrete shell perforated by over 1,300 openings of different diameters that collectively create a lace-like façade that is open to light, air, and views. This shell provides an efficient structural exoskeleton that frees the core from the burden of lateral forces and creates highly flexible, column-free open spaces within the building's interior. The variable openings that perforate the shell are modulated depending on structural requirements, views, sun exposure, and luminosity. The distinctly patterned fields resulting from these competing programmatic and structural demands were then parametrically negotiated and synthesized to produce a singular yet heterogeneous pixelated system that would operate simultaneously as a diagrid exoskeleton and permeable sun screen for the building. The holes punctuating this envelope were constructed by embedding computer numerically cut polystyrene forms, the shape of these voids, into the rebar matrix, that were then encased with modular steel slip forms prior to the pouring of the concrete. Super-liquid concrete was then poured over the fine meshwork of steel reinforcement and cast around these positive forms to produce the perforated monocoque exterior shell. A space nearly one meter deep between the shell and the main enclosure creates a so-called "chimney effect," a phenomenon whereby hot air has room to rise and effectively cools the surface of the glass windows behind the perforated shell. This passive solar technique essentially contributes a natural component to O-14's cooling system, thus reducing energy consumption and costs, just one of many innovative aspects of the building's design.

3.6f

3.6g

3.6h

Shenzhen Bao'an International Airport

RUR

Unuilt 2007
Shenzhen, China

3.7a

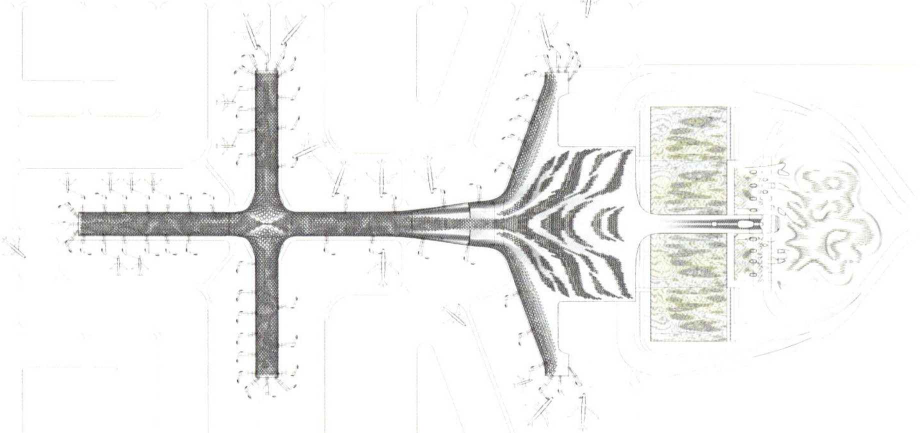

3.7b

In opposition to the monoculture of high-tech—a style that has emulated aviation technology of the 1960s, the Shenzhen Airport design proposes a twenty-first-century paradigm of intelligent environments that are locally diverse and unique yet globally coherent. These are spaces that humanize technology rather than merely represent it. Consequently, the space of Terminal 3 at the Shenzhen Airport has been rethought through the transmutation of a quintessentially earthbound material: concrete. Rather than the predictable pastiche of hi-tech materials, Shenzhen Airport employs a traditionally modern material yet embraces new conceptual paradigms in engineering and mass-customized technologies in the development of its formwork and fabrication. The shift from standardized construction to mass customization enables a range of architectural form, organization, and effect that is evidenced in the modulation of openings that punctuate the building envelope. The vaulted shell of the concourse building is embedded with a regular diagrid structure that is wed to a system of continuously varying openings. This pixelated surface enables the creation of a wide range of atmospheric and visual effects without changing either the structure or the basic form of the vault. On the exterior, the diagrid is entirely regular, allowing for the economy of standardized glazing and cladding units. Along the interior, however, the shape of the openings change. The modulation of light within this system is accomplished by locally and incrementally varying the cross-sectional angles of the openings by a range of degrees as these cut across the thickness of the building skin. This systematic flexibility allows the crown of the vault to be modulated with a cloud dapple pattern whose openings appear to change shape as travelers move throughout the concourse.

3.7c

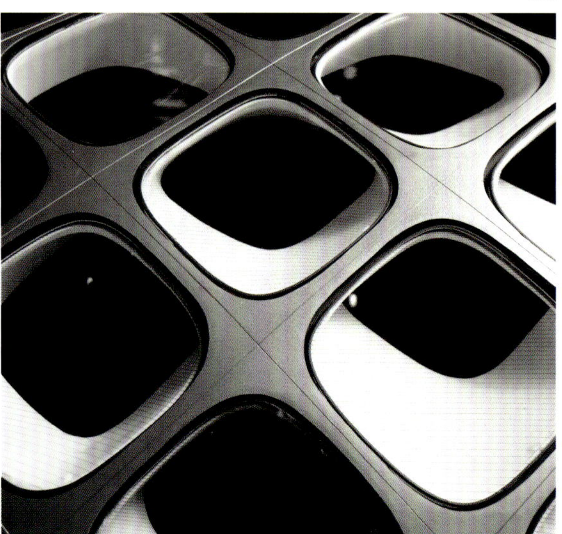

3.7d

3.7e

3.7f

Computational Chair Design

EZCT

Built 2004
Paris, France

In the CCD project, the two main mechanisms of natural evolution as defined by Charles Darwin—the variations which occur in genetic characteristics during their transmission from parents to children, and natural selection, which tends to favor individuals who, because of fortunate variations, are the most adapted to their environment—are translated into genetic algorithms used as generative design tools to breed a multigenerational "family" of chairs. To simplify the parameters of the process, the chair is initially defined as a simple geometric object—an orthogonal volumetric base and planar back—that is constituted by a three-dimensional field of pixels defined by a point field. This volume of voxels is then progressively eroded during the breeding process to produce the lightest chair that functions by withstanding the loads and deflections produced by a sitting body. Traits are transferred from one generation to another by hybridizing genetic material transcoded as the fusion of point fields that define the three-dimensional Voronoi cells out of which the chair is constructed. Here, evolutionary development is reduced to the positioning and number of points (determining the shape of cells) and a binary operation that controls whether cells are represented as solids or voids. Distinct "children" are thus generated according to automated computational procedures that synthesize these encoded point fields and their cell structures in different ways to allow for a range of variations in the offspring. The results of this breeding structure, which simulates the random mutations that occur during the evolutionary process, are then subjected to an algorithmic selection process that assesses the adaptive fitness of the individuals produced to their function and environment where fitness is defined by the chair's structural stability in relation to its material efficiency. This is determined by a structural evaluation of the ways in which forces—those that are imagined to be inflicted upon the chair by the body during the act of sitting—are resolved through the cellular structure during the progressive reduction of the chair's weight, volume, and density as measured by the number of voxels or cells out of which it is constructed. The intention is to genetically evolve a volume that resolves the forces inflicted upon it while simultaneously reducing its material weight with each generation, thereby developing a mechanization of the design process that simulates natural evolutionary behavior where the final results are deemed intelligent yet wholly unpredictable.

3.8a

3.8b

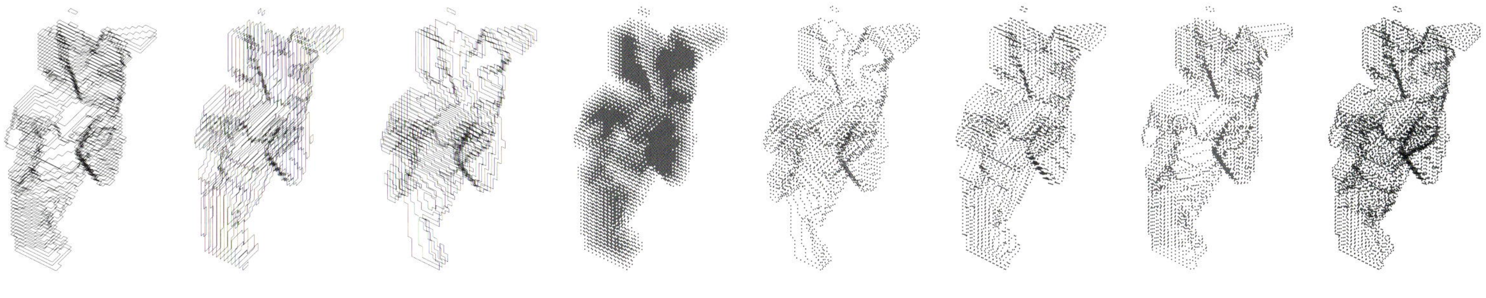

3.8c

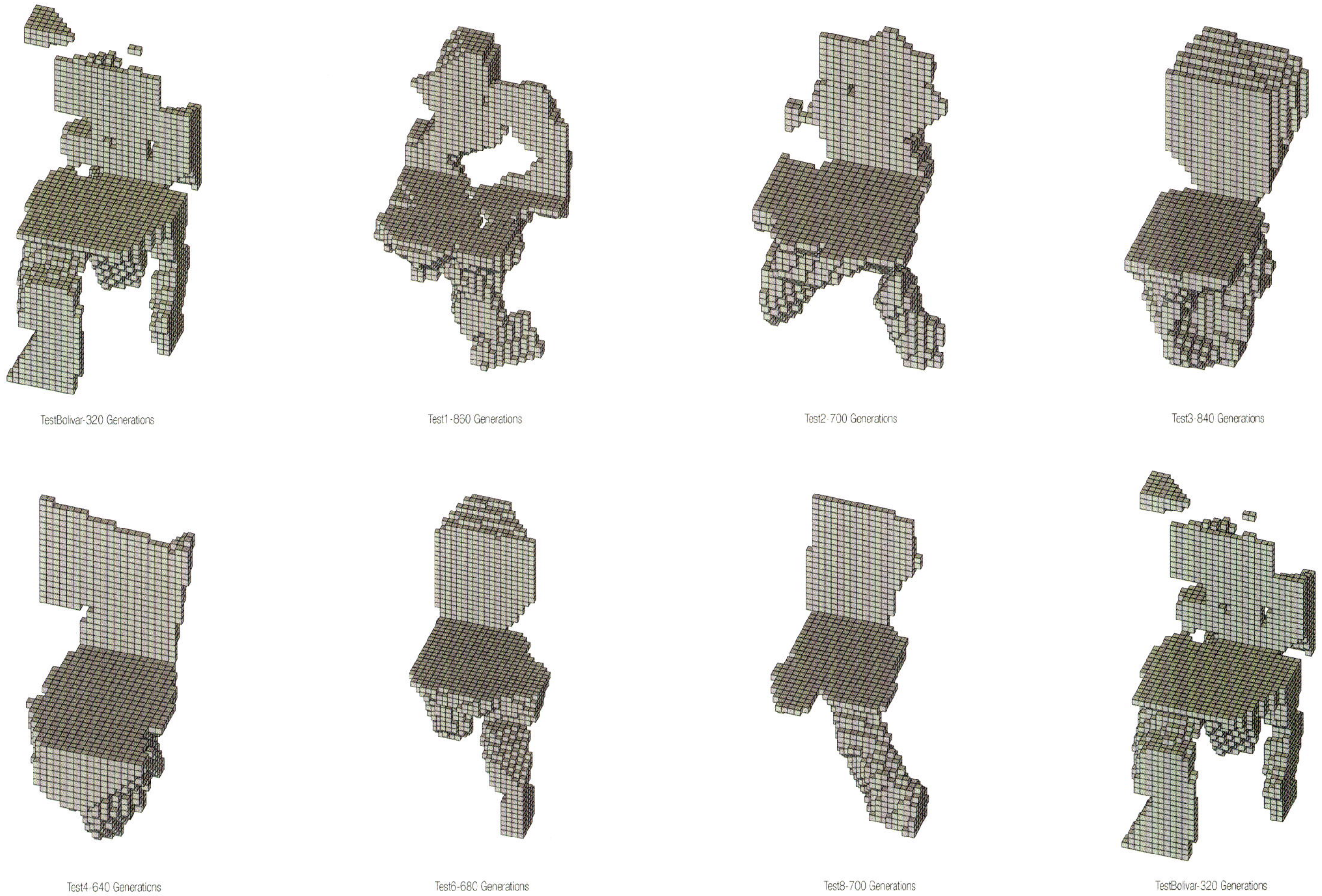

TestBolivar-320 Generations

Test1-860 Generations

Test2-700 Generations

Test3-840 Generations

Test4-640 Generations

Test6-680 Generations

Test8-700 Generations

TestBolivar-320 Generations

3.8d

3.8e,f,g

Rødovre Skyvillage
MVRDV
Unbuilt 2008
Copenhagen, Denmark

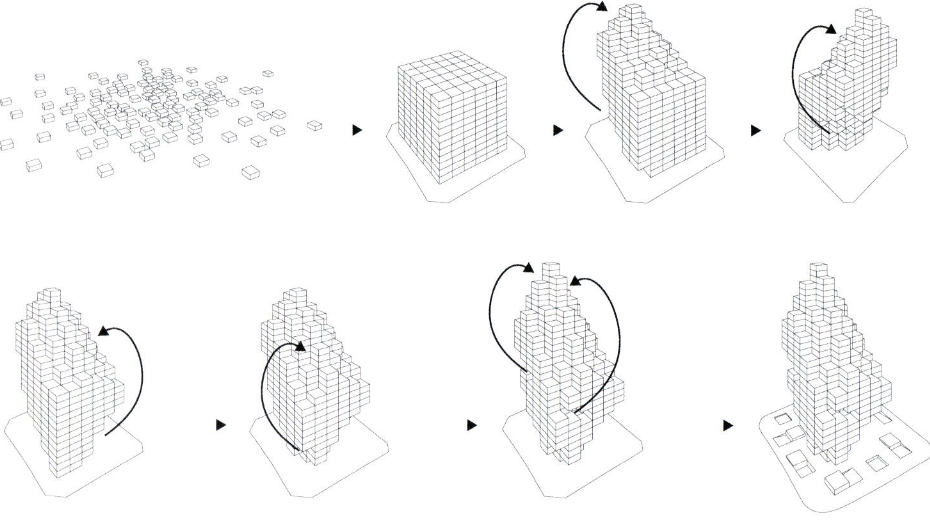
3.9a

The Rødovre Skyvillage, located on Roskildevej, a major artery east of the center of Copenhagen, is a pixelated 116-meter-tall tower with a total area of 36,000 m² that hybridizes residential apartments with a hotel and office facilities in addition to supporting retail space and public amenities at its base. The building's shape is intended to reflect an overlay of the historical spires of Copenhagen with contemporary high-rise buildings that define the skyline of the city. The project further combines two distinctive architectural typologies of Rødovre—the single family home and the skyscraper—in a vertical village comprised of a clustered constellation of cubic pixels, each of which operates to define the minimum space required for a housing unit, a hotel room or an office. These pixels, each of which are 60 m² based on a 7.8-by-7.8-m grid, are arranged around a bundled central core consisting of four individual shafts to allow separate access to the different program clusters. The pixels defining the overall building volume were then rearranged by removing and repositioning them to respond to different programmatic needs and environmental conditions. On the lower floors the volume is slim to create space for a public plaza. The lower cluster of pixels in the high rise are for offices, while the middle segment is comprised of pixels that are stepped back to create a variety of south-facing, terraced sky gardens—a stacked neighborhood with the amenities of a single family home. The top of the building is occupied by the hotel that takes advantage of the view towards the city center. As a response to the instability of real estate market forces, the overall structure is designed based on the aggregation of identical individuated units within a flexible grid that enables pixels to be programmatically altered over time. This allows the constellation to incrementally shift to accommodate different percentages and combinatorial permutations of the programs occupying this pixelated landscape according to the vicissitudes of the market and the changing needs of the population it serves.

3.9b

3.9c

PoroCity

MVRDV + The Why Factory

Built 2013
Cannes, France

3.10a

Initially exhibited at the 13th Venice Architecture Biennale, PoroCity is an ongoing study by the Eurohigh studio of The Why Factory on the potentials of porosity in relation to the development of the architecture of the skyscraper. Current cities consist of towers and blocks that are predominantly enclosed, distant, and introverted without the engagement of public urban life and the surrounding environment. The intention of the Eurohigh studio/PoroCity project is to render the skyscraper more permeable to enable open zones for social interaction and to expand the ecological potentials of an aerated, yet dense urbanity. Computation was used in this process through the development of scripts that applied and tested different methods of integrating variously programmed, scaled, and patterned voids into the standard tower structure to generate a range of urban typologies. The initial exhibition presented an extensive collection of 676 models at a scale of 1:1,000 that were made of one million LEGO bricks. The modeling bricks used provided a small-grain, three-dimensional pixelated framework for the project and a clear distinction between mass, as the generic program, and void, as the representation of public space within the building. As a first phase of this research, this exhaustive catalog presented an initial grid of twenty-six linear iterations which explored and foregrounded the qualities of porosity within the context of the dense city. The second phase of the project developed a more precise parametrization and deepened design process modeling nine skyscrapers at a scale of 1:100 exhibited at the Hong Kong Design Center (HKDC) at the 10th edition of BODW, Hong Kong's annual Business of Design Week.

3.10b

3.10c

3.10d

King Toronto

BIG

Built 2018–
Toronto, Canada

3.11a

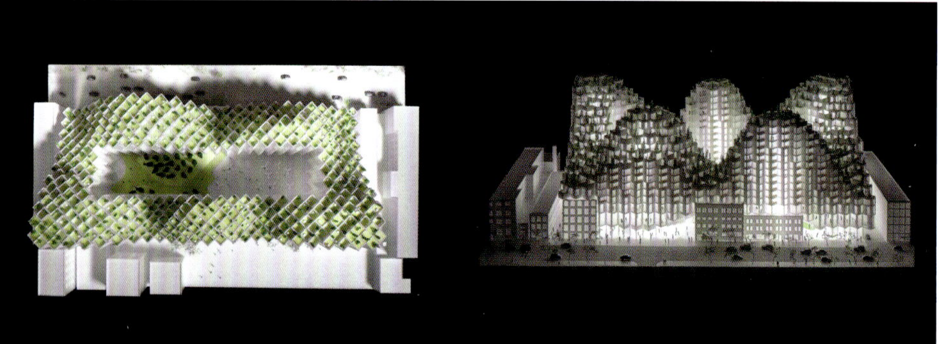

3.11b

3.11c

King Toronto is set in a transitional area of Toronto. From the tall towers of the Central Business District to the east to the low-rise neighborhoods in the northwest, the skyline is an indicator of the city's progress. Located at the meeting point of three neighborhood parks, King Toronto is a mixed-use housing development with an integrated public plaza creating a new attractor for the community while connecting the various pedestrian pathways that crisscross the area. The building is organized as a traditional perimeter block with a public courtyard in the center. The plaza itself is defined by two distinct atmospheres: a lushly landscaped forest paired with an urban, hardscaped court. The resulting balance between these opposing conditions reflects Toronto's current state of rapid redevelopment: the union of old and new, an open community atmosphere in an intimate setting, calming green scenery within a bustling urban context.

Surrounding the plaza, King Toronto rises as sets of stacked pixels or rather voxels (volumetric pixels) programmed for housing, retail, and boutique offices—avoiding the footprints of heritage buildings that already exist on the site. Each voxel is defined by the size of a room rotated 45 degrees from the street grid to increase exposure to light and air. The voxel individuates each unit and renders these legible such that the equation of voxels to inhabitants ensures that the aggregated assemblage of voxels is a reflection of the community that it houses. At the base the voxels are lifted to allow movement across the courtyard, while the roof surface is manipulated to form an undulating continuous topography, allowing sunlight to penetrate the entire building, while creating space for green terraces directly adjacent to each unit. The condition of the urban landscape, a synthesis of attributes drawn simultaneously from the architectonic and the natural, is thus repeated in the overlay of the perimeter block and rolling terrain, a voxelated green landscape that increases pedestrian circulation through the neighborhood while creating an abundance of greenery found only in urban parks and suburbs. Revisiting the revolutionary ideas of Moshe Safdie's Habitat, a utopian modular housing experiment built in Montreal for Expo '67 as an alternative to suburban sprawl, King Toronto offers high urban density with the amenities of suburbia while providing a new model to challenge the tower and podium typology.

3.11d

Serpentine Pavilion

BIG

Built 2016

London, United Kingdom

3.12a

3.12b

3.12c

The Serpentine Pavilion of 2016 by Bjarke Ingels Group (BIG) is configured to embody multiple attributes often perceived as opposites. It is a structure that is freeform yet rigorous, modular yet sculptural, and transparent yet opaque—simultaneously frame and fill, box and blob. The pavilion was designed starting with the idea of the brick wall, one of the most basic and fundamental elements of architecture. Yet rather than being constructed out of clay bricks or stone, the primary component of the pavilion's walls is a hollow extruded fiberglass frame, a rectilinear volume enclosed on four sides with open opposite ends. The wall is perceived as having undergone a formal metamorphosis, appearing to be pulled apart or unzipped. What begins at the top and at the outer ends as the linear edges of a single plane are transformed into the undulating surfaces of sine curves as the wall grows into a two layered volumetric enclosure containing an interior cavity within which the events of the Pavilion's programs are housed. In both plan and section these straight lines become sinuous curves, whose curvilinearity increases as one moves from the top toward the bottom of the pavilion where it forms a sheltered valley at the Pavilion's entrance and an undulating hillside adjacent to the park. The reading of the zippered edge is supported by the alternation of voxel-like boxes that seem to slip out from the vertical edge and become increasingly elongated in plan, appearing to stretch as they are morphed into the curving surfaces on either side of the wall. The unzipped wall creates a cave-like canyon lit through the fiberglass frames and the gaps between the shifted boxes as well as through the translucent resin of the fiberglass. As a result, the shifting overlaps as well as the movement and presence of people outside create a lively play of light and shadow on the cave walls within. The north and south elevations of the Pavilion are a perfect rectangle. The east and west elevations form an undulating sculptural silhouette. Towards the east and west, the Pavilion is completely opaque and material. Towards the north and south, it is entirely transparent and practically immaterial. This manipulation of the space-defining garden wall thus creates a presence in the park that changes as one moves around and through it, whereby presence becomes absence, the orthogonal structure becomes a curvilinear gesture, and the rectilinear wall built of voxel-like boxes becomes a sinuous and inhabitable blob.

3.12d

Generative Logic
Fields and Attractors

Transformations are divided into two primary categories. Euclidean transformations (such as translation, rotation, and reflection) only change the location or orientation, but not the geometry of the object. Affine transformations (such as uniform or nonuniform scaling, shearing, and projection) alter the object's geometry. When transformations are applied to a field of objects and the transformation factor is proportional or inversely proportional to the distance of some other object or entity, we call these attractor fields.

Translation Transformations

Translation + Single Attractor

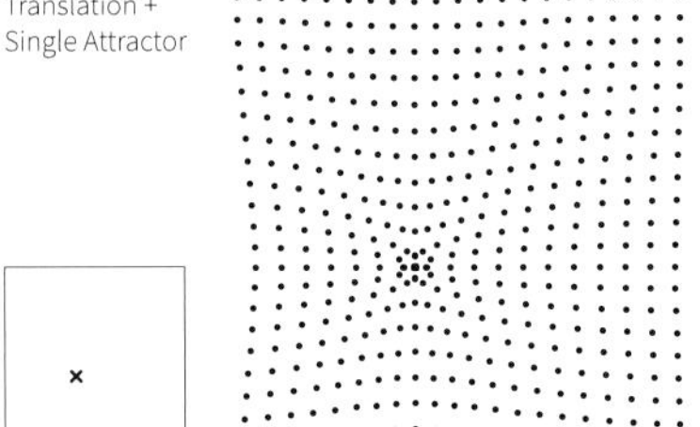

Translation + Multi Attractor

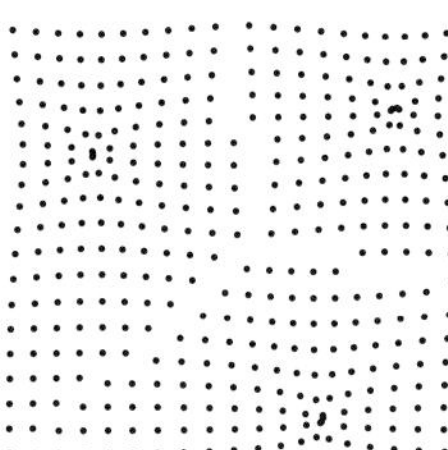

Translation + Curve Attractor

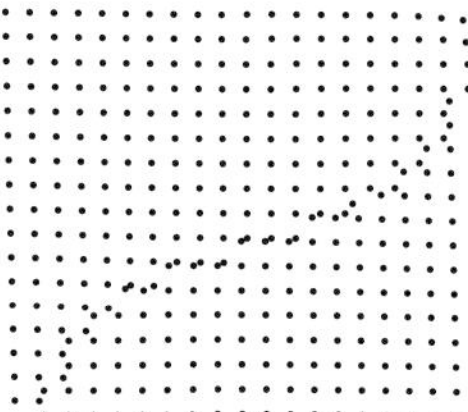

Translation + Image Attractor

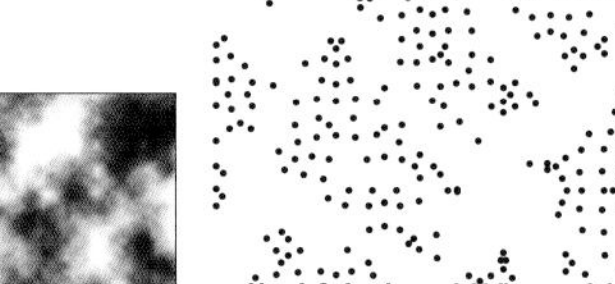

Rotation Transformations

Rotation + Single Attractor

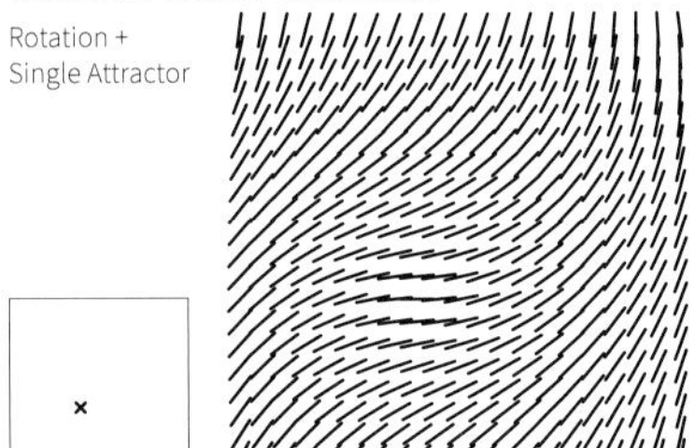

Rotation + Multi Attractor

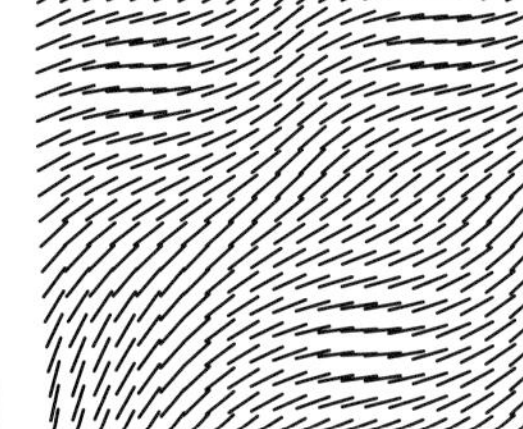

Rotation + Curve Attractor

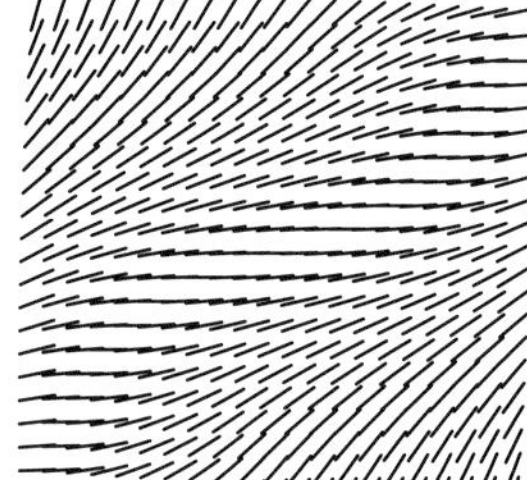

Rotation + Image Attractor

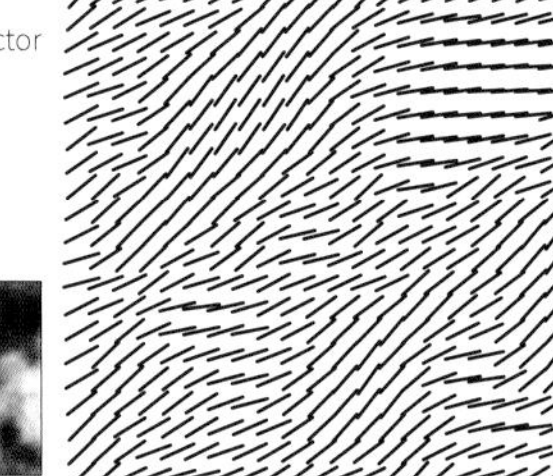

Scale Transformations

Scale + Single Attractor

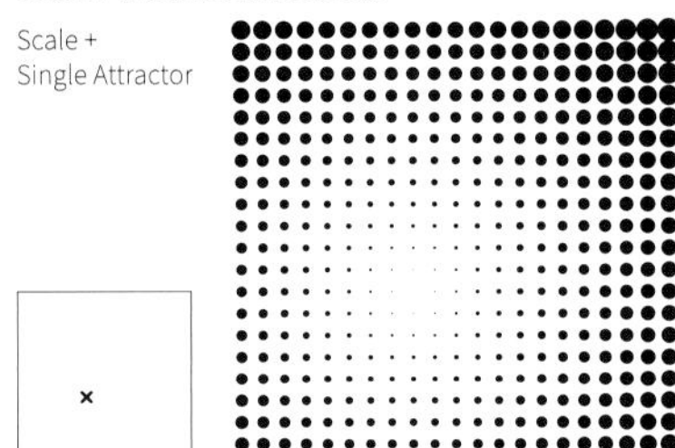

Scale + Multi Attractor

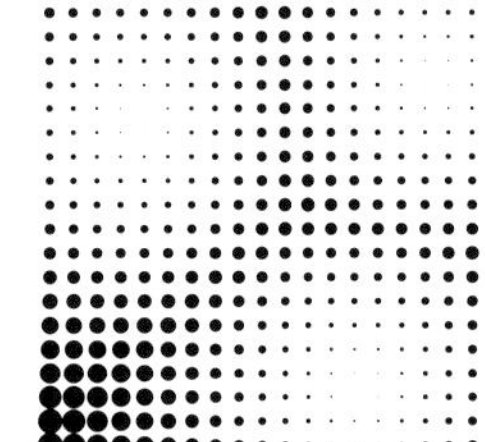

Scale + Curve Attractor

Scale + Image Attractor

Generative Process
Memorial to the Murdered Jews of Europe

The Memorial to the Murder Jews of Europe uses several field and attractor techniques to modulate the density, height, and tilt of the concrete stelae. First, nodes in the overall grid are randomly removed such that the density of stelae increases from the site edge to an interior threshold distance. Second, the height of the stelae increase and begins to undulate as the distance from the site edges increases. Third, the vertical orientation of each stela is randomly tilted around its X and/or Y axes.

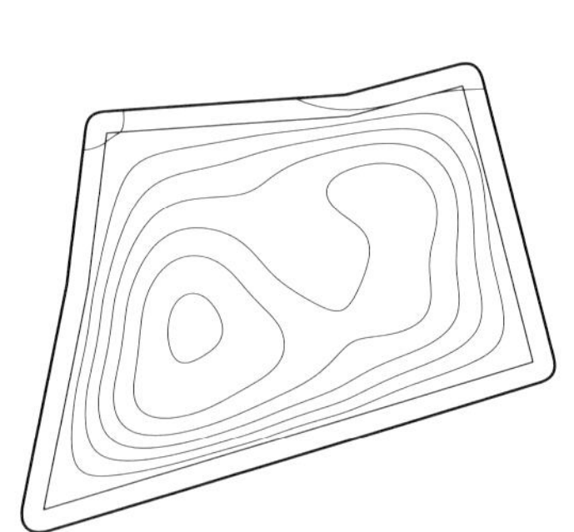

1. Define site boundary and topography

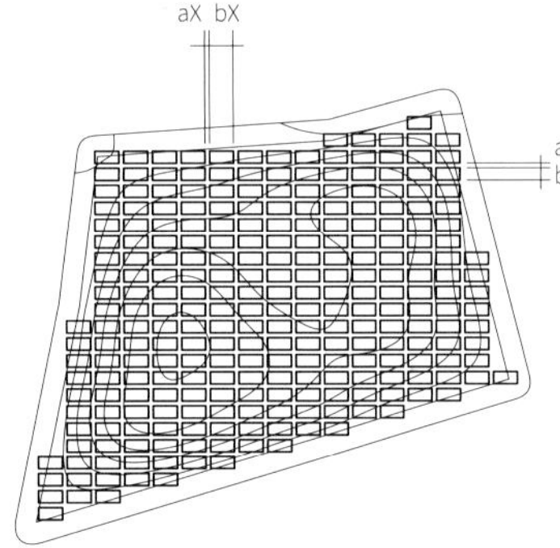

2. Overlay grid defined by block length (bX), width (bY), aisle width (aX, aY) and grid angle (ø)

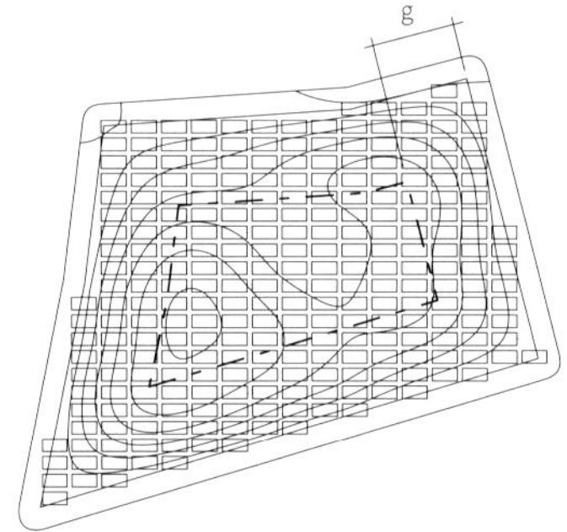

3. Define threshold for diffuse gradient

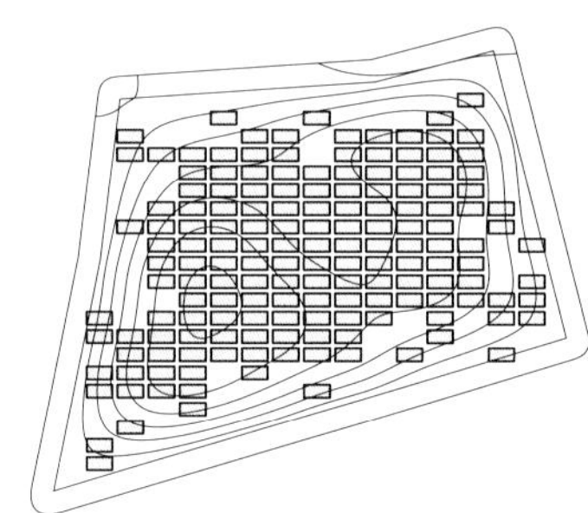

4. Apply diffuse gradient

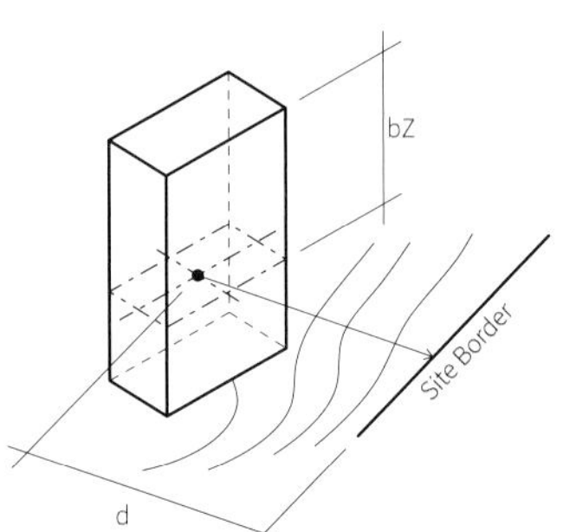

5. Define block heights (bZ) above site borders as a domain (hMin, hMax) relative to distance (d) to attractor geometry

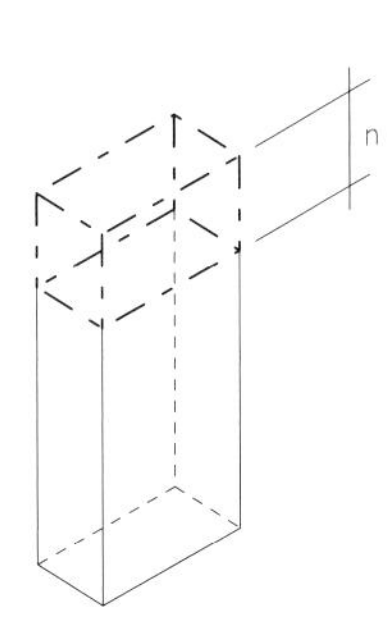

6. Define domain of height noise (n)

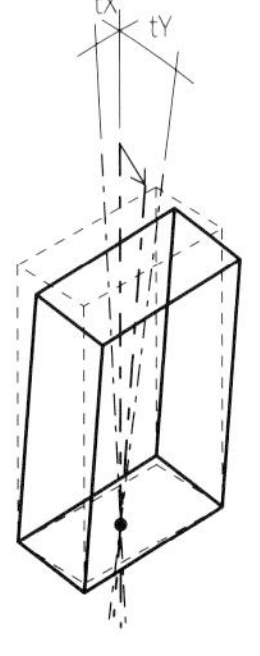

7. Define domain of tilt along X (tX) and Y (tY) axes

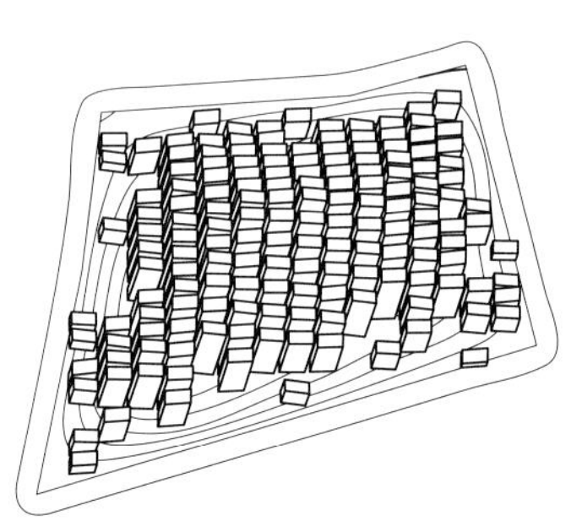

8. Apply block parameters to grid

Generative Matrix

bX = 2380 mm
bY = 950 mm
hMin = 200 mm
hMax = 4700 mm
aX = 950 mm
aY = 950 mm
θ = 0°
g = 30 m
Attractor = Site Border
n = 300 mm
tX = 5°
tY = 5°

Control Model

bX = 2380 mm
bY = 950 mm
hMin = 200 mm
hMax = 4700 mm
aX = 950 mm
aY = 950 mm
θ = 45°
g = 30 m
Attractor = Site Border
n = 300 mm
tX = 5°
tY = 5°

Site Conditions

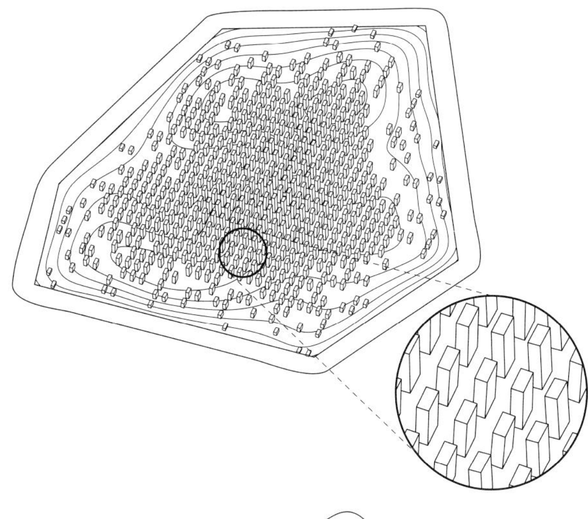

bX = 2380 mm
bY = 950 mm
hMin = 200 mm
hMax = 4700 mm
aX = 950 mm
aY = 950 mm
θ = 0°
g = 120 m
Attractor = Site Border
n = 300 mm
tX – 5°
tY = 5°

Diffuse Gradient

bX = 4760
bY = 475 mm
hMin = 200 mm
h**Max = 40**
aX = 950 mm
aY = 950 mm
θ = 0°
g = 30 m
Attractor = Site Border
n = 300 mm
tX = 5°
tY = 5°

Block Dimensions

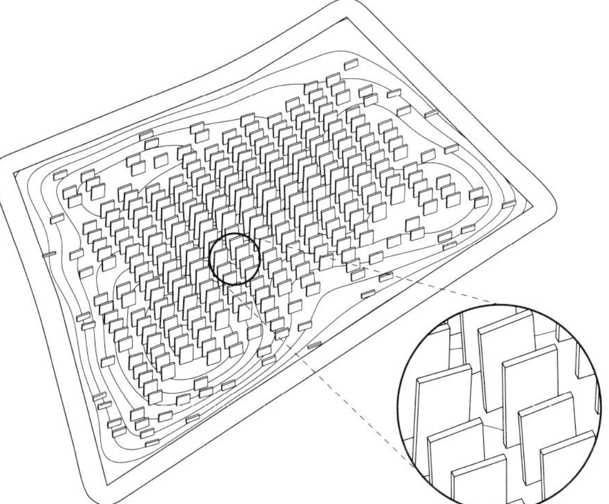

bX = 2380 mm
bY = 950 mm
hMin = 200 mm
hMax = 4700 mm
aX = 950 mm
aY = 950 mm
θ = 0°
g = 30 m
Attractor = Site Border
n = 3000 mm
tX = 20°
tY = 20°

Tilt / Noise

bX = 2380 mm
bY = 950 mm
hMin = 200 mm
hMax = 4700 mm
aX = 950 mm
aY = 950 mm
θ = 0°
g = 30 m
Attractor = Multiple Nodes
n = 300 mm
tX = 5°
tY = 5°

Multi Attractor

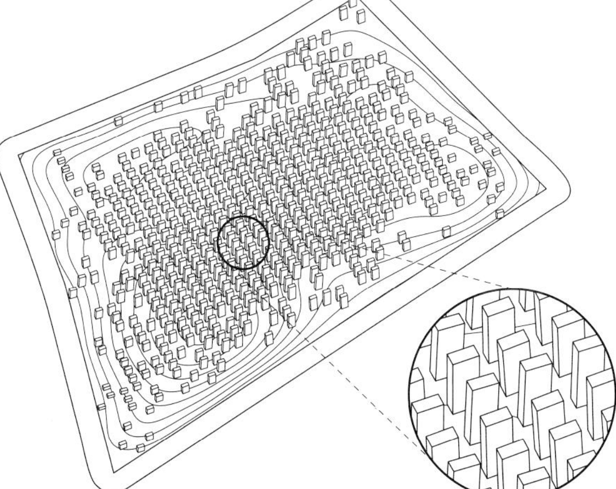

bX = 2380 mm
bY = 950 mm
hMin = 200 mm
hMax = 7620 mm
aX = 950 mm
aY = 950 mm
θ = 0°
g = 30 m
Attractor = Curve
n = 300 mm
tX = 5°
tY = 5°

Curve Attractor

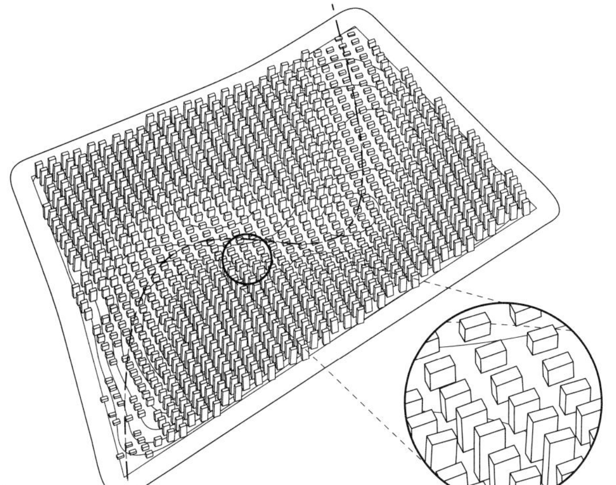

bX = 2380 mm
bY = 950 mm
hMin = 200 mm
hMax = 4700 mm
aX = 950 mm
aY = 950 mm
θ = 0°
g = 30 m
Attractor = Image Map

n = 300 mm
tX = 5°
tY = 5°

Image Attractor

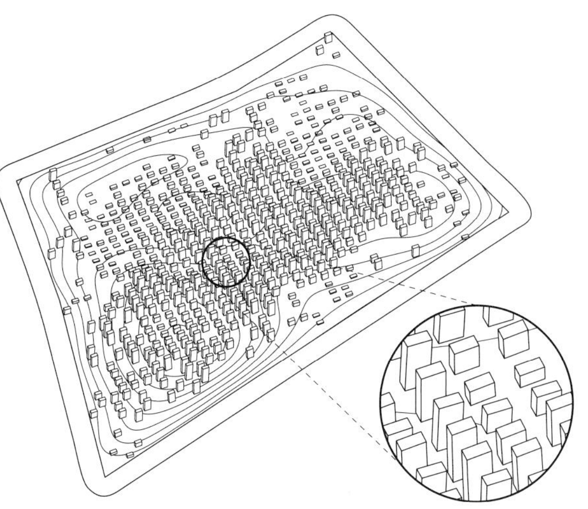

Generative Logic Point Distribution

The distribution of points on a plane or surface is a fundamental process in computational geometry. Activities such as producing a raytraced rendering or LiDAR scanning an environment rely on sampling values across a field of points. In many cases, if the point field is uniformly distributed (e.g., a square grid of points), artifacts of this regular distribution can appear or there may be not enough samples in certain areas and too many in others. Similarly, a purely random distribution often doesn't help as statistically there will be large voids or clumping of the samples. Numerous other methods exist that produces distributions that are neither too uniform nor too random.

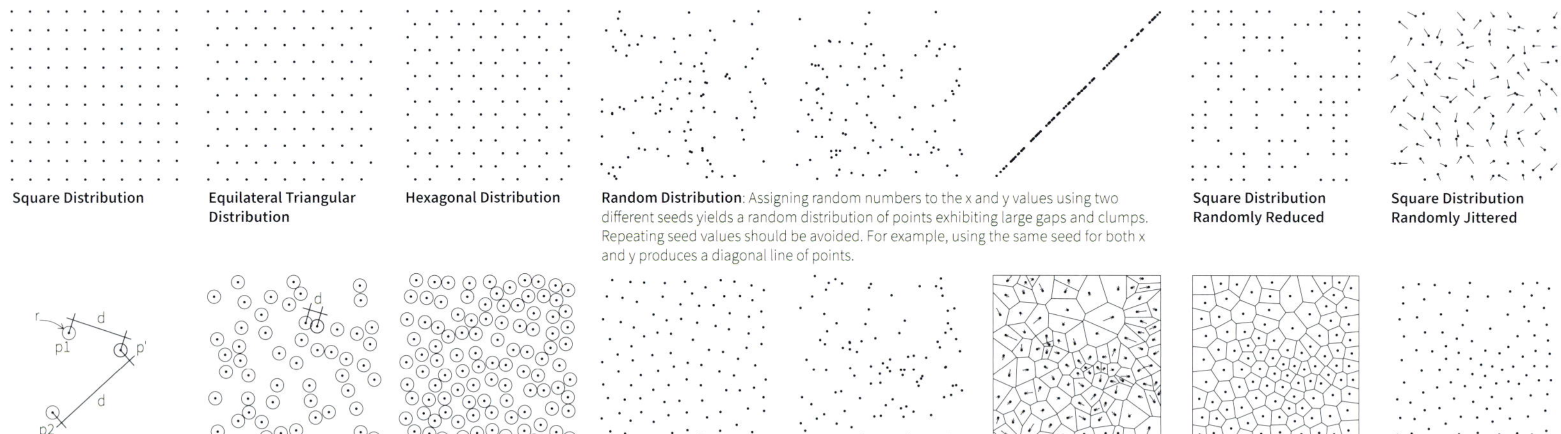

Square Distribution

Equilateral Triangular Distribution

Hexagonal Distribution

Random Distribution: Assigning random numbers to the x and y values using two different seeds yields a random distribution of points exhibiting large gaps and clumps. Repeating seed values should be avoided. For example, using the same seed for both x and y produces a diagonal line of points.

Square Distribution Randomly Reduced

Square Distribution Randomly Jittered

Poisson Disk Method: Start by adding a random point (p1) within the region. Try to add another random point within the region (p2). If the closest distance (d) between the point and all existing points is greater than a minimum distance (2r), add it to the list of points. If not, try with a new random point until no more points can be added to the region.

Lloyd's Algorithm: Start with a purely random distribution of points. Find the Voronoi diagram for the points and then find the centroid of each Voronoi cell. Find the Voronoi diagram of these centroids and repeat these steps several times until the points are more evenly distributed.

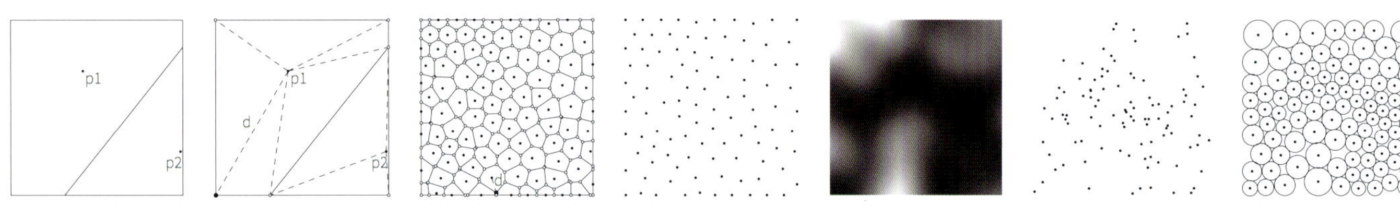

Farthest Neighbor Algorithm: Start by adding a random point (p1) with the region. Add a second random point far away from the first point. Find the Voronoi diagram of the set of points and select the cell corner that is farthest (d) from the set of points. Add this corner point to the list of points and repeat for the desired total number of points.

Image Based Distribution: The grayscale value of an image can be used to distribute points with variable densities. One method uses the grayscale as a probability map: the darker the value, the higher the probability that a point will be added. For a more even distribution, a circle-packing algorithm can be used with the radius derived from the image.

Generative Process KAIT Workshop

The KAIT Workshop by Junya Ishigami offers a good demonstration of some point distribution techniques. First, although the field of columns appears random, the clumping that occurs with purely random distributions is avoided by implementing some minimum spacing constraint. Second, column density is inversely proportional to high-activity programmatic areas.

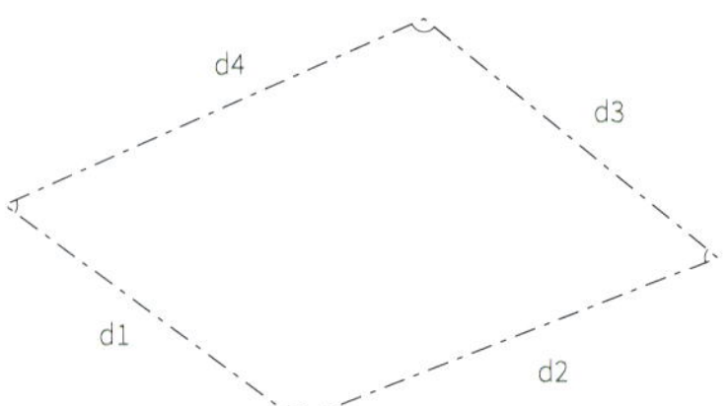

1. Establish a boundary curve.

2. Add void curves that represent areas that will have a lower density of columns.

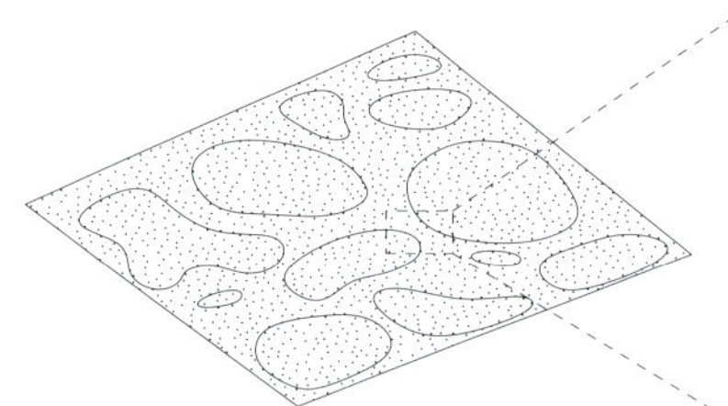

3. Add a random distribution of points (pts) that are no closer than a certain desired distance (dM)

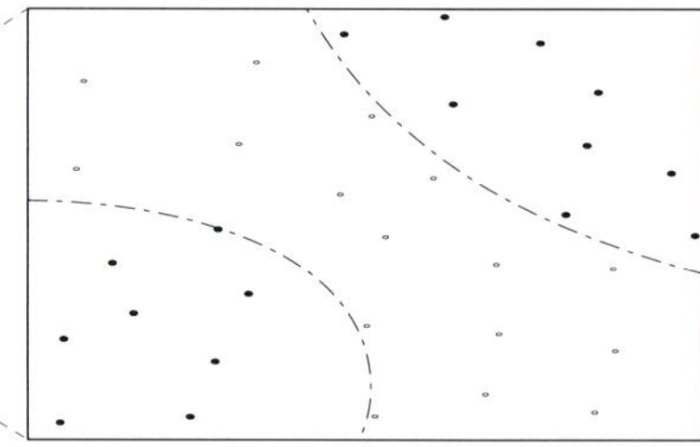

4. Determine if the points are inside or outside the void curves and split into two lists.

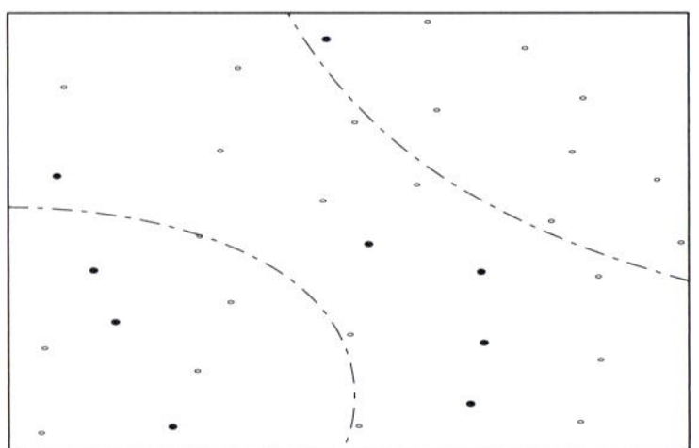

5. Randomly remove points from both lists based on desired density. Within the voids, remove more (k1%) while outside the voids, remove less (k2%). The remaining number of points is C_N.

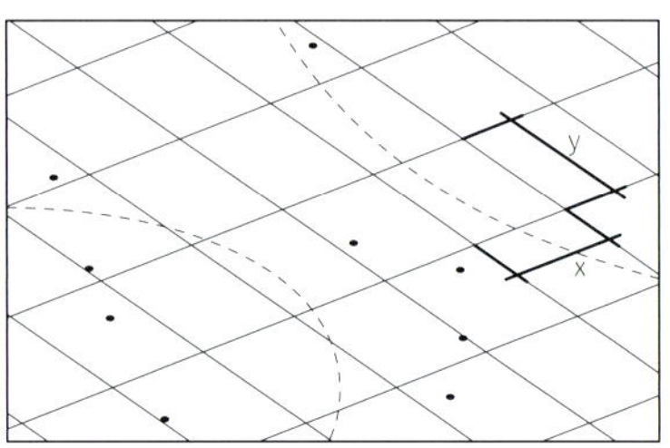

6. Establish a primary structural grid for the roof beams with spacing x and y.

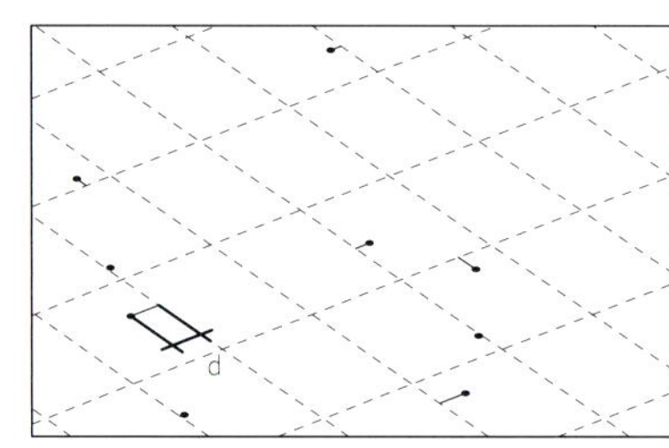

7. Measure the distance (d) between each point and its closest point on the structural grid.

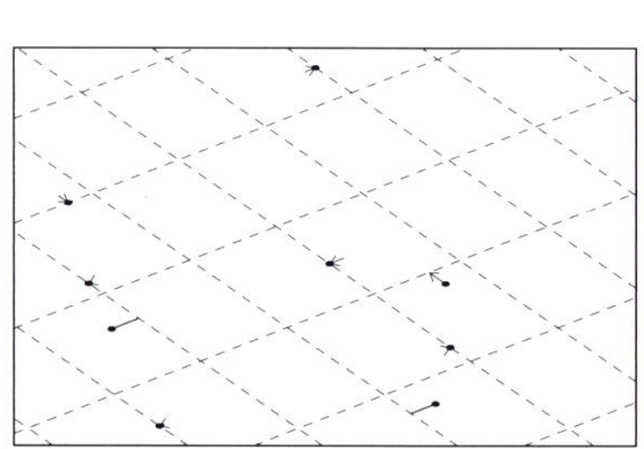

8. If the distance (d) is smaller than the minimum distance (cM), move the column location to align with the structural grid. If it is larger, do not move it.

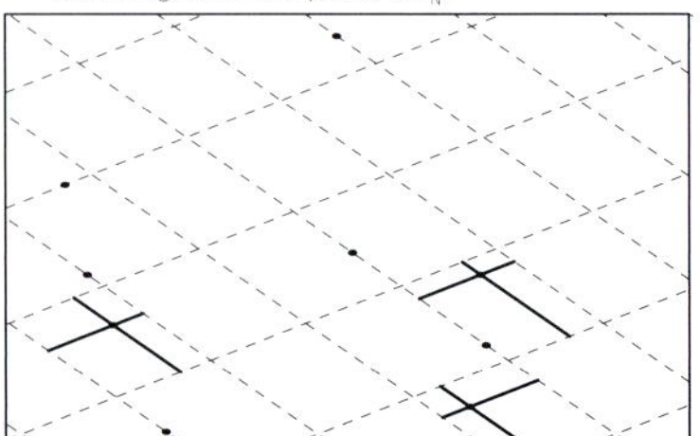

9. For the columns that are between the structural grid lines, add in a secondary grid.

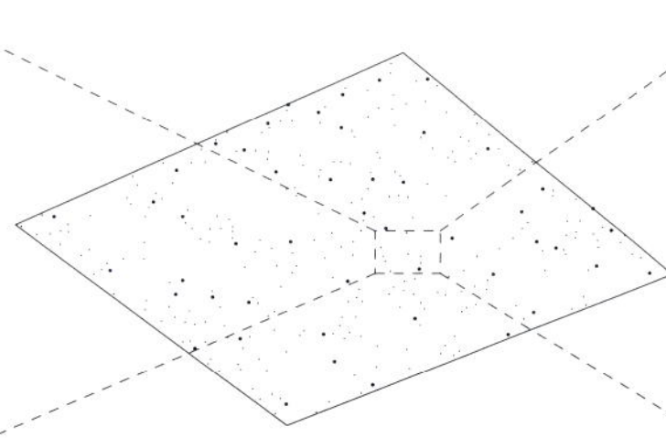

10. Based on structural calculations, a certain percentage of the columns can act in compression while the rest can be thinner and act in tension.

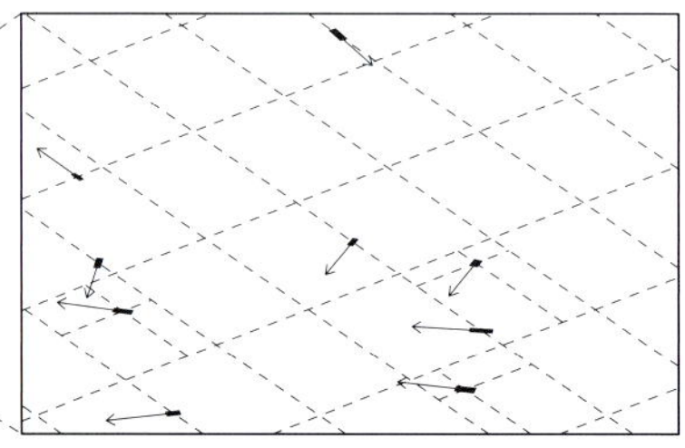

11. For each column, randomly rotate it in plan and add a rectangle with a width within the range cW and a thickness within the range cT.

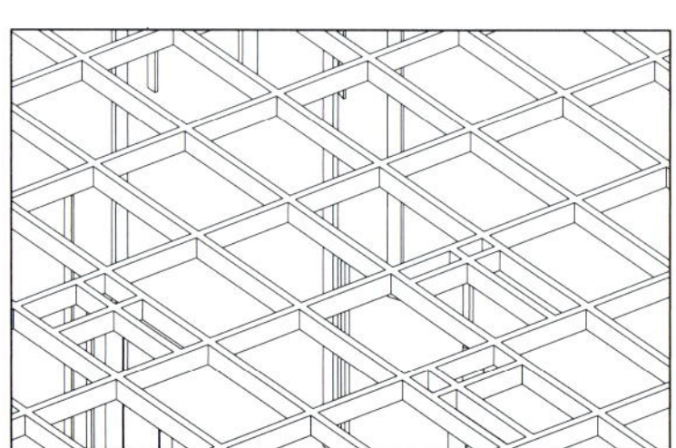

12. Extrude columns and roof grid to the desired height.

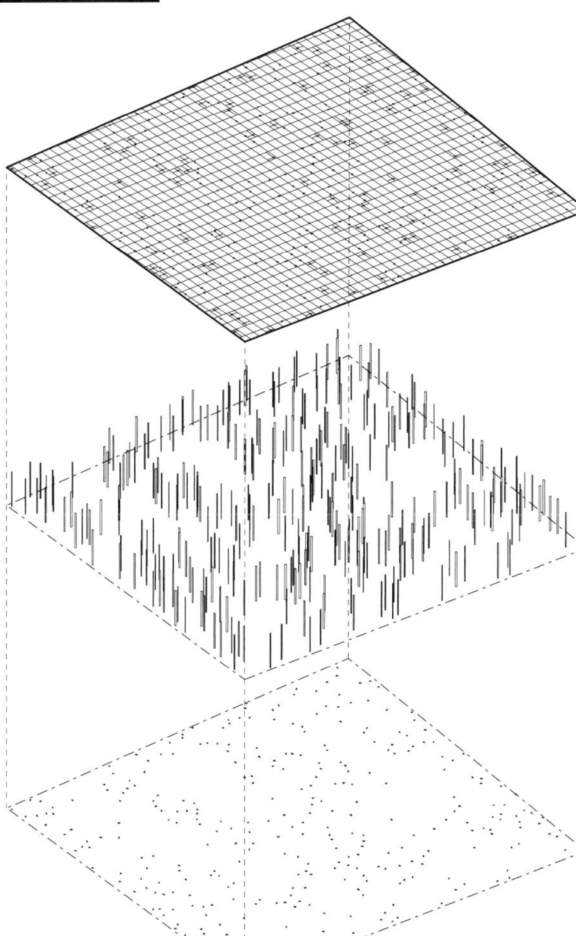

x = 1000 mm
y = 1500 mm
pts = 1745
dM = 1000 mm
k1 = 10%
k1 seed = 669
k2 = 30%
k2 seed = 229
cM = 250 mm
cT = 16 to 60 mm
cW = 80 to 190 mm
cN = 305
Boundary: Curve A
Voids: Set A

Control Model

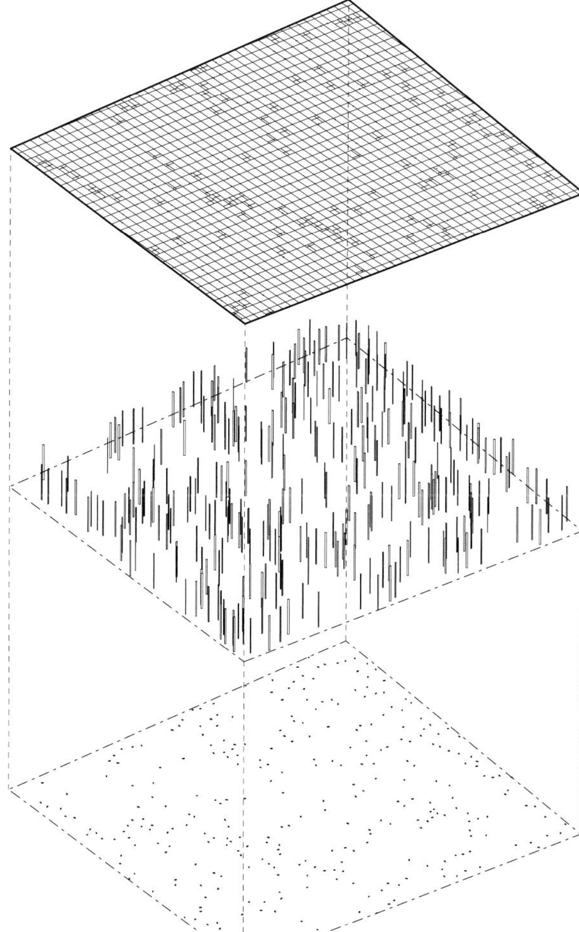

x = 1000 mm
y = 1500 mm
pts = 1745
dM = 1000 mm
k1 = 10%
k1 seed = 669
k2 = 30%
k2 seed = 229
cM = 250 mm
cT = 16 to 60mm
cW = 80 to 190mm
cN = 307
Boundary: Curve A
Voids: Set B

Rectangular Voids

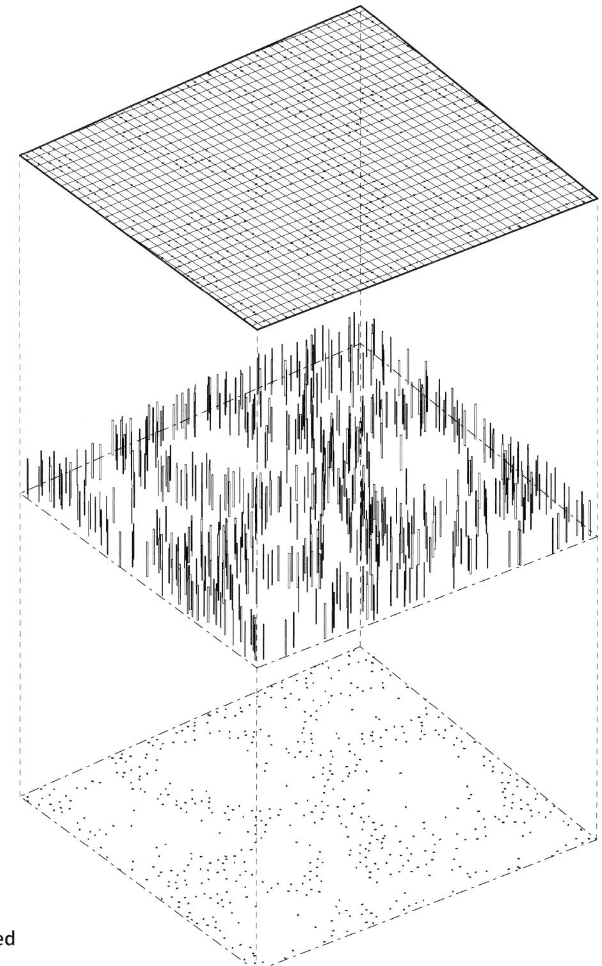

x = 1000 mm
y = 1500 mm
pts = 1745
dM = 1000 mm
k1 = 10%
k1 seed = 669
k2 = 60%
k2 seed = 229
cM = 1000 mm
cT = 16 to 60 mm
cW = 80 to 190 mm
cN = 557
Boundary: Curve A
Voids: Set A

High Density Columns Restricted to Primary Grid

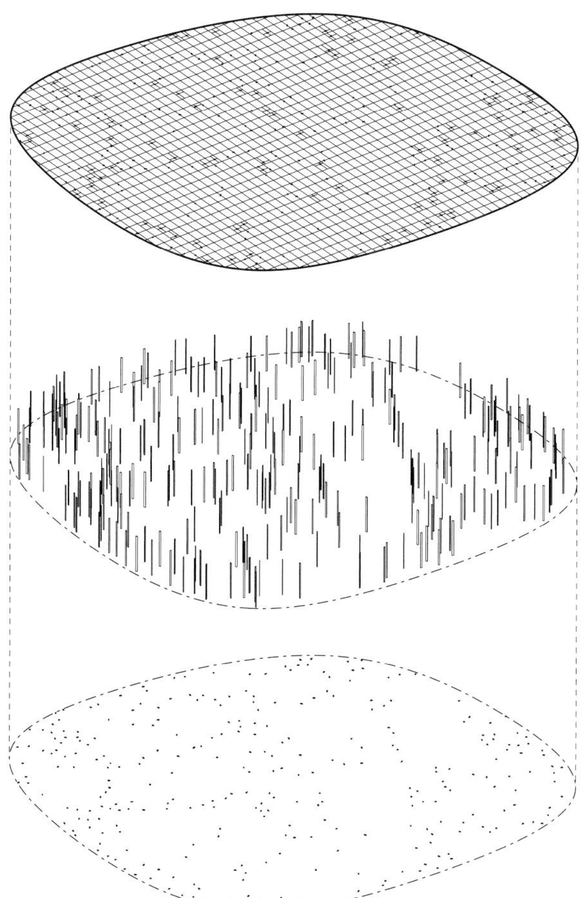

x = 1000 mm
y = 1500 mm
pts = 1745
dM = 1000 mm
k1 = 10%
k1 seed = 669
k2 = 30%
k2 seed = 229
cM = 250 mm
cT = 16 to 60 mm
cW = 80 to 190 mm
cN = 291
Boundary: Curve B
Voids: Set C

Curved Boundary

Generative Logic
Pixels, Voxels, and Sampling

One of the first representational concepts taught is the difference between vector and raster graphics. Raster graphics are made up of a fixed grid of pixels, typically used for images, while vector graphics are composed of paths defined by mathematical equations, allowing them to be scaled without losing quality, typically used for CAD drawing. Although often situated in relation to media formats, the topic is at the root of conversations about analog/digital, the directional/dimensional, the continuous/-discrete, and reality/representation.

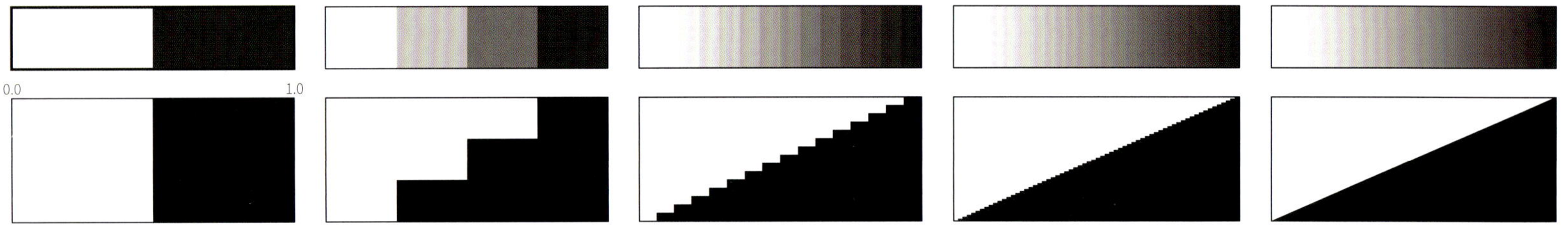

0.0 1.0

1-Bit Grayscale
2 shades/steps

2-Bit Grayscale
4 shades/steps

4-Bit Grayscale
16 shades/steps

6-Bit Grayscale
64 shades/steps

8-Bit Grayscale
256 shades/steps

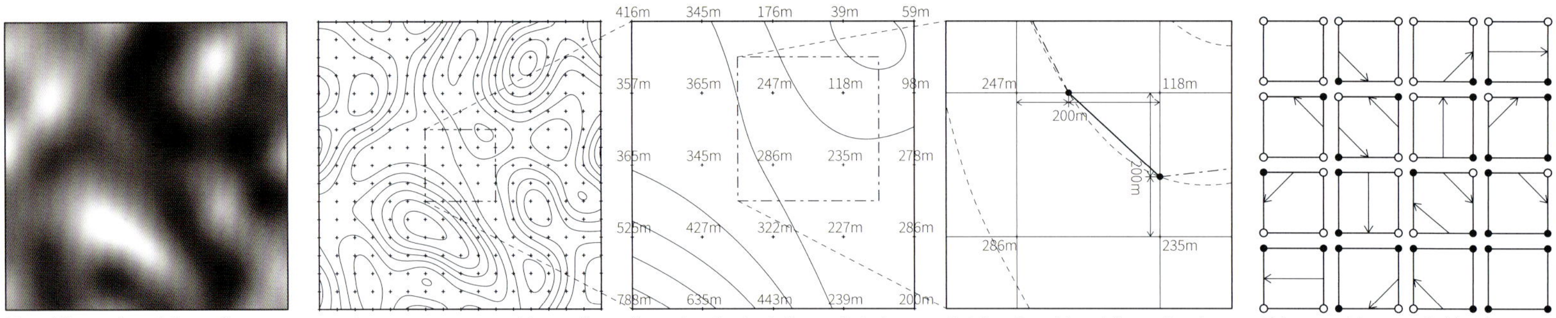

416m 345m 176m 39m 59m
357m 365m 247m 118m 98m
365m 345m 286m 235m 278m
525m 427m 322m 227m 286m
788m 635m 443m 239m 200m

247m 118m 200m 200m 286m 235m

Two-Dimensional Sampling
Imagine this is a landscape. The closer we look, the more we see.

In order to construct a topographic map of this landscape, we need to survey it at a certain resolution and get height samples.

If we enlarge the view to focus on just a few samples, we can see that a contour at 200m would cross somewhere between the points.

By doing a linear interpolation on the edges of a square made by 4 samples, we can locate the 200m contour with the square.

This process is known as the Marching Squares algorithm. There are 16 cases that describe the thresholds within a sample cell.

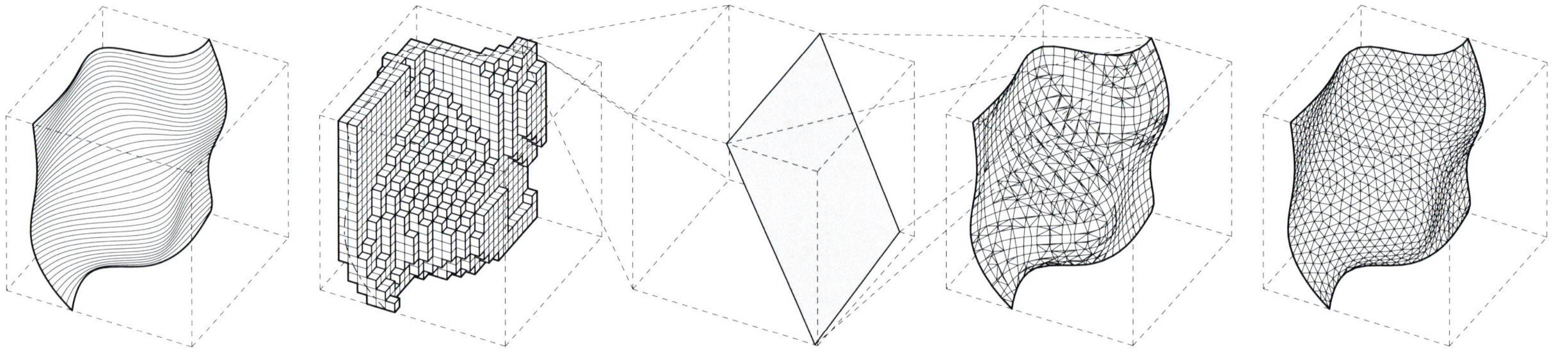

Three-Dimensional Sampling
Imagine a 3D field of scalar data such as the surface of a bone. In reality, it has infinite resolution, but its representation does not.

This field can be sampled at a certain (limited) voxel resolution. These voxels represent thresholds within the data (e.g., where a certain density is within range).

A common way to visualize these thresholds is to construct a discrete surface at each voxel using the Marching Cubes algorithm (see the fifteen primary configurations below).

The initial results of surface scans bear the traces of the voxelization process. Many of the mesh edges align with the sample grid.

The mesh is often processed further to make it more uniform and remove the artifacts of the voxel sampling.

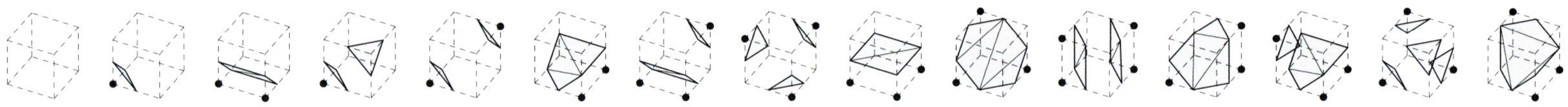

Generative Process
Rødovre Skyvillage

Similar to Hugh Ferriss's 1922 drawings "Four Stages of the Maximum Mass of the Zoning Envelope" for New York City, the Rødovre Skyvillage project by MVRDV carves away at the site's mass in response to environmental and programmatic design objectives. Although the smooth boundary condition satisfies these objectives, the voxelization of the volume facilitates a modular construction system and horizontal balcony surfaces. These voxel-based projects are part of a long tradition in architecture that emphasizes the discrete parts of a system over the continuity of the whole.

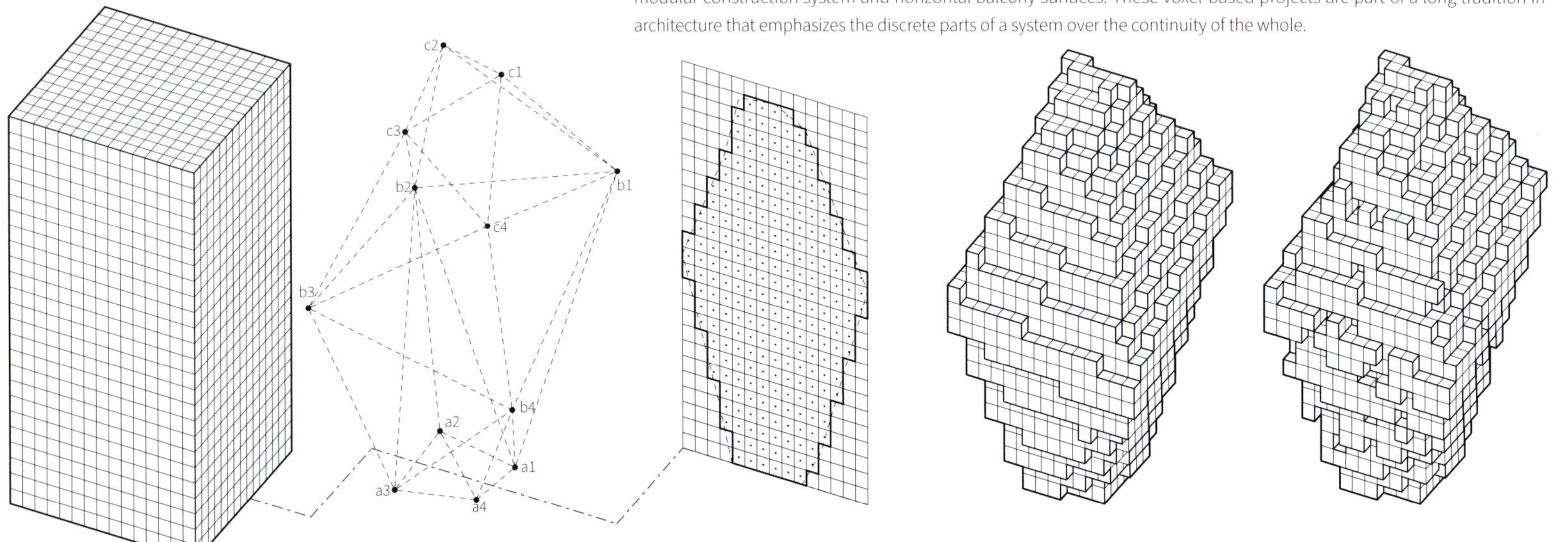

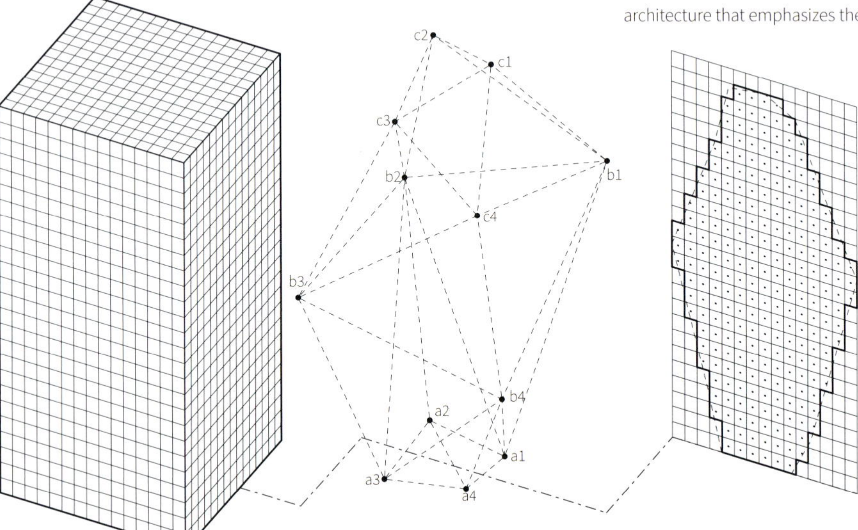

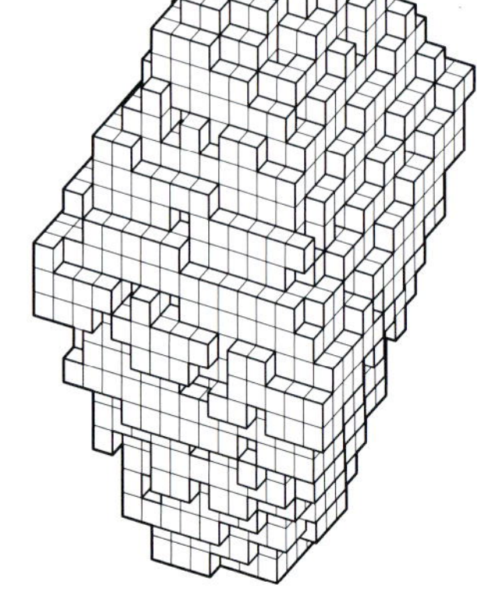

1. Create a matrix of voxels with the dimensions mX, mY, and mZ. Fill the site volume with the voxels.
2. Create a boundary frame by manipulating its vertices to approximate the mass of the desired structure.
3. Test if each voxel's centroid is within the boundary frame.
4. If the centroid is within the boundary volume, keep it. If it is not, remove the voxel from the matrix.
5. Remove a certain percentage (e%) of the voxels to further erode the surface of the structure.

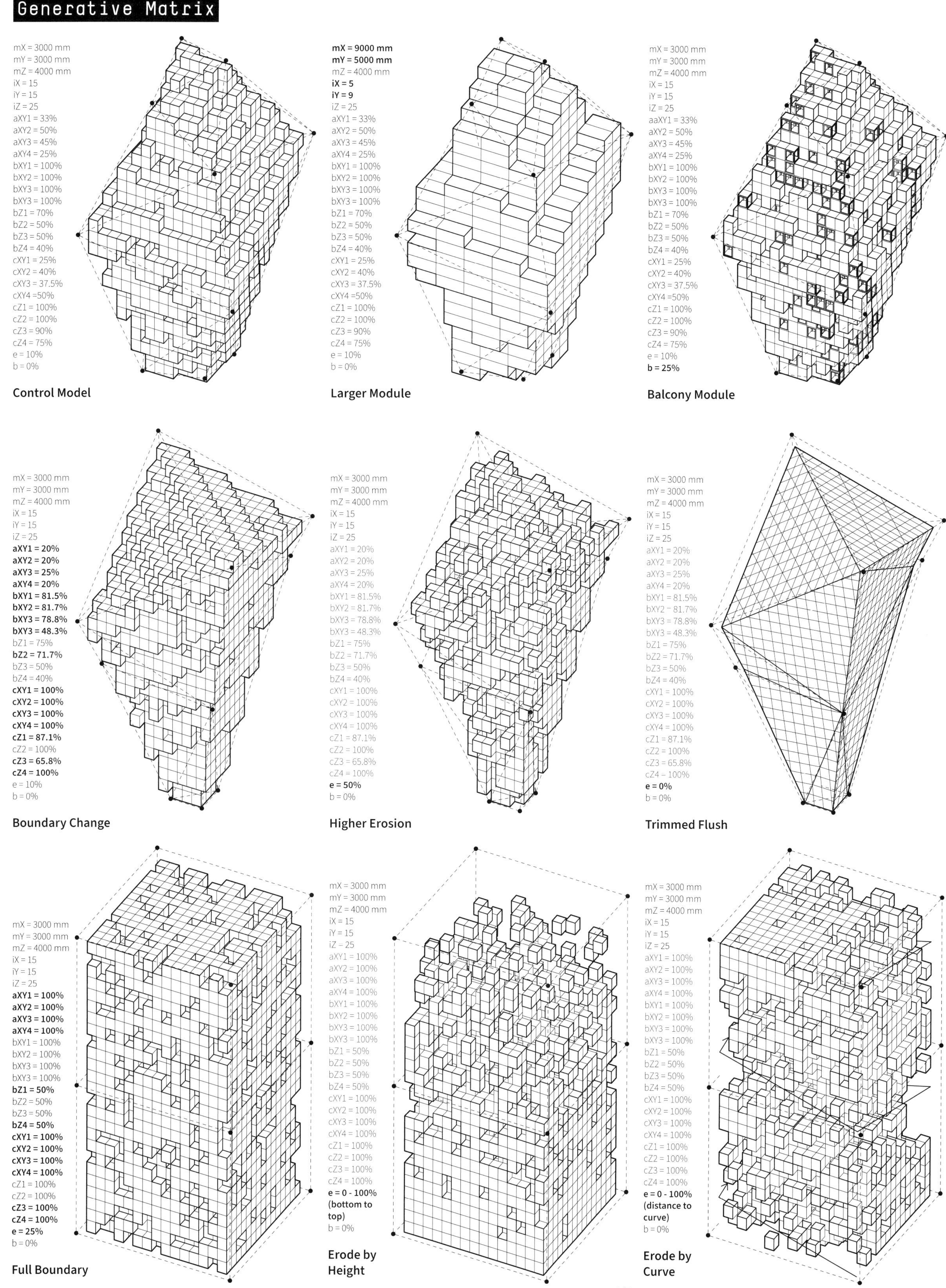
Generative Matrix
mX = 3000 mm
mY = 3000 mm
mZ = 4000 mm
iX = 15
iY = 15
iZ = 25
aXY1 = 33%
aXY2 = 50%
aXY3 = 45%
aXY4 = 25%
bXY1 = 100%
bXY2 = 100%
bXY3 = 100%
bXY3 = 100%
bZ1 = 70%
bZ2 = 50%
bZ3 = 50%
bZ4 = 40%
cXY1 = 25%
cXY2 = 40%
cXY3 = 37.5%
cXY4 =50%
cZ1 = 100%
cZ2 = 100%
cZ3 = 90%
cZ4 = 75%
e = 10%
b = 0%
Control Model
mX = 9000 mm
mY = 5000 mm
mZ = 4000 mm
iX = 5
iY = 9
iZ = 25
aXY1 = 33%
aXY2 = 50%
aXY3 = 45%
aXY4 = 25%
bXY1 = 100%
bXY2 = 100%
bXY3 = 100%
bXY3 = 100%
bZ1 = 70%
bZ2 = 50%
bZ3 = 50%
bZ4 = 40%
cXY1 = 25%
cXY2 = 40%
cXY3 = 37.5%
cXY4 =50%
cZ1 = 100%
cZ2 = 100%
cZ3 = 90%
cZ4 = 75%
e = 10%
b = 0%
Larger Module
mX = 3000 mm
mY = 3000 mm
mZ = 4000 mm
iX = 15
iY = 15
iZ = 25
aaXY1 = 33%
aXY2 = 50%
aXY3 = 45%
aXY4 = 25%
bXY1 = 100%
bXY2 = 100%
bXY3 = 100%
bXY3 = 100%
bZ1 = 70%
bZ2 = 50%
bZ3 = 50%
bZ4 = 40%
cXY1 = 25%
cXY2 = 40%
cXY3 = 37.5%
cXY4 =50%
cZ1 = 100%
cZ2 = 100%
cZ3 = 90%
cZ4 = 75%
e = 10%
b = 25%
Balcony Module
mX = 3000 mm
mY = 3000 mm
mZ = 4000 mm
iX = 15
iY = 15
iZ = 25
aXY1 = 20%
aXY2 = 20%
aXY3 = 25%
aXY4 = 20%
bXY1 = 81.5%
bXY2 = 81.7%
bXY3 = 78.8%
bXY3 = 48.3%
bZ1 = 75%
bZ2 = 71.7%
bZ3 = 50%
bZ4 = 40%
cXY1 = 100%
cXY2 = 100%
cXY3 = 100%
cXY4 = 100%
cZ1 = 87.1%
cZ2 = 100%
cZ3 = 65.8%
cZ4 = 100%
e = 10%
b = 0%
Boundary Change
mX = 3000 mm
mY = 3000 mm
mZ = 4000 mm
iX = 15
iY = 15
iZ = 25
aXY1 = 20%
aXY2 = 20%
aXY3 = 25%
aXY4 = 20%
bXY1 = 81.5%
bXY2 = 81.7%
bXY3 = 78.8%
bXY3 = 48.3%
bZ1 = 75%
bZ2 = 71.7%
bZ3 = 50%
bZ4 = 40%
cXY1 = 100%
cXY2 = 100%
cXY3 = 100%
cXY4 = 100%
cZ1 = 87.1%
cZ2 = 100%
cZ3 = 65.8%
cZ4 = 100%
e = 50%
b = 0%
Higher Erosion
mX = 3000 mm
mY = 3000 mm
mZ = 4000 mm
iX = 15
iY = 15
iZ = 25
aXY1 = 20%
aXY2 = 20%
aXY3 = 25%
aXY4 = 20%
bXY1 = 81.5%
bXY2 = 81.7%
bXY3 = 78.8%
bXY3 = 48.3%
bZ1 = 75%
bZ2 = 71.7%
bZ3 = 50%
bZ4 = 40%
cXY1 = 100%
cXY2 = 100%
cXY3 = 100%
cXY4 = 100%
cZ1 = 87.1%
cZ2 = 100%
cZ3 = 65.8%
cZ4 = 100%
e = 0%
b = 0%
Trimmed Flush
mX = 3000 mm
mY = 3000 mm
mZ = 4000 mm
iX = 15
iY = 15
iZ = 25
aXY1 = 100%
aXY2 = 100%
aXY3 = 100%
aXY4 = 100%
bXY1 = 100%
bXY2 = 100%
bXY3 = 100%
bXY3 = 100%
bZ1 = 50%
bZ2 = 50%
bZ3 = 50%
bZ4 = 50%
cXY1 = 100%
cXY2 = 100%
cXY3 = 100%
cXY4 = 100%
cZ1 = 100%
cZ2 = 100%
cZ3 = 100%
cZ4 = 100%
e = 25%
b = 0%
Full Boundary
mX = 3000 mm
mY = 3000 mm
mZ = 4000 mm
iX = 15
iY = 15
iZ = 25
aXY1 = 100%
aXY2 = 100%
aXY3 = 100%
aXY4 = 100%
bXY1 = 100%
bXY2 = 100%
bXY3 = 100%
bXY3 = 100%
bZ1 = 50%
bZ2 = 50%
bZ3 = 50%
bZ4 = 50%
cXY1 = 100%
cXY2 = 100%
cXY3 = 100%
cXY4 = 100%
cZ1 = 100%
cZ2 = 100%
cZ3 = 100%
cZ4 = 100%
e = 0 - 100% (bottom to top)
b = 0%
Erode by Height
mX = 3000 mm
mY = 3000 mm
mZ = 4000 mm
iX = 15
iY = 15
iZ = 25
aXY1 = 100%
aXY2 = 100%
aXY3 = 100%
aXY4 = 100%
bXY1 = 100%
bXY2 = 100%
bXY3 = 100%
bXY3 = 100%
bZ1 = 50%
bZ2 = 50%
bZ3 = 50%
bZ4 = 50%
cXY1 = 100%
cXY2 = 100%
cXY3 = 100%
cXY4 = 100%
cZ1 = 100%
cZ2 = 100%
cZ3 = 100%
cZ4 = 100%
e = 0 - 100% (distance to curve)
b = 0%
Erode by Curve

CELLULAR CLUSTERS

Whether derived from the tessellated subdivision of a surface or space, or the aggregative addition of individuated components, cellular clusters are essentially modular phenomena that are determined by local, rather than global ordering parameters. They are locally delimited while being globally open, yet they still operate at the scale of the whole as a collective and continuous multiplicity. While cellular structures derived from processes of tessellation operate through minimal surface enclosures and therefore maintain no gaps between cells since they are patterned according to the opportunistic occupation of space, clusters in general may establish different degrees of porosity. Cells can be in close contact or there may be wide intercellular spaces, depending on the stability, coherence, and density of the system.

Cellular Clusters

Generative Organicism and Polyhedral Patterning

Cellular clusters are locally additive or divisible systems made up of discrete components that produce a whole that has properties extending beyond the individual cell. The basic element of all biological systems, the cell is simultaneously related to, yet differentiated from the larger organizational structures it supports. Within geological systems, although the global form of a sand dune has attributes that distinguish it from the local forms of the crystalline mineral aggregates of which it is comprised, its ability to transform at the macro-scale in relation to external forces such as the sculpting power of the wind, is still a result of the micro-properties of each crystal and its relationship to its surrounding neighbors. Whether derived from the tessellated subdivision of a surface or space, or the aggregative addition of individuated components, cellular clusters are essentially modular phenomena that are determined by local, rather than global, ordering parameters. They are locally delimited while being globally open, yet they still operate at the scale of the whole as a collective and continuous multiplicity. Cellular clusters also perform simultaneously as both fill and frame to varying degrees depending on the relative contiguity of elements. As an aggregate of cells they form a field of individuated units, yet function as a frame in the way that they distribute forces through the aggregate, along edges or surfaces, in a nonlinear way. These clusters therefore combine the properties of discontinuity and continuity simultaneously in that they are composed of discrete and identifiable units, yet operate as a collective synthetic whole—a multiplicity that cannot be simply reduced to a grouping of single objects.[1]

Cells, bubbles, crystals, and honeycombs, such as those most evident in biology, chemistry, geology, and geometry, have varying degrees of contiguity and proximity, yet are all inevitably ordered according to their potential spatial juxtapositions resulting from their boundary conditions and geometry, in addition to the density of interrelated elements within the system. While cellular structures derived from processes of tessellation operate through minimal surface enclosures and therefore maintain no gaps between cells since they are patterned according to the opportunistic occupation of space, clusters in general may establish different degrees of porosity. Cells can be in close contact or there may be wide intercellular spaces, depending on the stability, coherence and density of the system. It is the proximity or sharing of edges and surfaces in fully packed aggregates that ensures the mutual diffusion of force and pressure as it moves across the system. Cellular systems may also be loosely formed or highly regular producing homogeneous or heterogeneous structures, yet they are all essentially repetitive unlimited systems that evolve through packing, filling or tiling strategies.

The renewed interest in cellular structures, that have certainly expanded the idealized terrain of Platonic solids and the closure and regularity of Euclidean geometries that are found at the foundational origins of architectural history, have emerged as a result of the ability of digital technologies to augment our capacity to visualize and parametrically inform, manipulate, and fabricate the complex spatial patterning of geometric structures. This new capacity has also motivated a shift in both the emphasis and application of these geometries to architecture as they move from the individual unit to the multiplicitous manifold system, from two-dimensionally patterned planar systems to complex cellular surface structures and multidimensional spatial aggregates, and from the regularity and symmetry of polyhedral structures to the progressive or rhythmic differentiation of variable systems. Whether these emerge from additive or divisive processes, or are understood through solid volumes, planar surfaces or the complex spatial lattices that frame and describe them, cellular clusters refer less to a single specific process of development, scale of operation or formal type than to a taxonomy that signifies the characteristic properties, organizational logics, generative strategies and conceptual underpinnings shared by a group of contemporary artifacts.

The appearance of cellular structures, evident in architectural projects such as the Water Cube project by PTW Architects with ARUP Engineering, or more experimental research endeavors such as the Grotto and Quasi-Table projects by Aranda/Lasch and the Chrysalis (III) installation at the Centre Pompidou by Matsys, can be understood to have their roots in two distinct yet geometrically related historical architectural trajectories. On the one hand, in the elaboration of ornamental surfaces found in Byzantine mosaics and the complex tessellated patterns of Islamic architecture. And, on the

1

2

3

other hand, in the geodesic domes and triangulated and hexagonal lattice shell structures developed by Buckminster Fuller in the pursuit of engineering efficiency and the technological advancement of architecture. Although very different in emphasis, scale, evolution and application, each of these trajectories drew from the potential of tessellating Euclidean geometries in the generation of patterned surfaces and systems.

Tessellation, also known as tiling, refers to the way in which a plane is subdivided and filled with a pattern of closed elements or "tiles"—typically geometric polygons—that aggregate to fill the surface without overlaps or gaps so that each tile shares its boundary with other tiles in the system. An edge thus constitutes the intersection between two bordering tiles, which is most often a straight line, and a vertex is the point of intersection of three or more bordering tiles. First comprehensively documented at the beginning of the seventeenth century by Johannes Kepler[2] and later developed in the nineteenth century by the Swiss geometer Ludwig Schläfli and Russian crystallographer Yevgraf Fyodorov among others, tessellation is dependent on a branch of mathematics that studies the patterned geometries of regular, semi-regular, and aperiodic tiling through different groups of isometries. Although the digital advancement of tiled surfaces in projects such as the Ravensbourne College by FOA have redefined the historical use of patterned ornament as it is applied to surface cladding, the expansion of tessellation to greater dimensions through the packing of crystalline polyhedral systems on the one hand, and its use to approximate curvature by reducing complex surfaces to triangulated or polygonal faceted systems (so that they might be constructed out of existing linear or planar materials) on the other, has augmented its architectural application across a broad range of phenomena.

An early example of the latter is the application of a triangulated lattice or planar system to approximate spherical curvature in the geodesic domes of Buckminster Fuller, such as in the one built for the 1967 Expo in Montreal. The geodesic dome—a triangular tessellation of the sphere—is produced by dividing the faces of an icosahedron into smaller triangles whose vertices are then projected onto the surface of the sphere, and whose edges form geodesic paths across its circumference. The degree of approximation of the initial sphere's curvature is therefore dependent on the fractal scaling of these triangles and the resolution of its linear or planar system in relation to the size of the spherical dome created. Fuller's initial dome structures exploited the intrinsic efficiency of the spherical shape, which like the soap bubble, "does more with less" by enclosing a maximal space using a minimal surface (whose differential increases as the diameter of the sphere increases), and combined this with the industrial and material efficiencies gained by constructing this surface using a homogenous cellular geometric pattern comprised of a repetitive interconnected system of straight line segments (struts) and flat panels.

Although revolutionary in concept, the limited application of the principles of the geodesic dome resulted most often from either technical and environmental issues or the resistance of its form to adaptation in relation to programmatic and cultural norms, some of which were successfully resolved in the use of these structures for stadia or the covering of large territories. This is evident in the Eden Project, known as the Biomes by Grimshaw Architects 2, a direct genealogical descendent of the geodesic dome that envelops an environmental exhibition encompassing a vast terrain of tropical and temperate regions. Here, the cellular cluster operates at two scales: in the double series of four interlinked soap bubble-like domes of varying sizes, and in the cellular surface geometry of these domes that consist of a double layer of hexagonal tessellated surfaces conjoined by a triangulated lattice structure, known as a hex-tri-hex space frame. The six tetrahedrons positioned at the vertices of each hexagon on the outer shell stabilize the structure while negotiating the scalar difference between tessellated cellular layers by embedding triangular cells at the meeting point of three hexagons along the inner surface. Emulating the intelligence found within natural systems (such as the hexagonal faceted eyes of insects) that provided its point of departure, this project capitalizes on the spatial efficiency of the cellular geometry and then combines this with the structural, material, and environmental efficiencies of employing an extremely lightweight, small, and easily assembled interior modular structure, with an exterior cladding of triple-layered, high-performance ETFE pillows.

The application of cellular structures to thickened surface geometries is further augmented in the Voussoir Cloud project by IwamotoScott Architects 1 that complexifies both the global form of the surface to be tessellated and the local geometry and modulation of aggregated cells that fill this surface. In this project, the homogenous spherical geometry of the dome is displaced by a heterogeneous system of intersecting catenary vaults whose surfaces are comprised of an array of packed triangulated cells that range in form, size, and distribution. The geometric logic of these cells and the structure that they produce through the variability of their packing however, although derived from a triangular surface tessellation tested to ensure the efficacy of its structural performance, tend to conceal and confuse, rather than reveal and elucidate, the implied structural forces of this vaulted system. In addition, although these voussoirs function in compression, like the tapered stone of arches to which they owe their namesake, the thinness of the material out of which they are constructed, the porosity of the surface they produce, and the fact that these cells meet not only along their skewed edges, but also at their vertices, further confounds the perceptual reading of the work. Here,

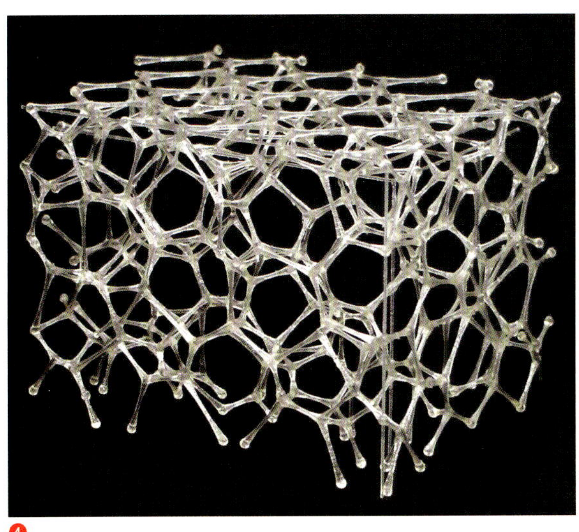

4

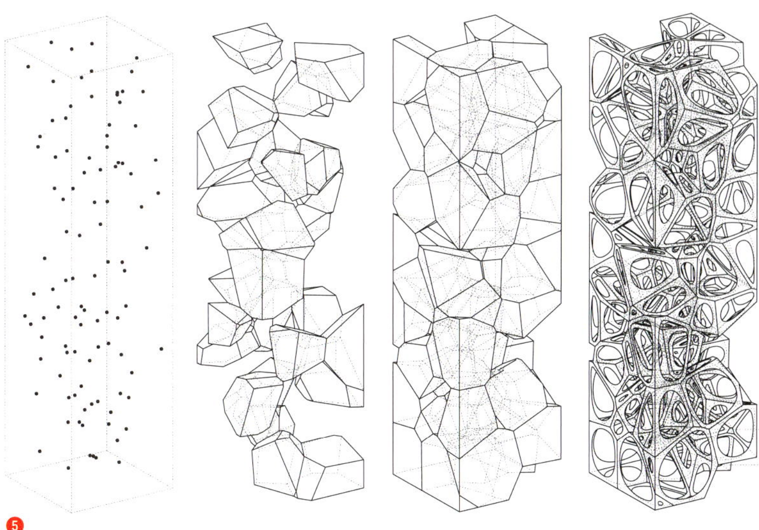

5

the thick material of typical voussoirs is displaced by thin wood laminate surfaces operating simultaneously in tension and compression. Structural depth is achieved by the folded flanges of each cell, which is further stiffened by the subtle inflection of the cells triangulated surface, and the curvature of its edges, specifically for voussoirs that are adjacent to open cells. Compressive stability is also achieved by variation within the cellular system. This occurs locally through the packing of cells when opposing lateral forces caused by the bowed flanges of neighboring cells push against each other because of the curvature along their seams and globally by the variation in size and distribution of cellular units across the whole. These decrease in size and increase in number and density toward the ribs of the vaults and bases of the columns to ensure stability, while increasing in size and porosity along the upper vault to both transmit light and physically and perceptually lighten its surface. The paradoxical nature of Voussoir Cloud and its capacity to produce a porous yet continuous stiffened surface out of a thin aggregative cellular geometry is in part, a result of the contradictions intrinsic to cellular systems that enable them to be simultaneously additive and divisive, discrete and continuous, and constituted by both local and global ordering systems.

The transformation of a thickened cellular surface geometry into a variable, complex spatial structure is perhaps best exemplified architecturally by the Beijing National Aquatics Centre, known as the Water Cube. Similar in strategy to the Digital Origami installation project by Chris Bosse of LAVA, one of the key designers of the project, the Water Cube is a volumetric cellular cluster that derives its structure from the condition of a foaming liquid suspended in an aggregative state. Perceived as a cube of water housing an aquatic program, the building is an orthogonal, three-dimensional volume whose interior spaces are carved out of a cluster of foam bubbles 3. Water and air thereby become the profound anti-materials out of which to construct their own container. This cluster of bubbles that comprise the building envelope's thickened skin are paradoxically ossified and materialized into a complex cellular structure whose micro-details are magnified to render evident the architecturalization of their form. Modeled on the structure of foaming water and exploiting a geometry based on the interface between soap bubbles, the packing of cells within this complex cluster is derived from the most efficient structural subdivision of space common to crystalline and cellular natural phenomena.[3] Space, structure, and façade are thus compressed into the same element. This cellular structure is then clad with an extremely thin, translucent, ETFE bubble-wrap perimeter envelope that acts as a passive solar collector, and that, like the structure, is composed primarily of air. This envelope dissolves the boundary conditions of the building while dematerializing its solidity through the scale, variability, and openness of the spatial lattice that acts as its support.

In the Water Cube, the diverse cellular structure of the whole is constituted using a variation of the Weaire-Phelan model, a regular repeating aggregation of two kinds of irregular polyhedral cells of equal volume, one an irregular dodecahedron and the other a tetrakaidecahedron, with twelve and fourteen faces respectively. Each of these is primarily comprised of irregular pentagonal faces (with the latter including two additional hexagonal faces to its geometry).[4] To generate an efficient structural lattice for the building, this packing model was then adjusted to reduce the number of types of structural elements in the system to three different faces, four different edges, and three different types of vertices or nodes that comprise the primary repetitive modular elements out of which the whole is constructed 4.[5] To further complexify the reading of this structure, however, these polyhedral bubbles were spatially packed and then rotated by 60 degrees so that the elevations revealed through the sectional slicing of the packed cells would appear to be far more erratic, referencing nature's ability to conceal the geometric coding of its cells, bubbles, and crystals behind the irregularity of their appearance. Although used in this project as a signifier of the protean characteristics of aqueous foam when moving between liquid and gas states within nature, the differentiation of cells and resultant heterogeneity is not an expression of randomness per se, but rather the key to its functional integration and performative optimization. In multicellular organisms, for example, cells pack together to form an intricate yet differentiated morphology of tissue structures whose functionality is dependent on this variability. The material response to external pressures and adaptation to specific environmental conditions—such as air, force, gravity or pressure—occur through the modulation and distribution of local cellular differentiation within particular zones or regions of the cluster while maintaining the continuity of the whole. Just as the variegated cellular structure of an insect wing refers to the range and distribution of forces necessary to enable the creature to fly,[6] the variation in the size and density of wood petals in the Voussoir Cloud installation is what enables its cells to negotiate between structural, functional, and aesthetic demands.

In natural cellular clusters, the hexagonal honeycomb of bees is the most famous of regular cellular systems. Here, each cell is connected to twelve others, six adjacent, three above and three below, constituting a packing system of twelve related cells. Latitudinal sections reveal its regularity which, like the soap bubble, is the product of equal pressure exerted by all sides contributing to the strength and stability of the system. Each cell within this system is a rhombic dodecahedron which, when tessellated, generates the densest possible three-dimensional array of packed polyhedral cells. In natural systems, such as soap bubbles and in cellular plant structures based

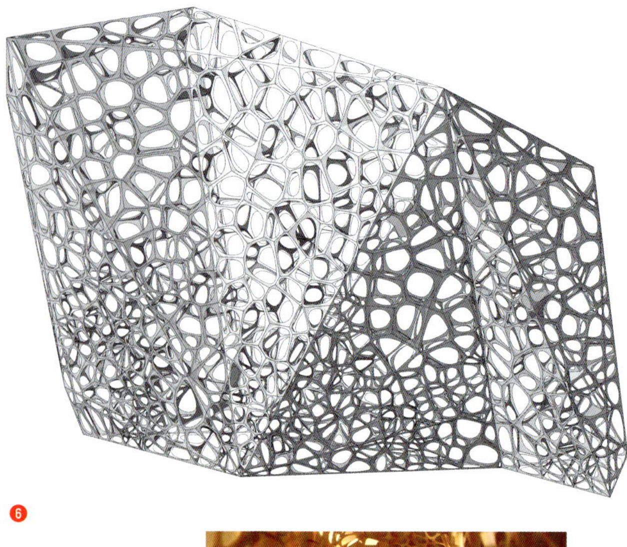

6

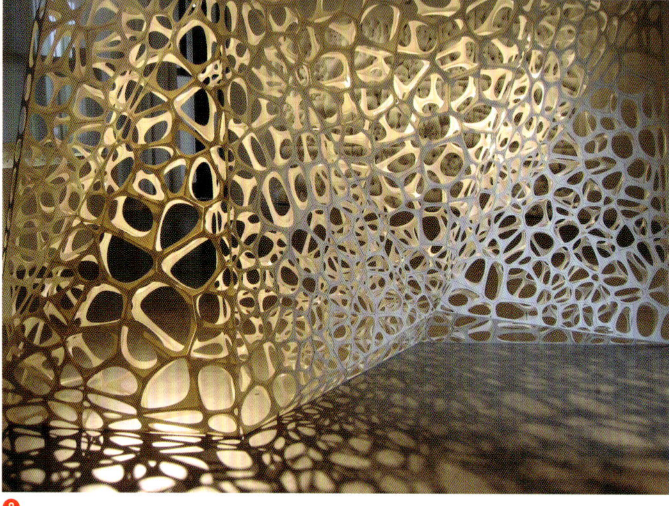

8

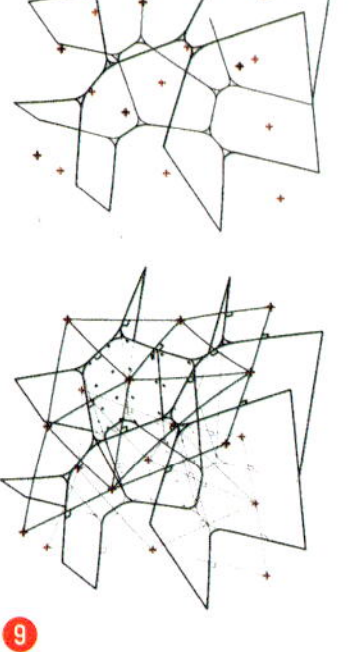

9

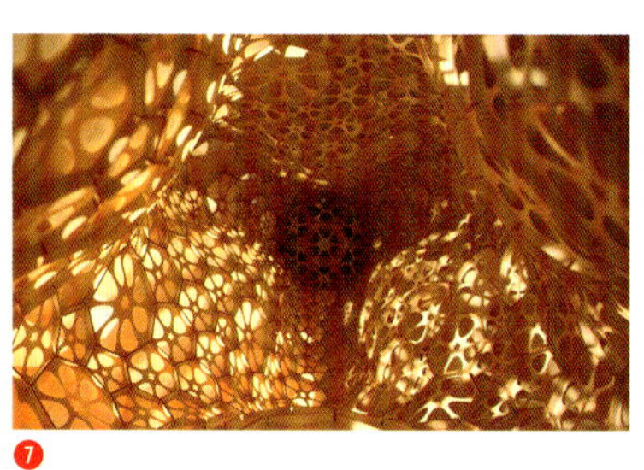

7

on the dense packing of spherical systems, the negotiation between the continuity of the cell and the continuity of the cell wall in relation to the structure of the larger aggregation occurs through a small intervening curved surface that bridges the line of contact, strengthens the joint at the vertex between cells, and mediates between the interior stability of the individual cell and the geometrical capacity of the unit to stack and aggregate.[7] In variegated projects derived from cellular morphologies such as C_Wall by Matsys, the difference between the geometries and the curvilinear voids cut into each cell is an expression of this principle that allows for rigidity and continuity in the system while minimizing surface material and enabling the porosity of the whole.

Expanded research in cellular aggregate structures such as the C_Wall and Chrysalis (III) have often been generated by the digital application of Voronoi tiling to the creation of architectonic surfaces, structures, and volumes 5. Voronoi diagrams derive their geometry from any given set of points, where the edges of each tile, or planar surface of each cell, will always be the perpendicular bisector of any line segment connecting two points within the field.[8] The region surrounding each point is therefore closer to that point than any other in the field, which is why these diagrams have been used in a range of applications from the determination of forest canopy growth patterns to the epidemiological modeling of the spread of disease. Since these points can be derived from any mapping of a population or information dataset and can produce any type of regular or irregular field condition, the patterns generated are therefore necessarily a result of local rather than global relations, and topological rather than geometric principles, that readily lend themselves to transformation in response to shifting parameters.

The variability of the C-Wall cellular system was thereby generated by applying a Voronoi tiling system to a point cloud array that was initially extracted from the differentiated tonal density of bit-mapped image. This point field was then projected onto the surface of a thickened and folded wall to parametrically generate a volumetric cellular structure derived from the tiling of this field, the voiding of its cellular polygons, and the panelizing of its double-sided structure 6,8. The unfolded cells, which were CNC-cut from thin paper and reassembled into a larger aggregate, exploit the high strength-to-weight ratio intrinsic to cellular structural morphologies by capturing space with minimal material effort. As an evolution of this earlier project, Chrysalis (III) 7 further expands the application of two-dimensional cellular structures to space. This is achieved, on the one hand, by the complex projection of the cellular morphology onto a wrapped volumetric enclosure that enables it to be unfolded as a developable surface, and on the other hand, through the spatial extrusion of these cells that create barnacle-like conical protrusions, which refer to the encrusted surface agglomerations found within aquatic environments. Although cut from planar wood veneer, the inner plates of these cellular clusters are each further divided into radially organized nonplanar cells. These are subtly folded cellular surfaces that, because of their local tendency to expand and contract, in combination with their networked connectivity across the whole, lead to competing movements within the surface that maintain its topological continuity while adjusting its geometry—a process that reveals the cellular cluster's capacity to continually self-organize in its search for greater equilibrium.

In Voroduo by Office dA 9,10,11 topological transformation and mutation is readily apprehensible through the progressive transformation of the sectional cellular series as this structural aggregate of connected yet pliable plastic tubes responds to its context like an animate object twisting back on itself in space. In the same way that a topological plane can mutate into a curved surface, here the flexibility of cells that compress, rotate and stretch in relation to a changing field of spatially positioned points used to describe its surface, enable the geometry of the installation to seamlessly morph and invert as it changes from a bowl at one end of the piece (or from a wall, in the case of its genetic offspring, Voromuro 12) into a vaulted dome at the other. Here, the plasticity of cells, which vary in shape, size, and direction and respond to changing forces, loads, and stresses distributed across the cluster, generate a family of forms that are specific to, and result from, their position within the larger whole. Just as natural variation in biological systems ensures the local adaptivity and optimization of global morphologies through the incremental differentiation of its cellular

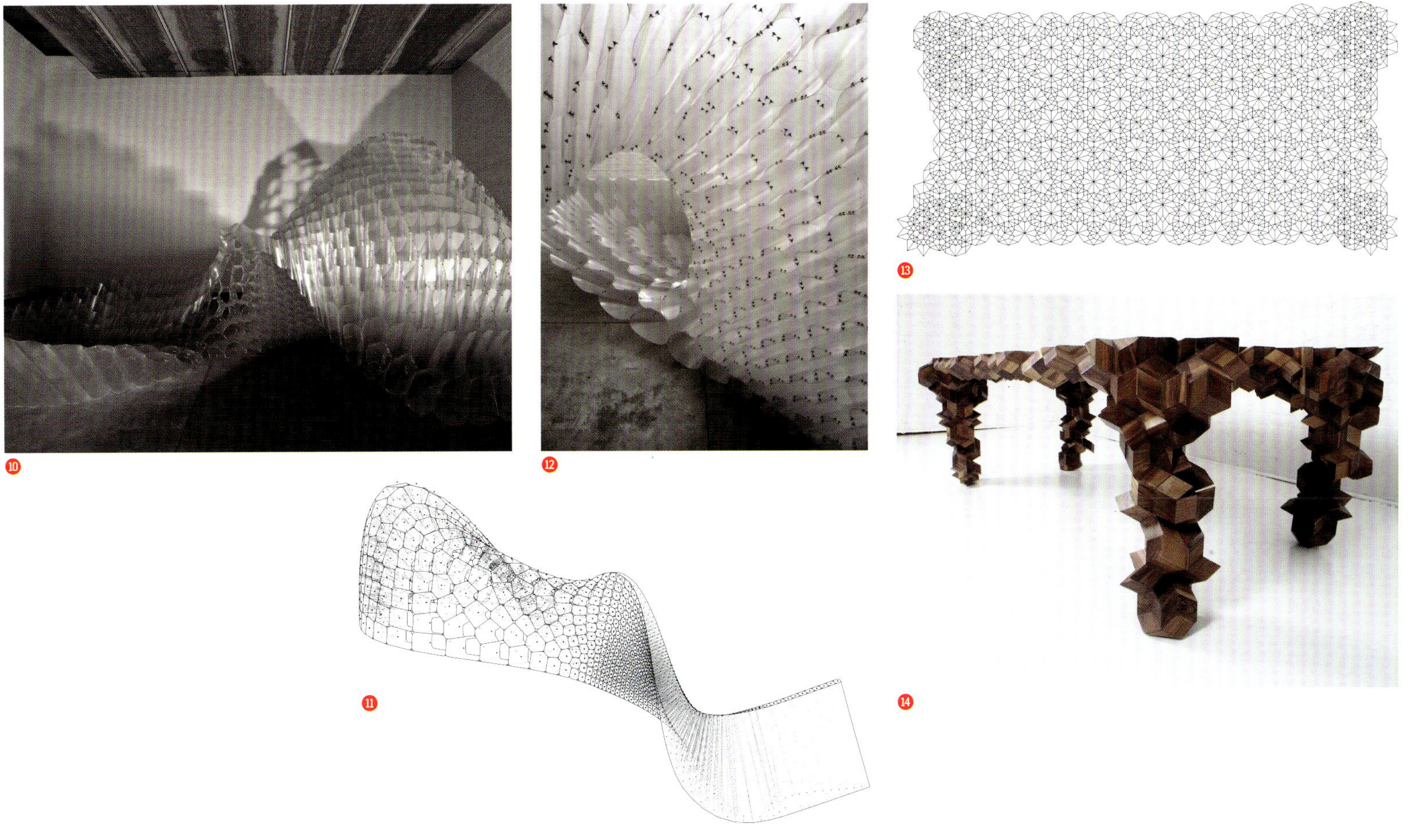

structures, this project indicates the larger applicability of such systems to architectural spatial strategies in search of a continuum between a dynamic global form and a pliant yet stable cellular morphology.

At the other end of this spectrum, the disjunction, rather than continuity between the global morphology of the whole and the local morphology of cellular structures is exhibited in projects such as the Quasitable 13, 14 and Fauteuil Chair by Aranda/Lasch that apply aperiodic polyhedral tiling to the creation of everyday functional objects. These projects evolved from the study of quasi-crystals—a complex phase of matter exhibited at the edge of its formation.[9] Although the molecular pattern of regular crystals is periodic and repetitive, when solids melt their crystalline pattern becomes aperiodic and endlessly uneven. Before computation, the study of the aperiodicity of cellular tiling was previously prohibitive because of the sheer quantity of information required to describe its endlessly changing patterns. It is not that the pattern is unstructured but rather that the complexity of its structure threatens our conception of order by combining local stability with long-range unpredictability. Theatricalizing the disjunction intrinsic to exogenous form-making, where form acts as a template that is arbitrarily filled with material substance, in the Quasitable the typological form of a table is literally carved out of what seems to be an overly coarse material substrate representing the complexity of a random system of Penrose tiling. The apparent growth and complex modular aperiodicity of the local cellular material substrate is scaled to visibly confront the semiotic stasis of the conventional global form that it seems to fill, questioning the difference between our understanding of microscopic matters in flux and our macroscopic perception of the stable forms to which these matters are applied, while embedding the complexity of our mathematical models used to describe the world within the very matters that they are intended to represent. Whether originating from the impulse to use emerging digital technologies to explore the intricate variability of biotic systems to expand the terrain of architectural practice as in the Water Cube and Grotto projects, or alternatively to materialize the complexity of higher order geometries in the everyday artifacts that surround us to embody this knowledge and render it palpable, recent spatial explorations in cellular morphologies radically shift the limits of our traditional spatial territories within architecture while bringing us closer to the remarkable versatility found within natural systems.

Notes

1. "Multiplicity must not designate a combination of the many and the one, but rather an organization belonging to the many as such, which has no need whatsoever of unity in order to form a system." Gilles Deleuze, *Difference and Repetition* (New York: Columbia University Press, 1994), 182. On the concept of multiplicity also see: Deleuze and Guattari, *A Thousand Plateaus*, 8–9.
2. Johannes Kepler, *Harmonices Mundi* (Harmony of the Worlds, 1619).
3. The Weaire-Phelan geometric model used for the structure is a contemporary evolution of the Kelvin problem (1887) that asks how space can be partitioned into an idealized foam structure of equally sized bubbles with the least amount of surface area separating them. This was a foam based on a uniform bitruncated, cubic honeycomb structure of aggregated, truncated octahedron. Lord Kelvin (Sir William Thomson) (1887), "On the Division of Space with Minimum Partitional Area," *Philosophical Magazine* 24 (151): 503. See also D'Arcy Thompson on "The Form of Tissues or Cell Aggregates" in *On Growth and Form* (New York: Cambridge University Press, 1945), 548–556.
4. For a summary description of the Weaire-Phelan model see Jane Burry and Mark Burry, *The New Mathematics of Architecture* (New York: Thames & Hudson, 2010), 79–81 and 266. See also Denis Weaire and Robert Phelan, "A Counter-Example To Kelvin's Conjecture On Minimal Surfaces," *Philosophical Magazine Letters* 69 (1994): 107–110.
5. Xueyi Fu et al., "Beijing Olympic National Swimming Centre: Structural Design." in *Structural Engineer* 85, No. 22 (November 2007): 27–33.
6. On the dragonfly's wing structure see Thompson, "The Form of Tissues or Cell Aggregates," 476.
7. Ibid., 470–471.
8. The Voronoi diagram, also known as the Dirichlet Tessellation, is named after the mathematician Georgy Voronoy. Franz Aurenhammer, "Voronoi Diagrams," (ACM Computing Surveys, 23, no.3 (1991): 345–405, and Atsuyuki Okabe et al., *Spatial Tessellations: Concepts and Applications of Voronoi Diagrams* (Chichester: John Wiley & Sons, 2000). For a summary of principles see: Burry and Burry, *The New Mathematics of Architecture*, 266, and Benjamin Aranda and Christopher Lasch *Tooling* (New York: Princeton Architectural Press, 2006), 76–78.
9. For a detailed account of these projects see Tomoko Sakamoto and Albert Ferré, eds., *From Control to Design: Parametric/Algorithmic Architecture* (New York: Actar, 2008), 196–205.

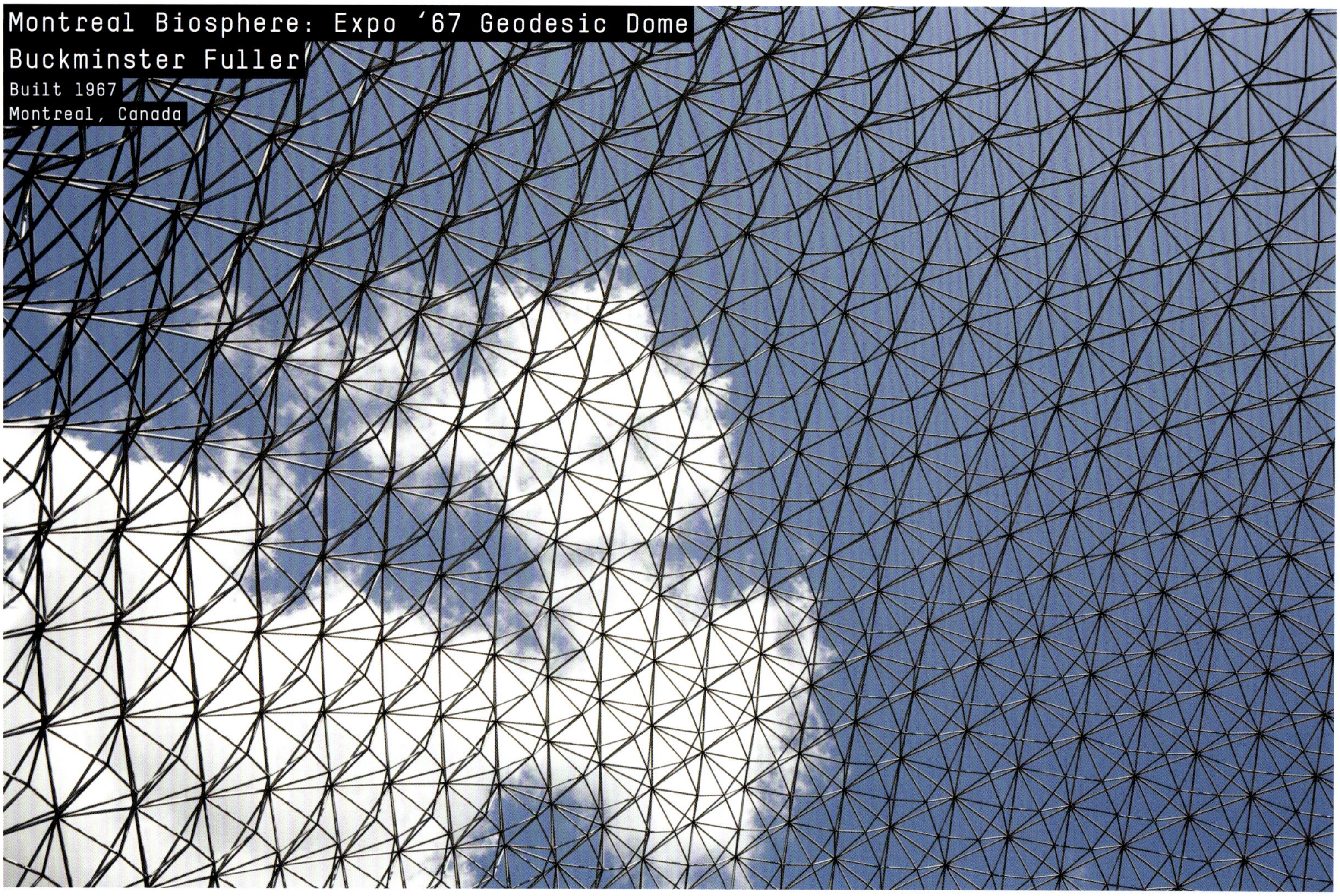

Montreal Biosphere: Expo '67 Geodesic Dome

Buckminster Fuller

Built 1967
Montreal, Canada

4.1a

4.1b

The Montreal Biosphere, designed as the United States' pavilion for the 1967 World Exposition, is a seventy-six-meter-diameter geodesic dome that originally enclosed a seven-story building of interconnected open platforms supporting the exhibition program. The geometry of the dome is based on the triangular tessellation of a sphere generated by dividing the twenty equilateral triangular faces of an icosahedron into smaller triangles whose vertices are then projected onto the surface of the sphere. The division of these faces produces a faceted surface structure of triangles, and as the frequency of divisions and number of facets increase, the structural geometry comes closer to the approximation of the spherical surface. The lines connecting the vertices on this spherical surface are the chords of the geodesic sphere which are then directly translated into the physical struts of the dome structure. Geodesic domes are inherently efficient structures because of their ability to enclose enormous volumes with minimal surface area, while distributing forces evenly across their surface. In Fuller's Biosphere, the structural stability of the dome is augmented by the transformation of the surface structure into a thickened tetrahedral lattice where each facet of the triangulated geodesic surface forms one face of a tetrahedron projected into the dome's interior. The interior vertices of these tetrahedrons are interconnected by a system of straight segments that form a hexagonal cellular network. This structural lattice, which is made up of metal tubes that are 9 cm in diameter, exploits the material efficiencies gained within the context of industrial production through the mass-production and technological prefabrication of repetitive elements. Although initially intended to be mechanically fastened together, in the final structure, these struts were welded together to ensure their stability—a condition that reinforced the dome's permanence by rendering it extremely difficult to dismantle. The complexity of this double-layered geodesic structure is now highly visible because of the dome's transparency resulting from its lack of enclosure, a consequence of the fire of 1976 (caused by welding repairs), which destroyed the acrylic skin in which it was originally sheathed. Restored from 1992–95, the dome is now an open-air structure containing a remodeled interior building for environmental observation dedicated to sustainable development.

The Eden Project: The Biomes
Grimshaw Architects

Built 2000

Cornwall, United Kingdom

4.2a

The Eden Project, which is known as the Biomes, houses the largest conservatories in the world, covering 2.2 hectares. A direct descendant of the geodesic dome in both structure and form, these vast and conjoined bubble-like domes provide a controlled environment for two exhibitions supporting tropical and temperate biomes that contain more than a thousand species of plants brought from around the globe. The Biomes is an immersive environment for the general public that also supports programs for environmental research and education. Sited on a former clay quarry, the project is comprised of two sets of four interconnected domes or geodesic half-spheres, the surfaces of which are constructed with a cellular lattice known as a hex-tri-hex space frame made of galvanized steel tubing. This space frame consists of a double layer of hexagonal tessellated surfaces linked together by a triangulated structure—six tetrahedrons that are positioned at the vertices of each hexagon on the outer shell and that form six triangles along the edges of the smaller hexagons on the inner surface that is implied by the bottom layer of the space frame. These tetrahedrons stabilize and connect the two faceted cellular surfaces, while negotiating the dimensional variations of their tessellated structures. The modular structure of the Biomes, which draws from the spatial and material efficiencies of the geodesic dome and further capitalizes on the larger efficiencies of the hexagonal cellular surface, is comprised of lightweight, straight segments that are prefabricated and easily transported and assembled on site. Although repetitive and relatively uniform for each layer of the structure, these segments have slightly different dimensions to accommodate the specificities of the site and negotiate the edge conditions where the structure meets the ground. Each hexagonal cell on the outer surface then acts as a frame for triple-layered, inflated pillows of high performance, lightweight, UV-transparent ETFE film that clad and enclose the structure, comprising a surface that encloses a maximal space with minimal surface area and that acts as a thermal blanket for the structure.

4.2b

4.2c

Sagrada Familia Church Ceiling, Clerestory and Rose Windows
Antoni Gaudi + Mark Burry
Built 1883-2001
Barcelona, Spain

4.3a

4.3b

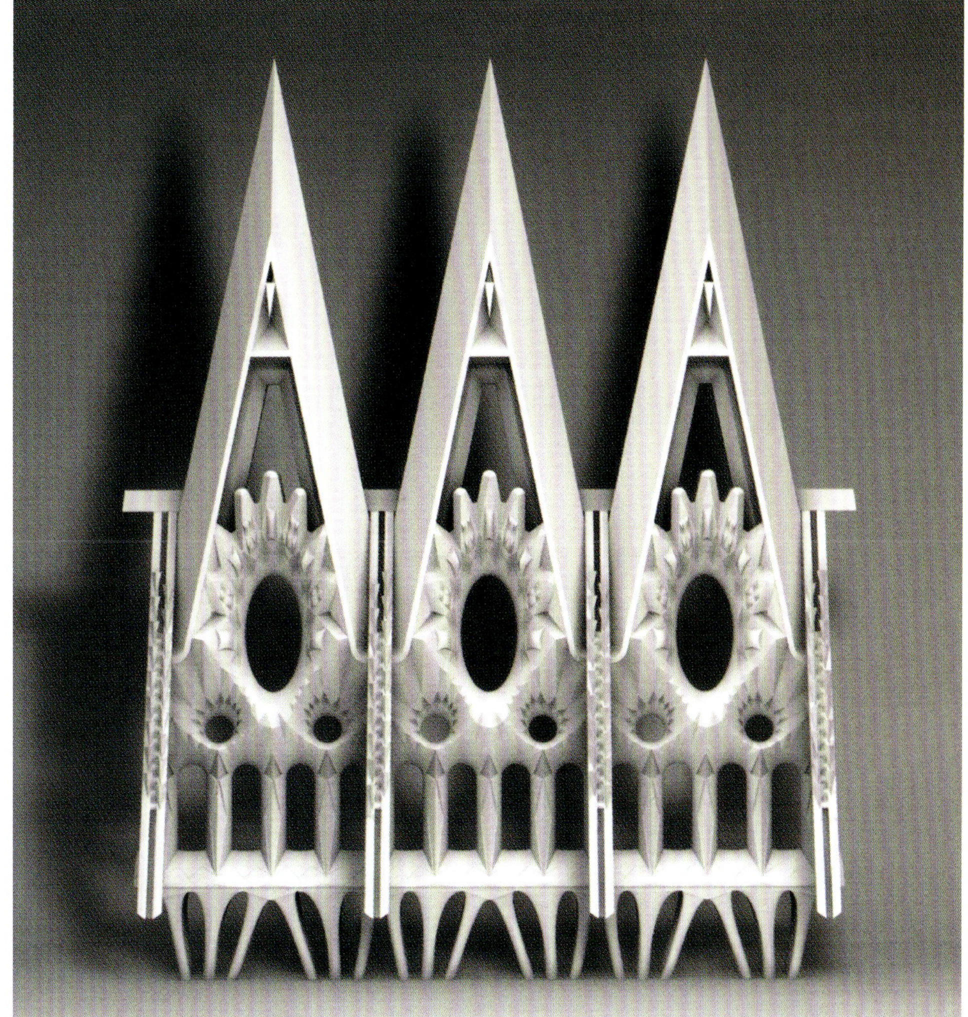

4.3c

The Rose Window on the west transept façade of Gaudí's Sagrada Familia is an 8-meter-wide-by-35-meter-high assembly of 15 openings, culminating in a huge, single elliptical opening that sits between the two towers of the west transept and throws west light into the central crossing. As there was no surviving restored plaster model from Gaudí's time for this element; the starting point for detailed design was provided by 1:25 scale plaster studies of this window carried out during the 1970s by Isidre Puig Boada and Lluis Bonet Gari, two of Gaudí's followers. The proportional system of the East Rose Window in the Nativity Façade, built during Gaudí's lifetime, and the lineage of 1:10 scale models for the lower and upper side aisle windows also informed the interpretation. Using a pointer on a 3D arm that locates points in Cartesian space, the Puig Boada and Bonet Gari model was digitized and converted into a corresponding virtual coordinate system in a 3D modeling program. This digital facsimile of the plaster model was used as the base for creating a precisely controlled flexible model using associative geometry and parametric design. This computer- modeling process involved the Boolean subtraction of a series of solids, primarily hyperboloids of revolution, from the notional solid of the wall. Each subtracted or sculpted form is digitally described by a geometrical definition with editable parameters, and with sequential geometrical relationships between each element, also governed by parameters. Such software results in a model that can subsequently be altered, subtly modifying the position or size of an opening or the proportional system governing the relationship of the openings. Making a single change to the geometry of one opening will impact on all the neighboring openings, and this way of modeling permits the whole 3D model to update without any need for erasure or remodeling. For the Rose Window there are 3,800 events in the parametric modeling history and thus any individual change involves the checking of all such events before the geometry of the model can be regenerated. The model was developed over six weeks and the design and construction, which involved traditional stone masonry and semi-automated construction methods, was completed in just over twelve months.

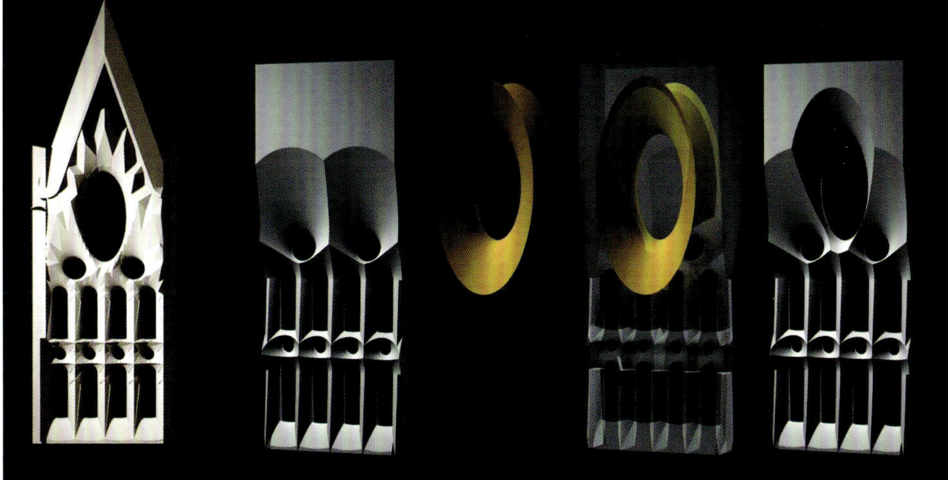

4.3d

4.3e

4.3f

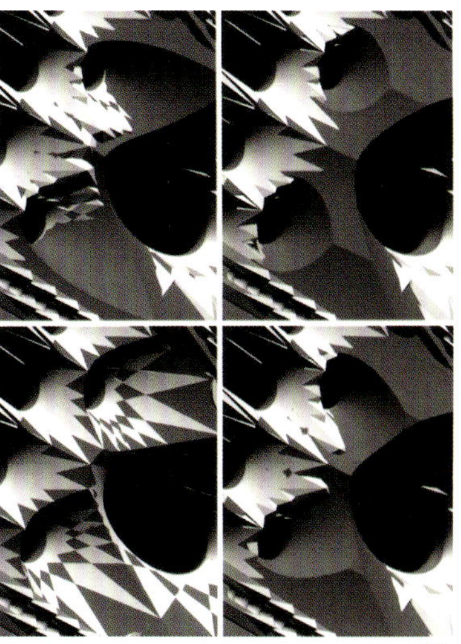

4.3g

Beijing National Aquatics Center / The Water Cube

PTW Architects / Arup

Built 2003-2008
Beijing, China

4.4a

4.4b

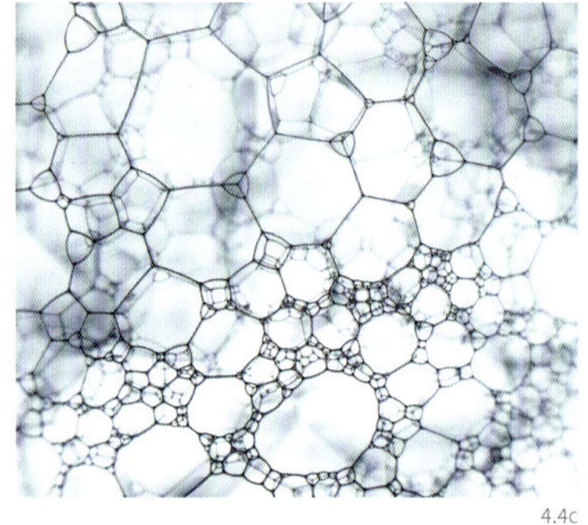
4.4c

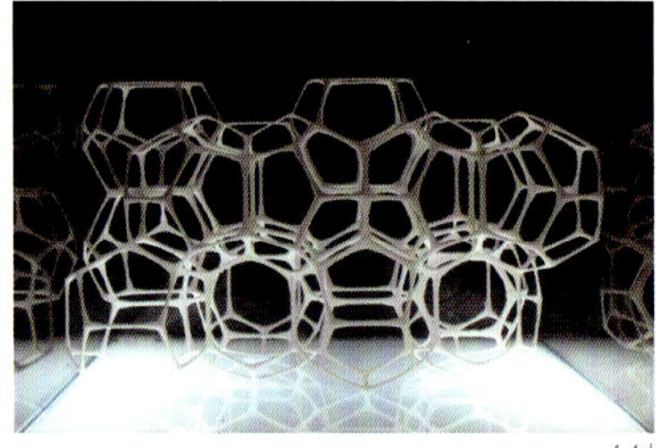
4.4d

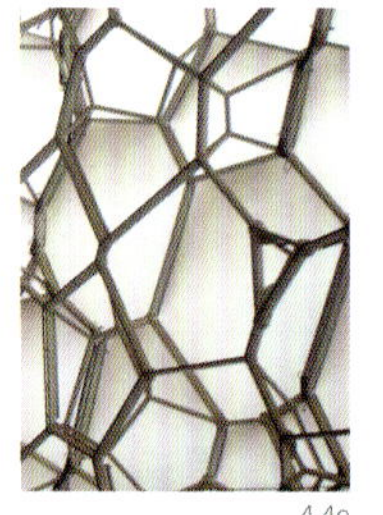
4.4e

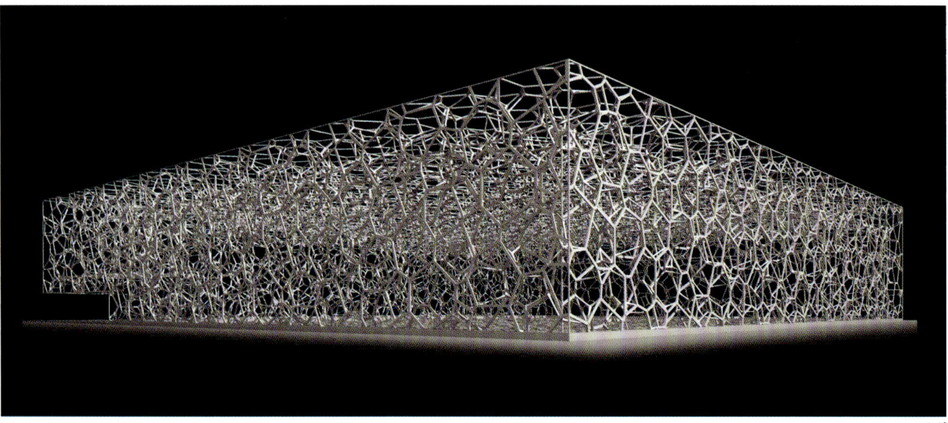
4.4f

The Beijing National Aquatics Center, commonly known as the Water Cube, was conceptualized as a cubic container filled with a cellular structure of bubbles representing foaming water. As a metaphoric overlay of the square (an important symbol in Chinese culture) with the aquatic program it was intended to house, the 70,000 m² project was built as a venue to support swimming, diving, and water polo competitions held during the 2008 Olympics. The Water Cube's thickened architectural envelope, which also functions as the structure for the building, is derived from the natural three-dimensional pattern of soap film that forms as an interface between gas bubbles suspended in a foaming liquid. This cellular pattern is considered to be the most efficient structural subdivision of space common to cellular phenomena found in nature and was the basis of Joseph Plateau's and Lord Kelvin's historic models studying aggregate soap bubble geometries. In the early 1990s, the computer simulations of Denis Weaire and Robert Phelan provided an improved solution to these earlier investigations, advancing a polyhedral geometry comprised of two cell types of equal volume—six tetradodecahedrons and two dodecahedrons—packed in a regularly repeating pattern, a variation of which was used to generate the cellular structural lattice for the Water Cube. This spatial topology is used to uniformly fill the volume, which is then carved away to provide the requisite space for the interior program. To achieve the perceived complexity, heterogeneity and irregularity of an aggregate of natural bubbles, the adjusted Weaire-Phelan polyhedral geometry was rotated in relation to the Cartesian orientation of the cube so that the skewed section of the structure, as it is revealed through the continuous series of planar surfaces forming the walls and roof, would operate to conceal the regularity of the cellular geometry. An iterative structural optimization script was then used to size all of the steel members and connections comprising the cellular lattice, which is made up of steel tubes welded to spherical nodes. The building structure is clad in an envelope of 4,000 inflated ETFE pillows—a secondary skin of bubble wrap, which, as a complement to the structure, is transparent, lightweight, and composed primarily of air. This combination of structure and cladding eliminates the need for a secondary structural system to support the envelope while operating as an insulated greenhouse that diffuses natural light throughout the space.

4.4g

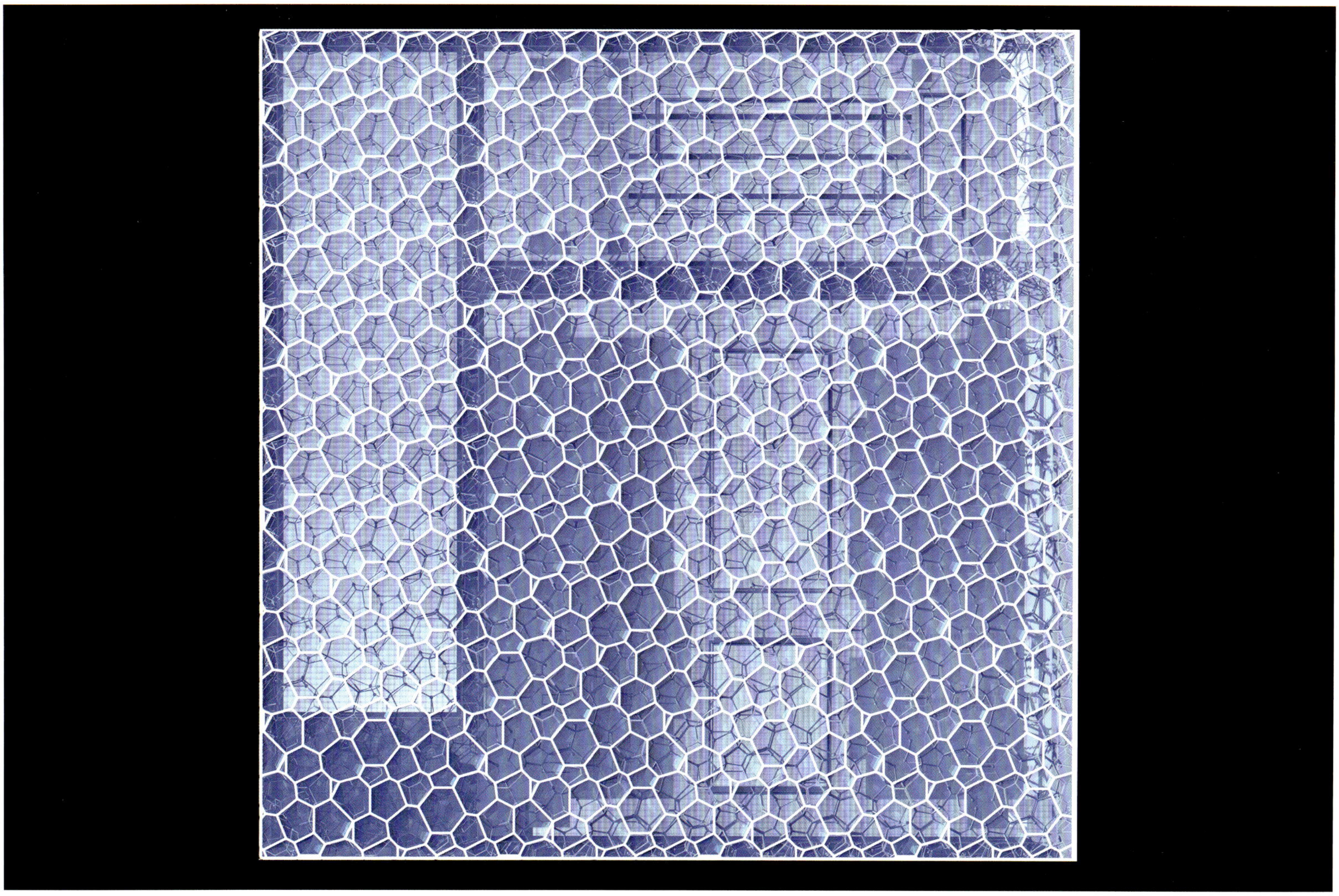

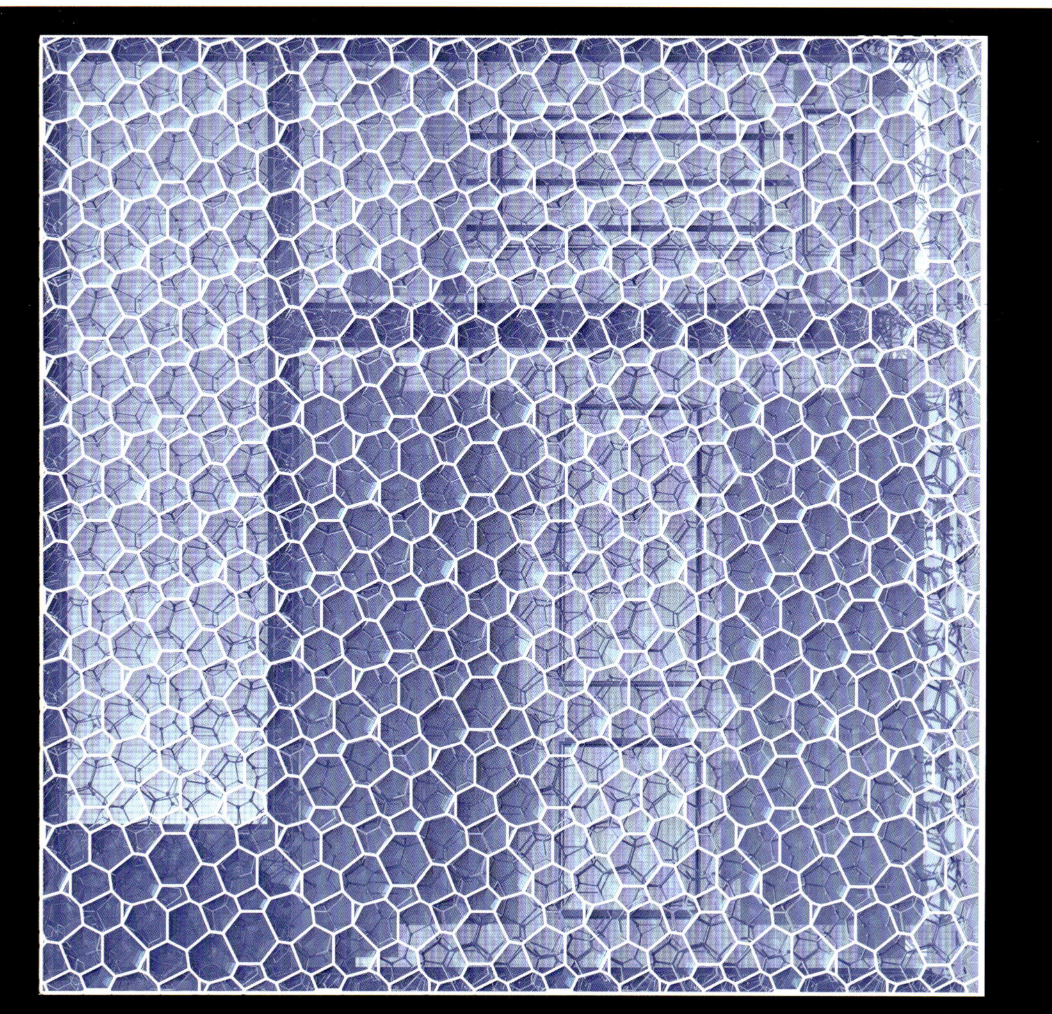

4.4h

1774 / Fauteuil Chair

Aranda/Lasch

Built 2007

New York, United States

4.5a

4.5b

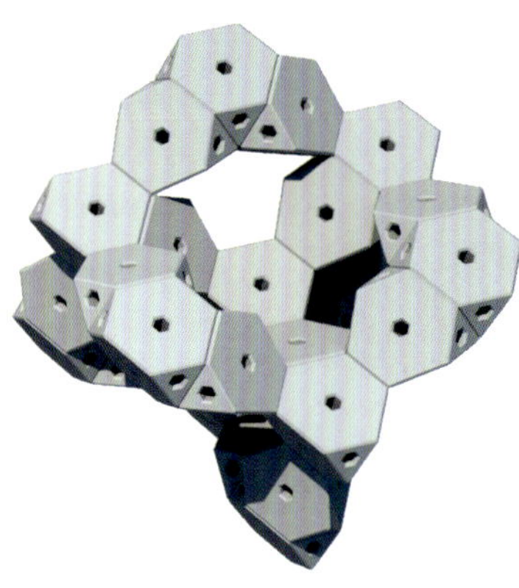

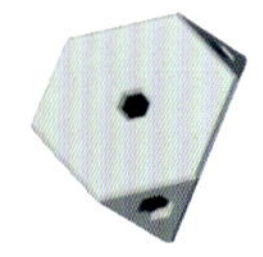

4.5c

In the year 1774, Louis XV died, the sunset of one of history's most lavish monarchies. In the same year, a young Swede named Johann Gahn, working in the deepest and wettest levels of a mine, fired a crucible lined with a mixture of charcoal, oil, and ore and discovered the metal manganese, a trace element critical for life processes in plants and animals. At a molecular level, when combined with oxides, the metal displays a striking "supercrystal" modularity. In the Fauteuil Chair, assembled from cellular polyhedral aluminum components, this nexus of events—the super-excess of Louis XV and the supercrystal of manganese—are fused into a single moment of design, where the geometric pattern of the lattice, a model defining the manganese oxide supercrystal, forms the substrate out of which the armchair and a broader series of Louis XV furniture can be found.

Louis XV, carved and gilt "Fauteuil."
Upholstered with Beauvais tapestry. Subject from La Fontaine's Fables.

4.5d

4.5e

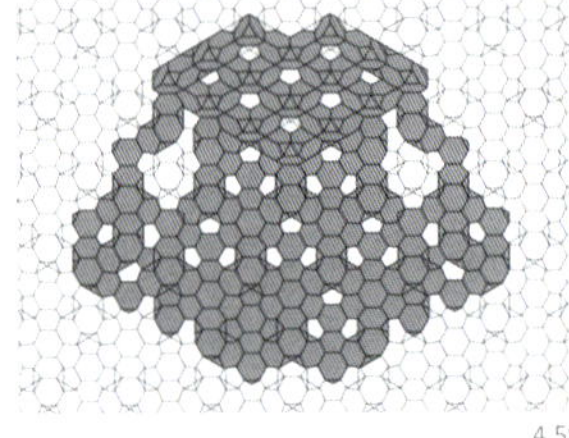

4.5f

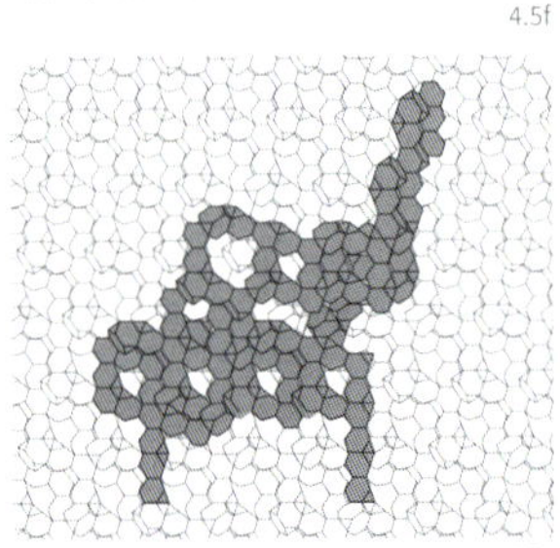

4.5g

4.5h

Quasitable
Aranda/Lasch

Built 2007
New York, United States

The Quasi-series is about the pursuit of orders that are rigorously modular but wild—almost out of order. Quasicrystals, a phase of solid-state matter discovered in 1982 by the material scientist Dan Schectman, represent this kind of material structure that hovers on the edge of falling apart. Like a regular crystal, it consists of densely packed molecules, but unlike a regular crystal, whose molecular pattern is periodic (or repetitive in all directions), the distinctive quality of a quasicrystal is that its structural pattern never repeats the same way twice. It is endless and uneven but can be described by the arrangement of a small set of modular parts. The key to quasicrystals' aperiodic structure is that it is organized by "forbidden" symmetries (such as five, eight or twelve-fold symmetries) that, until relatively recently, were not thought to be able to tile space without leaving gaps. In 1974, however, Roger Penrose was able to successfully tile the plane aperiodically with a pair of two specially shaped tiles. In 1980 Nicolaas de Bruijn then created an algorithm that turned Penrose's intuitive tiling into a method to describe a quasicrystalline order, which became the point of departure for the Quasi-series. The Quasitable, constructed from hundreds of individual walnut blocks, explores this aperiodic assembly in wood. Though the pieces come together in infinite combinations, there are only two kinds of rhomboid blocks. Although we understand the physical world to be constituted by a complex form of molecular matter, in the mundane world of objects such as furniture, the perception of such complexity remains invisible. In the Quasitable, this complexity operates as an experimental point of departure, such that the global form of the table that we recognize as a common element in our lives, is confronted with the burgeoning structural cellular matter out of which it is made.

4.6a

4.6b

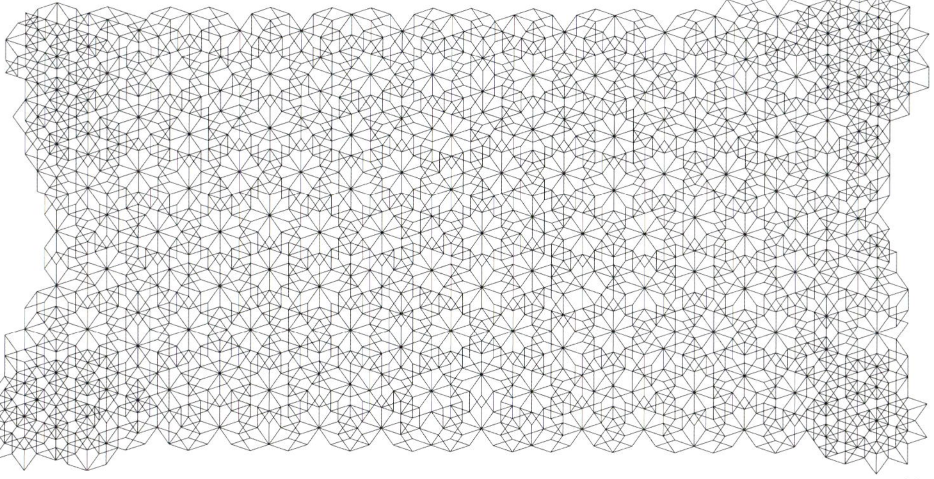

4.6c

4.6d

PS1 Grotto

Aranda/Lasch

Unbuilt 2004

New York, United States

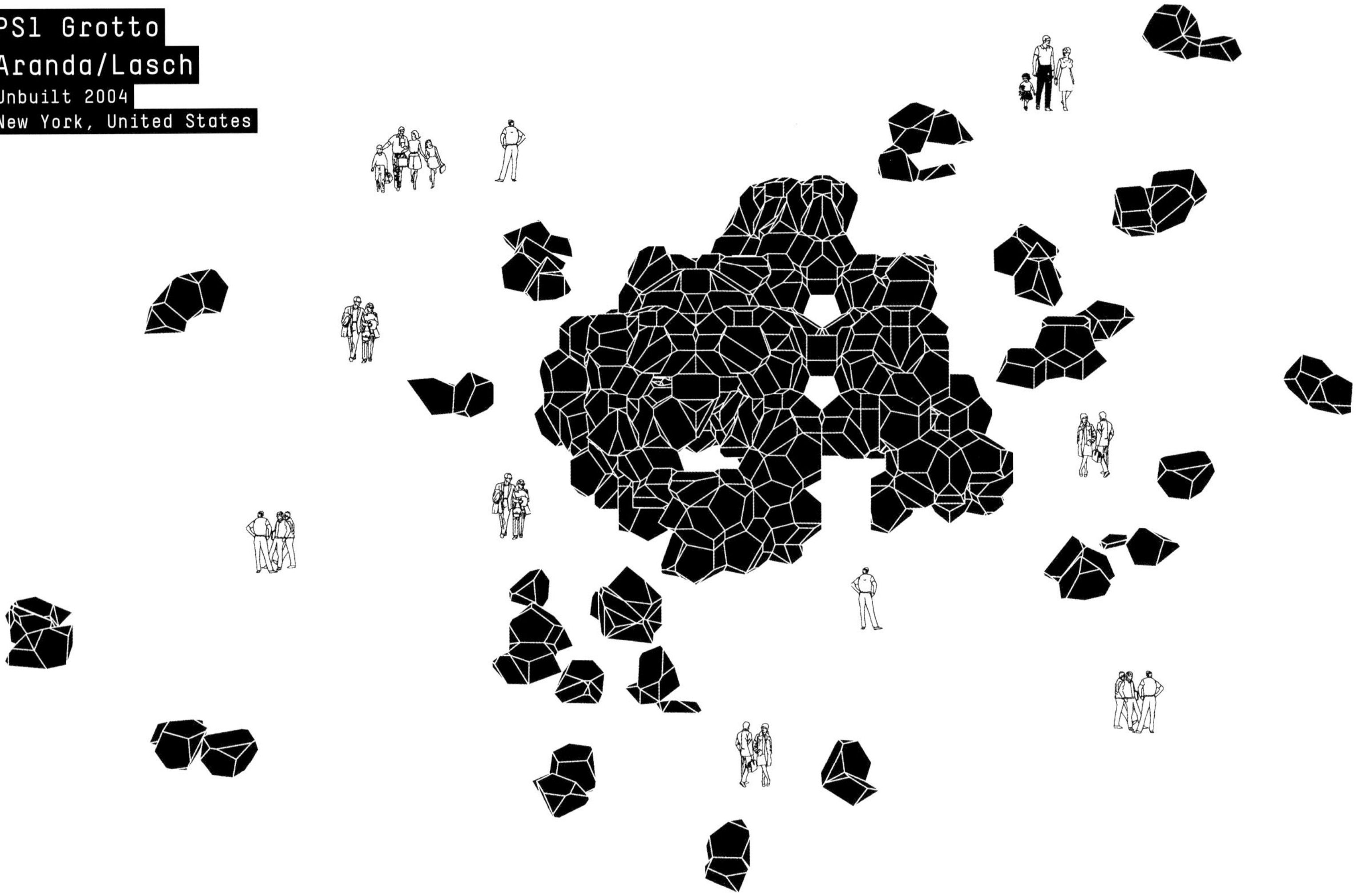

4.7a

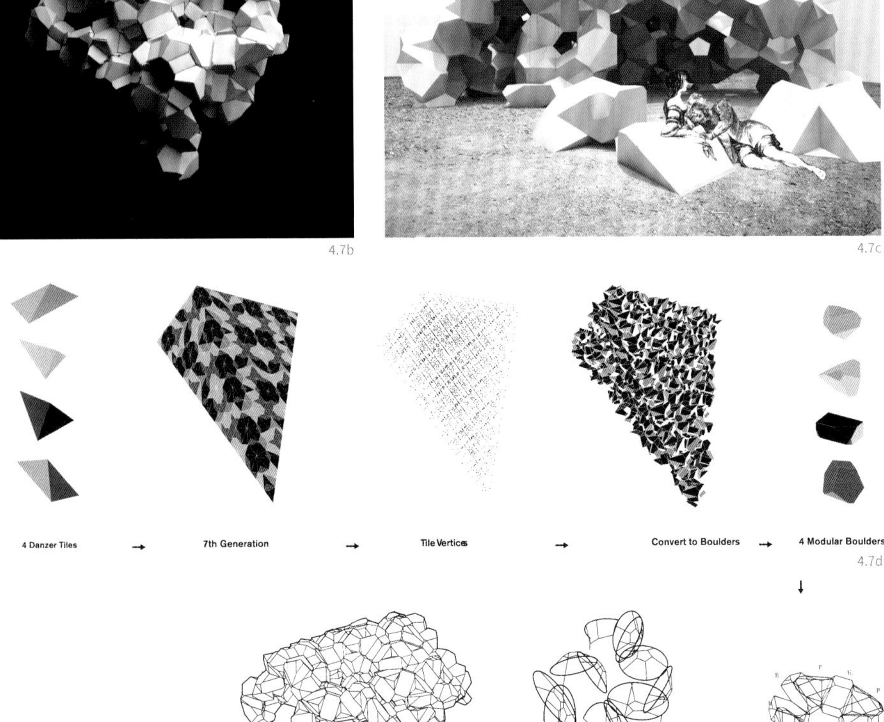

4.7b

4.7c

4.7d

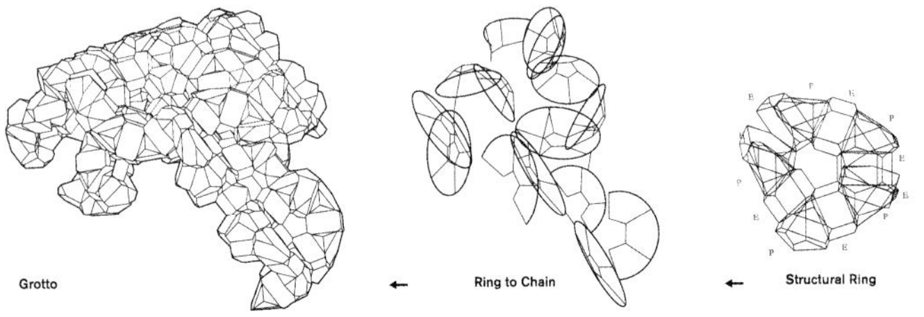

4.7e

The Grotto is an artificial structure or excavation in a garden made to resemble a cave. Since the structural unit of a grotto is the boulder, the challenge of the project was to develop a set of modular boulders that combine in a way that defies a conventional sense of order. The solution uses a combination of algorithms, based on cellular Voronoi geometries, that transfer modularity from a Danzer tiling technique (developed at Arup AGU) to a final set of four faceted tetrahedral boulders. These four expanded-polystyrene boulders fit together in a variety of ways using an underlying aperiodic logic. The result is a wildly ordered three-dimensional pattern that never repeats the same way twice. The Danzer tiling was carried out to the seventh generation to produce a tetrahedral packing of 11,382 triangles. Although triangles make great patterns, a triangle is not a boulder. In order to create the boulders—the structural unit of the grotto—it was necessary to strip the tetrahedral packing down to its vertices. This revealed a field of 3,066 points from which a boulder tiling could be derived. The result resembled a boulder mess that, on closer inspection, was actually highly structured and composed of only four types—the harmonies and modularity of the Danzer tiling translated. Each of these four types—referred to as Balls, Erasers, Plugs, and Monsters—behaves in its own way. Plug and Eraser boulders form a very stable ring configuration and became the basic structural unit of the project. These rings connect together to form arches and vaults. Since most of the spaces in the project would be made from purely compressive structures, a majority of the EPS foam boulders could simply be glued together. Only a few of the larger vaults, where rings are daisy-chained together, require any steel reinforcement. Finally, by excavating space out of this nonrepetitive three-dimensional pattern, a grotto space is formed and activated with program.

PS1 Loop
Howeler+Yoon Architects
Built 2006
New York, United States

4.8a

LOOP aspires to be a completely immersive social environment facilitated by computational design, digital fabrication, and interactive technologies. Through an atmospheric thickening of the ground plane, it provides a dense landscape and scaffold for activities and stimulates the unpredictable unfolding of social exchange. Rather than a discreet architectural object positioned as a feature within the courtyard, LOOP presents a "loose fill" of architectural form, simultaneously allowing for complete porosity and total coverage. The geometry is generated through an analysis of cellular aggregates, suggesting an uninterrupted lattice of form which outlines connections between spaces. There is no enclosure and no exposure, but a suggestion of continuous spatial division. In packing the single, continuous space of the courtyard with a network of smaller spaces, LOOP both encourages and defines the formation of discreet activity groupings to occur spontaneously during the Summer Warm-Up event at the PS1 Courtyard. The closely packed geometries housing closely packed activities form an infrastructure for recreation. Part landscape, part infrastructure, this pliable latticework is an interactive jungle gym featuring a number of programmed activity clusters including wading pools, waterfalls, bubble jets, and a collective trampoline. Its lower surfaces are sculpted for lounging while the upper canopy provides shade. Greater porosity at the center provides easy passage through highly trafficked areas, while greater material density promotes loitering around the periphery. The geometry of the fill was generated through a three-dimensional Voronoi cell-packing algorithm used to develop the loops. These were then digitally modeled, unfolded, and divided into segments so that they could be nested onto, and CNC milled from, half-inch-thick, 5-by-10-foot polypropylene sheets. Each segment was then heat-formed around a wooden mold and joined at the ends with a plastic welder to produce continuous loops to be mechanically fastened together onsite. The geometry of the project is controlled through computational tools that anticipate an optimized "output" using CAD CAM technologies. Its form, however, is also the result of a highly manual process that takes material properties—ductility, elasticity, and bending—and exploits them through computational techniques.

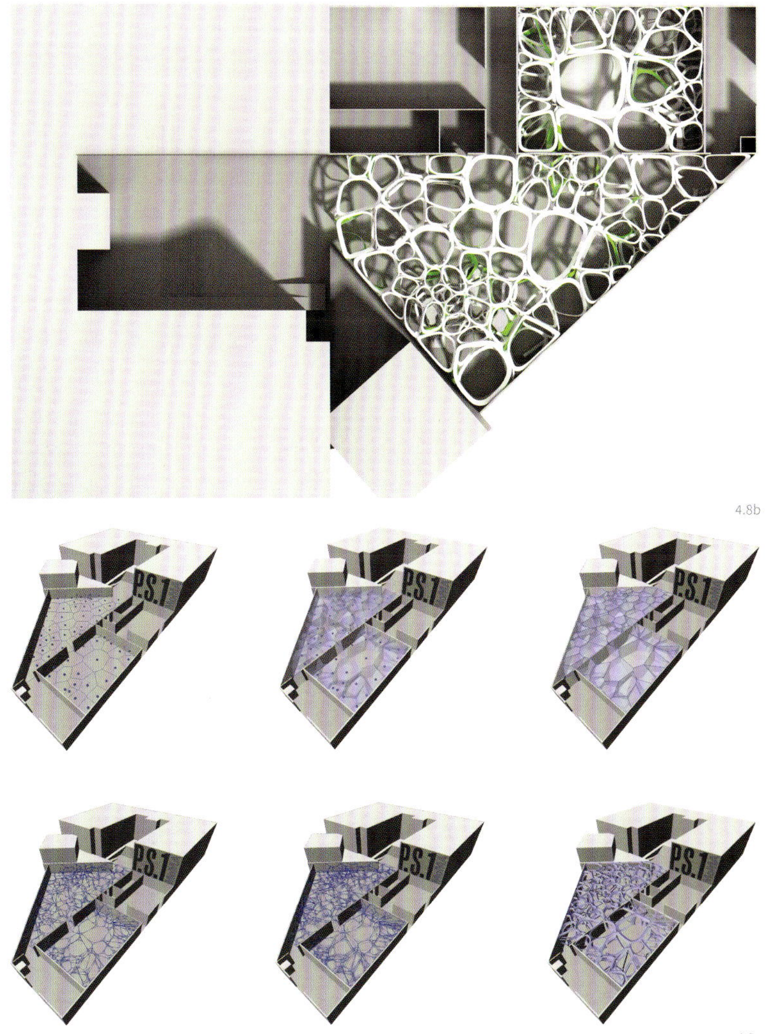

4.8b

4.8c

Voromuro

Office dA / NADAAA

Built 2007

Boston, United States

4.9a

The Voronoi diagram is adopted in this installation for the *Vita Brevis* exhibition due to its ability to establish a key reciprocity between its parametric and structural qualities. Located within the dark void of the Powder Magazine on Georges Island, the acrylic installation is conceived as a structural skin that appears to the eye only after its retina adjusts to the darkness. The form of Voromuro is generated from a preoccupation with structural shapes. Composed of two distinct structural systems—surface active and form active—the geometry of the installation unfolds seamlessly from an undulating wall to a vaulted dome, escaping traditional forms of typological classification. If conventional fabrication is based on material units—bricks or tiles—then the Voronoi offers a way to organize a cellular arrangement according to variable units that are the result of the dimensional and geographic particularities of the installation, specifically, the cellular organization that operates like structural coffering, yet finds a way to adapt to the varied tectonic requirements of ground, wall, arch, and dome. The cells are mass customized, ranging from cylindrical to cubic and polyhedral conditions in a continuous variable series, helping the form to arrive at structural stasis.

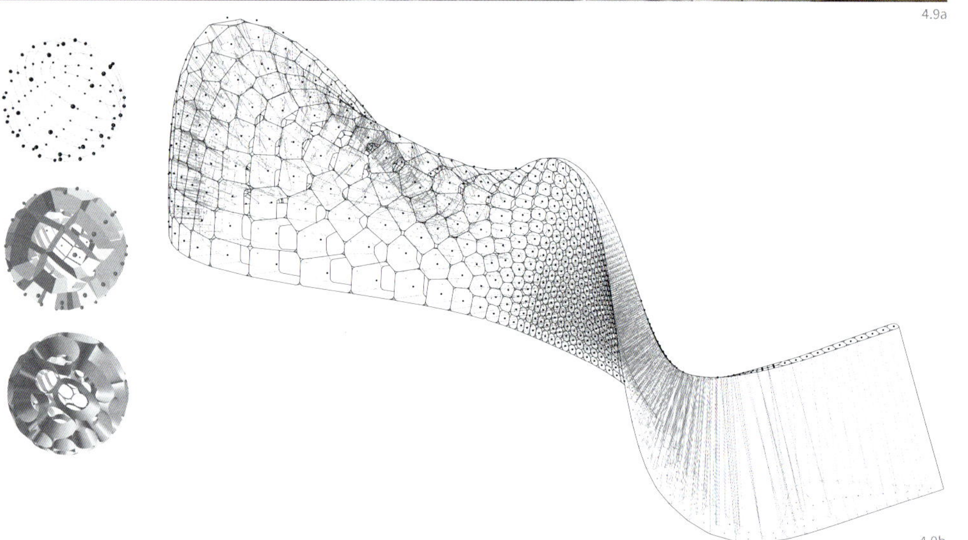

4.9b

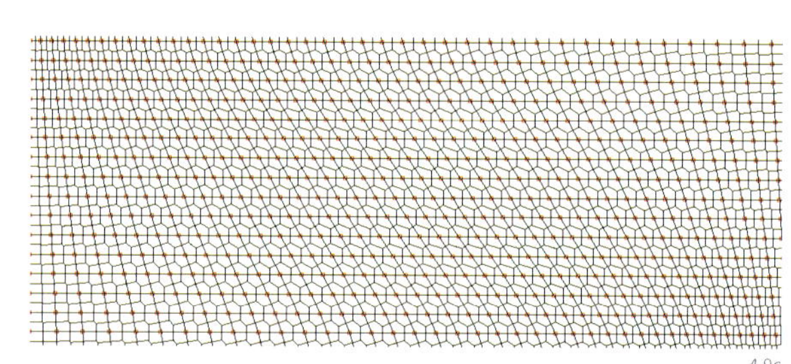

4.9c

4.9d

Nature Boardwalk Pavilion

Studio Gang

Built 2010

Chicago, United States

4.10a

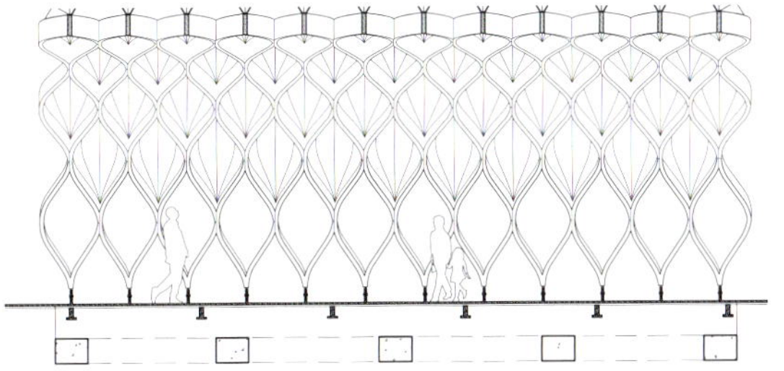

4.10b

4.10c

The South Pond pavilion at the Lincoln Park Zoo is part of the regeneration of a picturesque landscape into a thriving ecological habitat. The pavilion is situated along a new boardwalk that circles around the pond while circumnavigating the park as it passes through different educational zones used to explain the surrounding wildlife and its ecological environment. The pavilion provides shelter along this path while functioning as a multipurpose activity space and open-air classroom. Inspired by the geometric patterning of a tortoise shell, the cellular assembly of the pavilion is comprised of a prefabricated, glue-laminated, bent-wood, undulating frame made from repeating elements, each set of which surround a fiberglass dome. The cellular aggregation of these elements generates a continuous woven lattice formed into a barrel vault and adorned with fiberglass pods that form a bulbous field. Exploiting the pliability of wood, each member of the wooden lattice is curved in two directions simultaneously and connected laterally so that the joints between members are organized in a sequenced, alternating pattern to ensure continuity despite the discrete componentry of the system. The milling, bending, and lamination process of the making of each curved wooden rib, a technique used in boat building and furniture making, in addition to the doubly curved geometry of each element and its interconnection within a larger cellular lattice, increases the strength of the structure while minimizing its weight. This enabled the structure to be light enough to be assembled by hand eliminating the need for heavy machinery. The pavilion is open at the sides to enable a view to the surrounding environment, yet covered to provide shelter, the translucency of its cellular fiberglass pods allowing light to filter in while creating its own highly articulated floating terrain.

4.10d

4.10e

Voussoir Cloud
IwamotoScott
Built 2008
Los Angeles, United States

4.11a

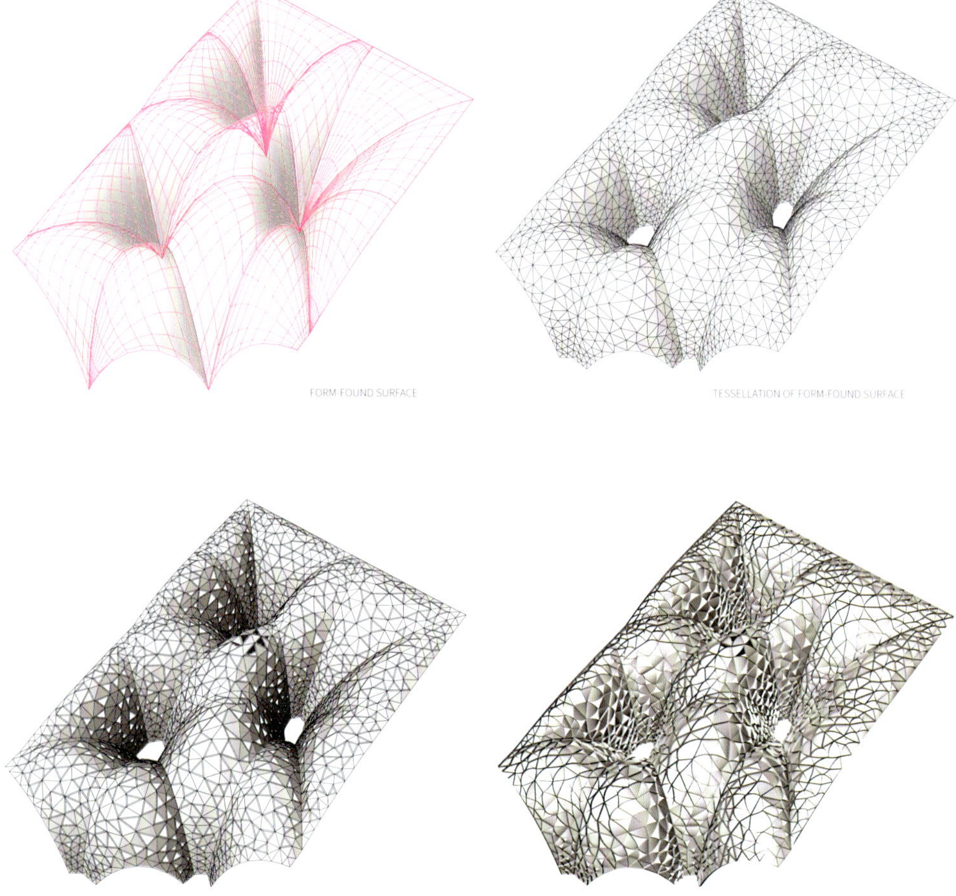

4.11b

Voussoir Cloud explores the structural paradigm of pure compression coupled with an ultra-light material system that is packed to produce a porous, tessellated surface. The design fills the gallery with a system of vaults, to be experienced both from within and above, creating a luminous and sensorial atmosphere within the space. These vaults are supported by five columns and delimited by the walls of the gallery and a soffit that together structurally maintain the compressive form of the work. In the development of the project, computational hanging chain models were employed to refine and adjust the profile lines of the vaults to become pure catenaries, and form-finding programs were used to determine the purely compressive vault shapes. Each vault, however, is also comprised of a Delaunay tessellation that both capitalizes on and confounds these structural logics. Greater cell density of smaller, flatter, more connective modules, or petals, gang together at the column bases and at the vault edges to form strengthened ribs, while the upper vault shell loosens and gains curvature and porosity. At the same time, the petals, or reconstituted voussoirs—those elements that are typically defined as the wedge-shaped masonry blocks that make up an arch—are reconsidered here using paper thin material, an attempt to defamiliarize both the structural and material logics of normative architectural typologies. The three-dimensional petals are formed by folding thin wood laminate along curved seams. The curve produces an inflected form that relies on the internal surface tension of the wood and folded geometry of the flanges to hold its shape. The flanges, which want to bulge out along their curved edges, are then packed together as compressive elements which, as a natural attribute of vaulted forms, is what gives the cellular structure its overall stability. There are four triangular cell types with zero, one, two, or three curved edges. Each cell behaves in a slightly different manner based on its size, edge conditions, and position relative to its neighboring cells (open or closed, straight or curved) and the overall form. Because the flange angles are dictated by the normal of the vaults rather than the cell itself, the curvature of each petal has a unique geometry that needed to be calibrated using a computational script to ensure its fit into the overall form.

4.11c

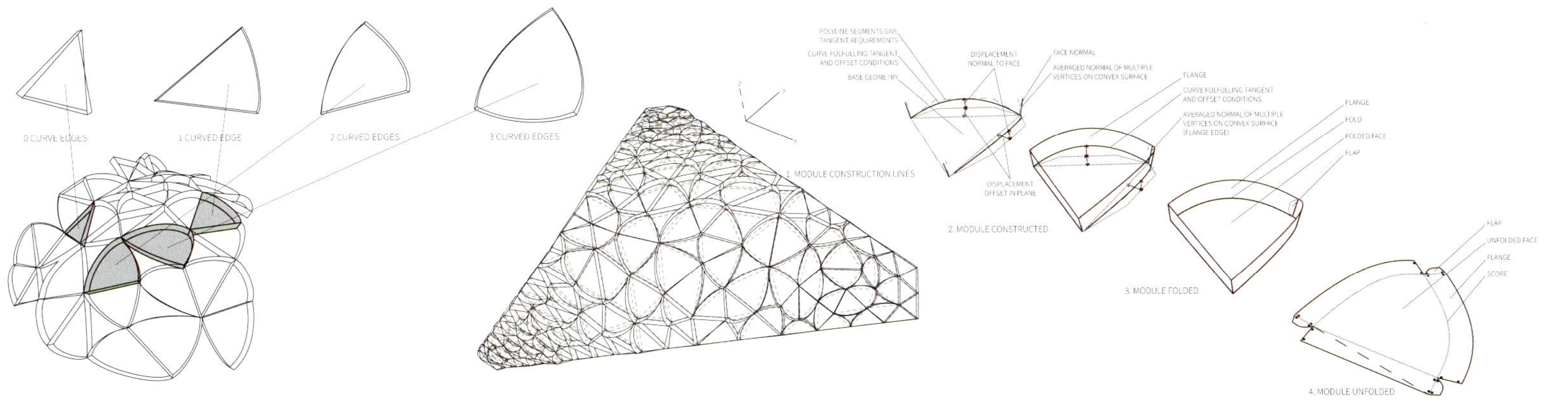

4.11d

4.11e

4.11f

Chrysalis |||

Matsys

Built 2011-2012
Paris, France

4.12a

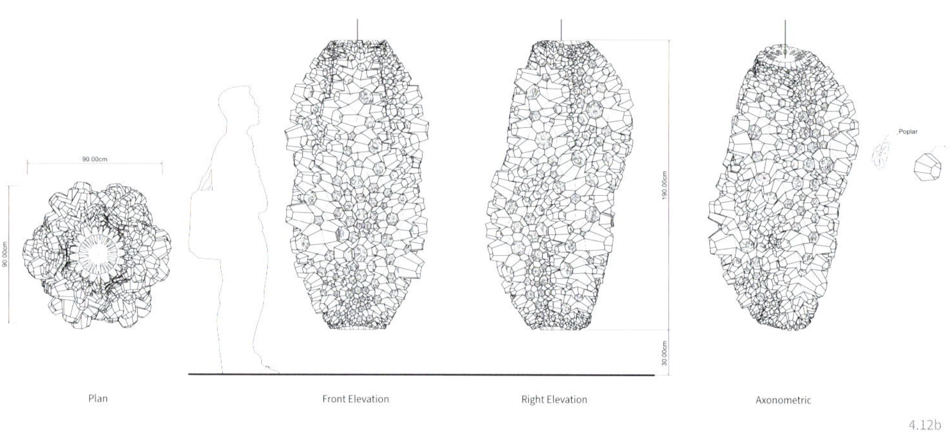

4.12b

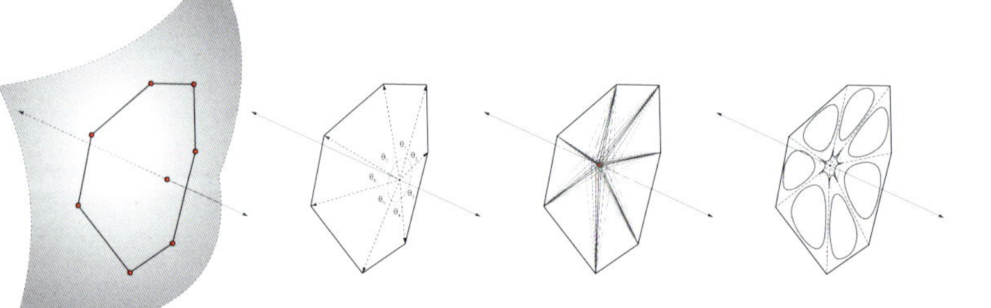
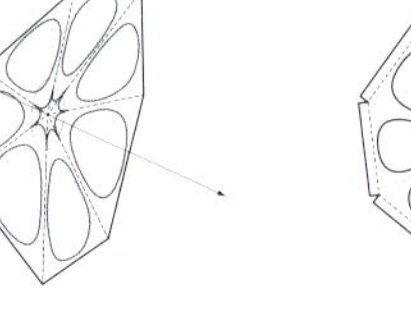

4.12c

Part of a series of projects exploring cellular morphologies using parametric tools and composite materials, Chrysalis (III) investigates the self-organization of barnacle-like cells across an underlying substrate surface, investigating the packing of a cellular morphology of irregular polygons as these are projected onto a vertically oriented volume whose surface is considered to be topologically continuous, yet flexible. The boundaries of the two-dimensional polygons filling this surface are spatially extruded to create individuated conical projections that render a thickness to the cellular cluster. These extruded cells are each filled with an inner plate that has been divided into a series of triangular segments and aerated by holes excavated from the center of each segment to allow light to move through the structure. Each cell is therefore composed of two parts: a cone-like outer surface made from cherry veneer and a nonplaner inner plate made from poplar veneer that stresses the outer cone into shape. As with a Voronoi cellular pattern, the centroid of each of these cells is initially determined by the position, orientation, and length of the cell edges and the vector running through this centroid that is normal to the curved surface. Vectors that connect this centroid to its edge vertices divide up the inner plate, whose segments are determined by iteratively moving the centroid along the normal vector until the total sum of all of the interior angles equals 360 degrees to ensure that the segments of the cell can be flattened into a plane. Each of the 1,000 cell components, both the polyhedral cones projecting from the structure and the inner plates, can therefore be unfolded flat in the digital model, to be digitally fabricated and then assembled by hand. The edge connectivity of the work's cellular structure, which uses a relaxed spring network constrained to the surface, ensures a system that is topologically continuous yet flexible in its geometry. This enables movement to occur within and across the cluster as the surface continuously reorganizes. The cells therefore shift and slide across the surface, amplifying their movements through the conical projections that radiate from the work, as they attempt to find a more balanced packed state in their continual search for greater equilibrium.

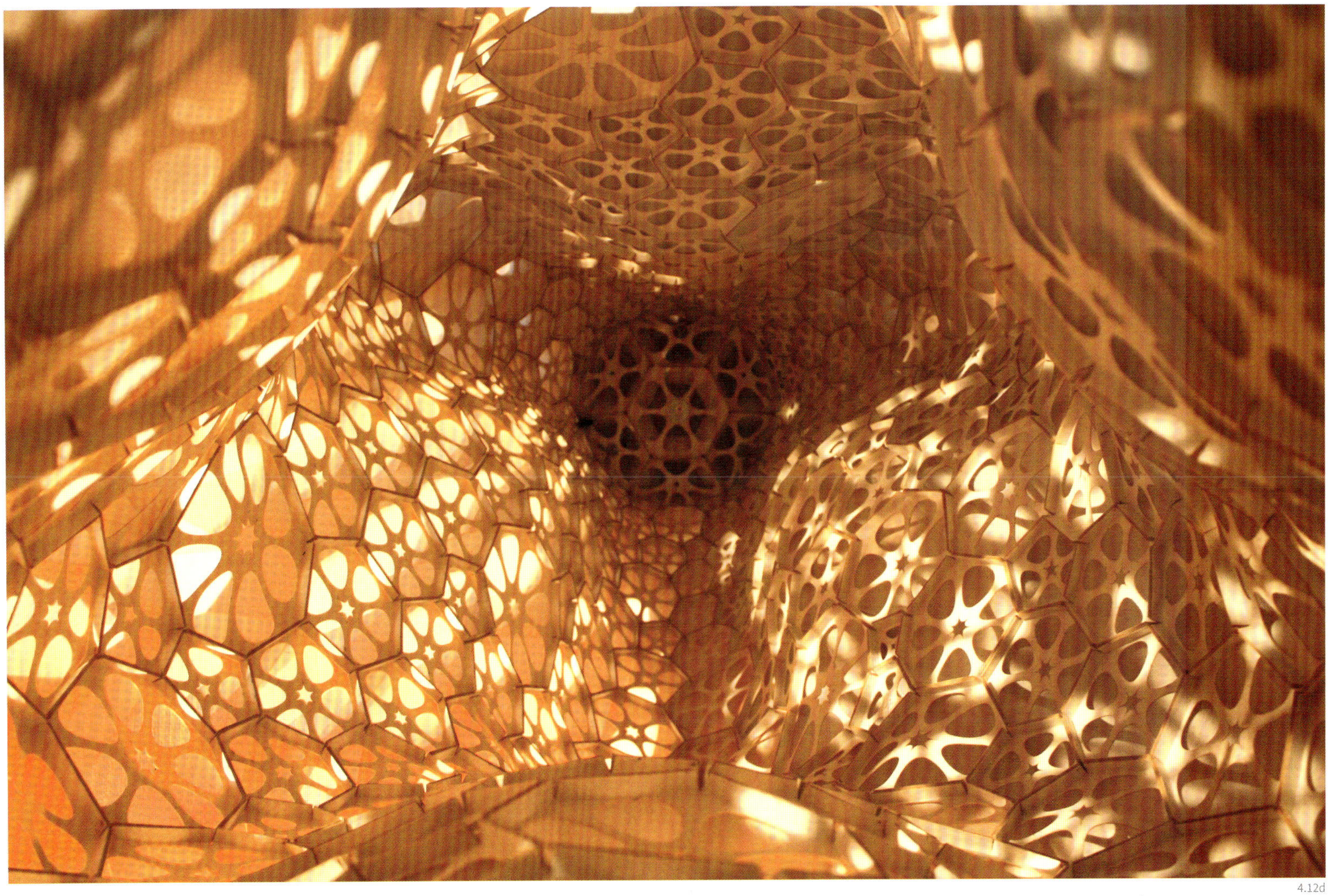

4.12d

4.12e

4.12f

Strand Screen
Matsys
Built 2016
Miami, United States

4.13a

4.13b

Inspired by the organic curves of art nouveau and the complex processes of wine making, the Strand Screen, like the Strand Table, is part of a series of works designed and fabricated for Maison Perrier-Jouët installed and exhibited at Design Miami. The three screens of eight-foot-tall, curved strands, evoking tree trunks or vines, mark out a central area and define the boundaries of a clearing such as one would find in a forest for respite and retreat. The piece, like those that are part of the Strand Garden collection, was inspired by the acculturated forms, materials, and landscapes intrinsic to the champagne-making process, from the twisting vines of the grapes to the strips of wood that form the oak barrels and wine presses.

Each of the three screens is generated from a cellular cluster of five-, six-, and seven-sided polygons, thirty in the largest cluster, that are extruded into twisting, curvilinear, tubular strands that expand into bulbous tubers near the top and contract as they taper toward the ground. The tubular strands, as they transform while moving through space, reference the environment and life of the vineyards themselves and the energetic and vital forms of the natural vegetal world whose plants, trees, and branches twist and turn as they grow toward the sun. These strands are clad in thin layers of CNC straight cut, 0.035-inch-thick, red oak wood veneers that are woven together at their edges with interlocking tabs integrated into their form. Appearing like solid yet limber tree trunks from a distance but becoming translucent up close, these tubular strands are illuminated from within, radiating a glowing warm light that gently emanates through the thin veneers revealing their natural grain overlaid with the intricacy of their connective micro-architecture.

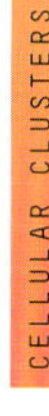

4.13c

4.13d

4.13e

2011 ICD/ITKE Pavilion
ICD/ITKE University of Stuttgart

Built 2012
Stuttgart, Germany

4.14a

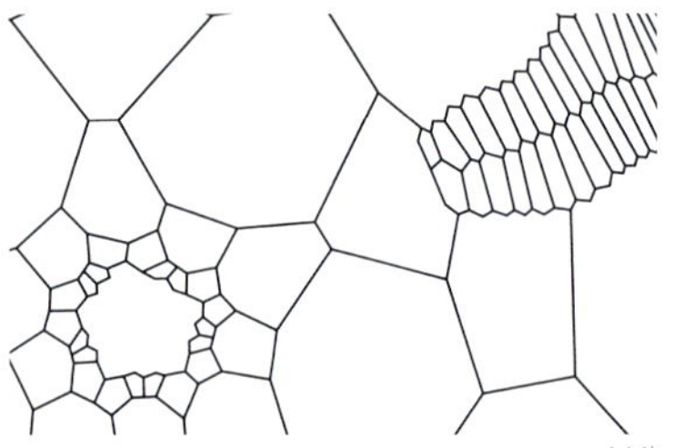

4.14b

The 2011 ICD/ITKE Pavilion project explores the architectural transfer of biological principles of the sea urchin's plate skeleton morphology by means of novel computer-based design and simulation methods, along with computer-controlled manufacturing methods for its building implementation. The project focused on the development of a modular system that allows for a high degree of adaptability and performance due to the geometric differentiation of its plate components and robotically fabricated finger joints. The plate skeleton morphology of the sand dollar, a sub-species of the sea urchin, provided the basic principles of the pavilion structure. The skeletal shell of the sand dollar is a cellular modular system of polygonal plates, which are linked together at the edges by finger-like calcite protrusions. High load-bearing capacity is achieved by the particular geometric arrangement of the plates and their joining system. This morphology, a fitting model for shells made of prefabricated elements, was therefore integrated into the design of the pavilion. Here, three plate edges always meet together at just one point, a principle that enables the transmission of normal and shear forces but no bending moments between the joints, thus resulting in a bending bearing but yet deformable structure. Unlike traditional lightweight construction, which can only be applied to load-optimized shapes, this new design principle, however, is applicable to a wide range of custom geometries. This enables the cell sizes to be heterogeneous as they differentially adapt to local curvature and discontinuities, and for the pavilion to be built out of extremely thin (6.5 mm) sheets of plywood, despite its considerable size. In addition, the traditional finger-joints typically used in carpentry as connection elements were developed as the technical equivalent of the sand dollar's calcite protrusions. The plates and finger joints of each cell were produced using a robotic fabrication system that employed custom-programmed routines to enable the economical production of more than 850 geometrically different components, as well as more than 100,000 finger joints freely arranged in space. Following the robotic production, the plywood panels were glue-joined together to form cells and then the prefabricated modules were assembled and mechanically fastened together to construct the pavilion.

4.14c

4.14d

4.14e

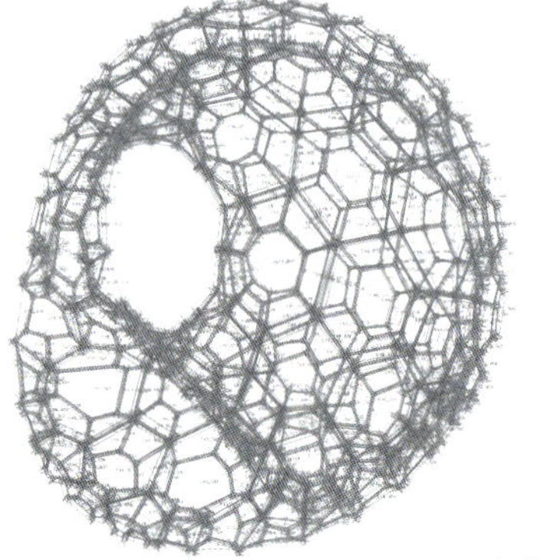

4.14f

4.14g

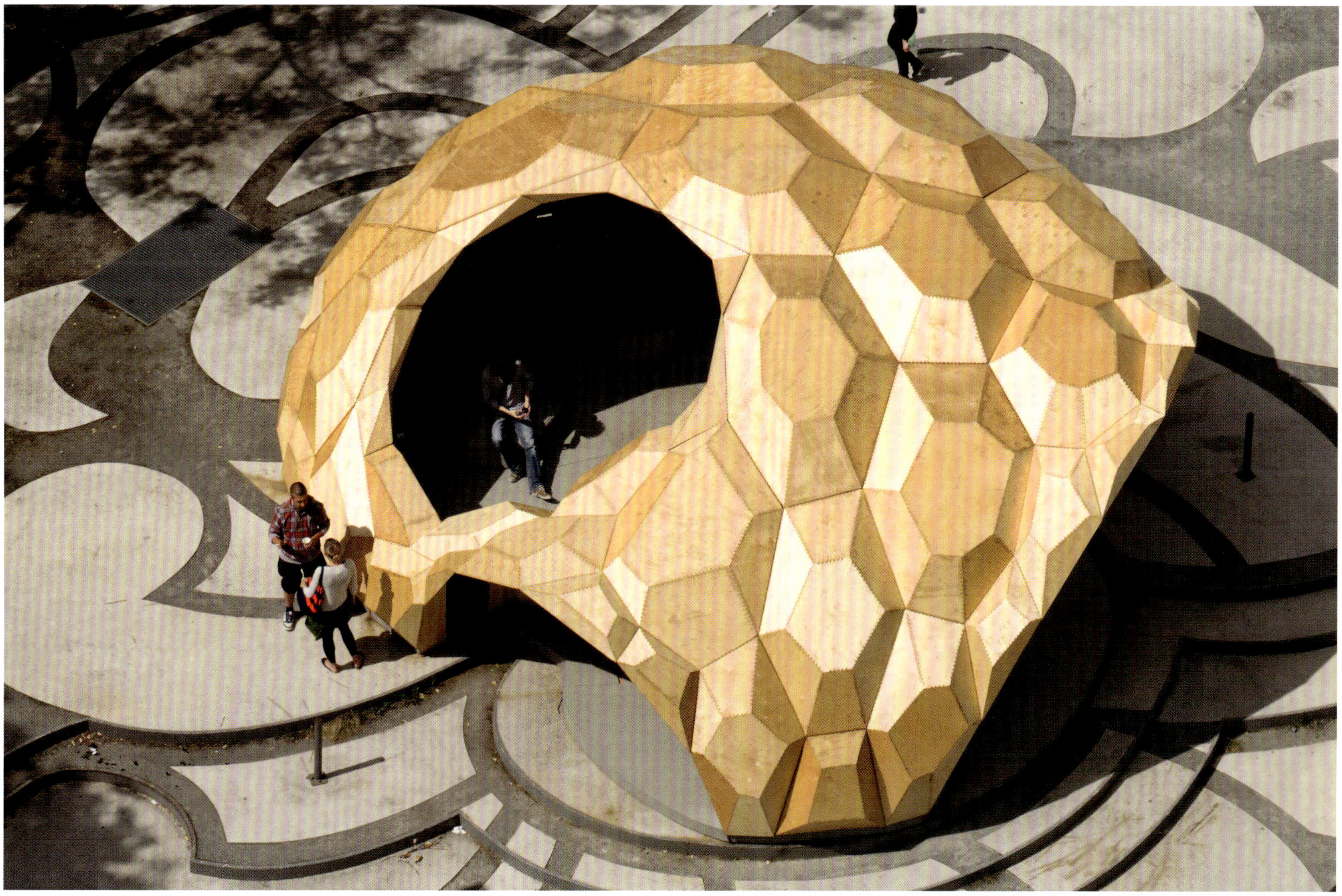

4.14h

Media-TIC
Cloud 9 / Enric Ruiz Geli
Built 2011
Barcelona, Spain

4.15a

The MEDIA-TIC building, designed by Enric Ruiz-Geli of Cloud 9, is in the 22@ district of Barcelona, an area of the city known as Poblenou that was once the productive center of Catalan industry, which in recent years has redeveloped to become a twenty-first century cultural hub for technology and innovation. In conjunction with the Barcelona Digital Foundation, MEDIA-TIC was developed to support, incubate, and accelerate businesses and research institutions focused on information and communication technologies (ICTs), as well as audio-visual and other forms of media, to increase the productivity and competitiveness of these sectors within the growing digital economy. The building was meant to not only house programs that advance information technologies and its range of media, but also to use these computational technologies in its design and fabrication while being emblematic of a new aesthetic grounded in the logics of these systems. The project thus sets up a dialogue between the industrial past of its historical context and its future aspirations. This is rendered evident in the dialectic between the building's steel structure and its ethereal, cloud-like, ETFE skin. The repetitive serial structure—four rigid braced frames consisting of trussed girders spaced fourteen meters apart from which the floors and cladding are hung—operates in contrast to the billowing, cellular cluster of triangular inflatable ETFE pillows that comprise the primary southeast Sancho d'Avila façade. This light, billowing, and seemingly immaterial surface, punctuated with openings and flower-like indentations that link interior spaces to the exterior, acts as an energy-efficient solar filter. The pillows have up to three air chambers so that they might be pneumatically inflated at different rates, triggered by thermal sensors embedded in the skin, to operate as a filter for the sun and improve the thermal performance of the cladding. Although the first layer of the cladding is transparent, the second and third layers, each imprinted with a pixelated pattern of dots, can be manipulated for varying degrees of shade. These two layers have inverted complementary patterns so that, in one configuration, when the pillow is fully inflated, the layers diffuse the light, and in another, the patterned layers align, creating a single opaque surface. The neighboring southwest façade has a vertically organized lenticular serial system of ETFE pillows filled with nitrogen where, like the clouds in the sky, the density of air particles is responsible for filtering sunlight.

4.15b

4.15c

4.15d

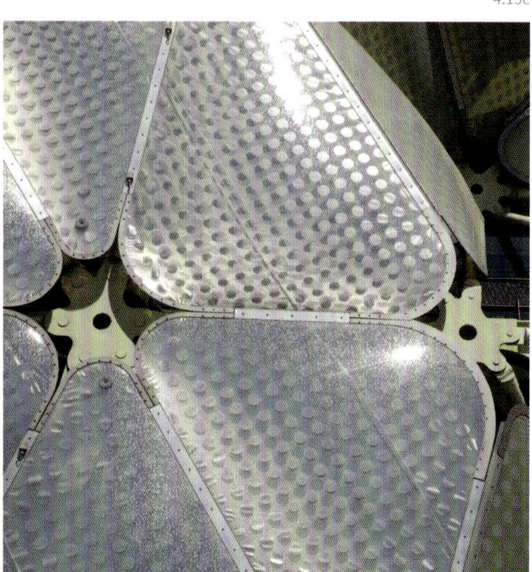

4.15e

4.15f

KAPSARC
Zaha Hadid Architects
Built 2009-17
Riyadh, Saudi Arabia

4.16a

Awarded with a LEED Platinum certification by the US Green Building Council, KAPSARC (King Abdullah Petroleum Studies and Research Centre) is a nonprofit institution for research into policies that contribute to the most effective use of energy to provide social wellbeing, developing policies and economic frameworks that reduce the environmental impact and costs of energy supply while enabling practical, technology-based solutions to use energy more efficiently. The 70,000 m² campus incorporates five buildings: the Energy Knowledge Center; the Energy Computer Center; a Conference Center with an exhibition hall and 300-seat auditorium; a Research Library; and the Musalla, an inspirational place for prayer. The primary organizing strategy of the design is a cellular, partially modular system that integrates different buildings into a single ensemble with interconnecting public spaces. Hexagonal prismatic honeycomb structures use the least amount of material to create a lattice of cells within a given volume while providing increased opportunities for connectivity. The project is thus organized as an amalgamation of crystalline forms emerging from the desert landscape that evolve morphologically to best respond to external environmental conditions and internal program requirements. The honeycomb grid is compressed towards its central axis, an extension of the natural wadi that runs toward the west. Configured to soften the strong light and minimize the extreme heat of the Riyadh Plateau, the buildings of the campus are organized to surround a large public courtyard shaded by canopies supported by a forest of highly crafted steel columns. Privileging the pedestrian, each of the buildings within the campus is entered through this central public courtyard that also serves as a meeting space and link between buildings while facilitating connections with the researcher's residential community to the west. The parametric sculpting of the cellular structure introduces porosity and connectivity into the whole while enabling the form to locally respond to its environment. The prismatic cells thus increase in height towards the south, west, and east to present a solid, protective shell to the harsh southern sunlight for heat mitigation while orienting the courtyards toward the north and northwest, with wind catchers integrated into roof profiles, to encourage prevailing northern winds to cool them while bringing indirect, softened light deep into the interior of the campus.

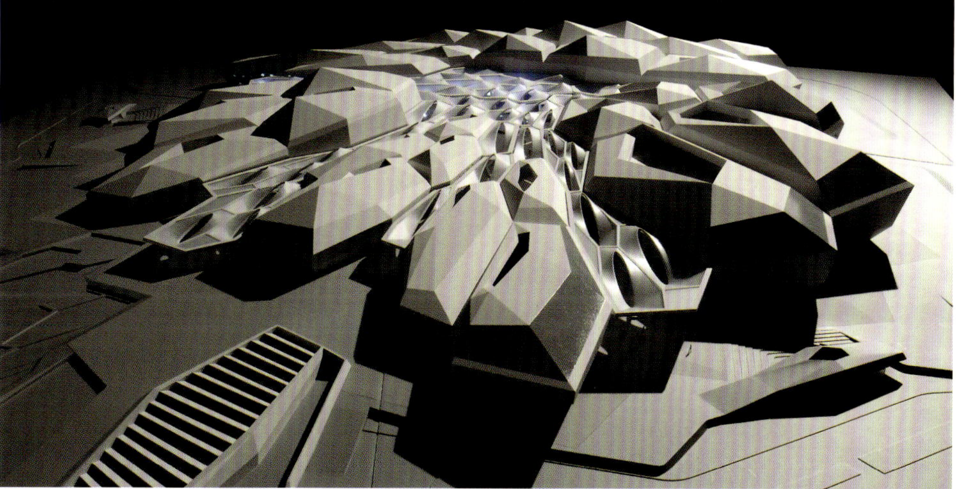

4.16b

4.16c

4.16d

Little Island
Heatherwick Studio

Built 2013-2021

New York, United States

Little Island, a response to the need to build a new pier on Manhattan's southwest riverside, is both a beautifully landscaped public park and world-class outdoor performance space with an outdoor theater for over 700 people and smaller performance space for 200. The identity of the project was initially derived from the site where hundreds of old wooden piles, the structural remains of older piers, jutted out of the Hudson River. These were the inspiration to generate a new field of concrete piles necessary for the new pier, while rendering them visible by extending them upwards above the water to support a new green landscape. The structure thus evolved into a foundation of 280 repeating piles that expand at the top into a cluster of cells. These completely fuse to tile the plane of the pier, dividing it into five-sided polygons except along the piers' orthogonal edges. These polygons are given depth to form cup-like concrete enclosures that are filled with earth to become planters for the thousands of tons of new soil required to sustain this landscape, consisting of more than a hundred different species of indigenous trees and plants suited to the harsh extremes of the New York climate. Every planter connects in a tessellating pattern, yet rather than constructing an earthen topography, these planters are positioned at different heights so that the artificial terrain undulates. Raising the park into the air not only counteracts the windswept quality of the large adjacent road but also works well with the need for outdoor theater spaces, as raked seating could be shaped into the landscape to give the audience better views. The resulting unique topography can be experienced as you walk underneath to enter, as well as from above, along the many pathways and viewing platforms that traverse the terrain, while hovering over the water.

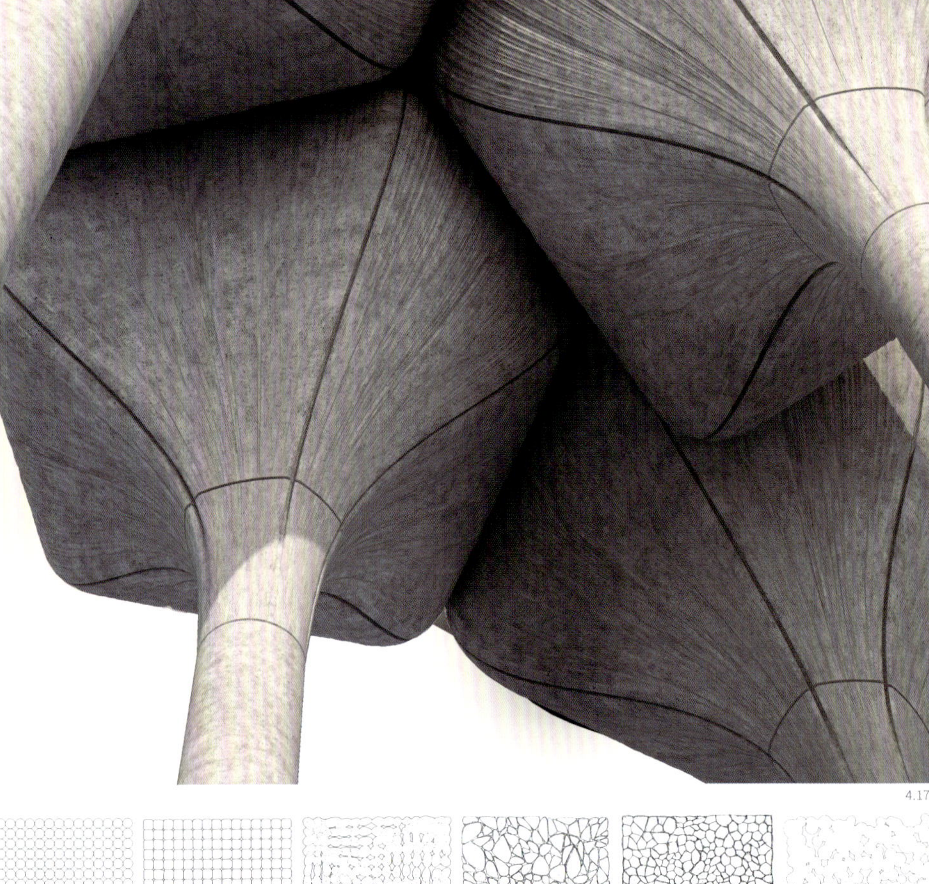

4.17a

4.17b

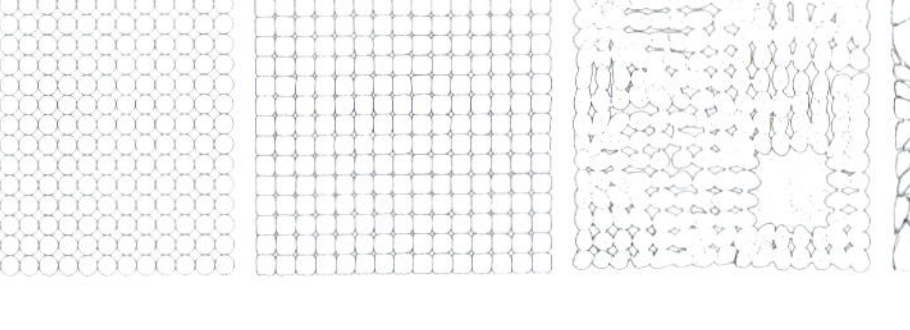

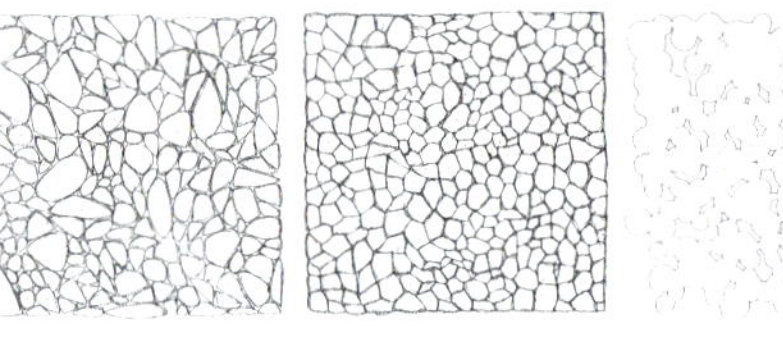

4.17c

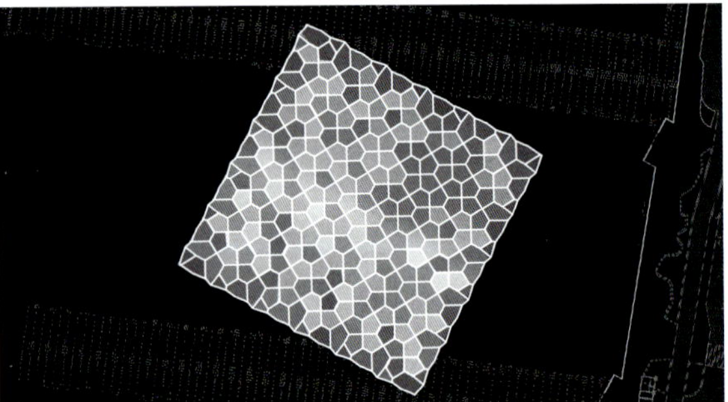

4.17d

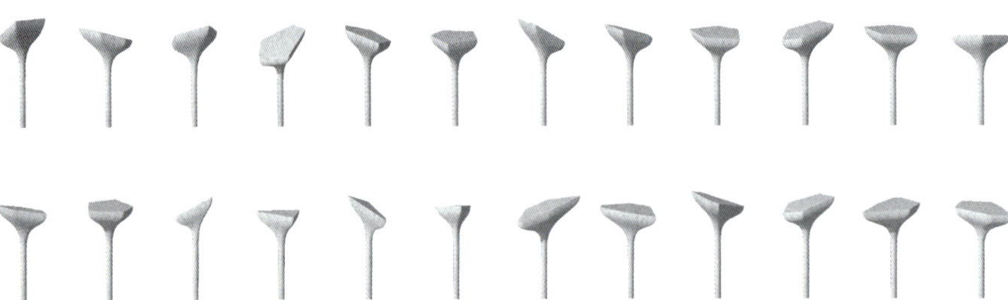

4.17e

4.17f

The Tide

Diller Scofidio + Renfro

Built 2015-2019
London, United Kingdom

4.18a

The Tide is a 5-kilometer network of public spaces and gardens embedded into the daily rhythms of Greenwich Peninsula. Both an elevated and at-grade walkway, with programming split across both levels, The Tide activates spaces above and below to provide a layered network of recreation, culture, and wellness. The Tide stitches together diverse ecosystems, emerging neighborhoods, and distinct cultural institutions, connecting north to south, east to west, center to periphery, and city to river. It is simultaneously a running track, a walking promenade, a series of quiet gardens, and a network of social and cultural hubs. The Tide is conceived of as a series of elevated, landscaped islands. Each island is distinct, defined by unique trees and planting, and by their surrounding views and sounds. These elevated gardens are designed as clusters of structural supports that create elevated planter beds, containing soil and channeling both gravity loads and water down to the ground. The sculptural structure supporting The Tide gardens above also frames and shelters the path below, creating arched pavilions that mark thresholds and passages at the ground-level public realm. The Tide's first phase is comprised of twenty-eight unique structural supports. These cluster together to form tripod-like structures that support the elevated gardens and walkways above while creating canopies for shelter and reflected illumination at the plaza level. Systems for lighting, electrical, data, and landscape (vegetation, soil, water supply, and drainage) are integrated seamlessly into the structural supports that are composed of welded plate steel inner ribs and outer skins forming an aircraft wing-like structure that is lightweight and minimizes impact to the London Underground station box directly below. The design of the structural elements was a special architectural and structural collaboration with AKTII using parametric software to maximize material efficiency and minimize fabrication complexity. The result is an integrated architectural and structural expression without superfluous cladding. The islands are connected by prefabricated steel bridges forming a continuous 2.4-meter-wide wide path with spans up to twenty-six meters. The first phase of the project is 1 kilometer long, and features a linear public walkway, elevated gardens, pocket cafes, and an architectural promontory overlooking the Thames River.

4.18b

4.18c

Generative Logic Polyhedra

Polyhedra are three-dimensional shapes composed of flat faces, straight edges, and vertices. There are many polyhedra that are convex and composed of regular faces. Most of these fall into one of three categories known as Platonic solids, Archimedean solids, or Catalan solids. Euler's Formula provides a useful relationship for all convex polyhedron: Vertices - Edges + Faces = x. For all regular polyhedra (the Platonic solids), X = 2.

Platonic Solids

The five Platonic solids are composed of faces that are regular polygons and have the same number of faces at each vertex. Named after Plato, these polyhedrons have served as the source for many architectural projects.

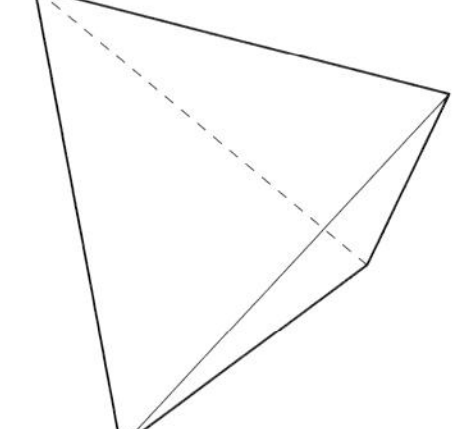
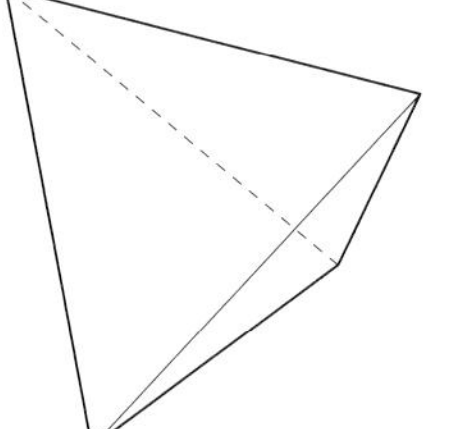

Tetrahedron (V:4, E:6, F:4)

Cube (V:8, E:12, F:6)

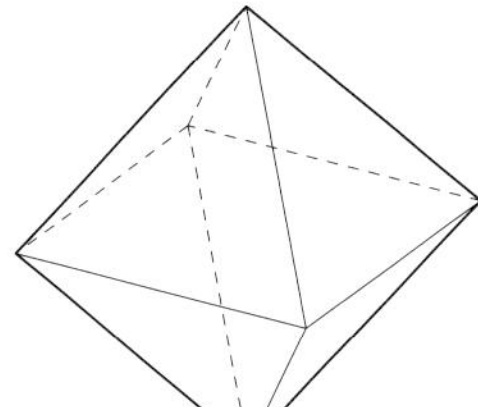

Octahedron (V:6, E:12, F:8)

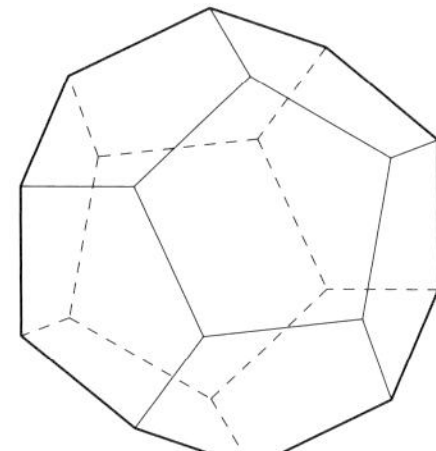

Dodecahedron (V:20, E:30, F:12)

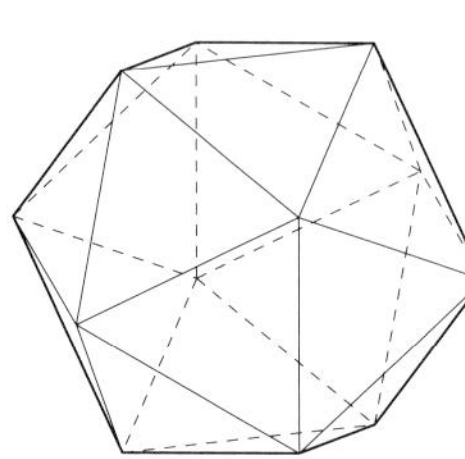

Icosahedron (V:12, E:30, F:20)

Polyhedron Duals

Each polygon and polyhedron has a dual that can be found by swapping the location of faces and vertices. Each Platonic solid has another Platonic solid as its dual. Tetrahedron's dual is itself, while cube/octahedron and dodecahedron/icosahedron are pairs.

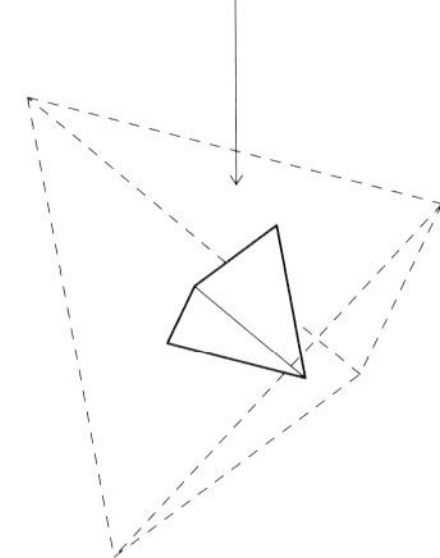

Tetrahedron's Dual is a Tetrahedron

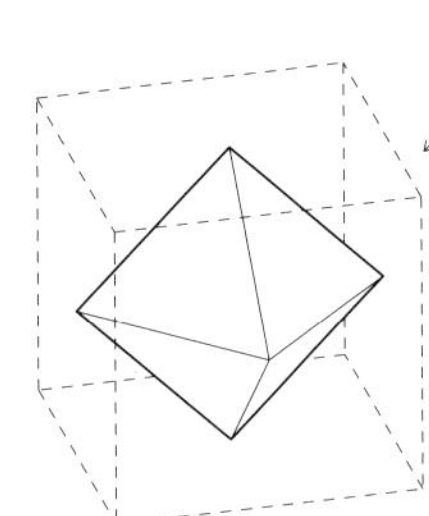

Cube's dual is a Octahedron

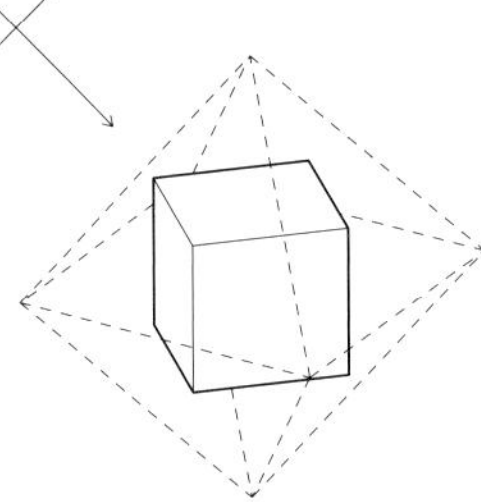

Octahedron's dual is a Cube

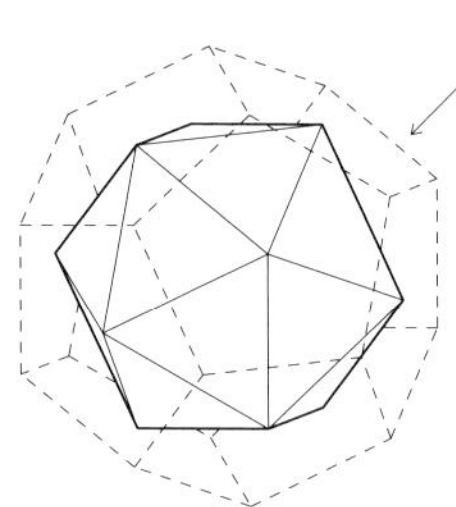

Dodecahedron's dual is a Icosahedron

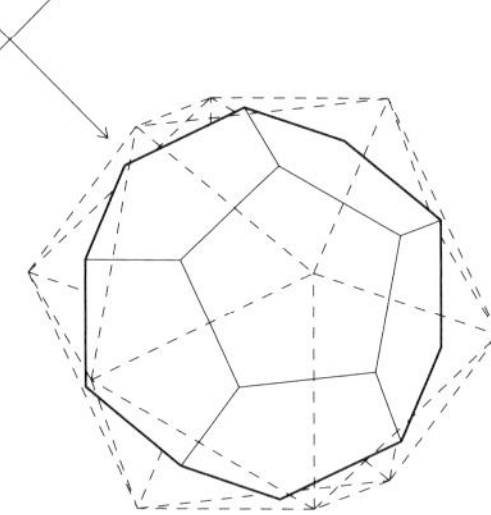

Icosahedron dual is a Dodecahedron

Spherical Polyhedron

While not technical polyhedron since their edges and faces are not straight or flat, spherical polyhedra can be created by projecting various polyhedra to the surface of a sphere. This technique is critical in the development of geodesic structures.

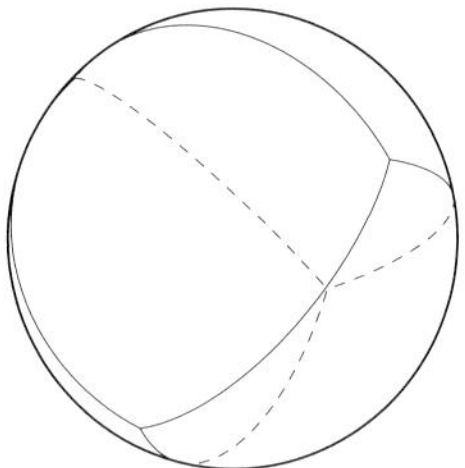

Spherical Tetrahedron

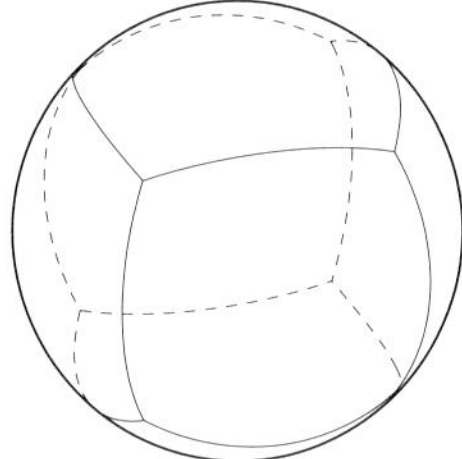

Spherical Cube

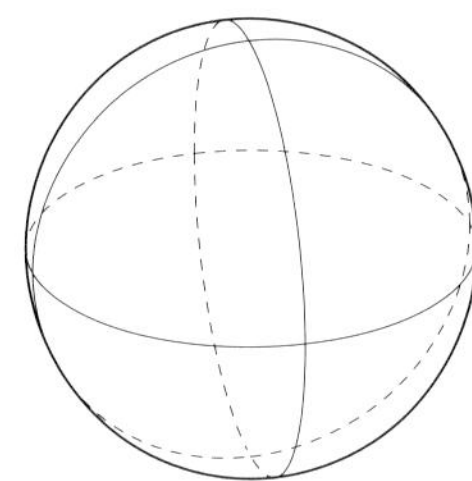

Spherical Octahedron

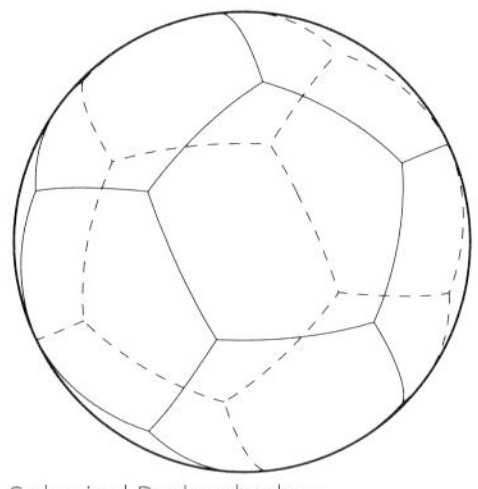

Spherical Dodecahedron

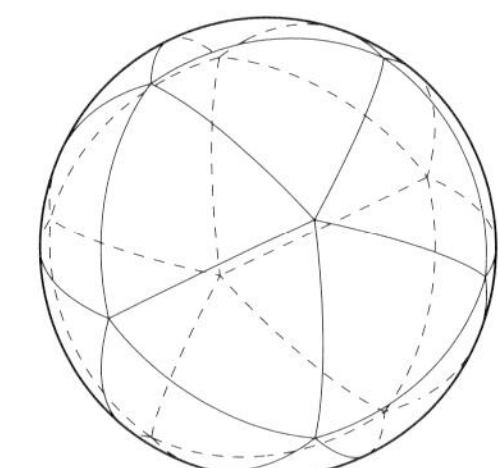

Spherical Icosahedron

Archimedean Solids

The Archimedean solids are quasi-regular polyhedra that have regular faces but composed of more than one face polygon type. For example, the truncated cube is composed of eight equilateral triangles and six octagons. Johannes Kepler rediscovered them by 1620 after centuries of being lost to history.

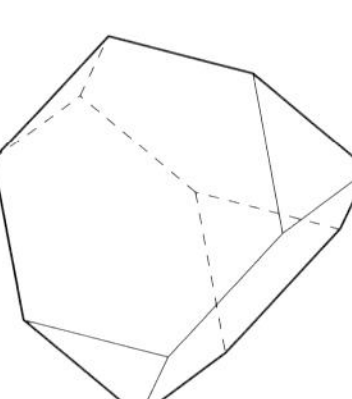

Truncated Tetrahedron
(V:12, E:18, F:8)

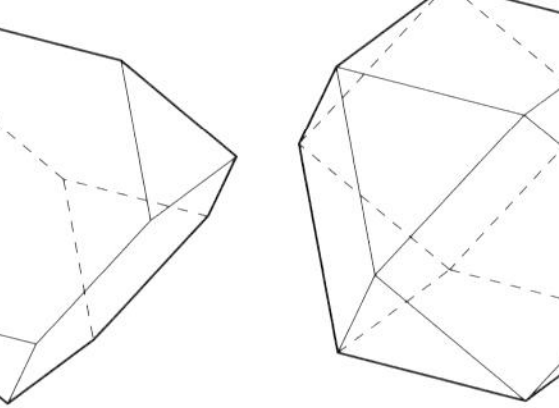
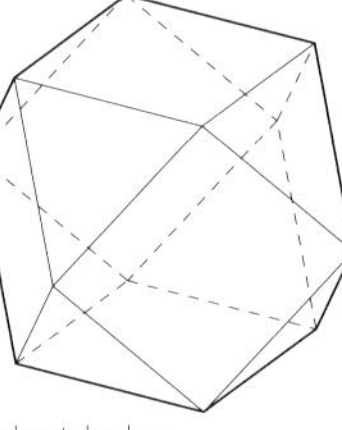

Cuboctahedron
(V:12, E:24, F:17)

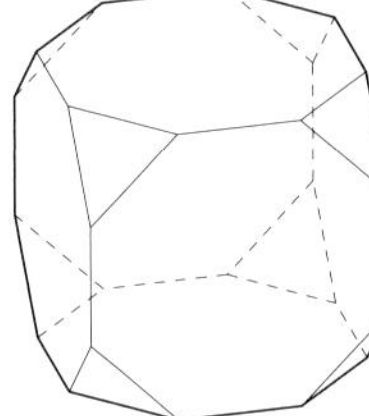

Truncated Cube
(V:24, E:36, F:14)

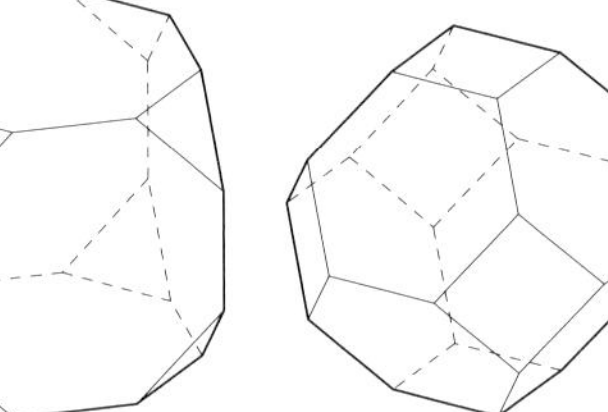

Truncated Octahedron
(V:24, E:36, F:14)

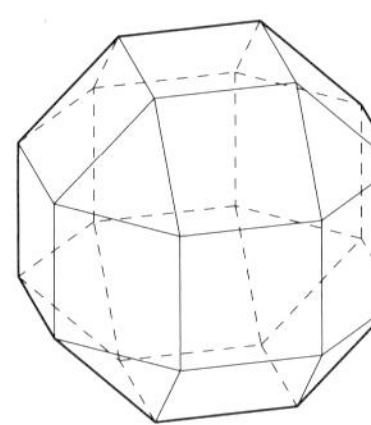

Rhombicuboctahedron
(V:24, E:48, F:26)

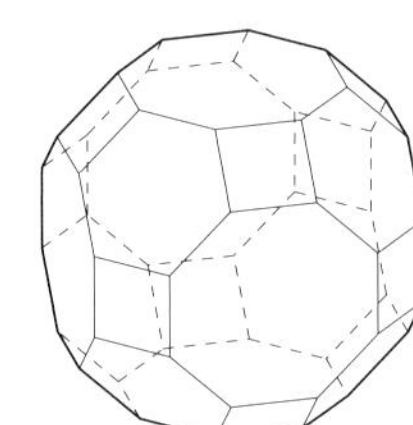

Truncated Cuboctahedron
(V:48, E:72, F:26)

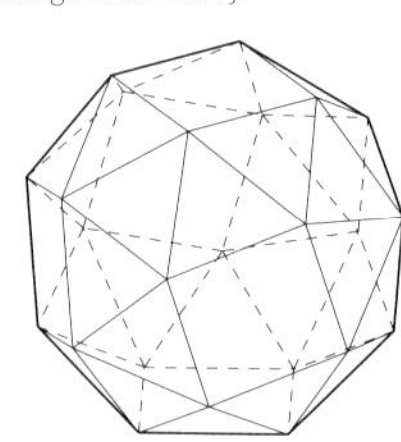
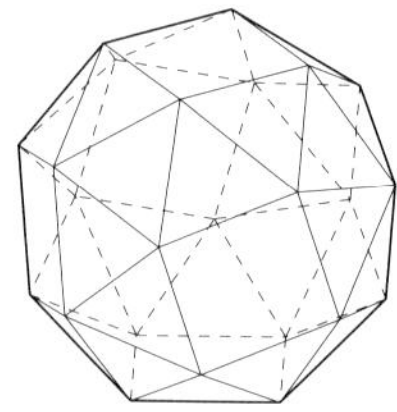

Snub Cube
(V:24, E:60, F:24)

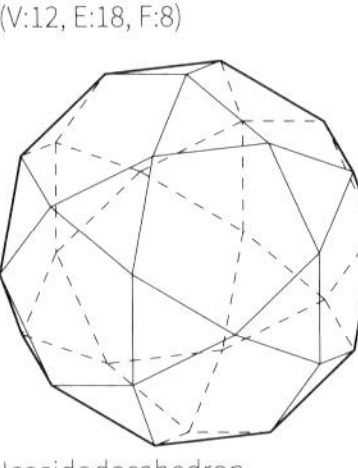

Icosidodecahedron
(V:30, E:60, F:32)

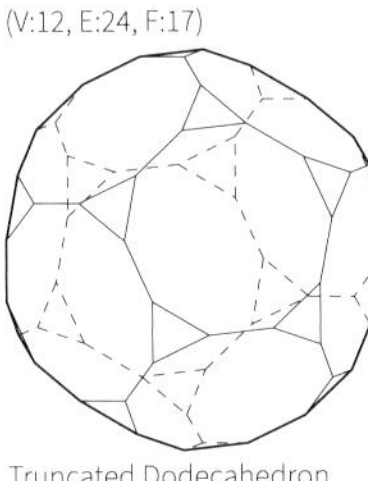

Truncated Dodecahedron
(V:60, E:90, F:32)

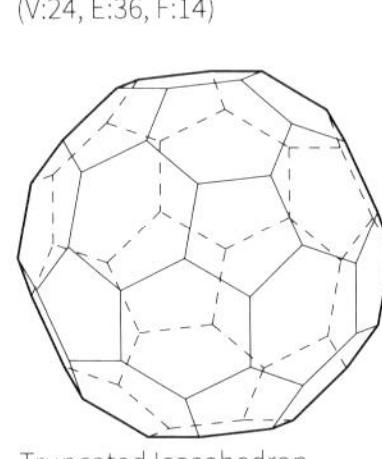

Truncated Icosahedron
(V:60, E:90, F:32)

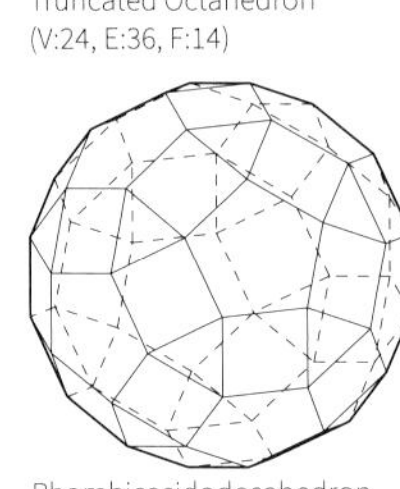

Rhombicosidodecahedron
(V:60, E:120, F:62)

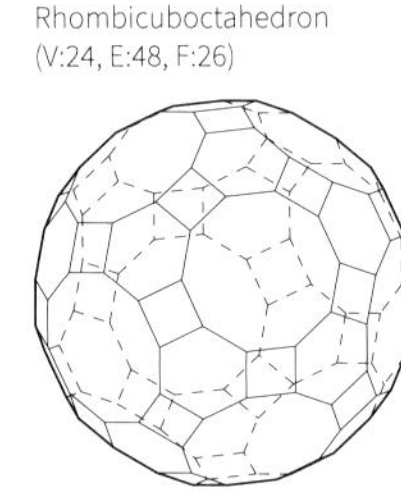

Truncated Icosidodecahedron
(V:120, E:180, F:62)

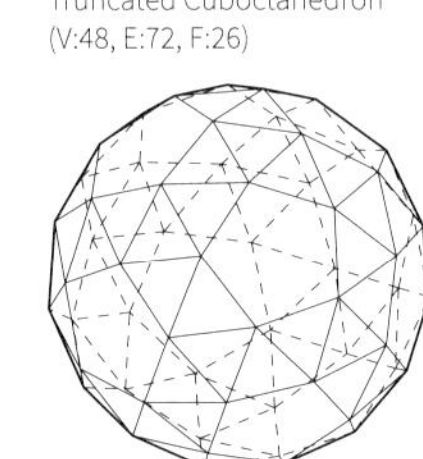

Snub Dodecahedron
(V:60, E:150, F:92)

Catalan Solids

The Catalan solids are the duals of the Archimedean solids. For each of the thirteen Archimedean solids, there is a corresponding Catalan solid with the opposite number of faces and vertices. They were discovered by Eugène Catalan in 1865.

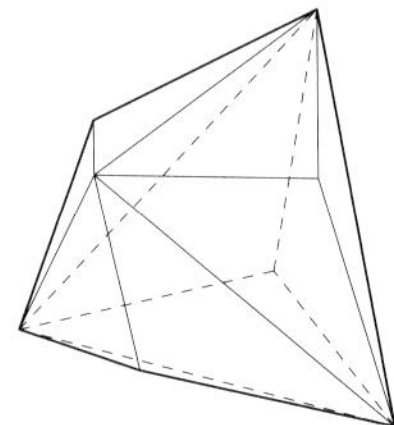

Triakis Tetrahedron
(V:8, E:18, F:12)

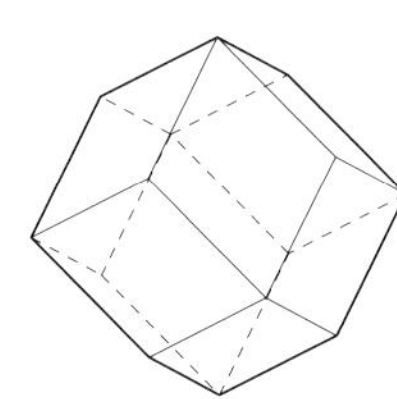

Rhombic Dodecahedron
(V:14, E:24, F:12)

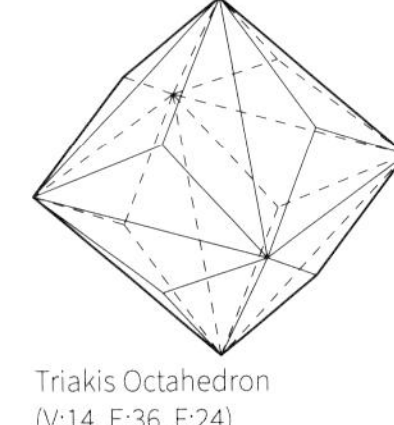

Triakis Octahedron
(V:14, E:36, F:24)

Tetrakis Hexahedron
(V:14, E:36, F:24)

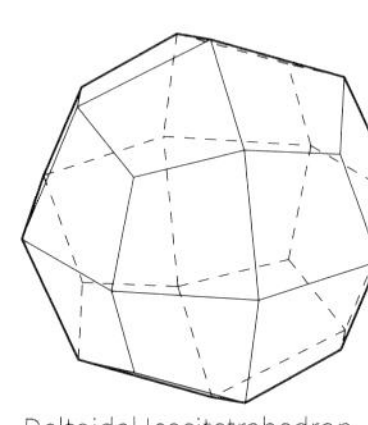

Deltoidal Icositetrahedron
(V:26, E:48, F:24)

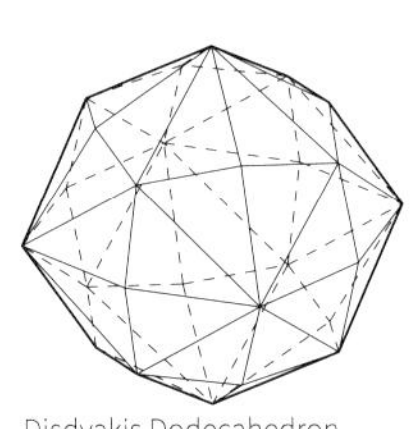

Disdyakis Dodecahedron
(V:26, E:72, F:48)

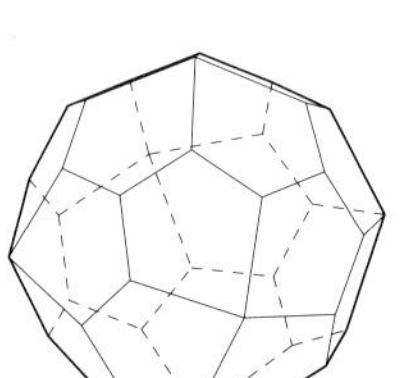

Pentagonal Icositetrahedron
(V:38, E:60, F:24)

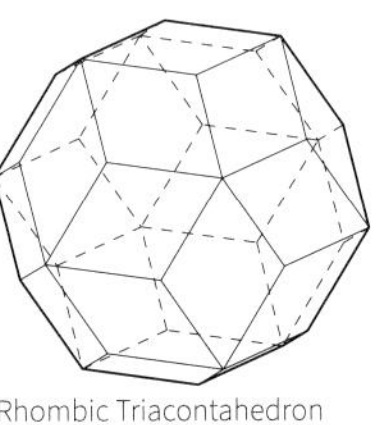

Rhombic Triacontahedron
(V:32, E:60, F:30)

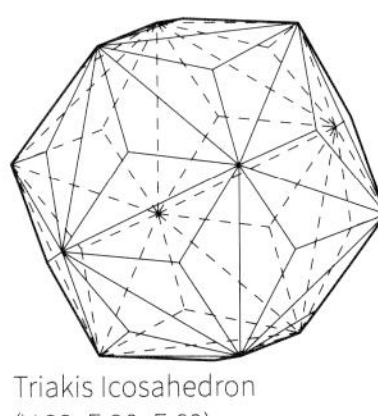

Triakis Icosahedron
(V:32, E:90, F:60)

Pentakis Dodecahedron
(V:32, E:90, F:60)

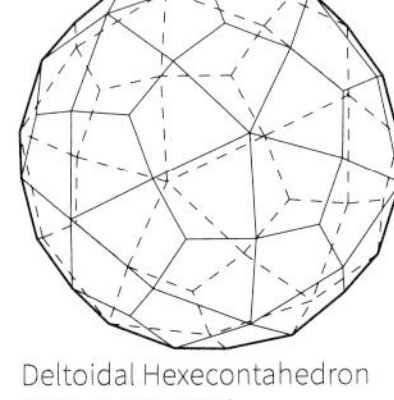

Deltoidal Hexecontahedron
(V:62, E:120, F:60)

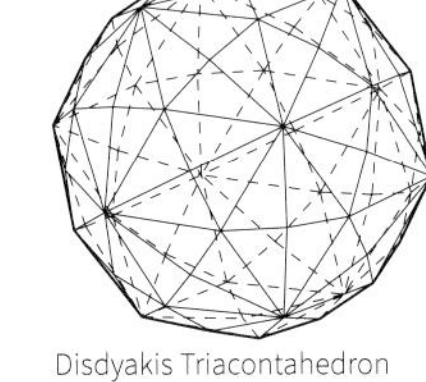

Disdyakis Triacontahedron
(V:62, E:180, F:120)

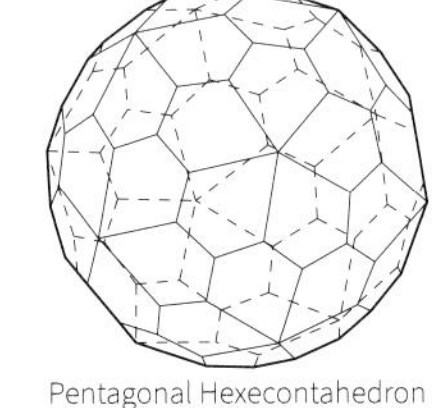

Pentagonal Hexecontahedron
(V:92, E:150, F:60)

Generative Process Montreal Biosphere

Buckminster Fuller developed hundreds of variations on how to translate between polyhedra and geodesic structures. The majority of these use an underlaying base icosahedron, however there are examples of other polyhedra used in both his built work and notes. The materials systems used to fabricated the structures varied from steel lattice works to fiberglass and wood.

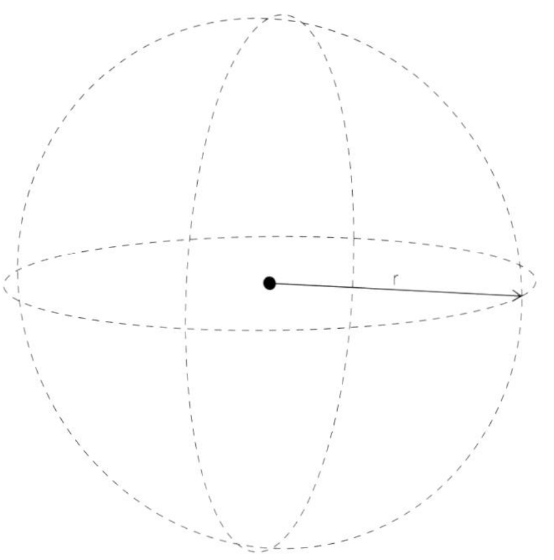

1. Create a sphere with radius (r).

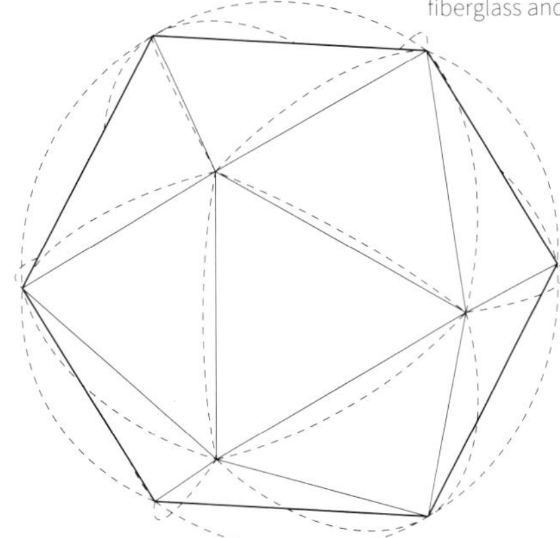

2. Create an inscribed polyhedron (p). In this example, an icosahedron is used.

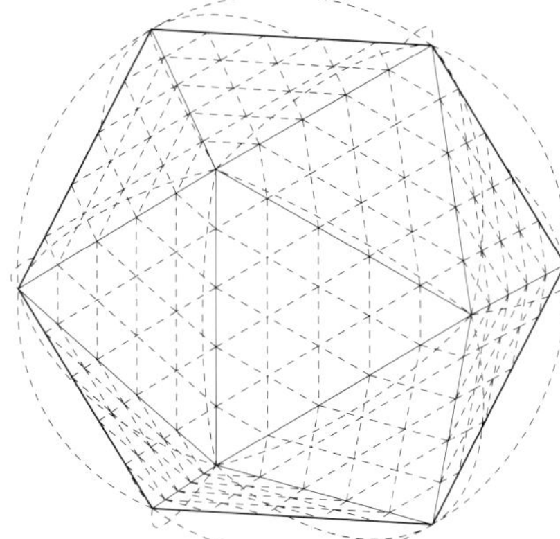

3. Subdivide the polyhedron's faces into smaller triangles. Various subdivision patterns can be used.

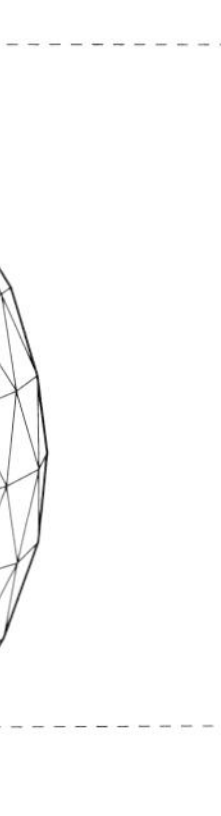

4. Project the subdivided edges to the sphere.

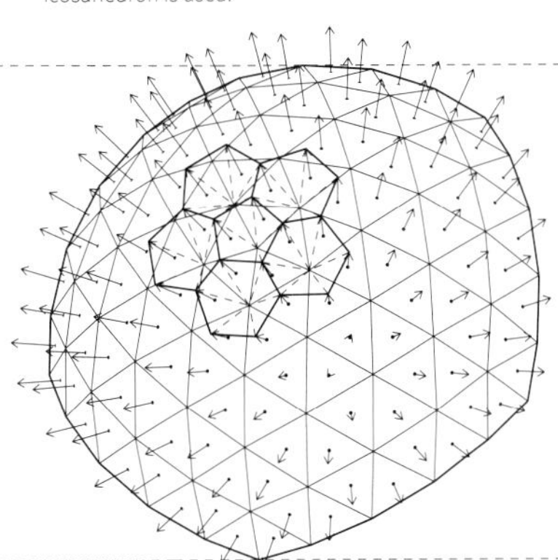

5. Find the center of each face at the normal vector at that point. Move the face centers in or out along the normals by the lattice depth (d). Connect neighboring faces to create the offset lattice layer.

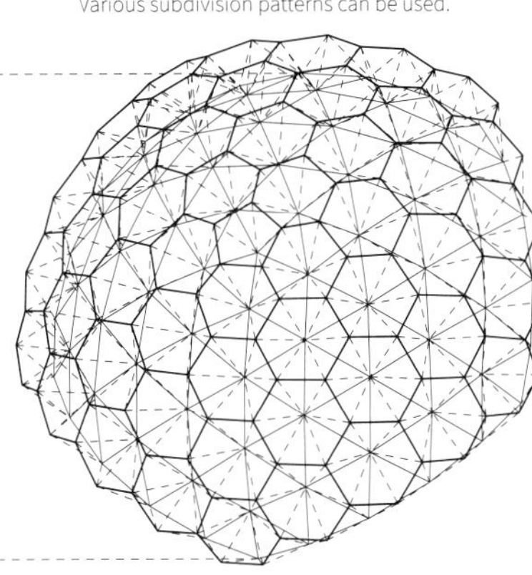

6. To create the lattice webbing, connect the inner face vertices with the offset face vertices.

Generative Matrix

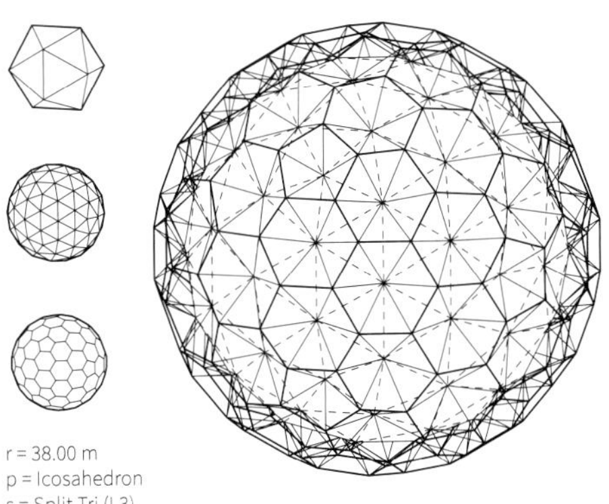

r = 38.00 m
p = Icosahedron
s = Split Tri (L3)

Control Model

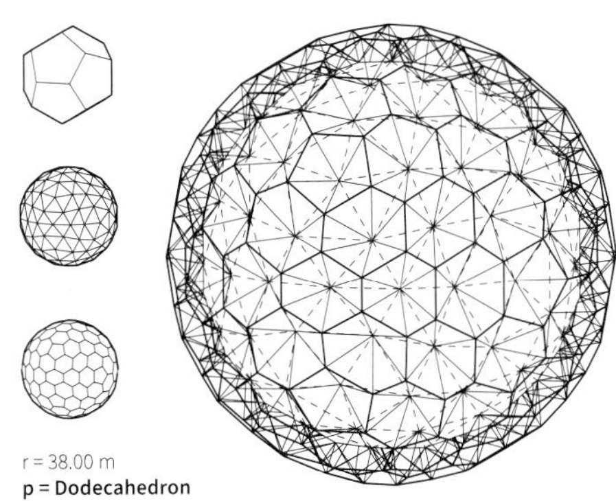

r = 38.00 m
p = Dodecahedron
s = Split Tri (L2)

Dodecahedron Base

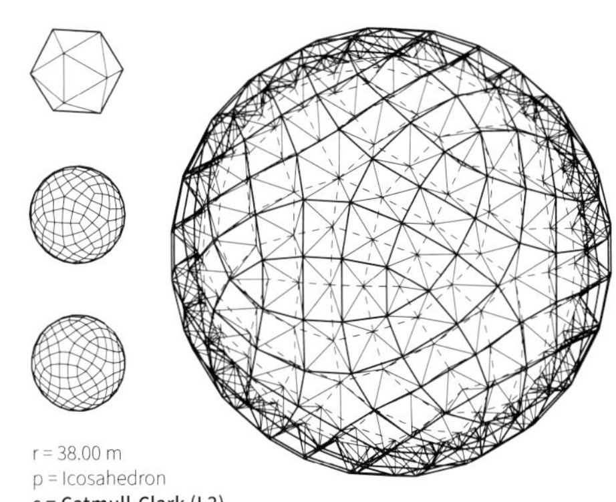

r = 38.00 m
p = Icosahedron
s = Catmull-Clark (L2)

Quad Subdivision

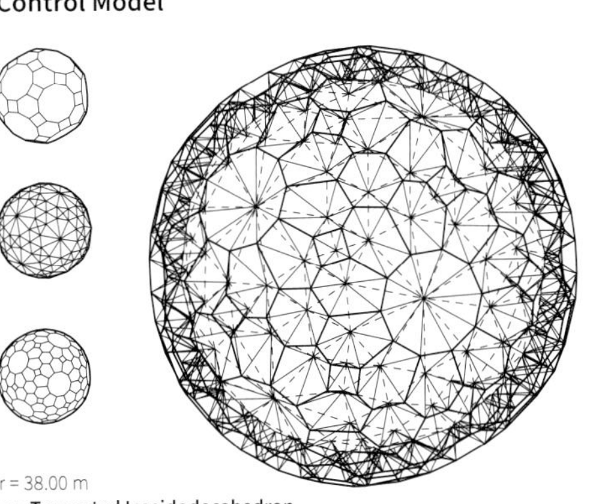

r = 38.00 m
p = Truncated Icosidodecahedron
s = Split Tri (L1)

Truncated Icosidodecahedron Base

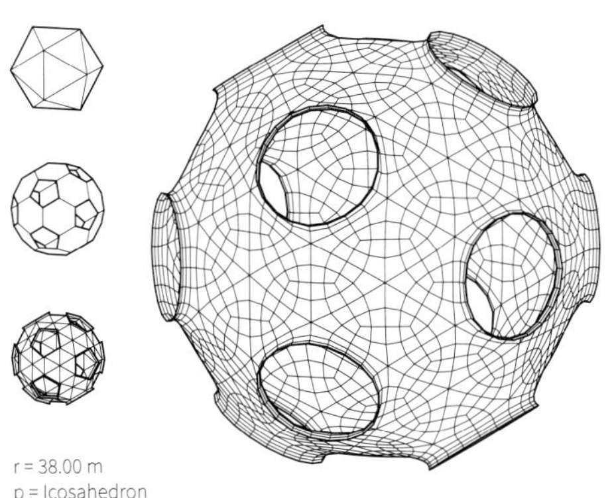

r = 38.00 m
p = Icosahedron
s = Catmull-Clark (L1)

Truncated Icosahedron Base With Holes

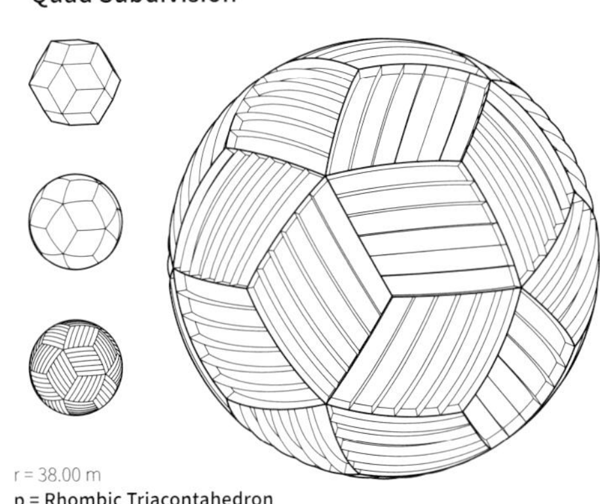

r = 38.00 m
p = Rhombic Triacontahedron
s = Linear Strips (6)

Rhombic Tricontrahedron

Generative Logic Cellular Morphology

The geometry of cellular structures has captured the imagination of scientists and designers for centuries. The cellular bodies such as soap bubbles are seemingly simple yet display fundamental principles of physical geometry. In the nineteenth century, Joseph Plateau proposed the rules that govern the formation of cellular intersections while others such as D'Arcy Thompson further developed these rules towards the relationships between form, growth, and behavior across living and non-living systems.

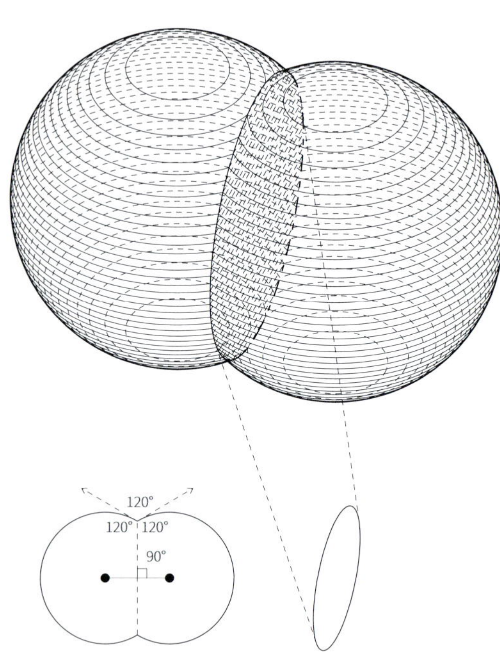

Plateau's Laws: Two Bubbles: Assuming Equal pressure, two cells intersect at a flat plane. The intersection points meet at an angle of 120°.

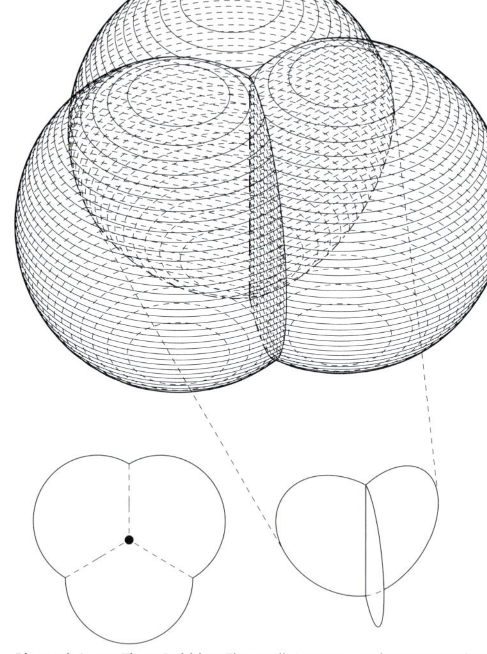

Plateau's Laws: Three Bubbles: Three cells intersect at a line at an angle of 120° (arccos(-1/2)).

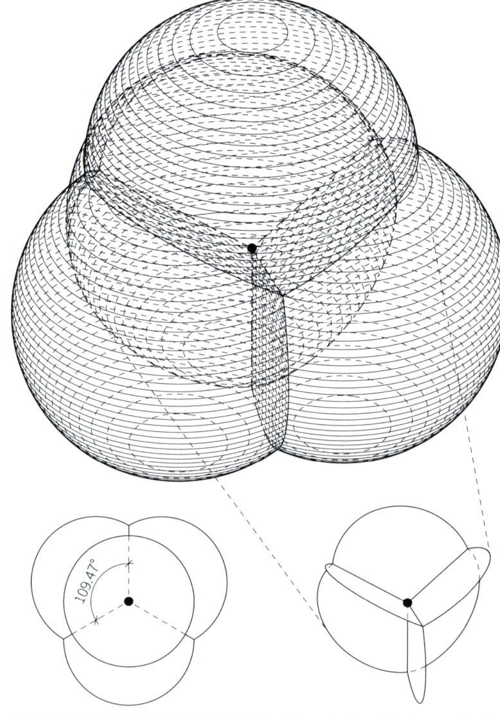

Plateau's Laws: Four Bubbles: Four cells intersect at a point at an angle of 109.47° (arccos(-1/3)).

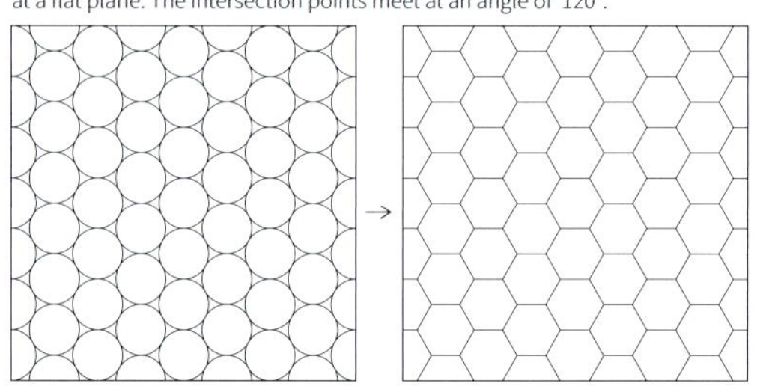

Circle-Packing: As circular bodies are compressed, their walls form hexagonal boundaries, the most efficient way to divide a surface into equal-area regions with the shortest total perimeter.

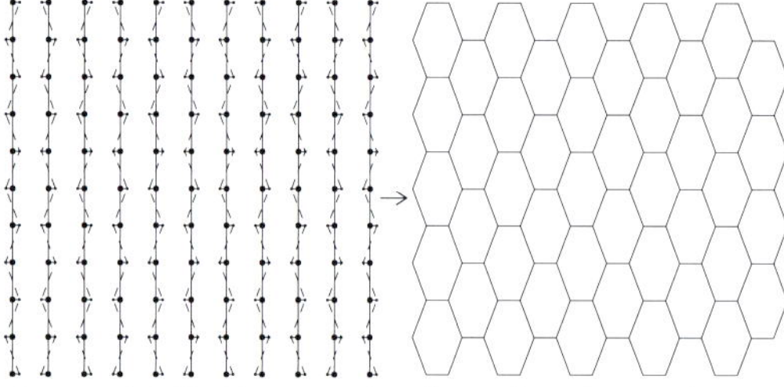

Honeycomb Guides: There are a variety of ways to form a honeycomb pattern. The technique here uses a series of guide curves that are subdivided into points and then offset in an alternating pattern to produce zig-zag polylines.

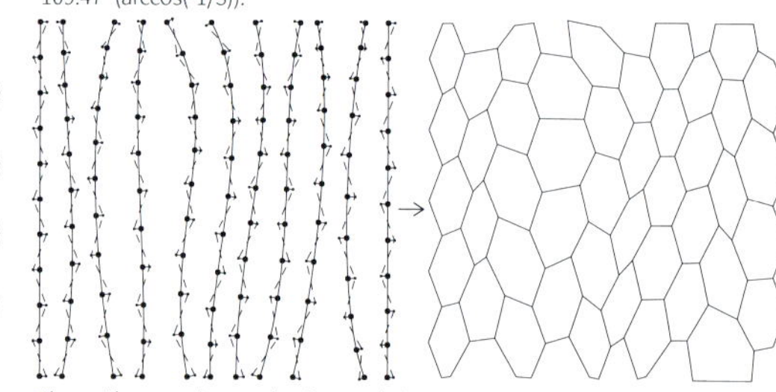

The guide curves' control points or their curve parameter space can be modified to produce less regular honeycomb patterns. This produces an anisotropic cellular morphology where cells are longer or wider in areas.

Generative Process KAPSARC

The KAPSARC project by Zaha Hadid Architects uses a complex cellular grouping of several large clusters of honeycomb cells with interstitial smaller cells that are a range of polygons with four to six sides. Each of the large clusters of cells have an orientation that radiates out into the surrounding site. By aligning the guide curves with the cellular orientations, it is possible to both individual cell's geometry as well as the overall configuration.

1. Establish the guide curves and zone curves for each cluster of cells. Subdivide each set of curves by the desired number of cells.

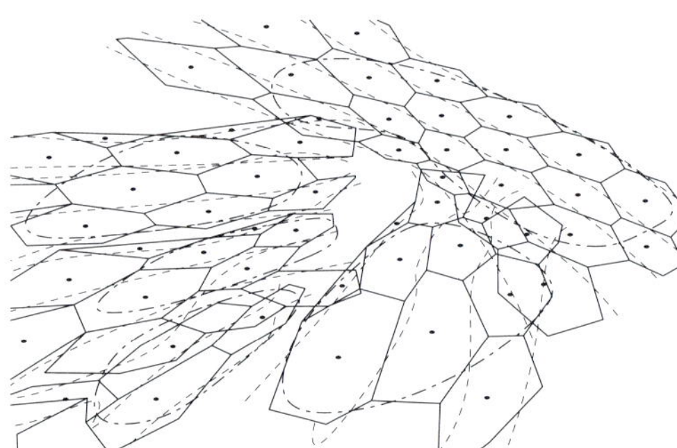

2. Generate the cells for each cluster by offsetting points tangent to each curve point. Find the center of each cell.

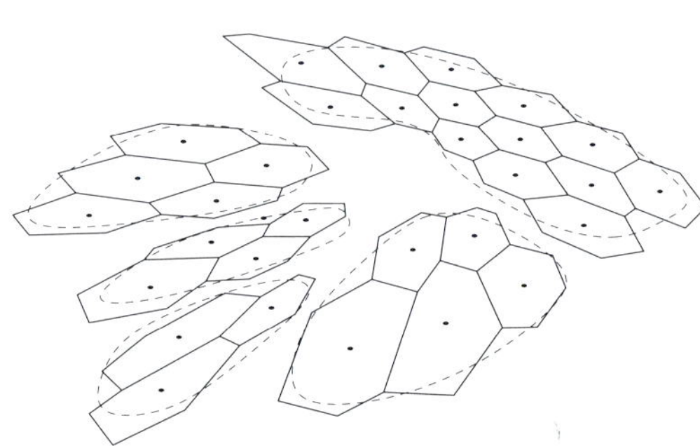

3. If the cell's center is within its zone curve, keep the cell curve. Otherwise, delete the cell curves if their center is not within the zone curve.

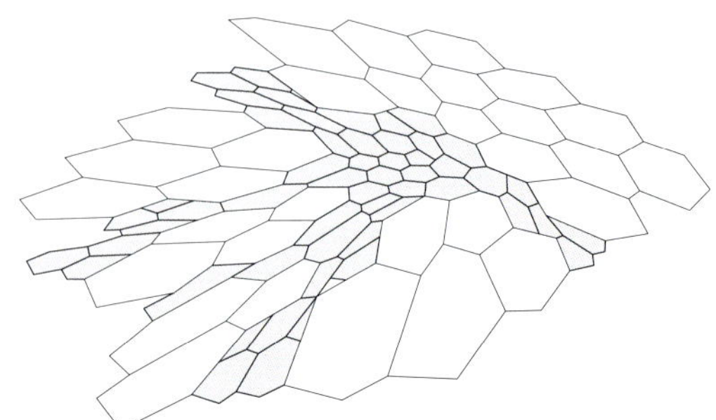

4. Create smaller cells that infill between the larger honeycomb clusters. These cells can have fewer or more sides to create the best fit.

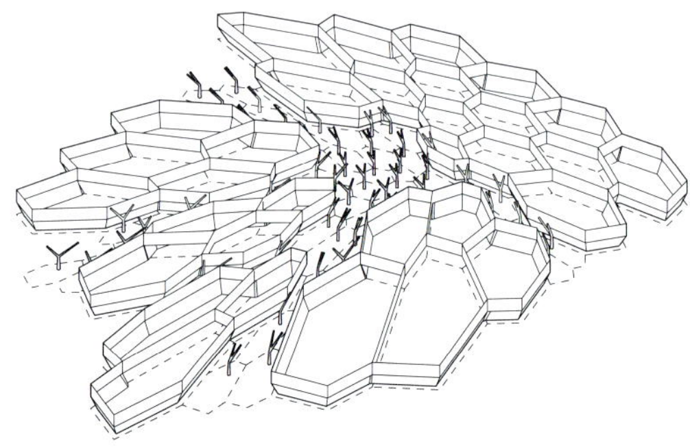

5. Generate the walls for the primary cell clusters and columns for the interstitial secondary cells.

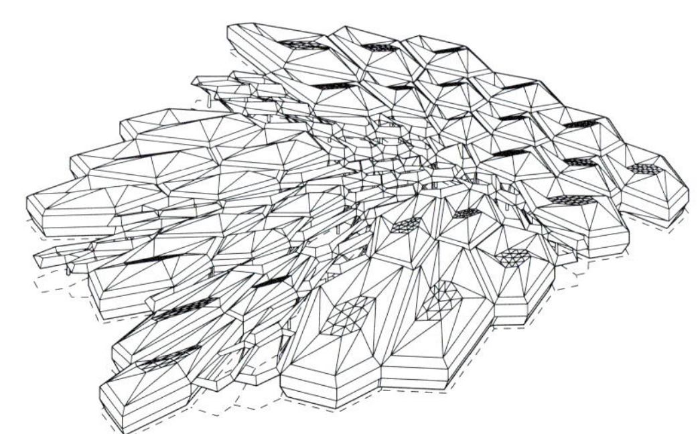

6. Generate roofs for both primary and secondary cells that tilt away from the sun to provide indirect light and better shading.

Generative Matrix

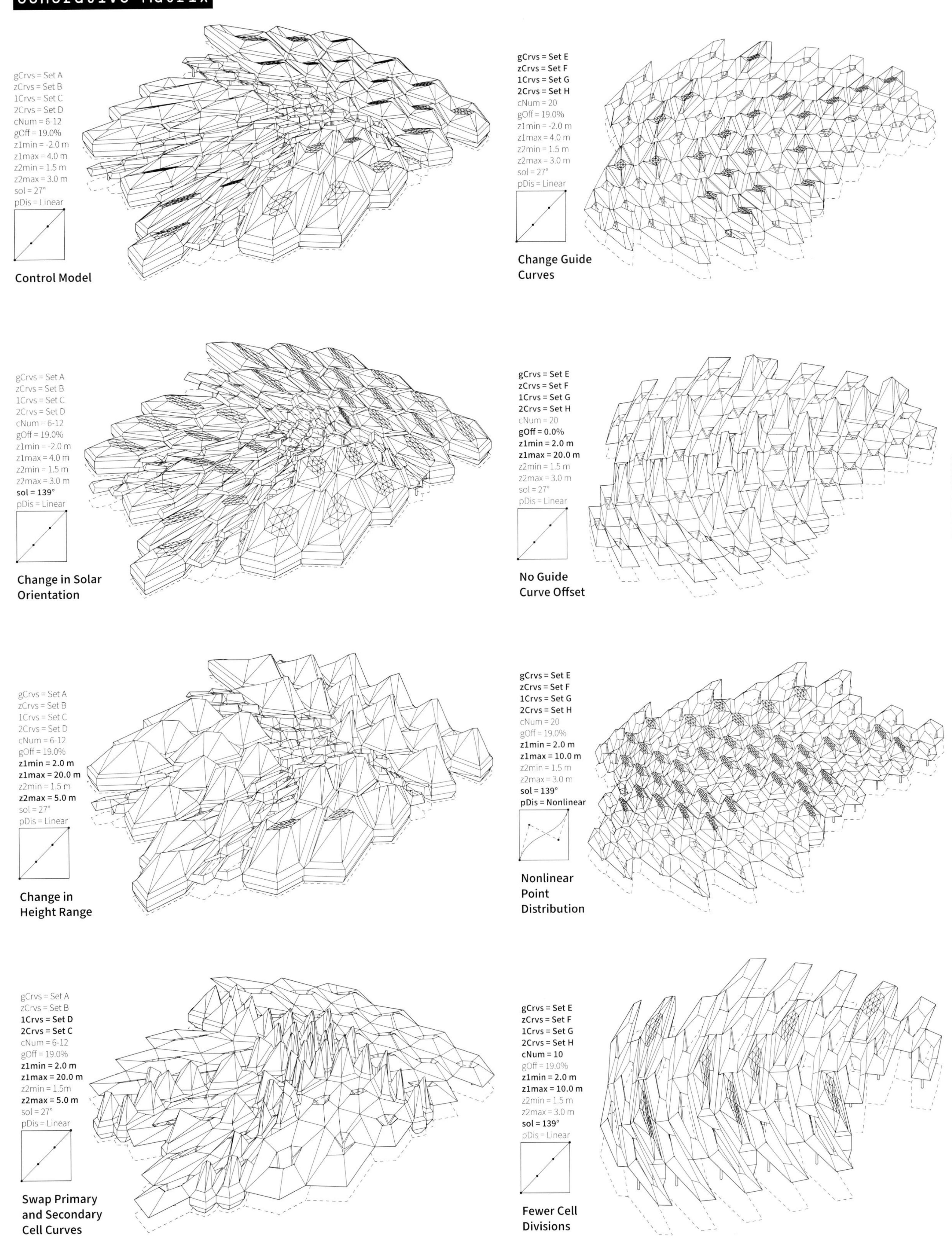

Generative Logic Voronoi Diagrams

Voronoi diagrams, named after Ukrainian mathematician Georgy Voronoy in 1908, represent a pivotal mathematical approach for partitioning space into distinct regions, contingent upon proximity to a designated set of points. Although Voronoy formalized the concept, its rudiments were preliminarily explored by notable figures such as Descartes and Dirichlet, along with the British physician John Snow. This algorithm plays a crucial role in various applications including spatial analysis, network modeling, and navigational systems. Witihn architecture, Voronoi diagrams are instrumental in the modeling of 2D and 3D cellular structures.

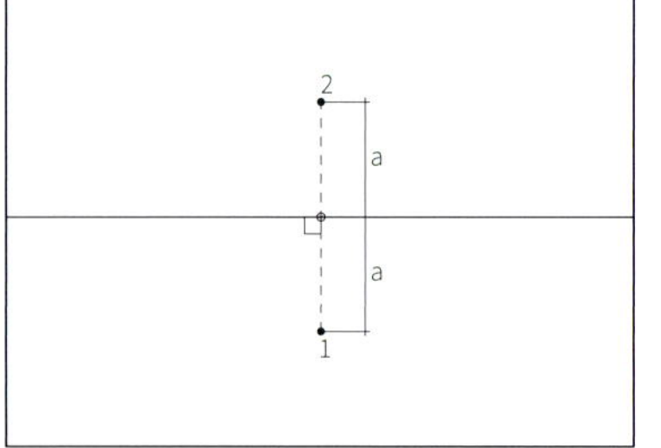

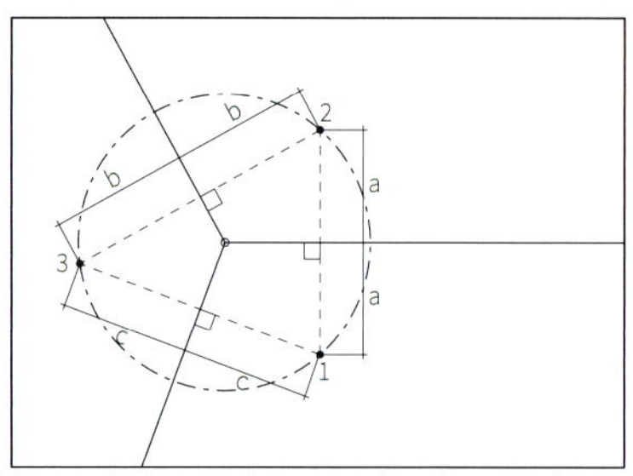

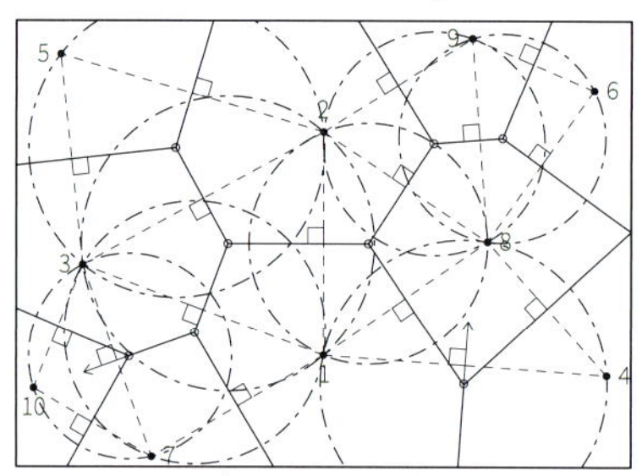

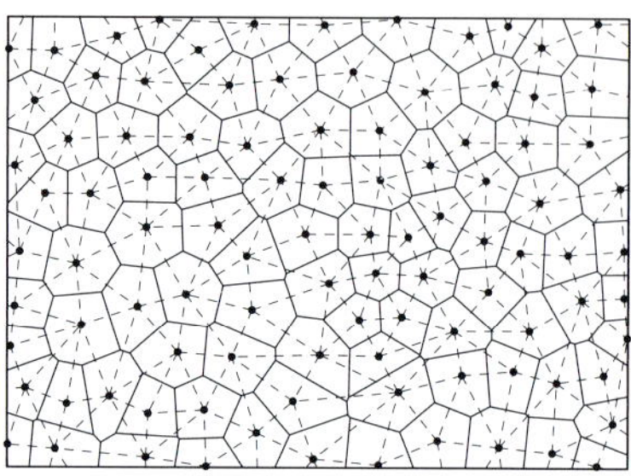

Voronoi Diagrams and Delaunay Triangulations: A Voronoi diagram divides space into regions based on a set of input points. For any point within a region, it is closer to that region's input point than any other. The dual of a Voronoi Diagram is called a Delaunay Triangulation. The circumcircle (a triangle passing through all three points) of any triangle in the triangulation are the vertices of the Voronoi cell and the perpendicular bisectors are the Voronoi cell edges.

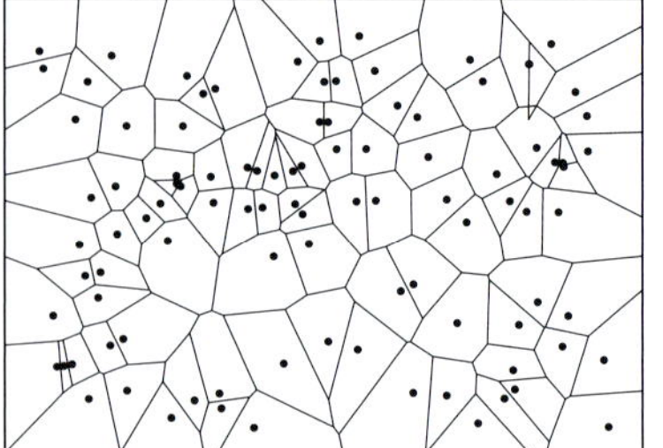

Pure Random Distribution: A purely random set of points produces more angular Voronoi cells.

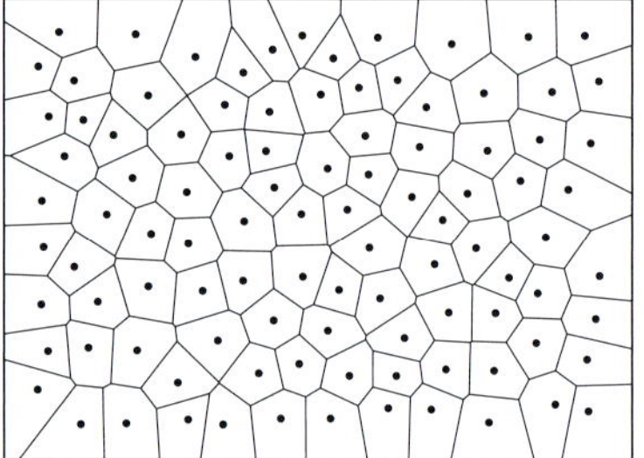

Randomly Even Distribution: Using a point distribution such as Llyod's algorithm produces more uniform cells.

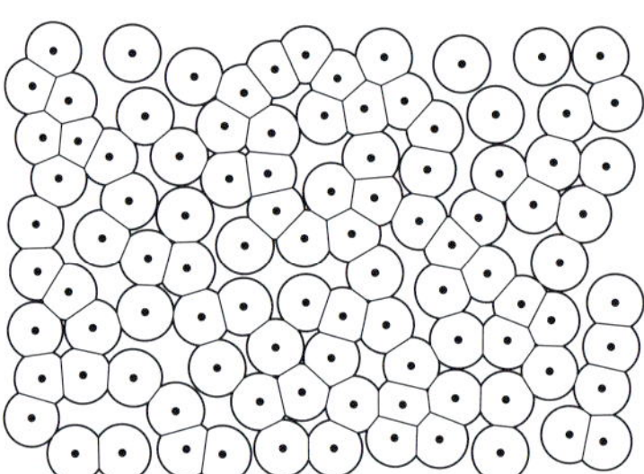

Maximum Radii: The appearance of soap bubble clusters can be created by setting a cell's maximum radii.

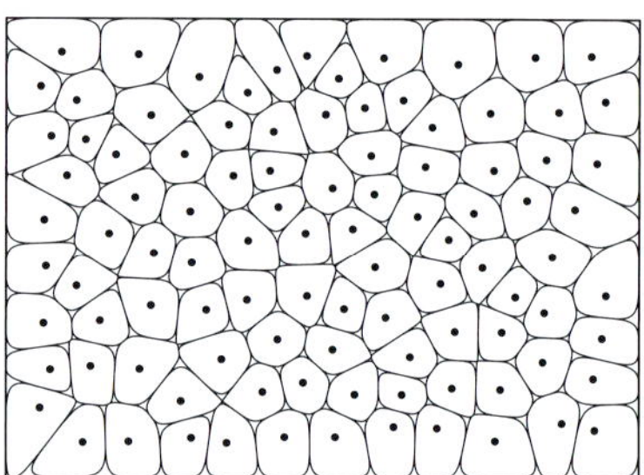

Polyline to Curve: Filleting the cell corners can make cells appear more compressed with physics simulation.

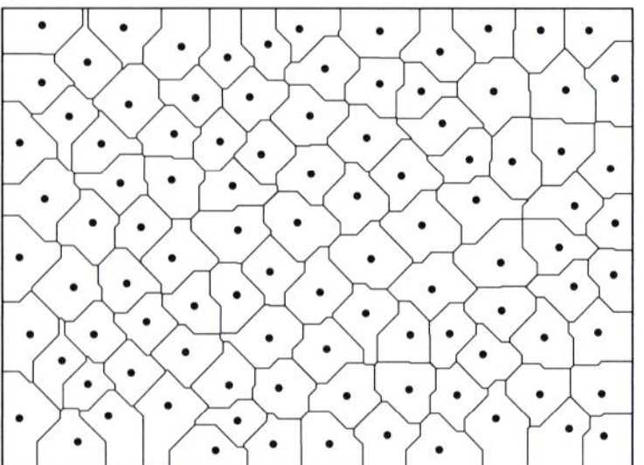

Manhattan Voronoi: The edges of cells can be forced to follow an underlying grid (hence the "Manhatten" name).

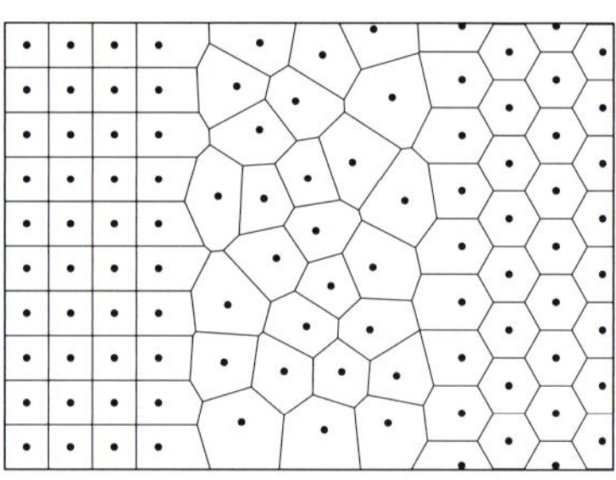

Square to Hexagon Transition: A square or hexagonal set of points leads to square and hexagonal cells.

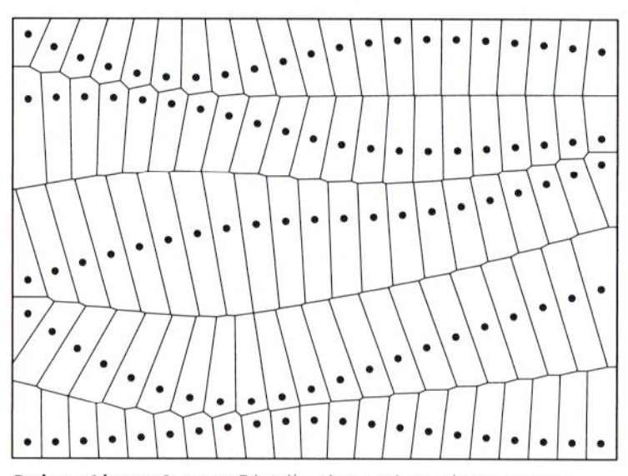

Points Along Curve: Distributing points along curves produces a pattern similar to a dragonfly's wing.

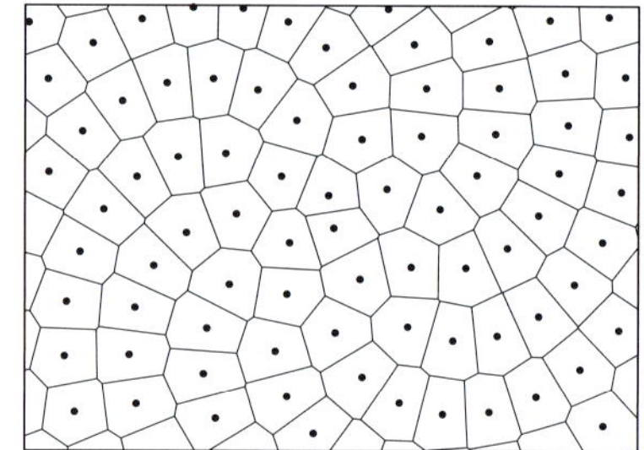

Spiral Phyllotaxis: Many plants and seeds use this spiraling or helical growth pattern.

Generative Process Little Island

Little Island navigates the spectrum between expensive mass customization and inexpensive repetitive uniformity through three different cellular systems. At the center of the site, below the largely flat central plaza, lies a rectangular grid of traditional concrete piers. Surrounding this standardized core is a ring of custom, but modular Cairo pentagonal columns. As these columns meet the site's boundary, more unique and irregular columns are used to mask the regularity of the interior. The diagrams below abstract this ito only two groups: a regular interior grid and an irregular Voronoi exterior grid.

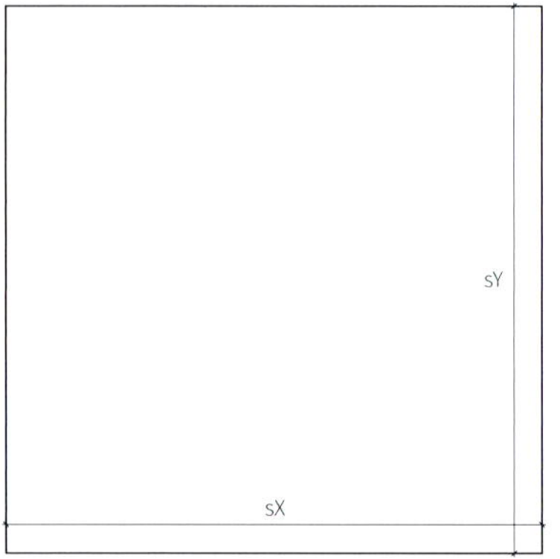

1. Create a rectangular site boundary with dimensions sX and sY.

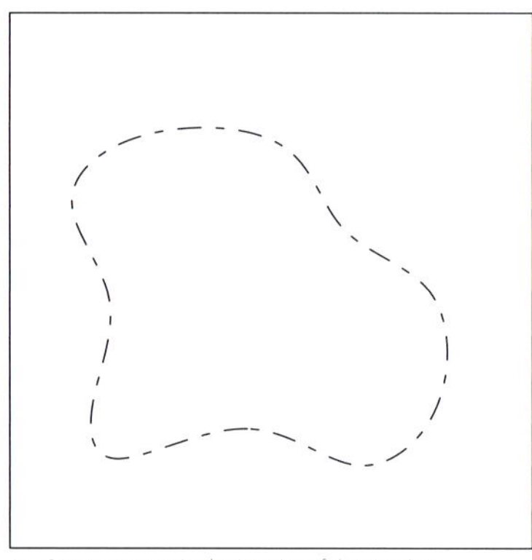

2. Create a curve in the interior of the site that represents the uniform grid zone.

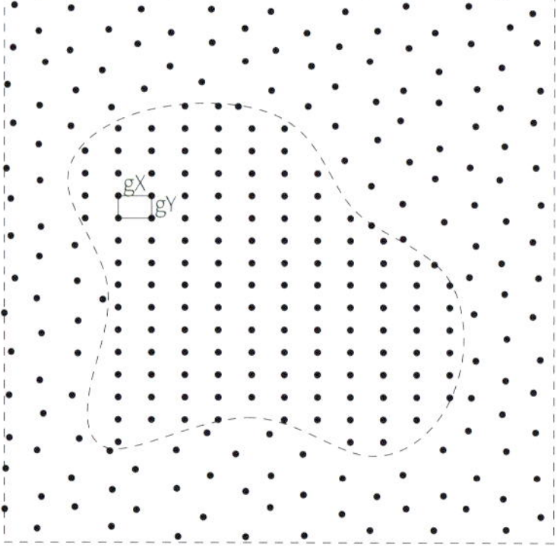

3. Populate the uniform and nonuniform zones with points.

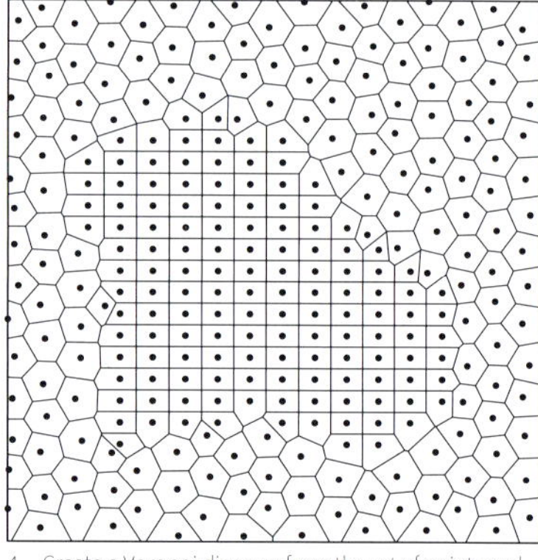

4. Create a Voronoi diagram from the set of points and the site boundary.

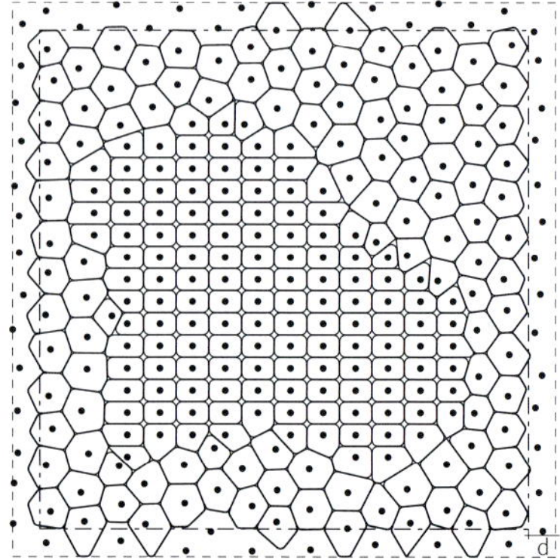

5. Cull any cells whose centers are within the distance (d) of the site boundary.

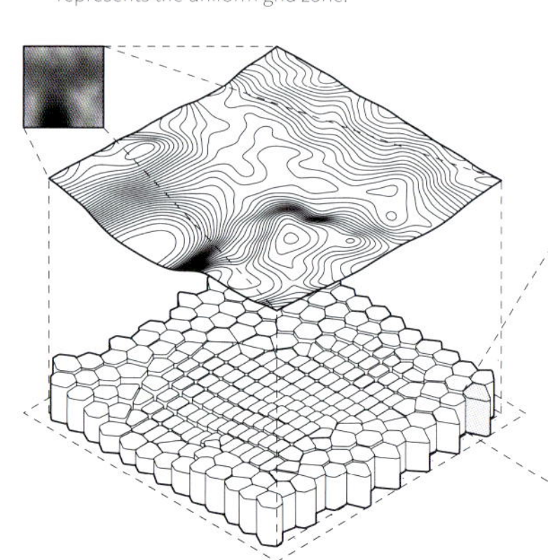

6. Using a heightfield image (i) that represents the desired topography, move the cell curves to their appropriate heights.

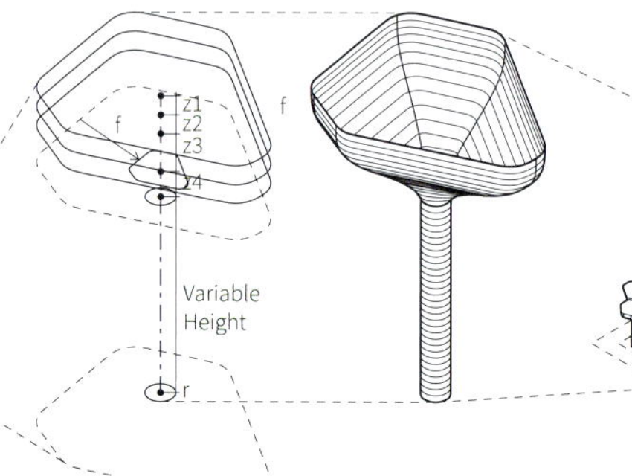

7. Scale and move a series of curves to create the source curves for the column loft.

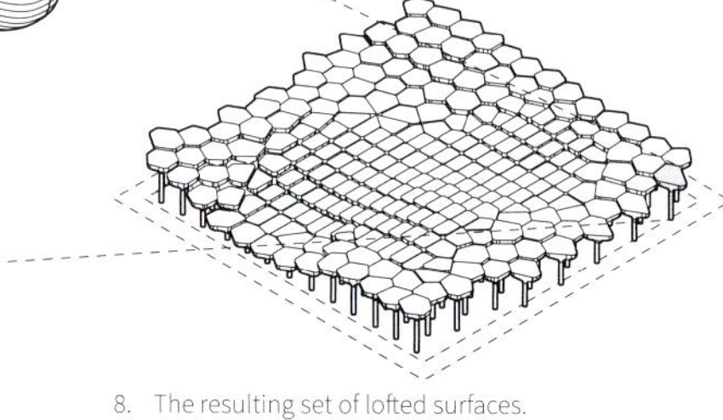

8. The resulting set of lofted surfaces.

Generative Matrix

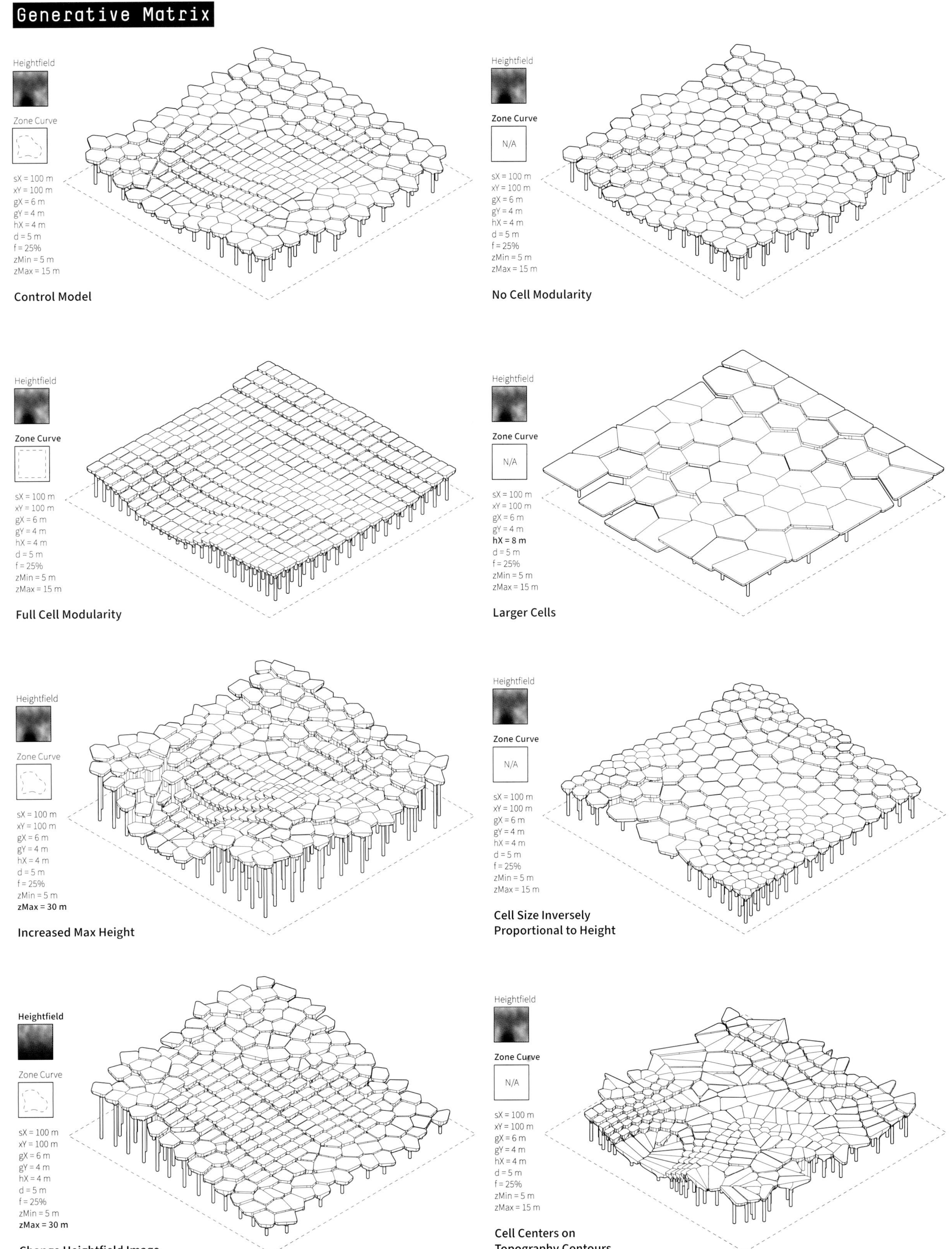

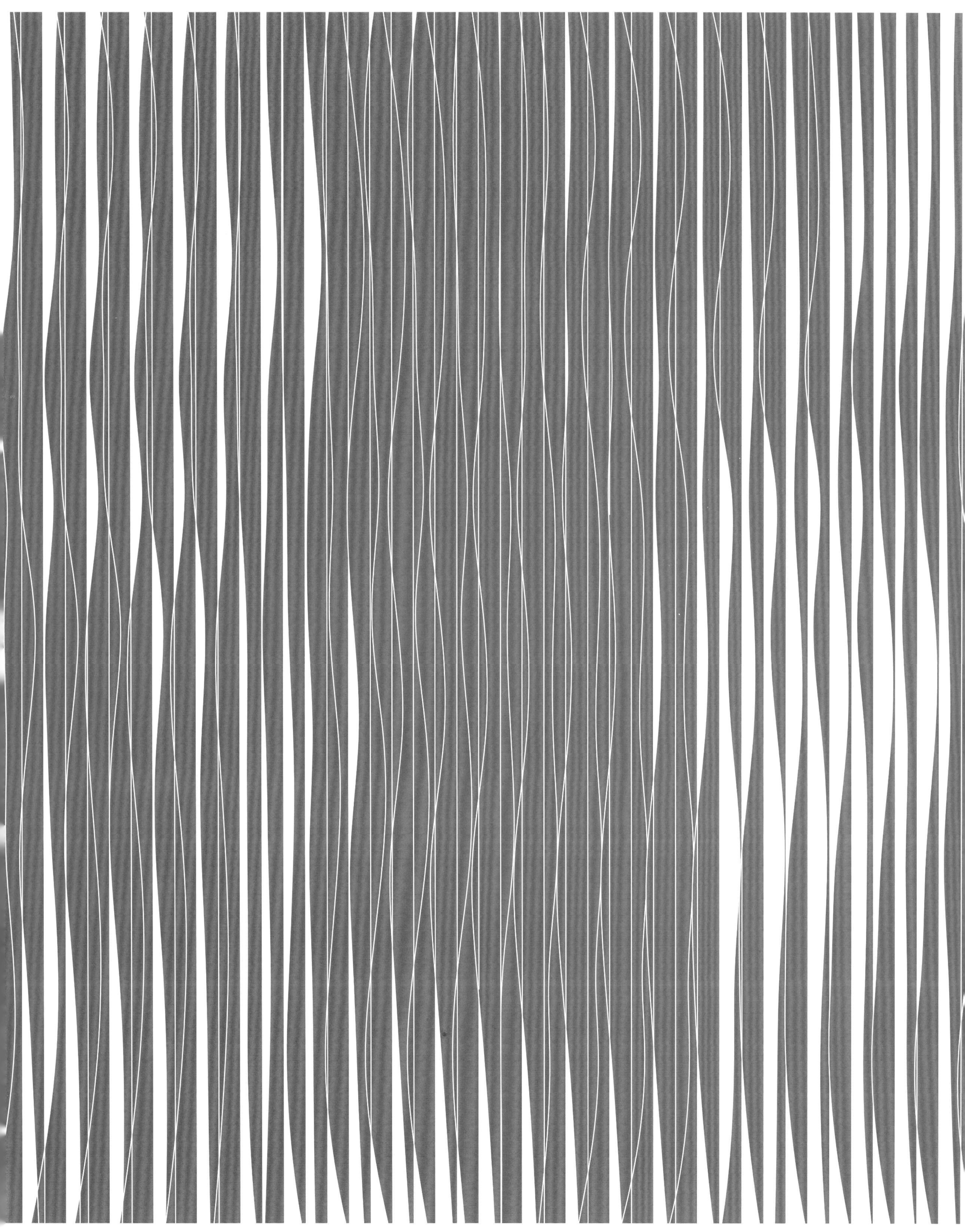

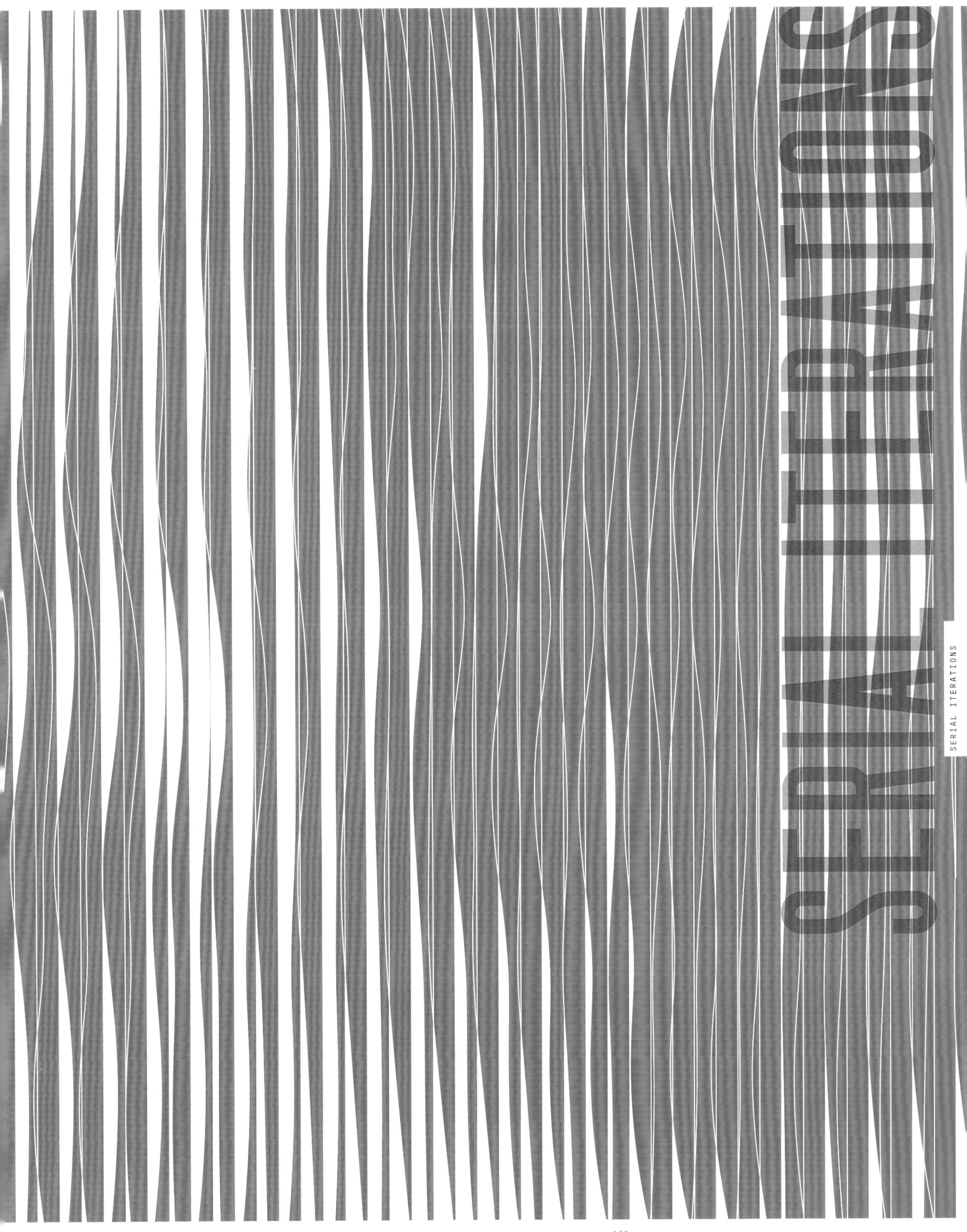
SERIAL ITERATIONS

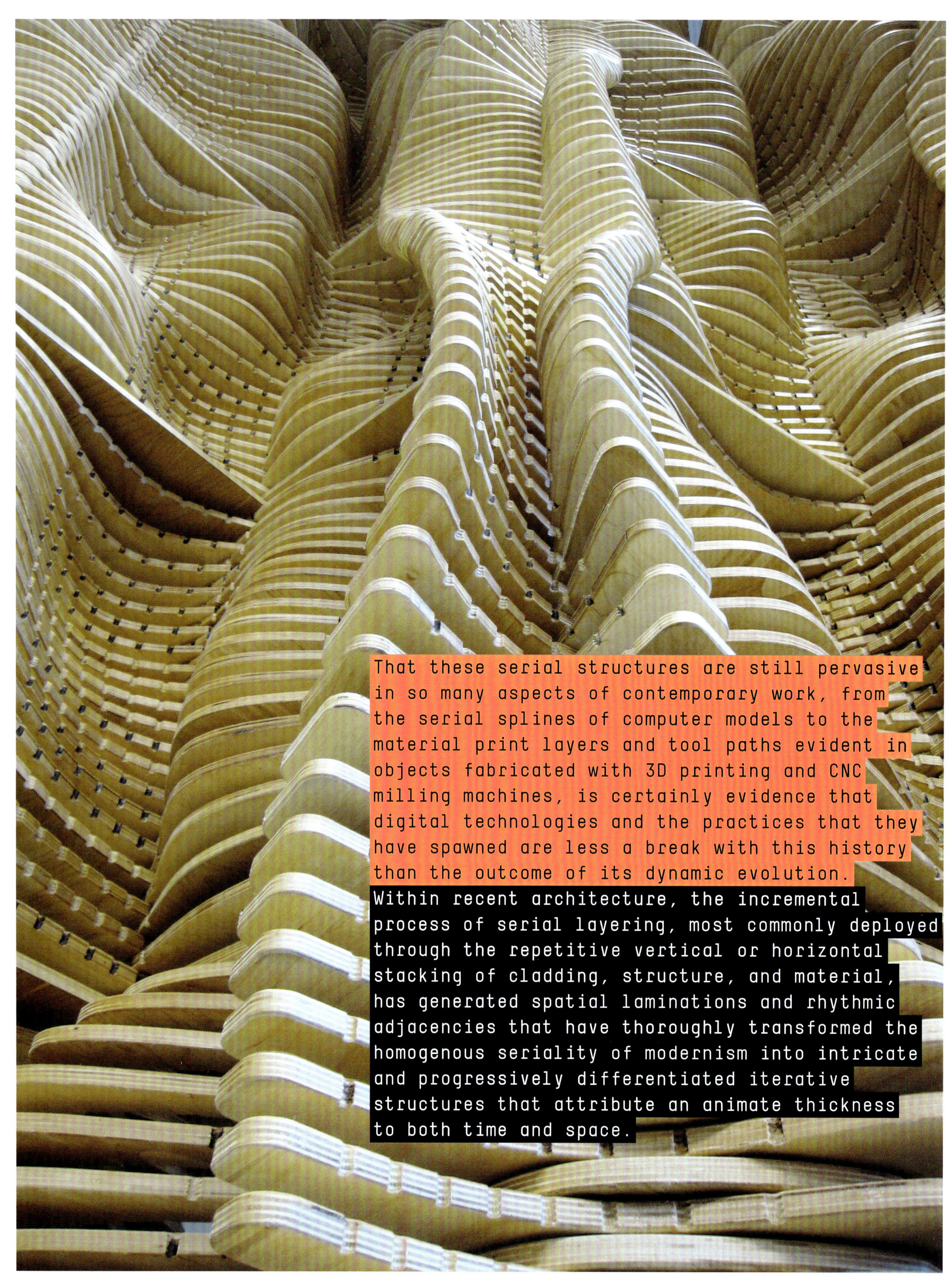

That these serial structures are still pervasive in so many aspects of contemporary work, from the serial splines of computer models to the material print layers and tool paths evident in objects fabricated with 3D printing and CNC milling machines, is certainly evidence that digital technologies and the practices that they have spawned are less a break with this history than the outcome of its dynamic evolution.

Within recent architecture, the incremental process of serial layering, most commonly deployed through the repetitive vertical or horizontal stacking of cladding, structure, and material, has generated spatial laminations and rhythmic adjacencies that have thoroughly transformed the homogenous seriality of modernism into intricate and progressively differentiated iterative structures that attribute an animate thickness to both time and space.

Serial Iterations

Continuous Differentiation and the Micro-Interval

Serial repetition was perhaps one of the most dominant models of modern thought. Distinct from the fixed boundaries and centered axial symmetries of Euclidean solids, the gridded repetitive structures of Cartesianism engendered a new mechanistic and cinematic world based on the idea that both space and time were homogeneous and infinitely extensive and could be framed and divided ad infinitum into an endless series of intervals. This concept unraveled the cyclical closure and ideality of classicism while projecting modernism toward an irreversible future. That serial structures are still pervasive in so many aspects of contemporary work, from the serial splines of computer models to the tool paths and print layers evident in objects fabricated with CNC millers and 3D printers, is evidence that these technologies and the practices that they have spawned are less a break with this history than the outcome of its dynamic evolution.

Within recent architecture, the incremental process of serial layering, most commonly deployed through the repetitive vertical or horizontal stacking of cladding, structure, and material, has generated spatial laminations and rhythmic adjacencies that have thoroughly transformed the homogenous seriality of modernism into intricate and progressively differentiated iterative structures that attribute an animate thickness to both time and space. Like the geomorphic layering of sediment in the natural landscape, these strata fill the spatial interval rather than framing it, just as the stacking of successive horizontal planes in the making of a topographical contour model are employed to fill, rather than frame, the interval of the site. In the filling of landscape rather than the framing of architecture, the intensive layering of material refers back to the micro-scales of matter. These layers index multiple and incremental changes, rather than singular moves, and reveal variation across the whole through the rhythmic distribution of difference.

In the Signal Boxes by Herzog & de Meuron, serial iteration is expressed in the incremental repetition, continuity, and progressive differentiation of the banded cladding, which renders the skin, rather than the space it encloses, dominant. These buildings are relatively simple orthogonal objects wrapped with eight-inch-wide copper strips that serve to protect the electronic equipment housed within from external electromagnetic fields on site while simultaneously referencing the form, scale, and color of the adjacent linear field of railway tracks ❶. There is obviously no architectural face to each of these buildings, not only because they lack the figuration and hierarchy of a façade but also because each architectural body is sheathed within a continuous striped armor that remains unbroken as it wraps and blurs the corners of the building, while masking the framed openings hidden behind the monolithic consistency of its serial skin. The repetitive bands of copper are perceived as a field of parallel horizontal lines that fill the plane and populate its surface, while also acting as a fine-grained perceptual metric that registers local differentiations as singularities emerging from within the field.

Intensifying the animation of the envelope, the attenuation and topological continuity of these copper-coiled bands perceptually amplifies the presence and directionality of the building surface while suppressing the boundary condition of the object and the geometry of the architectural frame. This privileging of directionality over dimensionality, topology over geometry, and surface over structure is supported in these works by critical local details that ensure that continuity remains dominant throughout. This is expressed in the repetitive serial structure and vertical overlapping of the layered bands, the folded detail of their bottom edges, the subtle curvature they produce in plan as they wrap the corners, and their continuous deformation in section as they twist along their lengths and rotate upwards to progressively open the cladding to light and air. These subtle inflections, whose local deformations thicken and animate the skin as it folds in and out of the plane—a strategy repeated yet ingeniously revitalized in the Lafayette 148 Global Headquarters—produce a rhythmic gradient across the surface that, like gills, enables the skin to breathe.

In the early part of the twentieth century, the futurist paintings of Umberto Boccioni and Giacomo Balla ❷ intended to capture the frenetic activity of metropolitan life through serial repetition, just as the photographic explorations of Eadweard Muybridge, Étienne-Jules Marey, and Harold Edgerton ❸ attempted to index the animate through the spatial unfolding of the cinematic series and the layered superimposition of its

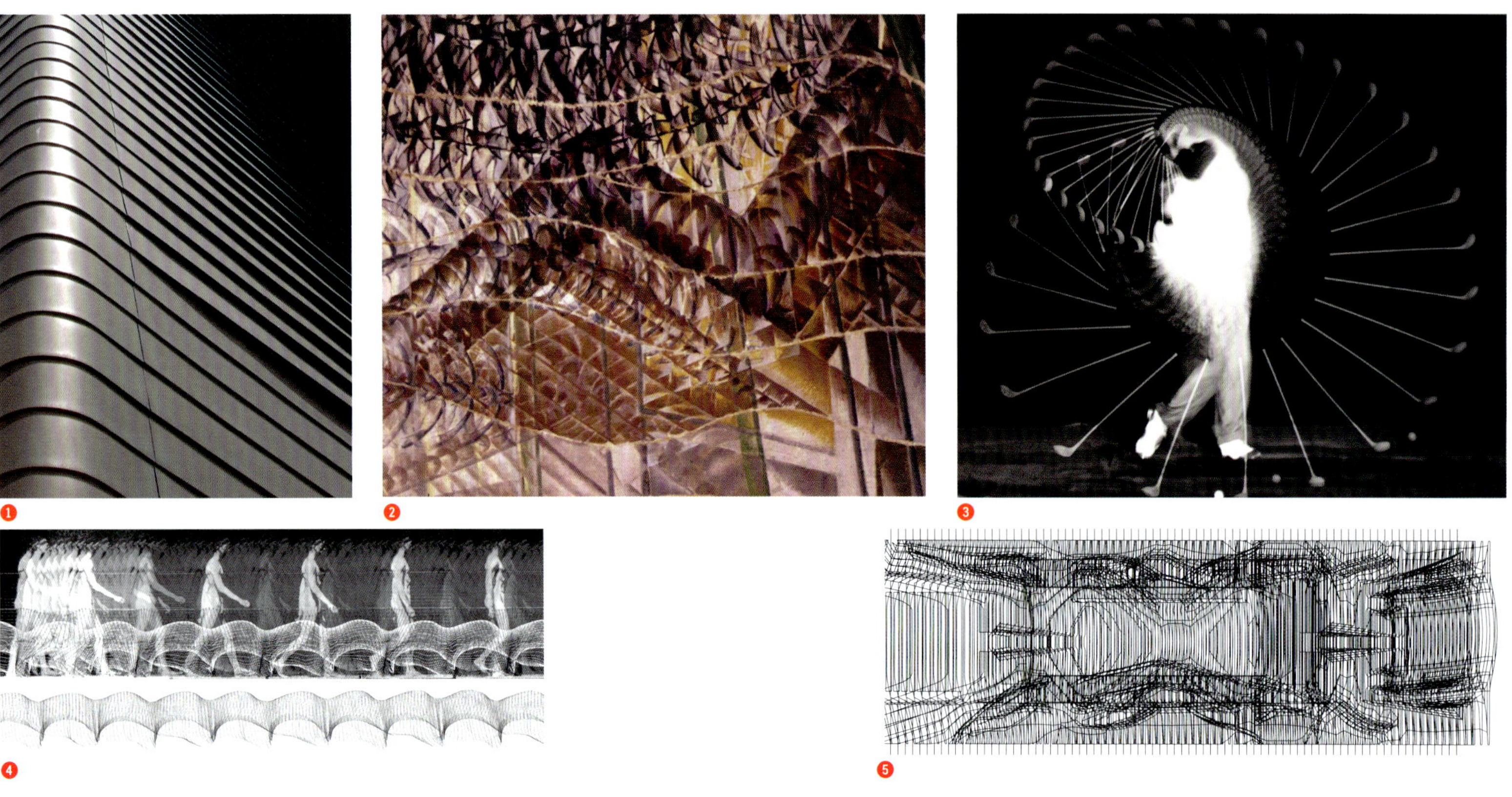

individuated frames. The cinematic and indexical capturing of motion in form registers incremental changes across the whole by synchronically revealing and spatializing a multiplicity of traces that each represent distinct instantaneous moments in a sequential and transformational series ❹. Their spatial juxtaposition furnishes an analytical reading of continuous material movement, while providing the perception of change as a process of progressive differentiation.[1]

Architectural projects dominated by seriality might be most closely aligned with the parameters of the cinematic shot, where repetition, as it is applied to an architectural frame, section, contour or interval, is the ordering device that enables the perceptual registration of difference within a continuous whole. A shot is a sequence of frames that contain multiple contiguous images that follow each other in space and time. In film, these frames are logically continuous because of the automated continuity of the filmic apparatus as the camera moves along a particular linear path through space (just as in architecture the continuity of serial sections refers back to the continuity of volume that is sliced) and simultaneously, also discontinuous because of the mechanical selectivity of the device as it extracts a limited set of "immobile sections" from the durational continuity of the real.[2] Bergson refers to this as the cinematographical tendency of perception and thought, which substitutes for the continuity of evolutionary change a series of juxtaposed unchangeable forms—perceptual frames—that follow each other in turn.[3] As the movement of the living behind the camera is selectively framed and rarefied, it is revealed through the progressive differentiation of individuated, yet successive sections dependent on the variability of the camera's movement along a specific trajectory.

Each of these immobile sections marks a singular state or threshold within the series, that can, like any contour or set of points, be conjoined with its adjacent sections in order to create the connective tissue between figures that generate a continuous morphology. In the boatbuilding and aeronautical industries, this method, traditionally referred to as lofting, enables the generation of doubly curved surfaces by connecting structural sectional profiles using continuous sheets of surface cladding. The process of lofting is what determines the shape of the surface's curvature when a series of profiles are aggregated and then connected to produce an uninterrupted surface. In architecture this is historically exemplified in the hidden structure of the roof of the Ronchamp Chapel by Le Corbusier, and in more contemporary projects, such as the Waterloo Terminal building by Grimshaw Architects, in the conjoining of progressively differentiated sectional trusses—both laterally in the making of the truss and longitudinally in the development of the entire roof. In film, however, a medium that is temporally extended although spatially compressed, it is our own perceptual apparatus that produces this continuity, which results from, yet conceals, the incremental sectional structure of the serial shot. This continuity is a product of our capacity to perceive multiplicitous wholes from incremental parts when an intrinsic formal relationship exists between their profiles, on the one hand, and when the difference between profiles and micro-scale of the temporal or spatial intervals that separate them are small enough to escape perceptual detection on the other. As the quantity and proximity of immobile sections is increased in both space a time, these aggregated serial sections transform from frame to fill as they approach the mobility and mutability of matter.

In the development of digital models of space, the serial sectioning of complex surfaces and volumes is what initially allowed for the overlay of Cartesian and topological models, by ensuring that these could be visually articulated through linear and planar systems that reference the longstanding planimetric and sectional artifacts of the history of architectural drawing and construction. Yet, where traditionally the plan and section were understood to be originary orthographic planes of projection—singular "privileged instants"—that preceded the making of architecture, the emergence of the serial section marked a critical shift in design practice.[4] As an inversion of traditional processes now enabled by the tools of modeling software, sectioning is used a posteriori as a method to instantaneously extract a successive series of parallel two dimensional slices from the surface geometry of any digitally modeled spatial form, such as was evident in the highly animated sectional drawings and models of the Yokahama Port Terminal project by FOA. ❺ This is done by prescribing in advance the orientation

6

8

9

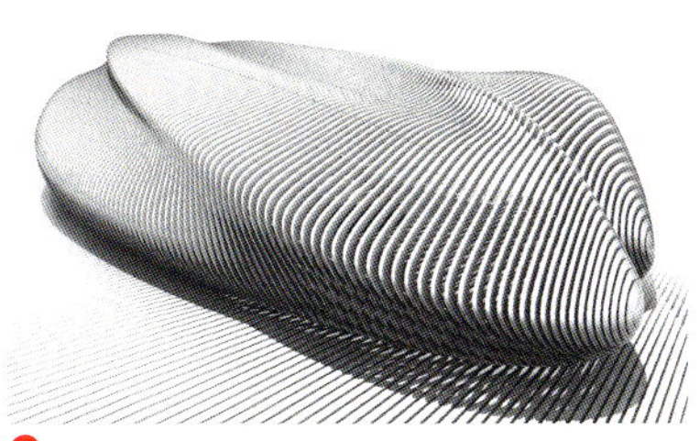
7

of the sectioning plane and either the measurement of the interval between sections or the quantity of sections to be cut within a limited dimension. Used as a descriptive rather than projective device, it has become either a method to incrementalize and therefore planimetrically or sectionally describe the spatial complexity of curvilinear surfaces and volumes (whose very spatiality renders them irreducible to orthographic projection) or, more importantly, a strategy to directly translate these spatial forms into a constructive logic by exploiting, reconfiguring, and redeploying existing industrial sheet materials—the planar residue of modernism—in an effort to generate a new landscape of artifice and matter.

Modernist models that highlighted the concept of seriality, evidenced in everything from the curtain walls of Mies van der Rohe's skyscrapers to the Tiller Girls in Berlin, invoked it as a symbol of the regulated, mechanistic, and repetitive processes and products of industrial production and the infinite divisibility of Cartesian space.[5] Yet, if the modern concept of seriality demanded the simple repetition of an unchanging element and interval deployed along a single straight axis thereby signifying the technologies from which it was derived, more recent projects grounded in serial iteration propose a variable sequence and rhythm of repetitive elements organized along a continuous, yet often spatially complex trajectory that reflects the evolution of these technologies in computationally driven practices. One Main 6 and the Galerie Miran 7 by dECOi and the *banq* design by Office dA 8 illustrate the progressive differentiation of the repetitive section as it is projected along a straight axis, a series enabled by the potential of digital design technologies to mass-customize a set of variable sections initially extracted from a single curvilinear surface. *Rip Curl Canyon* by Ball-Nogues studio 9 expands upon this process by introducing variations in the trajectory of the series along which these sections are deployed. Here, approximately 20,000 individual modular sections were die-cut from planar corrugated cardboard sheets and then horizontally laminated together and assembled into five undulating linear surfaces intended to emulate the twisted, rolling, and cavernous terrain of the American West. Each of the five landscape-like ribbons of laminated cardboard follows a curvilinear vector in space that directs the incremental yet continuous vertical offsetting of sections in relation to each other and combines this with their progressive rotation. Rather than generating difference through the uniquely contoured edge of each individual cardboard section, this project maintains a reduced set of four modular sectional types and instead exploits the increased variation of the trajectory in combination with both the quantitative repetition of the module and the differentiation already embedded in the curvature of a single section to introduce double curvature into the whole.

This solid yet fluid synthetic landscape is additively aggregated out of a limited set of profiles and cut from existing ready-made dimensional sheets of mass-produced materials. Yet rather than signifying the striated systems from which these emerged, the innovation of the project is in its capacity to find the geometric limits of these systems by intensifying the domain of their operation. Just as a continuous series of discrete points, if they are proximate and numerous enough, can be connected to produce a curved line in space, a set of discrete incremental axial translations and rotations, if they are individually small enough and collectively numerous enough, can also be aggregated to approximate what appears to be a spatial curvilinear path. It is not that the serial profiles of this project are actually deployed along a smooth spatial trajectory, but rather that the project uses other means to approximate this effect. In so doing, it exploits, if not the strategies, then certainly the hidden logics that are shared by both digital design technologies and the filmic apparatus.

Just as the striated Cartesian system that structures the bit-mapped digital field of the computer screen is hidden below the fluid intensity of its images, so too are the composite horizontal layers generated by rapid prototyping technologies rendered visually undetectable when embedded within the inflected topographical surfaces they produce. At relatively high resolutions, that is, when the scale of the structural plane of organization is extremely small in relation to the scale of the image or object it supports, the microscopic metric interval becomes an invisible matrix whose striated system is immediately contested by our experience of its smoothly articulated graphic and material products. The objective of this project, however, is not of course

10

11

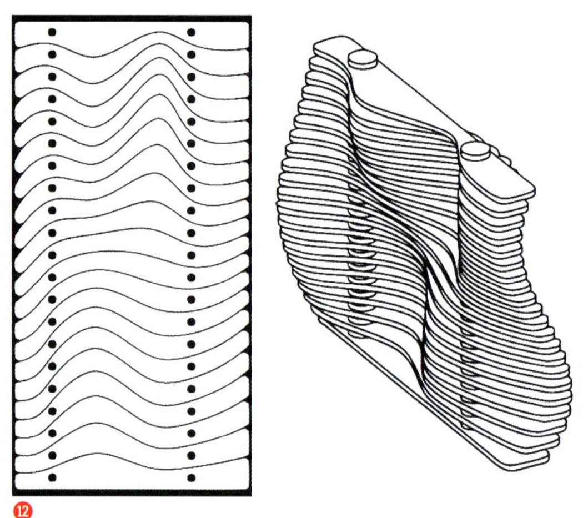

12

to simulate the fine-grain of a perfectly sculpted surface, but rather perhaps to problematize the issue of resolution within iterative serial systems by constructing an artifact that operates within the realms of both architecture and landscape that is simultaneously machinic and animate, dimensional and continuous, and part and whole. As the verticality and repetitive modularity of the architectonic section is countered by the horizontality and rhythmic continuity of the landscape it produces, so is the thinness of the surface (that functions concurrently as a ground, wall, and roof) contradicted by the thickness of the undulating topography and the density of its laminated material fill.

Although Henri Bergson had claimed that no matter how closely we bring together these instantaneous sections of matter, its events will always elude us (that is, they will still occur within the unrepresented interval),[6] there is a moment at which extreme forms of striation initiate qualitative perceptual fusions that are intrinsic to, and only manifest at, particular scales and/or speeds. Our interest here is in the ways in which striating machines have been placed in the service of smooth matters, not only in the representational methods that produce the intense sectional and spatial mappings of these projects, but more importantly in the generative processes and digital fabrication methods employed for their development. As a compelling example, for the *Inventioneering Architecture* installation, 10 DesignToProduction created a method to computationally script and digitally mill one thousand individually curved cross sections in the making of an abstract slice of Swiss topography. Employing a five-axis router, this was accomplished through the use of the "twisted cut." This is a technique that enables the milling tool to cut a double curvature out of planar MDF boards by rotating its axis in the third dimension while following the path of the two-dimensional, curvilinear contour defining the profile of each section in the series 11. The invention in this project is in its creation of a scripting technique that synthesizes these two distinct cutting paths, one in projection and the other in rotation, into a single variable trajectory, so that the continuity of the automated process of fabrication finds its correlate in the complex curvature of the resulting ruled surface of each segment. Once these segments are aggregated, the series generates a continuous, complex, curvilinear surface whose dimensionality is incrementally registered by the metric of parallel sections that define the rhythm and datum for the whole.

The capacity to exploit, and yet concurrently and strategically escape the limits of striation in the rhythmic iteration of serial structures, is exhibited most provocatively in the affective fluid surfaces of the Zero/Fold screen by Matsys 12. This is a wall prototype that transforms the limits of existing manufactured sheet goods in its quest for zero waste. When complex geometric shapes are cut from orthogonal planar sheets, the excess waste produced is necessarily a byproduct of the inability of these figures to be proximately packed when organized in the field, and their deviation from the rectilinear dimensions of the ground plane from which they are cut and extracted. Material waste is therefore often an unintentional consequence of the pursuit of formal complexity when derived from the redeployment of existing industrial products signifying the difference between the digital forms being fabricated and the logics of industrial production. This project, however, ingeniously addresses this issue by incorporating the dimensional and geometric parameters of the material stock into the generative design process. By collapsing figure and ground (and ensuring that the former fills the latter without remainder), the drawing surface and cutting plane are thereby synthesized into a single element that conflates the logics of design and fabrication. The complex curvilinear sections are thus inscribed into the plane from which they are to be extracted a priori, so that the negotiation between design and fabrication is reduced to the local mediation of lines traced upon this surface, and where seriality is intrinsic not only to the final prototype produced, but also to the configuration of the drawings that precede it. Here, every sectional cut is double-sided to intentionally generate the contoured face of two distinct, horizontally stacked components that are expressed in the double-sidedness of the wall. The transformation of the series occurs as a result of the progressive differentiation of the contours, both along the line of each curvilinear profile and between adjacent consecutive sections, to ensure that the implied surface continuity of the series (which reads as a limited swath cut from the flattened horizontal contours of a continuous landscape), is collapsed and

13

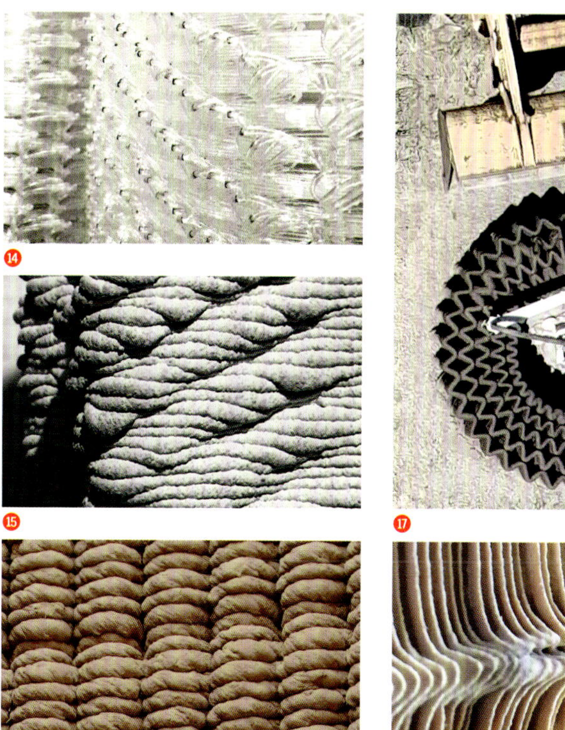

14 15 16 17 18

embedded into a single plane. These sections are then individually rotated by ninety degrees and stacked to produce segments of a double-sided vertical topography that is stabilized by the lateral weaving and interlocking of neighboring segments.

As a counter to Rip Curl Canyon's horizontal deployment of the unchanging unit along a variable trajectory, the Zero/Fold screen vertically stacks variable units along a simple trajectory, yet augments the complexity of this work by the attention paid to the progressive deformation of its contours, which are simultaneously animated both within the plane and along the edges of the serial stack.[7] The incremental vertical spacing of components by a dimension that closely approximates the depth of each section, emphasizes the fluid continuity of the wall's vertical surface, while enabling the weaving of the whole (13). This spacing allows for both the intertwining of stacked sections and the translucency of the screen, producing a moiré-like ,flickering rhythm along the surface that emerges from the resonance and intermodulation of the two patterned series as these converge within the thickness of the wall. These intersecting waves, which convert the overlay of intelligible ordering systems into the indistinct experience of the sensory pulse, create a rippling and undulating of the surface that attribute to the work a perceptual complexity that far exceeds the rationality of the parameters directing its development, transforming the machinic serial movements of individual components into the affective material vibration of the whole.

While the first generation of serial projects animated architecture by adding difference to repetition to produce variation, the next generation shifted the emphasis away from form to the inherent variability of material and its processes, amplifying the capacity for animation by exploiting the increasing complexity of evolving tools and the infinite degrees of information already encoded within matter. Adjusting the path, rhythm, and speed of material extrusion to exploit the micro-looping of bioplastic in the printing of the Strand Table (14), or the natural slumping of concrete in the making of the columns of Concrete Choreography (15), exposes and augments the serial layering of 3D printing once hidden behind the smoothness of the intricate volumetric forms it was able to produce. The material experimentation found in Casa Covida (16) and MUD Frontiers (17), which use natural, indigenous, and "wild" materials for ecologically compatible, full-scale, 3D-printed constructions, is thus complemented in the making of the Embodied Computation Lab at Princeton, which uses custom algorithms to detect, and CNC sand blasting to expose and make performative, the natural variable seriality already evident in the grain of wood, an index of the environmental history that animated the tree's growth and later, its decay (18). The layered repetition of the printing process in the one, or the industrially produced machined boards in the other, thus acts as a serial datum against which another entirely different form of life is exposed whereby traces inscribed within a thick surface structure reveal a "still life" of a once fully animate material world.

Notes

1. The embedding of time through the cinematic superimposition of frames as an implicit theme of modernism is discussed by Sigfried Giedion in *Space, Time, & Architecture* (1941) and *Mechanization Takes Command* (1948). It's elaboration and evolution in early digital modeling and fabrication, as well as its distinction from fluid material and morphological transformation, is discussed by Greg Lynn in *Animate Form* (New York: Princeton Architectural Press, 1999), 9–41.
2. The "immobile section" is a reference to Gilles Deleuze on Henri Bergson in *Cinema 1: The Movement-Image*, (Minneapolis: University of Minnesota Press 1991), 1.
3. Henri Bergson, *Creative Evolution*, trans. Arthur Mitchell (New York: Holt, 1911; Lanham, MD: University Press of America, 1983), 326. Although Bergson's critique is in relation to the difference between an immanent evolution that is embedded in duration and the discrete frames used to model it, the intention here is not to critique the accuracy of the method but to conceptualize serial sectioning as a creative operative device. See also Gilles Deleuze on Bergson in *Bergsonism*, trans. Hugh Tomlinson and Barbara Habberjam, (New York: Zone, 1988).
4. The concept of "privileged instants" is a reference to Bergson: "They are supposed, . . . to characterize a period of which they express the quintessence, all the rest of this period being filled by the passage, of no interest in itself, from one form to another form." (Ibid., 330–331).
5. On Kracauer, Hilberseimer, and the relationship between industrialization, seriality, and mass ornament see K. Michael Hays, *Modernism and the Posthumanist Subject* (Cambridge: MIT Press, 1995), 264–265.
6. "You cannot reconstitute movement with positions in space or instants in time: that is, with immobile sections. You can only achieve this reconstitution by adding to the positions, or to the instants, the abstract idea of a succession, of a time which is mechanical, homogeneous, universal and, identical for all movements. And thus you miss the movement in two ways. On the one hand, you can bring two instants or two positions together to infinity; but movement will always occur in the interval between the two, in other words behind your back. On the other hand, however much you divide and subdivide time, movement will always occur in a concrete duration; thus each movement will have its own qualitative duration." See Deleuze, *Cinema 1*, 1.
7. For a comparison of two distinct types of variability arising from the generic, see Reiser + Umemoto's *Atlas of Novel Tectonics* (New York: Princeton Architectural Press, 206), 52–53.

Figure credits

Fig. 4: Ila Berman, Bodyworks: Nomadic Body, *Bodyworks* exhibition, Contemporary Arts Center, New Orleans, 2001.

Waterloo International Terminal

Grimshaw Architects

Built 1994

London England

5.1a

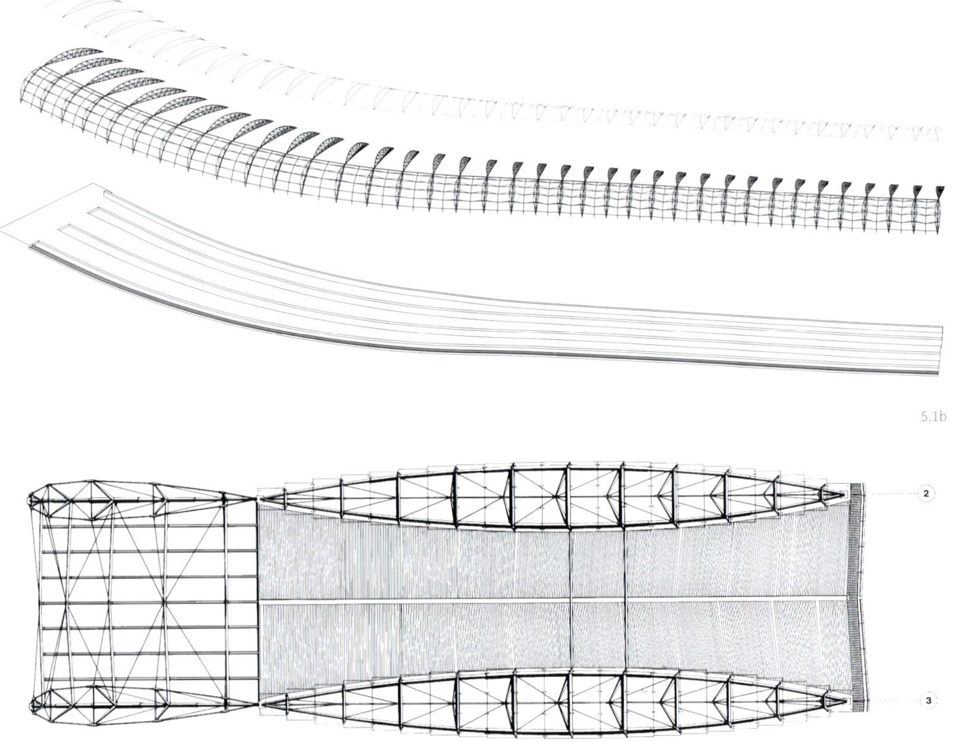

5.1b

5.1c

Designed to be a monument to the new age of transit heralded by the advent of cross-channel rail travel in Britain, the Waterloo International Terminal is a multifaceted transport interchange designed to support 15 million international rail passengers per year. The requirements of the program—which demanded a carefully calibrated choreography that included the security screening, immigration, and customs procedures typical of an international airport—in combination with the constraints of the urban site, demanded a highly streamlined building through which passengers could move quickly and efficiently. Located in central London adjacent to the existing national rail station, the site of the terminal was just wide enough to accommodate the necessary five tracks, being limited by electric rails on one side and the London Underground tunnels beneath. The project is primarily defined by the serial structure of its doubly curved roof, which incrementally varies in section along its 400 meter length. The asymmetrical form of the roof responds to the dictates of the site layout, specifically the westernmost track over which the roof must rise more steeply in order to accommodate the height of the trains. This western side is clad entirely in glass, with the structure of the roof clearly expressed. Facing onto the main access road, it provides arriving passengers with an impressive view of Westminster and the River Thames and passers-by with a panorama of the 400-meter-long Eurostar trains. Structurally, the roof takes the form of a flattened, three-pin, bow-string arch, with the center pin moved to one side (allowing for the undulation in height from west to east). It is a necessarily complex structure designed to a long, sinuous plan that narrows from 50 m at the concourse to 35 m at the platform end. The cladding system is accordingly flexible, with a limited range of variably sized sheets of glass placed in an overlapping con-figuration that can flex and expand in response to the roof's various twists and turns.

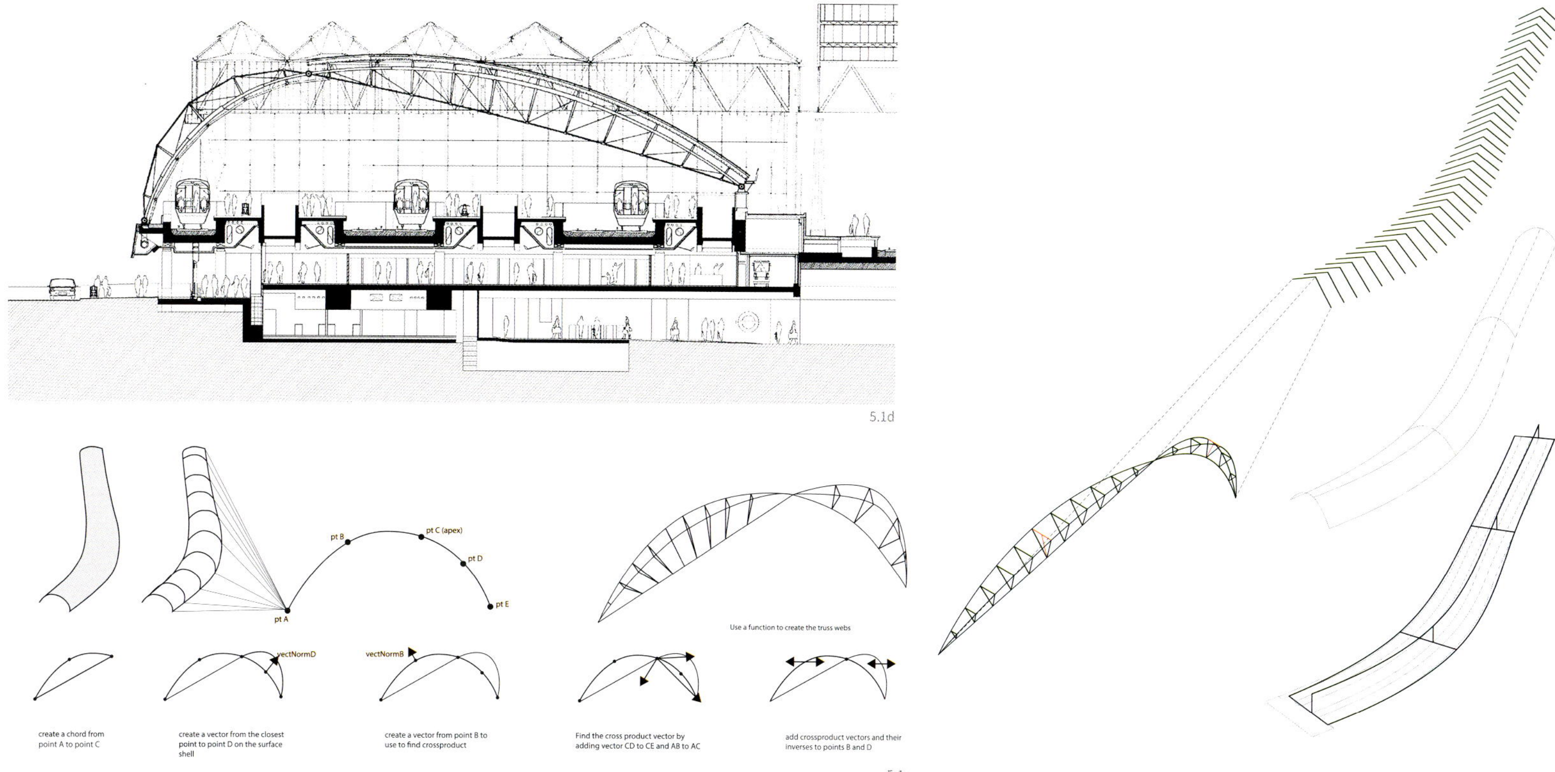

5.1d

5.1e

5.1f

5.1g

Ricola Storage
Herzog & de Meuron

Built 1986-1987
Laufen, Switzerland

The Ricola factory storage building in Laufen, which houses the company's Swiss herbal candies, is perceived as a singular and somewhat impermeable rectilinear monolith, clad in horizontally, serially stacked Eternit panels that appear to continuously wrap the building. This cladding is constituted by two primary linear planar elements generated from the same material. One of these is oriented vertically and acts as the building's cladding, and the other oriented horizontally as a louver protruding from the building. These two component types are repetitively stacked in an alternating pattern, the louvers giving sectional depth to the cladding while amplifying the serial rhythm of the skin as they cast shadows on panels below. The modulation of these shadows, the changing heights of the bands of cladding, which are larger at the top of the building than at the bottom, and the slight tilting of the vertical panels in section, which because of the changing gradient appear to splay to a greater degree as they approach the ground, generate the phenomenal experience of gravity, as if the building skin was being compressed by its own weight, an effect which at the corners also appears to split apart the enclosure. This insistent vertical stacking of horizontal layers of material and the seriality apparent not only in the banded cladding, but also in the repetition of exposed beams supporting the louvers that project from the façade, makes multiple visual and cultural references, not only to the stacking of palettes within the warehouse itself, and the traditional stacking of sawn timber boards around the many sawmills in the region, but also to the layering in the landscape and the adjacent geological quarry that forms its site. Seriality is used in this project to reveal not only the function of the building, which as a storage facility appears to store, in a stacked fashion, its own cladding components, but also to expose the implicit seriality intrinsic to the layering of elements in the process of construction itself.

5.2a

5.2b

5.2c

Signal Box
Herzog & de Meuron
Built 1989-1994
Basel, Switzerland

In its urban context, the Main Signal Box stands as a tower-like marker, entering into a relationship with the high-rise buildings of the surrounding district while, through its form and material detailing, referencing the rail site and its immediate environment. The building sits on a trapezoidal, almost triangular plot of land located between the railroad tracks and transforms from a trapezoid in plan to a rectangle moving vertically from the ground upward toward the roof of the building. An exterior skin of eight-inch-wide, horizontal, copper bands continuously wrap the building, concealing its framed edges and openings, while serving as a Faraday cage that protects the electronic equipment inside the signal box from the electromagnetic fields on the site. From the exterior, the horizontal continuity of the building's banded wrapper transforms the static solid of the building into a mutable geometry, so that its morphing shape is perceived as a direct response to its changing context—the position and organization of surrounding urban infrastructures and the competing movement of adjacent trains that crisscross the site. The repetitive serial banding of the cladding, which refers back, in both color and form, to the many parallel tracks inscribed across the site, attributes a cohesive consistency to the surface while acting as a datum that transforms incrementally in response to programmatic changes within the building. As these copper bands twist upward to become louvers, they express the location of fenestration behind the façade and momentarily open the envelope to light and air. Programmatic difference is thus responded to through the filter of an iterative architectural element that is simultaneously singular and multiple, regular and rhythmic. As individuated components, such as windows, are absorbed into this repetitive field of thickened lines, functional difference is visibly indexed through local variations that ripple across the skin.

5.3a

5.3b

5.3c

5.3d

Lafayette 148 Global Headquarters
Tsz Yan Ng + Mehrdad Hadighi of Studio for Architecture

Built 2008
Shantou, Guangdong, China

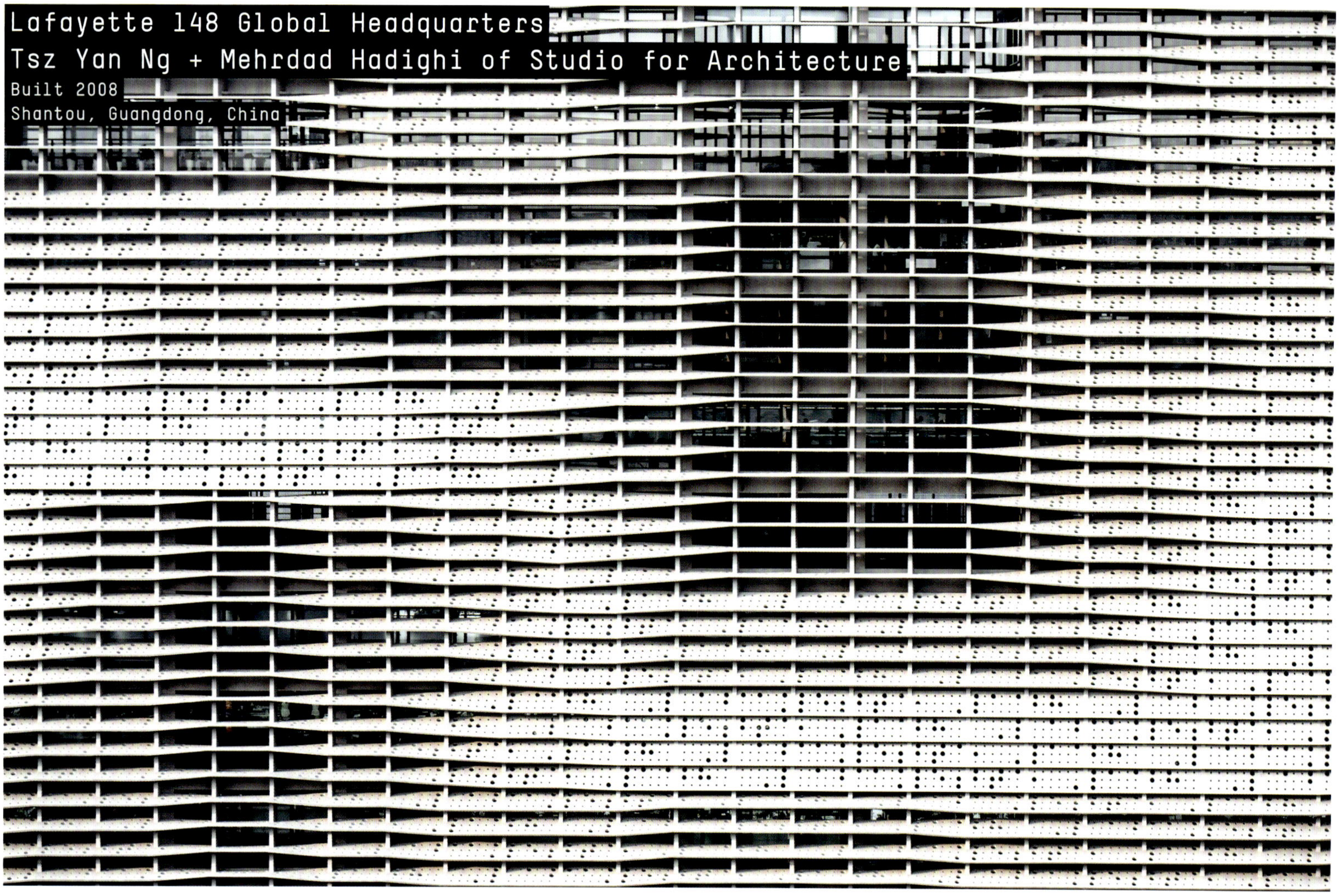

5.4a

Lafayette 148 Global Headquarters is an eleven-story, 226,257-square-foot building in Shantou, China, for a New York-based fashion label primarily supporting textile manufacturing and all the functions needed to support its clothing production. The program is stacked and stratified vertically with the factory levels sandwiched between nonmanufacturing spaces, the offices and design studios on the upper two levels, each stage of manufacturing and production located in the middle levels, and a double-height, ground-level showroom space that can be cleared out for runway shows off the entry space below. In addition, the building has been recognized for its concrete structure and highly innovative louvred cladding system. The need for an open, column-free space to support a wide range of functions is achieved with a post-tensioned structural system that provides an uninterrupted extended span. This unimpeded floor plate, combined with spaces carved out of the overall volume, allow light to penetrate deep within the building's interior, while creating a chimney effect that draws hot air out of the structure. Vertical circulation and other building amenities are organized in a service core located against the north façade, while the south façade, the highlight of the project, is a double-layered skin—an interior-glazed façade with operable windows that is enveloped in a sculptural, perforated, and twisted louvered skin. This engineered brise soleil fin structure operates like a continuous woven textile that wraps the south side (and part of the east and west sides) of the building, undulating in an orchestrated manner to selectively open the building to light and air while operating as an effective shading device to mitigate overheating and reduce energy consumption. These louvers, rather than being prefabricated, are poured-in-place concrete modules made with reusable formwork that take advantage of local skills and craftsmanship. Animating the façade with their synchronized movements at the scale of the architecture, these rippling serial fins reference the textiles and clothing being produced within the building that they so elegantly clad, while their patterned perforations, which somewhat clandestinely spell Lafayette 148 in braille, at another level of surface detail further articulate and enliven this so fashionable building skin.

5.4b

5.4c

5.4d

5.4e

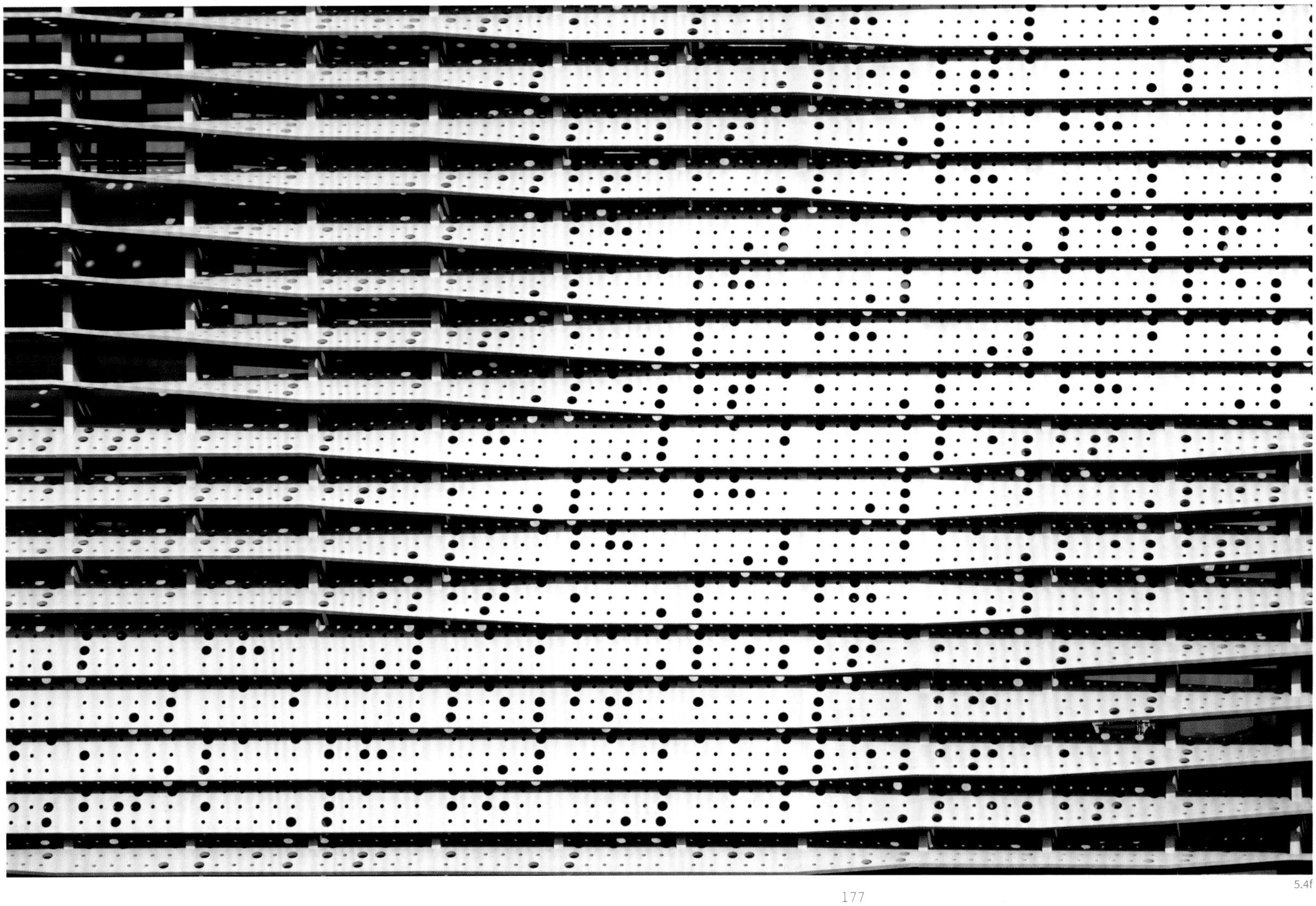

5.4f

Inventioneering Architecture
Designtoproduction and Instant Architects
Built 2005
Zurich, Switzerland

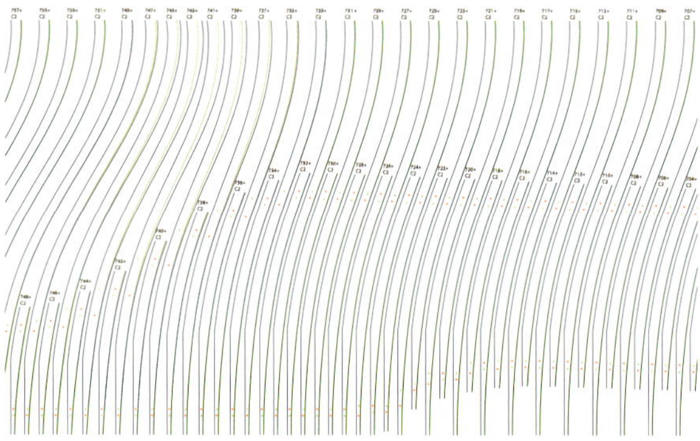
5.5a

5.5b

Inventioneering Architecture is a traveling exhibition on Swiss architecture that is mounted on a doubly curved platform resembling an abstract cross-sectional slice of the landscape in which these buildings are situated. A footpath meanders along the surface, crossing through and enabling access to the architectural models that float above it. The platform, which is three meters wide and 40 meters long, is divided into 1,000 individually curved cross-sections, each describing an incremental slice of the upper surface of the artificial topography. To generate a smooth rather than a stepped serial surface, designtoproduction employed the capabilities of a five-axis router and invented a method to simultaneously twist and cut each of the linear members of the landscape. The milling tool follows a linear path while rotating around it at the same time, thereby cutting a three-dimensional, doubly-curved, "ruled surface" out of two-dimensional sheet material that not only follows the topography of the platform both along and across the section, but also does this at a very low cost. The milled rafters are then connected by dowels and supported by perpendicular boards. One of the challenges of the project was to automate the translation of the overall geometry into the geometry of component parts and to transcode this into a steering script for the computer-controlled milling tool. This was accomplished by a serial set of scripts. The first script imports the original design defined as a NURBS surface into the modeling software Maya, reads the coordinates of each cross-sectional rafter constituting the platform's surface and determines the angles of its bank. A second script translates this information into the milling paths for all 1,000 rafters and also includes all drilling required for the dowels. A third script arranges and optimizes the rafters on the MDF boards and generates the G Code, which is the program controlling the five-axis CNC router. The entire surface, which used 120-by-4.2 meter boards, was thereby milled in fifty hours through an uninterrupted automated fabrication process that included detailing, optimized nesting, and the generation of machine code.

5.5c

Henderson Wave Bridge
IJP Corporation + AKT

Built 2004–2008
Southern Ridges, Singapore

5.6a

5.6b

5.6c

Springing from Mount Faber, the Henderson Wave is a pedestrian bridge spanning 36 meters above a six-lane freeway on the southern coast of Singapore. This location maximizes the visual impact of the structure over the gorge, while minimizing its length. The bridge, which was designed using a single proprietary set of parametric equations developed by IJP, is based on a sectional series of steel-framing elements that define a folded and undulating three-dimensional surface. This surface, which appears in elevation as a rolling sine curve of variable amplitudes, ascends and descends by 21 meters while remaining continuous in its form. The bridge is 284 meters in length and consists of seven contiguous arched segments—four curving above and three curving below the walkway—that trace the rhythmic heaving movements of the wave. Although the 1,500 m^2 timber deck that forms the primary walking surface of the bridge remains relatively flat to support pedestrians and cyclists (sloping upward as it moves from one end of the bridge to the other), at one of its outer edges the surface radically transforms. Here, it billows out and folds up and over the decking in order to enfold within itself sheltered niches for lounging and other temporary programmatic activities. From this side, the surface swells up like a wave and then descends again, offering dramatic scenic views for its occupants as it intersects with itself and plunges below the deck (an area that is physically inaccessible yet ensures the continuity of the structure). From the opposite side, the walkway forms a longitudinal datum—a horizontal centerline—against which the undulating wave is visually registered. The serial structure that defines this complex, doubly-curved surface is partially sheathed in a tapestry of 5,000 modular boards made of tropical hardwood, each incrementally varying by a single degree every 10 m, many of which are tapered to measure.

Rip Curl Canyon
Ball-Nogues Studio

Built 2006

Houston, United States

5.7a

5.7b

5.7c

Rip Curl Canyon is an installation developed for the Museum of Fine Arts in Houston as part of the exhibition *The Modern West: American Landscape, 1890–1950*. The installation is a formation of thick, landscape-like bands, which undulate through the space and converge at the back of the gallery, resembling the geological movements resulting from the earth's seismic activity as it shapes and molds the terrain. From its highest point, the installation's steep, crevice-like formations slope down and gain momentum before breaking apart to form ribbons of curling waves. Like rip currents—narrow, fast-moving belts of water—these segments twist and surge toward the front glass entry wall. The view through the glass provides only glimpses of the unfolding topography beyond and invites visitors to probe deeper, enticing them to climb onto, and walk upon, the installation and transform it into a traversable rolling playground. This eight-ton, twisting artificial landscape, which references a mythical location somewhere in the American West where land and water collide, is constructed out of 4,000 sheets of cardboard that are custom die cut into approximately 20,000 sectional contours. These differently shaped pieces are serially assembled and laminated into five larger wave-like ribbons that are then perched on top of a plywood structure. Each section is vertically offset and incrementally rotated in relation to its neighboring sections, in order to produce, through their serial aggregation, a doubly-curved, sculpted surface comprised of modular repetitive elements. In its assembly, the parts were held together by formwork, which was removed after lamination, enabling the relationship between cardboard sections to be shaped by a process akin to pouring concrete. Incredibly strong and capable of holding the weight of several people, these cardboard laminates operate as semi-monocoque shells needing only intermittent structural support from the plywood structure below. This wooden armature is made of 2-by-4 wood studs that were individually cut and CNC routered off site to conform to the varying dimensions and curvature of the undulating cardboard shells. A digitally developed language of slotting connections was also developed so that these nonstandard wooden parts could be assembled like a giant puzzle.

5.7d

SECTIONAL CURVE REPEATED ALONG SOURCE CURVE
SOURCE CURVE
SECTIONAL CURVE
ROTATIONAL CURVE
SURFACE

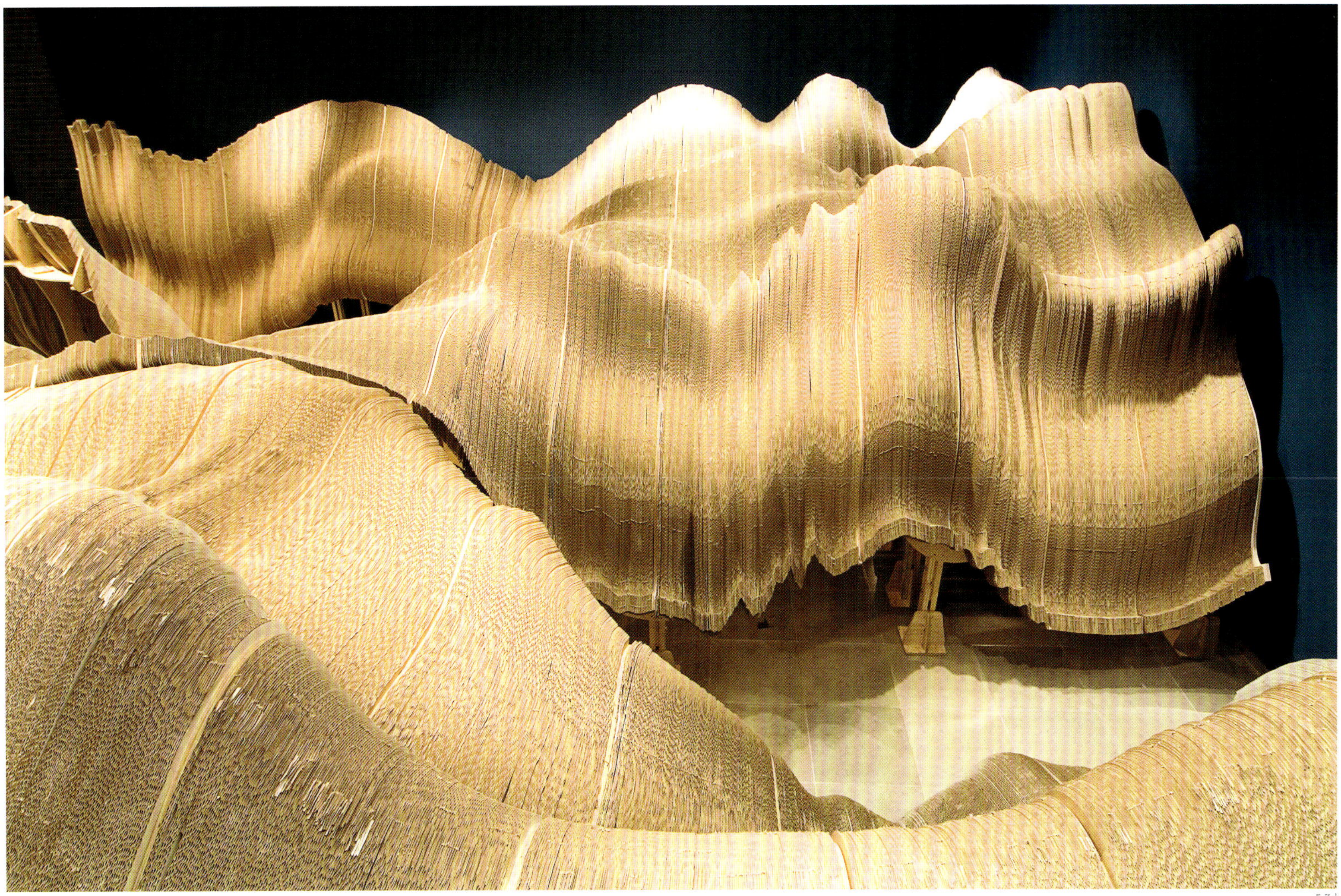

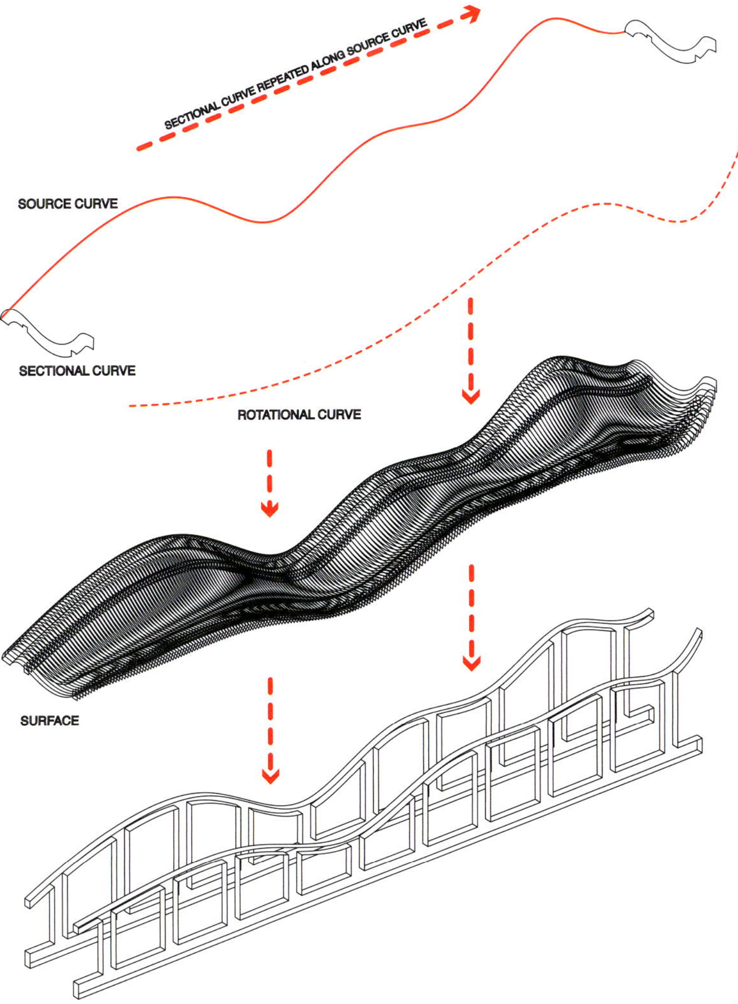

5.7e

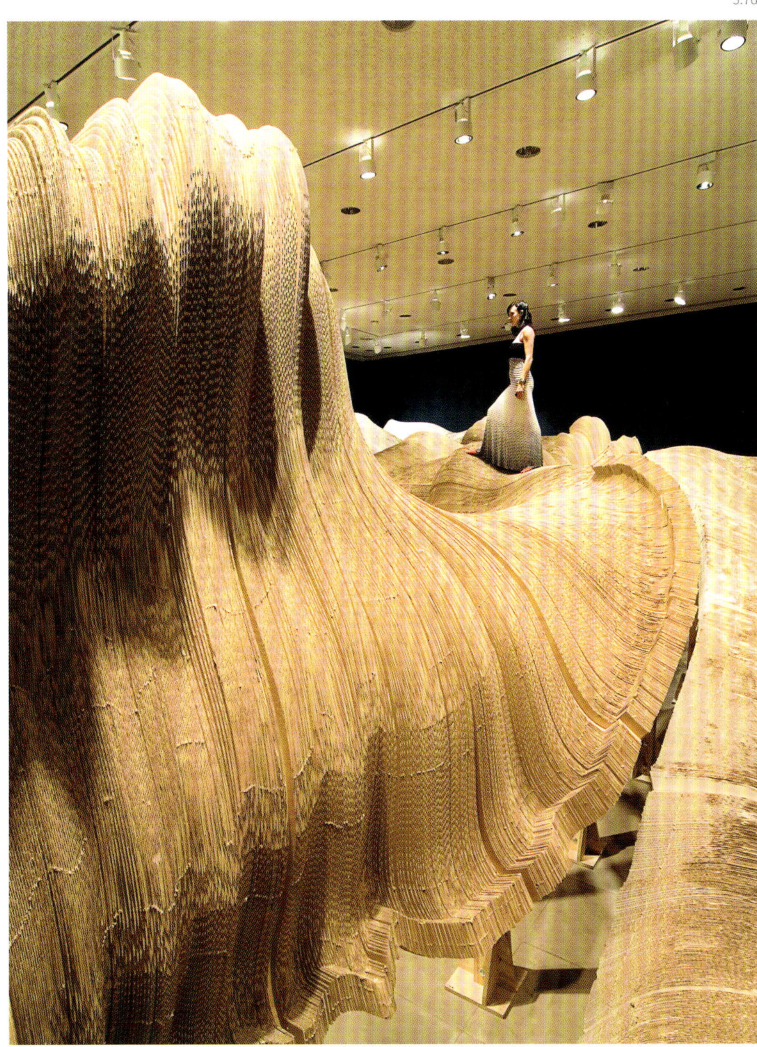

5.7f

FLUX Installation Armature

CCA mLAB

Built 2008

San Francisco, United States

5.8b

The FLUX installation is a serial iterative structure that explores the possibilities of parametric modeling and digital fabrication through the production of an exhibition armature. The piece is constituted by four white tubes that form a continuous linear installation whose undulating, twisting structure expands and contracts as its volume extends down the center of a long nave-like space. Each of these tubes is defined by a hexagonal cross-section and is made up of a repetitive series of approximately thirty vertical, structural, planar ribs made of ½-inch-thick, painted engineered fiberboard (MDF) that were individually cut using a digital CNC milling machine. These wooden ribs, each of which is slightly different in shape than its neighbor, form a continuous series of vertical sections that support an equal number of canted segments made of ⅛-inch-thick, sheets of white plastic—high-density polyethylene (HDPE)—that span between, and slot into, the ribs and support the exhibition. The hexagon cross-section, which is dominated by three elongated edges and therefore visually reads as being somewhat triangular in form, is parametrically controlled so that it incrementally rotates as its dimensions increase or decrease in length moving from one end of the modular tube to the other. The elongated edges are what define the horizontal base upon which the installation rests, and the two canted sides, which are positioned according to a spectrum of shifting angles, are oriented for the optimal viewing of the exhibition content. From the width of the ribs to the overall twisting geometry and perforated skins, the spatial form of the armature is controlled through a complex set of relationships defined by its formal, performative, and fabrication constraints. Each section in this series marks a singular state or threshold that is intrinsically and parametrically related to its adjacent sections so that the connective tissue between figures results in a continuous layered morphology whose rhythmic spatial laminations attribute an animate thickness to the work.

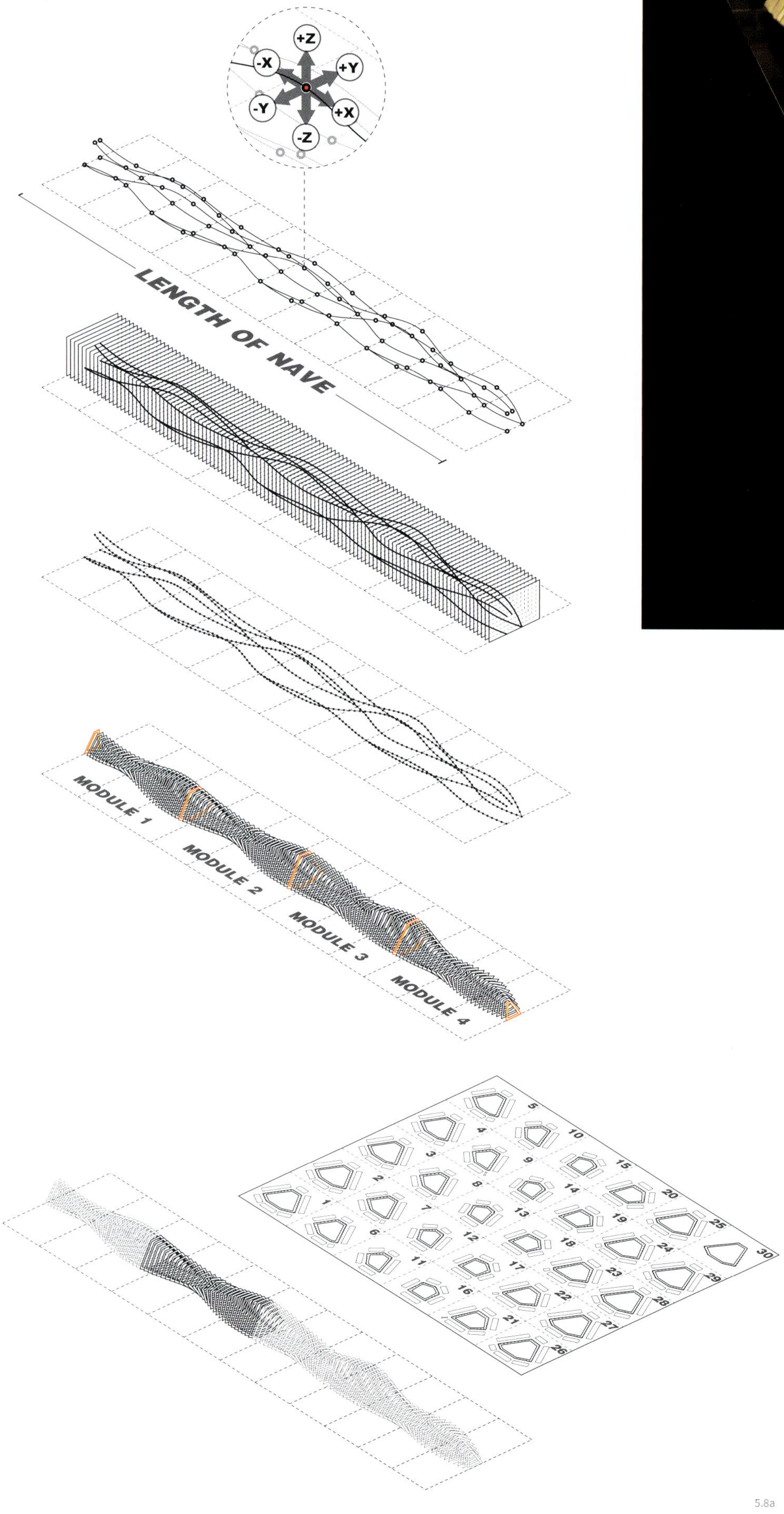

5.8a

5.8c

5.8d

5.8e

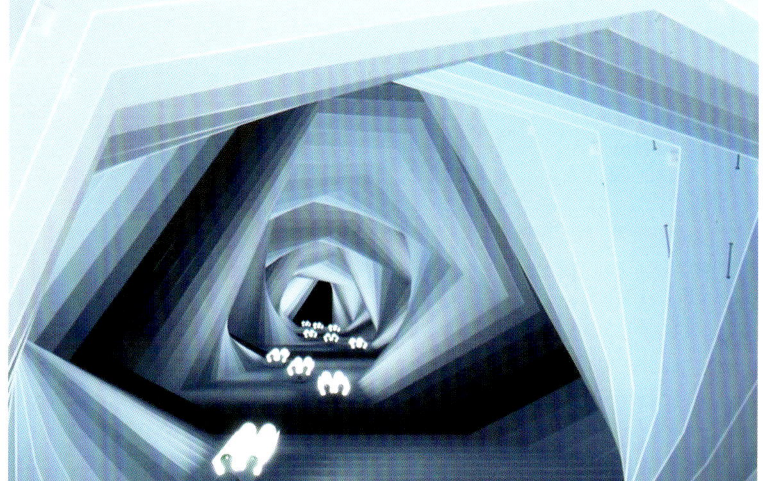

5.8f

Centennial Chromagraph

Variable Projects (Adam Marcus) + Daniel Raznick

Built 2013

Minneapolis, United States

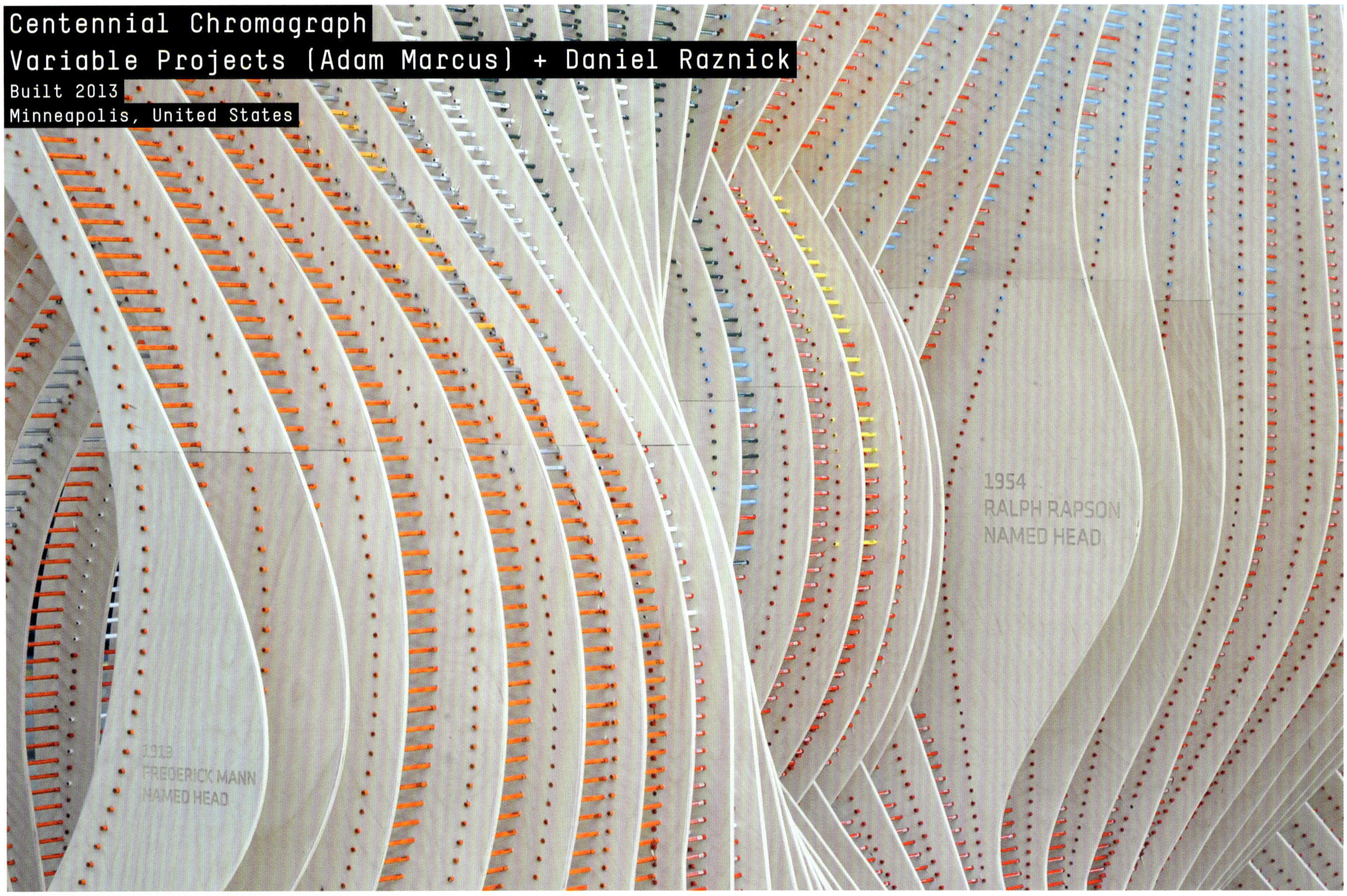

5.9a

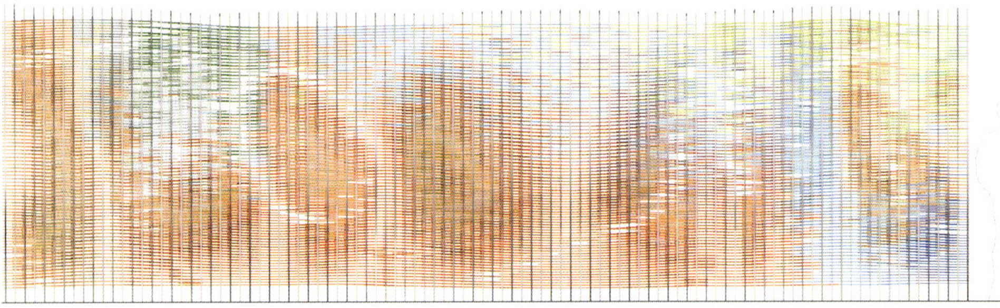

5.9b

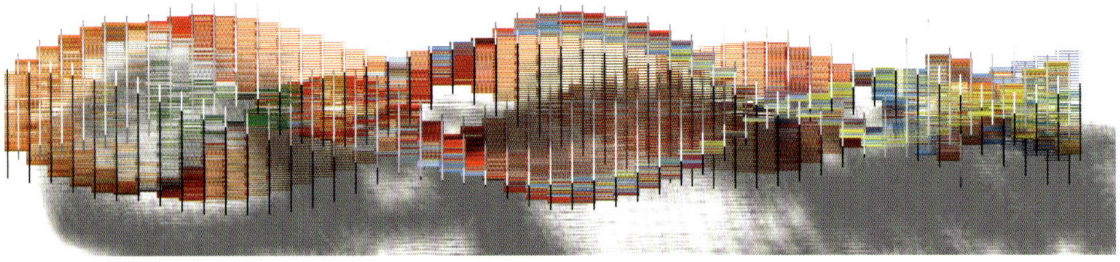

5.9c

Centennial Chromagraph is an installation designed to represent and celebrate the 100-year history of the University of Minnesota School of Architecture. An exercise in the materialization and spatialization of data, this project employs computational design tools to transcode the large quantities of data collected about the school during its century-long evolution into the tectonic elements of a free-standing synthetic structure. The installation consists of one hundred robotically-drilled and routed plywood ribs, joined together with 8,080 #2 colored pencils. These curved ribs, which are repetitively ordered along a straight trajectory, are bowed out to either the left or right side of the center axis of the piece, their alternation ensuring the overall stability of the structure. The curvature of the ribs expresses major historical eras and periods of the school—the tenures of its leadership, the buildings it has occupied, and the colleges it has belonged to—as these are represented, layered, and then diagrammatically transposed into three sets of symmetrical splines that together describe the parameters of the structure's implied envelope. These three distinct types of information are thus synthesized into a single continuous form, while the field of colored pencils reflects the changing composition of the school's degree programs and the geographic locations of its graduates over the past century. For example, the tenure of Ralph Rapson as head of the School of Architecture is evident in the large thirty-year curve that swells out in the center of the piece. Similarly, the prevalence of the bachelor of architecture degree, which began in the 1930s and lasted until the late 1990s, is legible in the large number of red pencils that extend across that sixty-year period. Each of the intervals between the ribs refers to an abstract increment in time that is perceptually measured in relation to the number of elements in the series and the length of the overall structure. When viewed from the side, the colored pencils form a three-dimensional datascape, making immediately evident, through the compression and superimposition of information, the school's shifting structures and programs throughout its evolution.

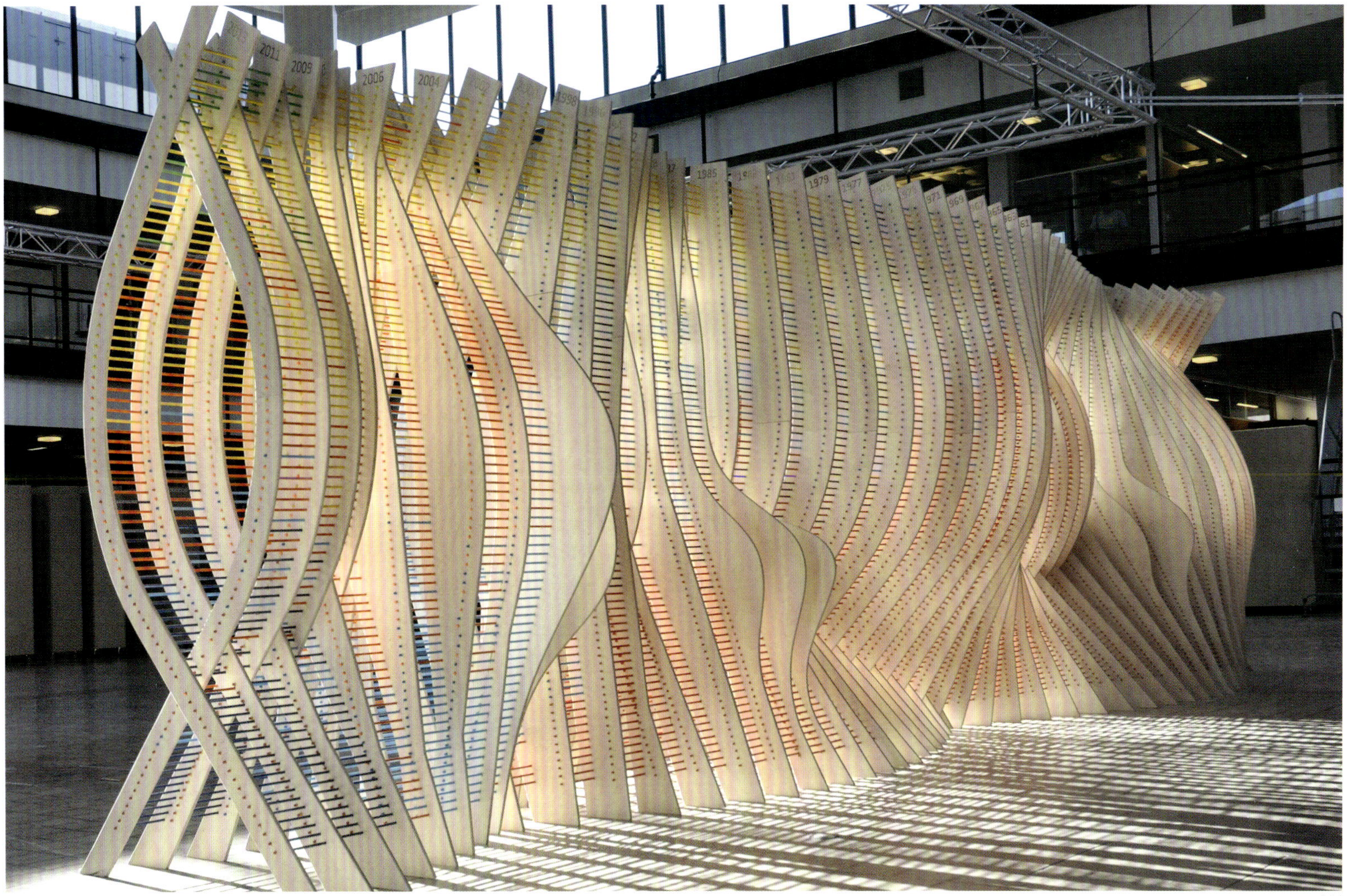

5.9d

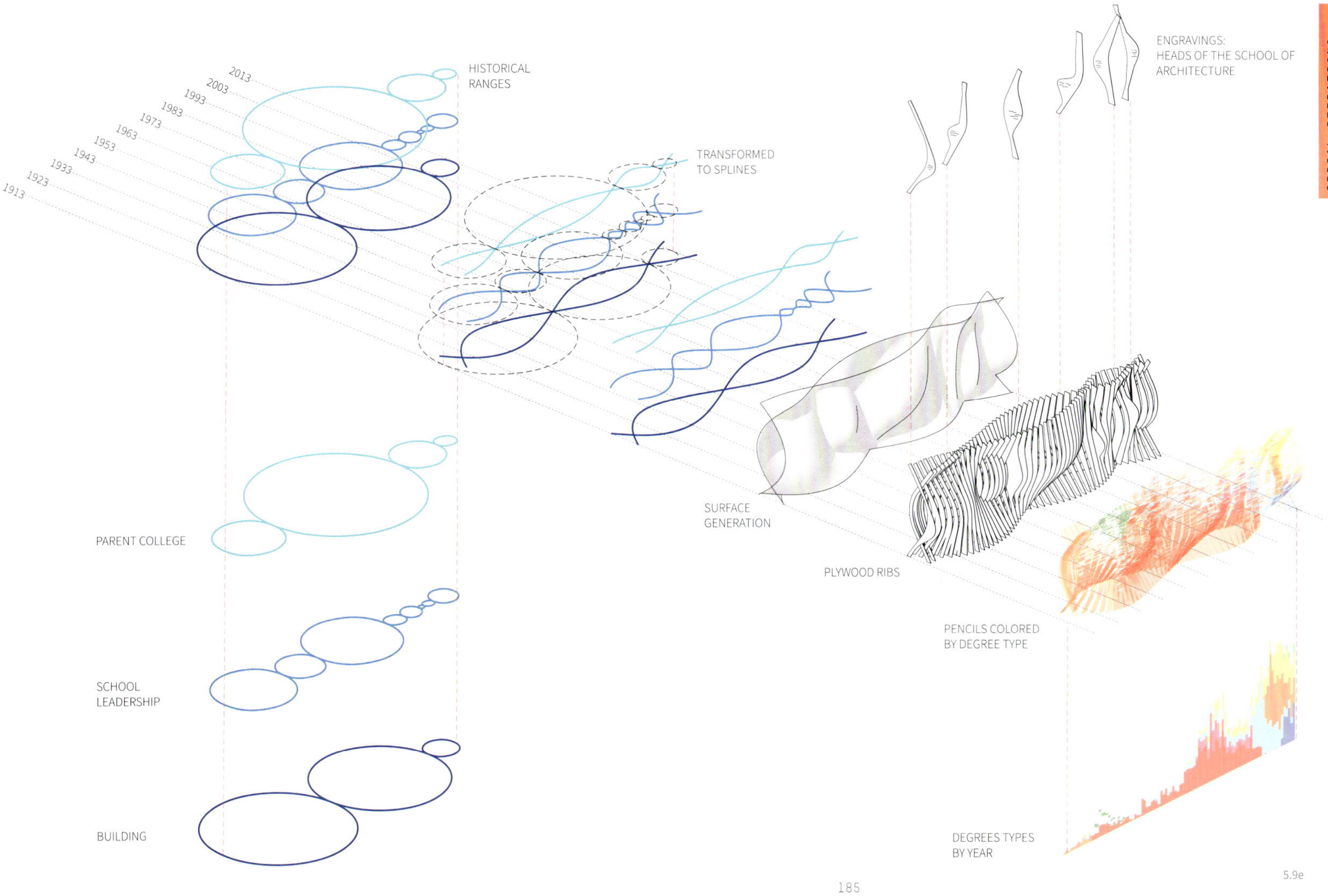
2013
2003
1993
1983
1973
1963
1953
1943
1933
1923
1913
HISTORICAL RANGES
TRANSFORMED TO SPLINES
ENGRAVINGS: HEADS OF THE SCHOOL OF ARCHITECTURE
SURFACE GENERATION
PLYWOOD RIBS
PENCILS COLORED BY DEGREE TYPE
PARENT COLLEGE
SCHOOL LEADERSHIP
BUILDING
DEGREES TYPES BY YEAR

5.9e

Aqua Tower
Studio Gang
Built 2010
Chicago, United States

5.10a

5.10b

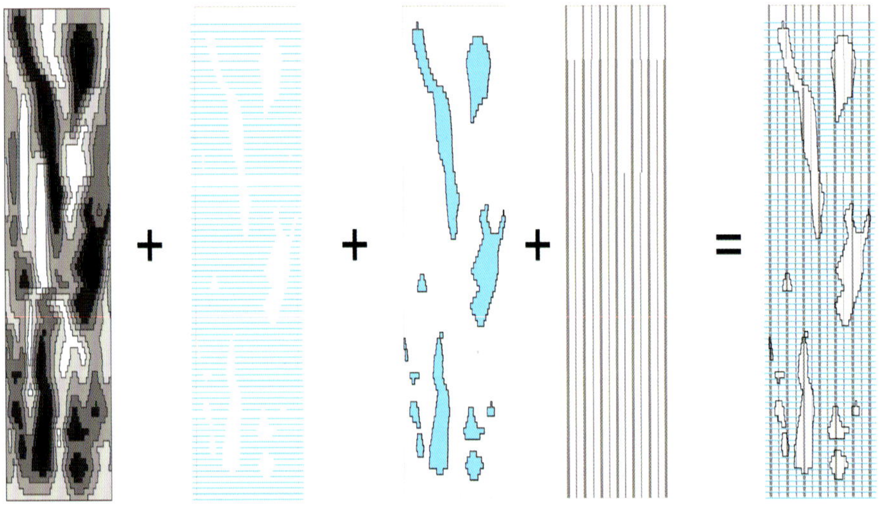

5.10c

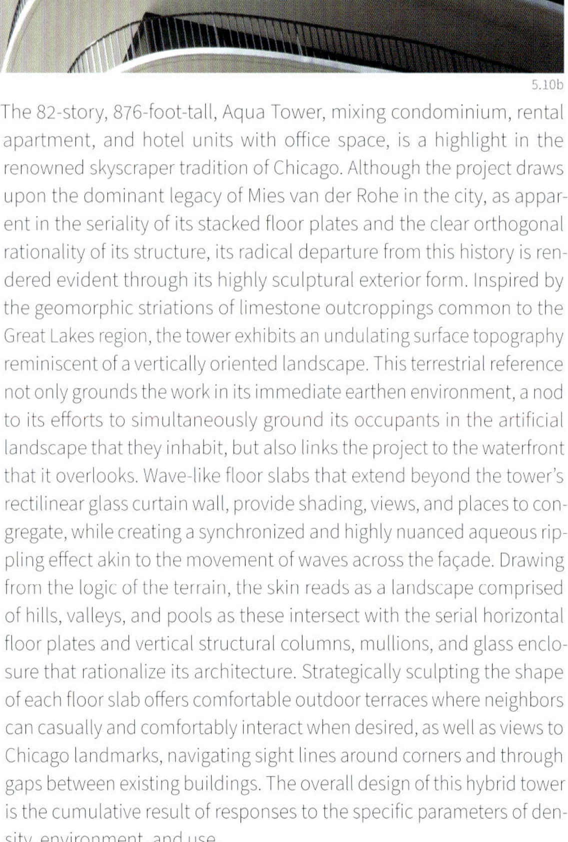

The 82-story, 876-foot-tall, Aqua Tower, mixing condominium, rental apartment, and hotel units with office space, is a highlight in the renowned skyscraper tradition of Chicago. Although the project draws upon the dominant legacy of Mies van der Rohe in the city, as apparent in the seriality of its stacked floor plates and the clear orthogonal rationality of its structure, its radical departure from this history is rendered evident through its highly sculptural exterior form. Inspired by the geomorphic striations of limestone outcroppings common to the Great Lakes region, the tower exhibits an undulating surface topography reminiscent of a vertically oriented landscape. This terrestrial reference not only grounds the work in its immediate earthen environment, a nod to its efforts to simultaneously ground its occupants in the artificial landscape that they inhabit, but also links the project to the waterfront that it overlooks. Wave-like floor slabs that extend beyond the tower's rectilinear glass curtain wall, provide shading, views, and places to congregate, while creating a synchronized and highly nuanced aqueous rippling effect akin to the movement of waves across the façade. Drawing from the logic of the terrain, the skin reads as a landscape comprised of hills, valleys, and pools as these intersect with the serial horizontal floor plates and vertical structural columns, mullions, and glass enclosure that rationalize its architecture. Strategically sculpting the shape of each floor slab offers comfortable outdoor terraces where neighbors can casually and comfortably interact when desired, as well as views to Chicago landmarks, navigating sight lines around corners and through gaps between existing buildings. The overall design of this hybrid tower is the cumulative result of responses to the specific parameters of density, environment, and use.

5.10d

5.10e

Zero/Fold Screen

Matsys

Built 2010

Calgary, Canada

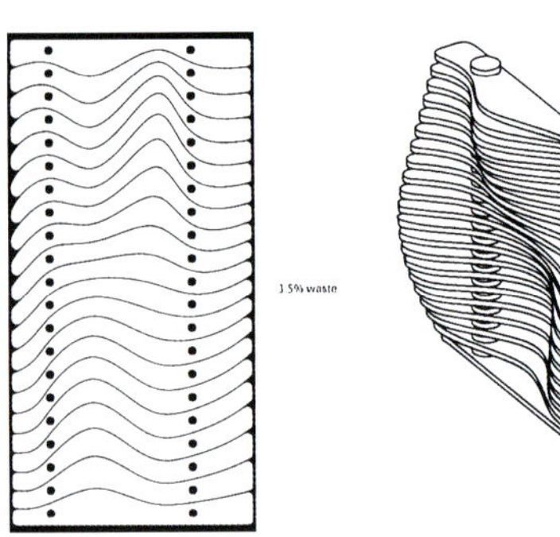

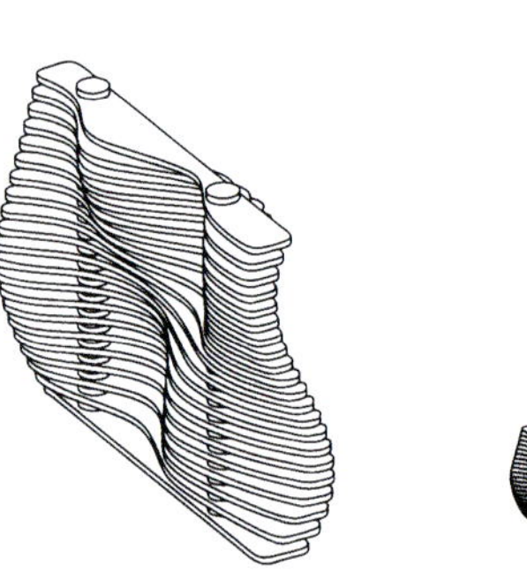

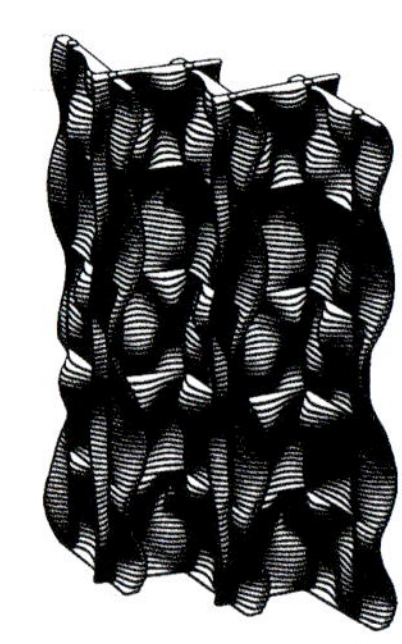

5.11a

The Zero/Fold and Foxtel Screens, which are developed based on the same set of strategies for design, fabrication, and assembly, are freestanding wall elements that operate to minimize material waste by incorporating the formal and material parameters specific to the fabrication process into the design of each work. As digital fabrication technologies have enabled architects and designers to explore more complex geometries, the difference between the complexity of the forms produced and the orthogonal geometries and typical sizes of the industrially produced material sheet goods from which these forms are cut and extracted, has unintentionally led to waste as a byproduct of the fabrication process. As a counter to the top-down, formal logics that often govern these processes, the Zero/Fold and Foxtel Screens incorporate the geometry and dimensions of the material stock used as generative parameters at the outset of the design. Each screen is developed by vertically stacking a series of horizontally oriented, linear elements that are CNC cut from sheets of plywood. In order to ensure that there is no waste produced, each cut in the plywood operates to simultaneously define the edges of two adjacent curvilinear, stacked sections. As these rib-like sections are initially traced upon the plane, they appear as a series of contour lines whose gradual deformation, moving from one edge of the sheet to the other, determines the degree of differentiation that is perceived along the surface of the wall. Once cut from the plywood, these contoured sections are rotated, stacked, spaced, and threaded together using metal rods to produce a continuous vertical topography. In order to both stabilize and visually complexify the work, the neighboring vertically stacked segments are then interwoven, producing a light-filtering, rhythmic screen of converging and intersecting wave-like undulations.

5.11b

5.11c

Foxtel Screens

Matsys

Built 2014
Sydney, Australia

5.12a

5.12b

5.12c

Roka Akor Bar Wall

Matsys

Built 2013

San Francisco, United States

The Roka Akor Bar Wall is comprised of a continuous series of contoured vertical wood ribs whose forms reveal the incremental transformations of a changing topography. The wall's highly articulated, yet gentle ripples and undulations are reminiscent of the movements of nature's landscapes—simultaneously inspired by Japanese screen paintings of cloudy mountain scenes in conjunction with the rolling hills, waves, and winds that are indigenous to the region within which the bar is situated. Similar to the Zero/Fold Screen, the Roka Wall minimizes material waste through the close-packing and alignment of adjacent vertical ribs that are nested onto amber grain bamboo plywood sheets as a single continuous series of sinuous contours. Once cut and rotated out of the plane, the back side of one rib becomes the front side of the next, forming a three-dimensional sculpted surface whose lighting dramatically exaggerates the landscape of waves and furrows that form a featured backdrop to the bar's seating areas.

5.13a

5.13b

Foxtel Walls
Matsys
Built 2014
Gold Coast, Sydney, & Melbourne, Australia

The three feature walls developed for Foxtel in Australia are based on the Zero/Fold Screen prototype, minimizing waste in the cutting of a continuous series of contours to produce a layered wall system comprised of vertical sections of bamboo plywood. A further variation of the Roka Wall, the Foxtel walls weave together two distinct series of undulating contours, each CNC cut from a different pattern and distinguished by their alternating colors. Akin to a sequence of overlapping waves, the outermost edges of these interwoven planar sections are exposed at their apexes, that is, the moment at which these undulant sections are the most highly differentiated. As the flowing edge of one contoured section recedes back into the wall, the contoured edge of the adjacent layer advances, producing a fluctuating rhythm within the series. Chromatic continuities perceived across alternating sections form a larger set of overall patterns that emerge from within this serial topography. Similar to the superimposition of regular patterns that produce a tertiary moiré, these interwoven patterns flicker and change depending on the position of the observer, amplifying the perceptual effects engendered by the serial system.

5.14a

5.14b

5.14c

5.15a

5.15b

5.15c

5.15d

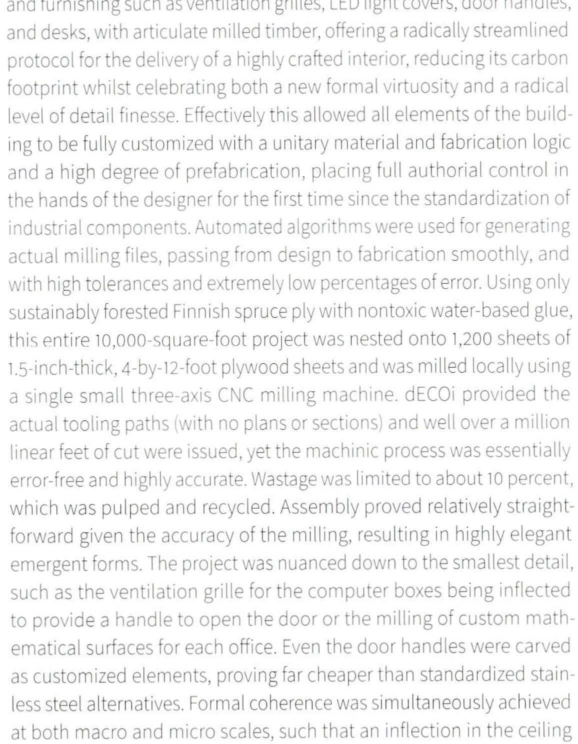

One Main, office space for a green building and clean energy technology investment firm, is essentially comprised of two planes—the floor and ceiling, articulated as continuous surfaces inflected by function, their curvilinearity expressing both their digital genesis and seamless fabrication logic. The ethos was to replace typical industrial components and furnishing such as ventilation grilles, LED light covers, door handles, and desks, with articulate milled timber, offering a radically streamlined protocol for the delivery of a highly crafted interior, reducing its carbon footprint whilst celebrating both a new formal virtuosity and a radical level of detail finesse. Effectively this allowed all elements of the building to be fully customized with a unitary material and fabrication logic and a high degree of prefabrication, placing full authorial control in the hands of the designer for the first time since the standardization of industrial components. Automated algorithms were used for generating actual milling files, passing from design to fabrication smoothly, and with high tolerances and extremely low percentages of error. Using only sustainably forested Finnish spruce ply with nontoxic water-based glue, this entire 10,000-square-foot project was nested onto 1,200 sheets of 1.5-inch-thick, 4-by-12-foot plywood sheets and was milled locally using a single small three-axis CNC milling machine. dECOi provided the actual tooling paths (with no plans or sections) and well over a million linear feet of cut were issued, yet the machinic process was essentially error-free and highly accurate. Wastage was limited to about 10 percent, which was pulped and recycled. Assembly proved relatively straightforward given the accuracy of the milling, resulting in highly elegant emergent forms. The project was nuanced down to the smallest detail, such as the ventilation grille for the computer boxes being inflected to provide a handle to open the door or the milling of custom mathematical surfaces for each office. Even the door handles were carved as customized elements, proving far cheaper than standardized stainless steel alternatives. Formal coherence was simultaneously achieved at both macro and micro scales, such that an inflection in the ceiling was echoed in the benches and carried down to the sinuous lines of the door handles. The formal exuberance of the space celebrates the indifference of digital tools to formal complexity and the precision and efficiencies gained in the fabrication process that also translated into the sustainability of material investment.

5.15e

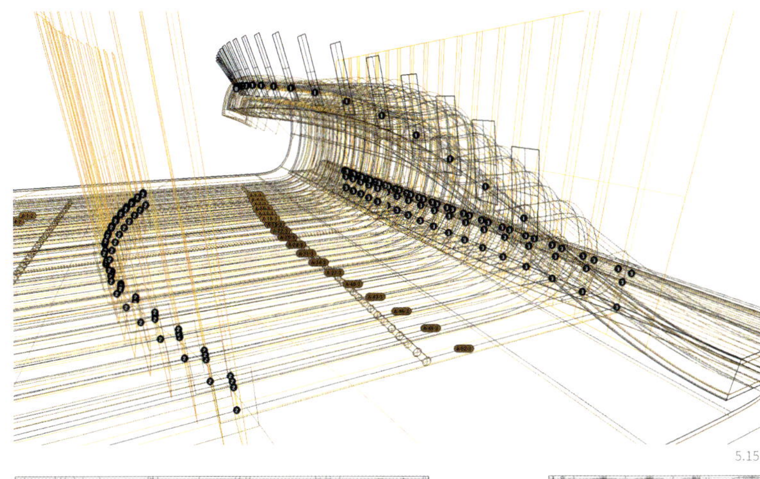

5.15f

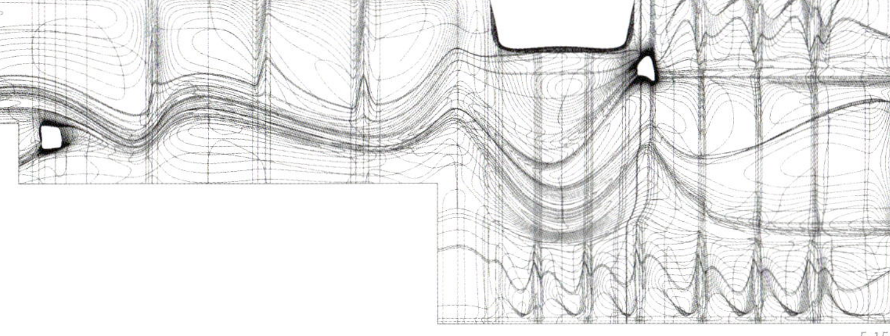

5.15g

Embodied Computation Lab Façade

The Living

Built 2017

Princeton, United States

5.16a

5.16b

5.16c

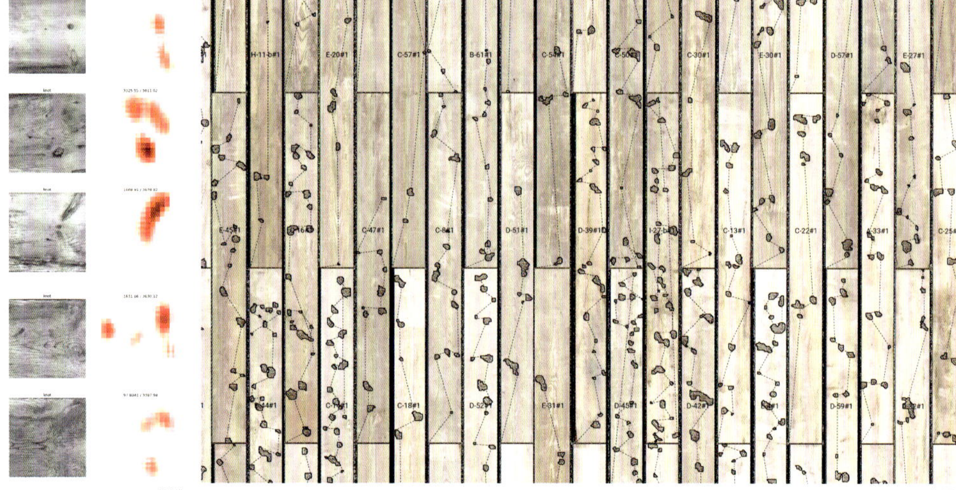

5.16d

The Embodied Computation Lab at Princeton University is an "open source building" to host research on the future of construction and computation. Just as biologists use an electron microscope to study organisms, architects will use this structure to study buildings. Research includes automated construction, embedded sensors, feedback systems, geothermal wells, energy harnessing, and wall and roof prototypes. The building itself is also a research project on multiple levels that integrates high- and low-tech attributes. It includes new sustainability and low-carbon features, and the façade, built from 900 salvaged scaffolding boards from New York City construction, involves the use of custom algorithms trained to detect knots in wood—bringing the power of machine learning to the physical world. Scaffolding boards are ubiquitous in construction but are typically discarded after a year of use rather than inspected for problems such as warping or cracking. Yet, more than offering a sustainable material, exploring the capacities of recycled wood led to revealing the natural variation in boards rather than suppressing it with a universal or lowest-common-denominator approach. Each board comes from a different tree with a different history of growth, indexed through its micro-contours that were exposed using a CNC sand blasting machine to create a unique façade. The resulting building envelope is thus both the final layer and the first research experiment of the building which is being used to study the potential of the serial grooves in the wood to offer performance benefits in terms of shedding water and trapping air to create an invisible layer of thermal insulation.

5.16e

5.16f

Ashen Cabin
Sasa Zirkovic/Leslie Lok
Built 2019
Ithaca, United States

ASHEN Cabin is a small building 3D-printed from concrete and clothed in a robotically fabricated envelope made of irregular ash wood logs. The 3x3 meter cabin lifts off the ground on 3D printed legs which adjust to the sloped terrain. All concrete components for the project were fabricated on a self-built large-scale 3D printer using a custom printing process used to explore how the layering of concrete, the relentless deposition of extruded lines of material, and the act of corbelling can suggest new expressive and functional methods for building. Challenging preconceived material standards in wood, the cabin utilizes wood infested by the Emerald Ash Borer for its envelope, a material widely considered as waste. Due to their challenging geometries, most infested ash trees cannot be processed by regular sawmills and are thus regarded as unsuitable for construction. Yet these infested and dying trees, considered to be a massive environmental problem, are an enormous untapped, abundantly available material resource to be upcycled for sustainable wood construction. Irregular tree logs can be sawn into naturally curved boards of various and varying thicknesses (up to 2 mm thin) using an industrial robotic arm with a custom band saw attachment. The boards are arrayed into interlocking SIP façade panels and solid off-cuts can be structurally integrated in the assembly which results in a minimum waste fabrication method. The SIPs are insulated, and the façade assembly is fully ventilated, detailed to manage shrinkage and does not require an additional rain screen. Balancing between the familiar and unfamiliar, the technological and ecological, these undulating wooden surfaces accentuate the building's program yet remain reminiscent of the natural log geometry from which they were derived.

5.17a

5.17b

5.17c

5.17d

5.17e

5.17f

Strand Table

Matsys

Built 2016

Miami, United States

5.18a

Strand Table is one of a series of works for the Strand Garden, designed and fabricated for the Perrier-Jouët champagne house as part of Design Miami. The piece, a seven-legged table that sits as if in a clearing surrounded by a forest, was inspired by the forms and materials—the strands, fibers, branches, and vines as well as the wood, chalk, glass, and grapes—specific to the champagne-making process. The table is constituted by seven strands each of which is comprised of a 3D printed, bioplastic base and a robotically milled oak top made of the wood that is traditionally used in wine presses and riddling racks. The seven strands are hexagonal in shape at the top, with smooth, rounded corners and are clustered together. The legs, reminiscent of inverted glass champagne bottles that glow from the inside, are wider at the top and narrow to a tapered base. Each leg or strand is differentiated by its height and defines its own tabletop, subverting the traditional subordination of the legs to the horizontal surface that they support. Here, the tabletop operates in multiple, a cluster of cellular individuated surfaces that are subservient to the legs that they complete. These are perceived as a cluster of tubular strands that swerve as they move upwards like the growth of the vines they emulate while swelling in diameter to become bulbous like the magnums to which they refer. Each stranded leg was 3D printed using a clear bioplastic that looks like glass, its serial making articulated as a rhythm that apparently transforms from a regular to a woven surface. Although the extruded layers of the printing process do not actually weave, the alternation of eight regular serial bands followed by four bands that create rhythmic micro loops of stranded liquid plastic protruding out from the surface in alternating but regular intervals, generates interruptions in the surface akin to the bubbly effervescence of champagne. This exploitation of the material used in the making of the strands and the parameters that define the form of their layering and the rhythm in which they are deployed expose the enormous potential for innovation in 3D printing at the level of its serial microarchitecture.

5.18b

5.18c

5.18d

5.18e

5.18f

Concrete Choreography

DBT ETHZ

Built 2019
Riom, Switzerland

5.19a

Concrete Choreography employs the column as a testing ground for computational design tailored to innovative fabrication, to demonstrate the remarkable architectural qualities achievable through 3D concrete printing not possible using other printing methods or conventional casting techniques. The challenge was to discover new formal expressions and material qualities by directly 3D printing exposed concrete elements without post-processing. The delivery of fine print resolution during high production speeds while ensuring process stability and robustness were key objectives, while investigating the extrusion layer as a design instrument for high-resolution and multiscalar material articulation. Digital fabrication can decrease the quantity of concrete used and eliminate unnecessary work sequences and materials used in temporary scaffolds and formworks, while simultaneously expanding the design space traditionally restricted through repetitive industrial models. Combining the ecological advantages of no-waste construction with digitized shape customization, the mold-less shaping of concrete shifts the focus from formwork production to controlling the properties and methods of material extrusion and deposition during its transition to cured concrete—a radical paradigm shift in concrete technology. The geometric freedom provided by 3D printing also enables the inclusion of internal features, facilitating a high degree of functional integration, such as space for reinforcement, lighting channels, and rainwater drainage, while site-specific customization, porous interiors, and surface ornamentation contribute to a novel design language. Each of the nine 2.7-meter-tall columns was designed as a double shell composition with a highly differentiated ornamental exterior and inner shell housing a cavity for reinforced concrete for increased stability and was entirely prefabricated using one industrial robot mounted on a three-axis gantry system. Internal bracing structurally supported the adjacent shell layers of freshly printed material and increased the achievable overhang for the column geometry. Trigonometric functions were also used to drive printpath deviations creating material-driven ornamentation calibrated at the limit of material stability from layer to layer. The characteristic dripping behavior of concrete thus became a powerful design tool, helping to subvert and evolve the seriality of the horizontally layered aesthetic.

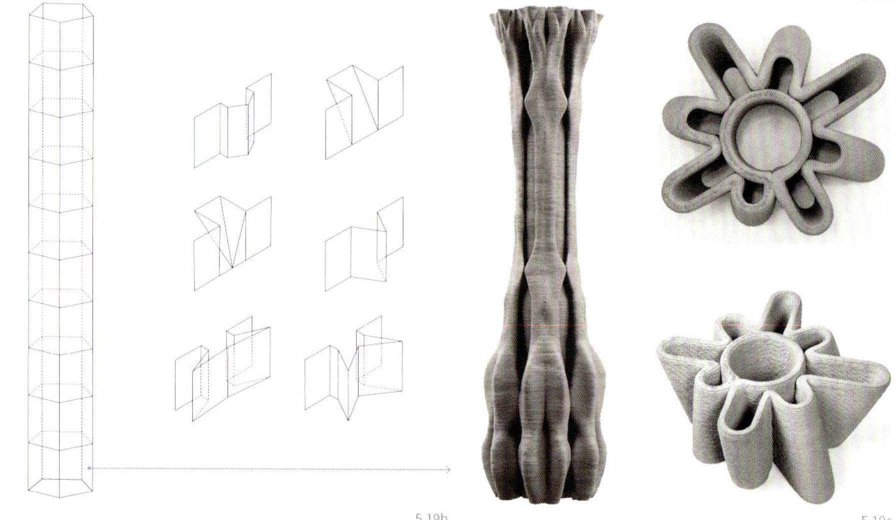

5.19b

5.19c

5.19d

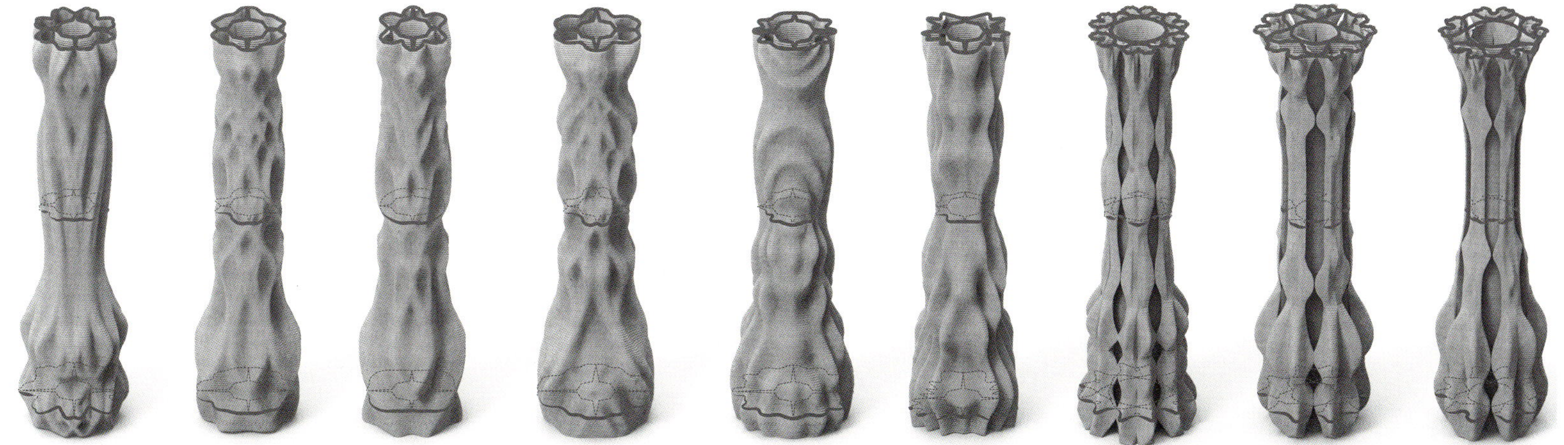

5.19e

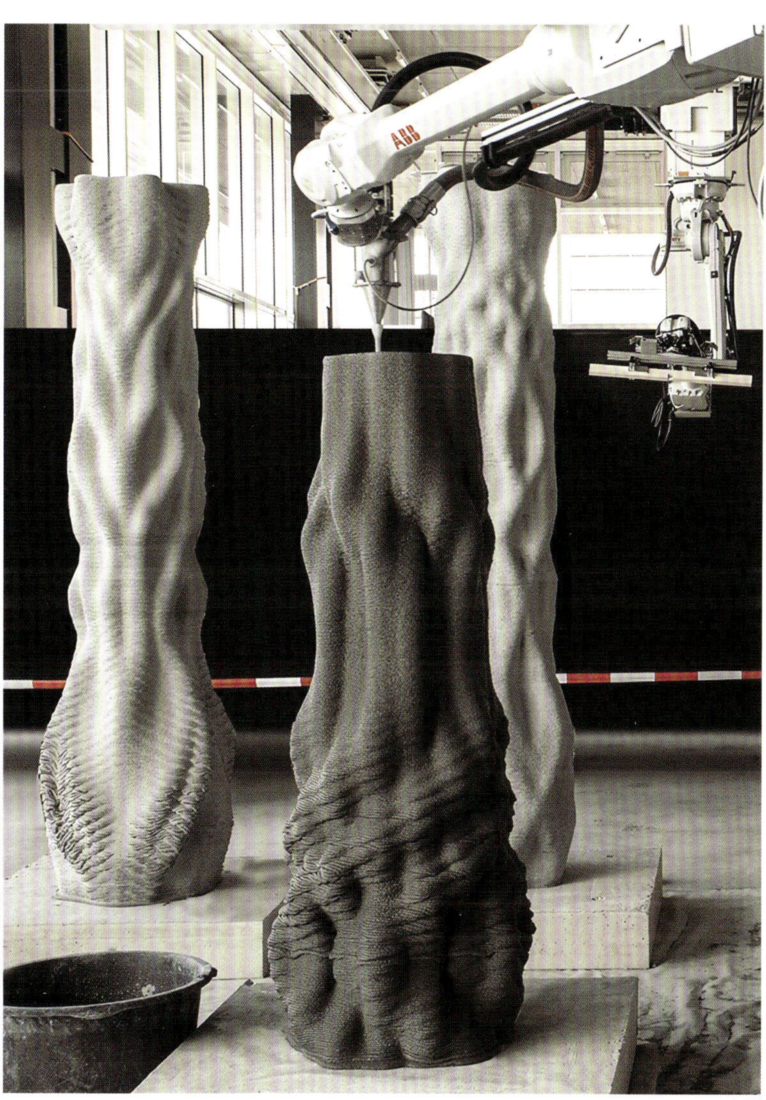

5.19f

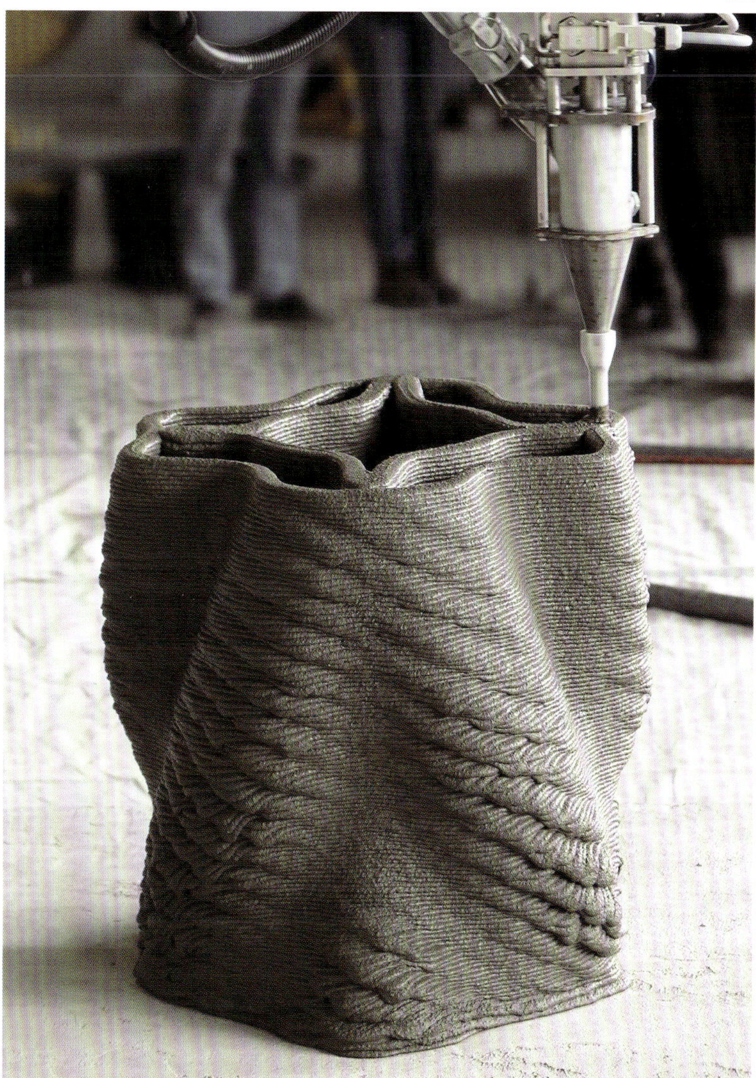

5.19g

5.19h

5.19i

5.19j

5.19k

Terra Performa
IAAC
Built 2017
Barcelona, Spain

5.20a

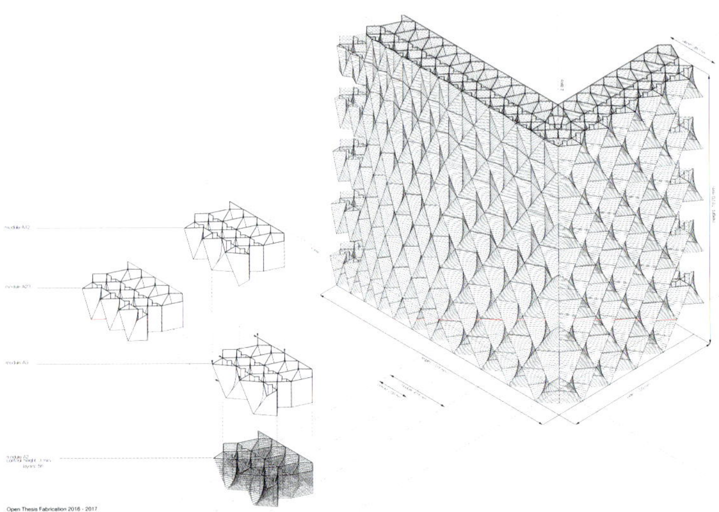

5.20b

5.20c

5.20d

5.20e

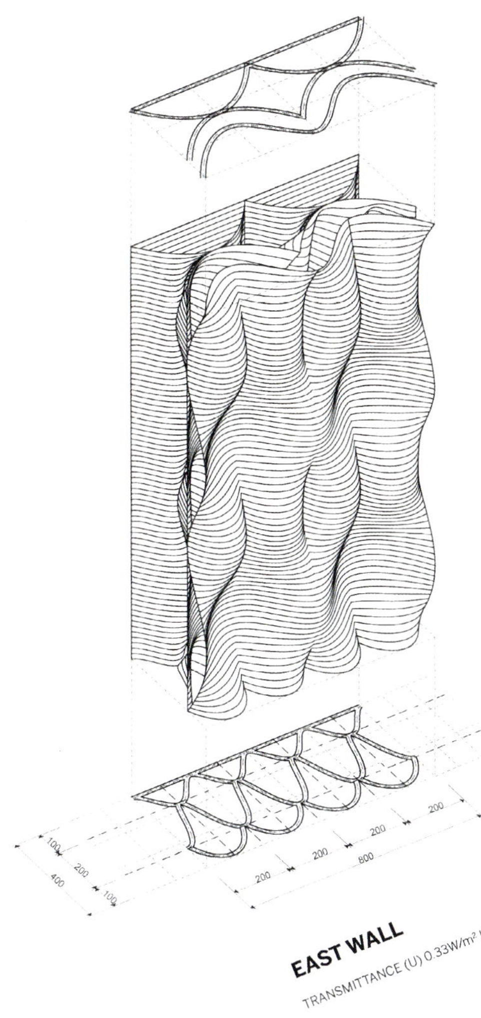

5.20f

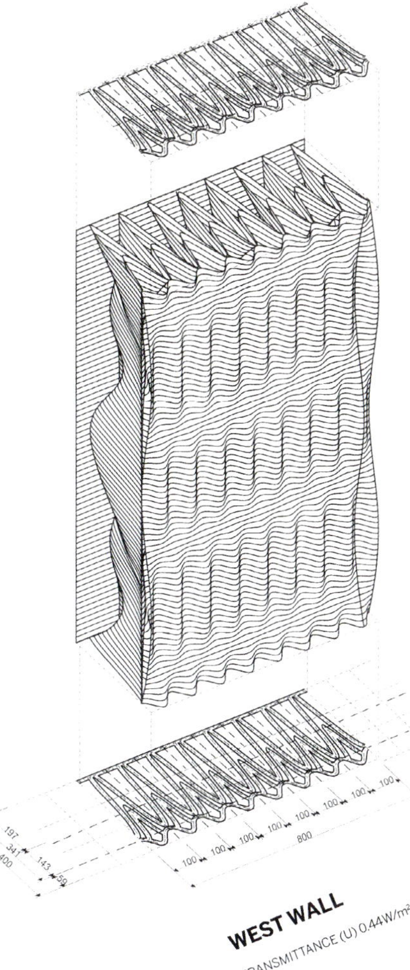

5.20g

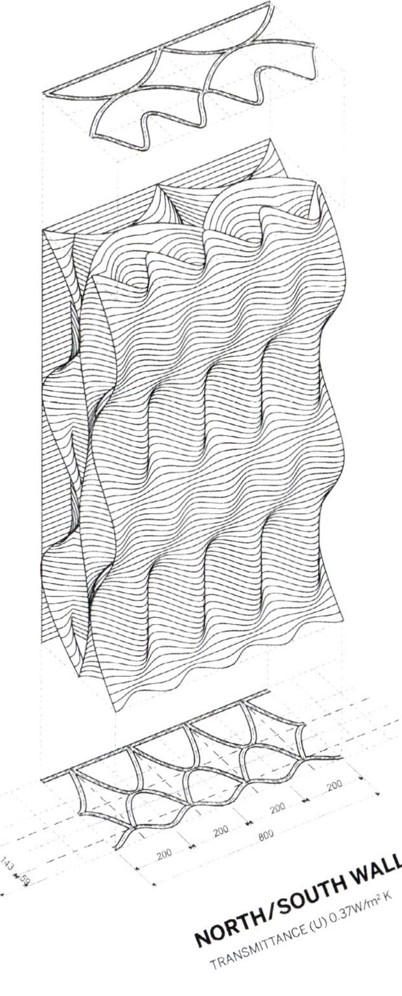

5.20h

Terra Performa focuses on research at the nexus of large-scale 3D printing, the influence of additive manufacturing on building with traditional materials and climatic performative design. Mud construction, an ancestral technique based on the use of local material, used for its rich environmental properties given that it has an ecological footprint close to zero, reduces the need for heating and cooling due to its intrinsic thermal properties and offers self-regulating environmental humidity. Given the capacity of 3D printing to generate infinitely complex geometries, the pairing of a low-tech environmentally sustainable material with such high-tech design and fabrication techniques aims at developing a prototype that can apply the design intelligence of performative formation achieved through simulation models, and their testing and analysis, to a material with long-term intrinsic ecological potential. The limitations of a full-scale 3D printing environment led to a modular approach where the modules are parametrically designed to optimize their performance in relation to solar radiation, wind behavior, and structural capacity as these intersect with the intrinsic logics of large-scale serialized 3D printing. The multilayered modules and their aggregated undulating façade enhance the structural capacity of the whole while enabling the self-shading of the wall from eastern and western sun exposures. Additionally, the modules are designed to incorporate various types of openings to maximize natural daylight and increase convection and airflow. These openings are strategically placed and vary from micro apertures embedded in each element, to larger openings between modules that produce light and wind channels. The extrusion technology and the material composition, which is a soil-based mixture with a natural additive specifically tailored for this printing process with an improved strength and viscosity, are based on the IAAC project Pylos using a Pylos extruder with a robotic arm. The open capacity of the printing technology and its direction using computational design technologies enables the seamless integration of elements at multiple scales within a single material and system. Here, the environmental performance of the design and its materials are complemented by the intrinsic beauty of its aesthetic, whose serial logics index the complex movements of the project's making, tracing its intricate and undulating path and the history of its material transformations.

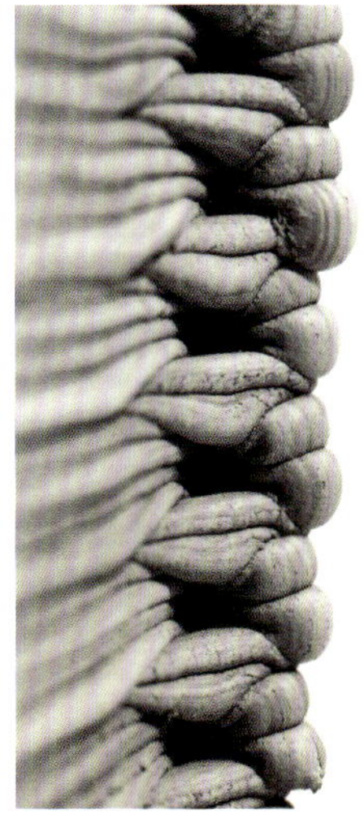

5.20i

5.20j

5.20k

Casa Covida and MUD Frontiers

Emerging Objects: Ron Rael/Virginia San Fratello

Built 2019-2020

San Luis Valley, Colorado, United States

5.21a

5.21b

5.21c

The MUD Frontiers and Casa Covida projects, both sited in the high alpine desert of Colorado's historic San Luis Valley, reexamine traditional indigenous building traditions and materials such as adobe—a combination of sand, silt, clay, water, and straw—using twenty-first-century technology and craft coupled with local labor to explore new possibilities for ecological and local construction techniques. The robotic 3D-printing of local soils shows promise for the rapid creation of robotically crafted, geometrically complex buildings that are durable and structural, using wild clays that have historically proven successful in building construction. As an elaboration of this larger research project, MUD Frontiers developed four individuated architectural typologies—the Hearth, Beacon, Lookout, and Kiln—using double-layered, 3D-printed, coiled earthen walls. The Hearth explores the decorative aspects of structure using local, rot-resistant juniper wood to hold the interior and exterior coiled walls together, while the Beacon, a study in lightness, both in illumination and weight, explores how texture and the undulation of the 3D-printed coil of mud can produce the thinnest possible structural solution for enclosure. These coils are then illuminated at night, contrasting the difference between the concave and convex curves that create the mud walls. Casa Covida, an experimental case-study house that continues this research, aggregates three distinct spaces—one for sleeping, bathing, and cooking/eating—each of which have openings to the sky, the horizon, and the ground. The central space contains a hearth surrounded by two *tarima*, or earthen benches, and the bathing space is filled with ancient waters from the deep aquifer below this mountain desert landscape with the retention of heat provided by the ground. The 3D-printing system combines a portable three-axis SCARA (Selective Compliance Articulated Robot Arm) purpose-built for on-site additive manufacturing that can construct structures larger than the printer itself, with a continuous flow and stator-driven mortar pump that delivers adobe material to the nozzle. The printer can be easily carried by two people and can be operated entirely by as few as one person using a cell phone that controls the printer. The design files are created by a robust software application that grows from Potterware, a ceramic 3D-printing software developed by Emerging Objects that was a by-product of the architectural aspirations for printing with clay.

5.21d

5.21e

5.21f

5.21g

5.21h

SERIAL ITERATIONS

Generative Logic Curvature

Although the geometry of a curve may appear simple, subtle distinctions can have large effects on fabrication processes and visual properties. One of the most important properties that a computational designer needs to understand is how curvature is created and controlled. The history of curves is a history of fabrication technologies and industrial design as the objectives of specific projects drove new mathematical descriptions for curvature such as Bézier and NURBS curves.

Polyline
A polyline is a joined collection of straight lines. Polylines have Position Continuity (G0) at each joint as their endpoints share location but nothing else. A polyline has no curvature graph as lines are curves with zero curvature (their curvature radius is at infinity). The zebra surface curvature analysis shows that a lofted surface from source polylines has discontinuities of surface curvature across the seams.

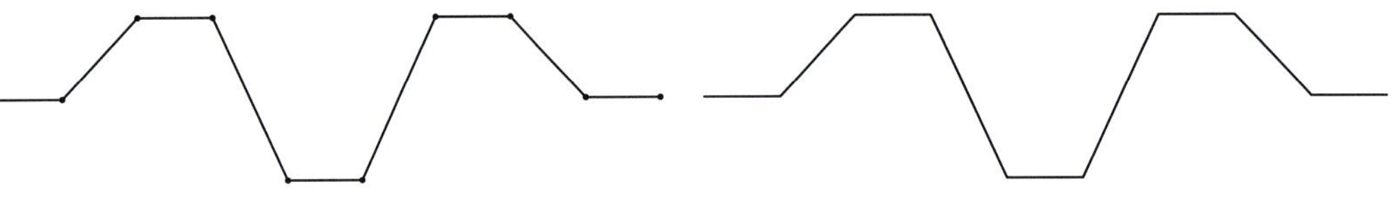

Filleted Polyline with Constant Radii
Many manufacturing processes require constant radii at corners due to the limits of materials or equipment. For example, a pipe bender can not bend a pipe at a sharp angle so jigs are used to bend at very specific radii that are above a minimum for that material and pipe diameter. Rounding the corners of a polyline is known as filleting its corners. The curvature analyses show significant discontinuities despite the appearance of smoothness.

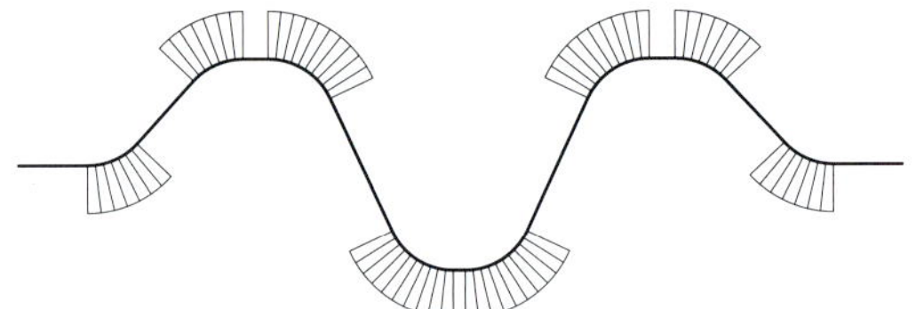

Filleted Polyline with Variable Radii
A smoother approach is to align the centers of radii such that there isn't a straight line with zero curvature between arcs. Although this decreases the abrupt shifts in curvature, curvature discontinuities can still be seen in both the curvature graph and zebra analysis.

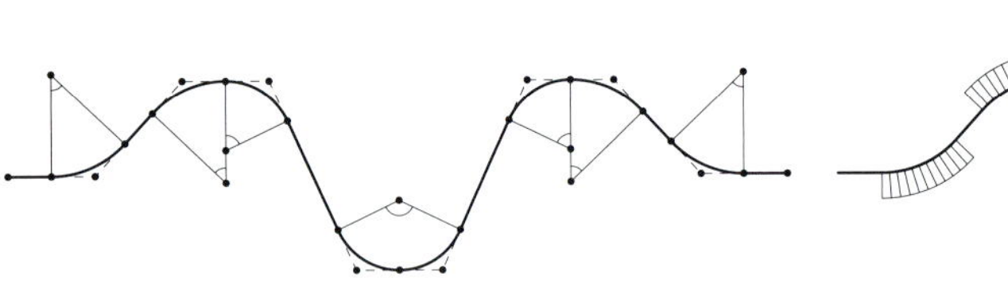

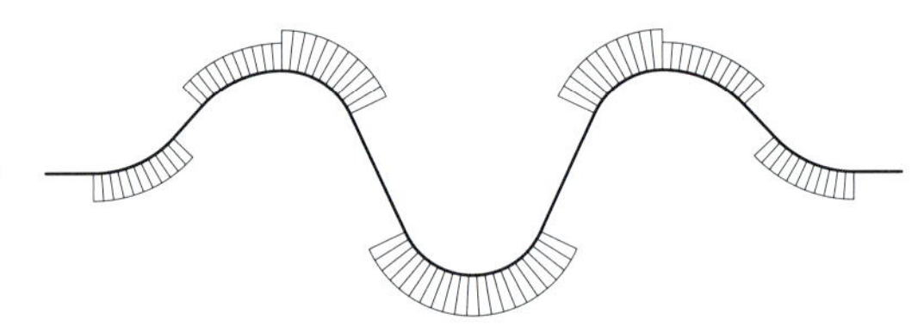

Polyarc
Pushing this concept further, a polyline's straight segments could be fully replaced by arcs and joined into a polyarc. Early automobile design used curved body panels that used arcs, however, when the panels were painted with a reflective autobody paint, the discontinuities were obvious and detracted from the designer's desire for the appearance of smoothness.

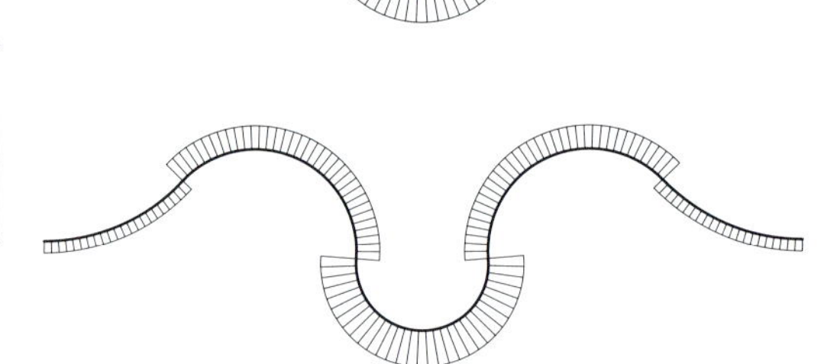

Bézier Curve
In the 1960s, an engineer working for the Renault car company, Pierre Bézier, popularized a mathematical description for a spline curve that had a smoother appearance developed earlier by Paul de Casteljau. Today, these "Bézier curves" are primarily used in graphic design. A series of control points with handles control the variable curvature.

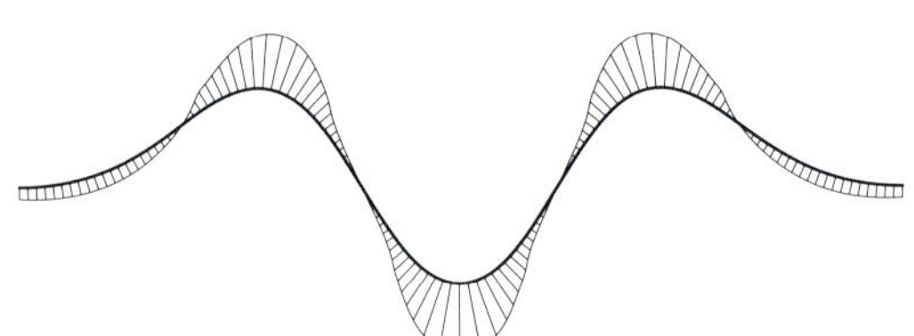

Interpolated NURBS Curve
Craftsmen building ships had used steam-bending jigs to create timber elements with continuous curvature. By bending the pliable steamed wood around fixed points and then clamping the wood while it dried, the wood became fixed in that shape. The interpolated curve simulates this technique by locating fixed points the curve must pass through. The curvature is continuous, however, it tends to produce less smoother curves than Bézier curves.

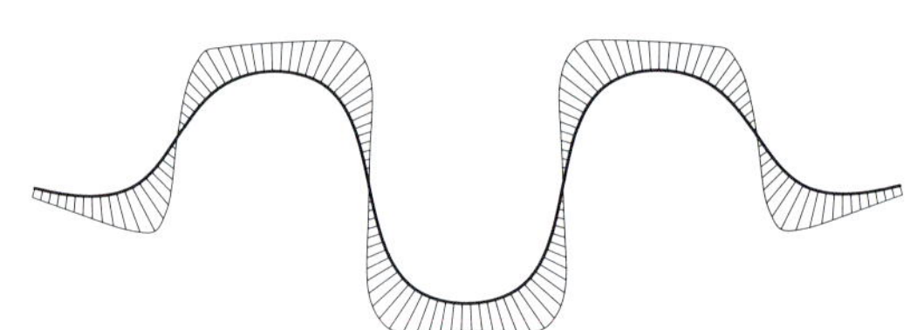

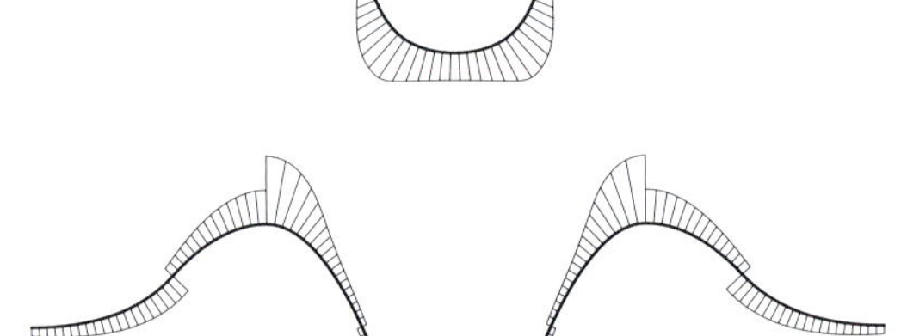

NURBS Curve Degree 2
NURBS, or Non-Uniform Rational Basis Splines, are an evolution of the Bézier curve that add more complexity. NURBS curves are described as having different forms of continuity. Polylines have G0 or Positional continuity. Filleted Polylines and Polyarcs have G1 or Tangent Continuity. Confusingly, a degree 2 NURBS curve also has G1 continuity as can be seen in the curvature graph with the abrupt breaks or the zebra analysis with the pointy stripes.

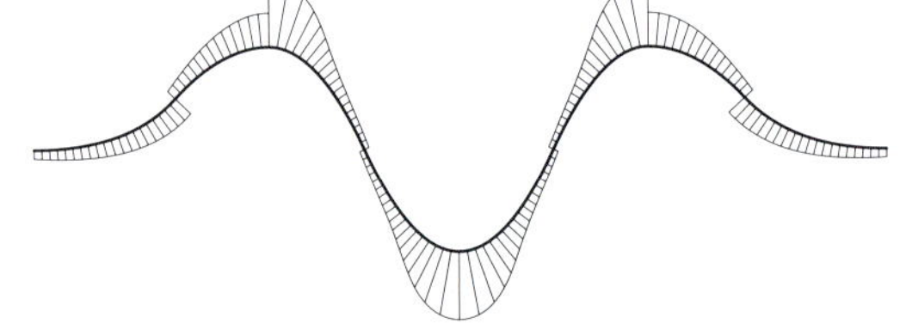

NURBS Curve Degree 3
A degree 3 NURBS curve has G2 or Curvature Continuity. Similar to Bézier curves, there are no abrupt breaks in the curvature graph or zebra surface analysis. You need at least four control points to make a Degree 3 curve. Degree 3 is the default for many drawing and modeling applications when making a NURBS curve.

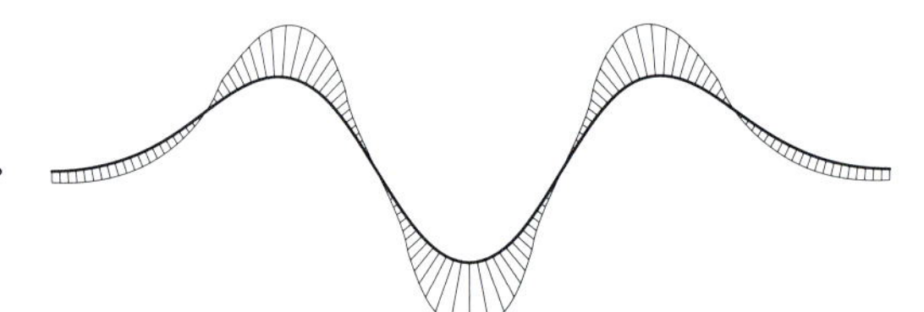

NURBS Curve Degree 5
Higher degrees of NURBS curves are primarily used within product and vehicle design where the reflections off the surface are of greater concern. The curvature graph and zebra surface analysis demonstrate the smoothness of the curve compared to the curves above.

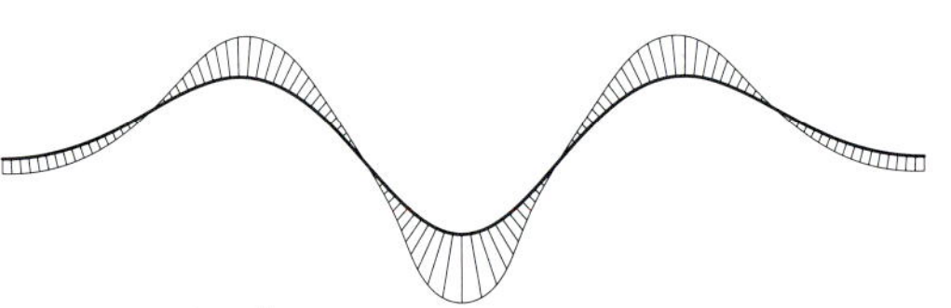

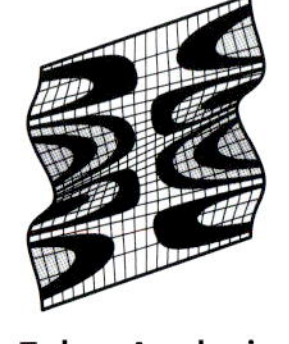

Geometric Descriptions **Curvature Graphs** **Zebra Analysis**

Generative Process Waterloo International Terminal

The Waterloo International Terminal was a seminal project in the history of parametric design as each truss was unique and had to be calculated individually. The project brought together several designers, engineers, and computational design experts who would later form the Smartgeometry group.

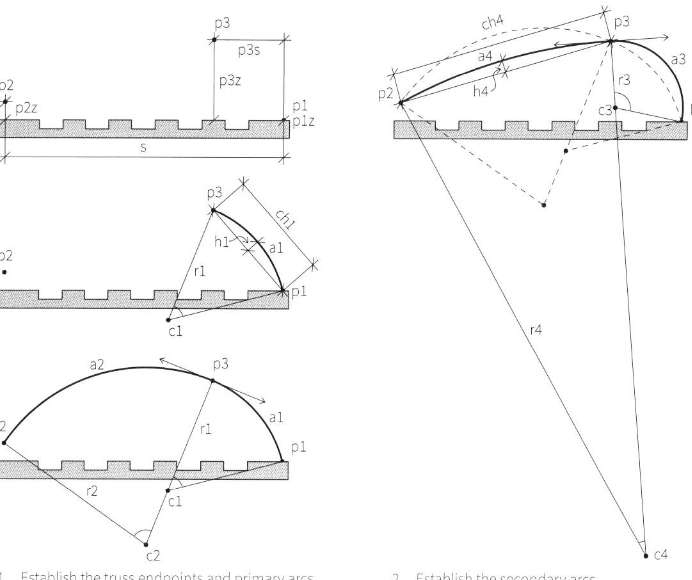

1. Establish the truss endpoints and primary arcs.

2. Establish the secondary arcs.

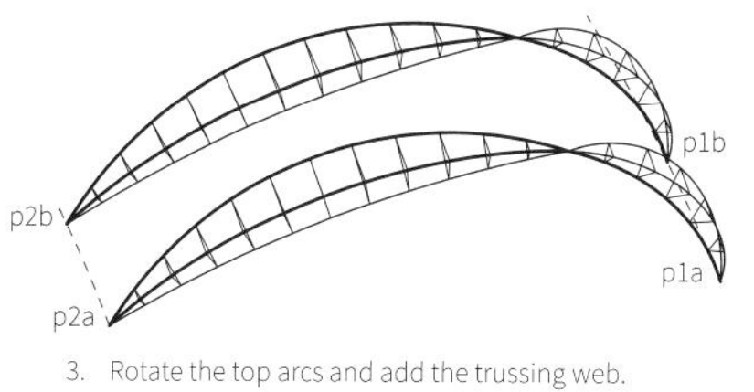

3. Rotate the top arcs and add the trussing web.

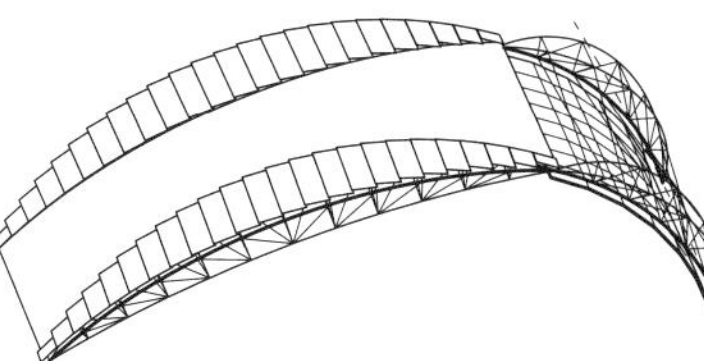

4. Add the roof panels, truss diagonals, and tension cables.

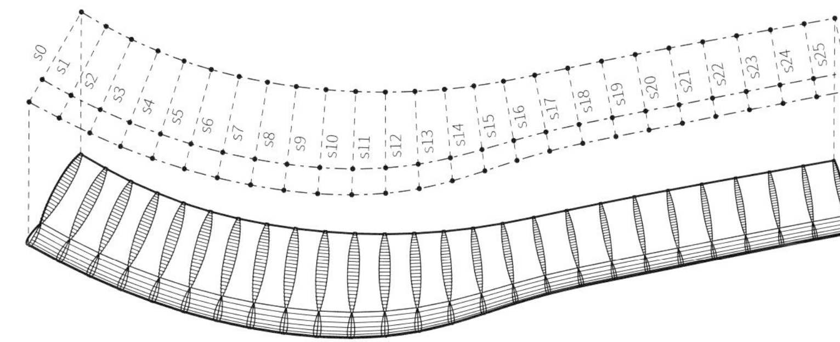

5. 5. For each bay span, calculate the truss and roof elements.

Generative Matrix

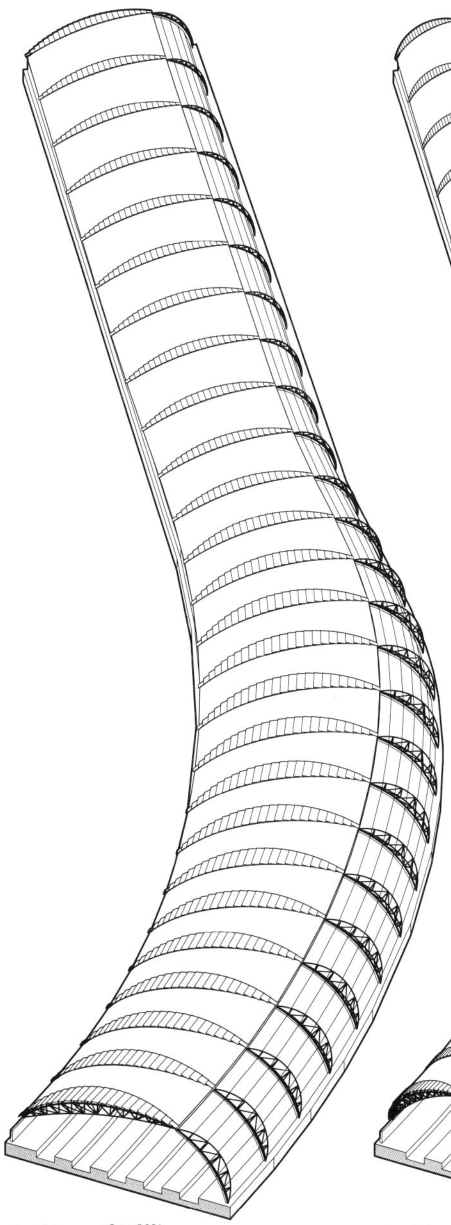

p1z = 0.0m
p2z = 3.0m
p3s = 25%
p3z = 30%
h1 = 6%
h4 = 11%
b = 25t
baseCrvs = Set A

Control Model

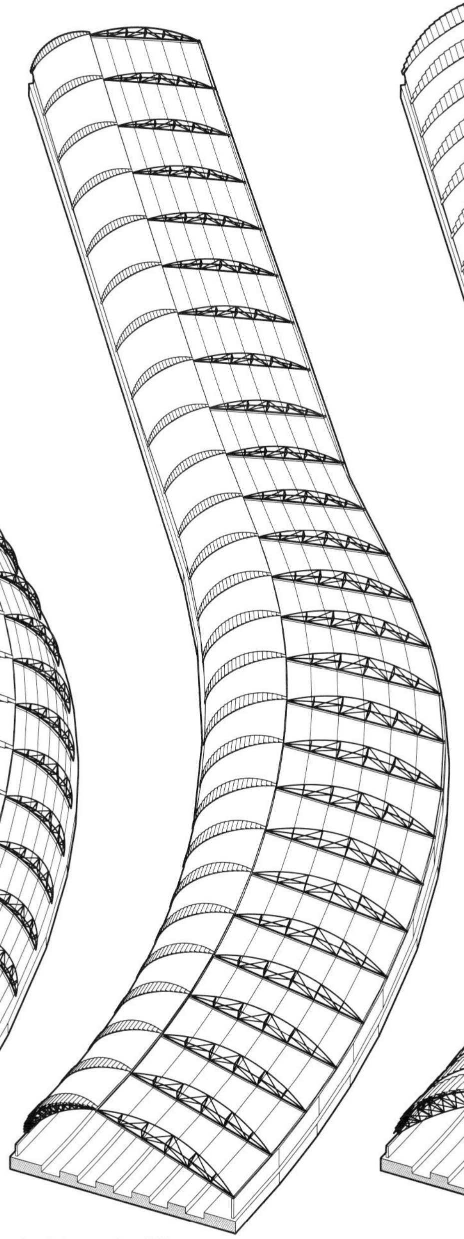

p1z = 5.0m
p2z = 3.0m
p3s = 67%
p3z = 30%
h1 = 10%
h4 = 6%
b = 25
baseCrvs = Set A

Change to Apex to Span Ratio

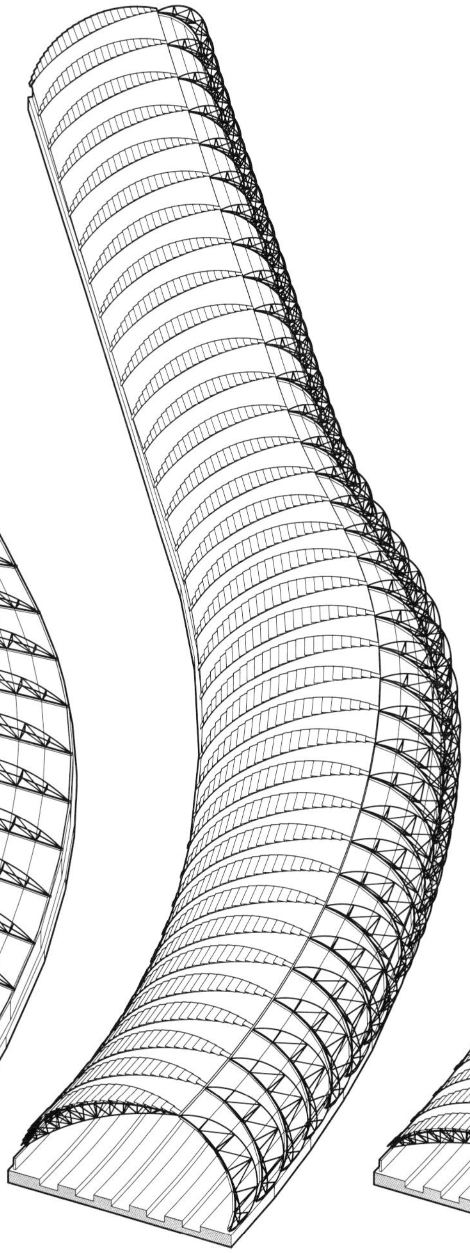

p1z = 0.0m
p2z = 3.0m
p3s = 25%
p3z = 50%
h1 = 15%
h4 = 11%
b = 35
baseCrvs = Set A

Change to Apex Height and Bay Count

p1z = 0.0m
p2z = 3.0m
p3s = 25%
p3z = 30%
h1 = 6%
h4 = 11%
b = 35
baseCrvs = Set B

Change to Base Site Curves

Generative Logic
Trigonometric Functions

Trigonometry is essential to computational design. It provides the mathematical foundation for precise manipulation of geometric elements, spatial arrangements, and angles. Understanding basic trigonometric functions allows the computational designer to move beyond descriptive geometry.

Degrees
Radians Expressed in Pi(π)
Radians Expressed in Tau(τ)
90°
45°
0°, 360°
315°
270°
225°
180°
135°
π/2
π/4
0, π/2
7π/4
3π/2
5π/4
π
3π/4
τ/4
τ/8
0, τ
7τ/8
3τ/4
5τ/8
τ/2
3τ/8

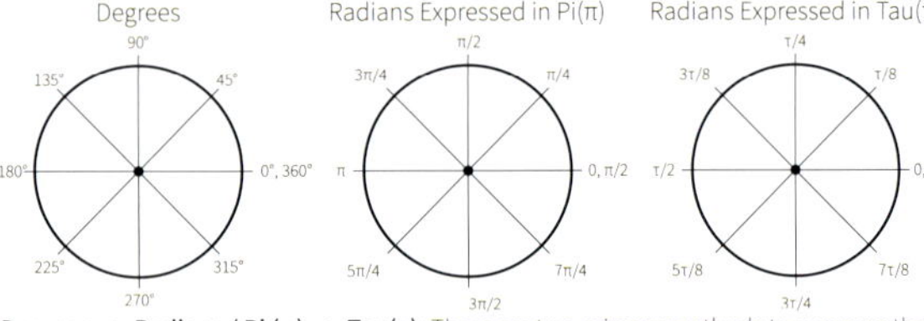

Degrees vs. Radians / Pi (π) vs. Tau(τ): There are two primary methods to measure the divisions of a circle: degrees and radians. However, radians are the preferred method as they lead to more succinct equations. In addition, although Pi (π) is the more commonly taught concept, Tau (τ) is more intuitive as τ = a full revolution around a circle (τ = 2π). For example, 75 percent around a circle (270°) can be expressed as 3τ/4 instead of 3π/2.

r
θ
r = 1
r
y
θ
x
0,1
√2/2, √2/2
1,0
√2/2, -√2/2
0,-1
-√2/2, -√2/2
-1,0
-√2/2, √2/2

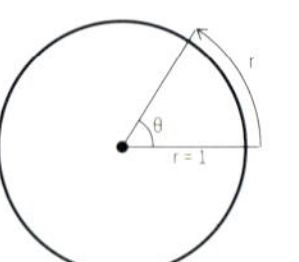

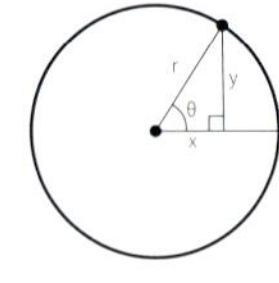

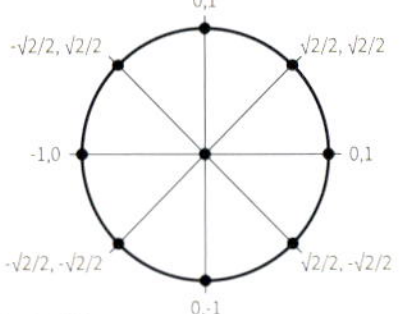

Unit Circle: A unit circle is a circle with a radius of 1. One radian is the angle that produces an arc length of 1 radius. A radian = 180/pi degrees, or roughly 57.3°.

Fundamental Trigonometric Ratios:

Sine:	sin θ = y/r = opposite/hypotenuse = SOH
Cosine:	cos θ = x/r = adjacent/hypotenuse = CAH
Tangent:	tan θ = y/x = opposite/adjacent = TOA

Unit circle equation: $x^2 + y^2 = 1$

1
0
-1
Crest
Trough
0
π/2
π
3π/2
2π

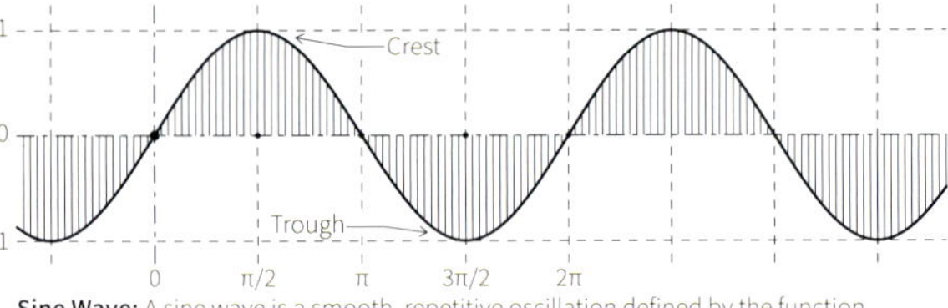

Sine Wave: A sine wave is a smooth, repetitive oscillation defined by the function y = sin(x) where x is the angle expressed in radians.

1
0
-1
0
π/2
π
3π/2
2π

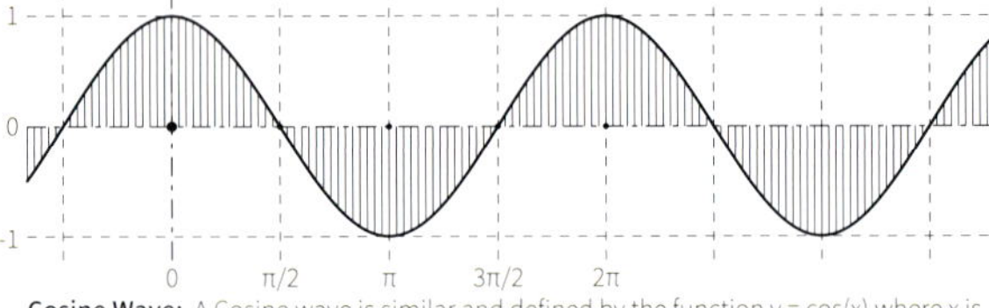

Cosine Wave: A Cosine wave is similar and defined by the function y = cos(x) where x is the angle expressed in radians. A sine wave starts low to high, a cosine goes high to low.

1
0
-1
Wave Height
Amplitude
0
π/2
π
3π/2
2π

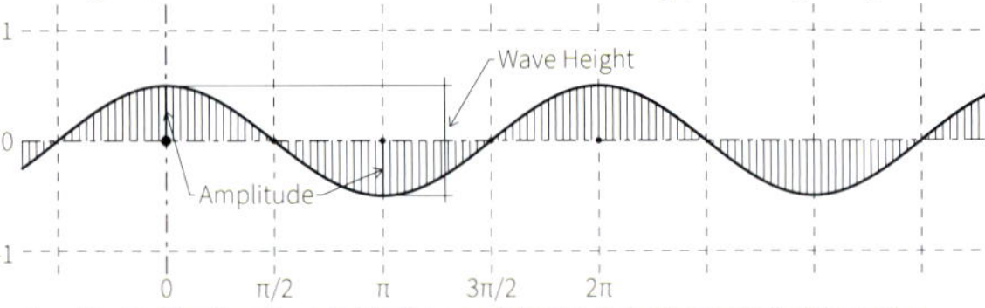

Amplitude: The Amplitude is 1/2 the wave's height. It can be controlled through a coefficient A in the function y = A * cos(x). Here, A = 0.5. The total wave height is 2A.

1
0
-1
Period
0
π/2
π
3π/2
2π

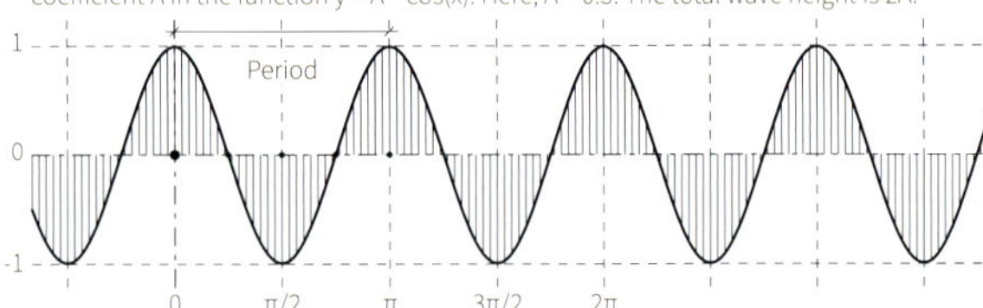

Period: The Period is wave's length from peak to peak. It can be controlled through a coefficient *b* in the function y = cos(*B*x). Here, *B* = 0.5 so two waves fit in the same length.

1
0
-1
0
π/2
π
3π/2
2π

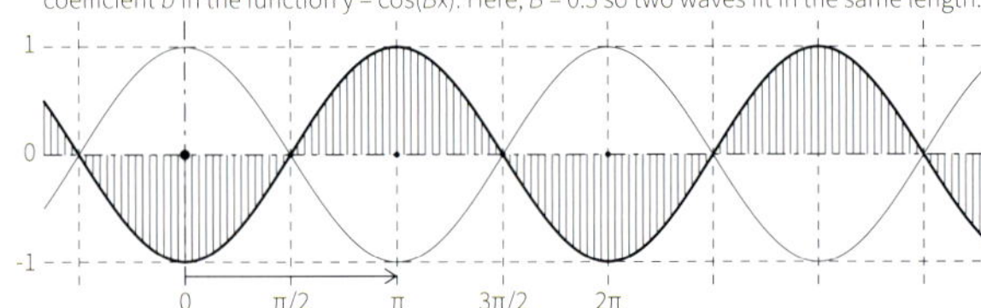

Phase Shift: The wave can be shifted left or right by the amount *C* in the function y = cos(x + *C*). Here, the wave has been shifted by π (or half its wavelength).

2
1
0
0
π/2
π
3π/2
2π

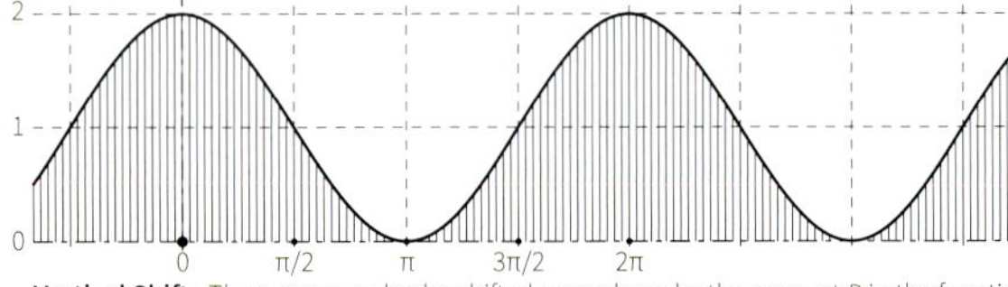

Vertical Shift: The wave can also be shifted up or down by the amount *D* in the function y = cos(x)+ *D*). Here, the wave has been shifted by 1 in the up direction.

Generative Process
Henderson Wave Bridge

The Henderson Wave Bridge by IJP Architects is composed of three hierarchical parametric functions. The primary function creates the cosine curve along a tilted plane; the second determines the heights of the spanning arches; the third creates the series of ribs.

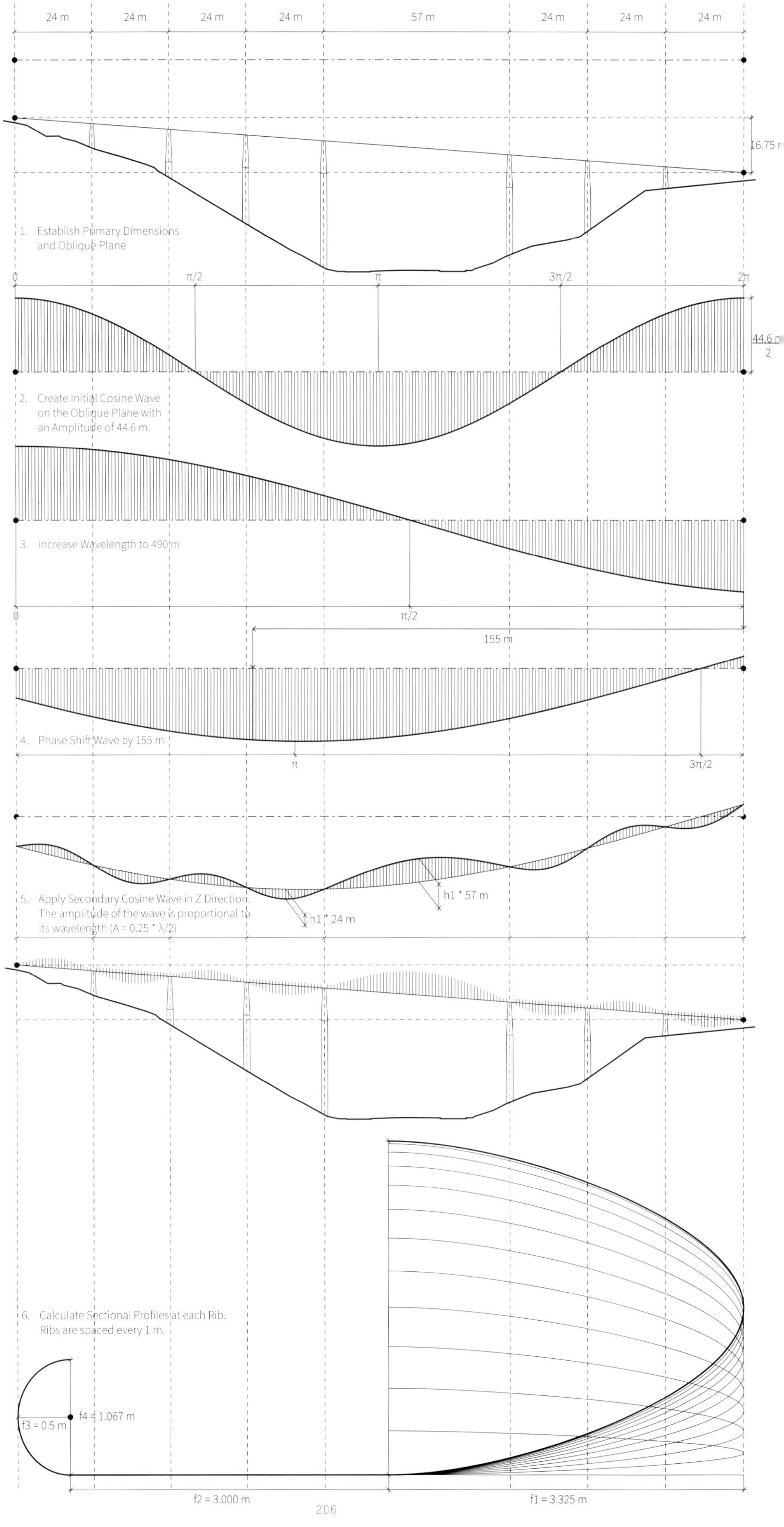

24 m
24 m
24 m
24 m
57 m
24 m
24 m
24 m
16.75 m
1. Establish Primary Dimensions and Oblique Plane
0
π/2
π
3π/2
2π
44.6 m / 2
2. Create Initial Cosine Wave on the Oblique Plane with an Amplitude of 44.6 m.
3. Increase Wavelength to 490 m
0
π/2
155 m
4. Phase Shift Wave by 155 m
π
3π/2
5. Apply Secondary Cosine Wave in Z Direction. The amplitude of the wave is proportional to its wavelength (A = 0.25 * λ/2)
h1 * 57 m
h1 * 24 m
6. Calculate Sectional Profiles at each Rib. Ribs are spaced every 1 m.
f4 = 1.067 m
f3 = 0.5 m
f2 = 3.000 m
f1 = 3.325 m

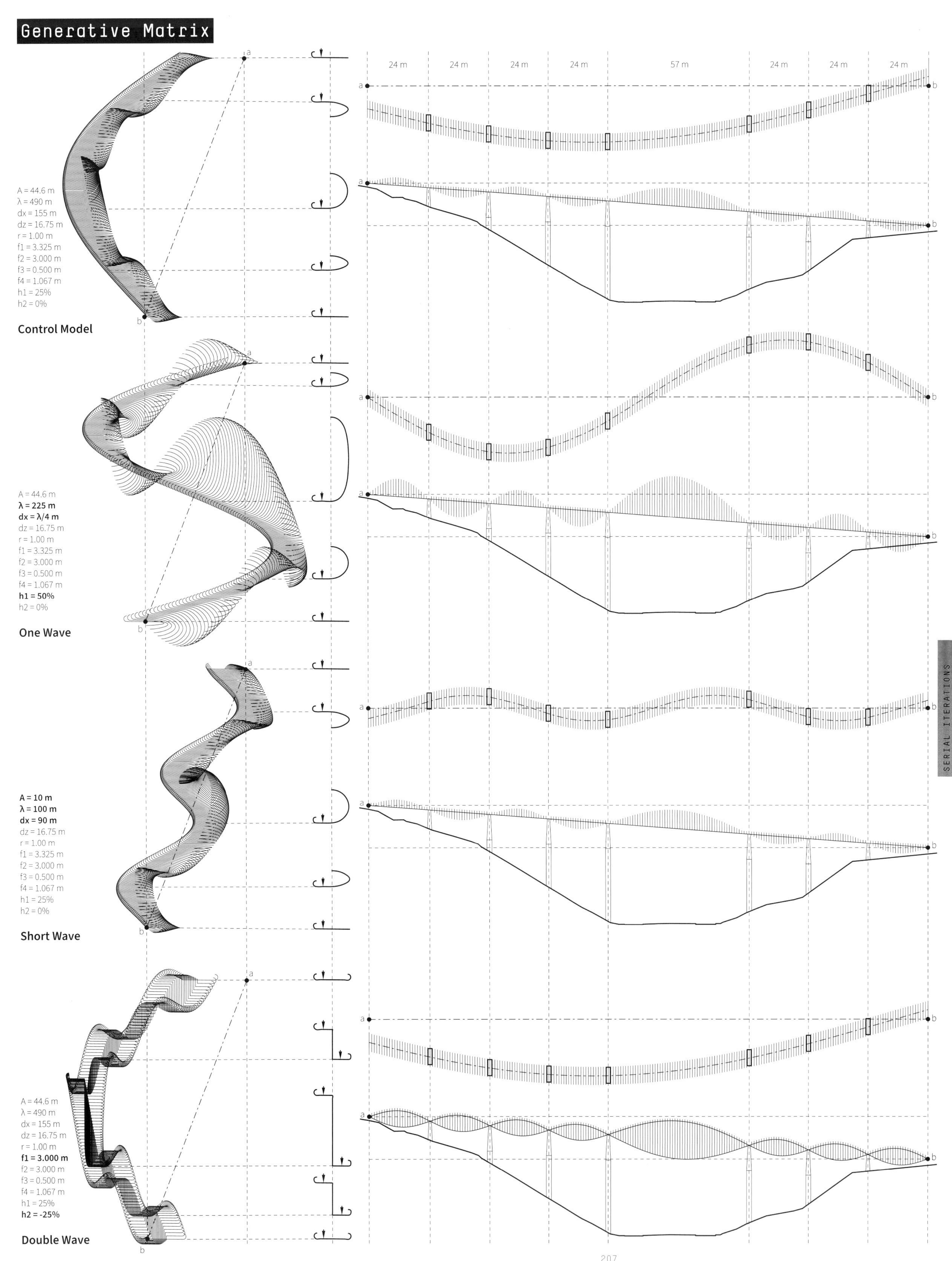
Generative Matrix
24 m
24 m
24 m
24 m
57 m
24 m
24 m
24 m
A = 44.6 m
λ = 490 m
dx = 155 m
dz = 16.75 m
r = 1.00 m
f1 = 3.325 m
f2 = 3.000 m
f3 = 0.500 m
f4 = 1.067 m
h1 = 25%
h2 = 0%
Control Model
A = 44.6 m
λ = 225 m
dx = λ/4 m
dz = 16.75 m
r = 1.00 m
f1 = 3.325 m
f2 = 3.000 m
f3 = 0.500 m
f4 = 1.067 m
h1 = 50%
h2 = 0%
One Wave
A = 10 m
λ = 100 m
dx = 90 m
dz = 16.75 m
r = 1.00 m
f1 = 3.325 m
f2 = 3.000 m
f3 = 0.500 m
f4 = 1.067 m
h1 = 25%
h2 = 0%
Short Wave
A = 44.6 m
λ = 490 m
dx = 155 m
dz = 16.75 m
r = 1.00 m
f1 = 3.000 m
f2 = 3.000 m
f3 = 0.500 m
f4 = 1.067 m
h1 = 25%
h2 = -25%
Double Wave

Generative Logic
Additive Manufacturing Methods

Although there are many different additive manufacturing technologies, almost all of them rely on slicing a 3D object into a series of layers and the discretization of the layer geometry into a series of lines, points, and/or pixels. Almost any material can be printed including plastics, clay, concrete, and various metals.

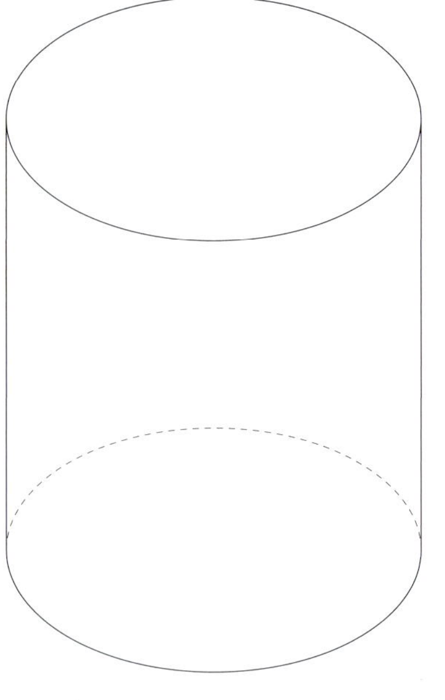

1. Start from a solid object.

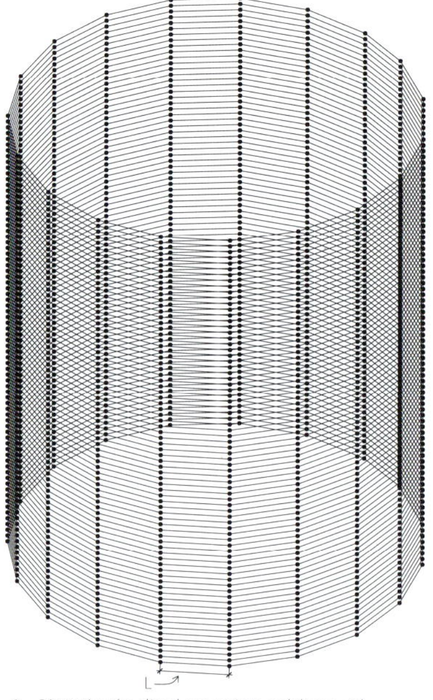

2. Slice the object by a layer height (h).

3. Discretize the sliced curves into polylines with straight segments.

$$E = \frac{h \times d_N \times L \times SF}{(\pi/4)d_f^{\,2}}$$

E = Distance the filament needs to be extruded
h = Layer height
d_N = Diameter of the nozzle
L = The straight distance between points (p_1 to p_2)
SF = Scaling factor to modify the flow (0.00 - 1.00)
d_f = Diameter of the filament

GCode Example = G1 X5.35 Y2.82 Z1.50 E0.176

4. Produce the GCode by calculating the distances between points and the extrusion rate.

Generative Process
Mud Frontiers

The Mud Frontiers project by Emerging Objects is exemplary of a range of innovative projects using additive manufacturing for full-scale construction. The project combines traditional a low-cost material (earth) with low-cost labor (robotics) while exploring the unique visual and structural properties of generative toolpaths. Rather than rely on default settings found within most slicing applications, the toolpath geometry is seen as a site for creative design investigations.

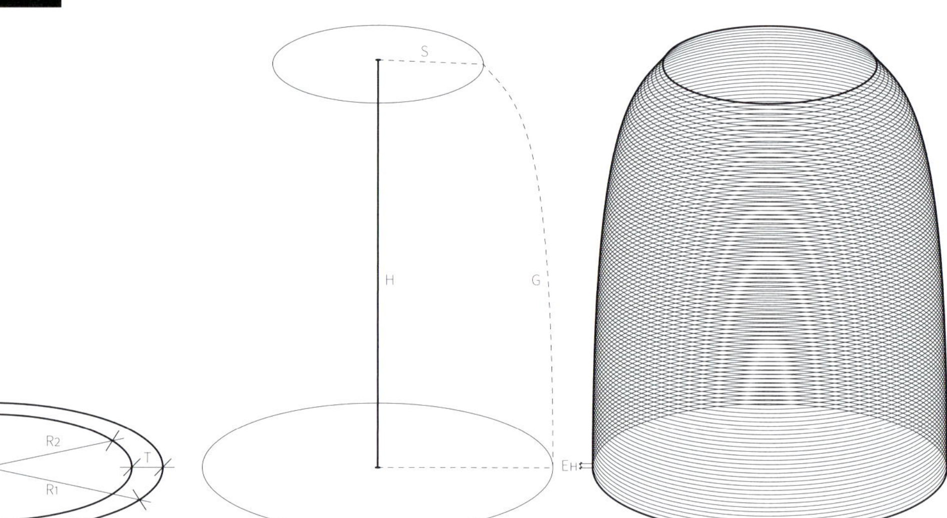

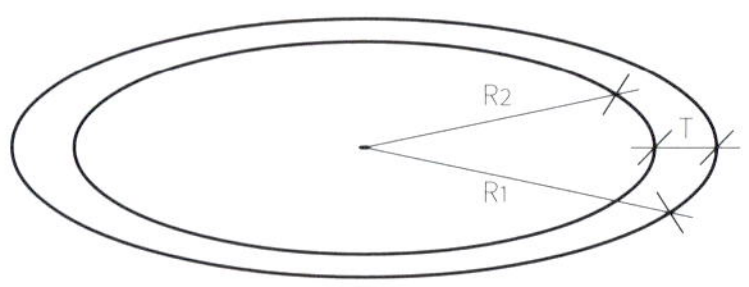

1. Create a circle with Radius (R1) that represents the nominal exterior of the structure. Subtract the nominal wall Thickness (T) to get the inner Radius (R2).

2. Move the outer circle up by the structure's desired total Height (H) and then apply a Scaling factor (S). Use a Graph (G) curve to interpolate the scale factor between the bottom and the top circles.

3. Produce a set of new circles between the top and bottom at the appropriate Extrusion Height (EH).

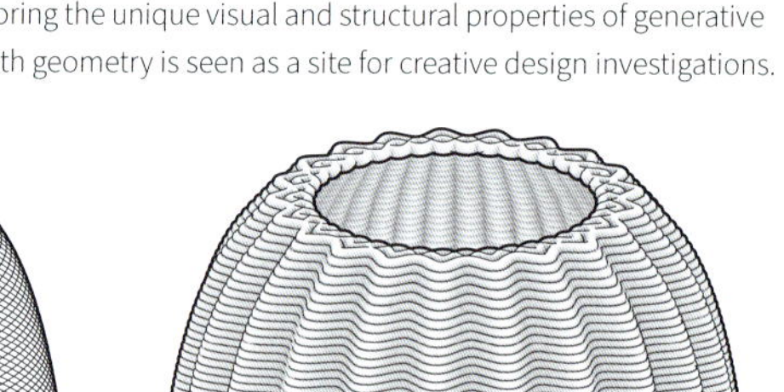

Enlarged sections on the following page

4. Divide each layer's initial circle (C1) into an even number of regions (UH). Depending on the number of Paths (C), add more base circles (C2, C3) between the wall thickness (T).

5. Develop a pattern (P1) between two or more series of points. For example, the undulating exterior path here alternates between the C1 and C2 circle points in the pattern 0-1. The amplitude of this wave is A1.

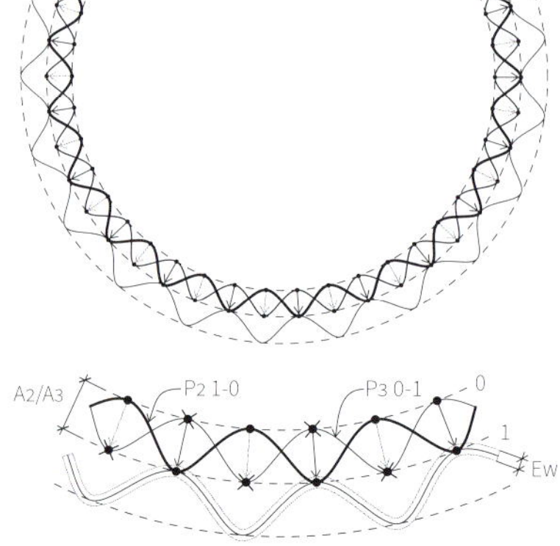

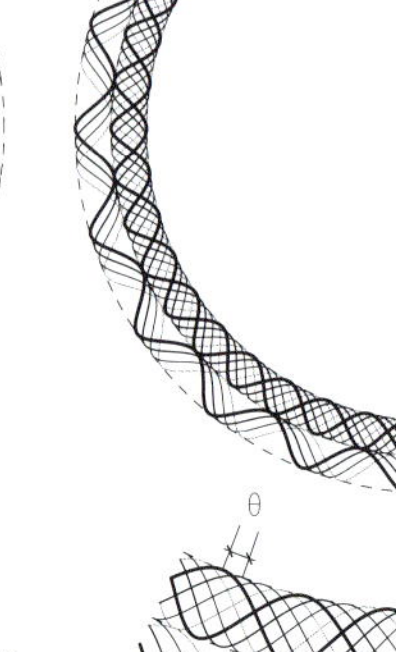

6. The inner wall is made of two paths (P2, P3) that cross each other. Additional adjustments may be needed based on the Extrusion Width (Ew).

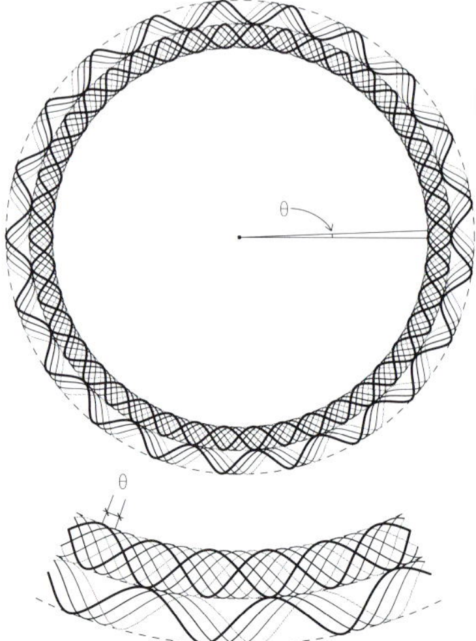

7. Each layer can be rotated in plan by an angle (θ) to produce twisting patterns along the facade. The toolpath can undulate vertically by applying a scaling factor over a certain number of layers (Uv).

Generative Matrix

R_1 = 3048 mm
T = 305 mm
E_H = 38 mm
E_W = 38 mm
H = 3658 mm
S = 60%
G = Curve A
C = 3
P_1 = 0-1
P_2 = 0-1
P_3 = 1-0
A_1 = T/2
A_2 = T/2
A_3 = T/2
U_H = 42
U_V = 0
R = 0°

Control Model

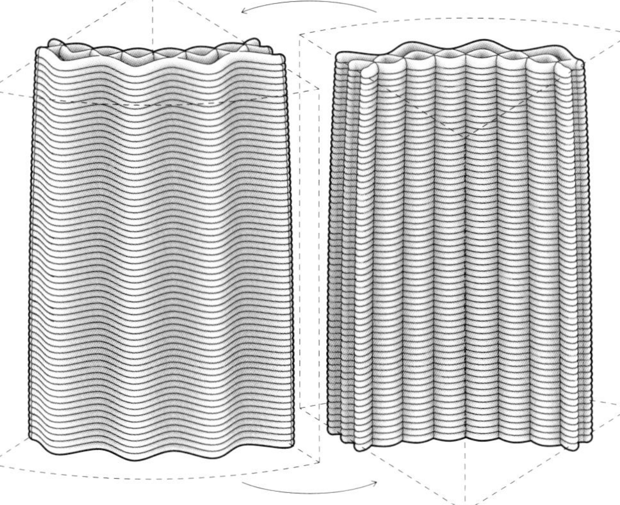

R_1 = 3048 mm
T = 305 mm
E_H = 38 mm
E_W = 38 mm
H = 3658 mm
S = 60%
G = Curve A
C = 3
P_1 = 0-1
P_2 = 0-1
P_3 = 1-0
A_1 = T/2
A_2 = T/2
A_3 = T/2
U_H = 42
U_V = 0
R = 2.14°

Rotated Layers

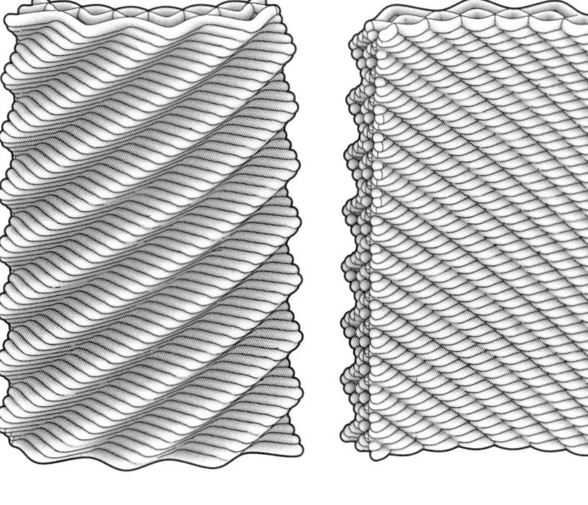

R_1 = 3048 mm
T = 305 mm
E_H = 38 mm
E_W = 38 mm
H = 3658 mm
S = 60%
G = Curve A
C = 1
P_1 = 1-0-0-1
A_1 = T
U_H = 42
U_V = 0
R = 0°

Wide Single Undulation

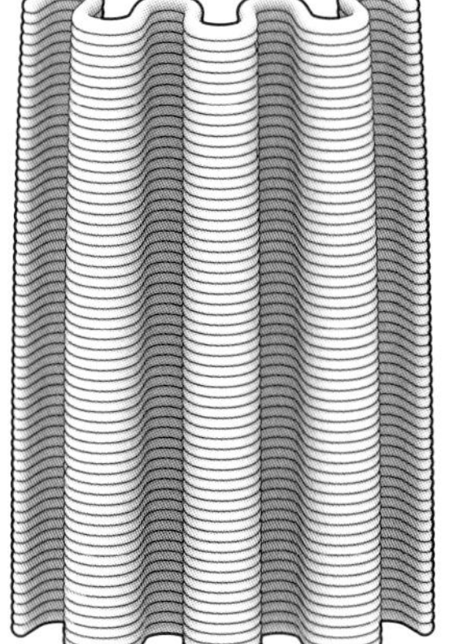
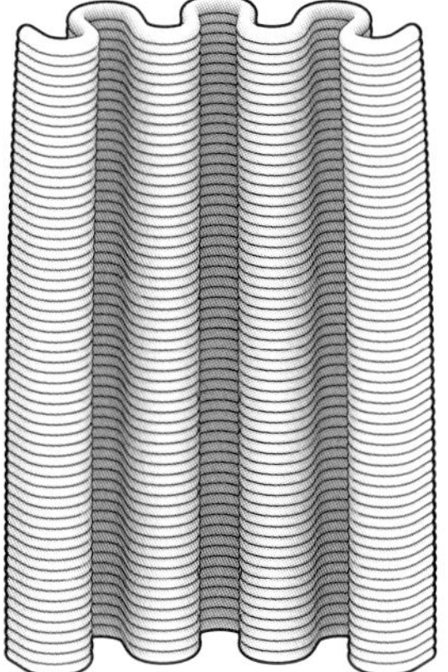

R_1 = 3048 mm
T = 305 mm
E_H = 38 mm
E_W = 38 mm
H = 3658 mm
S = 60%
G = Curve A
C = 1
P_1 = 1-0-0-1
A_1 = T
U_H = 112
U_V = 0
R = 3.21°

Dense Single Undulation

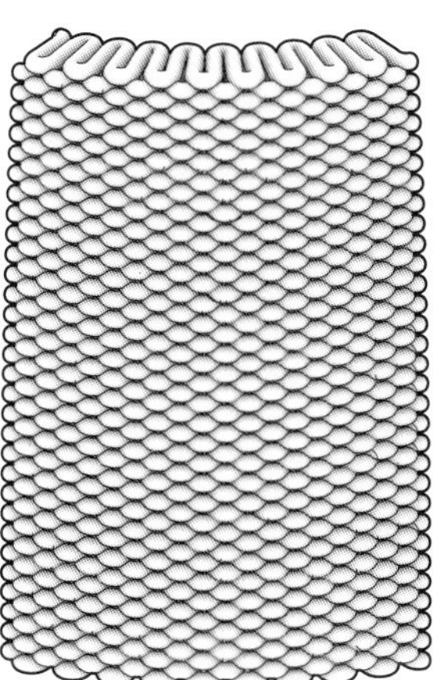
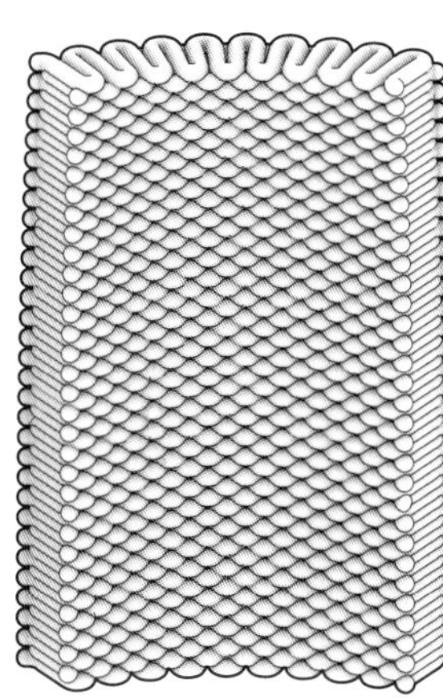

R_1 = 3048 mm
T = 305 mm
E_H = 38 mm
E_W = 38 mm
H = 3658 mm
S - 60%
G = Curve A
C = 3
P_1 = N/A
P_2 = 0-1
P_3 = N/A
A_1 = 0
A_2 = T
A_3 = 0
U_H = 42
U_V = 0
R = 0°

Standard 3-Layer Infill

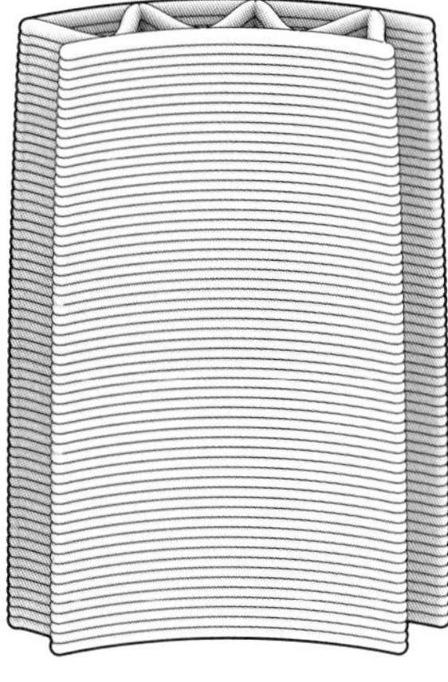

R_1 = 3048 mm
T = 305 mm
E_H = 38 mm
E_W = 38 mm
H = 3658 mm
S = 60%
G = Curve A
C = 3
P_1 = N/A
P_2 = 0-1-2-3-3-2-1-0 (every 4th layer)
P_3 = N/A
A_1 = 0
A_2 = 2*T
A_3 = 0
U_H = 42
U_V = 0
R = 1.07°

Alternating Loops

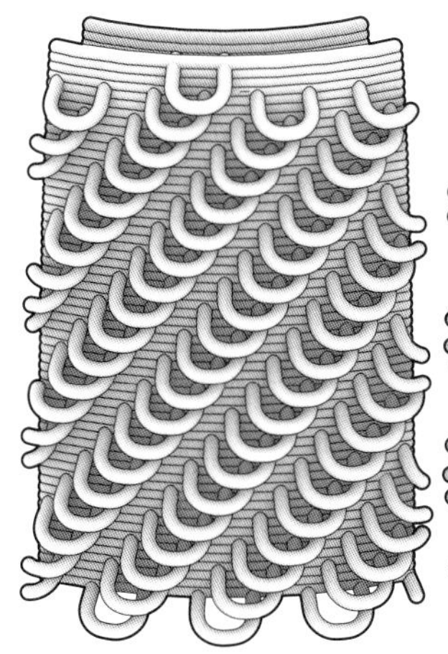
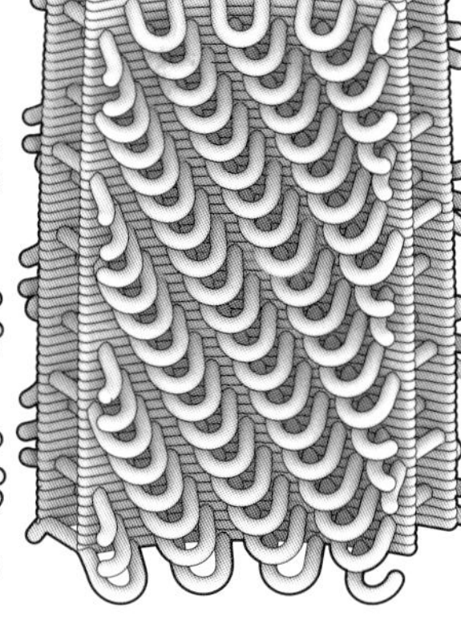

R_1 = 3048 mm
T = 305 mm
E_H = 38 mm
E_W = 38 mm
H = 3658 mm
S = 60%
G = Curve A
C = 2
P_1 = 0-1
P_2 = 1-0
A_1 = T/2
A_2 = T/2
U_H = 42
U_V = 10
R = 0°

Vertical Undulation

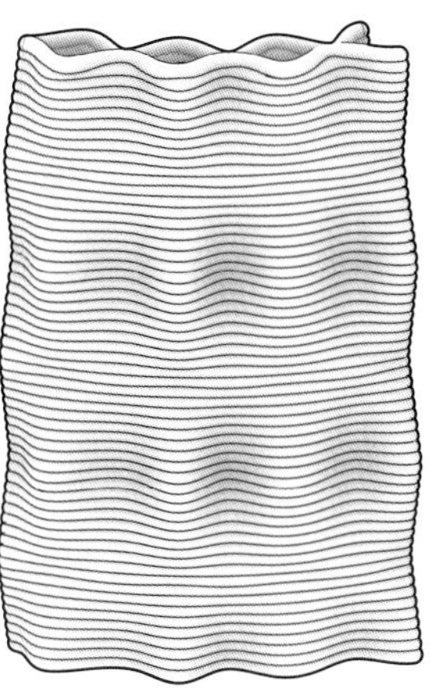
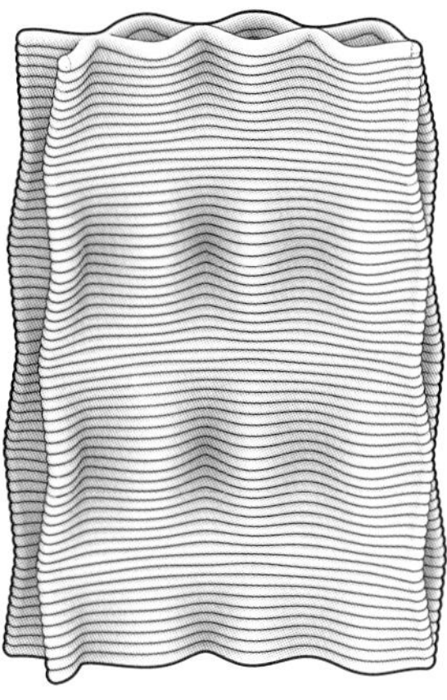

R_1 = 3048 mm
T = 305 mm
E_H = 38 mm
E_W = 38 mm
H = 3658 mm
S = 60%
G = Curve A
C = 2
P_1 = 0-1-1-0
P_2 = 1-0-0-1
A_1 = T
A_2 = T
U_H = 42
U_V = 10
R = 2.14°

Rotated Vertical Undulation

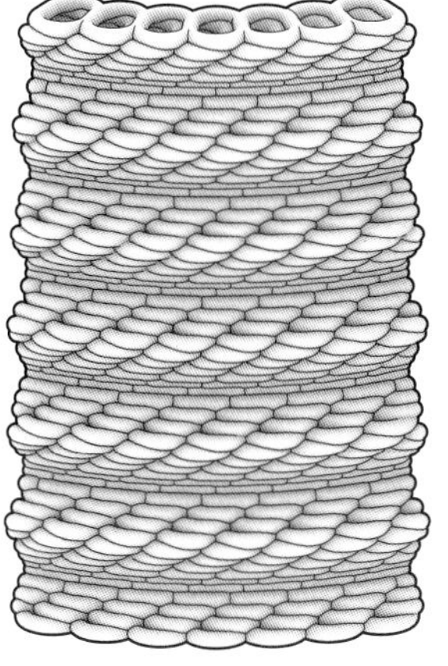
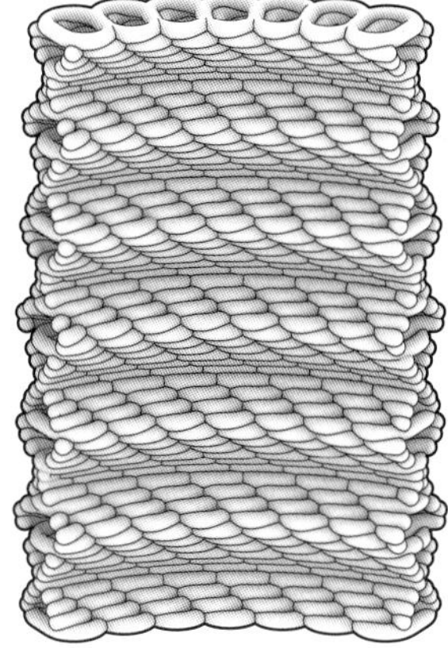

WOVEN MESHES

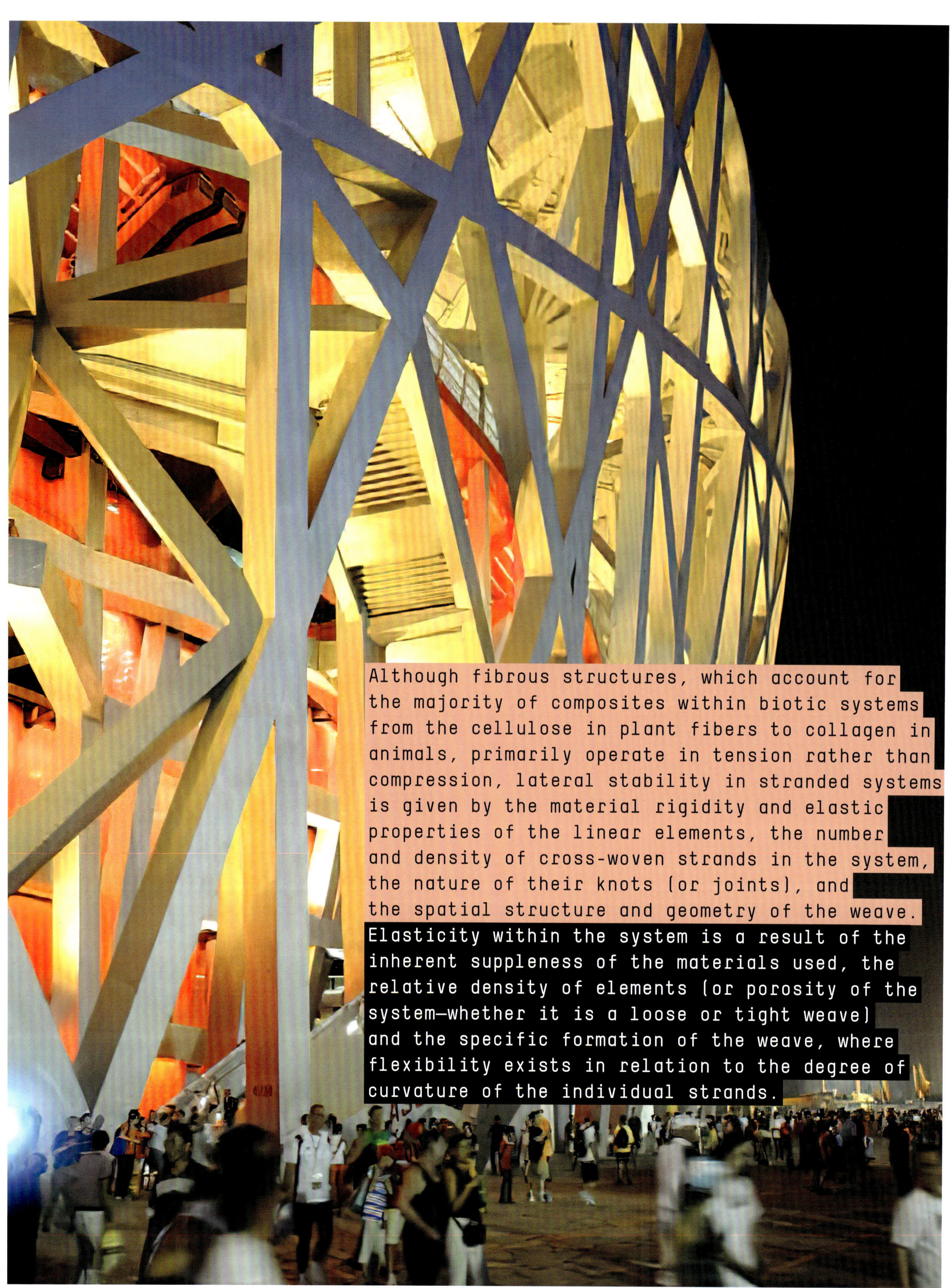

Although fibrous structures, which account for the majority of composites within biotic systems from the cellulose in plant fibers to collagen in animals, primarily operate in tension rather than compression, lateral stability in stranded systems is given by the material rigidity and elastic properties of the linear elements, the number and density of cross-woven strands in the system, the nature of their knots (or joints), and the spatial structure and geometry of the weave. Elasticity within the system is a result of the inherent suppleness of the materials used, the relative density of elements (or porosity of the system—whether it is a loose or tight weave) and the specific formation of the weave, where flexibility exists in relation to the degree of curvature of the individual strands.

Stranded Systems, Rhizomes and Meshworks

Weaving functions through interlocking—the intertwining of distinct strands within a system in order to stabilize individual linear elements that would otherwise lack coherence, rigidity or structure. It is a technique to produce a two-dimensional planar surface, or, when these move out of the plane as in basket weaving, a three-dimensional spatial surface, from one-dimensional linear elements. In traditional textiles, woven structures are produced through the interlacing of two distinct sets of threads known as warp and weft. Since cross-patterning is necessary to interlock woven structures, these sets of fibrous strands were traditionally positioned perpendicular to each other, the warp running longitudinally and the weft laterally, where the first set of strands is fixed and the second set mobile to enable it to wind sinuously above and below the fixed. In woven meshes, stability is achieved less by the regularity or irregularity of the system, than by the potential interlacing, entangling, and knotting of distinct fibers. Elasticity within the system is a result of the inherent suppleness of the materials used, the relative density of elements (or porosity of the system—whether it is a loose or tight weave) and the specific formation of the weave, where flexibility exists in relation to the degree of curvature of the individual strands. The straight and perpendicularly intersecting paths of traditional woven fabrics in combination with the tightness of the weave, for example, is what produces the relative fixity of the system which is biased to move only in the lateral direction. Taut longitudinally, the woven fabric is able to be stretched laterally when the parallel strands of the warp separate as the sine curve of the weft is straightened out. Knitted weaves[1] on the other hand, are based on meandering loops, rendering these surfaces flexible and allowing them to be stretched in different directions.

In his pioneering treatise on architecture, Gottfried Semper had argued that the beginning of building coincides with knotting as the first form of joinery and the intertwining of natural fibers that enabled branches and grasses to be transformed into woven walls. Although often reinterpreted either as an argument for the primacy of cladding or an allegory for the origins of tectonic construction, what is perhaps more compelling is the application of the principles of weaving to a range of architectural scales from the development of woven skin systems to the articulation of complex structural meshes. In architecture, trusses, lattices, and geodetics have conventionally operated as structural meshworks that distribute forces directionally, like a woven basket or fabric, according to the geometry of the weave. Although fibrous structures, which account for the majority of composites within biotic systems from the cellulose in plant fibers to collagen in animals, primarily operate in tension rather than compression, lateral stability in stranded systems is given by the material rigidity and elastic properties of the linear elements, the number and density of cross-woven strands in the system, the nature of their knots (or joints) and the spatial structure and geometry of the weave.

Architectural projects by Shigeru Ban such as the Japan Pavilion for the 2000 Expo in Hannover, a lightweight shell structure comprised of a geodesic mesh of lashed-together woven paper tubes, or the more complex tectonic hexagonal weaving of glue-laminated timbers in the Centre Pompidou Metz, simultaneously exploit, as in the making of a basket, the tensile strength and resilient flexibility of the stranded materials used in combination with the global stability given by the spatial curvature of the structure. The tubular paper lattice of the expo pavilion operates as textile-like meshwork that is redeployed according to the logic of geodesic framing systems to minimize distances, material, and energy while directing forces along the topological curvature of the surface. The lines of geodetic curves, such as those used in Fuller's domes, are established by finding the shortest path across a surface that establishes the shape of its equilibrium. These are redeployed by Foster + Partners and transformed into the diagonal spiraling radial geometry and continuously triangulated skin of the Swiss Re Headquarters in London. Similar to the mesh of the geodetic airframe based on a spiral crossing basket-weave of load-bearing members, this project exploits the self-similarity and structural efficiency of the geodetic weave, while modulating the internal reticulation of its surface to accommodate a changing global form. Computational geometry and advanced robotics have further expanded the application of these systems to highly differentiated structures by enabling the interactive modeling of vector fields across volumetric surfaces and expediting their translation

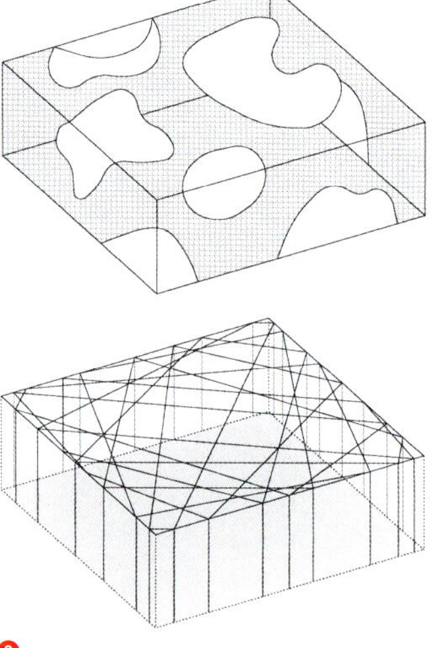

into geodetically informed patterns that optimize the elastic curvature of linear elements constrained to the surface.[2]

Architectural mesh structures such as the Alishan footbridge by Reiser + Umemoto ❶ extend the application of the woven mesh typology, while deviating from the principals of geodetic optimization to reflect the more complex negotiation of spatial, aesthetic, and structural demands. The bridge form, spatially derived from the differential unfolding of a tubular surface, and tectonically signifying the indigenous craft culture of the place, is delineated by a double-layered lattice of woven structural filaments that trace the geometry of its surface. If the goal of engineering is to minimize effort through the most efficient transfer of forces along a surface or through a structure, this project attempts to do the opposite by requiring a heightened intensity of material effort necessary to sustain its form yet demands that this be achieved with the apparent grace and poise of an aesthetic economy of means, while rendering visible, through the tracery of the mesh, the complex variability of its double-curved continuous surface.

In architectural systems, the assumption that optimized forms would represent universal truths ignores the true complexity of real material forces operating along surfaces or through a field by attempting to minimize rather than amplify their potential expression through the structural system. In contrast, heterogeneous or complex systems such as the Fenquihu footbridge, whose intention might be to delay, detour, or amplify the propagation of forces, or conversely, as in Toyo Ito's Sendai Mediatheque and Herzog & deMeuron's Beijing National Stadium, to paradoxically misalign the true functioning of the assembly in relation to its perceptual effects, often serve to undermine our expectations for a rigid and stable tectonic, while also signifying the intrinsic complexity of an energetic living matter. Pier Luigi Nervi's Gatti Wool Mill project, for example, is a clear manifestation of the relationship between matter and force as expressed in the isostatic rib structure of the waffle slab. Rather than either suppressing or neutralizing forces through a homogenous system, Nervi attempts to reveal the potential patterns of force concealed within the material system by expressing these forces in the differentiated (rather than homogeneous) pattern of the ribs. The internal modulation of this material structure is simultaneously abstract-descriptive and immanent-real in that it operates to impart dimensionality to flowing matter by translating the sensation of its forces into geometries of perceptible movement. These geometries are incarnated in the rib structure, formed to follow isostatic curves tangential to the bending moments that would be theoretically produced by stresses on the slab, that not only perceptually reveal and amplify these forces, but also, since forces necessarily flow along the vectors of matter, concurrently direct these forces along predetermined paths. Form paradoxically follows force at the same moment that force also follows form.

As a counter to the striated logics of woven systems, Deleuze had proposed felt as a form of smooth "anti-fabric," a supple solid that unlike the ordered, hierarchical and homogeneous patterned geometries of typical textile structures, operates only through "the entanglement of fibers obtained by fulling."[3] The structure of felt, which might be imagined to be a randomly produced formless overlay of lines, distills the mesh down to a single set of principals—the layering, intersection, and knotting or entangling of strands—that follow no spatial, geometric or patterned order other than their requisite density, crossing and interlocking within the surface. Toyo Ito's initial sketch for the Serpentine Pavilion ❷ might be imagined to follow a similar logic. The structure emerged from two primary conditions evident as initial design parameters: that the structure would be developed as a heterogeneous rhizomatic skin generated by the random, but evenly distributed, crisscrossing of straight lines to be projected onto an orthogonal box; and that the surface would be porous with integrated openings that would enable light and air to move through the pavilion. Rather than starting with a regular structure that gains complexity through a process of progressive deformation or differentiation in relation to the addition of information to the system, Ito begins with an irreducible multiplicity, a complex knotted mesh or anti-structural system as the basis of his architecture. The intention of this act, perhaps to undermine the culture of stasis to which architecture's foundations are wedded on the one hand and to contest the assumption that structural integrity is necessarily conjoined with the perception of clearly ordered systems on the other, proposes complexity and apparent randomness as a challenge to the structuring of material. Although perceptually unordered, the mesh operates through a different logic, where the layering and intersection of skewed lines that fill, rather than frame the surface are what paradoxically enable the structural entanglement necessary for its support.

Rather than simply attempting to build the random mesh, the Advanced Geometry Unit at ARUP engineers generated an internal algorithmic logic that would allow the heterogeneity of the mesh to evolve from a rule-based parametric system by finding a relationship between the rich complexity of the meshwork and a system that could rationalize its geometry, structure, and construction. Difference and order were simultaneously infused into the diagram by degrees. First, by establishing a relationship between the skewed line and the orthogonal plan of the pavilion by introducing an oblique ordering system that would not repeat the parallelism of the Cartesian system. Second, by employing a fractal geometry that connects the middle of one side of the square plan to the third of the adjacent side, yielding a laterally shifted, rotated and

4

6

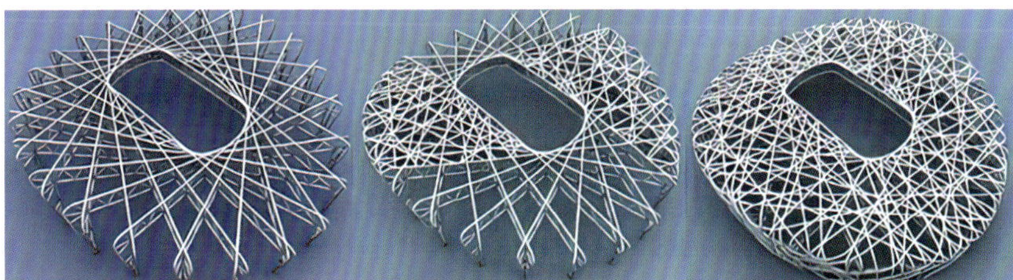

5

smaller truncated square partially inscribed within the initial boundary of the first, such that the extension of its sides would spawn a fractional duplicate of itself. And third, by recursively repeating and scaling these operations seven times according to the same logic so that the space produced by the smallest resultant square within the system would be relatively equivalent in size to, and therefore concealed within, the fractional divisions of the field.

Structural depth was then achieved through the perpendicular extrusion of the meshwork to produce a woven lattice of beams, and porosity introduced through the alternation of solid and void facets that are evenly, yet heterogeneously distributed throughout the field. Although the underlying spiral geometry of squares and hierarchical ziggurat structure are locally detectable within the subtle progressive thickening of the beams as one moves from the center to the periphery of the pavilion, these remain perceptually hidden within the consistency of the smooth, yet coarse-grained, thickened skin. The consistency of this permeable tectonic membrane as it wraps the entirety of the building's surfaces, conceals the global hierarchy, functional differentiation and semiotic distinctions of structure/skin, roof/wall, wall/window as these are conflated into a singular yet complex system emerging from a simple set of rules 3. Modularity and repetition preserve the intrinsic order required by the structure and its fabrication, yet, akin to natural systems, embed these within a locally constituted evolutionary genetic logic that underlies the heterogeneous complexity of the whole.

The Beijing National Stadium by Herzog & de Meuron 4, aptly described as the "bird's nest" because of its appearance as a tangled meshwork shaped into a bowl-like vessel, also conceals the regularity of its structure behind the heterogeneous superimposition of distinct linear systems that, similarly collapse roof, structure, and façade into a single interwoven stranded surface. The primary structure of the stadium is constituted by twenty four branching v-shaped columns evenly spaced around the perimeter of the building that define the plane of the façade 5. Each of these columns splits into three divergent tubular strands that move upward from the base, two of which cant both outward and sideways until they curve to form the fillets joining wall and roof, and then converge again and intersect each other to form the top chords of two splayed horizontal trusses that span the roof. The forty eight incrementally rotating trusses that connect to these split columns form a regular series of woven interlocking portals that crisscross each other along skewed pathways as they delineate the outer boundary of an opening over the athletic field located at the center of the saddle-shaped elliptical structure. These columns and trusses constitute a parametrically optimized three dimensional lattice of twisting box-shaped steel tubes that are formed to wrap the volume produced by the progeny of an elliptical extruded plan and a toroidal surface. This lattice is then overlaid with a complex irregular web of repeatable yet varied secondary and tertiary beams located along the outer surface that operate to conceal the regularity of the primary structure. The first of these sets of beams bisect yet rotate away from the primary structural elements, and the second set follow the programmatic spirals that move bodies throughout the stadium. By constructing all three systems as a continuously stranded wrapper, and by using identically sized square steel tubes (although of different plate thicknesses) and compressing their outer structural elements into a single doubly curved surface, the hierarchy and order intrinsic to the functioning of the primary system is undermined while creating the appearance that the stadium, like an enormous version of a weaver bird's nest, retains its form solely by the circumnavigation and woven entanglement of its stochastically banded web. Although evolving from an initially ordered structure, the sheer spatial complexity and continuity of this overlay of stranded systems demanded a parametric modeling strategy that could immediately compute enormous sets of data while propagating local design changes continuously throughout the meshwork.

The Sendai Mediatheque 6 repeats this strategy of misaligning structural and perceptual logics as it attempts to obscure the building's structural stability behind its fluid phenomenal affects. The shifting diameters, seemingly random placement, lateral deformation, slanting, and aeration of the woven mesh columns that support the building attribute to them a deceptive precariousness that undermines our expectation for structural order, fixity, and stability despite their actual earthquake resistant strength. Alternating between solid, liquid, and gaseous states, the structure of each column is diffused through the multiplicity of lines that constitute the mesh, dematerializing its solidity into an aerated cloud of matter. Intended to resemble seaweed undulating within a liquid substrate, these inflated and laterally moving columns simultaneously act as light wells and infrastructural conduits that appear to thread through, rather than sit below (and between) the floor plates, causing these thin horizontal strata to phenomenally float and shift in space, seemingly suspended in a fluid medium. The columns are constituted by a stacked vertical series of horizontal rings that are parametrically generated to incrementally vary in diameter and lateral displacement. These are conjoined by woven triangulated lattices that, similar to fish-net stockings, appear to locally stretch and compress as they follow the deformed surfaces and changing radii of the columns. Although the columns appear to thread through the holes in the slabs, at the points where each of the columns and floor plates intersect, the honeycomb structure hidden inside the slab morphs into a triangular pattern that is woven directly into the mesh of the tubular columns, and rigidly tied back to its rings. This connection produces an exceptionally strong structure in spite of its

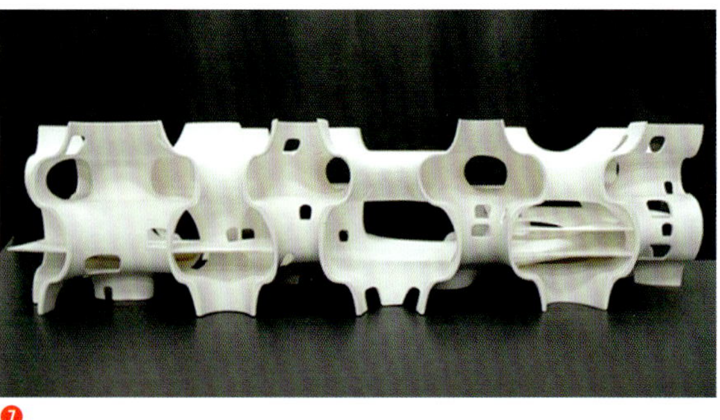

7

8

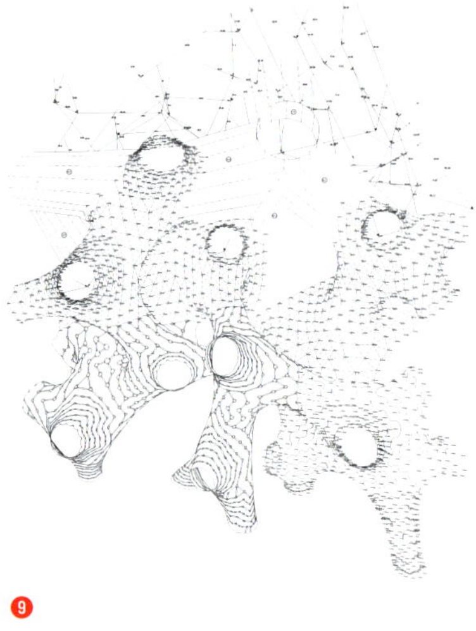

9

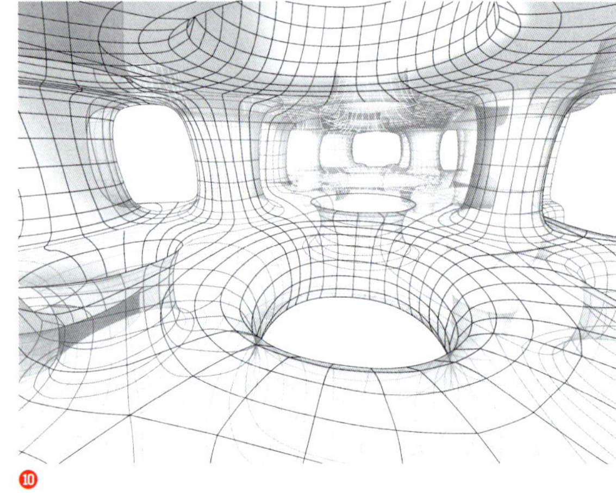

10

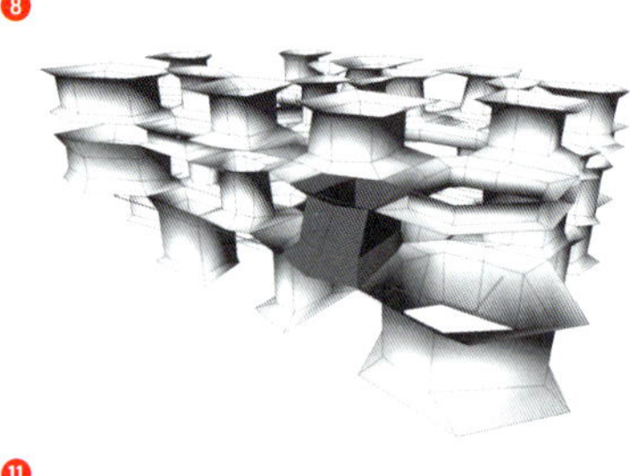

11

opposite perceptual effect, a condition directly attributable to the morphogenetic flexibility of the woven mesh.

The application of weaving to space through the topological continuity of tubular structures finds its evolution in projects such as Ito's Taichung Opera House 7 and the complex spatial network of interlaced surfaces in the Y/Surf/Struc and nonLin/Lin Pavilions by theverymany. Each of these projects translates linear meshworks into thickened tubular spatial lattices that shift the emphasis from the trajectories of the strands and the surfaces that they produce through their weave to the changing radii of ovoidal aperatures that are projected along these strands (like those in the making of a torus) and the contiguous curvilinear surfaces that they generate. In the nonLin/Lin Pavilion 8, a full-scale prototype resembling an architectonic version of sea coral, the nonlinear generation of its multidirectional branching morphology and doubly curved spatial surface is countered by the linearity of its developable geometry—that is, its ability to be unfolded into linear elements that can be cut out of planar aluminum sheets. Although the geometric description of these planar strips is subtly registered in the array of points projected as asterisks on the surface of these tubes, the complexity of both the network and surface provide a challenge to automated processes of unfolding, demanding a local, rather than global strategy of discretization 9.

In the opera house, these tubular networks become the actual space of inhabitation where the difference between the inside and the outside of the tube vanishes in relation to the density of the weave 10. Here, two three-dimensional spatial grids are interlocked, generating two sets of spaces each entirely continuous in both plan and section that although adjacent, remain spatially separated by the undulating surface of serial and stacked catenoids that both sets of spaces share.[4] The two grids are diagonally offset in plan, producing on each level a checkerboard pattern of polygonal spaces that tessellate the plan 11. These are then both differentiated to accommodate programmatic demands within the structure and algorithmically smoothed to generate ovoids that laterally grow and shrink as they move vertically through the building, following the sectional trajectories of the catenoids. The topological continuity produced by this truly volumetric woven space is wholly resistant to the Cartesianism from which it evolved and defies dimensionality such that its division into distinct levels is determined in one of two ways. Either, these are generated abstractly by the local placement of horizontal planar "plugs" that, like the plans, sections, and elevations, arbitrarily slice through the building and can therefore be positioned at potentially any height within an undulating spatial strand. Or alternatively, these are sited immanently, by indexing the points of inflection in the system—those moments of variable curvature connecting convex and concave sections of the surface that expose the original joints (or polygonal edges) of the catenoidal grid. As a thickened zone of occupation, rather than as a structure or surface, the woven mesh generates an extraordinary spatial experience where distinctions between movement and stasis, or inside and outside are reduced to the shrinking and widening of dimensions that either directly funnel, or spread and diffuse movement, or the degrees of concavity and convexity that might define a space as these are embedded in the changing inflections of its continuous surface.

The return to more literal forms of weaving stranded systems, yet those that radically expand the architectural paradigms to which these have been applied, is instantiated in the 2012 ICD/ITKE Research Pavilion in Stuttgart and the Polymorph project by Jenny Sabin. Each of these projects is dependent on the integration of rigid structures within the system—either globally as in the steel formwork for the ICD/ITKE Pavilion, or locally as in the digitally printed ceramic modules of Polymorph, that act as components operating in compression that complement the tensile capacity of the weave. In the pentagonal star-shaped ICD/ITKE research pavilion, a technologically advanced architectural transformation of the woven string sculptures of Naum Gabo, the triangulated steel frame structure acts as a lightweight mold onto which thirty kilometers of resin saturated glass and carbon fiber composites are wound 12. As an integration of computational, biomimetic, material, and robotic strategies, the project applies the chitinous micro-fibrous morphology of arthropodal skeletons to the development of a laminated fibrous structural building skin. The micro-differentiation of this semi-transparent material skin and its high tensile strength are achieved through the

12

13

14

geometric overlay and intersection of anisotropically directed filaments across the surface. In accordance with the biotic model that served as the point of departure for the project, these strands are organized in parallel in relation to the transfer of loads or are layered in different orientations to produce isotropic composites that accommodate uniform or multidirectional loads to optimize the pattern of the weave in relation to the flow of forces traversing the surface. Facilitated by the rotation of the structure and the programming of the robotic arm that controls the winding sequences, placement, and trajectory of fibers, the complex helicoidal layering of strands is guided by curvilinear grooved fins that project radially from the steel structure. These provide a minimal formwork for the hyperbolic paraboloid surfaces that are generated by the spinning of striated filaments around the structure, the final product of which is a four-millimeter-thick, automatically fabricated woven shell that is able to span a distance of eight meters.

Perhaps located at the opposite extreme of the ICD/ITKE's pavilion search for optimization, is the woven ceramic meshwork of *Polymorph* 13. An intricate fibrous floating cloud composed of over 1,000 interlinked modular ceramic components, this project is suspended in space and compels the eye to be immersed within the complexity of its entanglement while haptically tracing its intertwined linear trajectories. Polymorph exposes the relationships between a spatial surface or volume and its tessellated cellular division, on the one hand, and a linear, interlaced network that is organized by a triangulated geometry on the other. Concurrently plastic and rigid, the ceramic modules that are threaded together operate as preformed knots within the system. These act to direct the fibrous strands that are threaded within them, while operating as rigid components that, like beads on a necklace, function in compression to provide resistance and structural stability to the whole, enabling the meshwork to function in both tension and compression.

The module is a repeatable element that exposes the complexity of part to whole relationships within the weave, such that a family of three distinct but related ceramic modules are able to generate over 1,300 different connective combinations. This exposes one of the principal logics of weaving and crochet—how the incremental aggregation and serial repetition of varied loops and knots are able to integrate nonlinear modifications into the system and generate intricate and highly complex patterning across the whole. In other words, the structuring of complex global forms of order out of local differences that exploit two critical conditions of the weave: the statistical aggregation of patterned differences through the self-similar structure of its loops that are recreated in the ceramic modules of Polymorph, and the qualities achieved from sheer quantity when the intensive whole is irreducible to the sum of its parts.[5] In this case, complexity is already decisively embedded in the form of each single module that is then augmented by the double-layering of elements in the weave and the vast combinatorial permutations locally allowed by each knot within this system. Each component is a pinwheel- and trefoil-formed looped ceramic module that has been fabricated using 3D-printed molds and ceramic slip casting, where the ductility and pliability of the initial material enables the fluid morphological transformation between point, line, surface and volume both within each individual component and across the network. The specificity and internal differentiation of the knotted form of the modules, which permit three, rather than two, points of connection from each knot (doubled to six because of the layering of the weave), engenders the amplification of difference through the multiplication of connections offered from each node, the incremental rotation and mirroring of components, and the different modes of interlock that are facilitated when sets of modules are layered and then conjoined.

As a companion to Polymorph's floating volume, Mathematized Cloud by Alisa Andrasek 14 is a highly complex meteorological storm simulated from algorithmically weighted swarming vectors that replaces the intertwining of distinct fibrous strands with a voxel lattice made from a single robotically extruded thermoplastic filament. The necessity of the knot is eliminated by the ability of the thermoplastic material to fuse when heated, enabling a single 3D-extruded filament of matter, mobilized by the animate complexity of a robot to fill a poly-dimensional space. Simultaneously liquid and solid, the viscous material which moves through space like a vector as if being drawn in the air, delineates the edges and diagonal bracing struts of the voxelized lattice, fusing and turning at every vertex, while maintaining the topological continuity of a vector. Just as Polymorph had reinvented the weave by focusing on the spatial topology of its knots, Mathematized Cloud reinvents the architectonic geometry of the lattice by layering the complexity of highly mobile multi-agent systems with the intricacy of a robotically crafted high-precision micro-structure, bringing architecture closer to the performance found in natural systems through the innovative application of new forms of computational craft.

Notes

1. Although knitting and weaving are distinct procedures, the term "weaving" is used in a broad way throughout this text to refer to intertwined stranded systems.

2. Helmut Pottmann, Qi-Xing Huang, Bai-Lin Deng, Alexander Schiftner, Martin Kilian, Leonidas J. Guibas, and Johannes Wallner. "Geodesic patterns," *ACM Transactions on Graphics* 29, No. 4, (July 26, 2010): 1–10.

3. Gilles Deleuze and Félix Guattari, *A Thousand Plateaus*, trans. Brian Massumi (Minneapolis: University of Minnesota Press, 1987), 475–476.

4. A catenoid is a three-dimensional shape produced by rotating a catenary curve around an axis.

5. For a discussion on the qualitative aspects of intensive quantities see *Atlas of Novel Tectonics* (New York: Princeton Architectural Press, 2006), 46.

Gatti Wool Factory
Pier Luigi Nervi

Built 1951-1953
Rome, Italy

6.1a

An important project in the advancement of concrete construction systems, the Gatti Wool Mill employs an waffle slab system whose woven rib pattern follows the geometry of material forces—the isostatic trajectories of principal bending moments—embedded within the system. The design of the project, which required a wide-spanning floor system to support the heavy industrial machinery of the factory, is an evolution of Nervi's research on prefabricated concrete elements using moveable ferrocement formwork and Aldo Arcangeli's research on isostatic systems. Molding reinforced concrete ribs along the lines of force not only enabled a more efficient use of material by reducing the overall thickness of the slab and maintaining depth where it was needed, but also generated a form that clearly expressed and rendered evident the complexity of structural forces hidden within the materiality of a flat slab system. In the Gatti Wool Mill, the ribs are arranged as centric systems radiating around the points where the columns supporting the floor plates meet the slab. The radial vectors, which move outward from these points, intersect the centric rings and the larger orthogonal grid of beams that organizes the ceiling and defines the geometry of the outer edges of each 5-by-5-meter slab. These slabs, each of which is supported by a center column, are joined along their perimeters to form a monolithic whole. The trajectories of curved beams, which are the same depth as the perimeter beams, cut across this grid and link these columns into a fluid, continuous structural network—a geometric meshwork emerging from the physical forces within the system. This isostatic system for designing reinforced concrete structures was used in a number of other projects by Nervi including the Palace of Labor in Turin (1961) and the Large Sports Palace in Rome (1960).

6.1b

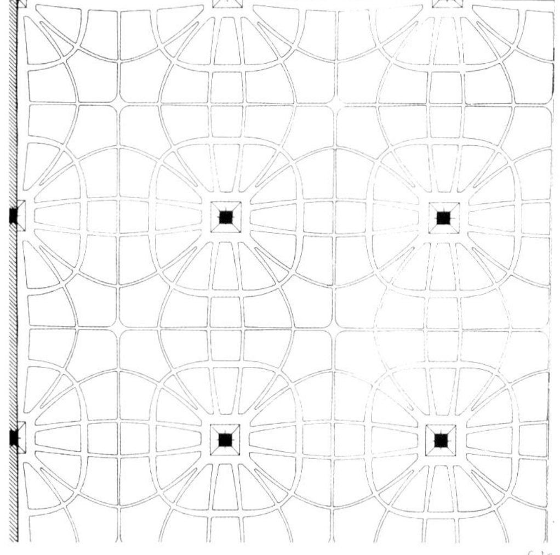

6.1c

6.1d

Continua Series: Design 1
Knoll International Showroom
Erwin Hauer

Built 1950
Mexico City, Mexico

6.2a

6.2b

The Continua Series of wall screens designed by Erwin Hauer are based on studies of repetitive continuities that enable the folding and weaving of doubly curved surfaces through the aggregation of complexly configured modules. Designs 1 through 5 of this series are based on an initial two-dimensional pattern that superimposes and overlaps two gridded fields of staggered circular forms. These diagonally oriented patterned fields are then interwoven by transforming the intersection of offset circles into a layered two-surface system whereby each surface has four points of connection, two of which cross above, and two of which cross below, the adjacent surface. This pattern of weaving renders solid the space between circular voids while transforming the area of overlap into openings so that the wall system becomes permeable to light and air. In Design 1, a further alteration of the surface occurs that conjoins the two layers at four additional points providing secondary segments that bridge across these openings. These secondary segments enable the edges of the stackable tiles—out of which this surface is physically constructed—to be continuous. The two diagonally oriented, opposing bridges that cross over and under each other and define the dominant pattern in this design are positioned at the center of each square tile, the regular aggregation of which, produces the modular wall system. Tiles are then fabricated by casting high-strength gypsum cement into molds. Akin to the sutured seam of a baseball, the edges of the curves embedded at the center of each of these tiles are topologically continuous enabling the weaving of the whole by exploiting the potential of conjoining two sets of fragmented spherical surfaces into saddle curves. The saddle shape, which combines concave and convex curvatures into a single continuous and spatial form, allows light to be diffused across the wall, whose gradients expose the subtle changes in its surface curvature. Adjusting the parameters of the system, such as the axes of rotation and the radius of curves upon which the design is based, enabled the emergence of a genetic family of related patterns that formed the basis of this wall series.

6.2c

6.2d

6.2e

30 Saint Mary Axe-Swiss Re
Foster + Partners
Built 1997-2004
London, United Kingdom

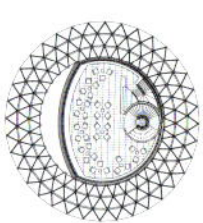
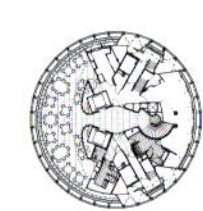
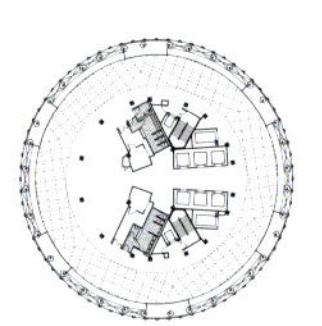
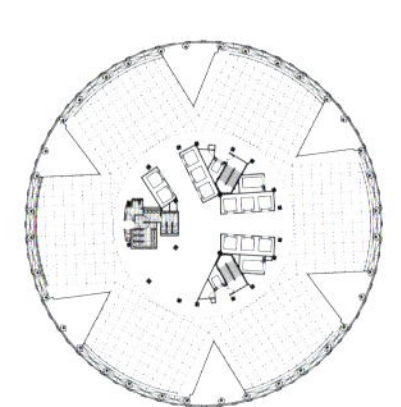
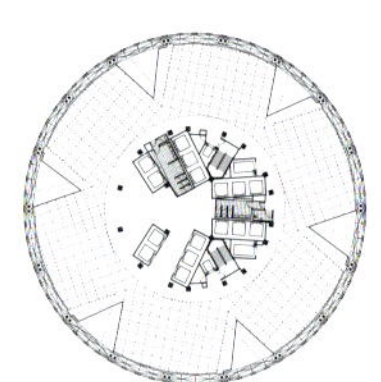
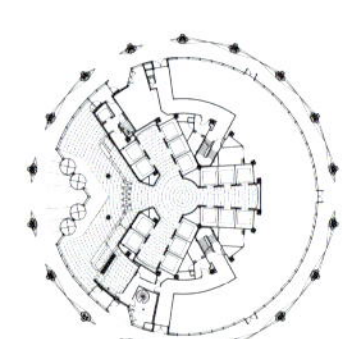

An instantly recognizable addition to the London's skyline, this highly innovative, forty-one-story tower provides 46,450 square meters of office space, in addition to retail space accessible from a public plaza at grade, and a 360-degree view of the skyline from its top floor. Generated by a circular plan with a radial geometry, the building widens in profile as it rises and tapers towards its apex. The tower's diagonally braced structure and triangulated skin allows column-free floors and a fully glazed façade, which opens up the building to light and views. Perimeter light wells, located between the radiating fingers of each floor, ensure access to light from within the core of the tower. These atria link vertically and are offset by 5 degrees on each successive floor to form a series of informal break-out spaces that spiral up the building. Besides contributing to the spaces for social interaction in the building, these spaces function as the building's "lungs," distributing fresh air drawn in through opening panels in the façade to reduce the energy consumed by the tower. The perimeter columns follow the helical path of the six-fingered floor plates up through the building, and a woven diagrid structure is formed by the pattern of intersecting columns that spiral in two directions. An additional series of horizontal rings connect the diagrid structure at its points of intersection resisting forces coming from the building's curvature and transforming the surface into a very stable tessellated triangulated structural shell. A parametric three-dimensional model was used to coordinate all interrelated components of the structure and facetted glazed cladding while optimizing its diagrid geometry. Responding to the constraints of the site, the building's form appears more slender than a rectangular block of equivalent size, and the slimming of its profile towards the base maximizes the public realm at ground level. Environmentally, its profile also reduces wind deflections, helping to maintain a comfortable environment at street level, while creating external pressure differentials that are exploited to drive its unique system of natural ventilation.

6.3a

6.3b

6.3c

6.3d

Sendai Mediatheque

Toyo Ito + Matsuro Sasaki

Built 1995–2000

Sendai, Japan

The Sendai Mediatheque is an eight-story structure that is located along Jozenji Street, a main avenue famous for its stately rows of Zelkova trees. The building, which contains 21,600 m² of occupiable floor area, combines a number of interacting programs including an art gallery, library, visual image media center, and service center for the hearing- and visually-impaired. The architectural proposal is comprised of three primary elements: a series of stacked floor plates, a field of structural tubes, and the outer skin of the building. The floor plates are thin horizontal layers that extend out to the glazed perimeter and are populated by patterned fields—of furnishing, library stacks (third and fourth floors), and movable gallery partitions (fifth and sixth floors)—each of which support the various programs distributed on the different levels. Thirteen vertical tubular columns that are set back from the building's perimeter penetrate the floor plates. Ranging from two to nine meters in diameter, these tubes are constructed as triangulated lattices of steel pipe and operate simultaneously as flexible structural elements and vertical conduits to enable the flows of energy, air, water, light, and people through the building. The columns, which appear to continuously deform as they move between and through the floor plates, are comprised of a vertically stacked series of horizontal rings that are parametrically generated to incrementally vary in diameter and lateral displacement. Despite their fluid appearance and seemingly random placement, these columns are structurally extremely stable and resistant to earthquake forces. Wrapping the plates is a glazed, double-layered envelope whose transparency enables the horizontal layers of the building to phenomenally extend beyond its boundary and for the interior structure and activities to be readily perceived from the street.

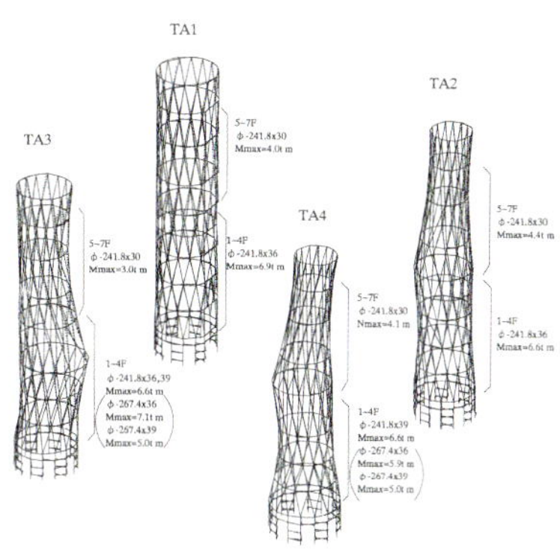

6.4a

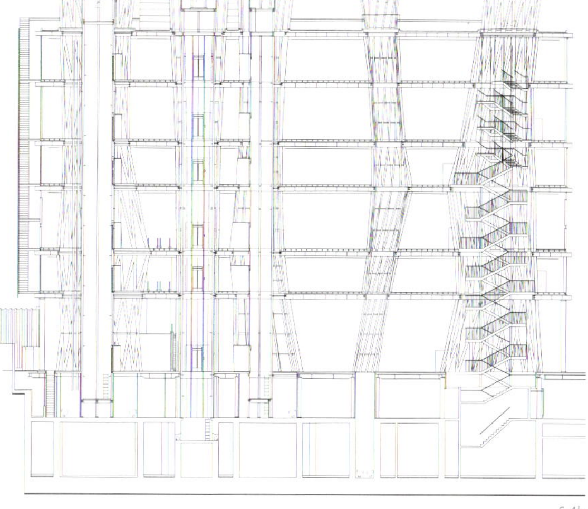
6.4b

6.4c

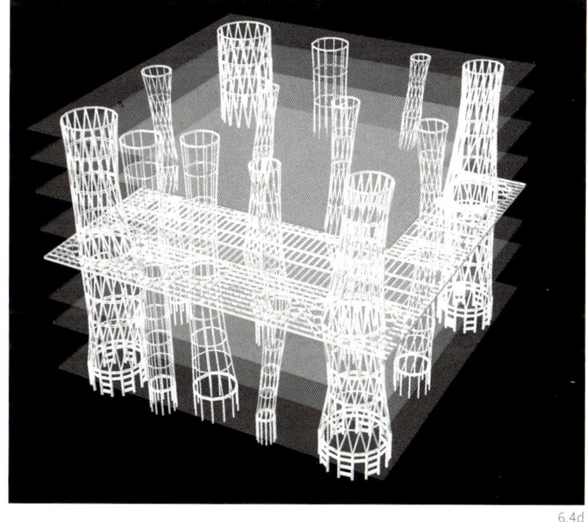
6.4d

6.4e

Serpentine Gallery Pavilion
Toyo Ito, Cecil Balmond + ARUP

Built 2002
London, United Kingdom

The 2002 Serpentine Gallery Pavilion is a porous white box with no internal columns—18-by-18 meters in plan and 4.5 meters high—that serves as a café during the day and is used for parties, debates, and lectures in the evening. The initial design proposal for the pavilion began with the overlay of two diagrammatic concepts: a random, yet evenly distributed set of intersecting skewed lines projected onto the orthogonal box that would operate as its structure and a field of large openings that would perforate the building's envelope to render it permeable to light and air. Although appearing as a random meshwork, the final structural lattice system for the project is a spiral pattern generated by a repetitive algorithm that progressively scaled, rotated, and truncated a proportional series of nested squares. The superimposition of these inscribed squares, and the extension and overlay their edges, results in a complex meshwork that conceals the structural pattern's regularity and hierarchy. This pattern is then folded from roof to wall in order to generate a continuous structural lattice that supports the building envelope. The structural stability of the lattice is achieved through the thickening of this linear meshwork, which is comprised of 550 mm-wide steel plates that vary in thickness from 12 to 50 mm depending on their position within the framework. Porosity is achieved across this envelope through the alternation of aluminum and glass infill panels that are suspended between the framing members of the lattice. These produce an abstract, polygonal, checkered pattern of solids and voids that defines the envelope's thickened skin, a consistent wrapper that operates simultaneously as structure and skin and that conflates the functions of roof, wall, and window.

6.5a

6.5b

6.5c

6.5d

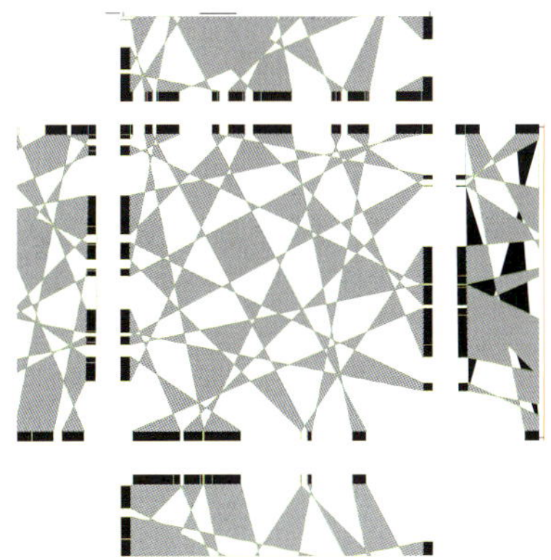
6.5e

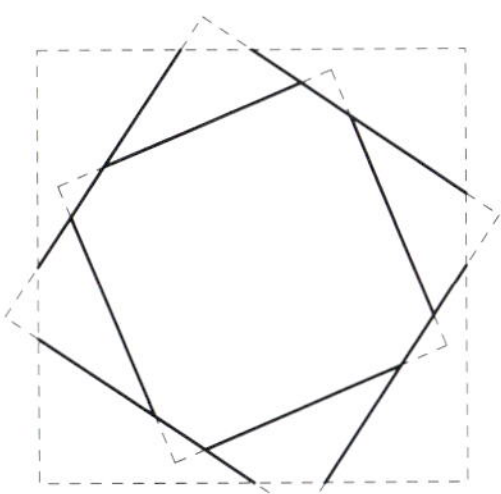
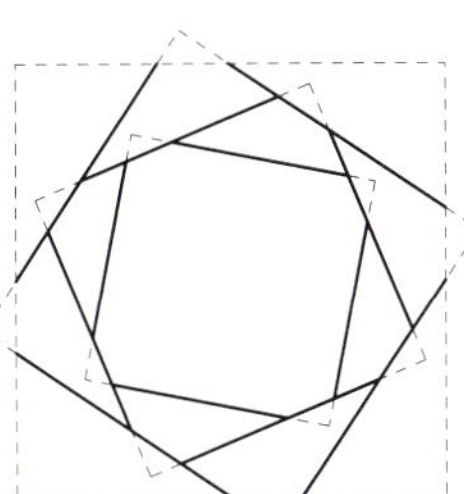
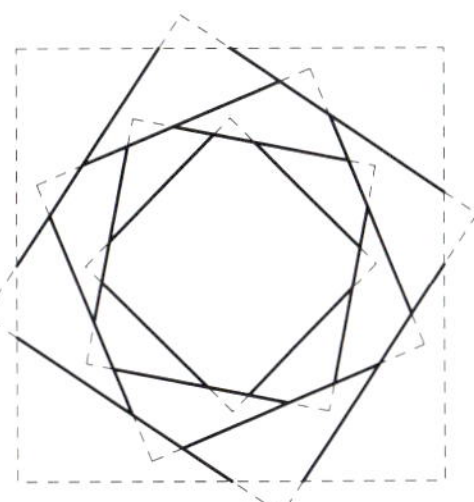
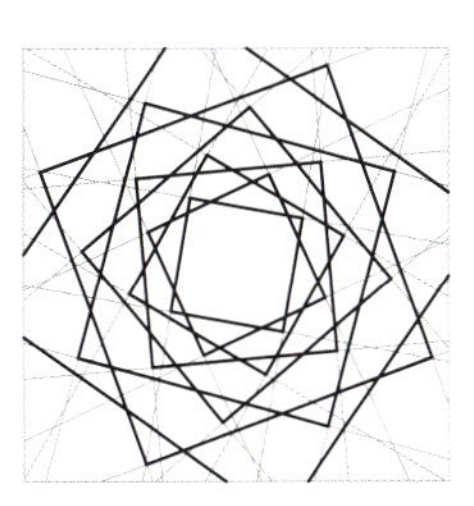
6.5f

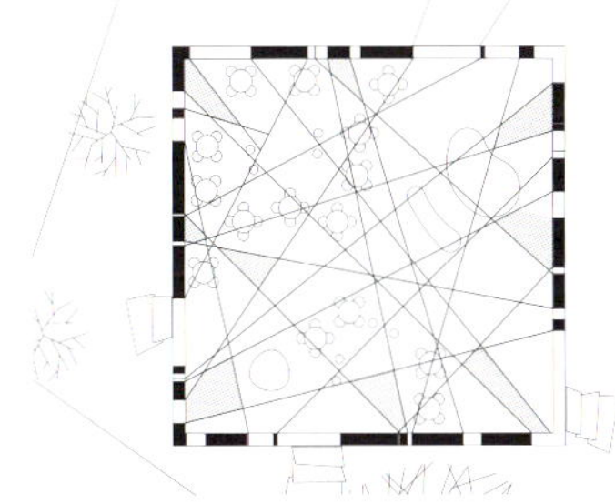
6.5g

6.5h

Beijing National Stadium
Herzog + de Meruon / Arup
Built 2002-2008
Beijing, China

6.6a

6.6b

6.6c

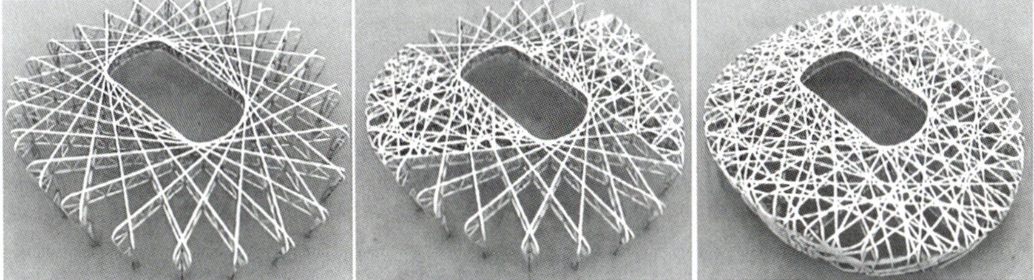

6.6d

6.6e

The National Stadium, commonly referred to as the "Bird's Nest" because of the complex interweaving of its exposed structure, is located at the center of the Olympic complex north of Beijing. Developed for the 2008 Olympic Games, the elliptical arena was conceived as a large collective vessel encased in a steel meshwork whose porosity, heterogeneity, asymmetrical curvature, and folded upper rim moderates the perceived scale of the whole. Sandwiched between the interior red concrete seating bowl that houses the audience for the games and the exposed exterior structure are the public spaces and stairs that connect the platforms and spiral up the sides of the stadium. Inspired by local art forms in China, in particular, the crackle-glazed pottery indigenous to the region, the stadium's woven meshwork operates as a layered system that conceals the regularity of its primary structure behind the seemingly random pattern that emerges when the three successive layers of its structure are superimposed. The structure is constituted by twenty-four canted double columns that are evenly spaced around the perimeter of the building and whose curvature at the top defines the folded edge of the roof. Each of these columns splits into a V-shape, branching into two trussed beams that intersect and then span across the roof. The forty-eight beams that crisscross the roof in this way tangentially define the perimeter of the opening above the field at the center of the stadium. A secondary system of mullions positioned at the outer layer of the façade and rotated to wrap the structure subdivides the primary structure to facilitate the panelized cladding, while a tertiary system follows the lines of the stairs that form a spiraling geometry that continues across the roof. The collapse of these systems into a single conflated layer of seemingly identically sized twisting steel tubes creates the appearance of a chaotic meshwork within which the programs of the stadium are housed. The roof of the structure is clad with a translucent ETFE membrane for weather protection that lets in natural light and that is positioned along the inner surface of the outermost exterior structure to ensure that the perception of the structural mesh remains dominant.

Tokyo Airspace

Faulders Studio + Process2

Built 2005-2007
Tokyo, Japan

6.7a

6.7b

6.7c

The project creates a 3,000-square-foot exterior building skin for a new four-story multifamily dwelling unit with professional photography studios in Tokyo, Japan. Located in the Ota-ku district, the site was previously occupied by the owner's family with a residence uniquely wrapped by a layer of lush vegetation that acted as a protective screen for the private dwelling. Since the entire site was razed to accommodate construction for the new larger development, the design invents an architectural system that performs with similar attributes to the demolished green strip and creates a new atmospheric space of protection. Conceived as a thin interstitial environment, the articulated densities of the open-celled meshwork that comprise the screen façade are layered in response to the inner workings of the building's program. The white porous screen, fabricated from an aluminum-faced composite known as Alpolic, defines a buffer zone that provides privacy from the street for the occupants living in the open-plan residences above while operating to unify the living units on the top floors of the building with the commercial spaces and landscaped areas below. Akin to a canopy of leaves, the layered screen mediates the building's relationship with its environment—shielding the glazed areas of the building behind a variegated foliage-like cover, while channeling rainwater away from exterior walkways via capillary action. The floating façade is constituted by four superimposed and overlapping patterned fields which were then paired and merged to create a double-layered skin. Each of these patterned fields is defined by a variegated cellular matrix, whose differentiation—in the size, shape, density, and distribution of its openings, for example—was generated as a response to specific parameters such as the need to engage or block daylight, or address customized views for the rooms positioned behind the screen. These differences were absorbed into a flexible computational system that enabled variation to occur within the consistency of a shared formal language while synthetically binding the multiplicity of requirements into a single continuous whole.

DAW/Double Agent White

theverymany

Built 2012

Sache, France

Double Agent White is a pavilion designed and built by Marc Fornes as part of the artist residency program at the Atelier Calder in Saché, France. It is a white perforated volume composed of nine differently sized partial spheres that are amalgamated and intersect to form one continuous surface. Conceptually the work aims to achieve a maximum degree of morphological freedom, structural continuity, visual interplay, and logistical efficiency using a minimal series of directives, components, and performative hierarchies in the production of an immersive architectural environment. The sphere is used as a primary element in that it encloses the maximum amount of space using minimal surface area. The introduction of smooth curvatures at the intersection of the sphere primitives enables a continuous double curvature across the surface of the piece to ensure the structural rigidity of the whole while simultaneously allowing the work to be broken apart into a series of geometrically related smaller decomposable subassemblies that can be optimally nested for efficient storage. When fully assembled the work occupies a space that is more than 20 feet in diameter by 11 feet tall, yet when partially dismounted for ease of reassembly, the spherical segments can be nested and packed into a single crate that occupies one third of this volume. Despite the curved geometric complexity of the larger surface, the spherical segments comprising it are tessellated and unfolded into strips so that they can be fabricated from flat sheets of aluminum that are CNC cut and then riveted together along their edges. The name of the piece is derived from the process of its development, given that its surface is generated by two parallel yet divergent sets of distributed agents. The first of these is a controlled macro set that defines the overall spatial geometry and describes this using the minimum number of developable elements that are able to be cut from flat sheets of aluminum within its dimensional constraints. The second of these defines the higher resolution ornament—the detailing of apertures that punctuate the surface and that are cut within the boundaries defined by the sphere's initial tessellation. These openings erode the materiality of the spherical surfaces, transforming them into a web-like mesh that enables the enclosed space to be filled with light.

6.8a

6.8b

6.8c

Taichung Theater
Toyo Ito + ARUP
Unbuilt 2005-2016
Taichung, China

Taichung Theater is the result of an international competition held in 2005. This 550,600-square-foot building, developed as a state-of-the-art facility for international performing arts, is sited in a park at the center of Taichung City's redevelopment district. Housing over 2,000 seats in its main theater, the building includes three performance spaces—a Grand Theater, an 800-seat Playhouse and a 200-seat Black Box Theater, rehearsal and workshop rooms, foyers, an Arts Plaza that stretches across the ground floor, a range of public dining facilities, and a roof garden. Contained within the larger dimensional limits of a single rectilinear volume, the geometry of the opera house is constituted by a complex horizontally and vertically continuous tubular network defined by the interweaving of two spatial grids that emerged from the spatial layering and offsetting of an irregular Voronoi cellular structure. This fluid network, which is constructed out of a continuous reinforced concrete shell intended to operate as an acoustic "sound cave," takes the form of an undulating topological surface that conjoins differently sized spatial cells—cave-like curvilinear volumes—that house the programs distributed throughout the building. As the tubes within this network swell and shrink in diameter, they produce a series of conjoined catenoidal, doubly curved surfaces that envelope individual program areas. To ensure the perceived continuity of this network, the elevations of the opera house appear as abstract vertical sections marking the point at which the internal tubular geometry intersects with the limits of the building's rectilinear enclosure. At grade, the planimetric pattern of the interior extends beyond the orthogonal boundaries of the building to enable continuities to exist between the architecture and its surrounding landscape.

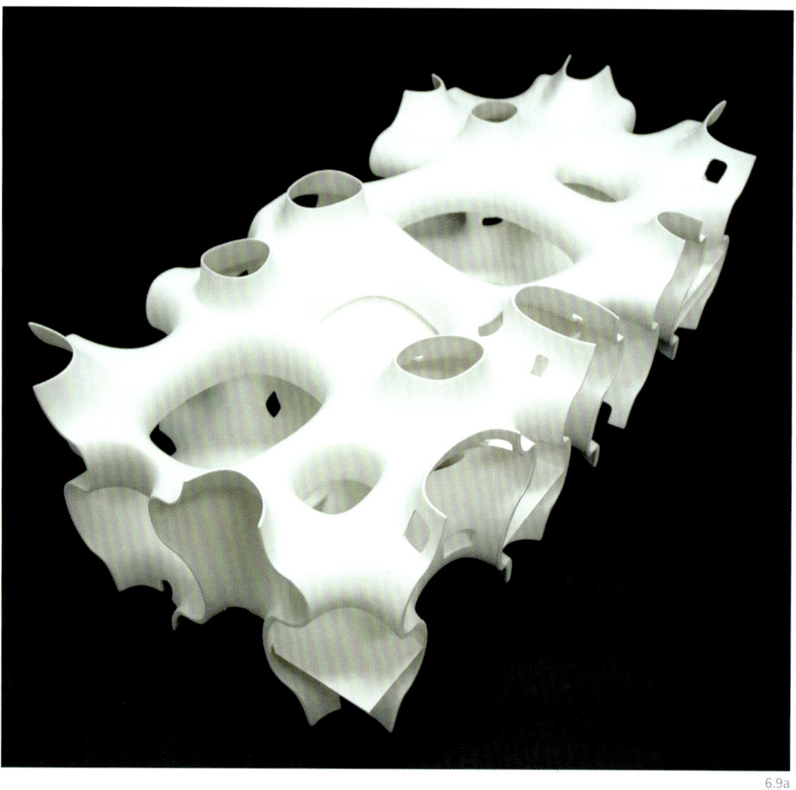

6.9a

6.9b

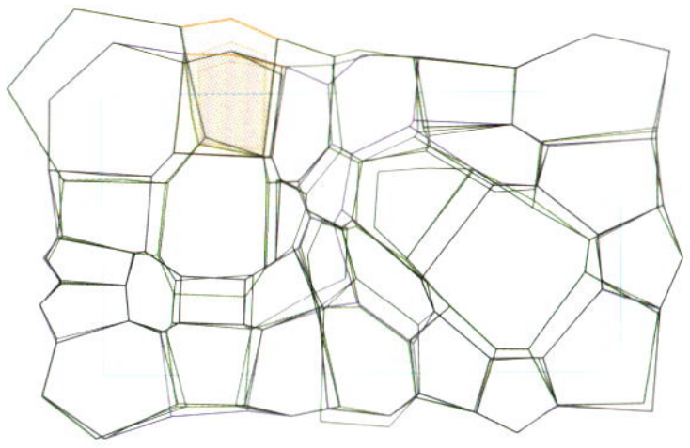

6.9c

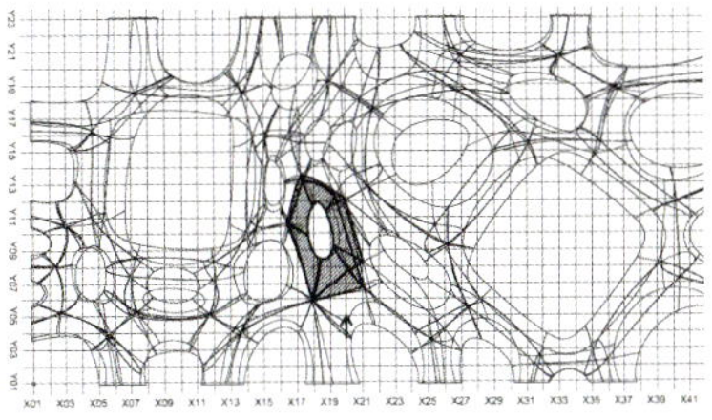

6.9d

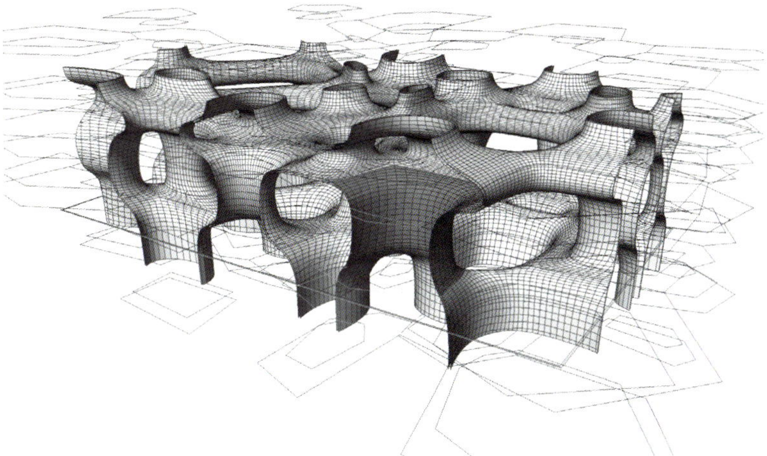

6.9e

6.9f

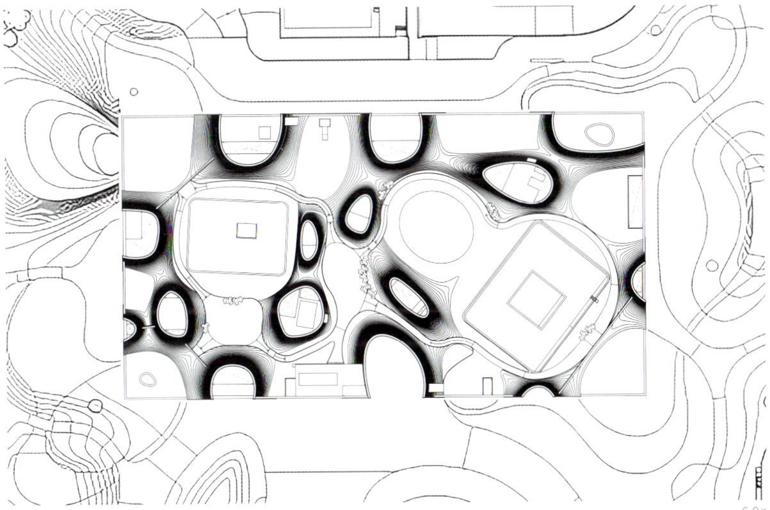

6.9g

6.9h

6.9i

nonLin/Lin Pavilion
theverymany
Built 2011
Orléans, France

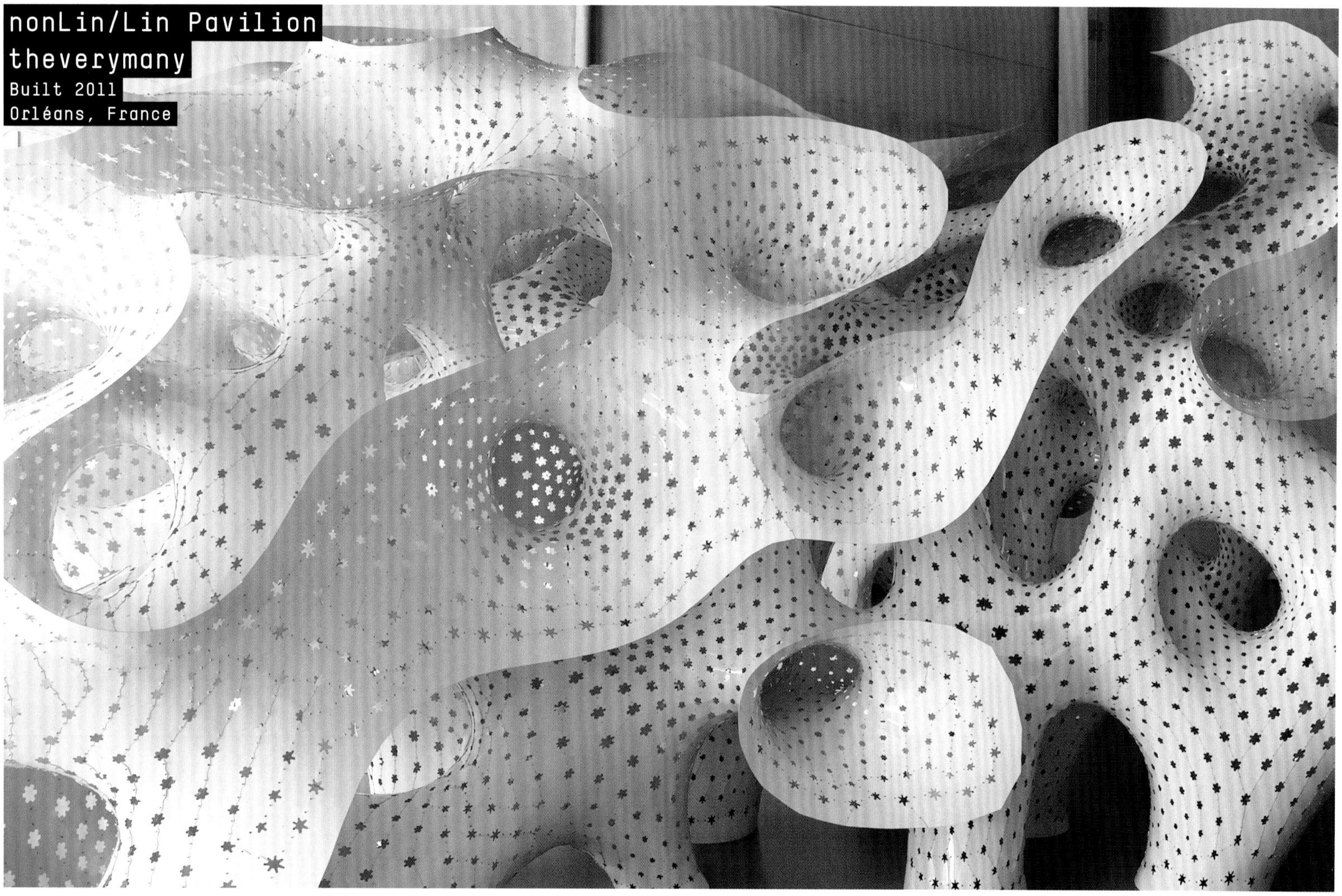

6.10a

The nonLin/Lin Pavilion constructed for the FRAC Centre is a full-scale and inhabitable, biomorphic, tubular structure that is generated using custom computational protocols. The parameters of these protocols are based on form-finding (surface relaxation), form description (composition of developable linear elements), information modeling (re-assembly data), generational hierarchies (distributed networks), and digital fabrication (logistics of production). The morphology of the pavilion conceptually and geometrically originates from a "Y" model, considered as the basic representation of multidirectional branching and the starting point for the pavilion's complex, nonlinear network of bifurcating and converging tubes. The computationally generated branching morphology is translated into a thick spatial lattice by "skinning" the trajectories along its network with tubes that grow or shrink in diameter as they either merge or bifurcate at different points within the system. The cross-sectional radii of the tubes are therefore varied based on local surface transformations resulting from their position within the network. Because of the complexity of the pavilion's doubly-curved surface geometry (due to the nonlinearity of its networked form), the discretization process—that is, its ability to be divided up into discrete units for fabrication—could not be globally applied to its morphology. Rather, it required the distribution of agents with local search behavior to trace its surface to determine the pattern of paths or cut lines along which the work could be unfolded and divided into flat, linear elements. The nonlinear generative process and morphological complexity of the work is thus countered by the linearity of its developable geometry to ensure its fabrication from planar aluminum sheets. Despite its assembly from a multitude of relatively thin elements, the continuity of the pavilion's monocoque shell and complexity of its double curvature renders it highly rigid and structurally stable.

6.10b

6.10c

6.10d

6.10e

WOVEN MESHES

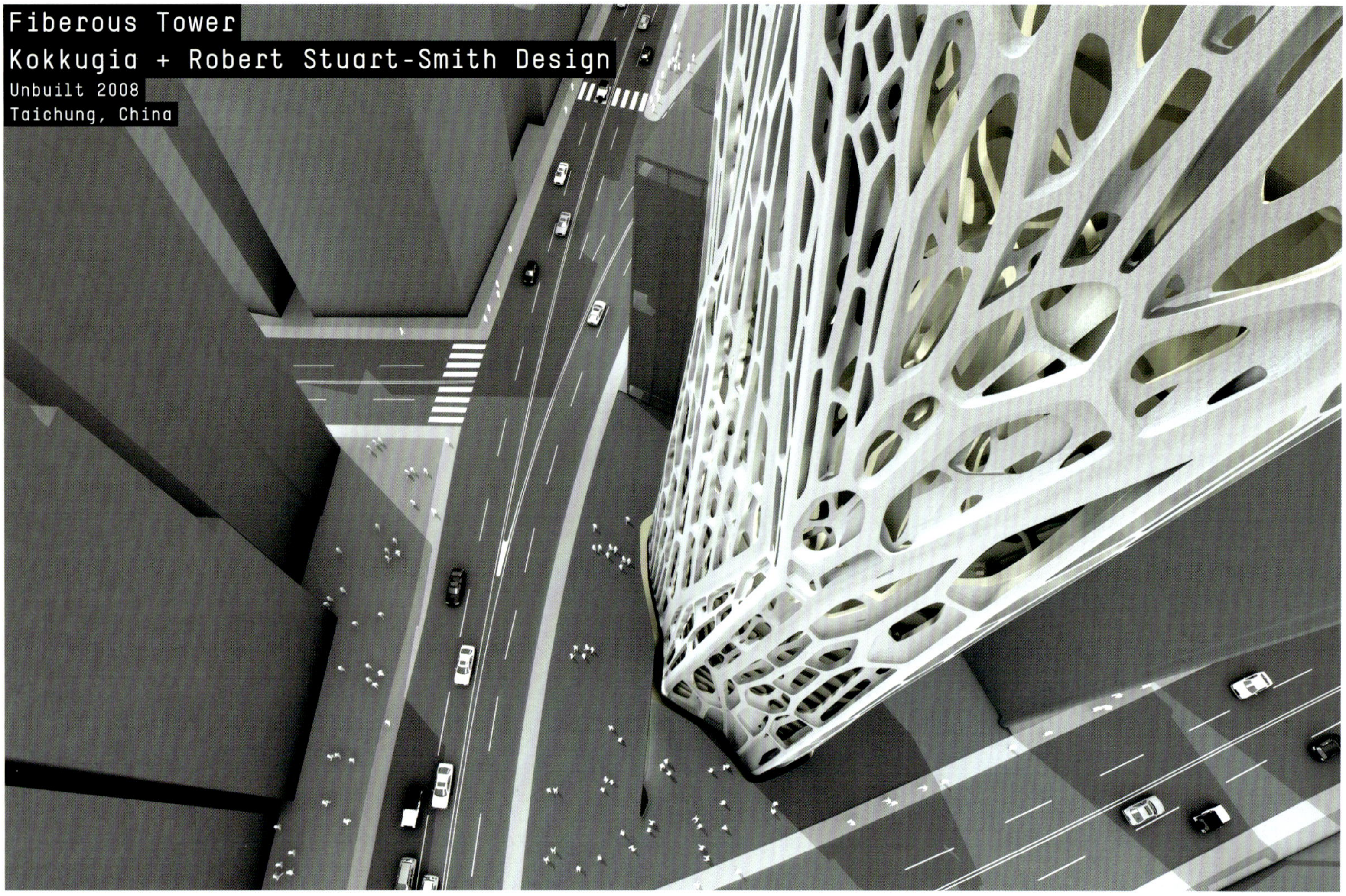

Fiberous Tower

Kokkugia + Robert Stuart-Smith Design

Unbuilt 2008

Taichung, China

6.11a

This fibrous tower compresses the structural and tectonic hierarchies of contemporary tower design into a single cast in situ concrete shell whose articulation, which is simultaneously performative and ornamental, is a synthetic response to multiple structural, environmental, and spatial imperatives. The project emerged from a series of earlier studies, done in collaboration with Rojkind Arquitectos, which were focused on exoskeleton tower typologies. These investigations explored the generation of structural, spatial, and surface ordering systems for towers using a self-organizing, agent-based algorithmic design methodology. Appearing as fibrous vegetative stalk, the continuous web-like scaffold of the tower operates as a nonlinear system that locally distributes loads through a heterogeneous network of paths while displacing the hierarchy of aggregated discrete elements typical of high-rise structural systems. It is a woven, load-bearing shell that absorbs and integrates distinct requirements into a singular complex geometry, operating simultaneously as a sun-shading device and framework for the building's envelope, while enabling the plan of the enclosed office spaces to remain open and column free. The varied pattern of this cellular, stranded shell also acts as an unique ornamental armature whose complexity creates distinctive characteristics for each space within the building. At different points along its surface, the shell is designed to thicken to house spaces for circulation, balconies, and vertical gardens. Although the articulation of the building skin is geometrically complex, it operates within the thickness of a comparatively simple shell geometry, enabling the use of conventional formwork techniques to construct a highly differentiated tower.

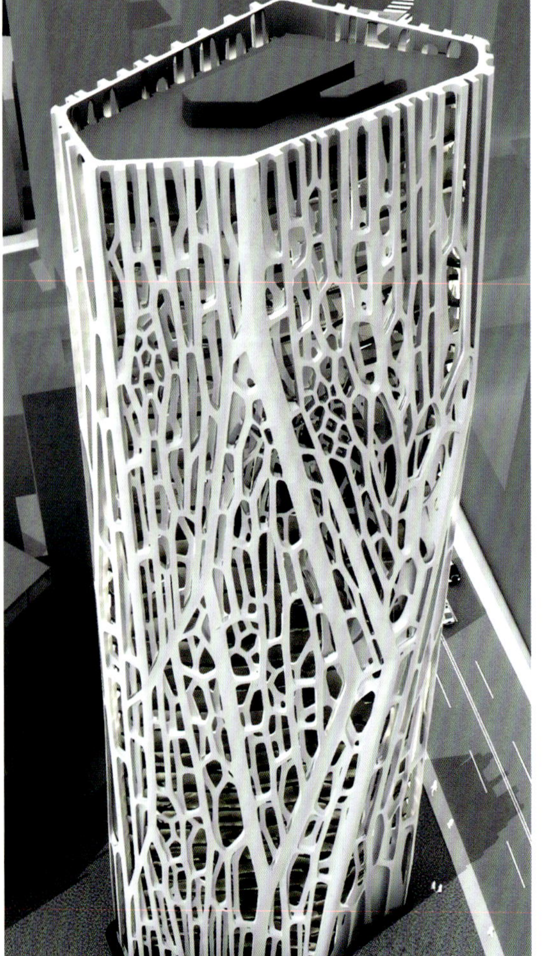

6.11b

6.11c

Polymorph: Digital Ceramics
Jenny Sabin Studio
Built 2014
Orléans, France

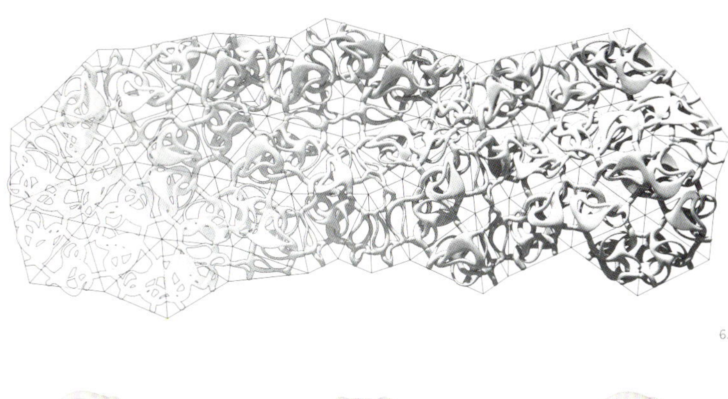

6.12a

6.12b

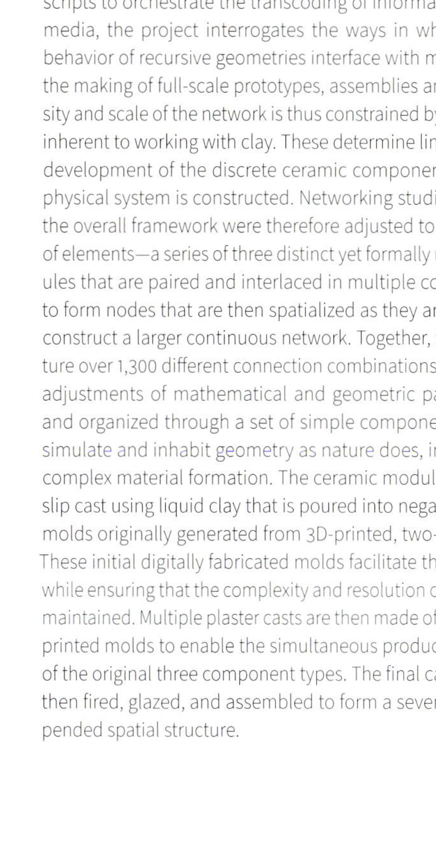

PolyMorph is an intricately woven floating cloud composed of 1,400 interlinked modular ceramic components that are threaded together to operate as a complex network. Using custom-developed computer scripts to orchestrate the transcoding of information across multiple media, the project interrogates the ways in which the networking behavior of recursive geometries interface with material properties in the making of full-scale prototypes, assemblies and systems. The density and scale of the network is thus constrained by material properties inherent to working with clay. These determine limits in relation to the development of the discrete ceramic components out of which the physical system is constructed. Networking studies used to generate the overall framework were therefore adjusted to integrate this family of elements—a series of three distinct yet formally related ceramic modules that are paired and interlaced in multiple combinatory patterns to form nodes that are then spatialized as they are strung together to construct a larger continuous network. Together, the components feature over 1,300 different connection combinations. Through the subtle adjustments of mathematical and geometric parameters designed and organized through a set of simple components, it is possible to simulate and inhabit geometry as nature does, in a constant state of complex material formation. The ceramic modules of PolyMorph are slip cast using liquid clay that is poured into negative two-part plaster molds originally generated from 3D-printed, two-part positive molds. These initial digitally fabricated molds facilitate the variability of parts, while ensuring that the complexity and resolution of each component is maintained. Multiple plaster casts are then made of the positive digitally printed molds to enable the simultaneous production of several casts of the original three component types. The final cast clay modules are then fired, glazed, and assembled to form a seven-foot diameter, suspended spatial structure.

6.12c

6.12d

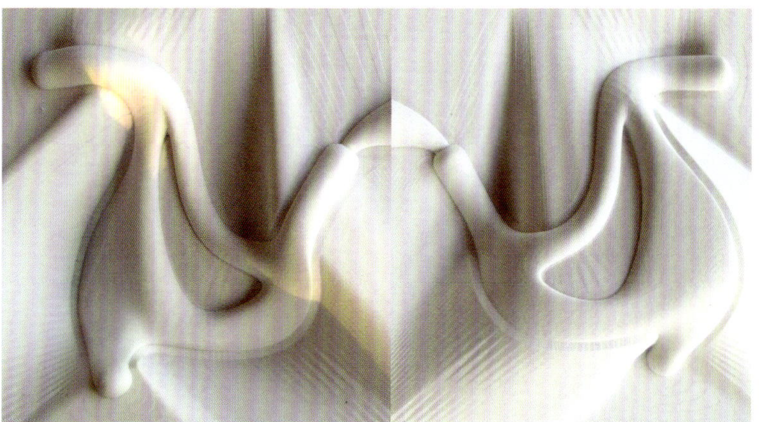

6.12e

2012 ICD/ITKE Pavilion
ICD/ITKE, University of Stuttgart

Built 2012

Stuttgart, Germany

The 2012 research pavilion is a woven structure robotically fabricated from carbon and glass fiber composites and developed using a digital information chain that linked all processes of design and its development to final construction. Influenced by the study of biomimetic principles and their potential application to architectural design, the project began with an investigation of the fibrous morphology of arthropodal exoskeletons—in particular, the ways in which chitin fibrils are embedded in a protein matrix in the shell development of lobsters. In this shell structure, fibers are incorporated in the matrix by forming individual unidirectional layers. Areas subject to directional stress distributions exhibit a unidirectional layer structure optimized for a directed load transfer. Where a nondirectional load transfer is required, individual layers are laminated together in a spiral (helicoidal) arrangement that allows a uniform load distribution in every direction. This local material differentiation within the shell leads to a highly adapted and efficient structure. The detailed analysis of the lobster shell's functional morphology was used as the basis of the pavilion's structure, which was constructed by directionally winding alternating layers of carbon and glass fibers over a lightweight steel frame. Six different filament winding sequences were used to control the variation of layering and orientation of fibers on individual layers at each point of the shell, designed to minimize material consumption while maximizing the structure's stiffness. The glass fibers are mainly used as a spatial partitioning element and serve as formwork for the following layers, while the stiffer carbon fibers contribute primarily to the load transfer and overall stiffness of the shell. In addition, functional fibers for illumination and structural monitoring can be integrated into the system. A six-axis robot, coupled with an external seventh axis, was used to place the fibers on the temporary steel frame, which was rotated on a pedestal by a robotically controlled turntable. As part of the fabrication process the fibers were saturated by running them through a resin bath directly prior to their robotic placement. The final, highly articulated, black-and-white, semi-transparent stranded structure—which was constructed by continuously winding more than 30 kilometres of fiber rovings—is approximately 8 meters in diameter and 3.5 meters high and weighs less than 320 kg.

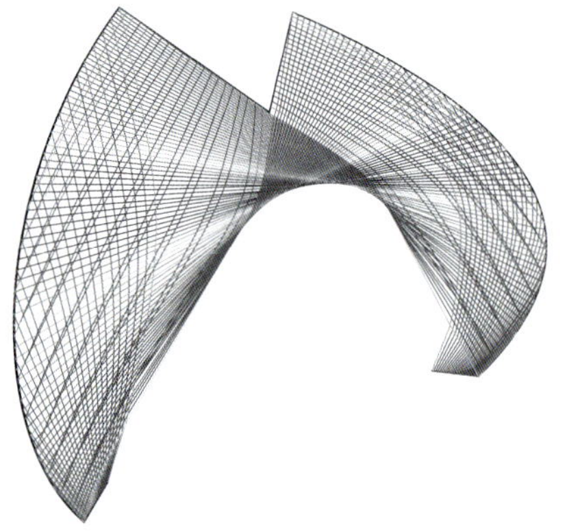

6.13b

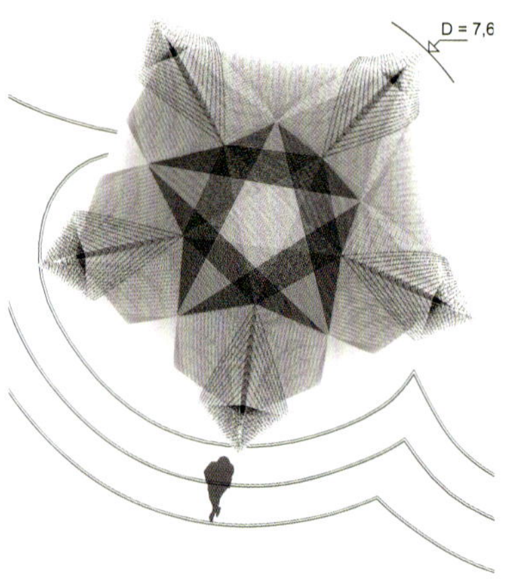

6.13a

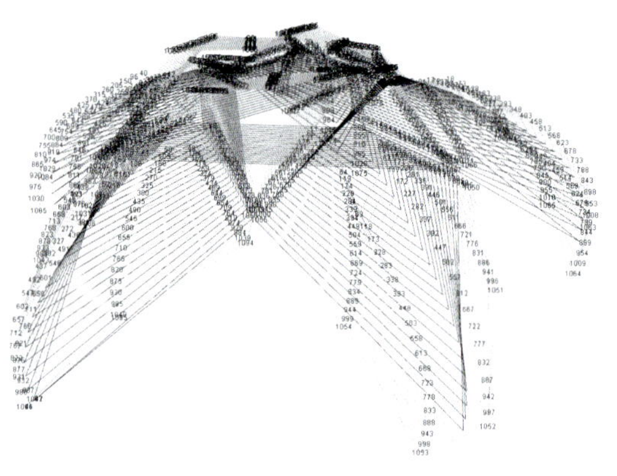

6.13c

6.13d

6.13e

6.13f

6.13g

2013/14 ICD/ITKE Pavilion

ICD/ITKE, University of Stuttgart

Built 2013-2014

Stuttgart, Germany

6.14a

6.14b

6.14c

6.14d

6.14e

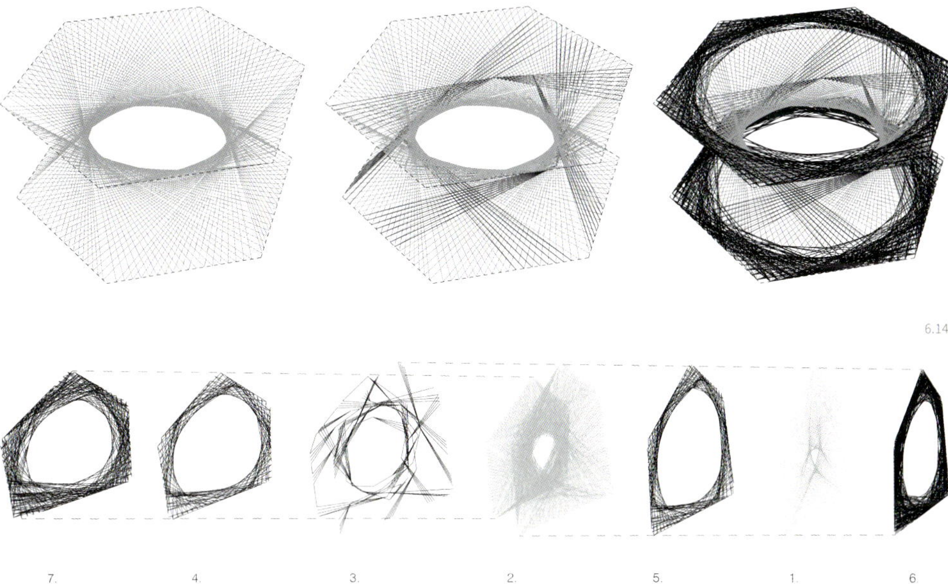

6.14f

6.14g

As an extension of the stranded shell structure research developed for the 2012 ICD/ITKE Pavilion, the 2013–14 pavilion is an investigation focused on the development of novel robotic fabrication methods for fiber-reinforced polymer structures that are developed through the transfer of biomimetic morphological principles to architecture. The project aims to develop winding techniques for the generation of modular, double-layered fiber composite structures that minimize the formwork necessary for the shell's development while maintaining a high degree of geometric freedom. The Elytron, a protective shell for beetles' wings and abdomen was used as a biological model in the development of the structure. The Elytra morphology is based on a double-layered structure that is connected by column-like, doubly-curved support elements known as trabeculae that merge the upper and lower shell segments with continuous fibers, the distribution and geometric articulation of which are highly differentiated throughout the shell. As these principles were applied to the development of the pavilion, they generated a double-layered, tessellated cellular structure that was constructed through the winding of six layers of resin-impregnated glass-and-carbon filaments. Each of the geometrically unique, doubly curved modules within the cellular structure is fabricated by the stretching of fibers across its two-layered structure using two collaborating six-axis industrial robots that each hold a custom-made steel frame defining the edges of the modules. The first set of fibers are tensioned between these two frames and act as a scaffolding for the subsequent layering of fibers. As these initial stranded layers interact they reciprocally deform generating doubly-curved surfaces from their initially straight fiber segments. These are then subsequently layered with carbon fibers that are highly differentiated across each module and act as structural reinforcement within the system. A computationally directed winding syntax determines the specific sequence, direction, and organization of fiber layering that is determined by structural requirements such as edge reinforcement and the paths of forces acting on each component and moving across the structure. In the final pavilion, the thirty-six lightweight composite components—the largest of which is 2.6 m in diameter and weighs only 24.1 kg—are conjoined along their edges to construct a woven shell structure covering a total area of 50 m² and a volume of 122 m3 with a total weight of 593 kg.

Cloud Pergola – Croatian National Pavilion

Alisa Andrasek

Built 2018

Venice, Italy

6.15a

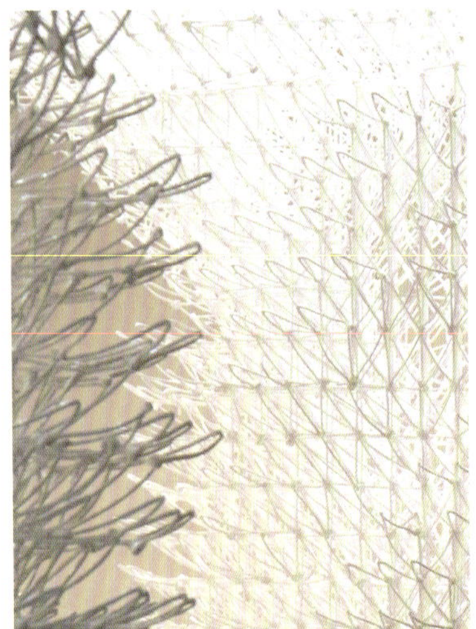

6.15b

6.15d

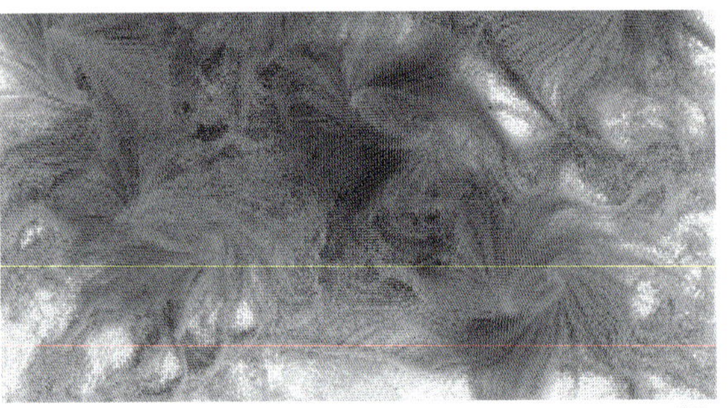

6.15c

6.15e

Mathematized Cloud for the Cloud Pergola installed at the Croation National Pavilion at the 2018 Venice Biennale builds on research on high resolution structures designed with algorithms and built by robots. It belongs to a family of structures that are information dense, extremely intricate, lightweight yet strong, and highly resilient. The structure is made from thermoplastics that are robotically 3D extruded into a complex spatial lattice. The robotic 3D printing used has the advantage of being a faster additive construction process able to generate highly intricate systems without unnecessary waste while enabling a high degree of tectonic and structural integrity that is differentiated and locally precise. The initial structure was designed using an algorithm for multi-agent systems (MAS), whereby agents operate as active discrete elements whose behavior is determined by a set of local rules, often based on stimulus-response logic. In Mathematized Cloud the algorithm used was based on Craig Reynolds's algorithms for swarming intelligence programmed using the attributes of alignment, cohesion, and separation. Agents are structured to address specific goals driven by design intent and specific constraints of the fabrication environment, collectively finding a solution. In this case, agents were conditioned to ascend from the ground up, with three simultaneous swarms spinning in counter directions in relationship to each other to achieve stronger and more balanced structure. This spinning behavior also leaves an aesthetic imprint in the lattice, with its diagonal struts shifting directionality, capturing such upward "streaming" behavior. When they reach a certain height, their behavior changes, radically slowing down in the vertical direction to privilege horizontal movement, which results in the ceiling sequence. Data extracted from these interactions produce information-rich fields, a collection of vectors whose values are captured through a poly-dimensional voxel space that is then transformed into a spatial lattice. Definition of every microstrut in such a high-precision structure is defined using the underlying agent-generated data, emulating the complexity and performance found in natural material systems, such as in our bones. In natural structures, we find material continuum without any mechanical joints. Using such a continuous and integrated system ensures that changes in the micro-arrangement of building blocks at the micro scale, yield different performances at the macro scale.

Flotsam and Jetsam Pavilions

SHoP

Built 2016

Miami, United States and Nairobi, Kenya

The Flotsam and Jetsam paired pavilions built for the 2016 Design Miami international fair, are novel, robotically fabricated 3D printed, extruded lattice structures, which, at the time of their making, were touted to be two of the largest 3D printed structures ever produced. Flotsam is an old nautical term for salvage found floating in the ocean, and jetsam, a reference to cargo intentionally thrown overboard to lighten a ship during a storm. The name is a playful reference to the sea and a nod to the impermanent nature of the installation, the translucence of its filament structure, and the way in which it, and those that inhabit it, seemingly "float" in space. The form of each of the pavilions, an amorphic, curvilinear double-layered structure, was also inspired by its coastal locale, each somewhat shaped like a jellyfish with a domed center and sinuous trailing tentacles that extend and morphologically transform into seating components. The pair of lattice structures, which are beached and surrounded by sand, were each assembled from contiguous 3D extruded lattice segments. These lightweight segments, which have a total surface area of 2,753 square feet, were prefabricated in just ten weeks by Branch Technology using two large-scale robotic arms and then erected and connected by hand on site in just four days. The footings and seating elements, as well as the central hub structure of one of the two pavilions, made by Oak Ridge National Laboratory, were 3D printed as hollow full-scale elements using a sustainably harvested biodegradable bamboo filament print medium developed by ORNL and printed on a large-bed 3D polymer printer. Following their installation in Miami, in 2019 the pavilions were relocated to Africa where they served as an entry environment for the first session of the UN-Habitat Assembly held in Nairobi, Kenya.

6.16a

6.16b

6.16a

Aguahoja I

Neri Oxman / Mediated Matter Group

Built 2018

Cambridge, United States

Aguahoja proposes a material alternative to plastic and a water-based approach to design, embodying a design approach extending from material formation to decay—from water to water. The work is derived from organic matter—biopolymers such as cellulose, chitosan, pectin, and calcium carbonate, which become printable once they are mixed with water. The objects are printed by a robot and shaped through hydration, using a technology that integrates material formation, digital fabrication, and physical behavior at a variety of scales that approach—and often match—that of the biological world. As a result, designers will be able to control properties of the substances they work with, which in turn become aspects of computational design and digital manufacturing through which they will be able to design an object's decay as well as its shape. In Aguahoja, intrinsic mechanical and extrinsic environmental properties drove the generated form. Vector fields encoded variation in structures interpolated into material deposition trajectories, and pressure, speed, and material concentration variations along structural streamlines were then encoded into real-time instructions sent to the manufacturing platforms. Hydration control maps then provided the evaporation-driven self-folding of the final three-dimensional structure. Aquahoja consists of a library of material experiments and a collection of hardware, software, and wetware tools and technologies. These culminated in a pavilion that demonstrates the architectural potential of the materials. The biocompatible objects were made from some of the most abundant biopolymers on our planet—crustaceans, bones, and apples, among others. The structures were thus designed as if grown: their form, which was induced based on previous tests and experiments, was guided by the process of their formation, and their construction required little to no assembly.

6.17a

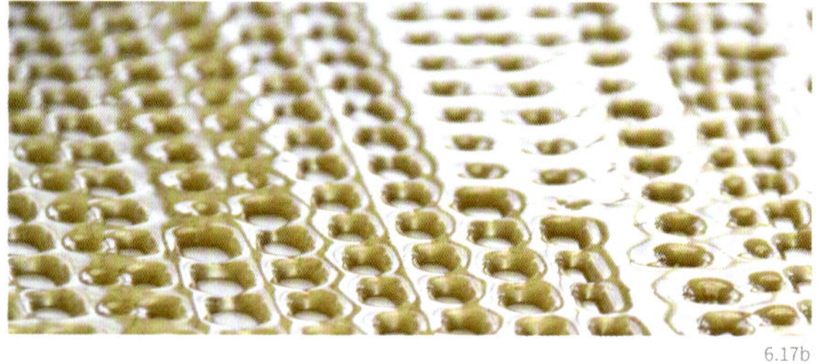

6.17b

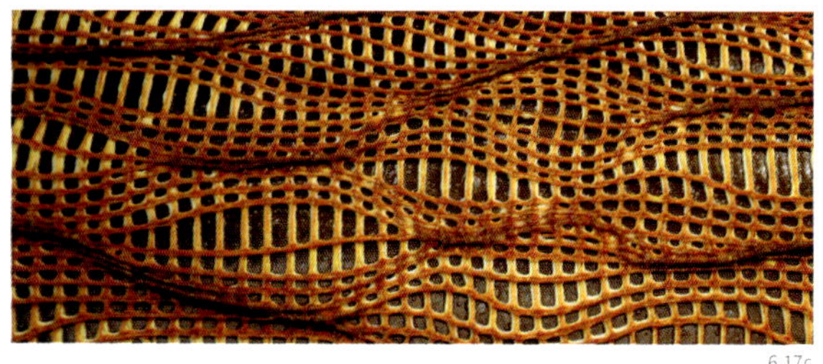

6.17c

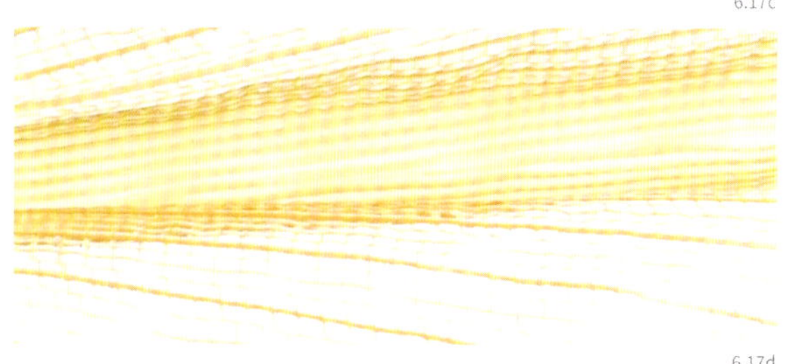

6.17d

6.17e

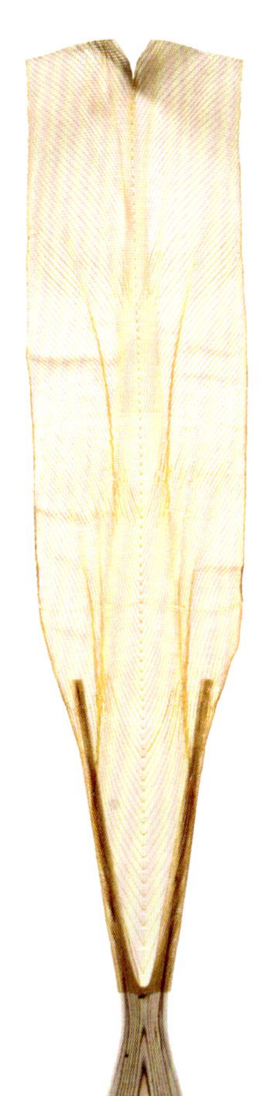

6.17f

Silk Pavilions I and II

Neri Oxman / Mediated Matter Group

Built 2013, 2020

Cambridge and New York, United States

The Silk Pavilion projects combine digital and biological fabrication, proposing a model that unites the biologically spun and the technologically woven. Inspired by the way silkworms generate a three-dimensional cocoon out of a single silk thread, the first Silk Pavilion project was developed in 2013: a dome in the shape of a large biological cocoon, the construction of which required both a robot and a swarm of 6,500 live silkworms. In the first phase of construction, twenty-six polygonal stainless-steel frames were used to create an underlying support structure. The frames were covered with a scaffolding of silk threads laid down by a computer numerically controlled (CNC) machine. An algorithm based on silkworm movement assigned the path of these continuous threads across the frames, creating various degrees of density and an overall surface geometry; the pattern also kept the silkworms from falling through the gaps. For the pavilion's interior, secondary structure, the silkworms were deployed as biological printers, filling the gaps among the machine-woven threads to create a dense habitable shelter. The worms, each of which spun a thread 0.6 miles (1 kilometer) long, were introduced into the bottom rim of the frame and then traveled over the structure, spinning flat silk patches and reinforcing the underlying structure. They underwent a healthy metamorphosis during the spinning phase and were removed from the structure following the pupation stage. As moths, they laid their eggs—about 1.5 million of them—enough for about 250 additional pavilions. Silk Pavilion II, developed for the *Material Ecology* exhibition at the Museum of Modern Art, added kinetic manufacturing to the mix of technological and biological construction methods explored in Silk Pavilion I.

6.18a

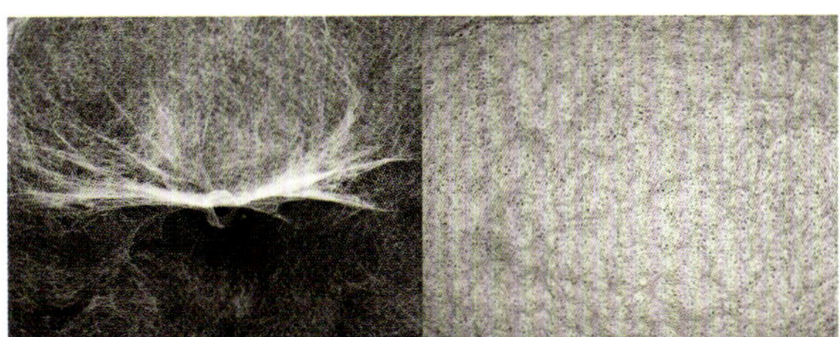

6.18b

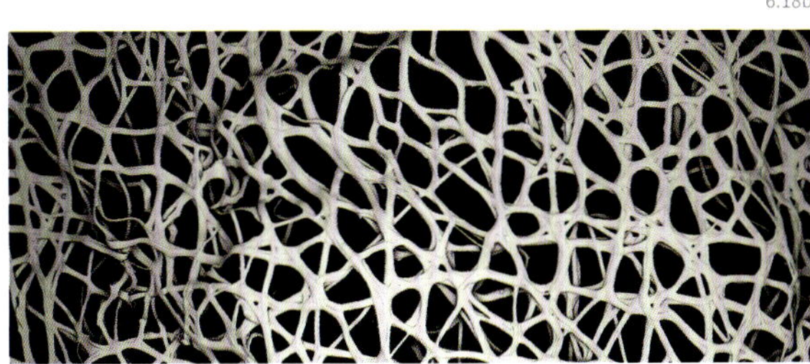

6.18c

6.18d

6.18e

6.18f

6.18g

Generative Logic Recursion

Recursion is a generative process in which the output of one step is used as the input for the next step. It is often used in computer science and mathematics, but it can also be found in art, architecture, and design. The process begins with a base case, which is then transformed iteratively through multiple generations until a stopping condition is reached. This stopping condition is important because recursive processes will continue indefinitely without some restrictions on when they should stop. It is important to carefully consider the base case and stopping condition when designing a recursive algorithm.

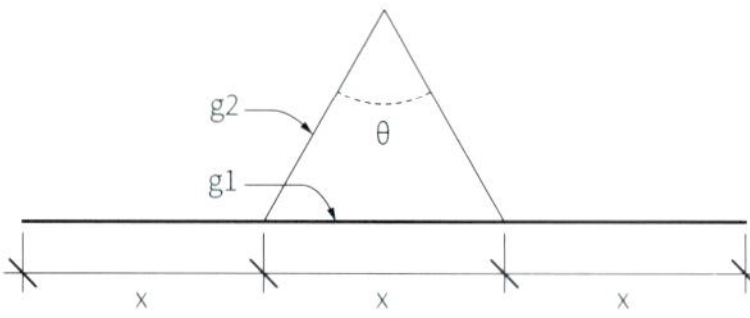

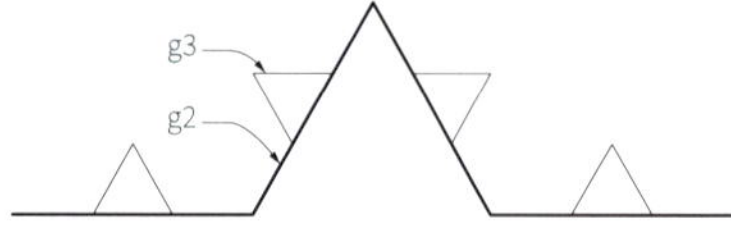

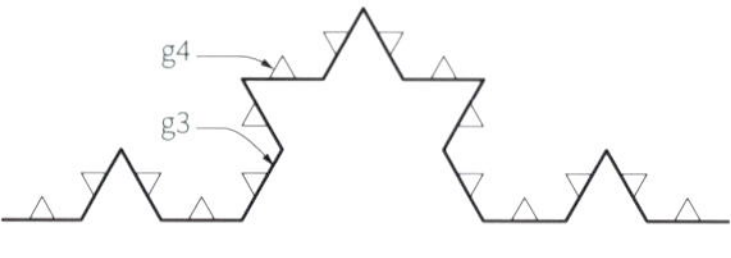

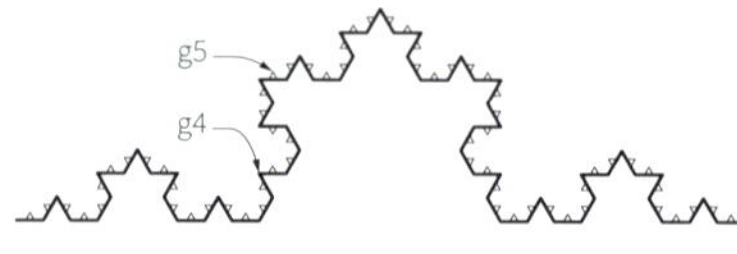

Koch Curve: The Koch Curve is a classic example of recursion. Introduced by Helge von Koch in a 1904 paper, the curve is created by iteratively replacing a simple line (g1) with four new lines that are each ⅓ the original length and meet at 60° and 120° angles (g2). As the new generation curve always has 4/3 the length of the previous generation, the curve's length tends towards infinity despite its bounds within a limited space.

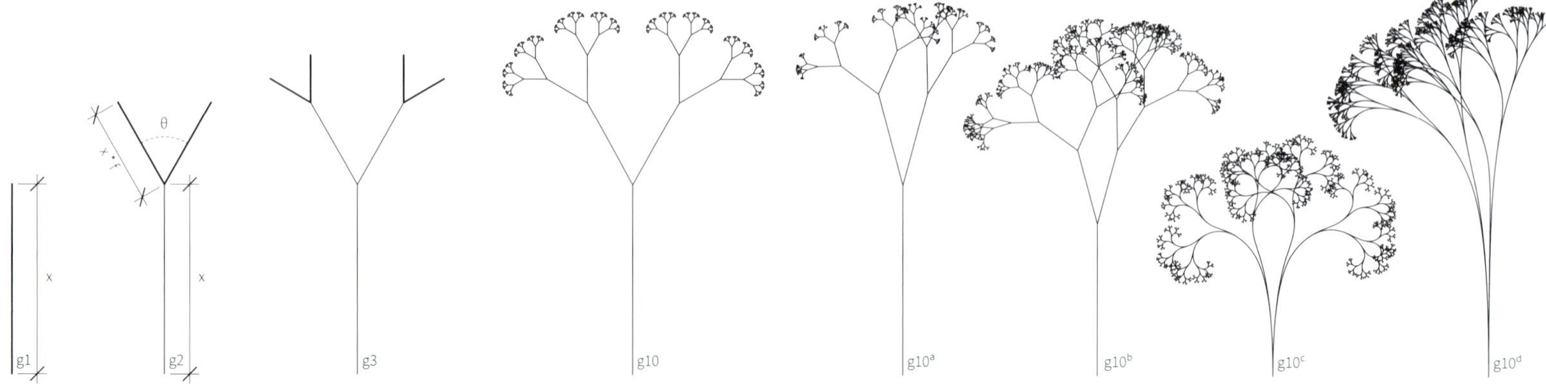

Fractal Tree: Another classic example of recursion is the fractal tree. At each generation, two new lines (g2) are added to the parent line (g1). These lines branch out from the parent line at an angle (θ) and at a fraction (f) of the parent's length. By the tenth generation (g10), a full canopy of branches has developed. By adding random noise to the branching angle and/or to the length ratio, more natural looking trees can be generated ($g10^a$ and $g10^b$). Furthermore, each generation can be connected via curves ($g10^c$ and $g10^d$) to create a more continuous geometry. Natural conditions such as a tree growing towards sunlight or away from the prevailing winds can be modeled by biasing the growth angles ($g10^d$).

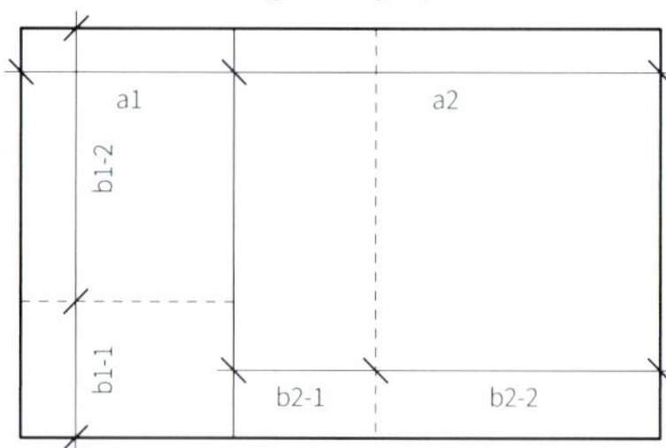

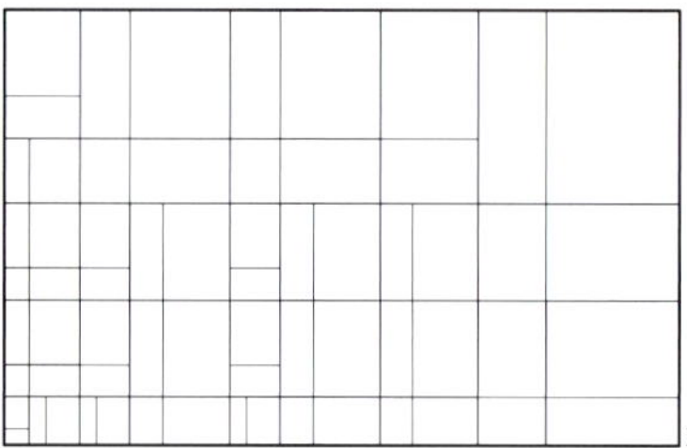

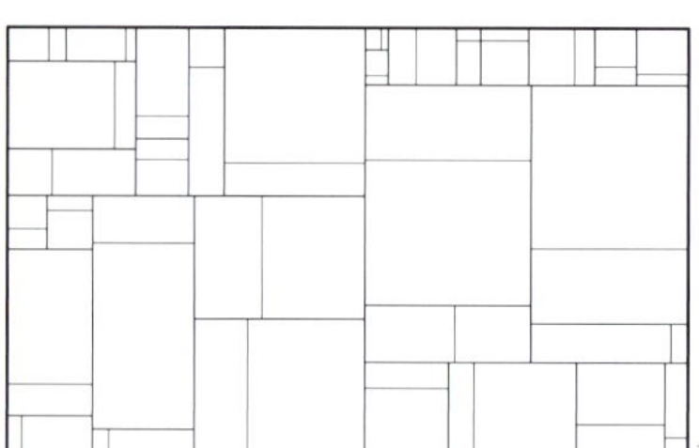

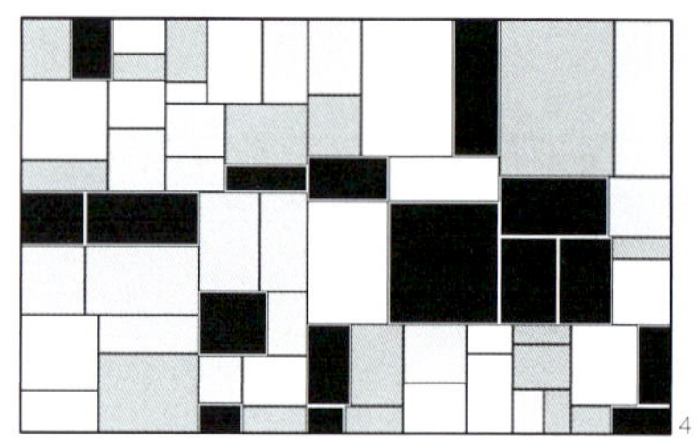

Recursive Spatial Partitioning: In the diagrams above (1 & 2), a simple rule is applied where a rectangular space is divided along its longer dimension into two new partitions with ⅓ and ⅔ of the parent rectangle's area. For example, in the second generation, a1 is divided into b1-1 and b1-2 along the vertical direction since it is the longest direction. By adding a random range along the longer dimension from 0.25 - 0.75 of the length, the partitioning of space displays more variability (3). By then applying a random tone, the overall subdivision of space begins to resemble patterns of human development such as agricultural fields or urban property boundaries (4).

Generative Process Serpentine Pavilion

The Serpentine Pavilion of 2002 by Toyo Ito and Cecil Balmond + ARUP used a recursive set of rules to develop a complex pattern that extends across the roof and folds down along the facades to form a cohesive structural lattice. The lattice is then further refined by alternating the subdivided polygons into solid (steel plate) or void (glass) infill materials.

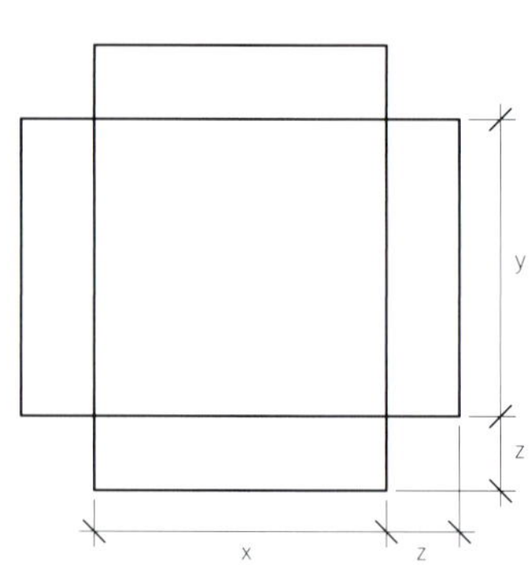

1. Layout the unfolded roof and facades based on the pavilion's interior dimensions.

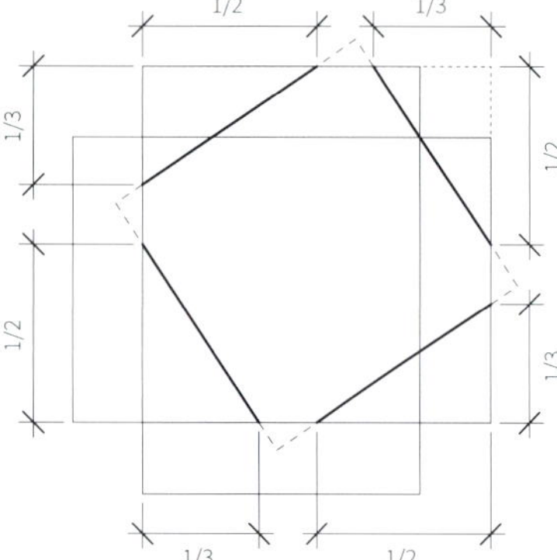

2. Using a generation shape (shaded area), connect points located at ½ of the side with points located at ⅓ of the next side.

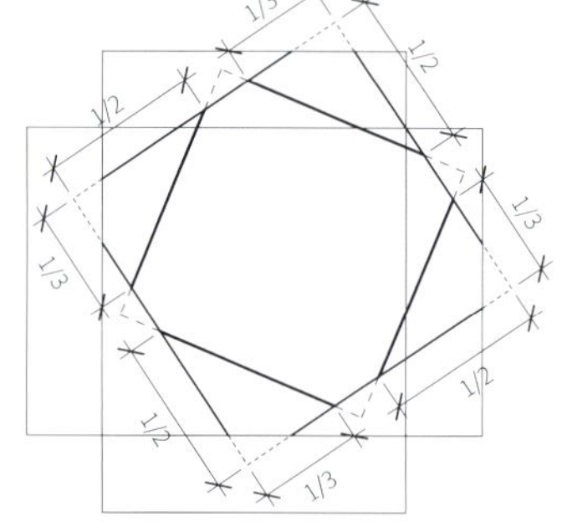

3. Repeat this process recursively by using the completed shape from the last step as the generation shape (shaded area).

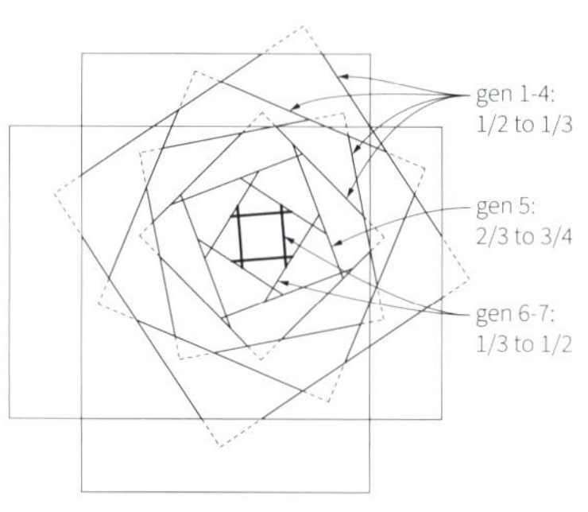

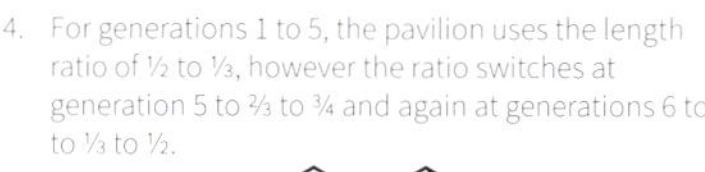

4. For generations 1 to 5, the pavilion uses the length ratio of ½ to ⅓, however the ratio switches at generation 5 to ⅔ to ¾ and again at generations 6 to7 to ⅓ to ½.

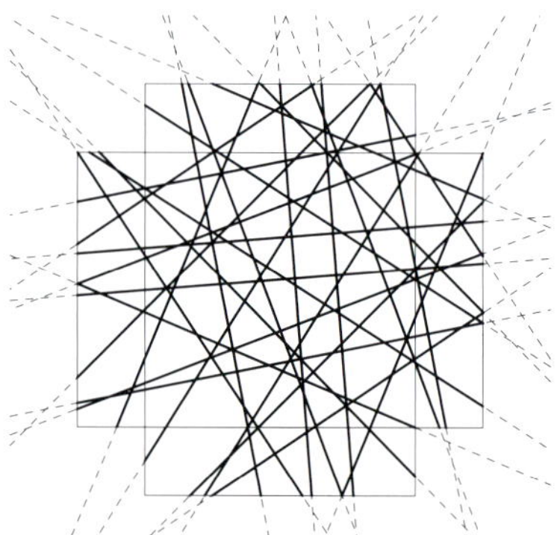

5. After seven generations, the recursive subdivision process is complete and the edges of each generations' shape are extended beyond the unfolded boundary.

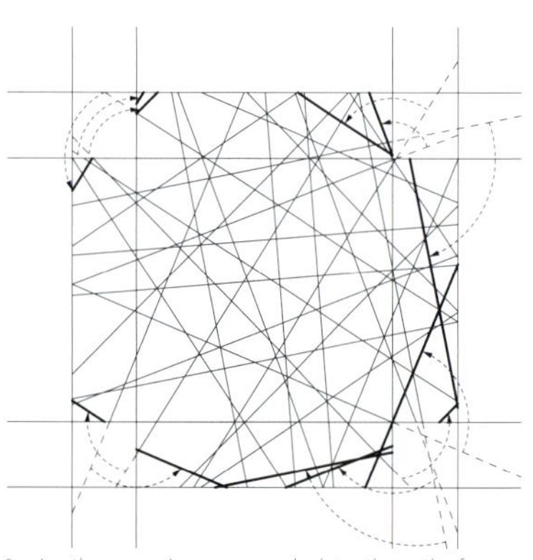

6. Another recursive process calculates the path of corner lines as they move across the facades and roof to produce the desired wrapping effect.

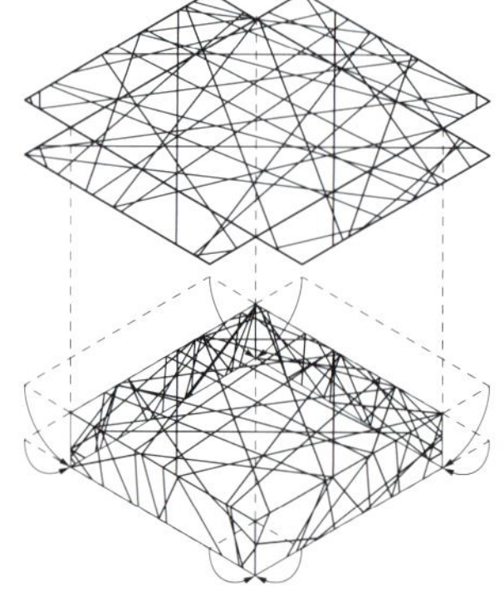

7. Once all lines end on one of the four ground plan edges, the facades are rotated down to their vertical positions.

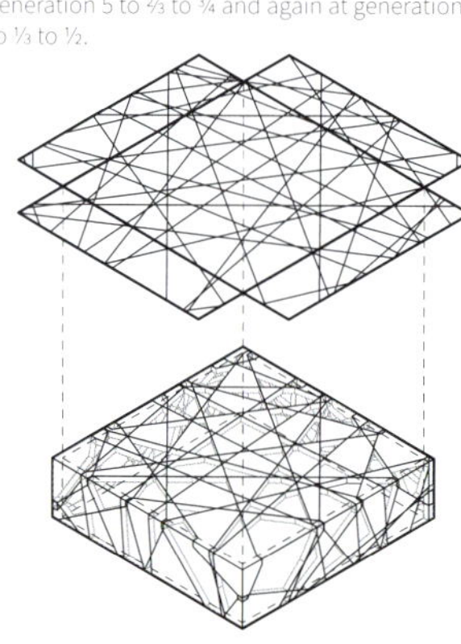

8. The structure is extruded and additional members fill in the hinged areas. The graph is sorted into solid and void areas as the intersection of lines always produces even partitions.

Generative Matrix

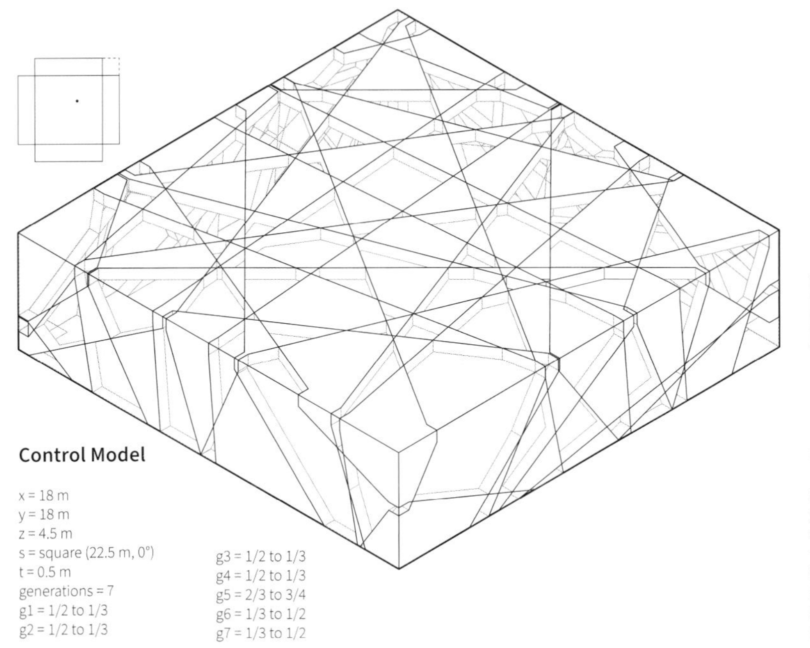
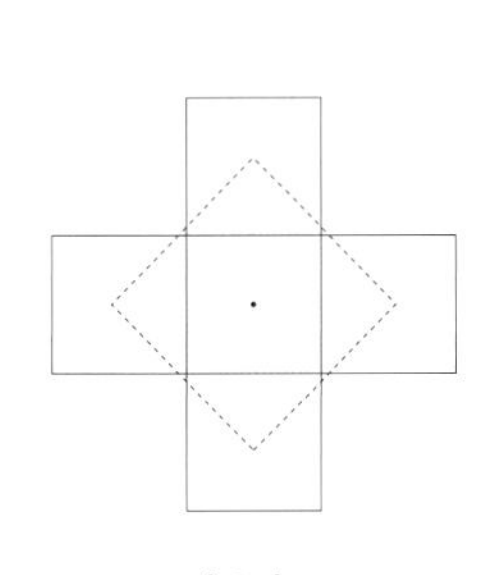
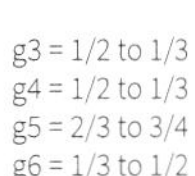
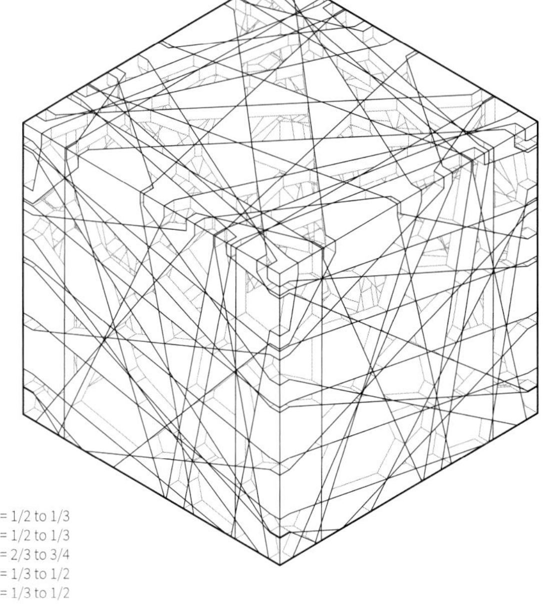

Control Model

x = 18 m
y = 18 m
z = 4.5 m
s = square (22.5 m, 0°)
t = 0.5 m
generations = 7
g1 = 1/2 to 1/3
g2 = 1/2 to 1/3
g3 = 1/2 to 1/3
g4 = 1/2 to 1/3
g5 = 2/3 to 3/4
g6 = 1/3 to 1/2
g7 = 1/3 to 1/2

Centered Cube

x = 12 m
y = 12 m
z = 12 m
t = 0.5 m
s = square (18 m, 45°)
generations = 7
g1 = 1/2 to 1/3
g2 = 1/2 to 1/3
g3 = 1/2 to 1/3
g4 = 1/2 to 1/3
g5 = 2/3 to 3/4
g6 = 1/3 to 1/2
g7 = 1/3 to 1/2

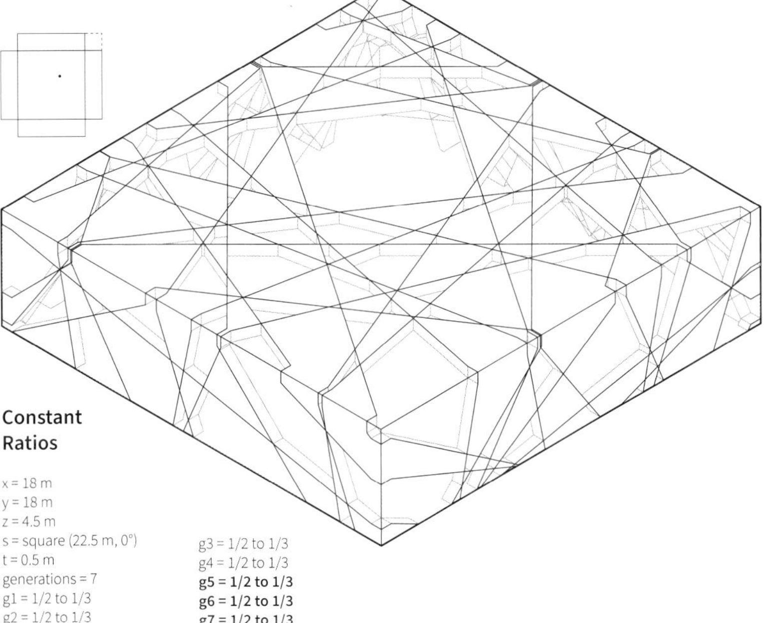
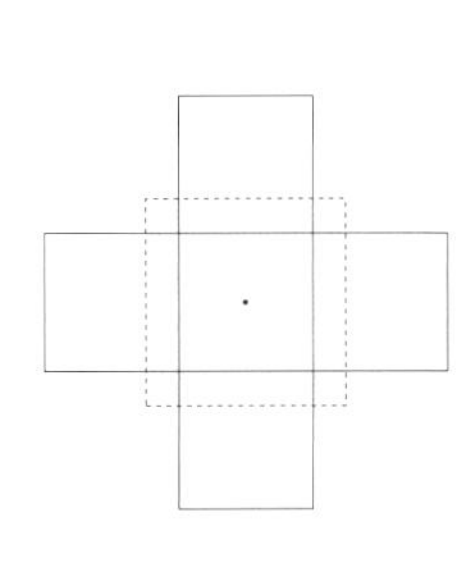
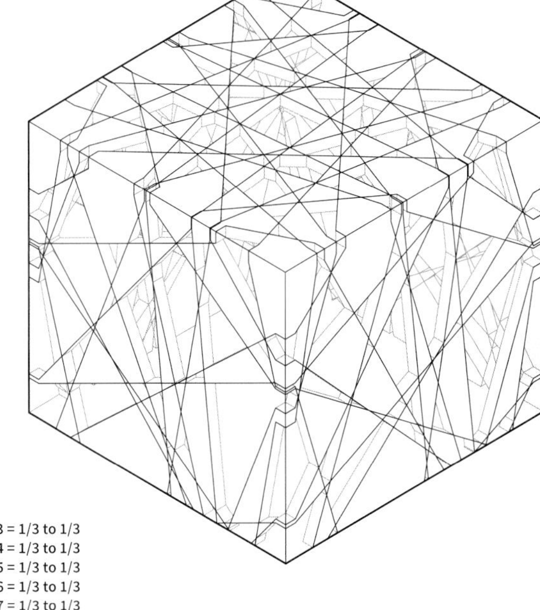

Constant Ratios

x = 18 m
y = 18 m
z = 4.5 m
s = square (22.5 m, 0°)
t = 0.5 m
generations = 7
g1 = 1/2 to 1/3
g2 = 1/2 to 1/3
g3 = 1/2 to 1/3
g4 = 1/2 to 1/3
g5 = 1/2 to 1/3
g6 = 1/2 to 1/3
g7 = 1/2 to 1/3

Equal Ratios

x = 12 m
y = 12 m
z = 12 m
t = 0.5 m
s = square (18 m, 0°)
generations = 7
g1 = 1/3 to 1/3
g2 = 1/3 to 1/3
g3 = 1/3 to 1/3
g4 = 1/3 to 1/3
g5 = 1/3 to 1/3
g6 = 1/3 to 1/3
g7 = 1/3 to 1/3

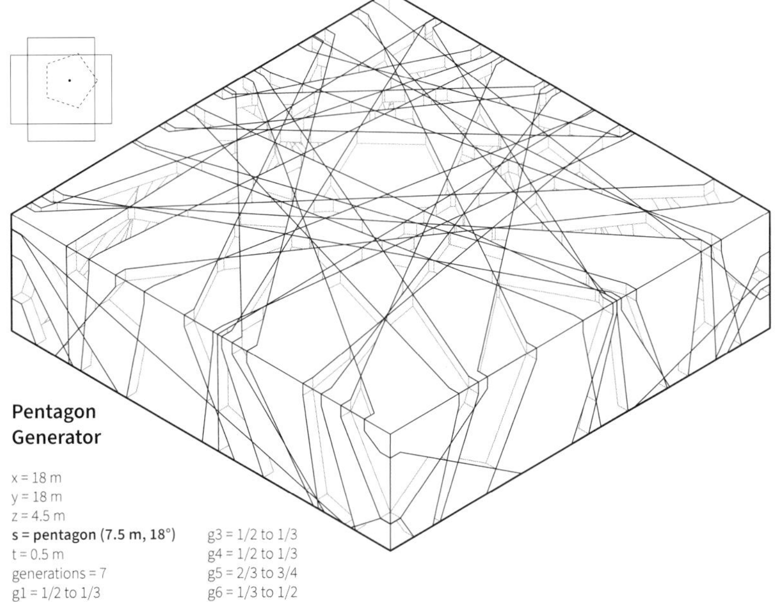
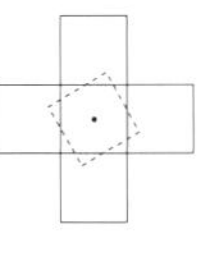
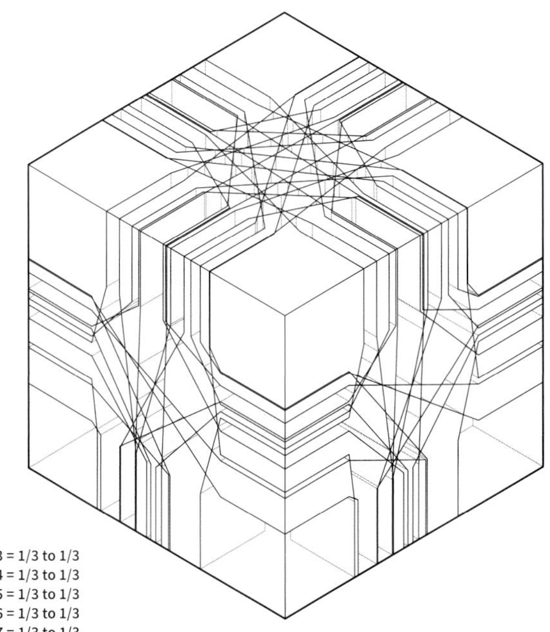

Pentagon Generator

x = 18 m
y = 18 m
z = 4.5 m
s = pentagon (7.5 m, 18°)
t = 0.5 m
generations = 7
g1 = 1/2 to 1/3
g2 = 1/2 to 1/3
g3 = 1/2 to 1/3
g4 = 1/2 to 1/3
g5 = 2/3 to 3/4
g6 = 1/3 to 1/2
g7 = 1/3 to 1/2

Thickened Cube

x = 6 m
y = 6 m
z = 6 m
t = 3 m
s = square (6 m, 30°)
generations =7
g1 = 1/3 to 1/3
g2 = 1/3 to 1/3
g3 = 1/3 to 1/3
g4 = 1/3 to 1/3
g5 = 1/3 to 1/3
g6 = 1/3 to 1/3
g7 = 1/3 to 1/3

Generative Logic
NURBS, Meshes, and Subdivision Models

The three primary forms of digital surfaces are NURBS, Meshes, and Subdivision Surfaces. It is critical for the computational designer to understand the differences between these types of digital surfaces. Each type was invented and implemented within various digital modeling platforms to solve specific issues within the manufacturing, simulation, and design disciplines. Each type has its own advantages and disadvantages for specific modeling or visualization tasks.

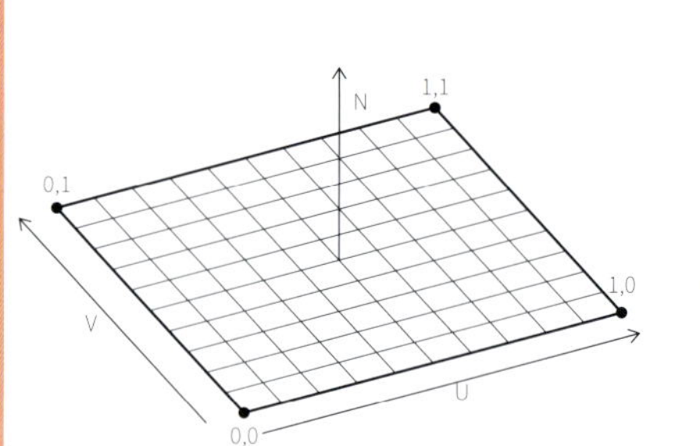

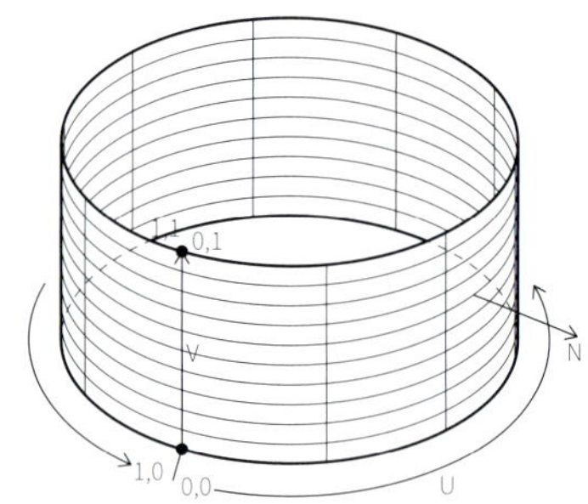

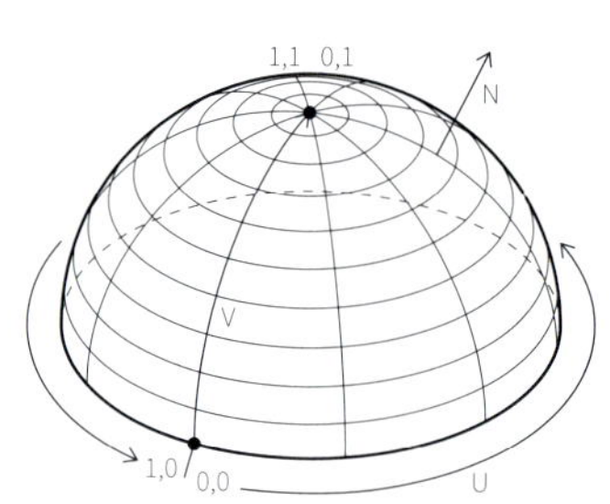

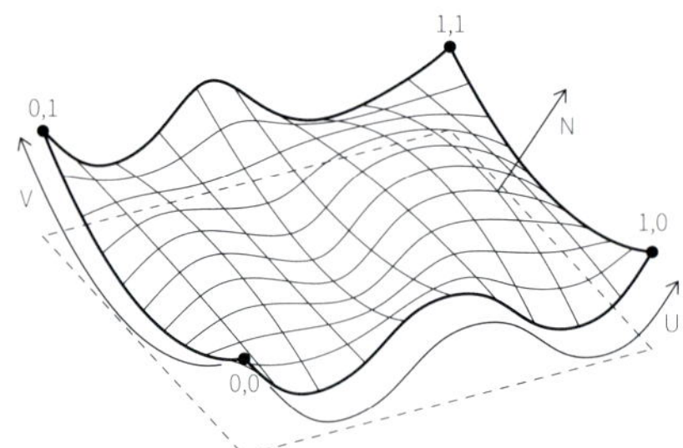

NURBS is an acronym for Non-Uniform Rational B-Splines. As described previously in the Curvature section, NURBS curves are mathematically defined curves consisting of control points and weights that are able to produce perfectly smooth curvatures. NURBS curves can be extended into surfaces through operations such as lofting, extruding, and revolving. However, the two biggest limitations of NURBS surfaces are their topology and their computational processing demands. Fundamentally, all NURBS surfaces can be understood as flat planes that have been warped and pinched into curved surfaces, which limits the complexity of their topology without trimming operations.

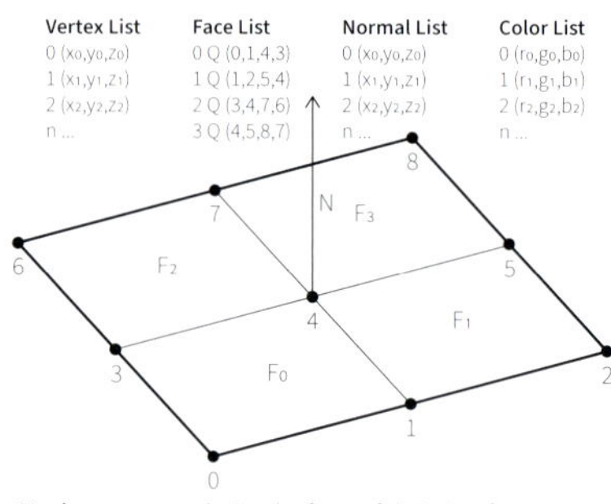

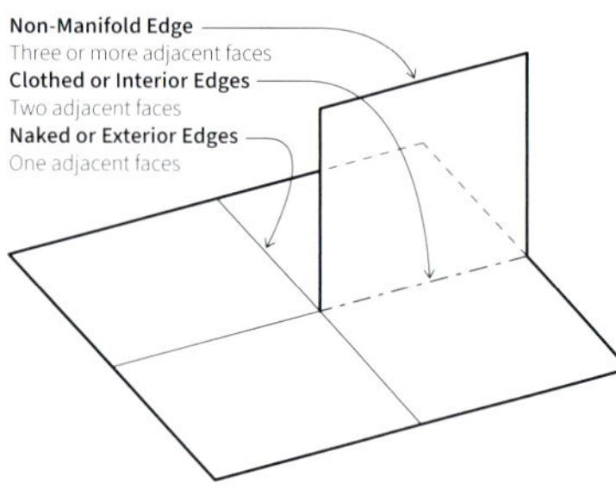

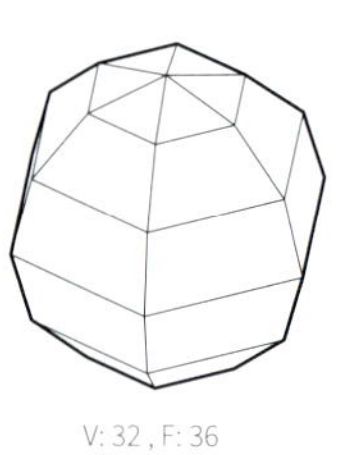
V: 32 , F: 36

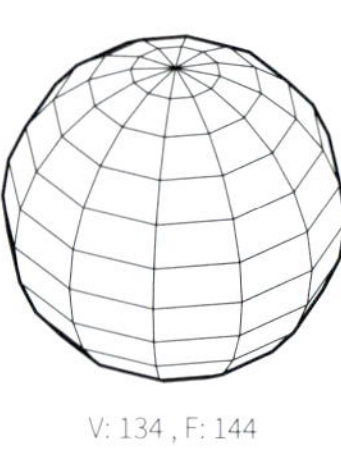
V: 134 , F: 144

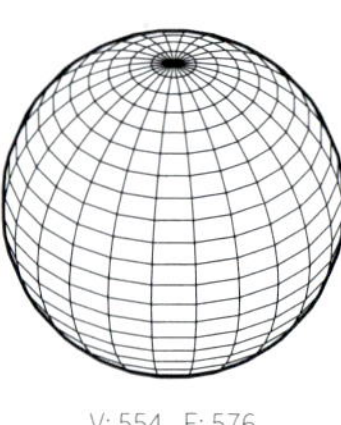
V: 554 , F: 576

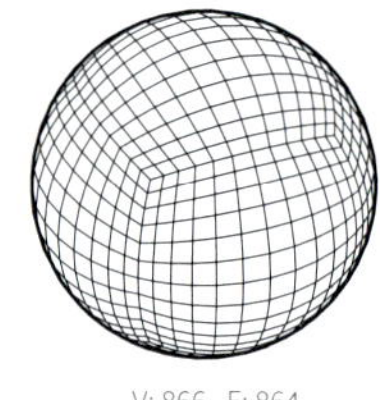
V: 866 , F: 864

Meshes are a much simpler form of digital surface compared to NURBS surfaces. Meshes are composed of four lists of information: a list with the Cartesian coordinates of each vertex, a list of face connectivity pointing to the vertex indices, a list of normal vectors for each vertex, and a list of RGB color values for each vertex. The simplicity of this data structure makes meshes ideal for computationally intensive processes such as visualization and simulation. However, although the discrete nature of meshes allows them to process quickly, it is also the source of their biggest limitation. As meshes are always made of straight lines connecting vertices, smooth surfaces can only be represented through many faces.

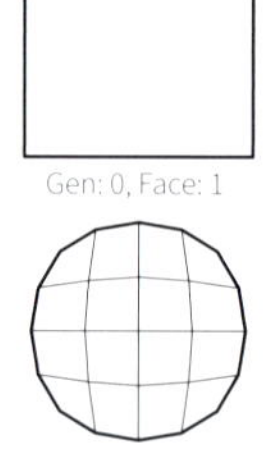
Gen: 0, Face: 1

Gen: 2, Face: 16

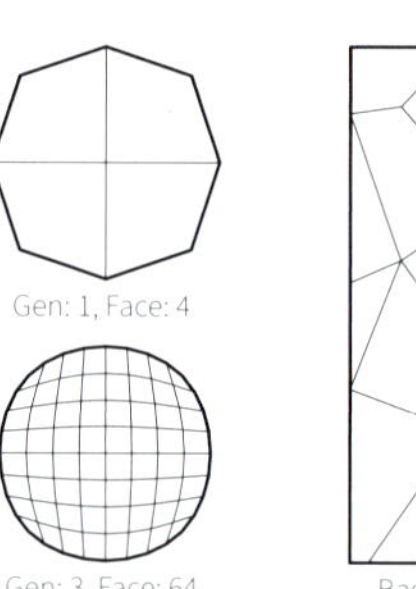
Gen: 1, Face: 4

Gen: 3, Face: 64

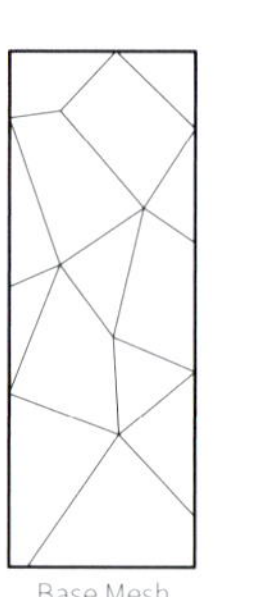
Base Mesh

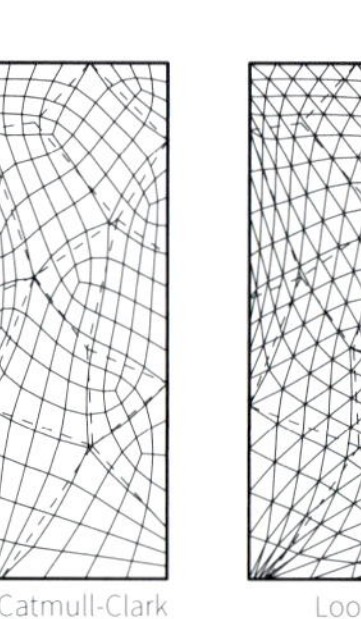
Catmull-Clark

Loop

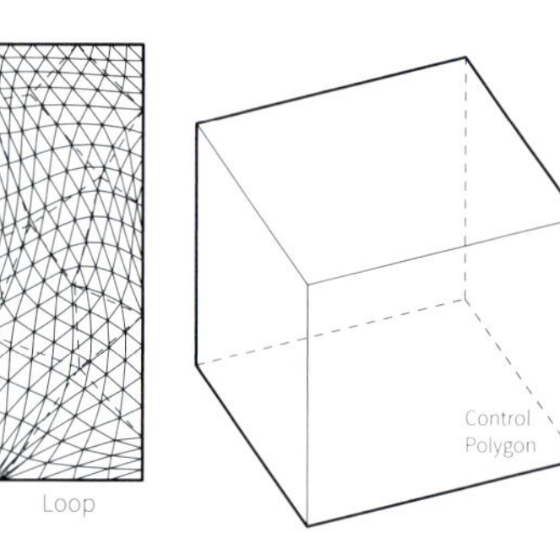
Control Polygon

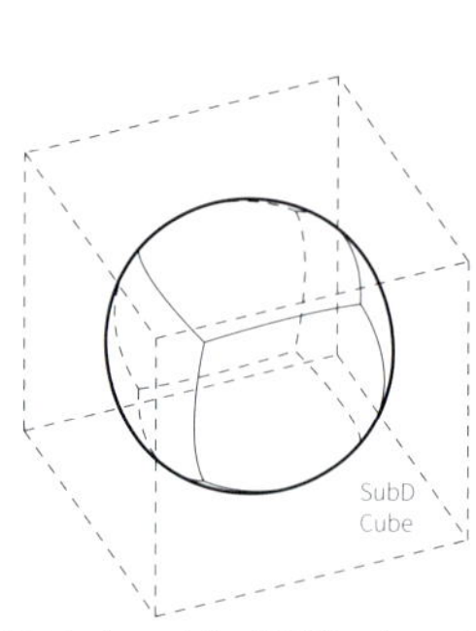
SubD Cube

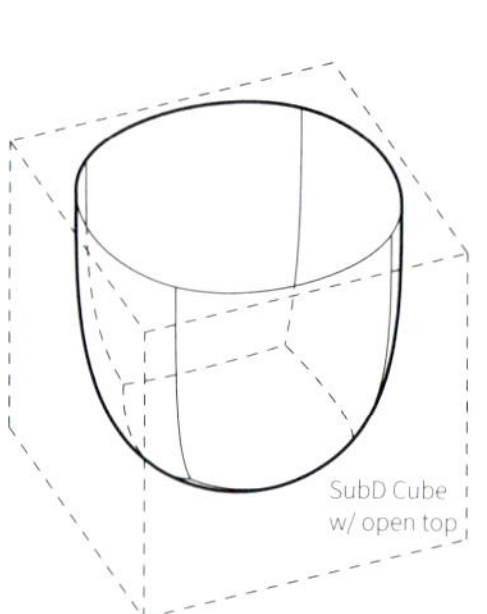
SubD Cube w/ open top

Subdivision Surfaces, or SubDs for short, can be thought of as an efficient compromise between NURBS and Meshes. Like meshes, SubD surfaces can have complex topologies and like NURBS surfaces, they can have smooth representations. SubD surfaces were original invented to facilitate the modeling of organic surfaces for the animation and film industry. SubD surfaces are typically modeled as simple polygon meshes. These low polygon count meshes serve as the control polygons for the smooth SubD surfaces many modeling platforms allow the designer to toggle back and forth between the rough and smooth representations of the geometry allowing rapid refinement of the geometry.

Generative Process
Taichung Theater

The Taichung Theater by Toyo Ito + ARUP is one of the clearest examples of the use of subdivision modeling in architecture. A series of Voronoi polygonal curves are lofted into faceted meshes and then these are converted into smooth SubD surfaces. Modeling this geometry with only NURBS or Meshes would have been very difficult as the surface has both complex topology and smooth curvature.

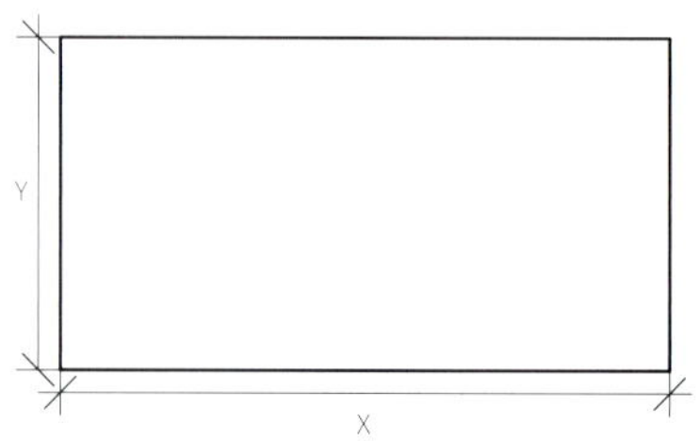

1. Establish the overall building volume's length (X) and width (Y).

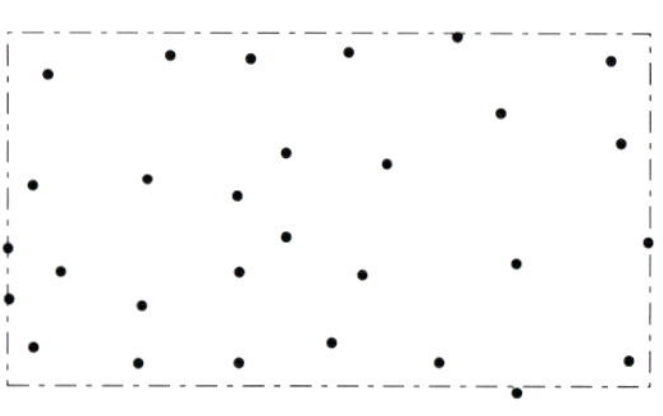
2. Place a series of points (PtN) within or near the site boundary using a pattern (PtP) such as random, grid, gradient, etc.

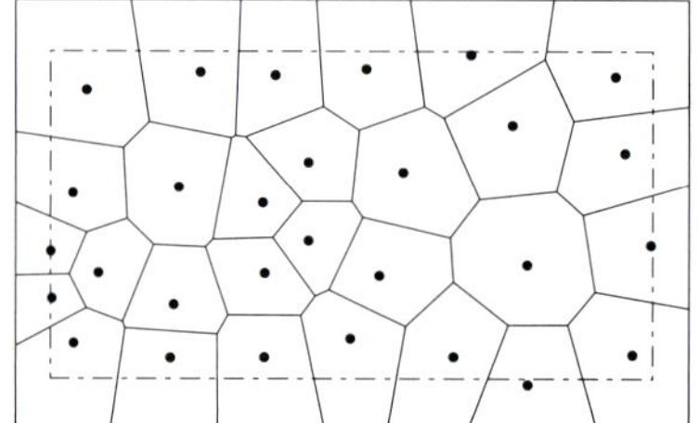
3. Calculate the Voronoi diagram for the points.

4. Scale each Voronoi cell around its centroid by two values: S1 and S2.

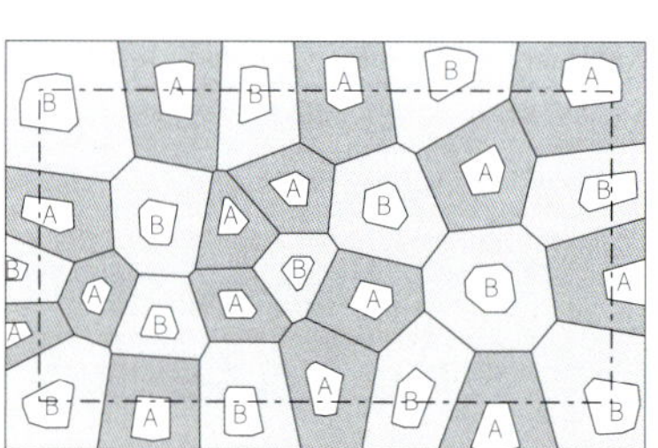

5. Split the cells into two groups, A and B. For exterior-facing cells, try to alternate the grouping pattern.

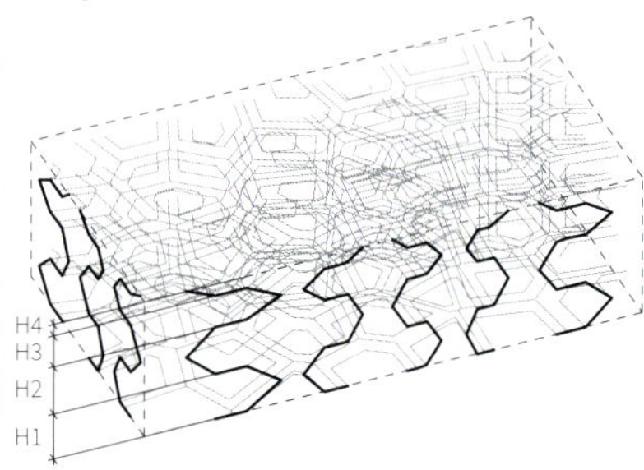

6. Move the original curves and the S1 curves to the floor heights (H1-H4).Move the S2 curves halfway between floors. Remove alternating curves for A + B.

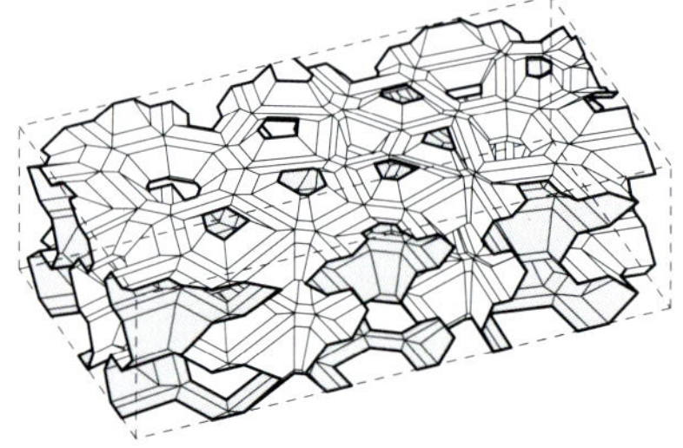
7. Within each A and B column sets, connect the remaining curves into polygonal mesh surfaces. These will serve as the SubD control polygons.

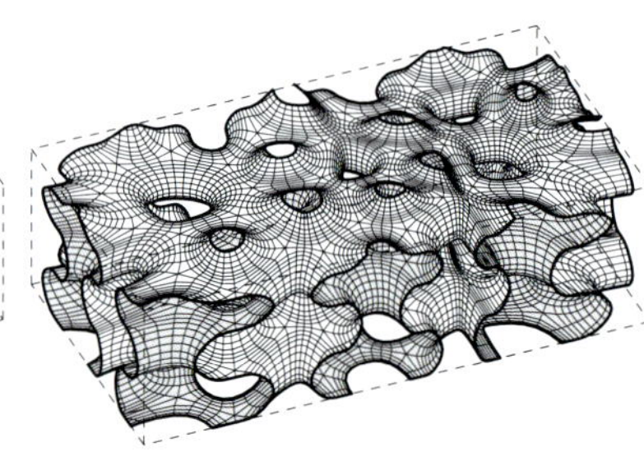
8. Smooth the control polygons to produce the smooth representation of the surface. Trim with the site boundary.

Generative Matrix

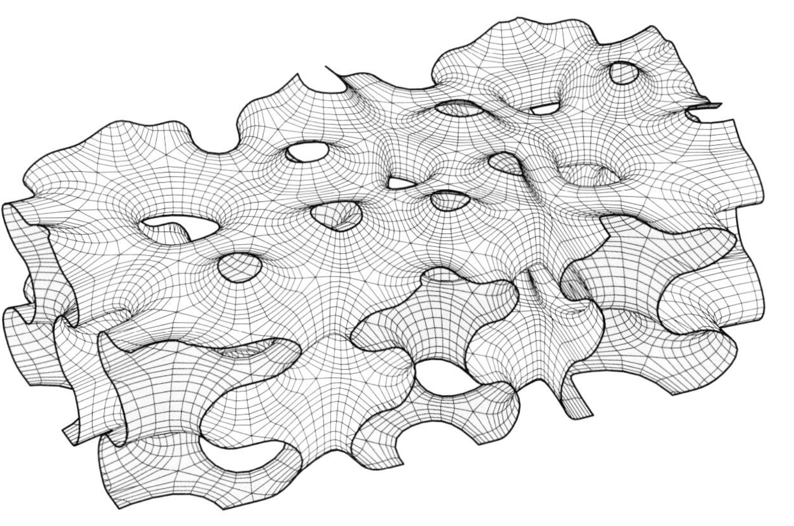

X = 123 m
Y = 66 m
H1 = 12.3 m
H2 = 13 m

H3 = 8.6 m
H4 = 6.5 m
Boundary = Box
PtN = 29

PtP = Random
PtS = 1
S1 = 75%
S2 = 37.5%

Control Model

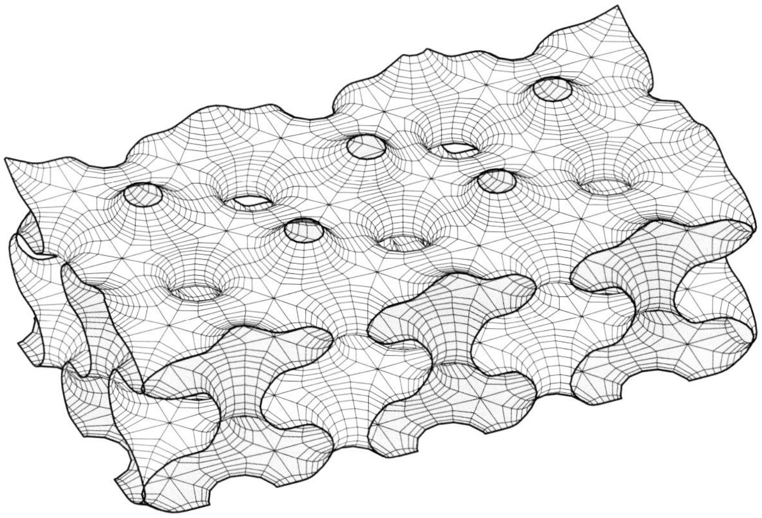

X = 123 m
Y = 66 m
H1 = 12.3 m
H2 = 13 m

H3 = 8.6 m
H4 = 6.5 m
Boundary = Box
PtN = 28

PtP = Grid
PtS = 2
S1 = 75%
S2 = 37.5%

Grid Pattern

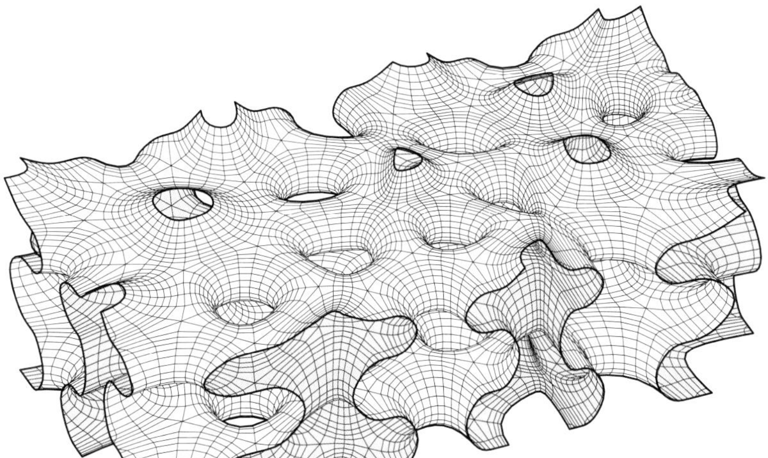

X = 123 m
Y = 66 m
H1 = 12.3 m
H2 = 13 m

H3 = 8.6 m
H4 = 6.5 m
Boundary = Box
PtN = 29

PtP = Random
PtS = -1
S1 = 75%
S2 = 37.5%

Inverted Pattern

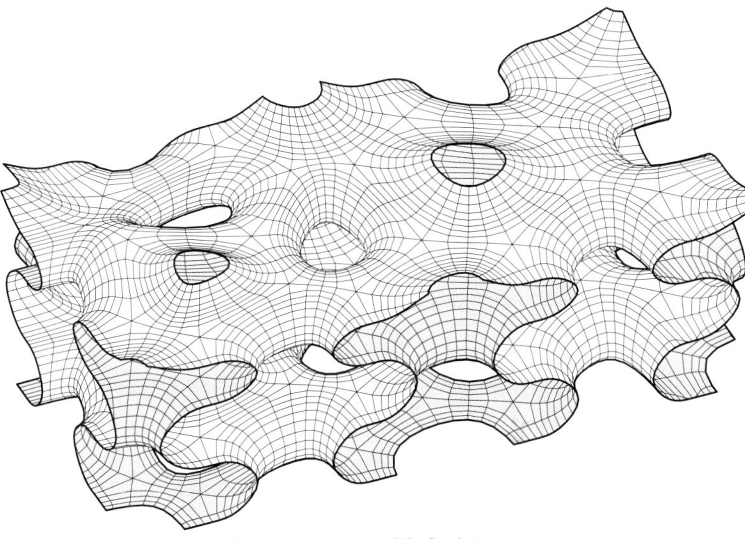

X = 123 m
Y = 66 m
H1 = 12.3 m
H2 = 13 m

H3 = 8.6 m
H4 = 6.5 m
Boundary = Box
PtN = 16

PtP = Random
PtS = 626
S1 = 75%
S2 = 37.5%

Decreased Input Sites

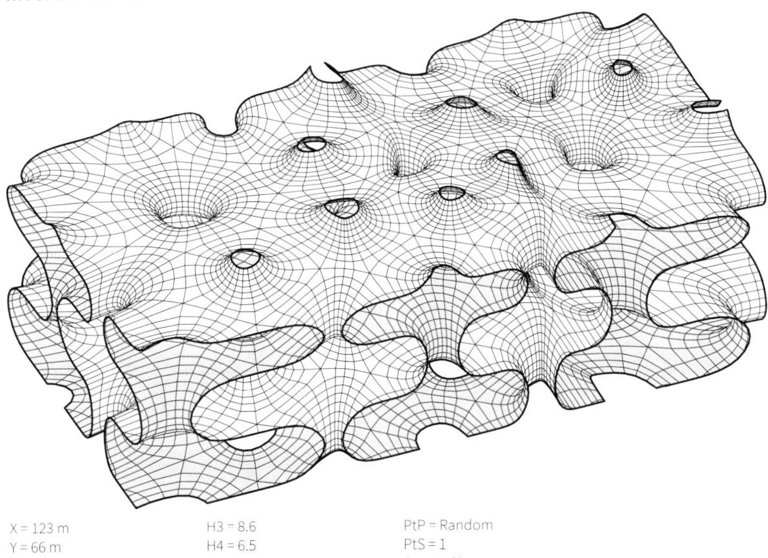

X = 123 m
Y = 66 m
H1 = 12.3
H2 = 13

H3 = 8.6
H4 = 6.5
Boundary = Box
PtN = 29

PtP = Random
PtS = 1
S1 = 50%
S2 = 25%

Decreased Scaled Factor

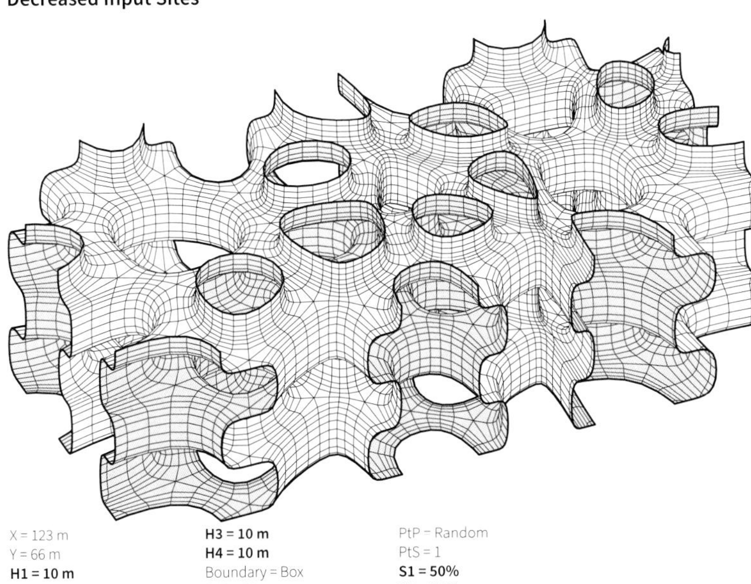

X = 123 m
Y = 66 m
H1 = 10 m
H2 = 10 m

H3 = 10 m
H4 = 10 m
Boundary = Box
PtN = 29

PtP = Random
PtS = 1
S1 = 50%
S2 = 50%

Equal Heights + Scales

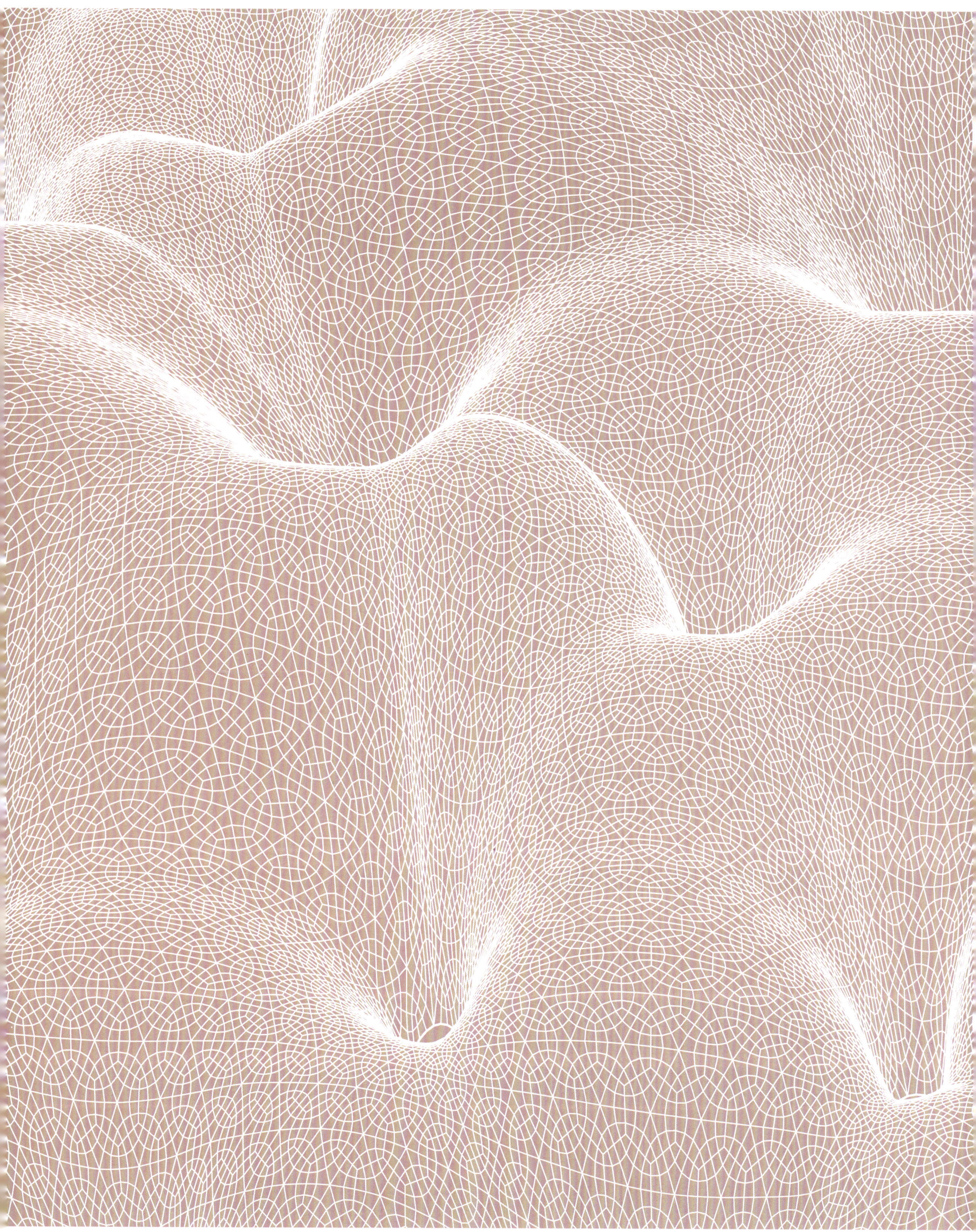

EMERGENT SURFACES

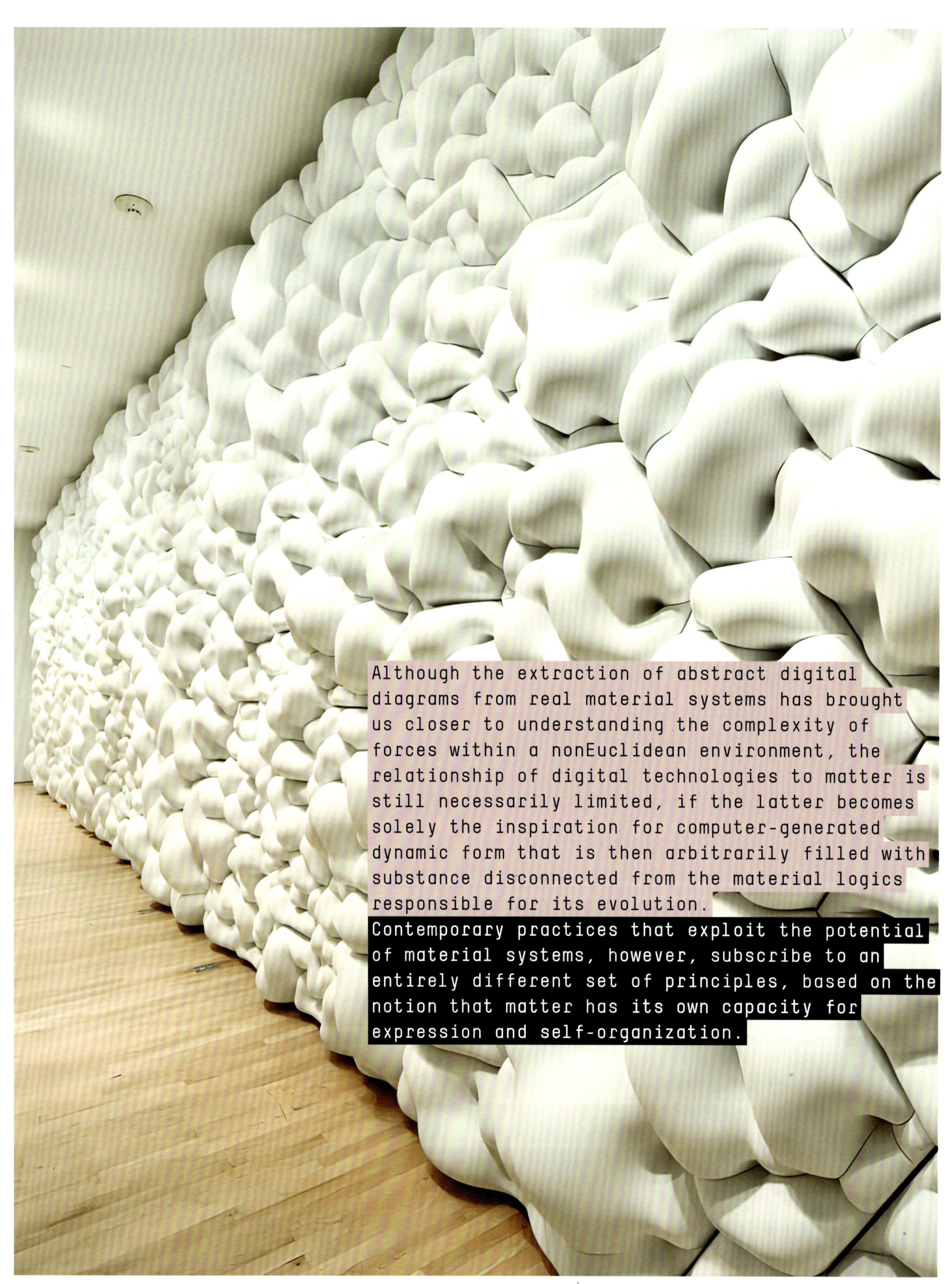

Although the extraction of abstract digital diagrams from real material systems has brought us closer to understanding the complexity of forces within a nonEuclidean environment, the relationship of digital technologies to matter is still necessarily limited, if the latter becomes solely the inspiration for computer-generated dynamic form that is then arbitrarily filled with substance disconnected from the material logics responsible for its evolution.

Contemporary practices that exploit the potential of material systems, however, subscribe to an entirely different set of principles, based on the notion that matter has its own capacity for expression and self-organization.

Emergent Surfaces

The Computations of Matter

If the abstraction of modern architectural systems constrained matter by subjecting it to the limits of an idealized geometry, it was an indication that the dominant ideology of modernism subscribed to the principles of a hylomorphic model: that matter ("hyle"), although a necessary constituent of all objects, is essentially homogeneous and formless, and it is the overlay of geometry that provides its formal definition and structure. Forms that are entirely geometrically derived are a function of shape generators rather than material forces, and as a consequence, architectures resulting from pure formal manipulation are inevitably unrelated to the matters that fill them. Although the extraction of abstract digital diagrams from real material systems has brought us closer to understanding the complexity of forces within a nonEuclidean environment, the relationship of digital technologies to matter is still necessarily limited, if the latter becomes solely the inspiration for computer-generated dynamic form that is then arbitrarily filled with substance disconnected from the material logics responsible for its evolution.[1] Within this context, if the emphasis is on the invention of the derived geometries and not the material forces that produced them, the relationship of digital form to the production of real architectural artifacts repeats the same traditional logic of exogenous form-making and the same hylomorphic conception of matter that has dominated Western consciousness for centuries.

Contemporary practices that exploit the potential of material systems, however, and that follow the experimental evolutionary trajectory of those such as Antoni Gaudi, Heinz Isler and Frei Otto, subscribe to an entirely different set of principles, based on the notion that matter has its own capacity for expression and self-organization. The deformation of material geometries in the catenary studies of Gaudi, the thin shell surfaces of Isler, or the tensile structures and soap bubble investigations of Otto, for example, reveal the potential of matter to express gravity and surface tension, along with the direction and magnitude of forces acting on the system, through material experimentation intent on exposing the pregnancy of form and structure already operating within dynamic material systems.

Catenary systems, for example, were originally based on hanging chain models,[2] where the geometric shape of curvature of a hanging chain is a direct expression of the material forces of the system—that is, the deformation of the chain by gravitational forces as it hangs under its own weight (1). Given that the curvature is therefore equal to the load path derived entirely from self-weight (in addition to any externally applied forces), it is thus considered to be an indexical model of self-equilibrium. The inversion of this analogical material model operating in pure tension, produces its equivalent in compression, a strategy used by Gaudi to develop the structural forms and masonry vaulting of the Crypt of the Church at Colònia Güell. By hanging cords from an inverted plan that marked the placement of columns, and then intermittently weighting these cords with small sacks of lead shot pellets representing loads located at specific points that were physically scaled to the model, Gaudi was able to construct a performative stereostatic model of catenary arches to be used as both a formal and physical material generator for the structure of the building. Here, architecture necessarily becomes an index of interacting material forces and constraints as well as a physical incarnation of a material diagram that is revealed through a process of form-finding directly engaged with the real properties of matter.

Form finding has been traditionally used primarily within engineering as a process of material and spatial optimization that eliminates bending and shear forces in a system by finding the way in which a structure generates and defines its own form based on its figure of equilibrium under applied loads. Before the use of computing, form finding was necessarily dependent on the use of material analogs—physical models such as the catenary models used by Gaudi that could accurately index the forces intrinsic to the system through the internal restructuring of its matter. The interaction of forces through the system are thereby resolved through the geometry of the form generated. As abstract machines, these analog systems for computing form therefore consisted of materials that were able to undergo physical transformation, yet whose degrees of freedom were necessarily limited so that the information generated by the system was rarefied and directed toward solving specific, and in the case of the catenary, vectorial problems.

1

2

3

The research of Frei Otto continued this trajectory of form finding in his development of lightweight tensile and pneumatic structures with minimal surface areas.[3] These evolved from his study of emergent material behaviors, in particular through his investigation of the properties of soap films and their application to the design of optimized tensile surfaces 2. Architectural projects such as the roof structure for the Olympic Stadium and Park in Munich co-designed with Gunther Behnisch, represents a culmination of this research. Suspended from a series of tall steel masts that are organized radially around the stadium, this expansive tensile membrane roof forms a continuous membrane that floats above and connects the primary buildings of the Olympic site. The dramatic undulations and sweeping curvatures of this highly sculptural surface are amplified by the differential range of points from which the membrane is held in tension and rendered legible by the gridded network of pre-stressed cables that constitute its internal structure as well as the patterned surface of thin acrylic sheets (originally a PVC-coated polyester textile) that form its uppermost layer. Within this system, the spatial shape of the surface articulated through the incremental divisions of the tensile gridded net, is an endogenously generated geometry that is informed by, and that co-evolves with, the matter that it also delimits. It is also a form that, despite its relatively fixed geometry, is variable, that is, flexible and locally adaptive within a specific range of intensive (elastic) and extensive movements. Given this new scale of operation, the quantity and complexity of calculations required for the building of the Olympic Park also led to the innovative development of mathematical computer-based procedures that were used concurrently with wire models. Whereas the latter were used to predict the evolution of the anticipated form and simulate the stresses embedded within its structure, the former were used to evaluate the data and calculate the dimensions of elements within the system.

The study of emergent behaviors through the nexus of material and computational models finds its evolution in contemporary work through a number of distinct trajectories. These range from the creation of generative digital tools such as CADenary and MOScat designed to simulate the material behaviors of catenary systems and RhinoVAULT, a software design tool to explore compression-based geometries developed by the Block Research Group on the one hand, to the multidimensional intensification of tensile suspended systems co-evolving through the overlay of material and computer modeling as in the early experiments of Reiser + Umemoto and the hanging projects of Ball-Nogues on the other. Intended as an intuitive software program to generate precise catenary systems within a three-dimensional digital environment, CADenary uses algorithms to simulate the physics of forces (such as gravity, lateral loads, tension, and compression) within a physical hanging chain system through "gravity-based string modelers." CADenary was intended to solve some of the issues with material analog models, in particular the difficulties of building such complex systems and simultaneously proportionally scaling mass to preserve accuracy across a broad scalar spectrum, the challenge of making iterative adjustments following local changes because of the sheer quantity of connected and mutually dependent elements, and the impossibility of simultaneous design editing and measurement.[4] The program uses linear "strings" of varying stiffness, weight, and dimension that can be hung from any point within the virtual environment. These strings are polylines constructed out of particles (points) and spring elements (straight segments between points that determine the stiffness and thus the deformation of the string) that approximate physical hanging model behavior when subjected to gravity.[5] These can then be interconnected and incrementally weighted along their length, allowing structures to emerge as the interacting forces within the artificial system seek a state of equilibrium. The digital models produced are therefore not only linear networks and meshed surfaces that can be geometrically described, but more importantly spatialized diagrams of the dynamic interrelationship of forces that can be translated into physical form operating in either tension or compression.

The incorporation of digital tools, such as CADenary, that are able to simulate the physics of membrane systems into the design process, has enabled the generation of a series of innovative projects that continue the legacy of Gaudi and Otto yet apply these to a wide range of spatial and material explorations. Ball-Nogues Studio's suspended vortical canopy entitled Maximillian Schell 3, for example, investigates the deployment of minimal membranes to an aggregated, rather than continuous, skin. This

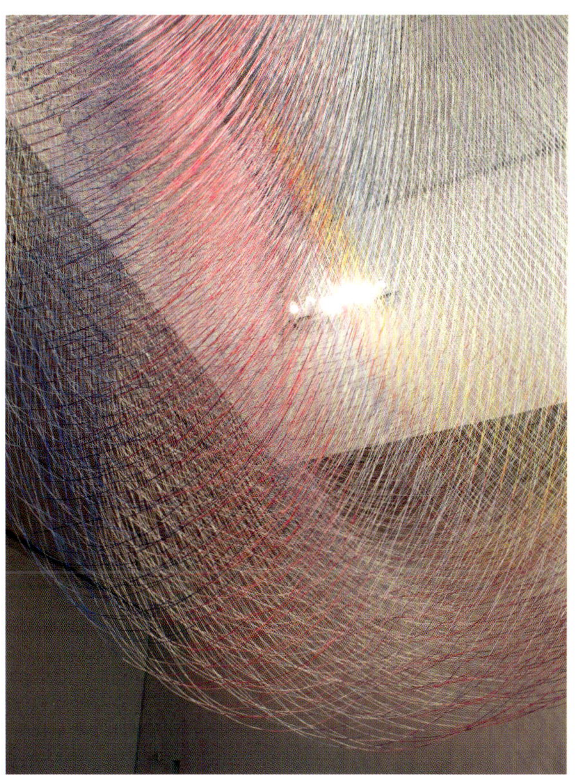
4

5

6

7

articulated surface, which operates simultaneously as structure and skin, is constituted by an assemblage of overlapping and interconnected amber-colored "petals" that are CNC cut from nylon and Kevlar-reinforced Mylar sheets. Since each petal is connected at three points, embedded within the surface of the vortex and hidden behind the chroma, shape, and overlap of the petals is a progressively differentiated triangulated geometry that represents the abstract structure of the meshed surface and the directed distribution of forces through the aggregated membrane. This meshed surface was modeled through computer software able to simulate the forces in the system using finite element analysis applied to the discretization of a continuous topological surface. A highly innovative overlay of tensile membrane form-finding with tessellated surface patterning, this project, through its geometry and materialization, both follows and diverges from the methods used to model surface optimization in simulating emergent behaviors in material systems. The multiplication of swirling triangulated elements generated by the overlapping of the petals and the translucency of the materials used also incorporates a perceptual thickness to the work that maximizes the visual and atmospheric effects of its material incarnation in a way that far exceeds the rational search for optimization that inspired its evolutionary legacy.

The transformation from the digital simulation of hanging systems and optimized surface structures to the qualitative effects emerging from the "resolution of maximal optima" occur when the number of elements within the system and complexity resulting from their interconnectivity is substantially amplified.[6] The catenary experiments of Reiser + Umemoto used to supplement the simulated digital models generated for the design of the Graz music theater, for example, and the interconnected vaults of Afterparty designed for PS1 by MOS, reflecting the heterogeneous complexity of the urban multitude, expose the material relationships that emerge from multidimensional force fields, when the quantity of hanging strings and number of connections along each path within the system are increased such that the secondary local interactions between laterally connected elements start to become dominant within the system. For Reiser + Umemoto, like Otto, the material model, akin to its digital counterpart, is a generative rather than a representational design tool that enables the evolution and expression of emergent behaviors within the system. Yet, unlike the digital simulation, the physical model's added value is in its capacity to resolve fine-grained interactions within the system through intrinsic material computations, arising from matter's capacity for endogeneous self-organization, that can, despite the precision of mathematics, escape the finite approximations of geometric analysis.

The paradoxical maximization of minimal systems through the convergence of material and digital models finds its apotheosis in the atmospheric catenary fields of Suspensions, a series of ephemeral spatial works by Ball-Nogues Studio 4. Unseen Current, one of the initial installations in this series, is a three-dimensional array of catenaries comprised of close to 3,000 hanging colored strings that are suspended across the space of the gallery. The sheer multitude of these catenaries shifts the emphasis from the delineating striations of optimized forces to the smooth gradient fill of a floating cloud of matter. Notwithstanding its vague appearance and intrinsically fluid nature, this billowing mass is precisely formed by the anticipatory relationship between microscopic, gridded fields that situate each of the catenary endpoints and collectively define the organizing sections of the project, and the changing lengths of the strands that are suspended from these punctuated fields and that define each string's curvature. The density of this highly striated system, however, approaches a threshold along the form/matter continuum after which point the system is seemingly inverted. Here, extensive catenary structures used to geometricize, rarefy, and optimize matter are redeployed as intensive fluctuating force fields that perceptually thicken and rematerialize space while re-incarnating its gradient geometries. Within this context, quantity becomes a parametric limit through which emergent formations are realized and where the statistical and the numeric begin to assume their own qualitative values.

One of the most compelling examples of emergent behavior evolving at the nexus of matter and computation that also capitalizes on the "maximizations of the minimal" is the series known as P_Wall by Matsys 5 that has undergone an iterative process of

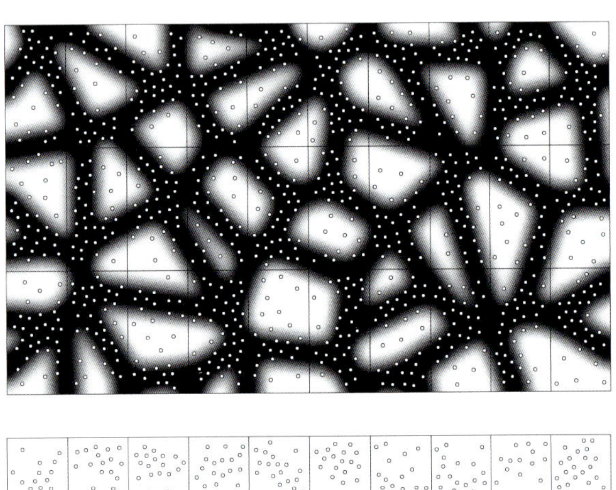

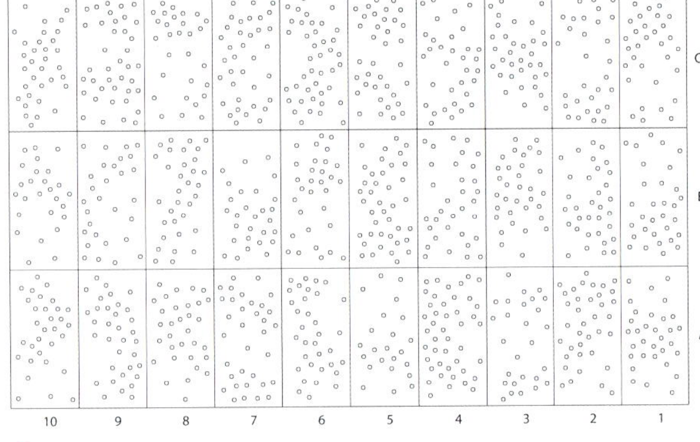

❽

❾

transformative development since its first installation in 2006. In the tradition of casting using flexible formwork, a process referencing the earlier experimental façades of Miguel Fisac ❻, the bulbous and creased, yet smooth undulating skin of P_ Wall reconceives the planarity and immateriality of the typical architectural surface. Each wall in the series is composed of a tessellated pattern of cast tiles, individually generated by pouring plaster (and in later versions, concrete) into modular flexible forms comprised of spandex lycra fabric stretched across a field of vertically oriented wooden dowels ❼. The position of dowels within each mold forms a random field of extruded points. These constitute a fragment of a larger field generated by transcoding the gradient tones of a patterned bitmapped image into an atomized array of points, a process that intentionally disarticulates the image's figuration while extracting a heterogenous ordering device for the whole ❽. As this punctual field is superimposed on the geometry of tiles, it is further parametrically adjusted to ensure that no intersection occurs between the fill of points, and boundaries that delineate the divisions of this surface. The superimposition of the field of points and geometry of tiles (which ultimately represent two distinct methods of tessellating the plane) provide continuity across the entire system, while maintaining the distinction between the heterogeneous variability of the material surface and the rhythmic regularity of its modular division.

The emergent formation of the wall's material surface occurs through the pouring of its individual tiles. As the weight of the plaster interacts with the elasticity of the fabric, a voluptuous topography emerges that, by its ability to index the process of its own fluid material deformation, releases the sensory from the figuration of the geometric and the stronghold of form ❾. We sense the emergence of matter at the moment that form is released and unbound, seemingly overwhelmed by the corporeal forces it strives to domesticate, just as weight is perceived when flesh is affected by the force of gravity, countering surface tensions (local surface structures accounting for the tautness of the skin) that resist deformation. The capacity of matter to self-organize within this system and reach a state of equilibrium is in relation to multiple parameters. These range from the height and positioning of the dowels, that, like buttons on upholstered cushions, constrain the size and form of each topologically curved surface, to the flexible weave of the fabric and its capacity for deformation, as these interact, not only with the influence of gravity on the liquid slurry, but also with the temporality of the plaster's changing state as it transforms from liquid to solid while curing. This slows, and eventually halts both the material and formal evolution of individuated components in the system.

Neither in search of the neutrality and rationalism signified by the abstract white walls of modernism, nor of the technological thrift governing the engineered economies of structural optimization, *P_Wall* intentionally maximizes the affective potential of its material system through a number of conditions intrinsic to the development of the work. These include the progressive layering of strategies and synthesis of their communicating parameters, the exponential multiplication of elements that, like *Afterparty*, converts the single catenary into the bulging undulations of a heterogenous kaleidoscopic field, and the relaxation of the optimal through the elastic surface that amplifies, maximizes, and captures, rather than contracting and minimizing, the gravitational forces that are propelled through the system. The level of internal complexity of the resultant system is therefore proportional to the density of information and degrees of difference generated by the relationships between these sets of material diagrams and the procedures that govern the project's development.

As in many contemporary works, the quest for the single optimal path pursued by Otto is thus subverted in favor of the proliferation of a variable field of matter, whose images of equilibrium, indexed by the material formations of the system, refuse to signify the harmonious, minimal, or universalizing geometries from which they so obviously depart. Yet, distinct from related projects such as *Soft Cast* by Minimaforms that revels in the dynamic differentiation generated by engaging multiple uncontrollable agents external to the system, *P_Wall* establishes clear constraints through continual feedback loops that capitalize on the ability of an animated geometry to both direct and follow the protean qualities of matter, in conjunction with a parametric digital flexibility that enables selections to be made from within a range of predicted

11

12

10

13

14

possible design outcomes as part of a fluid generative process.

The lineage of Otto and Candela, extended by new computational design tools and fabrication technologies is perhaps best exemplified in the full-scale experimental projects by the Block Research Group (BRG), where, for example, Otto's cable net tensile structures and Candela's shells find their progeny in Knit Candela 10 and the HiLo roof 11, freeform concrete shells constructed using a suspended cable net falsework system and fabric formwork 12 to support and mold the shell. Computationally driven knitting minimizes the need for cutting patterns to produce complex spatial surfaces allowing form generation at the macro-level to emerge as a result of customization occuring at the micro-material level of the stitch structure of the membrane. Whereas P-Wall experiments with the material deformation of a homogeneous membrane controlled by the heterogeneous placement of dowels that operate in compression to constrain the system, the knit membranes of Isoropia by CITA, the Mobius Rib Knit by Sean Ahlquist 13, and the KnitCrete formwork of Knit Candela are heterogeneous knitted fabrics designed to generate highly specific spatial surfaces when deployed under tension.

One of the most compelling developments by the BRG has been the creation of graphically intuitive, interactive computational form-finding design tools such as RhinoVAULT, a plugin based on Thrust Network Analysis (TNA). These tools extend traditional 2D graphic-statics methods to three dimensions that, when combined with computation and parametric modeling software, can be used as design tools with real-time feedback that expose the relationship between a spatial form and the distribution and magnitude of forces moving through it as the form is dynamically manipulated. As an extension of material models for resolving the movement of forces along paths in a surface or system, graphic statics, a nineteenth-century invention, make visually explicit the relationship between a structure's shape and the equilibrium of its internal and external forces. By linking form and force diagrams to an interactive three-dimensional model, a structure can not only be evaluated in terms of its structural performance, but also be designed using these tools by directing and controlling the geometry of its forces. The displacement of numerical calculations and endless iterations with data-informed, interactive geometric visualization aligns the tool more directly with intuitive formal and spatial design processes.

Such an approach might seem to be anti-computational in nature, in that it highlights the graphic and geometrical rather than the numerical, yet this approach ensures that the interface is readily apprehensible while leaving the calculable to the computational machine dedicated to this task. This process has been used by BRG in the building of a number of complex compression-only funicular vaults and surface structures such as the truly spectacular Armadillo Vault 14 constructed for the 2016 Venice Biennale. This structure, a freeform doubly curved vault made of mortar free, dry-assembled, discrete pieces of stone with a thickness proportional to less than one-half that of an eggshell, is an explicit material manifestation of not simply the primacy of geometry, but rather its potential, when linked with the intrinsic capacity of matter to endogeneously self-organize through the alignment of form and force, to expose what a truly expressive and encoded matter-based architecture might become. These projects are perhaps arguments for experimentation that operates in direct relation to real, acknowledging not only the capacity of material computation to express geometries of force buried within the thickness of matter, but also the role of the real, of matter, as a site of invention from which new logics, organizational systems, and perceptions arise.

Notes

1. The introduction of NURBS (NonUniform Rational Basis Splines) into architectural computer modeling software and the pervasive use of weighted control points that can be moved to deform curvilinear lines and surfaces are often used to simulate vectorial forces acting on these forms. As an immaterial plastic system, however, these lines can be infinitely stretched and have no material resistance to deformation. Although often used as material analogs, unless computationally simulating true gravitational loads or material forces acting within a system, these are graphic representations only and are therefore distinct from the material forces responsible for the true physical deformation of objects.
2. The term "catenary" is derived from the Latin term catena, which means "chain."
3. Frei Otto and Bodo Rasch, *Finding Form: Towards an Architecture of the Minimal* (Germany: Axel Menges, 1995).
4. Axel Kilian, "Linking Hanging Chain Models to Fabrication," *Fabrication: Examining the Digital Practice of Architecture*. Proceedings of the 23rd Annual Conference of the Association for Computer Aided Design in Architecture and the 2004 Conference of the AIA Technology in Architectural Practice Knowledge Community. (Cambridge: ACADIA, 2004), 110–125.
5. Ibid., 115.
6. Reiser + Umemoto, *Atlas of Novel Tectonics* (New York: Princeton Architectural Press, 2006), 152.

La Sagrada Familia / Church at Colònia Güell

Antoni Gaudi

Built 1898-1906

Barcelona, Spain

7.1a

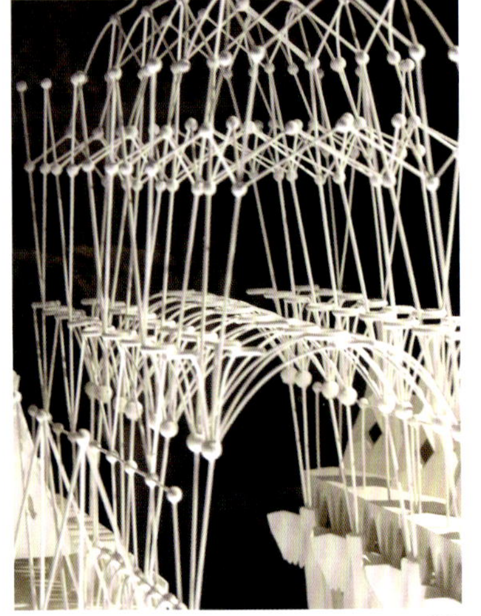
7.1b

7.1c

7.1d

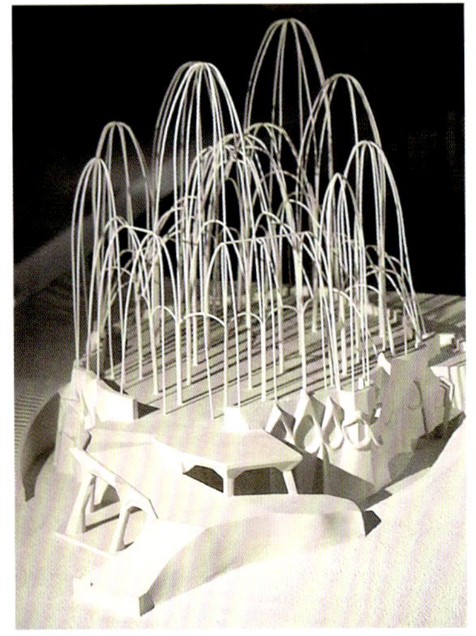
7.1e

As a pioneer in the area of architectural form-finding, Antoni Gaudi, a Spanish Catalan architect, created a new architecture based on principles found in nature that optimized the relationship between form and material. His understanding of the use of inverted catenary curves in the design of arches and his appreciation of, and desire to build upon the structural developments of Gothic churches, led him to use complex hanging scale models made of chains or weighted strings to develop the structures and masonry vaulting of the Crypt and Church at Colònia Güell and the enormous nave space—a volume conceived as a forest canopy supported by tree-like columns—of the expiatory Church of La Sagrada Familia. By hanging cords from an inverted plan registering the placement of columns, and then weighting these cords with small sacks of lead shot pellets representing loads located at specific points that were scaled to the model, Gaudi was able to construct a performative analog to aid in the structural design of these buildings. Hanging chain models deform under the influence of gravitational forces and distribute loads evenly along the chain. The shape of their curvatures in equilibrium is a direct expression of the material forces or load paths operating along the chain as these are derived from its self-weight under tension. Gaudi complexified this physical parametric system by hanging multiple strings asymmetrically from other strings, and supplementing these with weights representing additional point loads to be accounted for within the structure. Each adjustment in relation to the length of a member, its points of connection with other strings in the system, or the weight or position of a point load, would therefore activate an immediate material re-computation of the catenary system and engender an altered form. By then inverting the catenary form of these hanging systems, Gaudi was able to produce a mirrored structure operating in compression that provided the structural form for these churches.

Los Manantiales Restaurant
Felix Candela

Built 1958
Xochimilco, Mexico

The Los Manantiales Restaurant shell structure, originally sited alongside floating gardens in the Xochimilco area of Mexico City, is one of Felix Candela's most seminal works. The thin concrete structural shell is an eight-sided, groined vault composed of four intersecting hyperbolic paraboloid saddles. The project is an evolution of Candela's full-scale, form-finding experiments on thin-shell hyperbolic structures—doubly curved forms that can be geometrically generated using straight line segments and constructed using straight boards as formwork. The building encloses a large radial symmetrical space that is marked at the center of the ceiling by the intersection of the four hypars whose centrifugal, upwardly canting, parabolic edges conceal the octagonal floor plan of the interior while dramatically accentuating the shell's spatial sculptural form. The double curvature of the shell, which enables the roof surface and structure to be entirely continuous, houses a large column-free space that is 139 feet in diameter and that is supported at eight points radially positioned at 106-foot intervals along the building's perimeter where the saddle-shaped vaults intersect with each other and meet the ground. These points sit on inverted umbrella footings that are linked below the earth's surface to counter the outward thrusts of the roof's structure. The 1.5-inch thick concrete shell is thickened at the intersecting axes of the hypars to conceal v-shaped steel beams that stiffen the vaults and reinforce the roof's structure along the lines of greatest stress enabling the profile of the cantilevered, outwardly thrusting free edges of the shell to remain extremely thin. These lines of intersection between hypars are smoothed over with concrete to produce a seamless and continuous undulating shell—a form that was intended to appear to float, like a lotus flower, on the water.

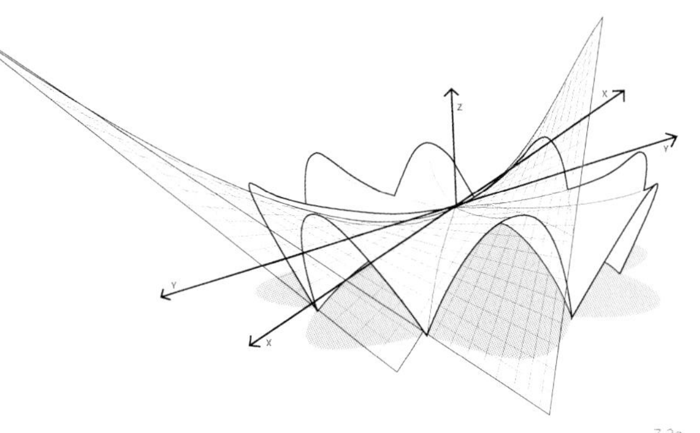
7.2a

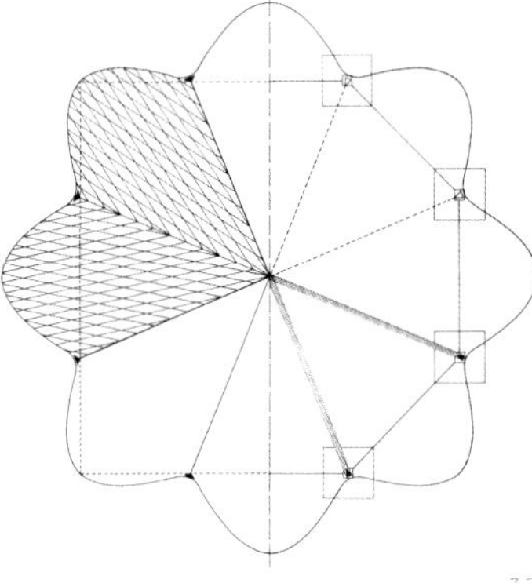
7.2b

7.2c

7.2d

7.2e

Olympic Stadium
Frei Otto + Günther Behnisch

Built 1972
Munich, Germany

7.3a

7.3b

Following projects such as the cable-net music pavilion in Kassel, Germany and the German pavilion at Expo '67 in Montreal, the Munich Olympic Stadium and Park designed by Frei Otto and Gunther Behnisch evolved as part of Otto's oeuvre dedicated to the design of lightweight, high-performance tent structures, emerging from his experimental research on the "form-finding" behavior of materials—in particular, his studies of the minimal surfaces of soap films and their application to the optimization of membrane surfaces. The Olympic Stadium roof is comprised of a sequence of floating, tensile structures that are hung from cables supported by large steel masts organized radially around the site. The doubly curved, tensile surfaces hover above the seats of the stadium while also operating as a continuous series of translucent tents covering the arena, gymnasium, and swimming areas that form the Olympic Park. The curves and undulations of the roof membrane, which are formed by a series of interlinked saddle-shaped surfaces that simultaneously sweep downward from the points from which they are suspended and upward from the massive struts and foundation anchors that connect them to the ground plane, self-organize as they follow the structural forces flowing through the system.

The curvature of the roof's form is made visible by the gridded cable system that operates as a flexible structural net supporting a patterned surface of thin, polymethyl methacrylate sheets (PMMA) that form its uppermost layer. The roof was designed using hanging wire structures and other physical models to simulate the behavior of the material system and predict the evolution of its form. These models were measured photogrammetrically using double exposures to determine the spatial displacement of the cable net in its loaded and unloaded states. The scale and complexity of the roof structure also led to the generation of groundbreaking geodetic, mathematical, and computer-based procedures used to calculate the shape and behavior of the membrane's surface, analyze its numerical data, and determine the dimensional properties of its components. Using these highly sophisticated modeling and computational techniques, Otto and his team at the Institute for Lightweight Structures produced some of the most innovative tensile structures of the twentieth century.

7.4a

7.4b

Sergio Musmeci's bridge across the Basento River that links the industrial and residential areas of the city of Potenza is primarily distinguished by the highly sculptural surface positioned below the flat, horizontal traffic deck that slightly tilts toward the city. The dynamic undulations of this lightweight surface reflect the fluidity of the river below while acting as the traffic platform's structural support. This continuous concrete shell structure composed through the manipulation of a single plastic surface folds both upward and downward at its edges, both supporting the planar deck of the bridge and meeting the ground at narrowed points akin to a contiguous series of hands with outstretched fingers. The alternation of these complex convex and concave forms produces a single doubly curved continuous surface that is distributed along the length of the bridge as four longitudinal arches, each spanning approximately 70 meters. Designed using soap films, tensile rubber membranes, and other analog models and form-finding techniques, the minimal surface supporting the platform is materialized as a 30-centimeter-thick shell of reinforced concrete whose form was designed to eliminate bending stresses while optimizing the distribution of compressive forces evenly throughout the shell. The singularity of the form also renders the bridge particularly resistant to differential settlement and seismic vibrations common to the region in which it is built. In addition to its structural role, the infrastructure supporting the bridge operates as its own sculptural promenade situated within the landscape—an artificial rolling terrain and hard parkscape for pedestrians that is suspended between the cars above and the river below.

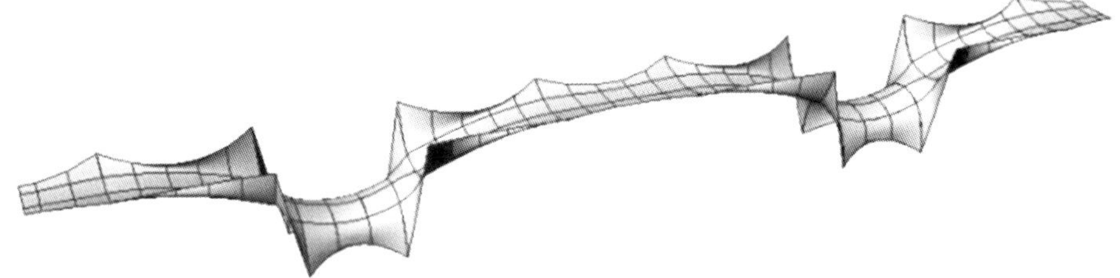

7.4c

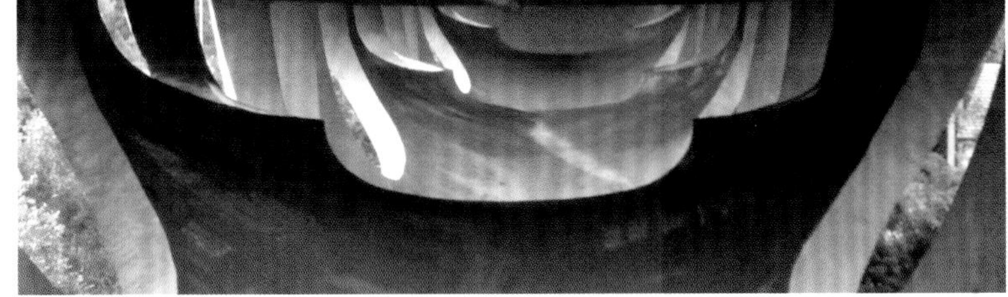

7.4d

7.4e

CADenary Software
Axel Kilian
Built 2002-2005
Cambridge, United States

Originally inspired by Antonio Gaudi's suspended catenary structures, CADenary is a simulated hanging chain modeler in Java that was developed to provide a computationally enhanced design tool to generate catenary forms within a digital modeling environment. The tool was intended to be used for both the construction and analysis of catenary forms in addition to grid shells and enables a correspondence between fabrication schemas for physical mockups of the digitally simulated hanging chain or meshed surface and real time form-finding simulations. The software program is developed to simulate physical forces such as gravity and lateral loading, tension and compression within a physical hanging chain model based on a particle spring system and was intended to resolve some of the limitations of material analog models, such as the ability to proportionally scale mass in complex material systems while maintaining accuracy across a wide range of scales. CADenary also enables iterative adjustments in form-finding, a more difficult process in analog models because of the large number of interlinked and mutually dependent elements, the continual shifting of form that occurs with the changing of loads, and the impossibility of simultaneous design creation, editing, and measurement. The digital model uses linear "strings" of varying stiffness, weight, and dimension that can be hung from any point within the virtual environment. These strings are polylines constructed out of particles (points) and spring elements (straight segments between points that determine the stiffness and thus the deformation of the string) that approximate physical hanging model behavior when subjected to gravity. These can then be interconnected and incrementally weighted along their length, allowing structures to emerge as the interacting forces within the artificial system seek a state of equilibrium.

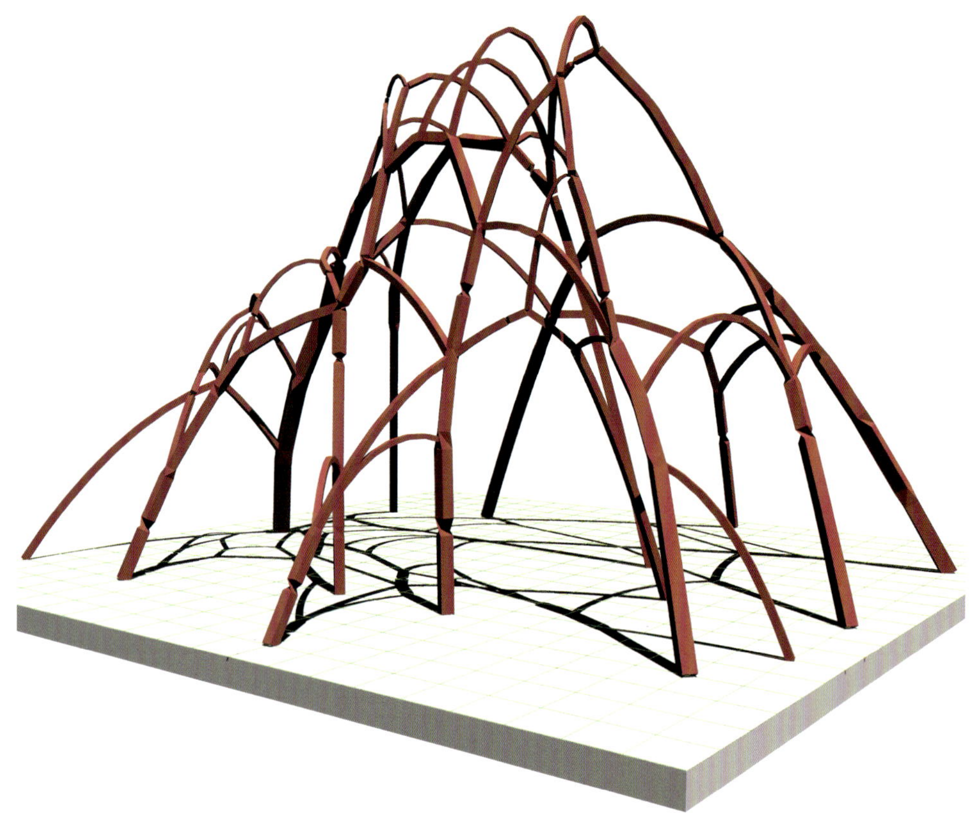

7.5a

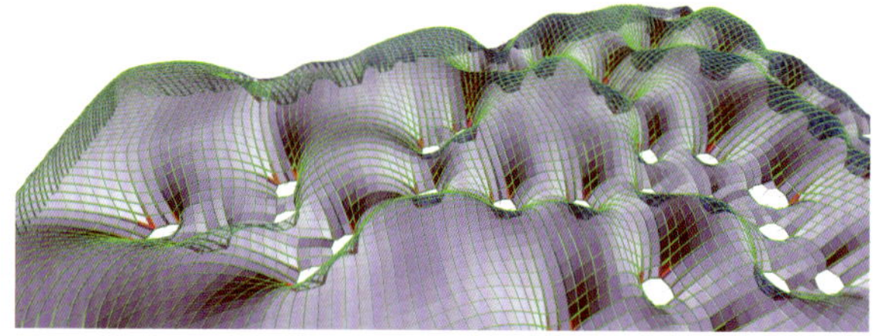

7.5b

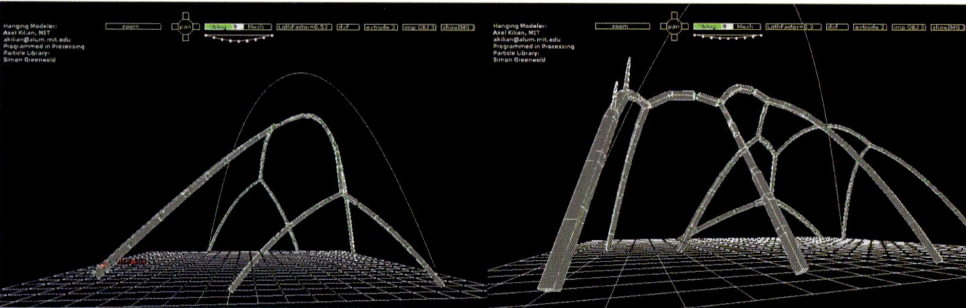

7.5c

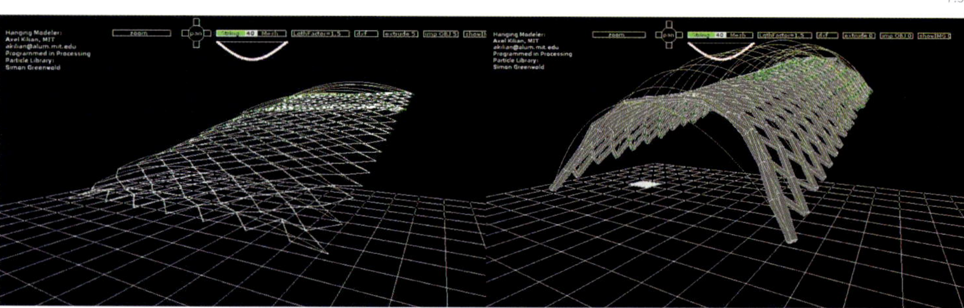

7.5d

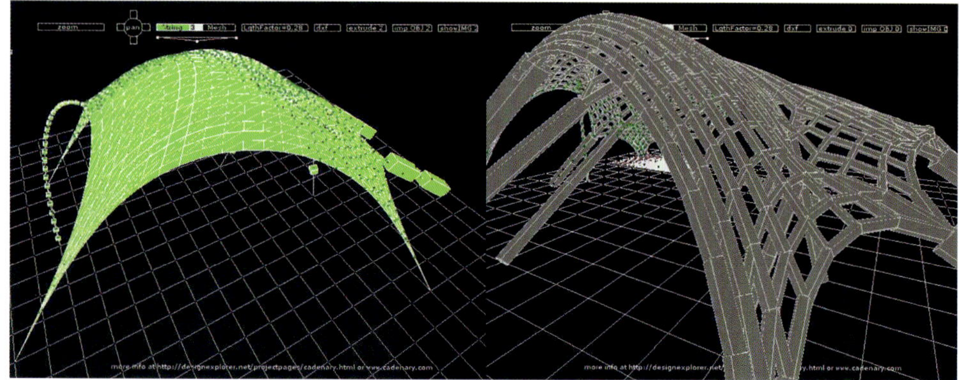

7.5e

7.5f

PS1 Afterparty + MOScat

MOS

Built 2009
New York, United States

7.6a

MOScat simulates the action of interconnected catenary structures. As the structural system grows, the software is capable of flattening the structures it produces, generating design plans that facilitate its physical construction. MOScat was implemented through a number of projects, including Arcade, a temporary pavilion for Convent Garden in London, and Afterparty, MOS Architects' summer installation in the PS1 courtyard in New York.

In Arcade, the pavilion system consists of two components: interconnected variable steel arches and a soft panelized shingled surface. The project reworks spatial and structural typologies drawn from the vaults of Roman baths, Gothic churches, and Arab souks to shape something much less well-defined: the urban multitude. The contemporary crowd lacks a singular purpose and unifying hierarchy or the closure defined by these historic forms. Arcade responds to this through its inflected serial structure with local kaleidoscopic symmetries, operating simultaneously as a figure and field that provides cohesion without hierarchy. Afterparty continues this exploration, conflating basic arch, vault, and dome geometries through a multitude of clustered catenary volumes of varying heights and diameters—high-tech "primitive huts"—that are continuously sheathed in a dark, furry skin (a shaggy Indonesian geo-textile) rendering the whole perhaps more mammalian than architectural. Each of these aggregated and variable enclosures is also truncated and sliced open at the top to render the shade structure of the canopy more permeable. These oculi cast a field of circles of light upon the ground while simultaneously cooling the courtyard through passive ventilation via a stack effect as the vertical stretching of these spaces into chimneys also functions to move hot air upward. The exterior membrane is stretched over a recycled tubular aluminum frame structure with vertical struts linking the circular openings at the roof of each vaulted component with arches that support the whole while providing a continuous series of openings at grade. The shifting proportions of the large-, medium-, and small-scale catenaries allows them to operate as individuated rooms each with its own scale and view to the sky that provide spaces for different degrees of intimacy while simultaneously acting as a continuous, vaulted canopy structure that conjoins these spaces and provides shade to the courtyard.

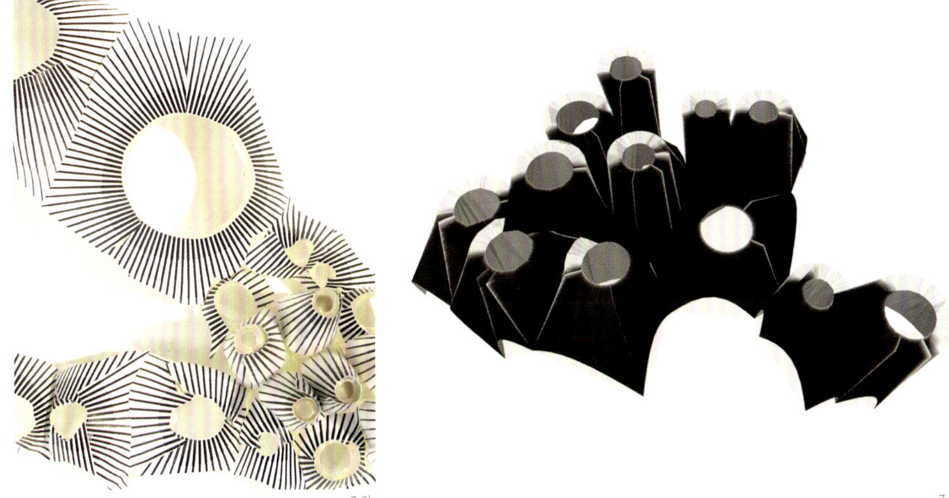

7.6b

7.6c

7.6d

7.7a

7.7b

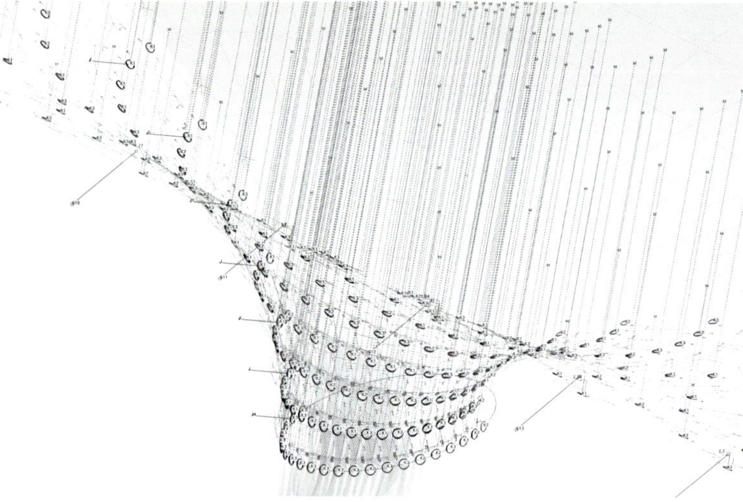

7.7c

7.7d

Located in the Materials & Applications exhibition venue in Los Angeles, this vortex-shaped, temporary outdoor installation warps the flow of space with a featherweight rendition of a celestial black hole. Constructed from tinted Mylar resembling stained glass, the piece pays homage to a character played by actor Maximilian Schell in a forgotten Disney sci-fi adventure entitled *The Black Hole* that follows the protagonist's monomaniacal quest to harness the power of the vortex. Swirling overhead, this immersive installation creates an outdoor room for social interaction and contemplation that functions as a summer shade structure while changing the space, color, and sound of the courtyard gallery. As the sun passes overhead during the day, the canopy casts colored fractal light patterns onto the ground while a tranquil subsonic drone from the integrated ambient sound installation by composer James Lumb entitled *Resonant Amplified Vortex Emitter* lightly rumbles below the feet of the viewer. In the evening when viewed from the exterior, the vortex surface, which is both reflective and transparent, glows warmly while both obscuring and allowing glimpses of the building behind it. The canopy, an assembly of 504 Mylar petals each cut and labeled using a CNC machine, operates as a tensile minimal surface matrix that integrates structure and skin similar to a tent or cable net structure. Each petal is connected to its neighbors at three points using clear polycarbonate rivets to form the overall shape of a vortex. As though warped by the gravitational force of a black hole, the petals continually change scale and proportion as they approach this central attractor. The project was generated through a form-finding process combining modeling and computation that negotiated between the detail development of the individual petals and their aggregation into a smooth vortex-shaped canopy. This process also involved the creation of several material prototypes, the final version of which was achieved by reinforcing an amber-colored Mylar film that offered UV-resistance through its laminated golden metallic finish with bundled Nylon and Kevlar fibers for strength. From the exterior, the minimal surface structure gives the canopy a smooth appearance, while from the interior, the piece resembles an enormous transparent flower with its petals lightly draping and curling downward with gravity.

Unseen Current / Venice Project

Ball-Nogues Studio

Built 2008

Chicago, United States

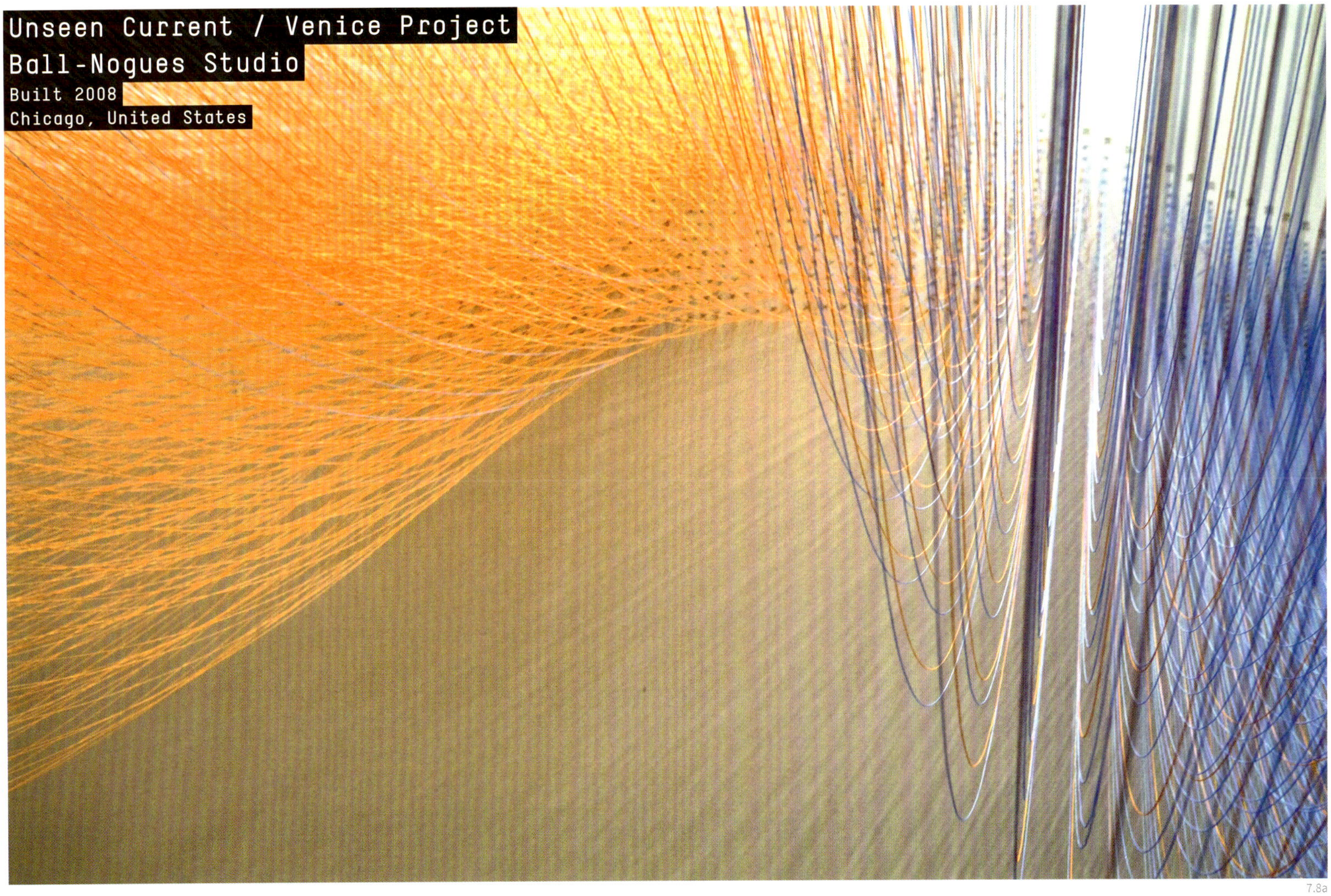

7.8a

Unseen Current—one of the first of a series of catenary projects by Ball-Nogues—is a navigable billow of fog flowing through Extension Gallery. Three thousand hanging strings or catenaries totaling 10 miles in length span between the walls of the gallery in precise arrangements. From a distance, this three-dimensional array of catenaries suggests a surface or volume as the individual strands become subsumed in the multitude of elements that define the floating mass. Upon moving toward its center, the mass becomes a rolling fog. The strands are individually colored so that the changing hue—inspired by the smoggy sky of Los Angeles—is perceived as subtle gradations of color that shift from a rich orange to sky blue.

Each hanging strand is precisely positioned in space, defined by the location of its endpoints connected to the walls of the gallery and the length of the string. Custom software was developed to explore the overall modeling of the form and the surfaces that would be generated, define the lengths of string and numerical parameters for the project, and produce the sectional drawings to act as templates for the installation. The complexity of the whole and its emergent form is thus dependent on the exact pattern of the stippled sectional field of points at each end of the multitude of catenaries, and the changing lengths of string that define the surface and thickness of the swelling and undulating mass. Like a pointillist painting of overlaid clouds, this stippled field demarcates a series of sine curves of varying amplitudes and thicknesses—fluid rolling waves that, when projected into space, become an inhabitable billowing mass of shifting color that fills the space of the gallery.

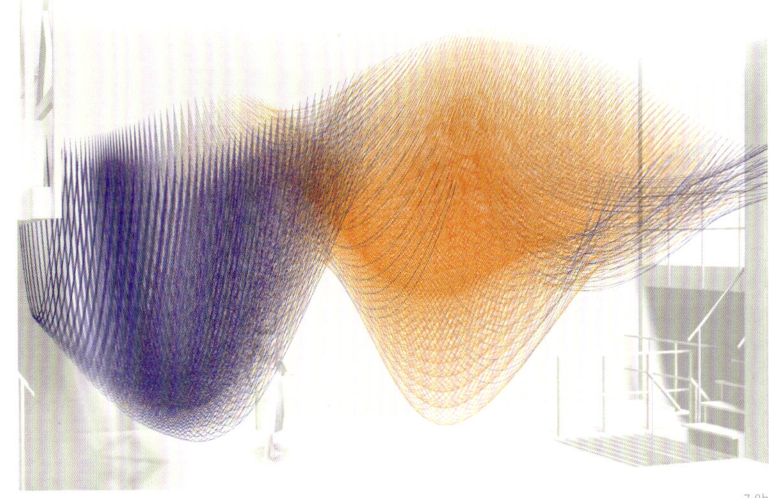

7.8b

7.8c

7.8d

SensoryPLAYSCAPE

Sean Ahlquist

Built 2016

Carbondale, United States

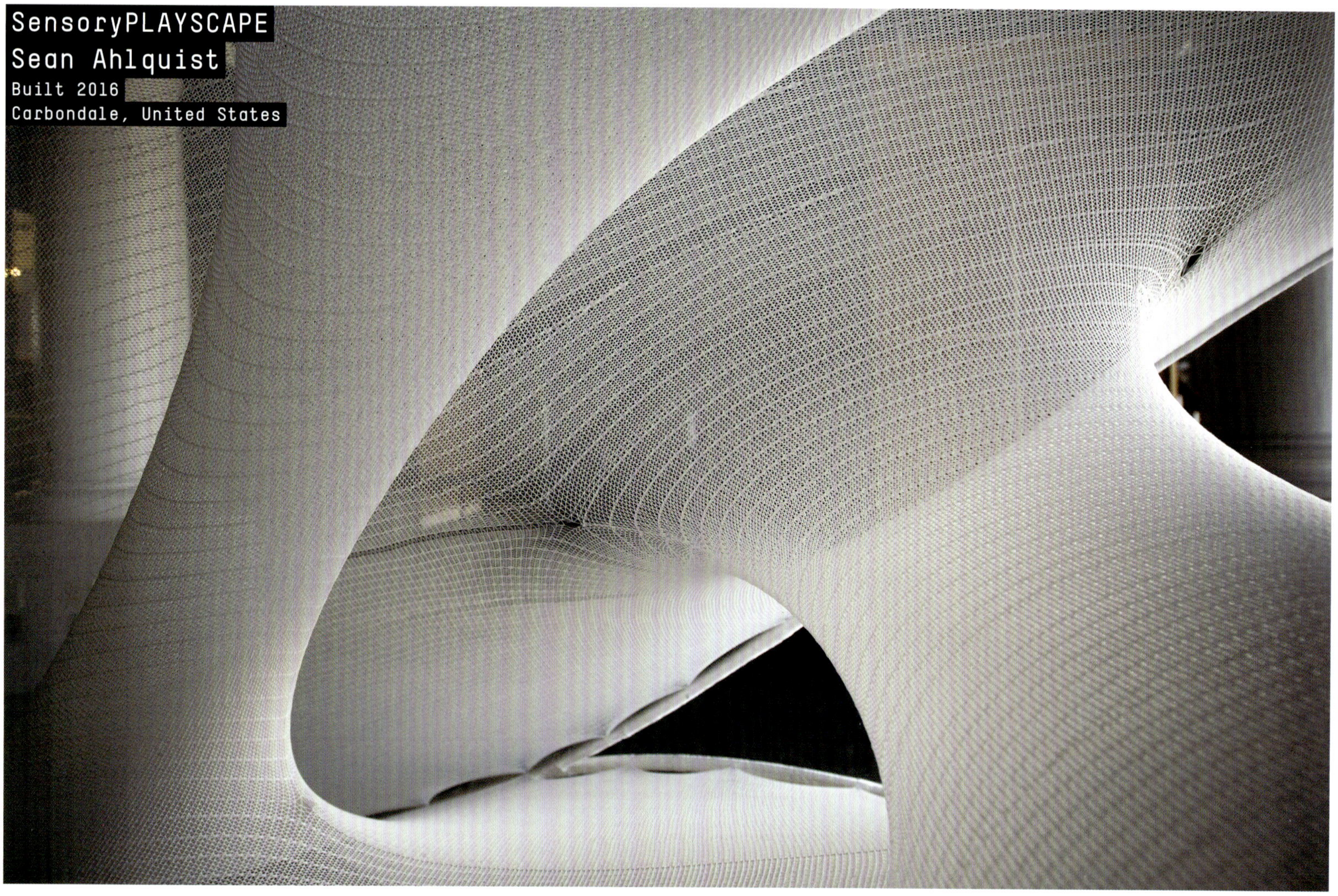

7.9a

7.9b

7.9c

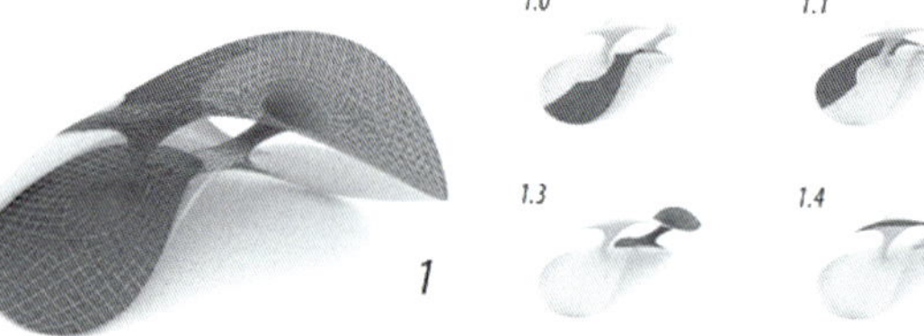

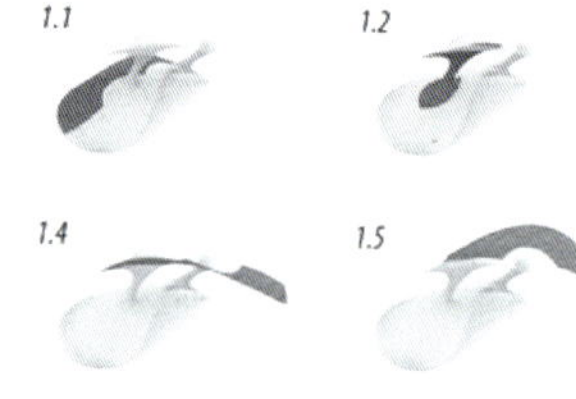

7.9d

The SensoryPLAYSCAPE is a textile membrane hybrid structure that operates as a multisensory tactile and responsive playscape environment for children, in particular, for those with autism for whom physical stimulation and proprioceptive feedback is most critical. The prototype is a hybrid system comprised of a stable, curvilinear, and contiguous looping boundary structure across which are stretched CNC-knitted textiles. The structure is constructed out of glass fiber reinforced polymer (GFRP) rods that are bundled, bonded, and sleeved to produce curved laminated structural beams. This technique not only allows for a wider range of curvature in the boundary using smaller diameter GFRP rods, but also strengthens the structure while ensuring a continuous system (resisting sheer stresses) provided by the overlap of distinct rod segments. The knitted structure is a complex computationally generated textile that transitions seamlessly from surface to tubular geometries, transforming a plane into a cylinder through the knitting process. The morphological shaping and contouring of the surface is thus dependent on the logic of the stitching process and pattern as these are controlled by the computationally programmed knitting machine. Tubular forms are knitted by a continuous movement from the back to the front needle bed, while their change in diameter is achieved by altering the number of stitches from one row to the next. The overall form of the textile is developed by extrapolating geometry and relative force calculations using a springFORM simulator, while simultaneously doing full-scale material testing with knitted swatches. Further, the prototype embeds visual and auditory interactivity using the Microsoft Kinect and interface design developed the programming environment Unity.

Mobius Rib-Knit Textile Hybrid
Sean Ahlquist
Built 2014
Ann Arbor, United States

The Mobius Rib-Knit prototype is a lightweight tensile membrane structure that uses computationally controlled knitting to produce a highly differentiated textile that, when held in tension stretched across a continuous bent rod with embedded "leaf-shaped loops," generates a seamless topological form despite the contortions of its guiding geometry. The textile hybrid structure integrates two distinct behaviors: the elastic bending of the glass-fiber reinforced rods that define the structural frame and edge condition of the prototype at the macro-level, and the form-active behavior that operates at the micro-level of the variegated stitch structure of the knitted textile. The rod is initially positioned as a continuous boundary along the edges of a plane across which a four-sided, seamless, knitted textile is stretched. This rod is then deformed in opposing directions at four locations along the boundary's edge, generating four inverted alternating "leaves," connected by a central ring. Through this process the rod is transformed into a series of tangentially contiguous, curved, looped beams that gain structural stiffness through their reconfiguration. The textile is then affixed to, and suspended from this undulating boundary, transforming the initial plane into a doubly curved, mobius surface where the inside and outside of the textile remain continuous. The textile is made using a large-scale CNC weft-knitting machine. Weft-knitting (as opposed to warp-knitting or weaving) creates a textile formed by the looping of yarn fibers in a horizontal direction which, given the flexibility of the loop when pulled taut, gives the textile its multidirectional elasticity. The alternating black and white serial structure of the rib-knit further complexifies this deformability by balancing the recoiling tendencies of the textile, while providing a means to perceptually register the activation of the topological surface.

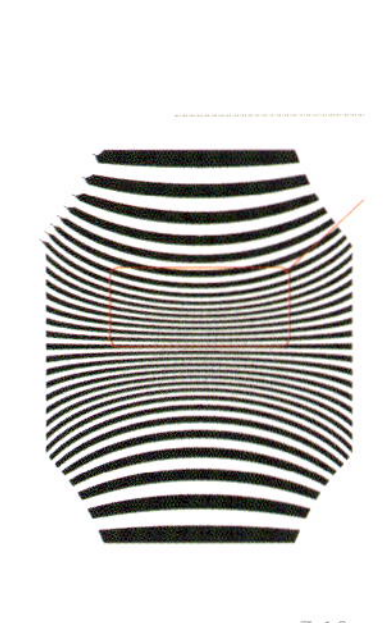
7.10a

7.10b

7.10c

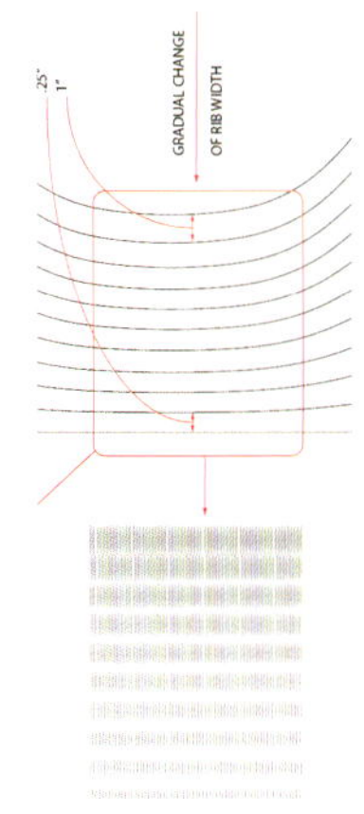

7.10d

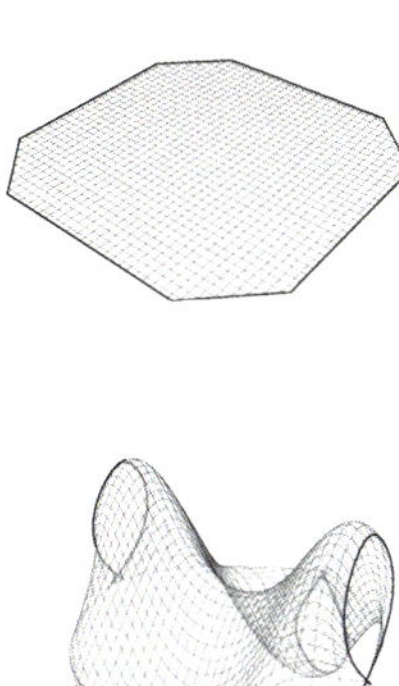
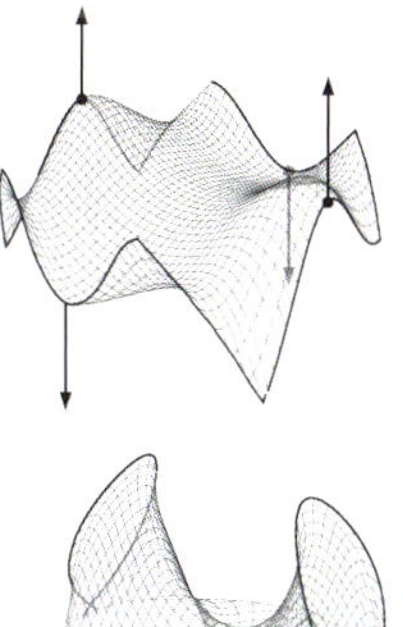
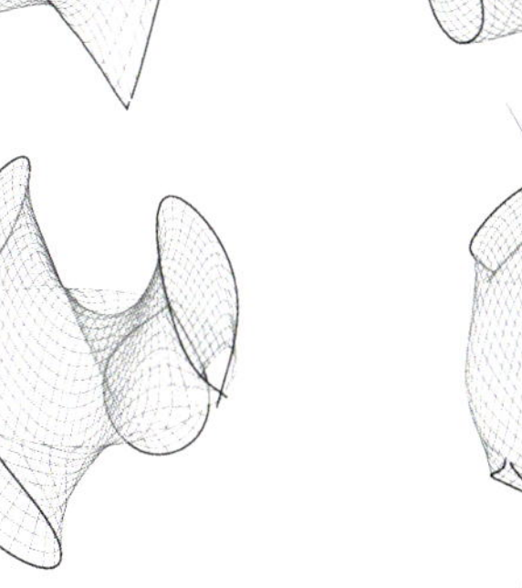
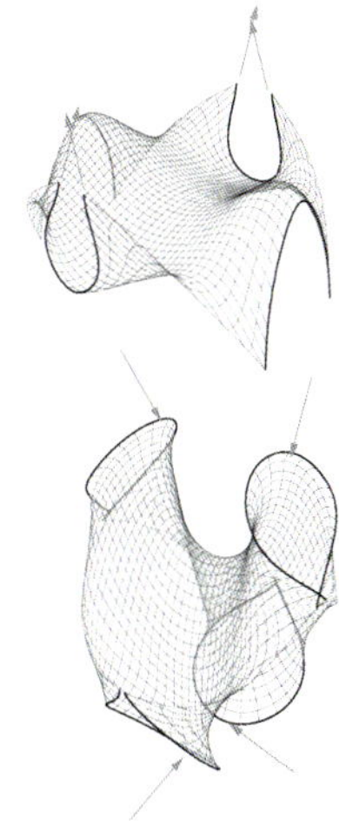
7.10e

7.10f

7.10g

Shellstar

Matsys + Riyad Joucka

Built 2012

Hong Kong, China

7.11a

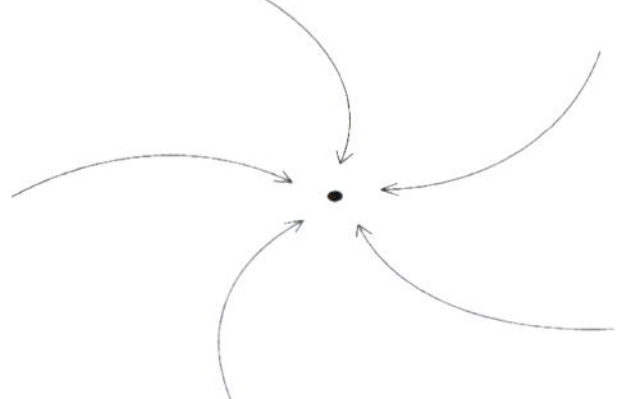

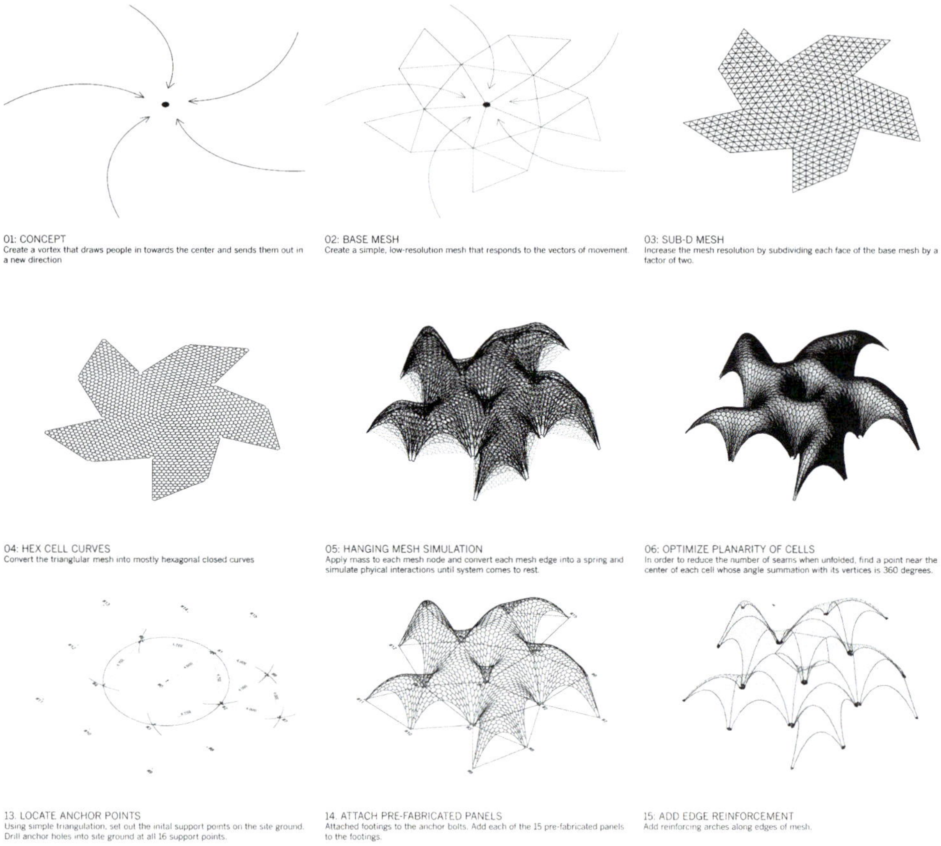

01: CONCEPT
Create a vortex that draws people in towards the center and sends them out in a new direction

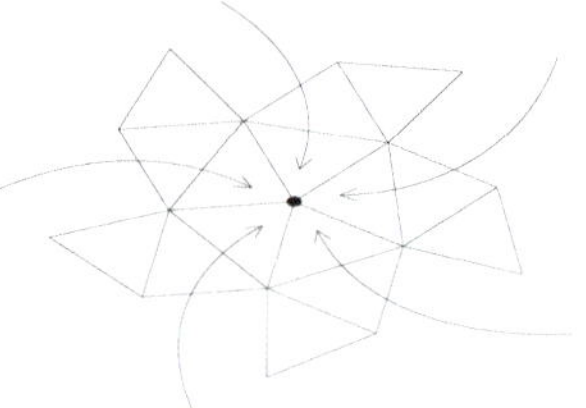

02: BASE MESH
Create a simple, low-resolution mesh that responds to the vectors of movement.

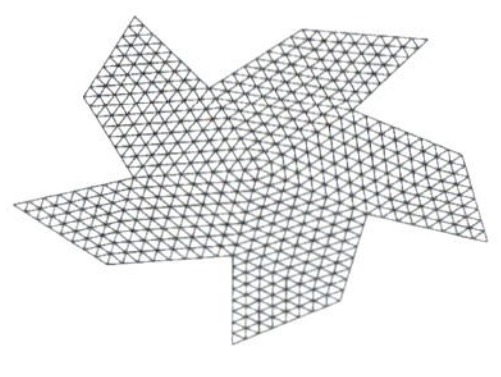

03: SUB-D MESH
Increase the mesh resolution by subdividing each face of the base mesh by a factor of two.

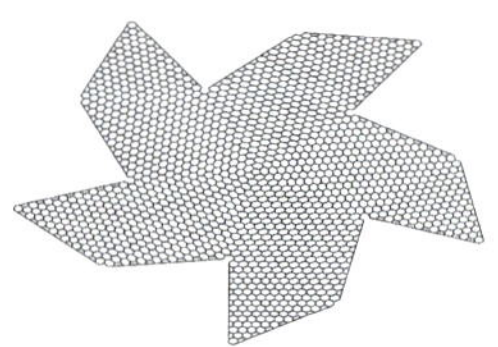

04: HEX CELL CURVES
Convert the trianglular mesh into mostly hexagonal closed curves

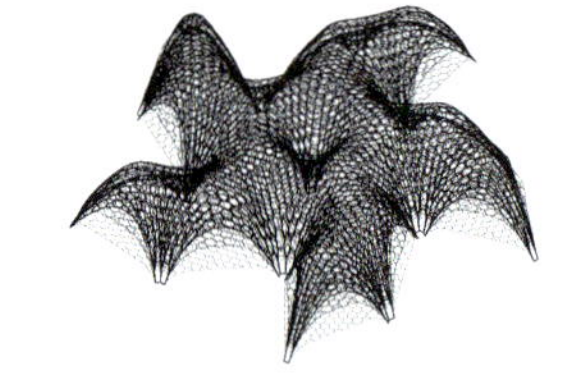

05: HANGING MESH SIMULATION
Apply mass to each mesh node and convert each mesh edge into a spring and simulate phyical interactions until system comes to rest.

06: OPTIMIZE PLANARITY OF CELLS
In order to reduce the number of seams when unfolded, find a point near the center of each cell whose angle summation with its vertices is 360 degrees.

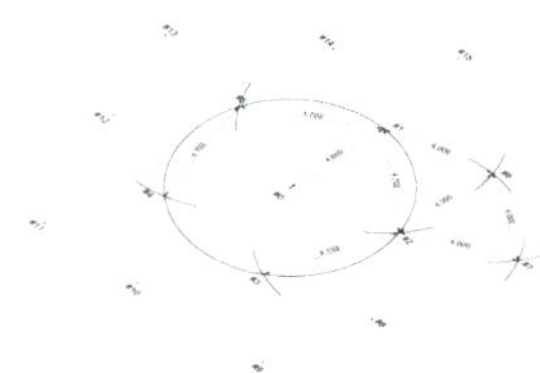

13. LOCATE ANCHOR POINTS
Using simple triangulation, set out the inital support points on the site ground. Drill anchor holes into site ground at all 16 support points.

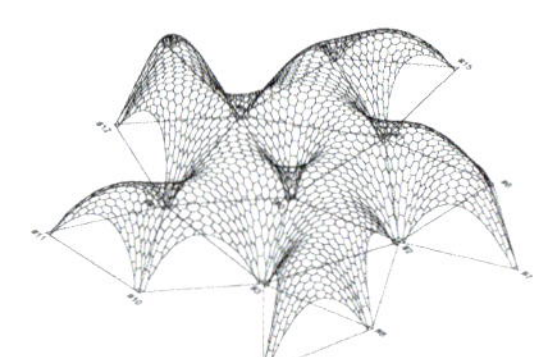

14. ATTACH PRE-FABRICATED PANELS
Attached footings to the anchor bolts. Add each of the 15 pre-fabricated panels to the footings.

15: ADD EDGE REINFORCEMENT
Add reinforcing arches along edges of mesh.

7.11b

Shellstar is a lightweight, temporary pavilion that maximizes its spatial performance while minimizing structure and material. Commissioned for Detour, an art and design festival in Hong Kong in December 2012, the pavilion was designed to be an iconic gathering place for the festival attendees. Located on an empty lot within the Wan Chai district of Hong Kong, the design emerged out of a desire to create a spatial vortex to draw visitors into the pavilion center and subsequently drawn them back out into the larger festival site. Working fully within a parametric modeling environment, the design was quickly developed, iterated, fabricated, and assembled within a six-week time period. The design process can be broken down into three distinct processes that were enabled by advanced digital modeling techniques: form-finding, surface optimization, and fabrication planning.

Form-Finding: The form emerged out of a digital form-finding process based on the physical modeling techniques developed by Antonio Gaudi and Frei Otto, among others. Using Grasshopper and the physics engine Kangaroo, the form self-organizes into catenary-like surfaces that are aligned with the vectors defining the position and orientation of structural forces, thus allowing for minimal structural depths.

Surface Optimization: The structure is composed of nearly 1,500 individual cells that are all slightly nonplanar. In reality, the cells must bend slightly to take on the global curvature of the form. The cells, however, cannot be complexly curved (too nonplanar) as this would make it difficult to cut them from flat sheet materials. Using a custom Python script, each cell is optimized to eliminate any interior seams and ensure that it is as planar as possible, greatly simplifying fabrication.

Fabrication Planning: Additional custom python scripts were also used to enable each cell to be unfolded flat and prepared for fabrication. The cell flanges and labels were automatically added, and the cell orientation was analyzed and then rotated to align the flutes of the Coroplast material with the principal bending direction of the surface.

7.11c

7.11d

La Voute de LeFevre

Matter Design

Built 2012

Columbus, Ohio

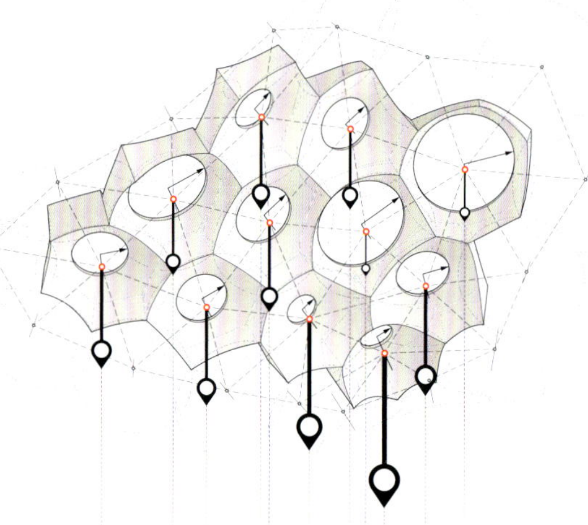
7.12a

La Voûte de LeFevre, installed in the Banvard Gallery, synthesizes methods drawn from ancient stereotomic vault construction with contemporary digital practices. The project is inspired by the stone, cutting techniques and thick material masses intrinsic to these historic vaults as these are reconsidered through the complex spatial and surface variability enabled by advanced computational, modeling, and fabrication techniques. The 15-by-20-foot vaulted structure, which hovers above the space and is supported by three slender columns, is built out of individually milled hexagonal tiles of Baltic birch plywood, each a nonstandard volumetric unit that is unique in diameter, thickness, and sectional profile. Each unit is produced using a five-axis Onsrud router that carves the thickened plywood block into a six-sided hexagonal form, with angled scalloped edges, a concave face, and an opening at its center. As with traditional stone carving, whereby a drawing method was established to ensure that each individual stone would be cut to exactly align with its neighbor, the perforated hexagonal blocks out of which La Voûte is assembled are defined using a custom simulation program able to determine the size and shape of each unit and its central opening, while adjusting the mass, volumetric form and position of each relative to its neighbors. As the openings in the tiles increase in size, the weight of the blocks decrease, dematerializing the vault as it moves upward so that the compressive forces moving through the structure—now able to be computationally modeled—are perceived in the shifting density of elements and the continuity of its form. Although the column is a single solid unit, carrying the loads from above, the patterning of its surface topology ensures a continuity with the discretized units of the vaulted ceiling and the consistency of the whole. The terrain of this project produces something that is simultaneously familiar and yet not. A new architecture that is seemingly ancient yet contemporary, heavy and light, and familiar yet alien.

7.12b

7.12c

7.12d

7.12e

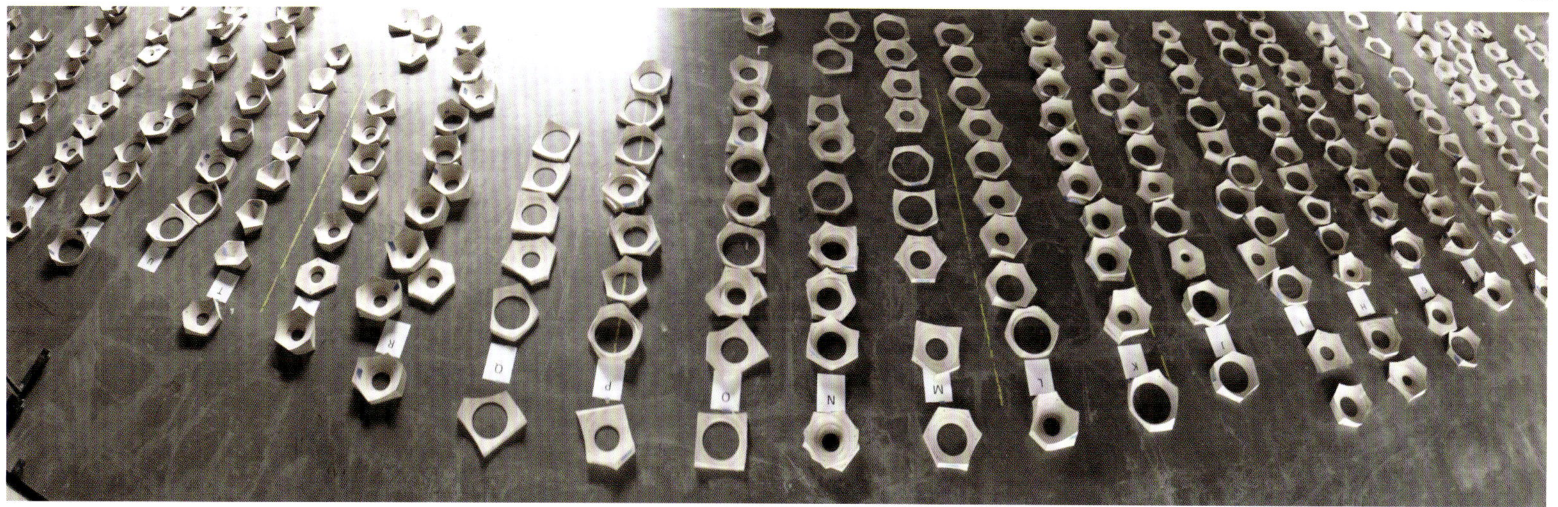

7.12f

7.12g

7.12h

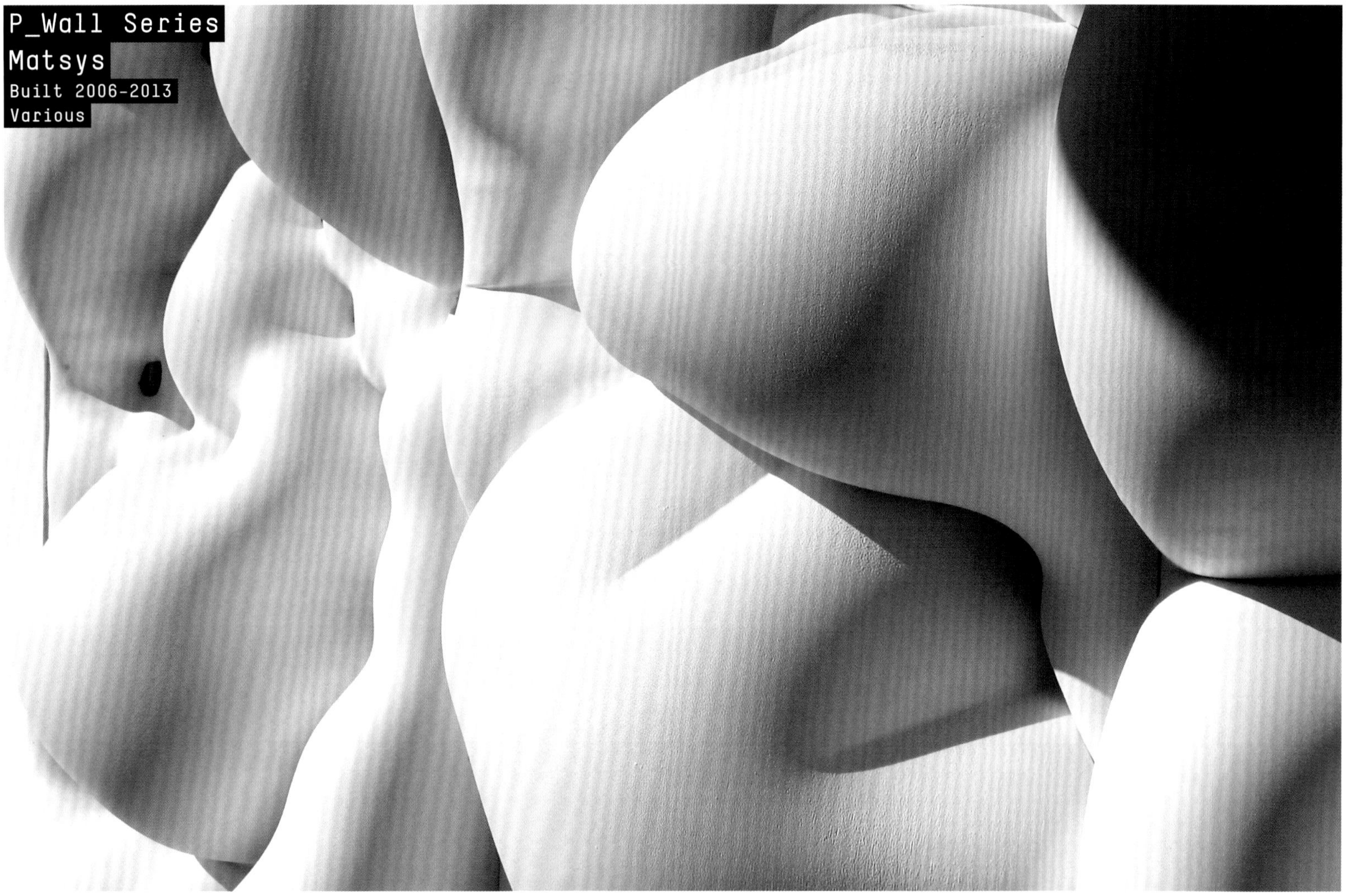

P_Wall Series

Matsys

Built 2006–2013

Various

7.13a

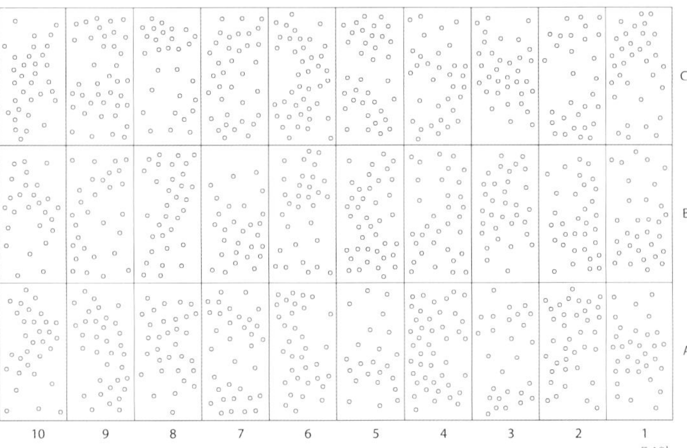

7.13b

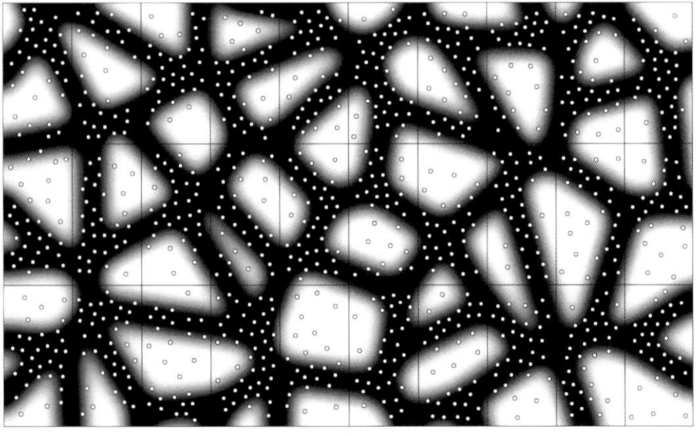

7.13c

This project investigates the self-organization of two materials, plaster and elastic fabric, to produce evocative visual and acoustic effects. Inspired by the work of the Spanish architect Miguel Fisac and his experiments with flexible concrete formwork in the 1960–70s, P_wall attempts to continue this line of research and add to it the ability to generate larger and more differentiated patterns. Each wall in the series is constituted by a tessellated pattern of cast tiles, each of which is produced by pouring plaster into modular flexible forms. The project begins with two superimposed layers: the pattern of tiles that divides up the surface, and a cloud of points that is generated by transcoding the tonal density of image—its grayscale values—into an abstract stippled field. This field of points is used to mark the positions of vertical dowels which sit below, and thus constrain the elasticity of the fabric formwork (while ensuring that no intersection occurs between the points and the boundaries that define the edges of the modular tiles). When plaster is then poured into the mold, the fabric expands and deforms under the weight of the fluid material slurry producing a bulging and seemingly voluptuous surface that finds resistance and is therefore indented at the points where it meets the dowels. The resultant plaster tile thus finds a certain resonance with the body as it sags, expands, and stretches, expressing its own relationship between matter, gravity, and structure. Assembled into a larger surface, a pattern emerges between the initial image's grayscale tones and the shadows produced by the wall.

7.13d

Heap Tiles
Rhett Russo
Built 2015
New York, United States and Hertogenbosch, Netherlands

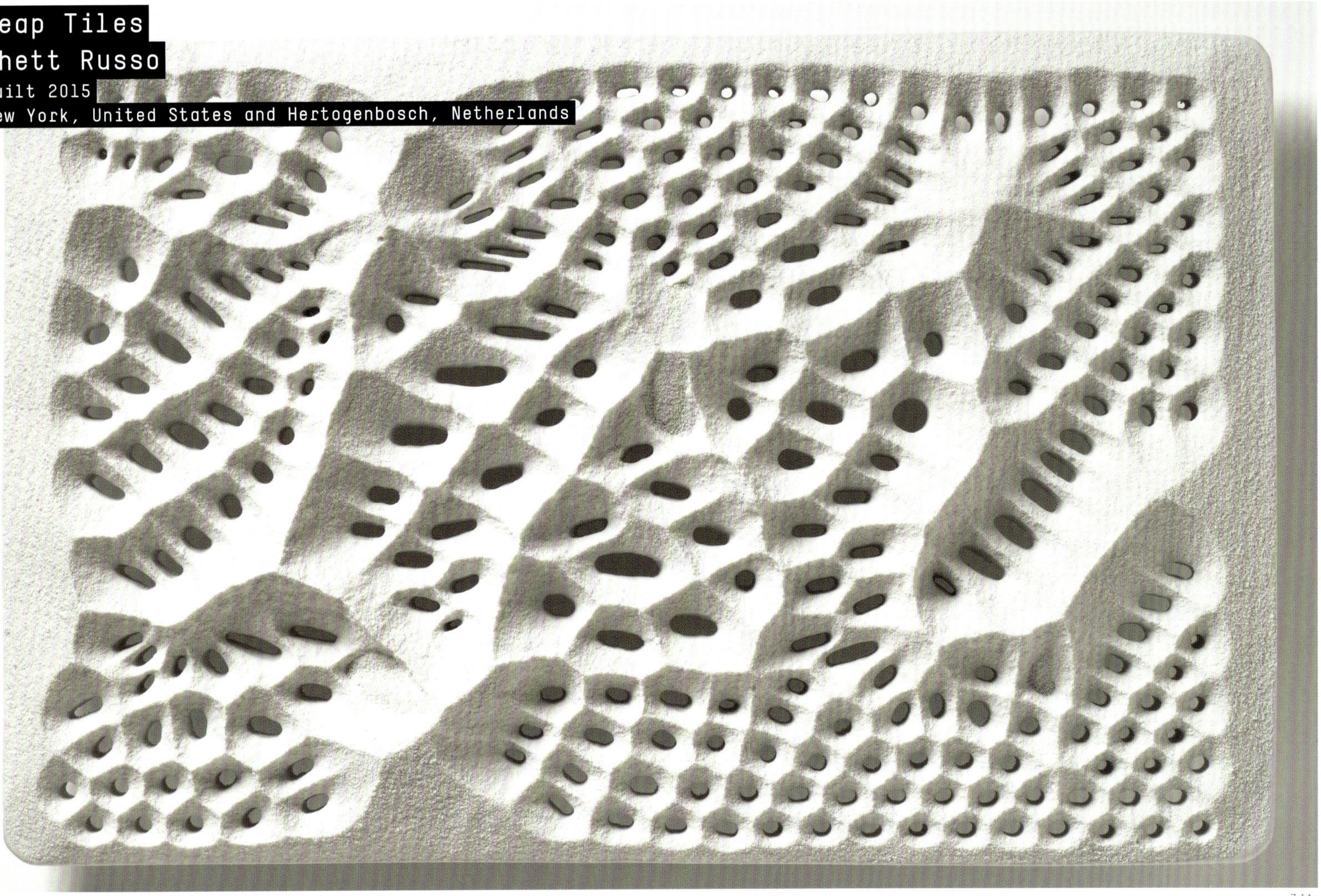

7.14a

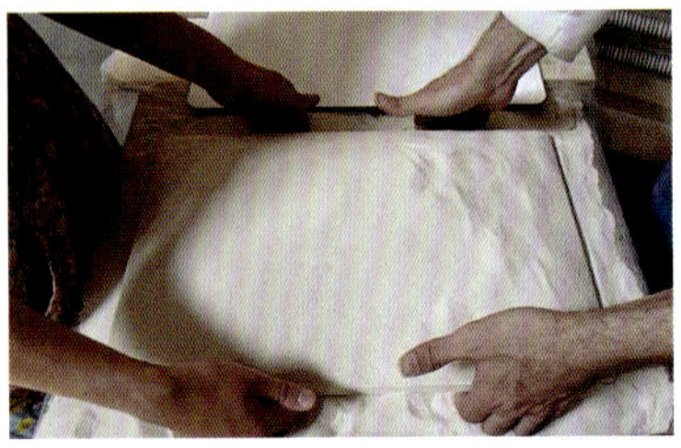

07-04-14h59m25s

07-04-14h59m43s

07-04-15h00m02s

07-04-15h00m17s 7.14b

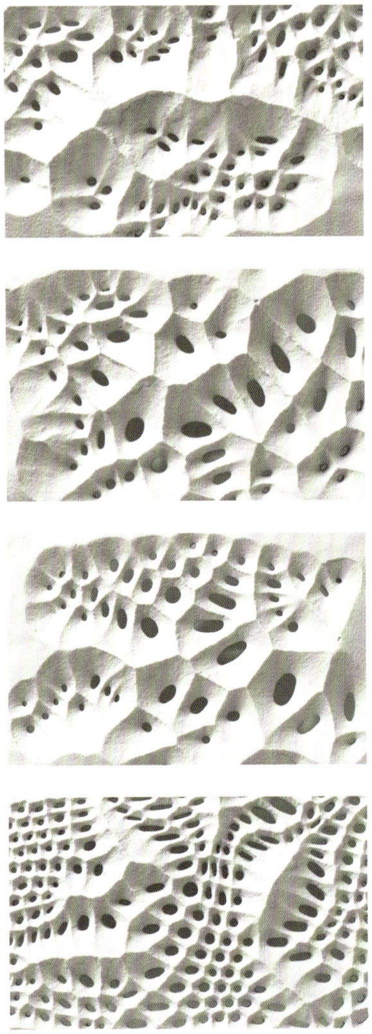

7.14c

7.14d

7.14e

Heap is a project that investigates the sintering of granular ceramic derived by grinding up used china and controlling the process through which it is "heaped" onto a surface. It explores the properties of self-organization within granular formations. A similar lineage was developed in Japanese swordsmithing where the crystalline structure of steel was chemically modified to produce signature markings. Similarly, the formation of the tiles is a product of the chemistry of the material out of which is made, in combination with its physical and geometric properties. Tiles are formed without using molds by simply circuiting heaps of this material through a series of holes, where, like sand, the resulting grains self-organize into distinct formations. The refined granular porcelain is not something that exists in a natural state, but rather a material whose manufacture into spherical grains gives it a fluidity and special set of technical properties. When it is fired at high temperature it bonds. The process relies upon the spherical properties of the engineered porcelain grains to produce consistent morphologies. As a granular flow the grains obey the same angle of repose when they come to rest, and the resulting cascades can be repeated. While the flow of the heap produces sharp concave features on the top of the tile, the excess material that flows through the holes produces convex features. Repeating the process on sloped surfaces expands the potential of the granular morphology so that the holes and the pitch of the surface can introduce a new set of forces. Because the axis of gravity is straight down, the heaps develop at oblique angles to the curved surface. Using the computer to investigate and encode these formations allows for a more calibrated process to generate different hole patterns and varying densities whose patterns are then tested using templates to understand the correlation between the pattern of holes and the corresponding three-dimensional surface produced.

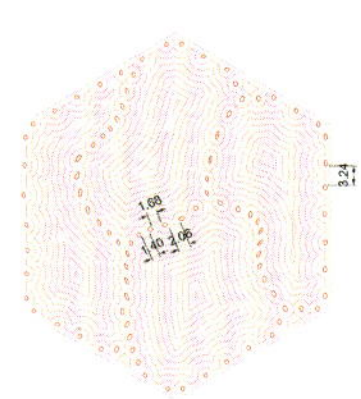

M1
91 oval attractors
max height (full scale) 11.19 cm
contours 1 cm intervals

2d surface Area = 2304.47262 cm2
91 ovals Cumulative Area = 33.7959669 cm2
3d surface Area = 3237 cm2

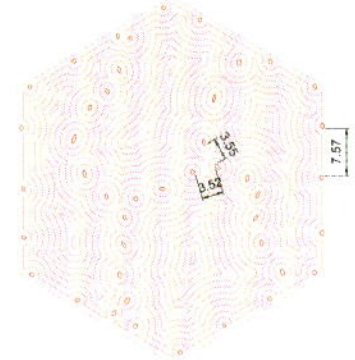

M2
44 oval attractors
max height (full scale) 11.35 cm
contours 1 cm intervals

2d surface area =2321.76472 cm2
44 ovals Cumulative Area = 16.503873 cm2
3d surface area = 3265.9 cm2

M3
98 oval attractors
max height (full scale) 9.49 cm
contours 1 cm intervals

2d surface Area = 2300.23498 cm2
98 ovals Cumulative Area = 38.0336072 cm2
3d surface Area = 3224.3

7.14f

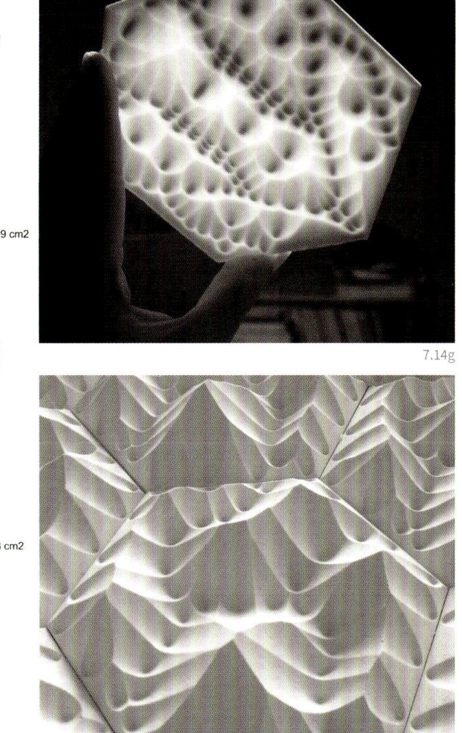

7.14g

7.14h

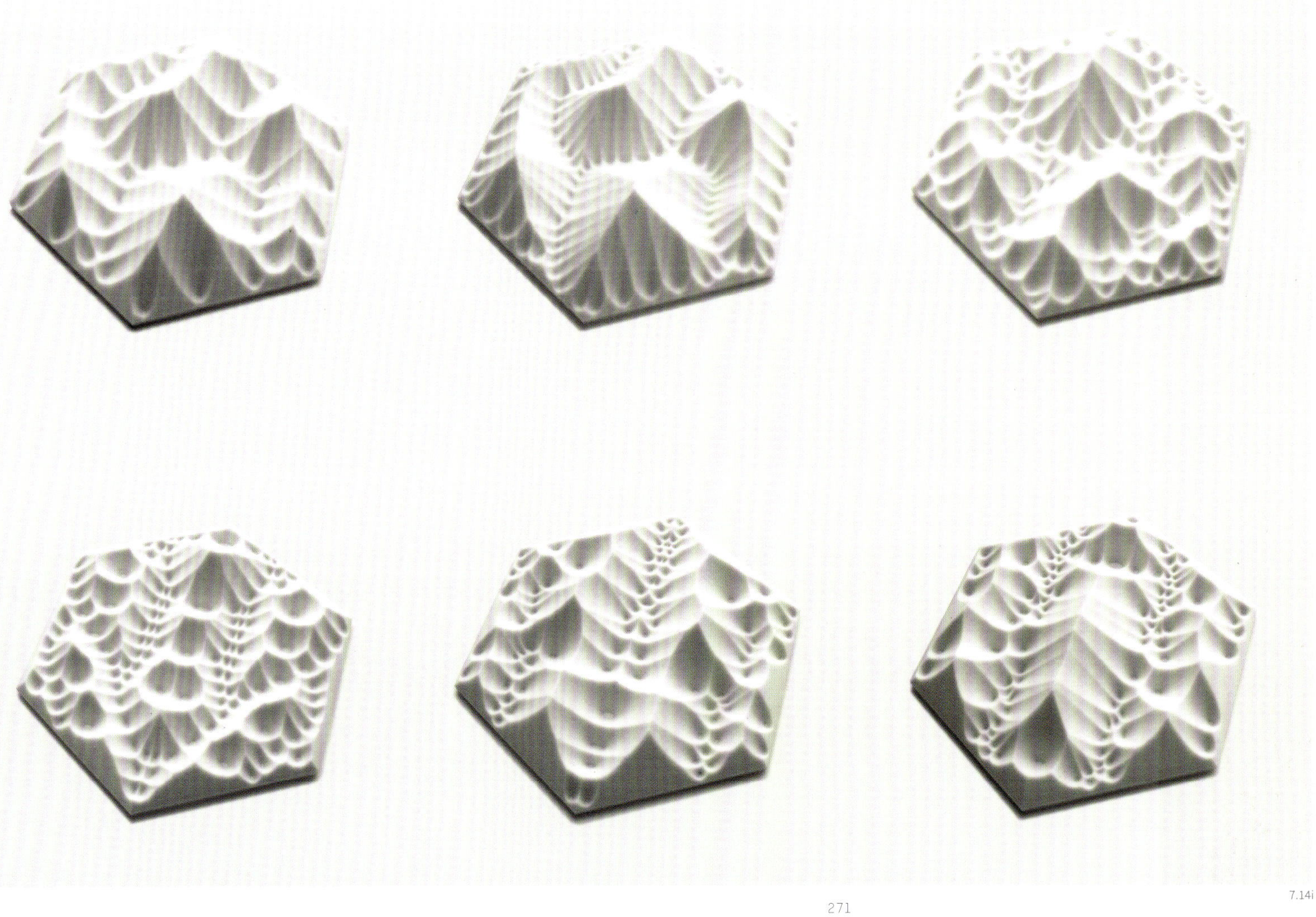

7.14i

EMERGENT SURFACES

Softcast
Minimaforms

Built 2012

London, United Kingdom

7.15a

7.15b

7.15c

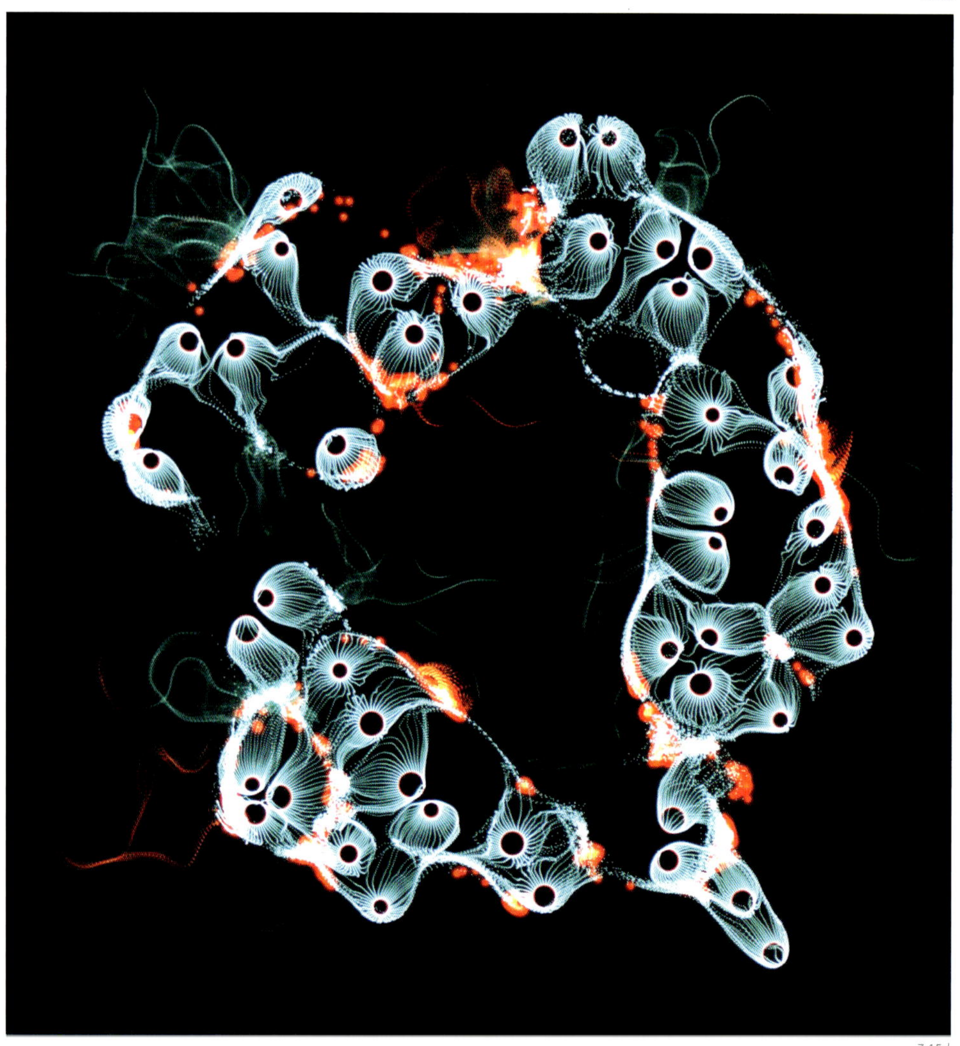

7.15d

Soft Cast explores the idea of a behavioral architecture, capable of adapting and transforming through the active coupling of advanced computational tools and material and human behavior. This experimental project uses a full-scale, flexible formwork system—a continuous tensile membrane network that is suspended within a larger rigid framework—to cast material prototypes whose generative process and configurations are determined by the interaction between multiple agents and influences. These include the parameters and digital techniques used to shape the form in addition to simulating, analyzing, and forecasting its material self-organization, the behavior of populations and the spatial organizations and distributive patterns that they collectively create, and the material performance of the tensile membrane and the casting medium used to render visible the expression of interacting forces. The textile formwork, which is supple rather than rigid, allows material surfaces to emerge as the cast is generated that exploits both the fluidity and changing states of the concrete to be cast and the adaptability of the formwork—its ability to stretch, deform, and mold, in relation to changing local forces that collectively render the resultant prototype unpredictable.

Digital techniques use parametrically controlled systems and computational models to define the patterning of the surface, which includes the determination of points of pressure and tension, the geometries and types of connections between a double-sided textile formwork, and the pouring points that might vary in location and number. In this system, the self-organization of the flexible membrane in relation to the liquid casting material as it sets and becomes rigid is therefore brought into relationship a range of configurative controls that are responsible for the patterning of the surface allowing formation to be understood as operating simultaneously at the scale of material processes and at larger architectural and environmental scales that determine the prototype's spatial organization and surface articulation. It's final geometry is thus the result of continuously changing, interacting parameters that are human, digital, and material—where matter is a computable and life-like agent—and whose active feedback loops allow architectural conventions of control, formation, and form to be radically readdressed.

7.15e

KnitCandela
Block Research Group ETH + ZHCODE
Built 2018
Mexico City, Mexico

7.16a

7.16b

7.16c

KnitCandela, an homage to Félix Candela, reimagines his spectacular concrete shells through the introduction of novel computational design methods and the KnitCrete formwork technology. The shell's dynamic geometry is inspired by the fluid forms of the traditional colorful dress of Jalisco, Mexico, while paying homage to Candela's work. While Candela relied on combining hyperbolic paraboloid surfaces (or "hypars") to produce reusable formworks and thus reduce construction waste, KnitCrete allows for the realization of a much wider range of anticlastic geometries. With this cable net and fabric formwork system, expressive, freeform concrete surfaces can be constructed efficiently, without the need for complex molds. KnitCandela's thin, doubly curved concrete shell with a surface area of almost 50 m^2 and weighing more than five tons, was applied on a KnitCrete formwork of only 55 kg. This hybrid and ultra-lightweight knitted fabric formwork is also easily transportable, such that it was brought to Mexico from Switzerland in a suitcase. KnitCrete formworks use a custom, 3D-knitted, technical textile as a lightweight, fixed shuttering, coated with a special cement paste to create a rigid mold and are supported by additional falsework elements such as a tensioned cable net or bending-active splines. Compared to conventional weaving, knitting minimizes the need for cutting patterns to create spatial surfaces, allows for the directional variation of material properties, and simplifies the integration of channels and openings, for example, for the insertion of additional formwork elements, insulation, reinforcements, electrical components, and technical systems for heating and cooling. The 50 m^2 of textile shuttering of the formwork for KnitCandela is made up of four long strips ranging from 15 m to 26 m in length. Each of the four pieces is a seamless, double-layered textile, its two surfaces fulfilling different tasks. The visible inside is an aesthetic surface that displays a colorful pattern and reveals traces of the supporting cable-net falsework system. The backside fulfils technical needs by including features for inserting, guiding, and controlling the position of additional formwork elements. Once completed the formwork remains, its striped pattern on the interior visualizing the rows typical of the knitting fabrication process and expressing the radial symmetry of the shape, whereby the soft, colorful fabric of the interior contrasts the monochromatic and hard exterior of the concrete shell.

7.16d

7.16e

7.16f

Freeform Tile Vault
Block Research Group ETH
Built 2010
Zurich, Switzerland

7.17a

The Freeform Tile Vault is BRG's first built vaulted masonry prototype designed with advanced computational methods but constructed with traditional timbrel, or Catalan, thin-tile vaulting techniques. Compression-only shell structures have the advantage of requiring very low material strengths while still being able to efficiently span large spaces. Part of an ongoing exploration of advances in timbrel vaulting, this project was made possible through innovation in form finding, guiding formwork systems, and construction methods. Using a new form-finding methodology—Thrust Network Analysis (TNA)—to generate compression only, spatial vaulted surfaces, the BRG explored innovative possibilities to build a freeform thin-tile vault with unreinforced masonry. The vault was fabricated in situ using a recyclable eggcrate cardboard formwork that was precisely CNC cut, glued, and assembled on site (supported below by stacked shipping pallets), dramatically reducing the labor and material costs for construction. Although the surface is a double-curvature, the prototype organizes the tiles in one direction only, relying on the mortar joints between tiles to produce the second curvature along the opposing axis.

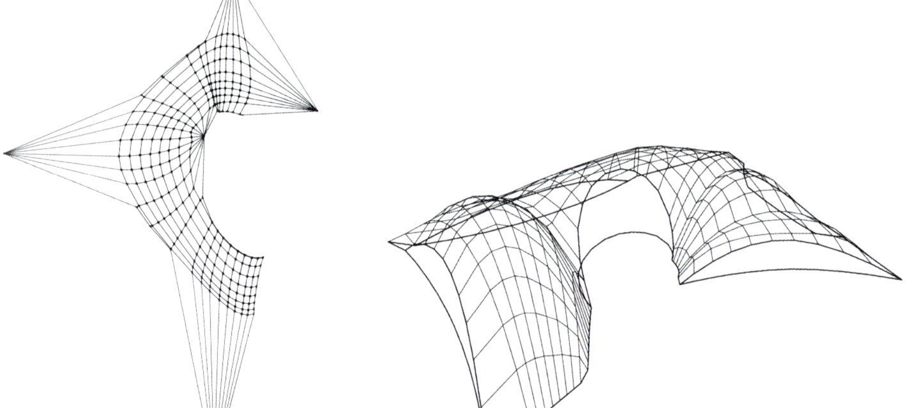

7.17b

7.17c

7.17d

Droneport Prototype
Block Research Group ETH / Norman Foster Foundation

Built 2016

Venice, Italy

The Droneport shell, a full-scale earthen masonry structure exhibited at the 15th Venice Architecture Biennale, is a prototype for the "Droneport"—a small airport for drones for the future Red Line project in Rwanda that seeks to create a drone network to deliver medical supplies and other necessities to places in Africa with limited access to roads. The objective, set by Norman Foster, was to make the design available as a "kit-of-parts" with a construction manual for the safe, efficient, and repeatable construction of droneport modules by local workers using primarily local resources. A tile vault with a simple, foolproof formwork system was proposed since a tile vault is inexpensive to construct and requires very little formwork if it has a well-designed shape and stresses are low, allowing the use of locally available materials such as nonfired soil bricks. This minimizes the carbon emission of the entire building process and reduces the need to import large amounts of expensive materials such as steel or cement. With its tools for compression-only form-finding, the BRG developed a masonry shell that addresses the structural and construction requirements for a safe building in Rwanda, while supporting the original architectural concept. The prototype vault spans 10 m by 8 m with only three layers of bricks, an inner layer of traditional clay tiles, and two outer layers of "DuraBric"—a naturally cured building block made of compressed earth and cement developed by the LafargeHolcim Research Centre. The structure is designed such that it is stressed uniformly by its own weight and has sufficient double curvature to be stable in compression under all other loading conditions. In addition, because of the geometry of the openings, concatenated modules create a continuous and smoothly undulating surface.

7.18a

7.18b

7.18c

Armadillo Vault
Block Research Group ETH

Built 2016
Venice, Italy

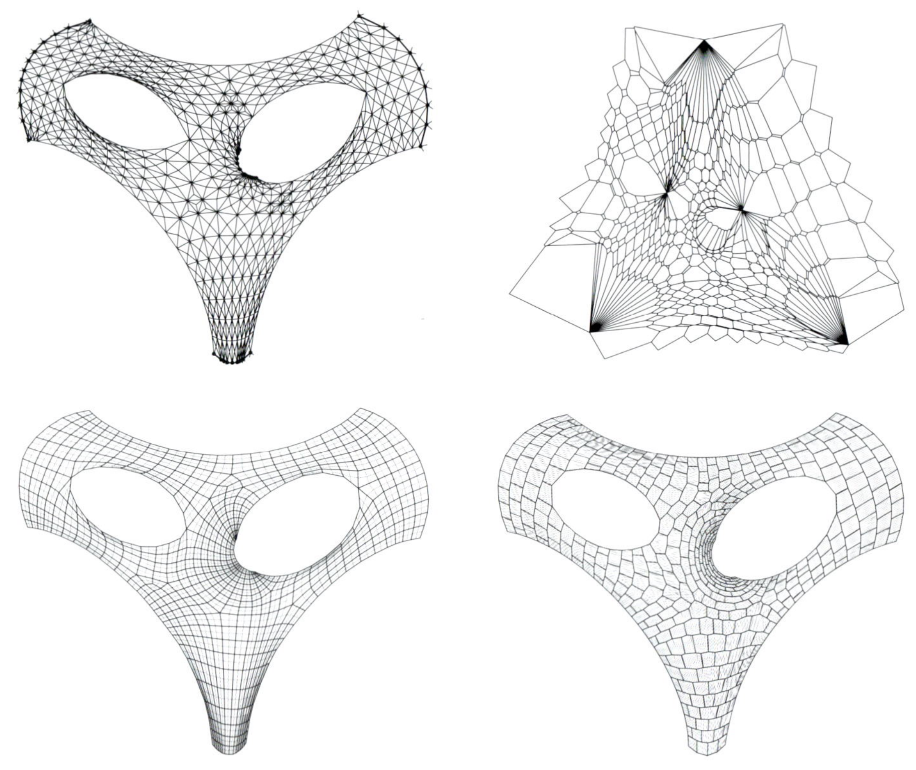

7.19a

The Armadillo Vault was the centerpiece of the *Beyond Bending* exhibition at the 2016 Venice Architectural Biennale. The vault, which spans 16 meters with a minimum thickness of only five centimeters, is comprised of 399 individually cut limestone pieces, unreinforced and assembled without mortar. Akin to the spectacular Gothic vaults, this cut-stone vault is stable because of its funicular geometry, which allows it to stand in pure compression, while tension ties equilibrate the form. Starting from the same structural and construction principles as historic stone cathedrals, this sophisticated form emerged from novel computational, graphic statics-based design and optimization methods. The engineering of the discrete shell also used innovative computational approaches to assess stability under various load conditions. The dominant self-weight of the vault was taken as the design load to define the funicular geometry of the middle surface of the structure, which directed the form-finding process. As the weight itself is a function of the geometry of this surface and locally assigned nonuniform thicknesses, this was an iterative process during which the overall design of the vault was continuously refined, from the generation of a thrust network using form and force diagrams to the generation of a smooth control mesh to allow for more sculptural modifications to the geometry, while maintaining compression-only equilibrium and ensuring a high positive double curvature everywhere in the shell. Each stone voussoir is thus informed by structural logic, as well as the need for precise fabrication and assembly, the constraints of a historically protected setting, and limitations on time, budget, and construction. The voussoirs are designed to be planar on the exterior to avoid the need to flip the stones during machining, their interior sides' doubly curved geometry resulting from initial rough cutting. Rather than milling away the excess material left by this process, it was instead hammered off, leaving the resulting grooves as an expressive feature, aligned with purpose to serve as visual reminders of the force flow. The shell's dual appearance, scale-like on the outside and softly curving on the inside, is thus a direct materialization of, and response to, the project's constraints. Proportionally as thin as an eggshell and standing without reinforcement, the expressively flowing surface structure challenges the inherited idea that complex, freeform geometry is structurally inefficient while being less authentic in its use and application of material.

7.19b

7.19c

7.19d

7.19e

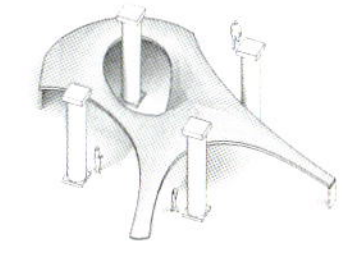
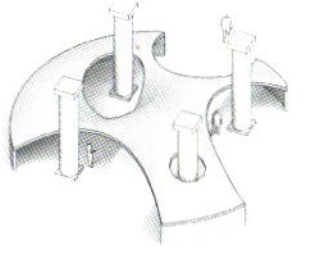
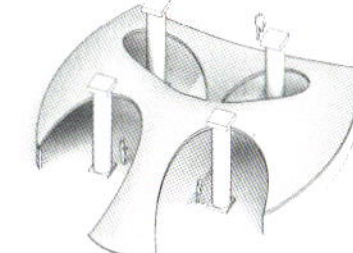
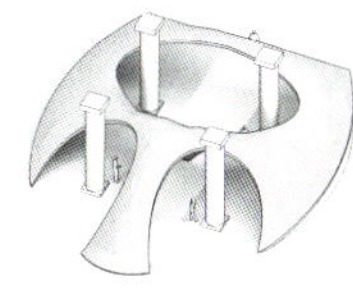
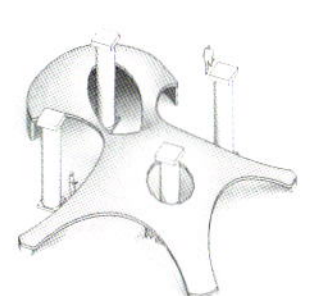
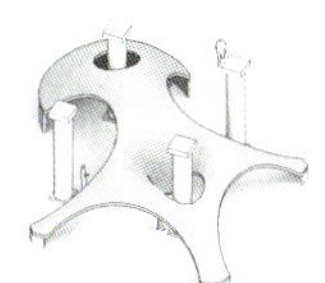
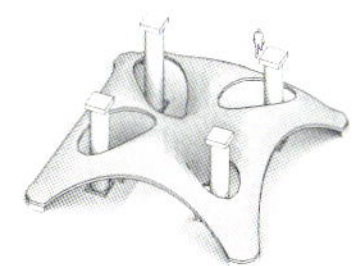
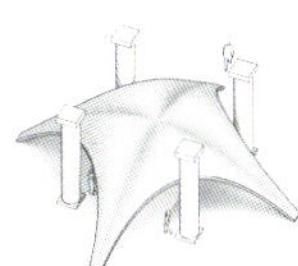
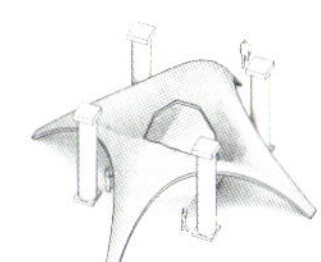
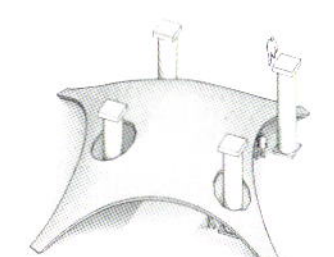
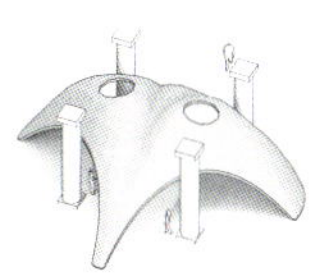
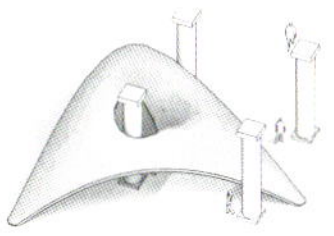
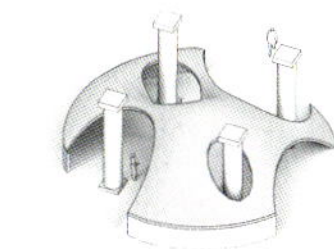
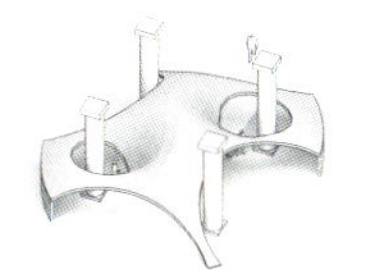
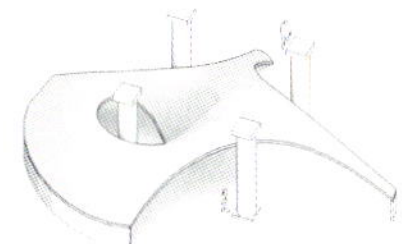
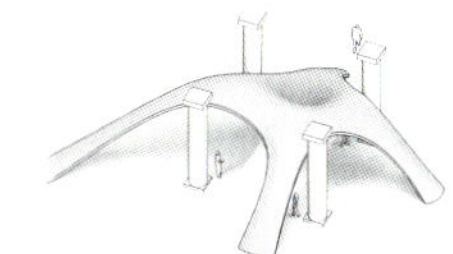
7.19f

Isoropia

CITA: Centre for Information Technology and Architecture

Built 2018

Venice, Italy

7.20a

Isoropia is a form active, knitted, hybrid structure, a textile vault, designed for the 16th Venice Architecture Biennale. Creating a structural continuum that transitions between two different canopy structures on the two outer sides and a vaulted space in the interior, Isoropia shifts from a cable net system on the exterior, which pre-stresses and stabilizes the structure, to a tensegrity-like structure in the interior in which compression elements pre-stress the knitted membrane. This differentiation poses specific challenges to the form-finding and analysis process as well as to the specification and fabrication process. Isoropia—meaning balance, equilibrium, and stability—is a finely tuned balance of tension and compression. The central aspect of the design is the discretization of the structure into independent, bow-like modules that act autonomously while tied together into a continual structural system. Each bow-module acts as a spatial beam in which the three-dimensional cones create the depth of the beam. Each module consists of two bent, glass-fiber reinforced plastic beams inserted into a connecting membrane which is pre-stressed by a cable net or set of compression rods. The bow module is variegated across the structure, changing both the shape and width of the textile membrane as well as the length and thickness of the tube-beam thus creating a family of modules all optimized but with a differentiated structural identity, shape, and expression. Isoropia occupies a multiscaled design space in which performance at the macro level is informed by its micro materiality, requiring a bespoke customization method for creating textile specifications that interface with fabrication. An automated process was developed in which the mesh geometry is relaxed and re-sized, and the detailing of channels and cone centers are superimposed. Further, a strategy for the functional grading of the membranes was generated by composing patterns of differentiated stitch structures around the center points allowing the cones to protrude and become more spatial, which augmented the structural performance of the bow module. Finally, Isoropia is an ultra-light, resilient structure designed to deflect under environmental impact. To understand the structural behavior of this deflection, an integrated simulation was developed to calculate impact and allow feedback into the design process.

7.20b

7.20c

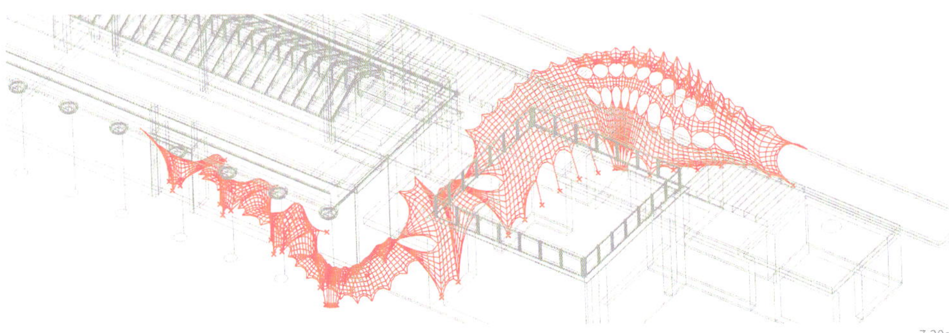

7.20d

NEST HiLo Roof
Block Research Group ETH

Built 2017, 2019-20
Zurich and Dübendorf, Switzerland

The HiLo Roof prototype, later realized in Dübendorf, Switzerland, is built with a cable net and fabric formwork system, designed to dramatically reduce the material waste that is typically involved in the construction of concrete shells. It improves on traditional formwork structures for doubly curved surfaces, which would be comprised of custom timber carpentry or milled foam by using mostly reusable components. The cable net is spanned within a reusable timber boundary supported by conventional scaffolding and is designed to deform under the weight of the wet concrete into the desired shape of the HiLo Roof. This is achieved by the nonuniform distribution of forces in each one of the cables, a distribution that is planned by customized computational form finding tools. The constrained form-finding and optimization methods used in the design of the cable net were able to negotiate structural requirements, architectural and fabrication constraints, while minimizing the number of cables and nodes. The node was designed to ensure that the cable had the required degrees of freedom for the shaping of the net. The node also facilitates the placing of the fabric and the textile reinforcement in their intended locations, while providing a guide for the correct concrete thickness at any point in the doubly curved shape. In collaboration with the ETH Automatic Control Laboratory, an algorithm was implemented with the purpose of determining the amount of tension to be applied at each boundary cable to best direct the shape of the cable net towards the intended design. The prototype also tested the spraying of a thin layer of concrete through the carbon-fiber reinforcement onto the fabric shuttering, resulting in a solid concrete shell that varies in thickness from boundary to support locations.

7.21a

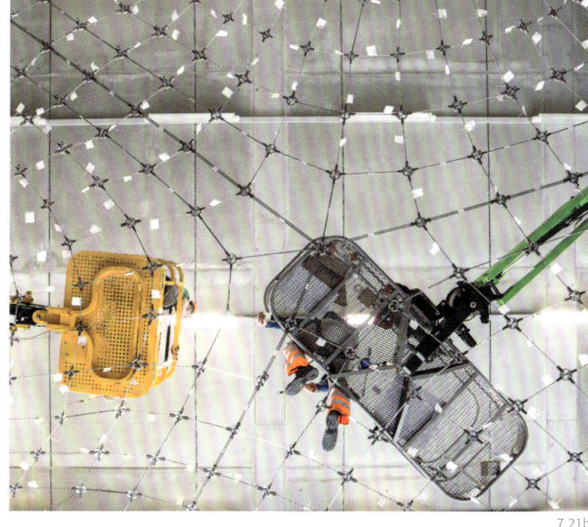

7.21b

7.21c

7.21d

Confluence Park Pavilion
Matsys + Lake/Flato+
Built 2014-2018
San Antonio, Texas

7.22a

Located along the Mission Reach section of the San Antonio River, Confluence Park is an educational park focusing on the critical role of water in the regional ecosystems. The 6,000-square-foot central pavilion of the park is composed of twenty-two concrete "petals" that form a network of vaults to provide shade and direct the flow of rainwater, funneled through the petals' columnar bases into an underground cistern used for the park's irrigation. The design of the pavilion was inspired by the way many plants in the region direct rainwater to their root system through harnessing the structural efficiency of curved surfaces. The design uses the Cairo tile, an irregular pentagon, as the underlying base grid in order to resolve the tension between cost-effective modularity and the desire for nonrepetitive spatial richness. The pentagon is subdivided into five triangles in a way that results in only three unique modules: two asymmetrical triangles that are mirrors of each other and one equilateral triangle. From this irregular triangular base grid, a parametric model was used to create the three-dimensional solids of each doubly curved petal. Structurally, each petal is half of an arch, which starts out as a 16-inch-thick column and tapers to a 4-inch-deep curved roof. The double-curvature of the surface geometry helps with the structural rigidity of the petal. Each petal is connected to its paired half-arch by two structural pin joints. The petals' capacity to shed water in the proper direction was tested through water flow analysis using particle simulations. The three petals' formwork was fabricated using five-axis CNC milled forms. After milling the foam forms, a 2-inch-thick composite structure composed of inner and outer layers of fiberglass composite with a central core of balsa wood was applied. The formwork was then shipped to the site and positioned in a way that it could be cast as a modified tilt-up wall construction. This avoided the need for a fully enclosed form, which decreased the cost and allowed the top and bottom surfaces to have radically different finishes: the bottom is cast against the smooth fiberglass while the top is broom-finished with the broom strokes aligning with the direction of the water flow. The Cairo tile geometry was reused at a much smaller scale for the thousands of concrete pavers used throughout the park. Four different inlay patterns were developed for the pavers such that a larger network of branching curves is created. This network is aperiodic and references the bifurcations and deltas of the local watershed.

7.22b

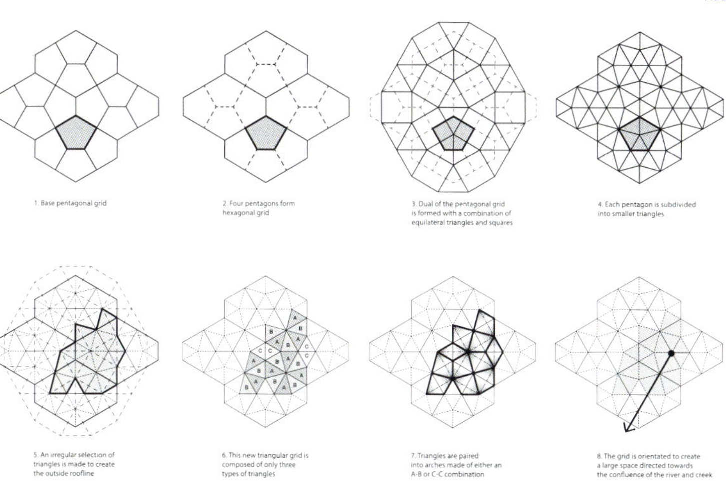

7.22c

7.22d

7.22e

Generative Logic
Ruled Surfaces

Architects and engineers have been using various forms of curvature to create stronger and larger structures for thousands of years. Understanding the various forms of curvature and how to design and build with them is critical for an computational designer. While some forms of curvature are hard to build with one materials system, they can be easy with another. For example, while surfaces like domes that have synclastic curvature are difficult to build, saddle shapes or hyperbolic paraboloids with anticlastic curvature are much easier to build out of simple, straight segments.

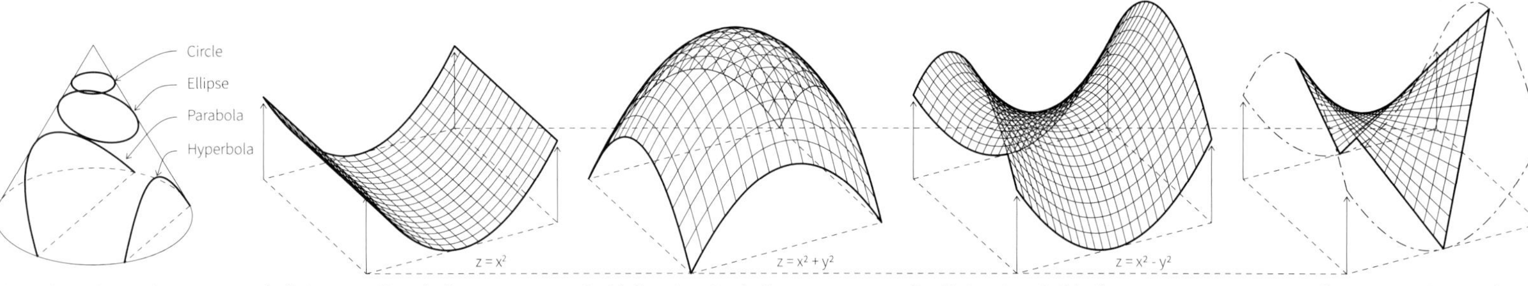

The Conic Sections are the curves obtained by intersecting a cone with a plane. They are the basis for understanding mathematical surfaces and curvature.

Single Curvature: Monoclastic
A Parabolic Cylinder is parabola that has been extruded and is a example of monoclastic or single curvature. The surface curves in only one direction. All lines in the other direction are straight so this is called a Ruled Surface. The surface also has Zero Gaussian Curvature.

Double Curvature: Synclastic
A Circular Paraboloid is an example of a surface with double curvature. For any point on the surface, its principal curvature directions lay are on the same side of the surface making it synclastic. This is also known as Positive Gaussian Curvature.

Double Curvature: Anticlastic
A Hyperbolic Paraboloid is another example of a surface with double curvature. However, for any point on the surface, its principal curvature directions are on the opposite side of the surface making it anticlastic. This is also known as Negative Gaussian Curvature.

A **Hypar Surface** is a trimmed section of a infinite hyperbolic paraboloid surface. When trimmed as shown above, it is easier to see the straight lines on the surface.

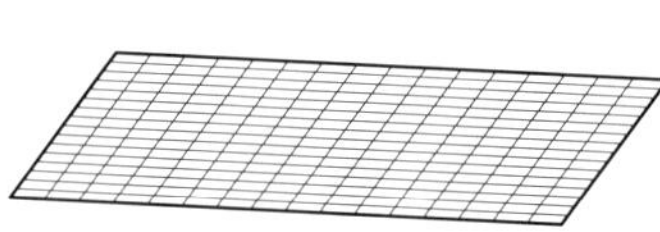

A hyperbolic paraboloid can also be made by starting from a flat surface.

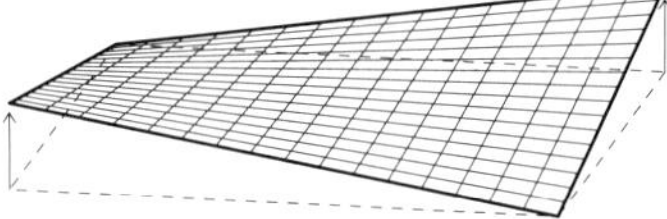

Certain materials can be pushed into slight double curvature by pushing on opposite corners.

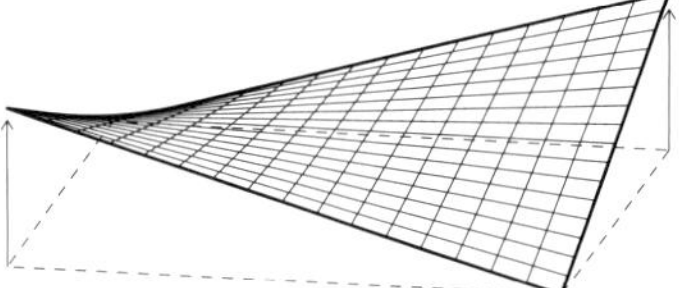

Despite the curvature, the surface can also be understood as being composed of an infinite number of straight lines.

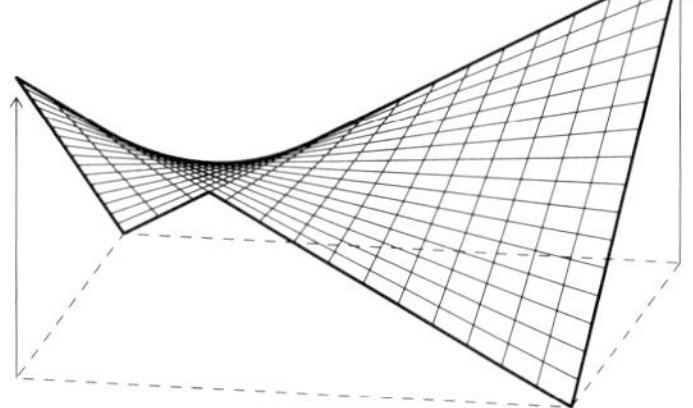

Many complex forms can be created through a series of straight lines. These are known as a ruled surface.

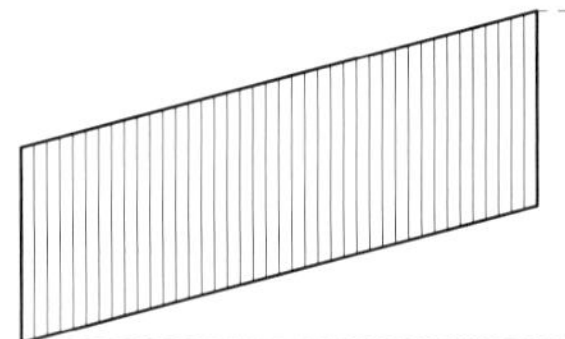

Starting from a vertical surface...

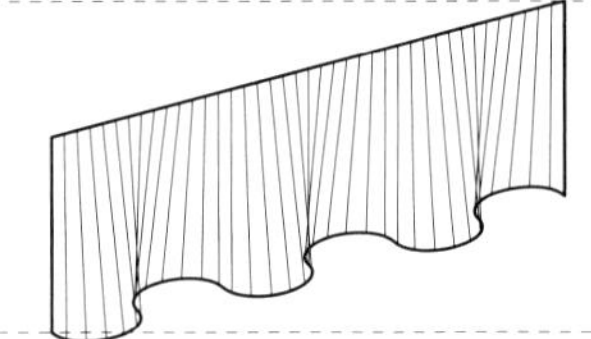

...one edge can begin to undulate to form a ruled surface.

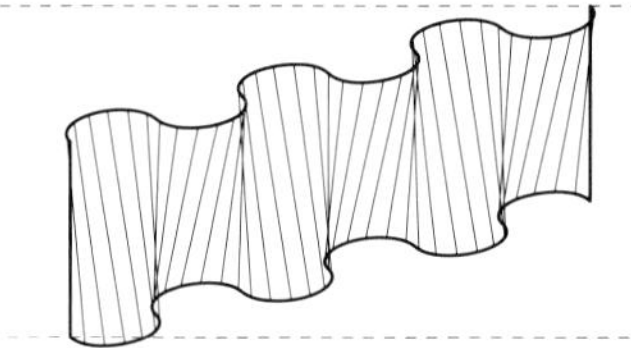

The top edge can also undulate and the surface is still a ruled surface.

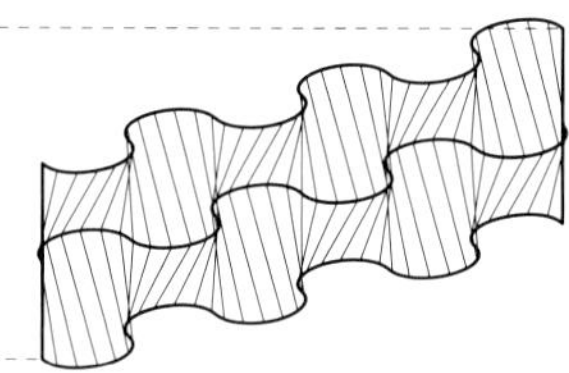

A break in the curvature continuity occurs when multiple ruled surfaces are joined together.

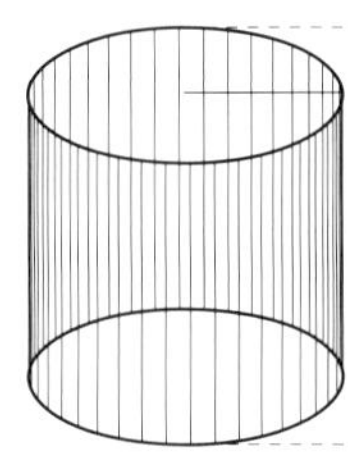

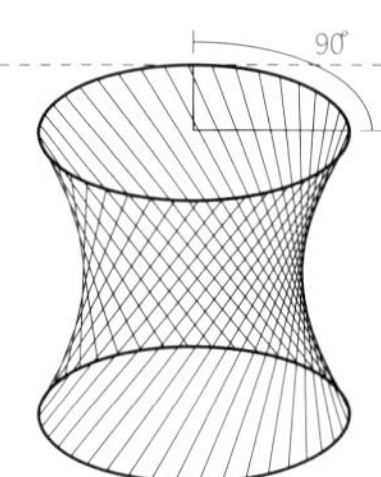

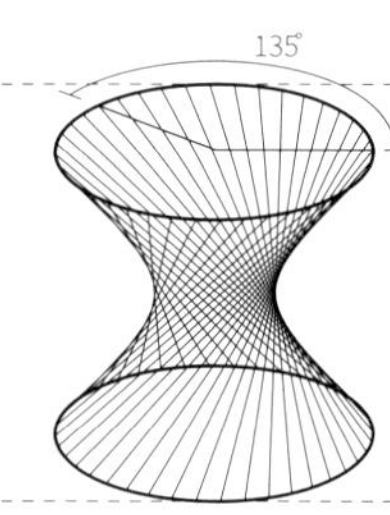

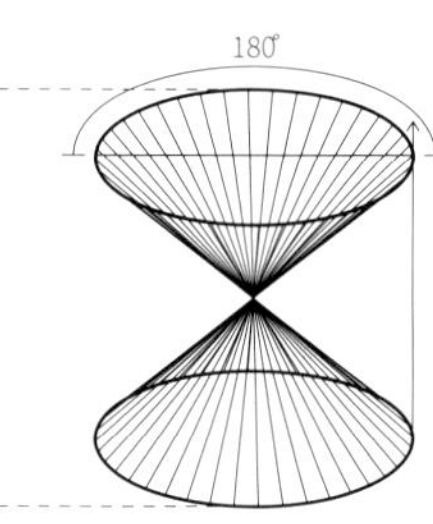

A Hyperboloid of Revolution can be created by rotating two circles and drawing straight lines between their points. Once the circles are rotated 180°, a double cone is formed.

Generative Process
Los Manatiales Restaurant

The Los Manatiales Restaurant by Felix Candela makes exemplary use of ruled surfaces and hyperbolic paraboloid geometry to create both a structural marvel and an elegant space. Composed of a series of vaults radiating out from a central point, the structure was constructed from straight lengths of wood used as formwork for reinforced concrete.

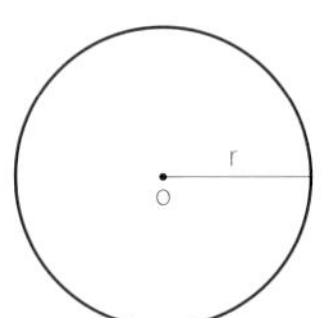

1. Create a boundary curve (C) from origin (o). The boundary curve can be circular (radius: r) or can be a non-uniform curve.

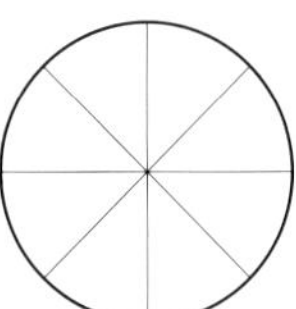

2. From the center point, divide the boundary curve into (n) number of sections.

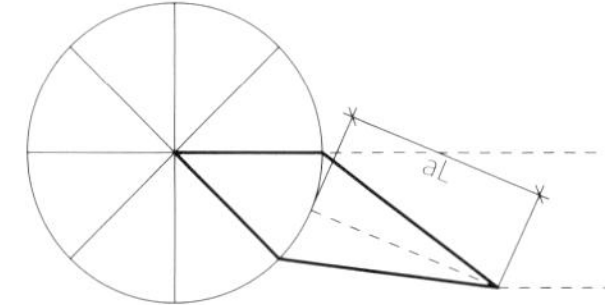

3. For each segment, the two points along the boundary curve represent the vault bases. Move the midpoint between these points away from the center by the apex length (aL) distance.

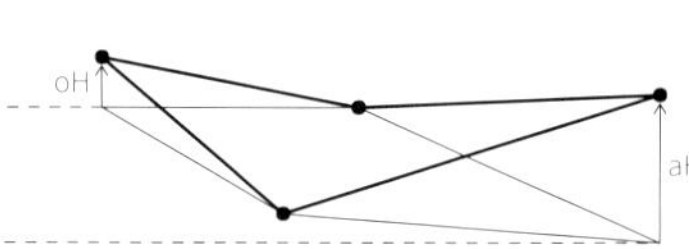

4. Lift center point by the center height (oH) and the apex point by the apex height (aH).

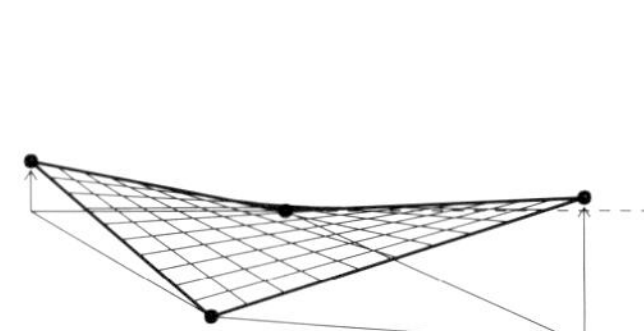

5. Create surface from the center point, the two base points, and the apex point. This surface will be a hyperbolic paraboloid.

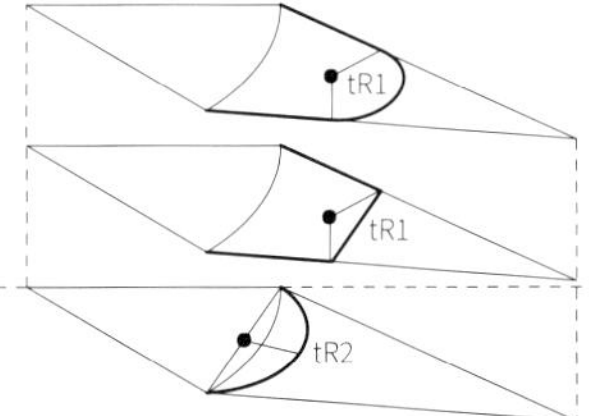

6. Select one of the trim types (tT): fillet, chamfer, arc, or untrimmed. Create the trim profile flat on the XY plane.

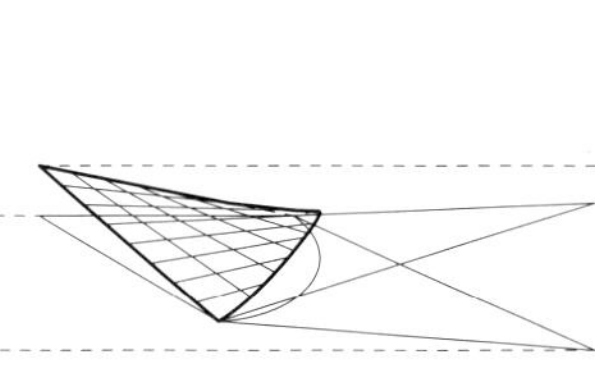

7. Project the trim profile curve up to the hypar surface and trim the apex corner to create the final trimmed surface.

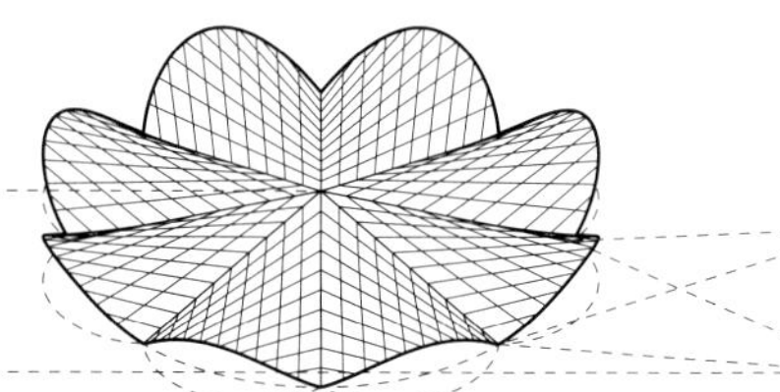

8. Repeat steps 3 to 7 for each section of the boundary curve to create the full series of vaults.

Generative Matrix

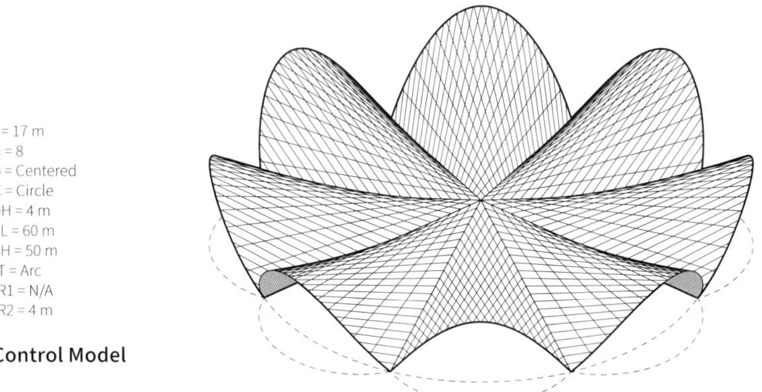

r = 17 m
n = 8
o = Centered
C = Circle
oH = 4 m
aL = 60 m
aH = 50 m
tT = Arc
tR1 = N/A
tR2 = 4 m

Control Model

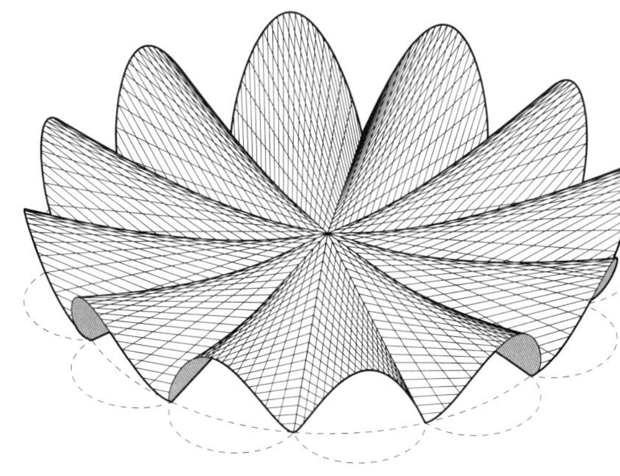

r = 17 m
n = 12
C = Circle
o = Centered
aL = 60 m
aH = 50 m
oH = 4 m
tT = Arc
tR1 = N/A
tR2 = 4 m

More Segments

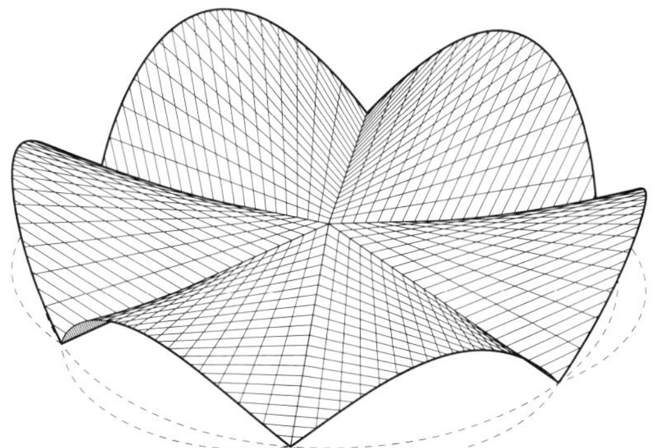

r = 17 m
n = 6
o = Centered
C = Circle
oH = 4 m
aL= 60 m
aH= 50 m
tT = Arc
tR1 = N/A
tR2 = 4 m

Fewer Segments

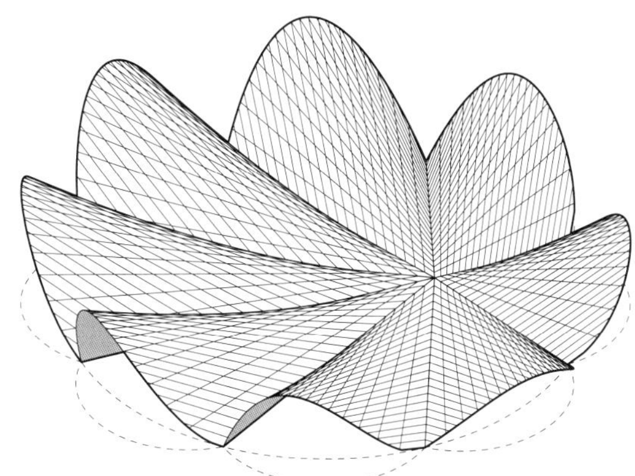

r = 17 m
n = 8
C = Circle
o = Off-Centered
oH = 4 m
aL= 60 m
aH = 50 m
tT= Arc
tR1 = N/A
tR2 = 4 m

Off-Centered Origin

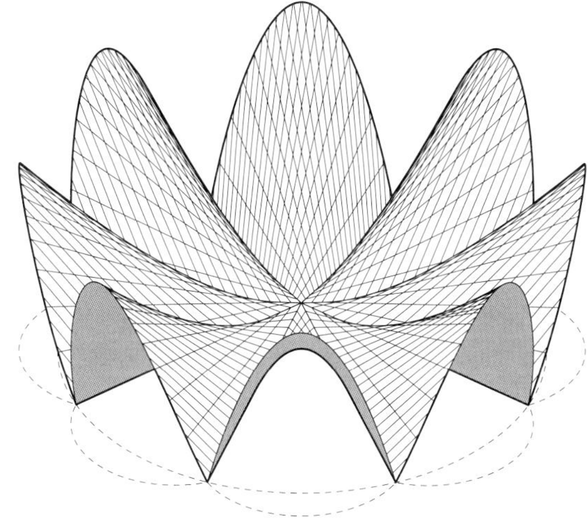

r = 17 m
n = 8
C = Circle
o= Centered
oH = 4 m
aL = 60 m
aH = 100 m
tT = Arc
tR1 = N/A
tR2 = 4 m

Steeper

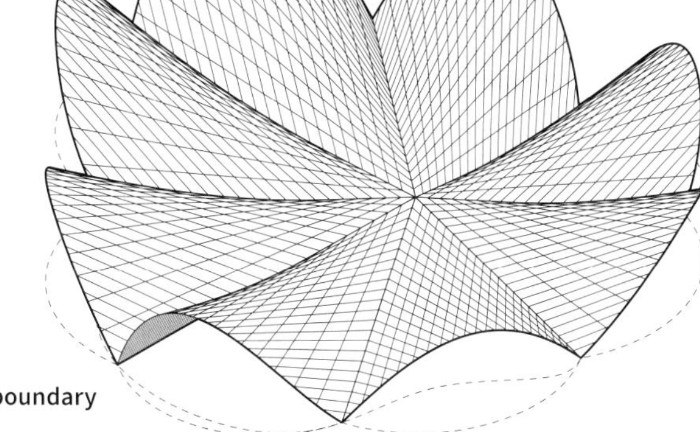

r = 17 m
n = 8
C = non-uniform
o = Centered
oH = 4 m
aL = 60 m
aH = 50 m
tT = Arc
tR1 = N/A
tR2 = 4 m

Non-Uniform boundary

r = 17 m
n = 8
C = Circle
o = Centered
oH = 4 m
aL = 60 m
aH= 50 m
tT = Chamfer
tR1 = N/A
tR2 = 7 m

Chamfered

r = 17 m
n = 8
C = Circle
o = Centered
oH = 4 m
aL = 60 m
aH = 50 m
tT = Untrimmed hypar
tR1 = N/A
tR2 = N/A

Untrimmed

Generative Logic
Minimal Sufaces

In addition to ruled surfaces, curvature is also an important consideration for the development of structures using minimal surfaces, an open surface that has minimized its area between fixed constraints at points or along edges. Although a sphere like a soap bubble is often referred to as a minimal surface as it has minimized its surface area in relation to its volume, it has differential pressures on the inside and outside and is not strictly a minimal surface in the mathematical sense.

Gaussian Curvature and Mean Curvature: To calculate these values at any point on a surface, the principle curvatures values must first be extracted. The principal curvatures are calculated as the reciprocal of the minimum and maximum radii of the circles passing through any point on the normal planes. Gaussian curvature is the product of the principal curvatures ($k_1 \times k_2$) while mean curvature is the sum of the principal curvatures divided by two $(k_1 + k_2)/2$. If a surface's mean curvature is zero, it is considered a minimal surface. Zero-mean curvature surfaces are a subset of constant mean curvature surfaces where the mean curvature is the same at every point such as spheres and catenoids.

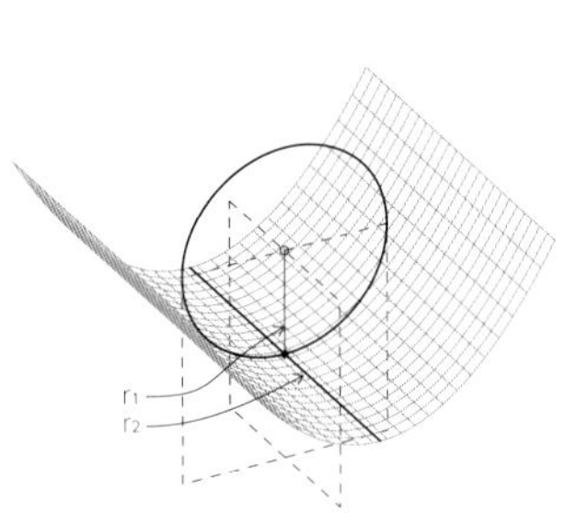

Zero Gaussian Curvature (Developable Surface)
$r_1 = 10 \rightarrow k_1 = 1/10 = 0.1$
$r_2 = \infty \rightarrow k_2 = 1/\infty = 0$
Gaussian Curvature = $0.1 \times 0 = 0$
Mean Curvature = $(0.1 + 0)/2 = 0.05$

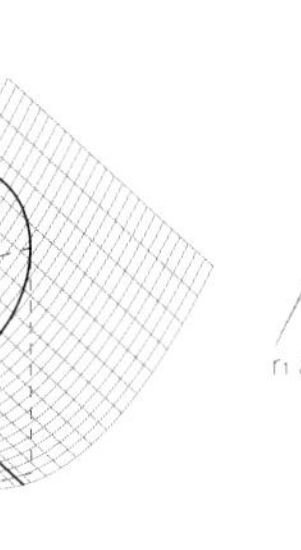

Positive Gaussian Curvature (Synclastic Curvature)
$r_1 = 10 \rightarrow k_1 = 1/10 = 0.1$
$r_2 = 10 \rightarrow k_2 = 1/10 = 0.1$
Gaussian Curvature = $0.1 \times 0.1 = 0.01$
Mean Curvature = $(0.1 + 0.1)/2 = 0.1$

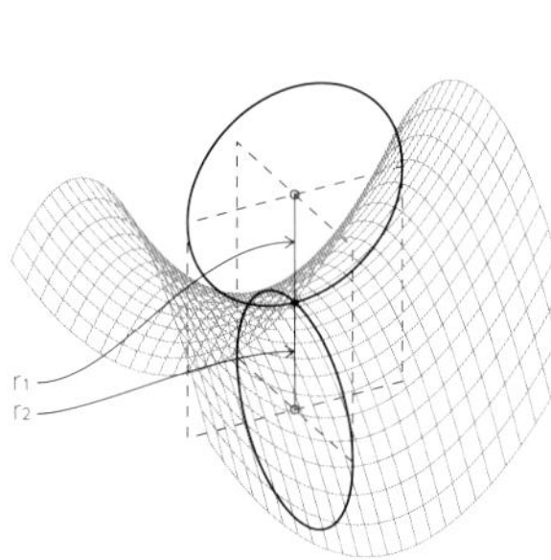

Zero Mean Curvature (Minimal Surface and Anticlastic Curvature)
$r_1 = 10 \rightarrow k_1 = 1/10 = 0.1$
$r_2 = -10 \rightarrow k_2 = 1/-10 = -0.1$
Gaussian Curvature = $0.1 \times -0.1 = -0.01$
Mean Curvature = $(0.1 + -0.1)/2 = 0$

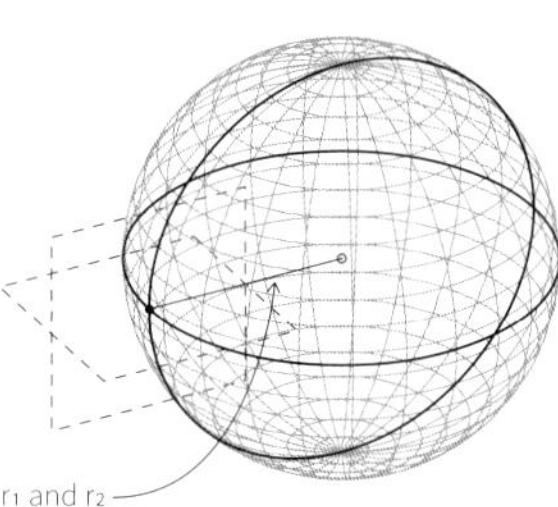

Constant Mean Curvature (CMC)
$r_1 = 10 \rightarrow k_1 = 1/10 = 0.1$
$r_2 = 10 \rightarrow k_2 = 1/10 = 0.1$
Gaussian Curvature = $0.1 \times -0.1 = -0.01$
Mean Curvature = $(0.1 + 0.1)/2 = 0.05$ (at all surface points)

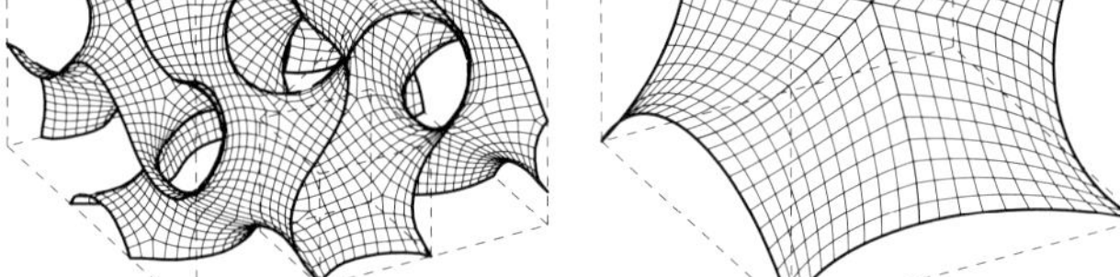

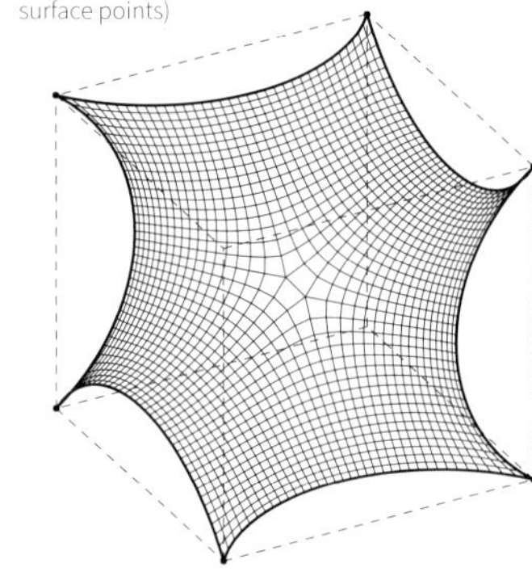

Minimal Surfaces can be created through several techniques. A classic example of a minimal surface is the Gyroid with the parametric equation:

$\sin(x) \cdot \cos(y) + \sin(y) \cdot \cos(z) + \sin(z) \cdot \cos(x) = 0$

Minimal surfaces can also be simulated through a process of form-finding by the minimizing the tensile stress within the mesh edges. If each edge of a mesh is thought of as a spring under tension, the edge wants to get smaller, and it pulls on its neighbor. With all edges simultaneously pulling on each other and against selected anchor points, the system eventually finds an equilibrium. The same gyroid patch can be created through this form-finding technique.

Generative Process
The Basento Viaduct

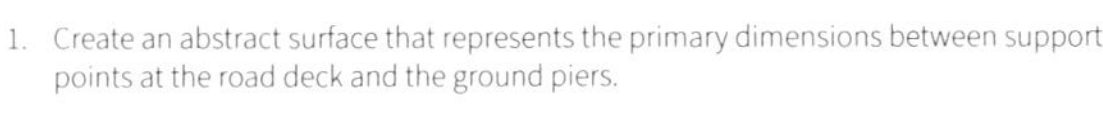

Similar to the physical form-finding experiments by Antonio Gaudi and Frei Otto, the design for the Basento Viaduct by Sergio Musmeci was developed through physical models made with tensioned fabric. The objective was to avoid internal bending stress within the concrete structure which allowed for the efficient use of material in carrying the structural loads.

1. Create an abstract surface that represents the primary dimensions between support points at the road deck and the ground piers.
2. Convert these surface planes into simple meshes and then subdivide each mesh into a higher density simulation grid.
3. Apply physical simulation properties to the various mesh components: The original support points are converted into fixed anchors that are not allowed to move during the simulation. All other points are given a magnitude and direction for a gravity force. A minimizing length force is applied to all of the mesh edges.
4. The simulation is run iteratively such that at each stage, the mesh edges and vertices move according to the applied forces until an equilibrium is found. After the average movement of the vertices is less than a certain threshold value, the simulation is stopped.

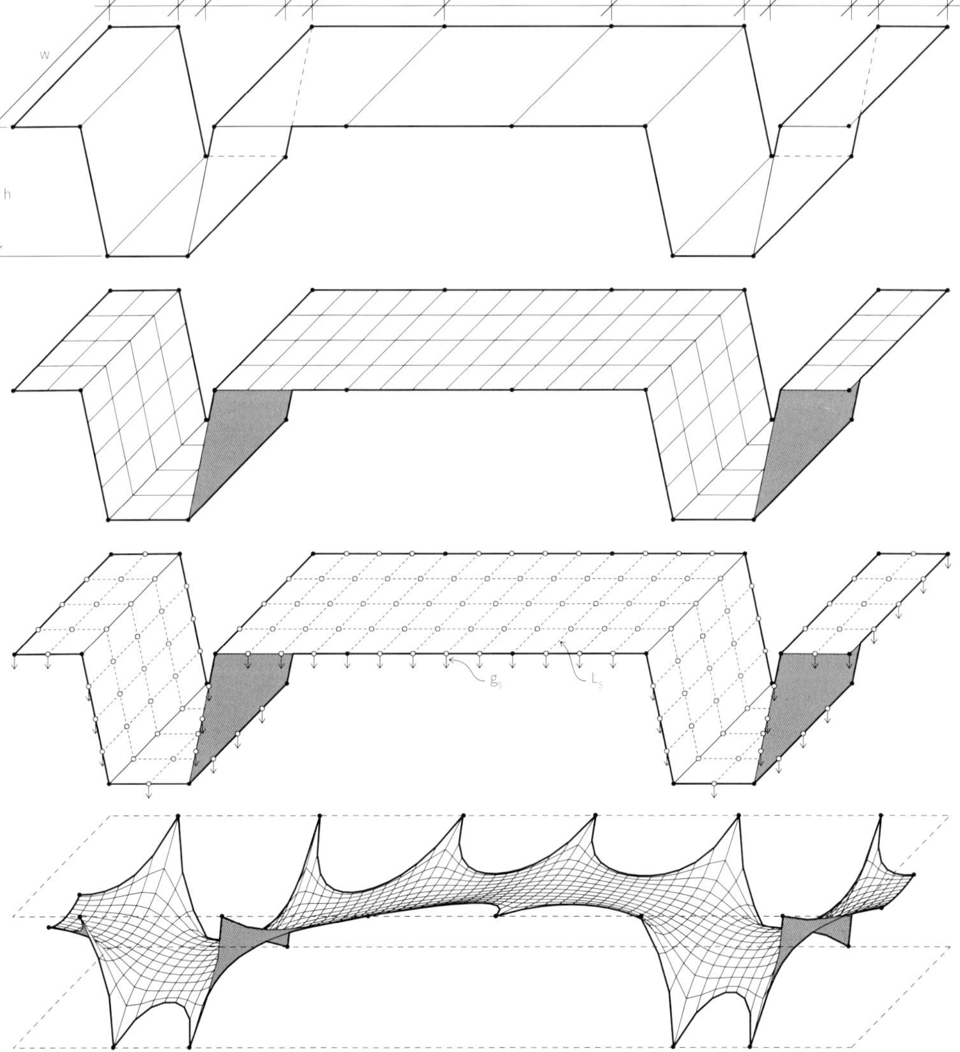

Generative Matrix

h = 16 m
w = 17.5 m
$s_1 = s_4/2$ m
s_2 = 3.46 m
s_3 = 10.38 m
s_4 = 17.30 m
s_5 = 10.38 m

g_S = 100
g_D = 0, 0, -1
L_F = 1
L_S = 1500
pat =2 low, 4 high

Control Model

h = 16 m
w = 17.5 m
$s_1 = s_4/2$ m
s_2 = 3.46 m
s_3 = 10.38 m
s_4 = 17.30 m
s_5 = 10.38 m

gS = 200
g_D = 0, 0, -1
L_F = 1
L_S = 1500
pat =2 low, 4 high

Increased Gravity

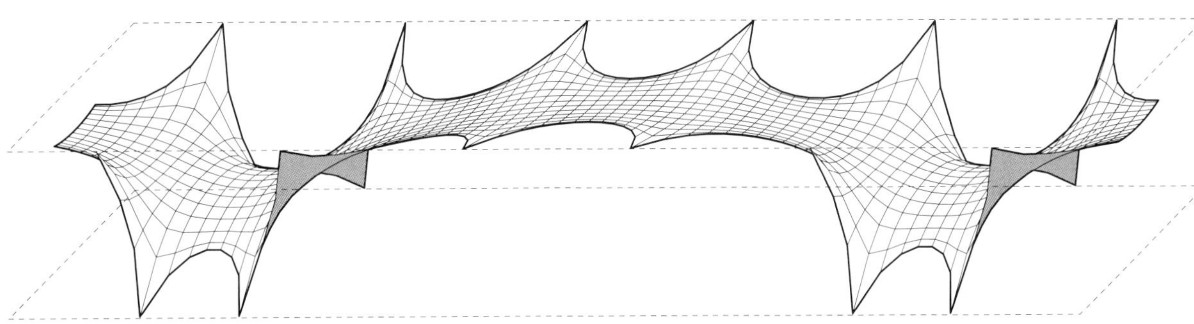

h = 16 m
w = 17.5 m
$s_1 = s_4/2$ m
s_2 = 3.46 m
s_3 = 10.38 m
s_4 = 17.30 m
s_5 = 10.38 m

g_S = 100
g_D = 0, 0, -1
L_F = 1
LS = 10,000
pat =2 low, 4 high

Increased Edge Stiffness

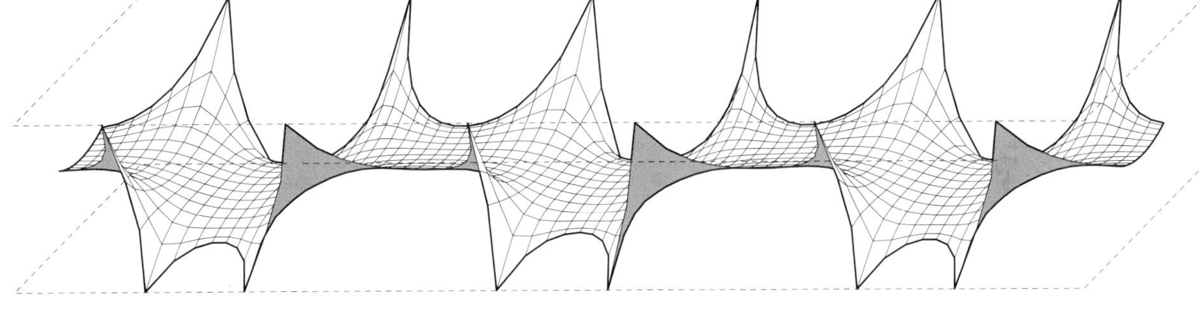

h = 16 m
w = 17.5 m
$s_1 = s_4/2$ m
s_2 = 3.46 m
s_3 = 10.38 m
s_4 = 17.30 m
s_5 = 10.38 m

g_S = 100
g_D = 0, 0, -1
L_F = 1
L_S = 1500
pat =2 low, 2 high

Additional Ground Supports

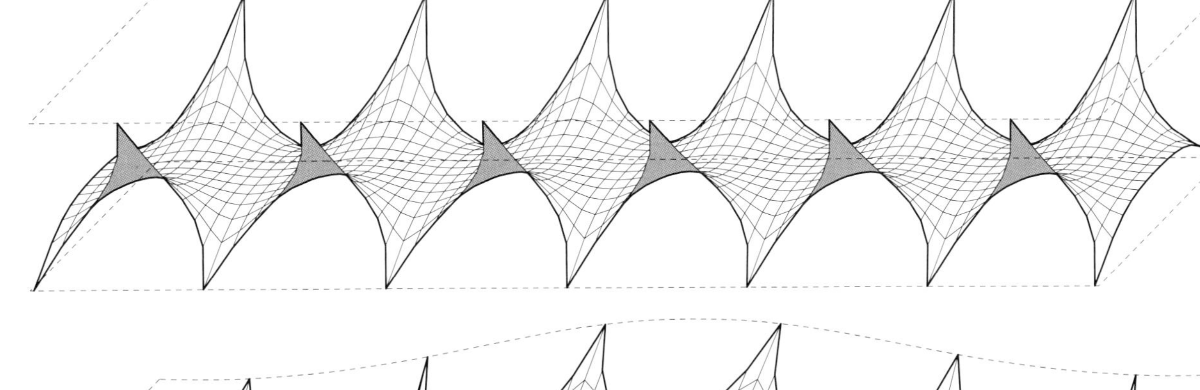

h = 16 m
w = 17.5 m
$s_1 = s_4/2$ m
s_2 = 3.46 m
s_3 = 10.38 m
s_4 = 17.30 m
s_5 = 10.38 m

g_S = 100
g_D = 0, 0, -1
L_F = 1
L_S = 1500
pat =1 low, 1 high

Alternating Supports

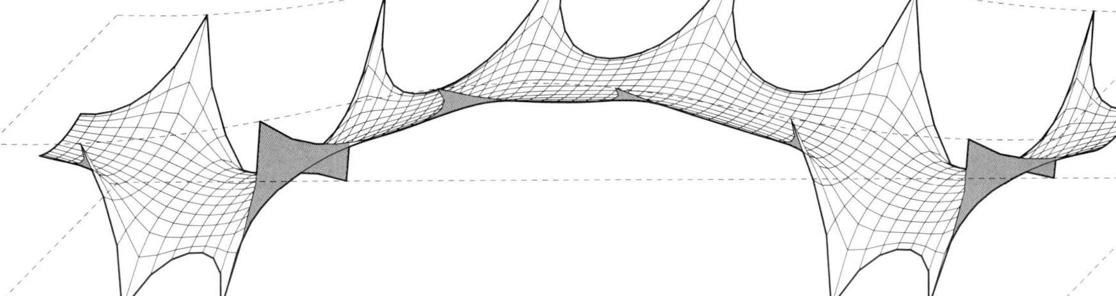

height = 16 m - 20 m
w = 17.5 m
$s_1 = s_4/2$ m
s_2 = 3.46 m
s_3 = 10.38 m
s_4 = 17.30 m
s_5 = 10.38 m

g_S = 100
g_D = 0, 0, -1
L_F = 1
L_S = 1500
pat =2 low, 4 high

Arched Roadway

Generative Logic
Catenary Curves and Surfaces

Catenary curves describe the shape of a chain (*catena* in Latin) hanging under its own weight and anchored at both ends. Architects and engineers have used this shape through the inversion of a pure tension system into a pure compressive system. Examples include Antonio Gaudi's *Casa Mila* and Eero Saarinen's *Gateway Arch* in St. Louis.

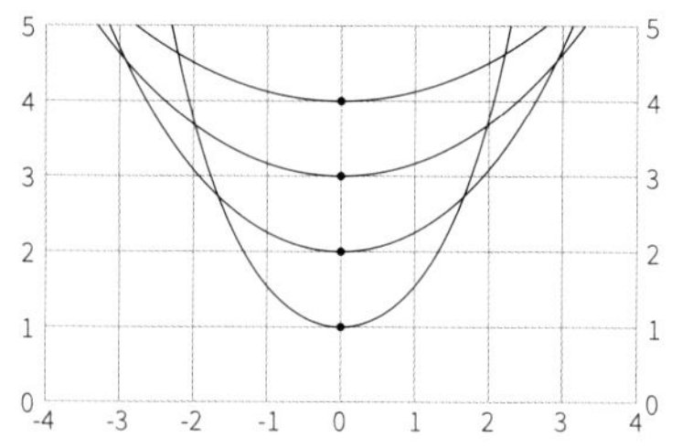

1. The equation in Cartesian coordinates for a Catenary curve is $y = a^{*}cosh(x/a)$ where a is the distance of the lowest point of the curve above the x-axis. Although similar, a parabola and catenary are not identical.

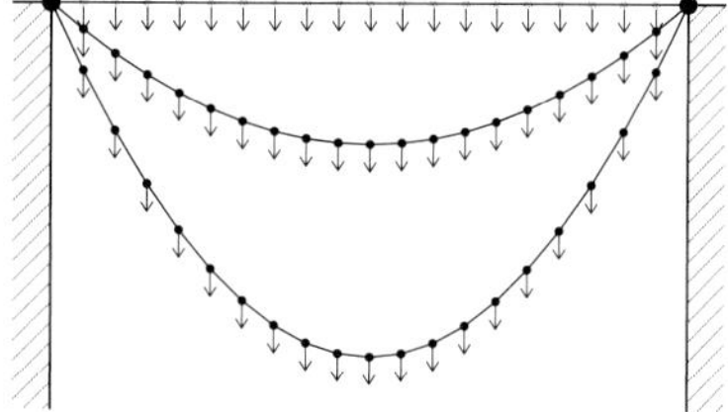

2. A Catenary curve can also be simulated as a series of elastic line segments spanning between two anchored points. When gravity is applied to each node, the segments extend and the catenary forms.

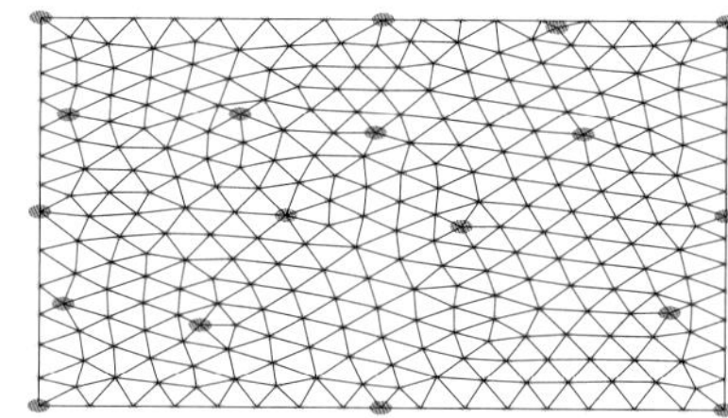

3. This concept can be extended from 2D to 3D and with a field of points and connected segments. Instead of gravity being applied down, it can be applied up to simulate a pure compression vault.

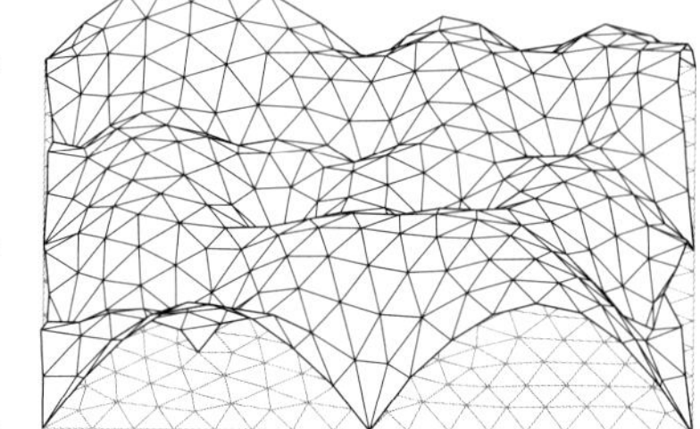

4. The system finds an equilibrium between the mass of the nodes and the elasticity of the elements.

Generative Process
Confluence Park

Although the Confluence Park Pavilion appears as a singular vaulted surface, it is composed of eleven structurally independent arches. Each arch is composed of two half-arches, or "petals," that both provide shade and direct rainwater to collection drains located at each column base. Using a Cairo pentagon, the structure uses only three modular forms to cast the twenty-two petals.

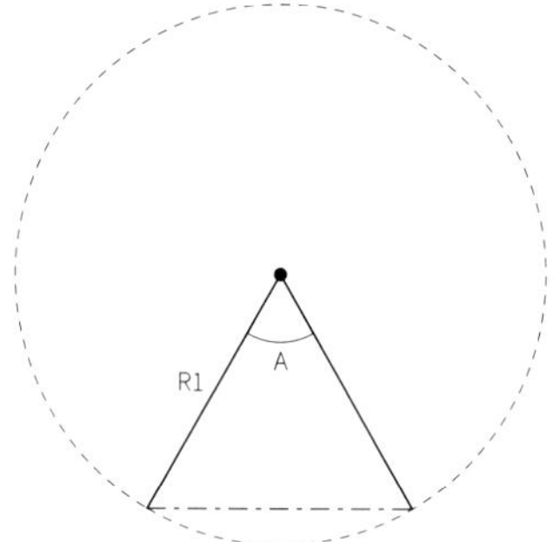

1. From a central point, create two lines with radii R1 . Separate the two lines by angle A. In this example, A equals 60° and it forms an equilateral triangle.

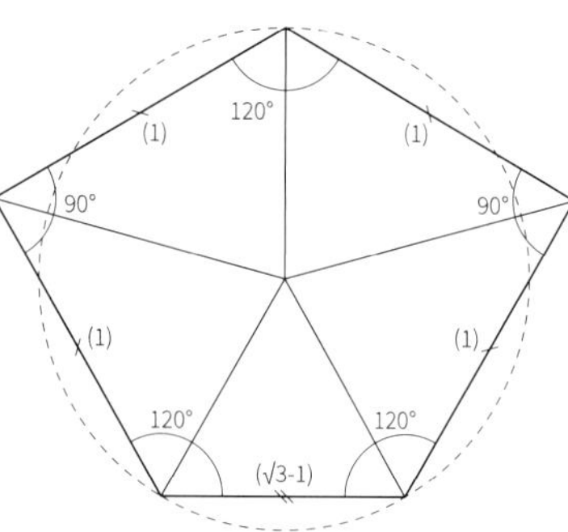

2. Continue to add three more points with the angles and length ratios above to make what is known as a bilaterally symmetric Cairo pentagon.

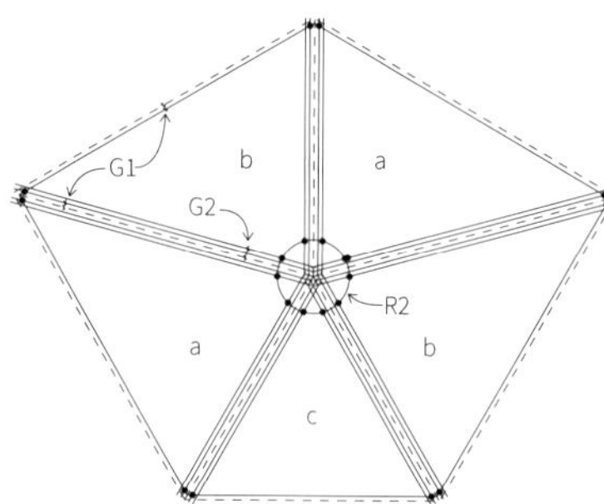

3. Offset the pentagon by the distance G1 and radiating central lines by both G1 and G2. Create a circle at the center with radius R2. Find their intersections.

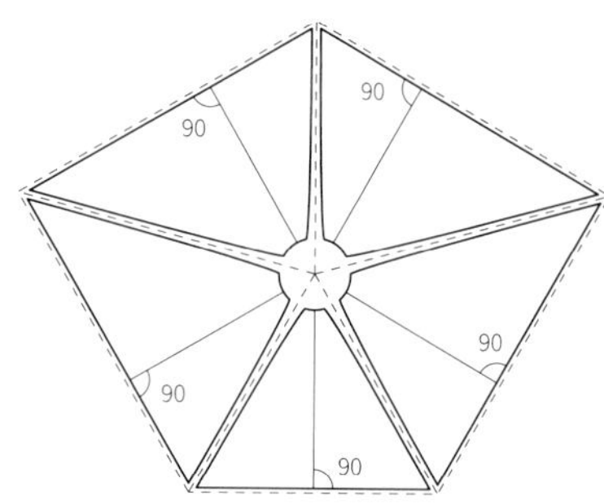

4. From the center point, draw the perpendicular bisector of each triangle. This will be the central valley of each petal.

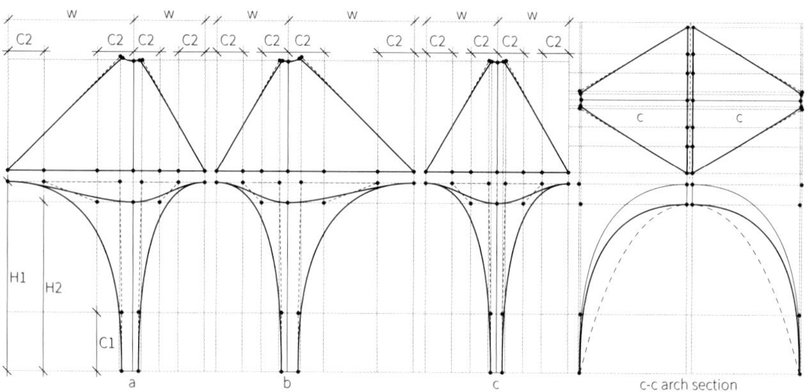

5. This makes a total of five petals made up of two "a" petals, two "b" petals (that are the mirror of the "a" petal), and one "c" petal. Construct the sectional profiles of each petal such that there is tangency continuity to the surrounding petals. The variable C1 is a percentage of H1 or H2 while C2 is a percentage of the distance from the perpendicular bisector of each triangle and the outer points. The arches are not true catenary curves as shown in the section above (dashed line is a catenary).

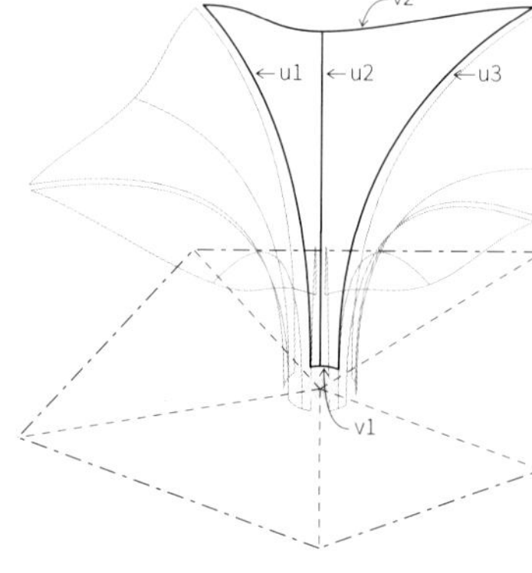

6. This should produce a total of five curves: three longitudinal profiles(u1, u2, and u3), and two transverse profiles (v1 and v2).

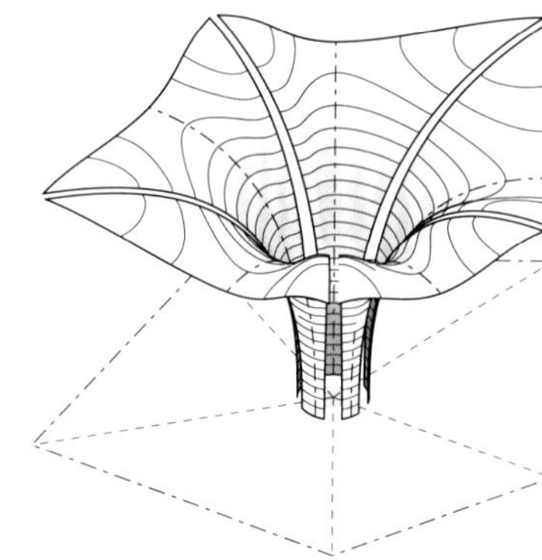

7. Create a networked surface between these U and V curves to produce each petal. Manipulate the C1/C2 and H1/H2 parameters to adjust the curvature.

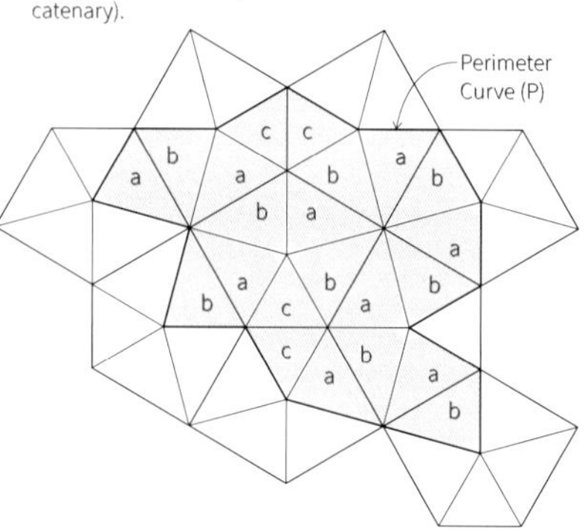

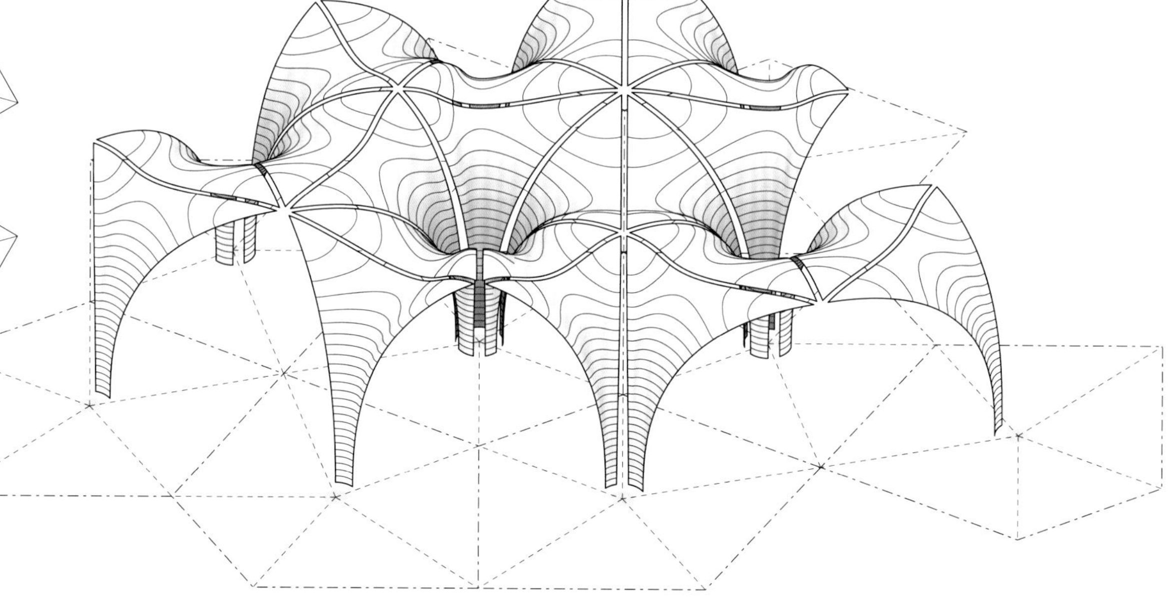

8. To make the final arches, each "c" petal is paired with another "c" petal and each "a" petal is paired with a "b" petal. This pattern can tile a plane infinitely, so determine the specific number of arches needed for the program and site requirements. For Confluence Park, only one center point is completely surrounded by five petals. At the base of each column is a drain that collects the water flowing down petal valleys.

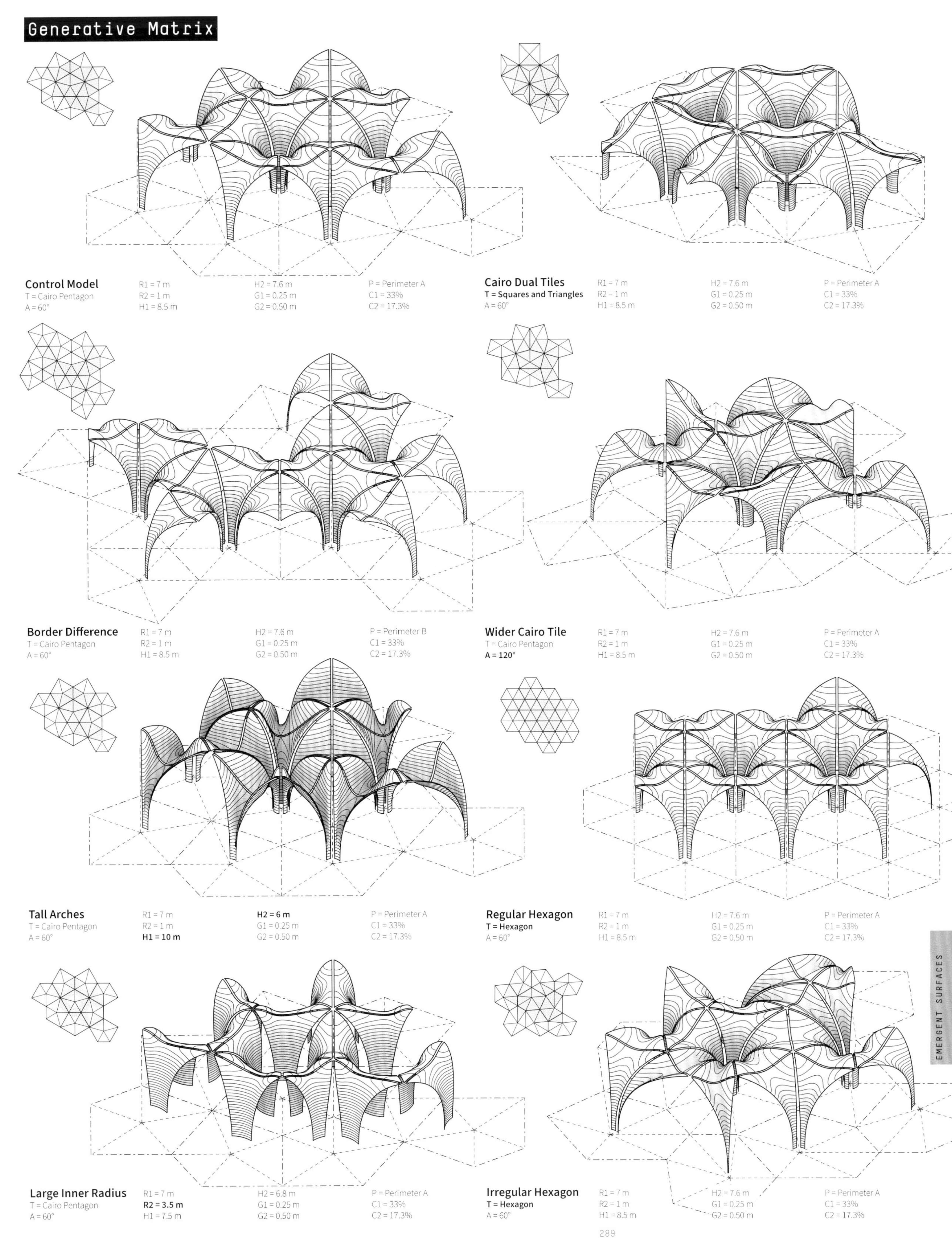
Generative Matrix
Control Model
T = Cairo Pentagon
A = 60°
R1 = 7 m
R2 = 1 m
H1 = 8.5 m
H2 = 7.6 m
G1 = 0.25 m
G2 = 0.50 m
P = Perimeter A
C1 = 33%
C2 = 17.3%
Cairo Dual Tiles
T = Squares and Triangles
A = 60°
R1 = 7 m
R2 = 1 m
H1 = 8.5 m
H2 = 7.6 m
G1 = 0.25 m
G2 = 0.50 m
P = Perimeter A
C1 = 33%
C2 = 17.3%
Border Difference
T = Cairo Pentagon
A = 60°
R1 = 7 m
R2 = 1 m
H1 = 8.5 m
H2 = 7.6 m
G1 = 0.25 m
G2 = 0.50 m
P = Perimeter B
C1 = 33%
C2 = 17.3%
Wider Cairo Tile
T = Cairo Pentagon
A = 120°
R1 = 7 m
R2 = 1 m
H1 = 8.5 m
H2 = 7.6 m
G1 = 0.25 m
G2 = 0.50 m
P = Perimeter A
C1 = 33%
C2 = 17.3%
Tall Arches
T = Cairo Pentagon
A = 60°
R1 = 7 m
R2 = 1 m
H1 = 10 m
H2 = 6 m
G1 = 0.25 m
G2 = 0.50 m
P = Perimeter A
C1 = 33%
C2 = 17.3%
Regular Hexagon
T = Hexagon
A = 60°
R1 = 7 m
R2 = 1 m
H1 = 8.5 m
H2 = 7.6 m
G1 = 0.25 m
G2 = 0.50 m
P = Perimeter A
C1 = 33%
C2 = 17.3%
Large Inner Radius
T = Cairo Pentagon
A = 60°
R1 = 7 m
R2 = 3.5 m
H1 = 7.5 m
H2 = 6.8 m
G1 = 0.25 m
G2 = 0.50 m
P = Perimeter A
C1 = 33%
C2 = 17.3%
Irregular Hexagon
T = Hexagon
A = 60°
R1 = 7 m
R2 = 1 m
H1 = 8.5 m
H2 = 7.6 m
G1 = 0.25 m
G2 = 0.50 m
P = Perimeter A
C1 = 33%
C2 = 17.3%
EMERGENT SURFACES
289

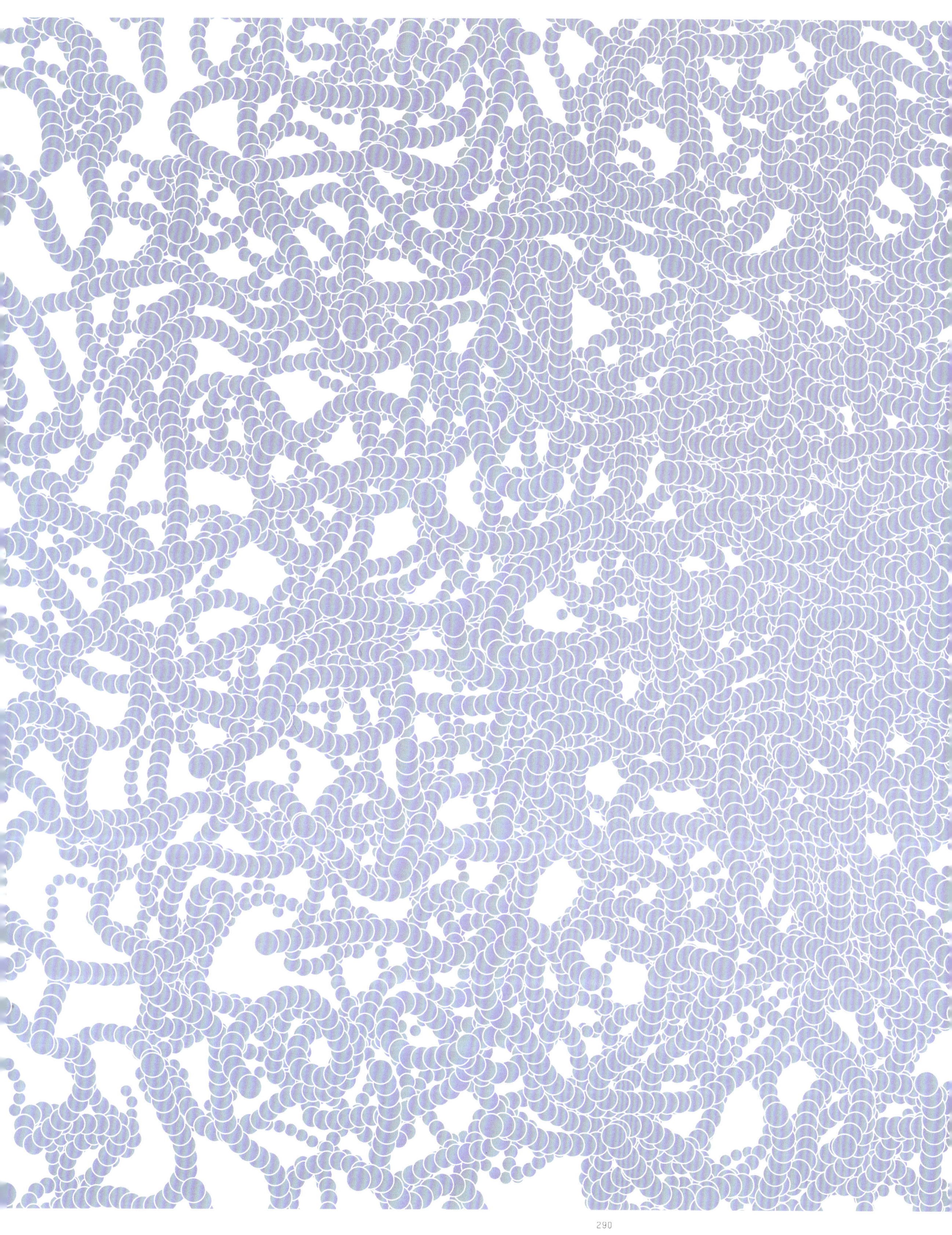

MULTI-AGENT NETWORKS

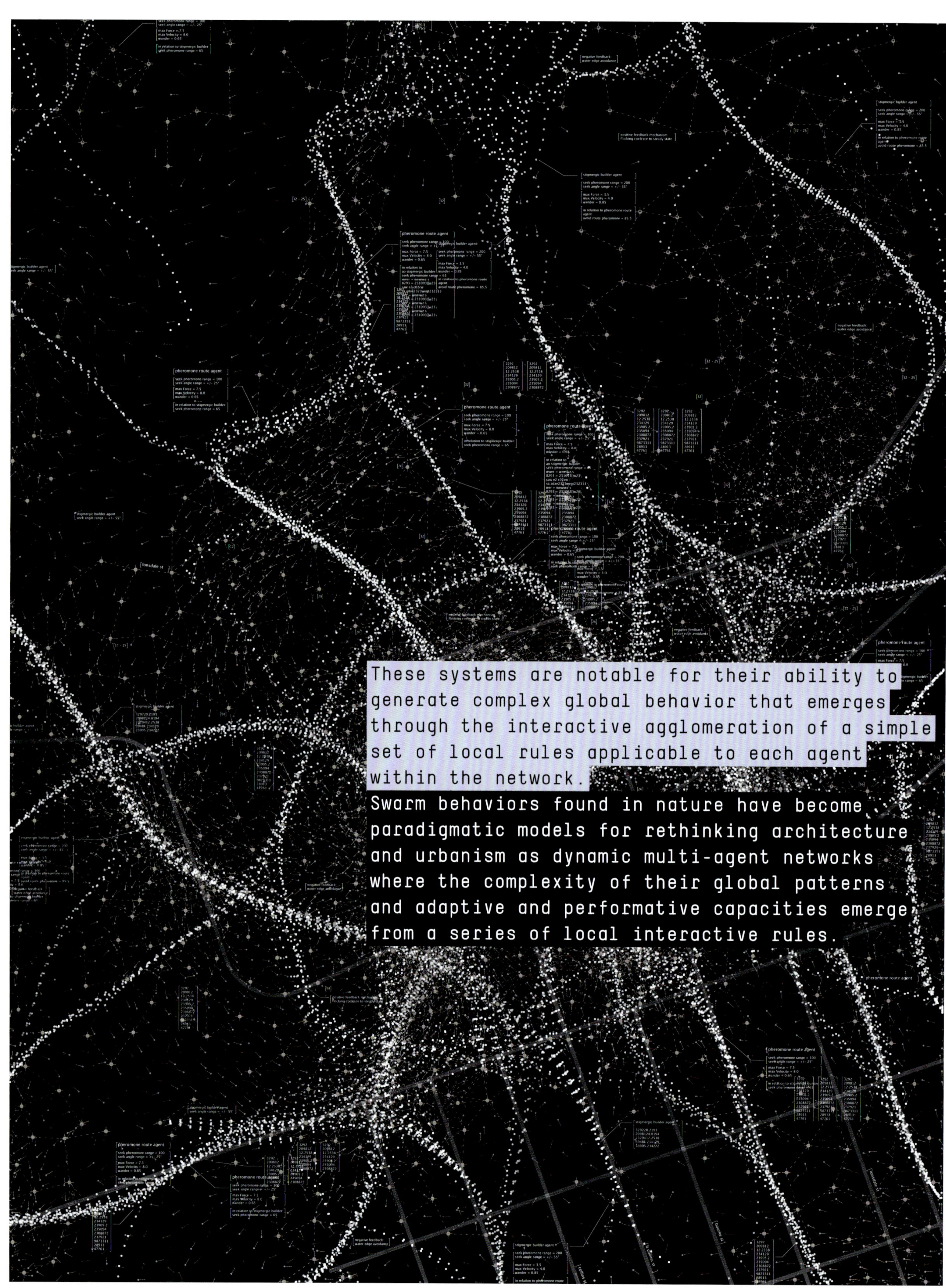

These systems are notable for their ability to generate complex global behavior that emerges through the interactive agglomeration of a simple set of local rules applicable to each agent within the network.

Swarm behaviors found in nature have become paradigmatic models for rethinking architecture and urbanism as dynamic multi-agent networks where the complexity of their global patterns and adaptive and performative capacities emerge from a series of local interactive rules.

Multi-Agent Networks

Collective Behaviors and the Intelligence of Populations

Multi-agent networks refer to intelligent, decentralized systems that are composed of relatively discrete elements each of which operates as an independent actor within a larger dynamic collective. These systems are notable for their ability to generate complex global behavior that emerges through the interactive agglomeration of a simple set of local rules applicable to each agent within the network. Initially evolving from the computer simulation of swarming, schooling, and flocking activities found in insect, fish, and bird migrations such as the early *boids* program developed by Craig Reynolds,[1] multi-agent networks have been used to model a wide range of phenomena ❶. These include the behavioral life of ecosystems, the diffusion of global innovation in economics, the spread of disease in epidemiology, the cultural transmission of populations in anthropology, and the mapping and anticipation of traffic patterns in urban infrastructure. In addition, the intensive application of swarm behavior simulations to more continuous self-organizing systems, such as multicellular processes in biology, have transferred their deployment to the realm of artificial life and the study of self-assembly, morphogenetic growth and development, and evolutionary and ecological dynamics.

Within the design disciplines, swarm behaviors found in nature have become paradigmatic models for rethinking architecture and urbanism as dynamic multi-agent networks where the complexity of their global patterns and adaptive and performative capacities emerge from a series of local interactive rules. Given their dependence on open-ended algorithmic procedures that define relationships between individual elements rather than prescribing a larger set of formal types, the application of such networks to architecture have produced a wide range of practices many of which fall into three broader categories: multi-agent matters, urbanisms, and systems. The first of these are comprised of architectural projects imagined as a form of artificial life constituted by self-organizing elements whose local parameters determine behaviors that simulate generative patterns of form growth and development. Here, components within the system are both created and arrayed using a mode of swarm logic applied to a continuous matter, such as the process developed by Alisa Andrasek to model Mathematized Cloud ❷. This logic parametrically adjusts each element within the system in relation to its neighbors such that the architecture created, which subscribes to no overarching global geometric order, is a residual material trace of the morphogenetic evolution of the system over time. The second category refers to a form of swarm urbanism focused on the collective emergence and behaviors of discrete populations, vehicular infrastructures, building clusters, and territorial elements whose origination and interaction are determined by algorithms applied to programmatic directives and parametrically calibrated environmental influences. These can instigate a range of potential settlement scenarios and adaptive urban topographies or, as in projects such as Edible Infrastructures, locally adjusted metabolic structures and food distribution networks for the productive city.[2]

Ultimately, the distinction between these first two groups is highly relative. This distinction is dependent on the architectural or urban scale of operation of the system, the degree of discretization or continuity of its components, that is, whether the behavior of the swarm generates a continuous material growth or aggregate of distinct cells or elements, and the way in which temporality is defined within the system. This last qualifier is perhaps the most critical given the categorical difference between the fluid formal or material movements of a generative process that ultimately produce a reified fixed and immobile artifact (no matter how perceptually animate it might appear) as was evident in early projects by Greg Lynn, such as the Port Authority Gateway project, and a multi-agent system that retains the trajectory of time within the potential multitude of projective scenarios that it might produce as in continuously transforming, evolving, or interactive systems. In the first case, time is registered in the procedural traces of the final architectural artifact, which is no longer fluid, mobile or adaptive, just as the growth of natural objects retain the traces of material events within their very formation. In the second case, time is maintained as the performative environment of the multi-agent network, just as a game's virtual envelope refers not only to the categorical rules and distributing hypotheses of the game, but also to the temporality and plurality of all possible plays and aggregated outcomes determined by the rules of interaction and constraints of the system.[3] In this sense the

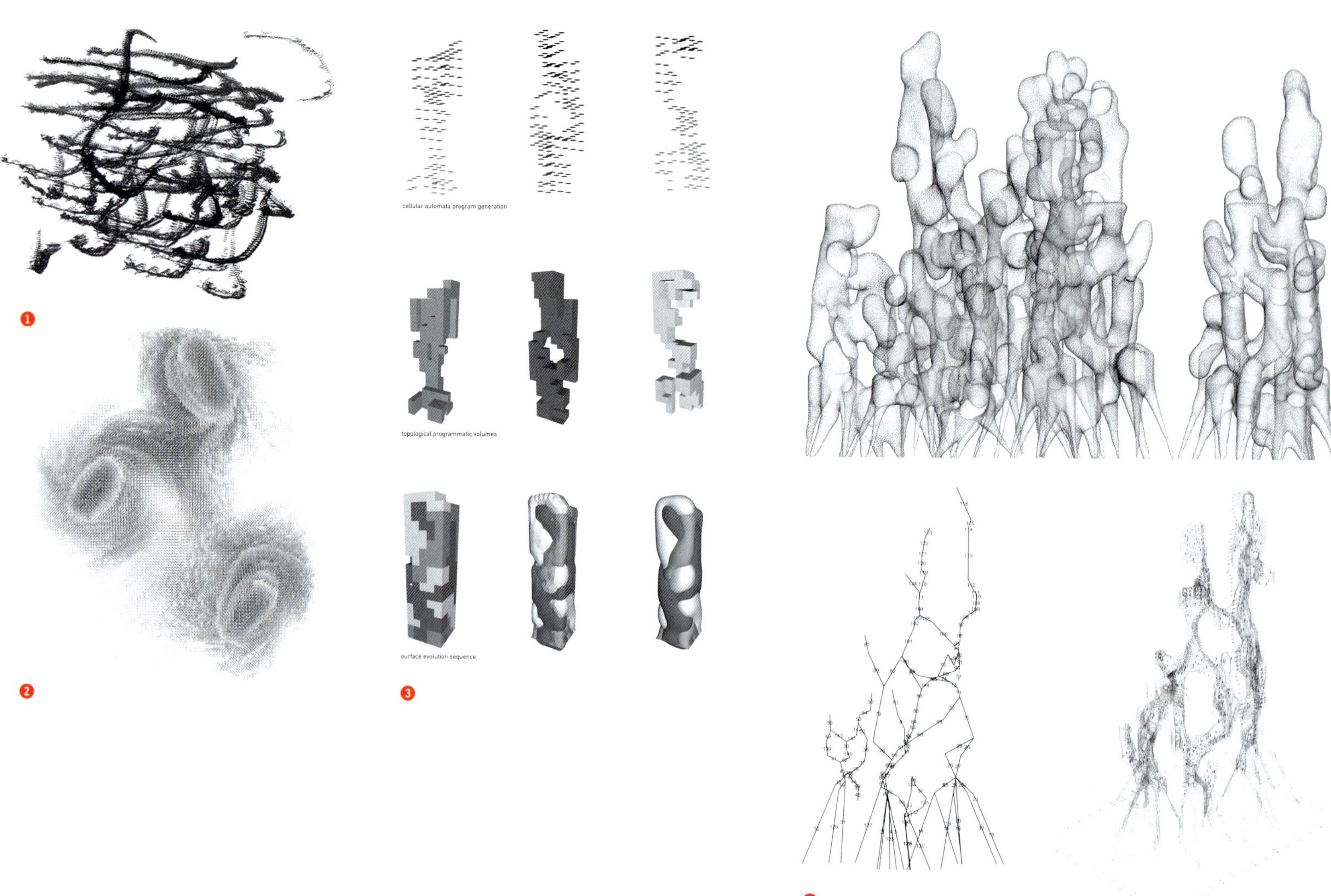

network can be understood to constitute a multidimensional manifold that contains within itself all possible states intrinsic to the dynamic behavior of the system.[4] This latter condition is complex in that temporality might be virtually evident in the larger parameters that determine an infinite range of possible outcomes without those outcomes being actually evidenced in the selection of a limited range of final products. Finally, the third group is comprised of interactive multi-agent systems that are programmed to operate continuously in time and are thus performative and adaptable within a prescribed set of limits. These endow surfaces, structures, and spaces with a sensory intelligence and actuating capacity facilitated by a multitude of locally responsive elements that collectively enable the production of mediated or artificial atmospheric environments.

The first type include projects that engage software to set up a dynamic parametric event space directed by variable attractors and constrained by rule-based limits that together steer the architecture's generative development. In Highly Evolved ❸ by Kokkugia, for example, the spatial position of cellular living or commercial units are pre-programmed with desires that respectively attract them to such things as optimal access to light and views or urban density. Program is thus redefined as an interactive encoded rule set operating on a set of selected entities—elements and spaces that are represented by nodes and vectors in the system—that simulates and animates the growth of form using computation to spatially model information within a temporal framework. In this process, both the mimetic typologies of classicism and the structural models of modernism are replaced by dynamic digital diagrams made possible by parametric modeling intended to reinterpret the architectural in relation to the fluctuations of programmatic, environmental, and other contextual matters. Typological stasis and structural closure are thereby supplanted by a topological model that permits infinite mutability and differentiation within the design process. Complexity is generated through the synthetic growth of this topological envelope or system, which acts as a material index of the mediation of encoded internal and external parameters—internal programmatic directives and external environmental forces and constraints that, through their local interaction, lead toward the generative development and diversification of the architectural form.

A contemporary reinvention of the exquisite corpse, which integrates the indeterminacy of chance yet displaces collagist differentiation with the formal continuities assured by the consistency of mechanisms operating within the network, *I've Heard About* by R&Sie(n) ❹ is another type of multi-agent architecture that purports to be an endlessly adaptable living environment. This project is a fantastical colonizing communal habitat and growing swarm of matter that, like a mollusk, integrates the constructive methods of its fluid architecture into the very processes of its formal and material emergence. Similar to the evolution of a termite mound that is simultaneously generated by the individual agency of the termites and the contiguity of material traces formed by their collective movements, this project's inhabitable biostructural landscape immediately registers the local negotiations of its citizenry through its own responsive protocols and adjustable material behaviors.[5] In addition, as the local biotropic growth of branches seeking space and sunlight are nevertheless connected to a continuously developing infrastructure that assures their stability and the transit of water and nutrients, this project grows according to arborescent vectors determined by the interaction of individual contingencies and incorporated situational data sets that are intended to ensure the cooperative intelligence and democratic nature of its evolutionary form. These inputs are processed through computational growth scripts and open algorithms that transcode human desires and relationships (conflicts and transactions), spatial requirements and external information (such as the morphology of the surrounding urbanity, the availability of natural light, or the tectonic limits of the structure), into modifiable variables and operating rules for their behavior. The definition of these becomes the locus of design. The reticulated structure defined by these mobile vectors, is then designed to be digitally and materially fabricated by a construction engine called Viab that is programmed to be open to ongoing external inputs. Inspired by coral growth deposition on the one hand and the spider's process for extruding silken webs on the other. Viab is an integrated biomechanical, architecturally scaled 3D printer meant to literally secrete the project's structure and contour-crafted enclosure in response to variable conditions of occupancy, load, and use.

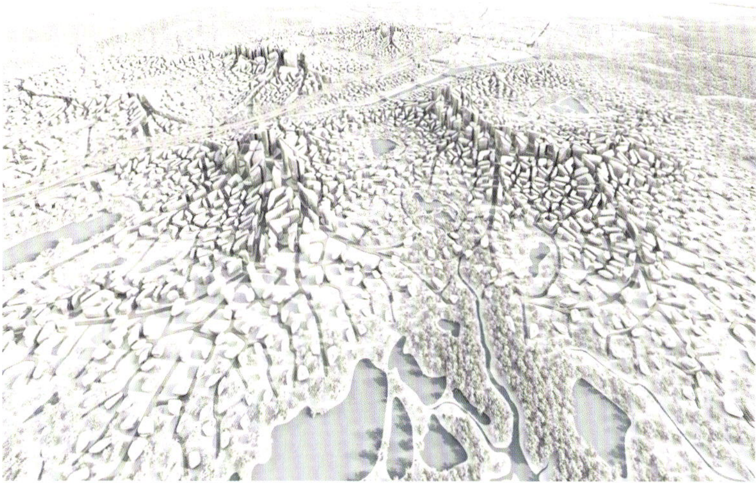

5

We might imagine that such forms of swarm intelligence that reflect the local interactions, negotiations, and feedback loops of diverse populations are already in operation in the everyday metropolis and responsible for its continuously emerging form. In addition to indigenous models of local aggregation or patterns of informal settlement that precede, or occur within and alongside the making of cities, real urban life, its physical evolution, and ongoing events already exhibit complex forms of swarm behavior. What distinguishes contemporary computational models from these, however, is the embedding of design intentionality into this system through integrated and scripted algorithmic protocols such as those evident in I've Heard About or in Kokkugia's Swarm Urbanism—a multi-agent network developed for the Melbourne docklands in Australia. These operate through the interaction of individual agents as in Reynold's early flocking simulations dependent on local rules determining the relative separation, cohesion, velocity, and alignment of "boids," as well as in the stigmergic coordination mechanisms used by termite colonies, which communicate through the emission and tracking of chemical traces in the making of their aggregative mounds. In these projects, multiple individuated agents representing different variables or urban particles in the system are encoded with desires or behavioral imperatives that define their ability to self-organize into the inhabitable clusters and infrastructural networks of urbanity. The decentralized and nonhierarchical structure generated through this process is an interconnected field that operates as both a representation and a material index of the interacting agents within the urban system that are imagined to continue to unfold and coevolve over time.

Despite the scale and ambition of these systems, their true complexity and relevance in relation to the multilevel dynamics of the urban environment is ultimately dependent on the selection, number, and definition of variables represented by agents within the system; the part-to-whole relations or nested hierarchies that are intrinsic to urban morphologies and populations and that elaborate the concept of agency within the system; the quantity and complexity of spatial, demographic, programmatic, and environmental inputs and forces that the system is able to absorb and respond to; the way in which these internal and external stimuli are coded; and the programmed rules that govern local behaviors in the network and that are ultimately responsible for the production of its architectural and urban morphology.

In Urban Field—Adaptive Urban Fabric by Ursula Frick and Thomas Grabner designed for Navi Mumbai 5, such generative systems are applied to structural planning variables such as connectivity and modes of territorial occupation as these are influenced by a range of environmental and economic factors. These influences, which include the level of noise pollution, physical and visual access to water and greenery, relative adjacency to less desirable urban areas, topography, buildable density, and land value, for example, are established as parameters that are then weighted relative to location and attributed numerical values. The superimposition of these different layers of influence and their values are spatialized across the territory as a gradient field to which optimized systems of distribution—such as the branching network establishing infrastructural connectivity or the cellular allocation of building plots—are adapted. As these parameters and gradient fields change, so do the morphologies of the architectural envelopes they effectively influence. This algorithmically driven design process generates a spatialized urban master plan that is potentially infinitely adaptable in relation to an unlimited set of influences. The perceived organicism and smooth, seductive internal consistency of the final form, however, results from the digital transcoding of information that translates qualitative differences in kind, those cultural and material differences intrinsic to the messy operations of the real city into abstracted differences in degree.

The application of swarm behaviors to multi-agent systems that operate within real time (rather than its generative or virtual counterparts), is evident in a range of interactive projects that are equipped with an integrated and embedded responsive capacity. From The Living's underwater Amphibious Architecture installation (that enables us to communicate with urban fish) to Howeler + Yoon's Windscreen 6, which provides a changing luminous index of air movement, our expanded culture-nature interface, mobilized through multi-agent interactive systems, has inserted

6

7

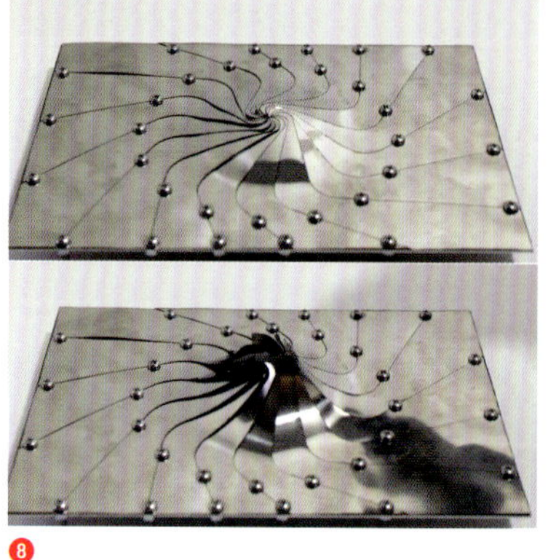
8

a protean environmental wilderness and feedback loop into architecture's domestic terrain. Beyond dissolving the boundary between human and animal territories, these practices point to an environmental response to post-industrialization, where technology's apparent physical absence—its disappearance into the atmospheric—has prompted architectural territories to be transformed into ambient meteorological events. In our world of digitized information and intelligent matters, our explorations of atmospheric environments, those defined by fluid continuous qualities often deployed across mobile fields of discrete components, have called into question architecture's cultural role as a provider of spatial stability and material permanence. This is exemplified in the projects HygroScope by Achim Menges 7 and Oculus by DOSU, each of which draws upon inherent material behavior to "re-compute" its form based on shifting environmental parameters. Whereas HygroScope exposes the unseen fluctuations in the humidity of Paris (as perceived against the highly controlled environment of the interior space of the Pompidou) through the opening and closing of its meteorosensitive wooden petal morphology, Oculus 8, made of thermobimetal, operates as a self-ventilating screen whose apertures curl open in response to increases in temperature.

Interactive responsive fields, such as Howeler + Yoon's White Noise White Light field sited at the base of the Acropolis in Athens, Cirriform by Future Cities Lab, or Urban Syncopation by Scaleshift, generate animate illuminated atmospheres that respond to their living occupation. In these projects, emergent environments are the result of interactive programming embedded into the potential functioning of the space, such that its affects are dynamically revealed and experienced through direct engagement and immersion. Responsive systems are used to express the choreography of inhabitation, or render evident and respond to environmental transformations, through the filter of an interactive gradient field in continual flux. These are technologized spatial environments employed to amplify, rather than constrain, the gestural excesses of animate biotic behaviors or provide locally networked responses to the fluidity of meteorological change. Architecture is deployed as an infrastructure that organizes a variable spectrum of potential material responses to parametrically defined inputs, and that, through the organization of local rules and collective behaviors, dynamically stimulates the expressive production of a multitude of artificial atmospheric effects.

In White Noise White Light 9, for example, four hundred gridded flexible fiber-optic stalks are equipped with passive infrared sensors to detect proximate movement. These are programmed to respond to this movement with varying degrees of white light and sound where the degree of response is directly proportional to the distance of a body from any single stalk. In addition, the stalks are flexible and therefore, like a field of tall grasses, bend and move when lightly touched by a passing body. The collective system not only provides an animated indexical mapping of the wake of occupation by rarifying, transcoding and rendering both aural and visible a previously silent and, at night, invisible activity, but also, through the multiplicity and arrangement of elements, amplifies the perceived spatial domain of occupation while architecturalizing its effects. These proliferate with the increased number of bodies within the space, enabling the changing occupation of visitors to be a protagonist in the making and material animation of the architecture, where the architecture acts as filter to both organize and synthesize the local movements of a population into a larger patterned whole.

The transformation from animated territory to dynamic atmospheric surface occurs in Cirriform 10, a proposal for an interactive façade. Drawing from changing cloud formations that refract light through their crystalline structure, Cirriform is constituted by a field of geometrically defined "crystals" that rotate and pulse ambient light in relation to the presence of the body. Using overlapping web cams connected to a machine vision program, the installation continuously senses and transcodes the movements of those walking past or approaching the façade into distinct values that determine the changing degrees of vertical rotation and light intensities of each rhomboid-shaped crystal, generating a constantly fluctuating spectrum as these are relayed across its surface. The longitudinally stretched shape and perforated covering of each cell amplify the changing porosity of the screen as these rotate, while their

9

10

11

positions within the field, because of the vertical displacement of cells relative to each other, produce an incremental wave-like geometry that translates locally instigated movement into an undulating, glowing swarm.

In the Windscreen project, we find a shift from the digitally induced atmospheres of Cirriform to the ambient visualization of meteorologically driven data. Operating as a distributed series of micro-turbines, this project directly translates the velocity of wind into a kinetic radiant pattern that, through the changing intensity of light driven by the rotation of each turbine, visually registers the effects of invisible air currents. In addition, this project acts a didactic device that, through its immediate production and consumption of renewable resources, exposes the potential untapped energy of the wind. Energy use (and its production and consumption) is thereby directly and simultaneously translated into both legible information and immersive affect, both of which are mediated by the architecturalization of the specific form of each device—calibrated in size and porosity—and their distribution and patterning within the field.

The shift from highly localized to more extended, networked interactivity is exemplified in the Urban Syncopation installation 11, where each of the six horizontal, pixelated strata that constitute the wall receives data from a different downtown Toronto site. The wall system, whose arrangement corresponds to the sequencing of streets from which this data was collected, references the layered streets, urban grid, and shifting topography that constitute the fabric of the city, while concurrently extracting sensory information drawn from the city's public spaces as an index of the dynamic conditions of their inhabitation. The city, a multi-agent network itself, is understood to be simultaneously material and performative: a physical artifact as well as an infrastructure or stage for the more ephemeral activities and events of urban life to take place. These more fleeting conditions of urbanity are captured in the piece in two distinct ways. Through the wall's materiality and geometry, as its folded, mirrored surface passively reflects, refracts, and fragments the surrounding motion of visitors who become both actors and audience within the gallery space, and by urban sound data, collected using sound sensors located along five primary east-west urban corridors, which is transcoded into a streaming flow of syncopated bands of pulsing light.

Although many of the projects within this volume refer to a form of networked information used to drive the generation of architecture, multi-agent systems are specifically those that foreground local interactivity and adaptation in their design evolution or performance that result in complex collective behaviors and structural formations constitutive of a larger intelligent whole. These decentralized organizations operate as multiplicities that are irreducible to the aggregation of individual acts. Notwithstanding the fact that from the perspective of architecture much of this research is still in its infancy in relation to the complexity of biotic, social, and ecological living systems it hopes to emulate, the vast range of scales and potential applications of responsive systems and multi-agent networks indicate the many territories within which such research and design is currently unfolding.

Notes

1. Craig Reynolds' computer program was one of the first simulations of flocking and swarming behavior developed in 1986. It was a mathematical animated model demonstrating the complex global behavior of a large number of interacting autonomous agents based on three local rules applicable to each individual within the system: 1. cohesion/attraction: remain close to neighbors and steer toward their average position; 2. alignment: move in the general direction of the flock while matching the velocity of neighbors; 3. separation: avoid collisions with nearby flockmates. See Craig Reynolds, "Flocks, Herds, and Schools: A Distributed Behavioral Model," *Computer Graphics* 21 no. 4, (July 1987): 25–34.

2. Edible Infrastructures is a project developed by Darrick Borowski, Nikoletta Poulimeni, and Jeroen Janssen that uses swarm behavior models and algorithms as design tools in the creation of multiscalar distributed food networks for urban-agricultural landscapes. See www.edibleinfrastructures.net.

3. On the theoretical model of games see Gilles Deleuze, *The Logic of Sense*, ed. Constantin V. Boundas, trans. Mark Lester (New York: Columbia University Press, 1990), 58–59. According to Deleuze, "[t]he characteristics of normal games are therefore the preexisting categorical rules, the distributing hypotheses, the fixed and numerically distinct distributions, and the ensuing results. These games are partial in two ways: first, they characterize only one part of human activity, and second, even if they are pushed to the absolute, they retain chance only at certain points, leaving the remainder to the mechanical development of consequences or to skill, understood as the art of causality." Although Deleuze refers explicitly to games, the theoretical model itself implicitly registers other activities, such as design, which are not games, yet whose principles and conditions are correspondent. The skill of design is the art of causality understood within the discipline as intention presiding over material, while the rules that preexist design are its conventions and methods, a set of established skills that determine its overriding competence, and that regulate the potential performativity of the system by retaining chance at particular intervals.

4. For a discussion of manifolds see Manuel DeLanda, *Intensive Science and Virtual Philosophy* (New York: Continuum, 2004), 13.

5. See Francois Roche, "I've Heard About . . . (A Flat, Fat, Growing Urban Experiment): Extract of Neighborhood Protocols," *Digital Cities*, Neil Leach, ed. *Architectural Design* 79, No. 4 (July/August 2009): 40–45.

Stranded Sears Tower

Greg Lynn FORM

Unbuilt 1992
Chicago, United States

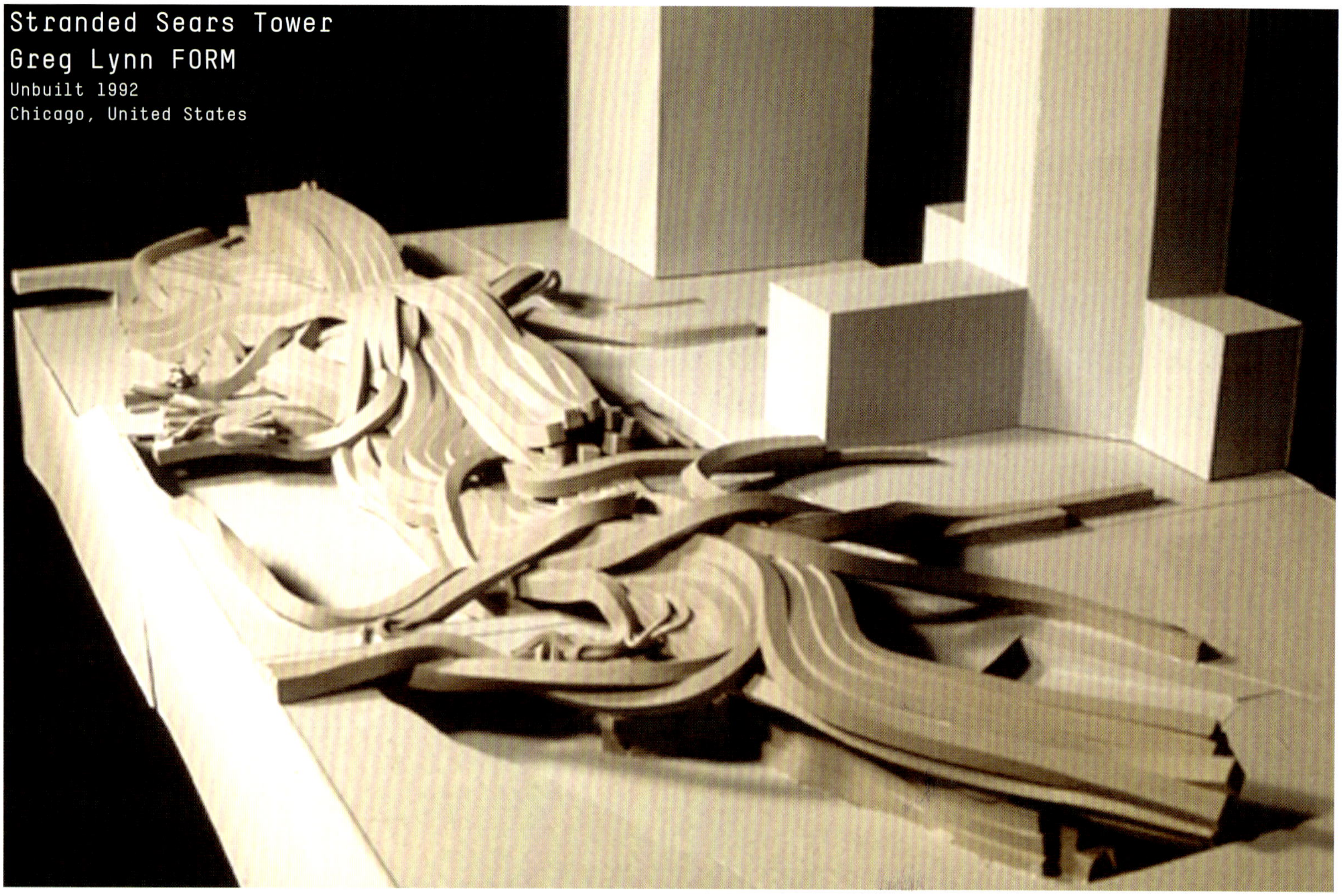

8.1a

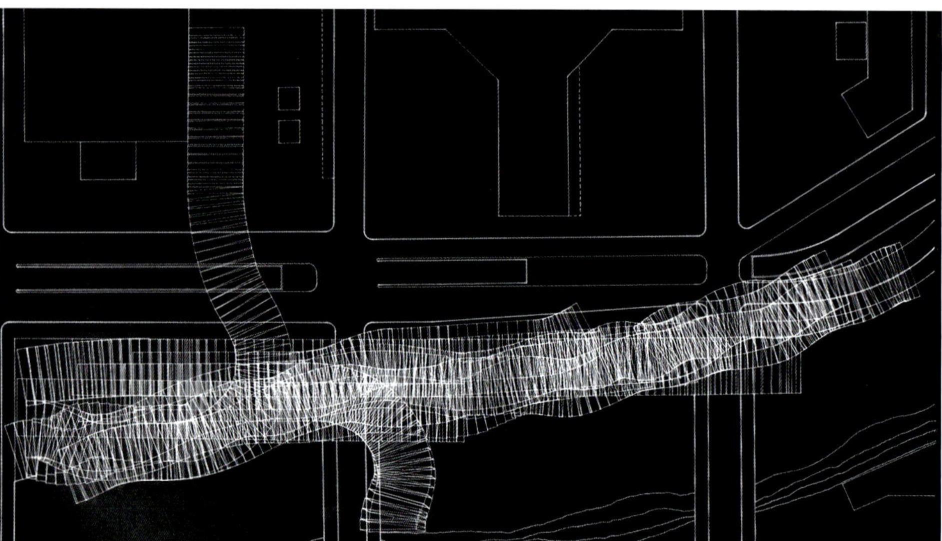

8.1b

The Stranded Sears Tower was part of an exhibition asking architects in Chicago to relocate and reenvision landmark buildings in the city. In the reformulation of the skyscraper's monumental form, the organization of the Sears Tower and its nine-square typology undergo a twofold deterritorialization, to internalize its particularities and extend its influence outward into the city. The project reformulates the vertical bundle of nine tubes horizontally along an adjacent riverfront site—a strip of land between Wacker Drive and the Chicago River—to emulate the fluidity of the river and generate new types of social interaction by linking these now separated tubes with movements flowing along and across the site. The contiguous tubes, which operate as a stranded collection of interwoven twisted or plaited filaments thus accommodate themselves to the multiple and often discontinuous borders of the site, while also engendering affiliations with particular local events—adjacent buildings, landforms, sidewalks, bridges, tunnels, roads, and the river's edge—that would have been repressed by a more rigid and reductive geometric system of description. Although the increments of the floor plates are generally oriented perpendicularly to the surface of the drawings, the particularities of the site often deflect any single ideal orientation in favor of multiple oblique orientations. The deformations of twisting, plaiting, and bending are not accidental but unpredicted, as they result from the combination of over two thousand bundled tubes with local conditions. The resulting image is neither monolithic nor pluralistic but belongs to the now supple and flexible internal order of the bundled tube that is differentiated by the external forces of the river's edge, the city grid, and the vectors of pedestrian and transportation movement. The bundled tube is an assembly of microsystems, becoming a paradigm for multiplicitous movement. The unified image of the monument thus unravels into heterogeneous local events that participate in the multiple external systems of its surrounding urbanism. The Stranded Sears Tower is neither discrete nor dispersed, but rather turns from any single organizational idea toward a system of local affiliations outside itself.

Port Authority Triple Bridge Gateway

Greg Lynn FORM

Unbuilt 1994
New York, United States

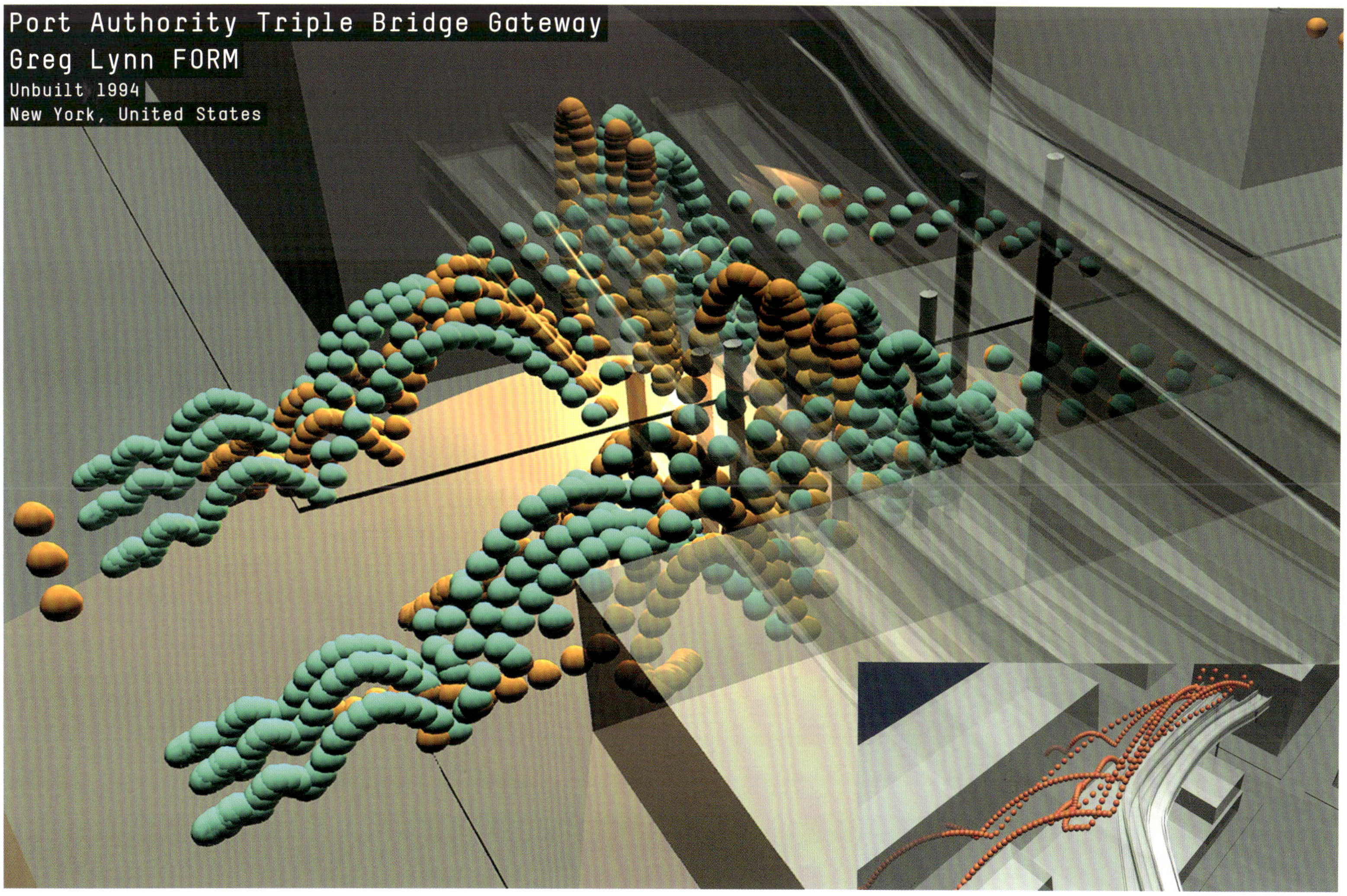

8.2a

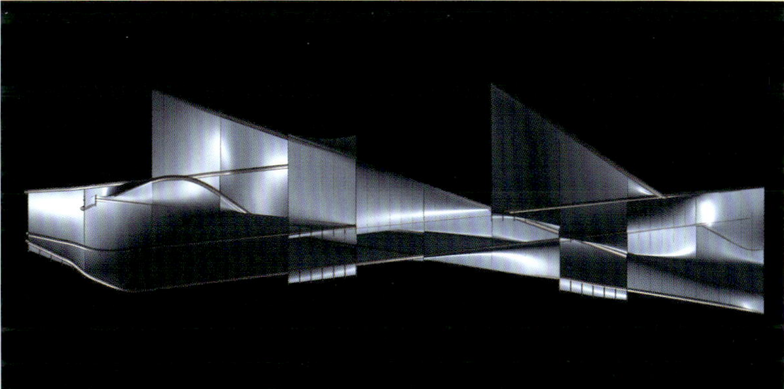

8.2b

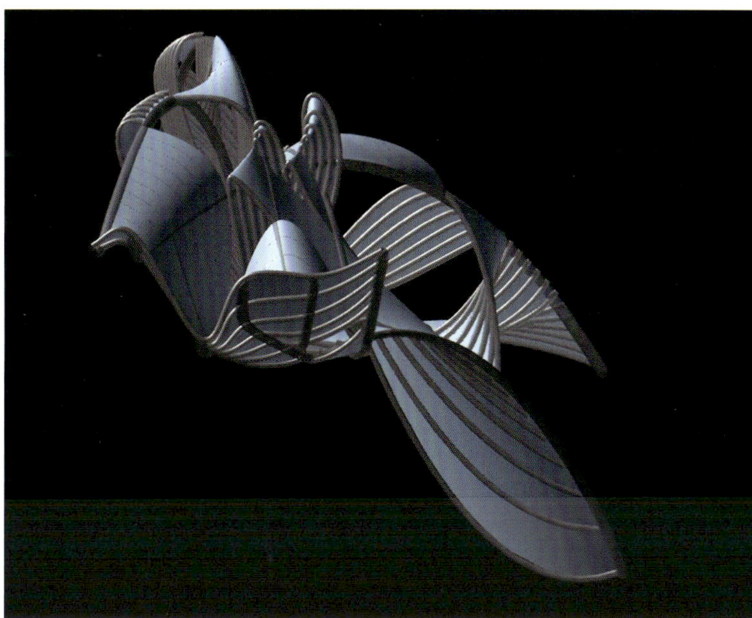

8.2c

The Gateway competition involved the design of a protective roof and a lighting scheme for the underside of the bus ramps leading into the Port Authority Bus Terminal. The site was modeled using forces that simulate the movement and flow of pedestrians, cars, and buses across the site, each with differing speeds and intensities of movement along Ninth Avenue, 42nd and 43rd Streets, and four elevated bus ramps emerging from below the Hudson River. These various forces of movement established a gradient field of attraction across the site. To discover the shape of this invisible field of attraction, geometric particles were introduced that change their position and shape according to the influence of the forces. Through their density and location, the particles enable the visualization of movement, speed and direction as they are attracted by different motion forces on the site. From the particle studies, a series of phase portraits were captured that expose the cycles of movement over a period of time. Instead of freezing a single instant of the particle study, an animation "sweep" technique captures a sequence of positions through a phase of their motion. Particles released both from the west façade of the bus terminal and on the street level of Ninth Avenue are the source of these sweeps. Because these particles have elasticity and density, and because they move in a space with gravitational force, the paths take the shape of the gravity-resistant arches. These phase portraits are then threaded by curvilinear vectors. These vectors became the center lines for a secondary structure of tubular beams that link the ramps, existing buildings and the Port Authority Bus Terminal. Eleven tensile fabric surfaces were then stretched across these tubes as an enclosure and protective surface. The tensile surfaces provide a screen for the projection of transportation information visible to pedestrians and passengers while providing a surface for the diffusion of light from below.

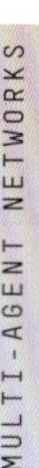

I've Heard About
New Territories/R&Sie(n)
Unbuilt 2005
Paris, France

8.3a

8.3b

8.3c

I've Heard About by R&Sie(n) is an endlessly adaptable living environment whose indeterminate and interminable form is locally defined by the behaviors of its collective citizenry. Operating akin to a termite mound whose material traces engender a series of local responses from other agents within its system, this communal habitat grows as an ever-evolving swarm of matter that integrates the constructive methods of its fluid architecture into the very processes of its formal and material emergence. The project is an architectural urbanism—architectural in its concentration and dense clustering of adjacent units—and urban in its scale and the potential diversity and local behavior of its infrastructure. Operating as an inhabitable biostructural landscape, its ability to grow in relation to environmental conditions such as light and air, material parameters such as the structural and tectonic limits of its branching morphology and programmatic demands, such as its capacity to adapt to the desires, relationships, and contingencies of its inhabitants, is controlled by algorithms that determine the ways in which these various and often conflicting inputs are transcoded and interact and by growth scripts that prompt a response to these inputs through changes in its evolving physical biotropic structure. This structure literally grows through a form of additive manufacturing—the ongoing accretion and deposition of material—that is controlled by Viab, an autonomous construction machine and architecturally scaled 3D-printing robot that is responsible for secreting the architecture's contour-crafted enclosure. Similar to the polyptych growth of coral, the project's architectural construction by Viab does not precede its inhabitation, but rather lives along side it, operating as a responsive machine that is in sync with its collective occupation.

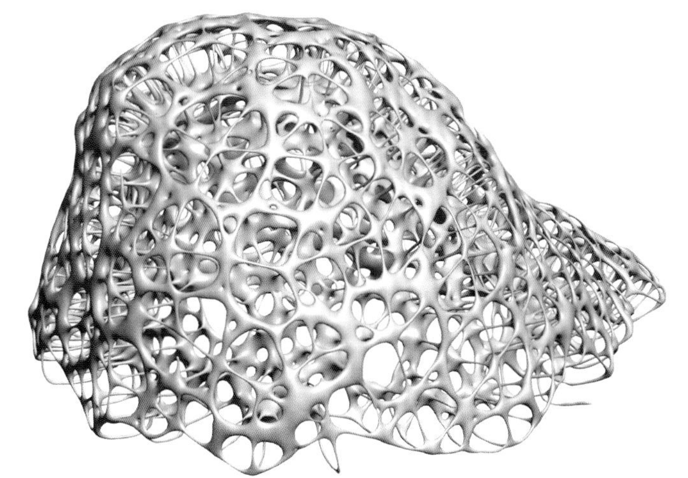

8.3d

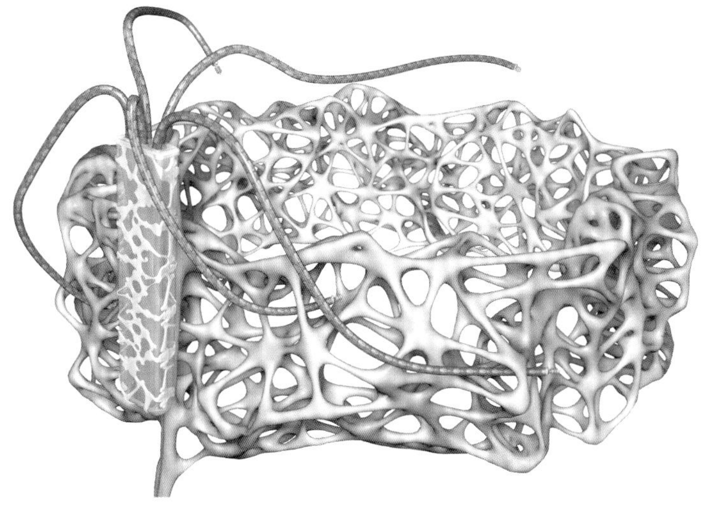

8.3e

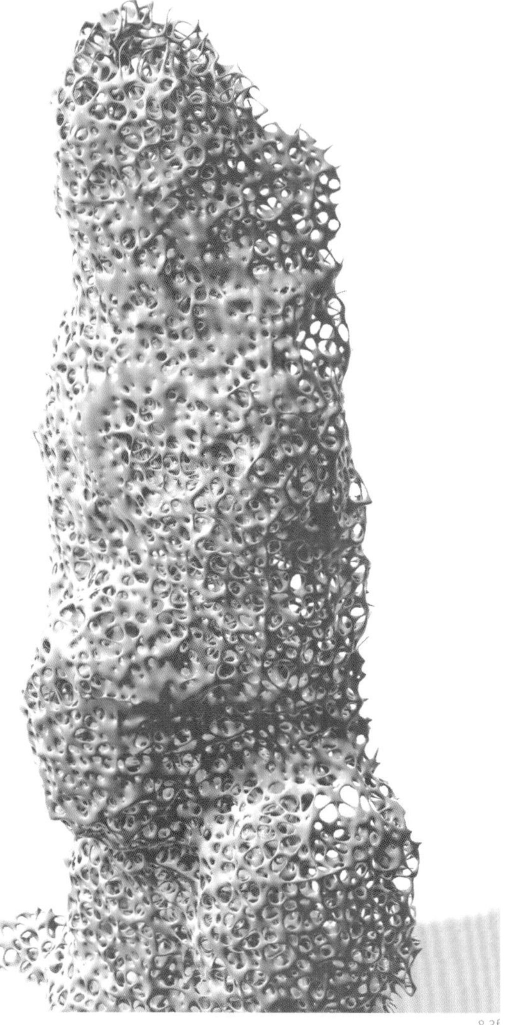

8.3f

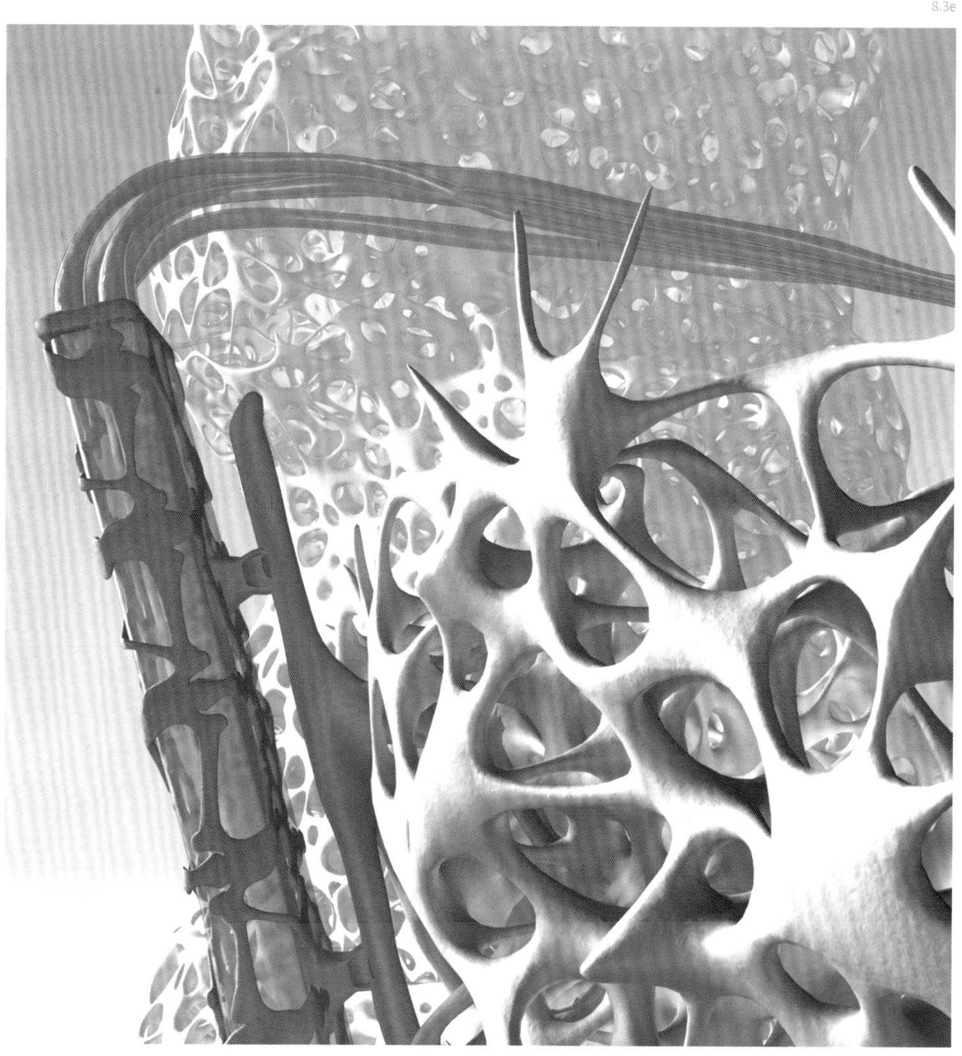

8.3g

Smart Town

New Territories/R&Sie(n)

Unbuilt 2007

Korea

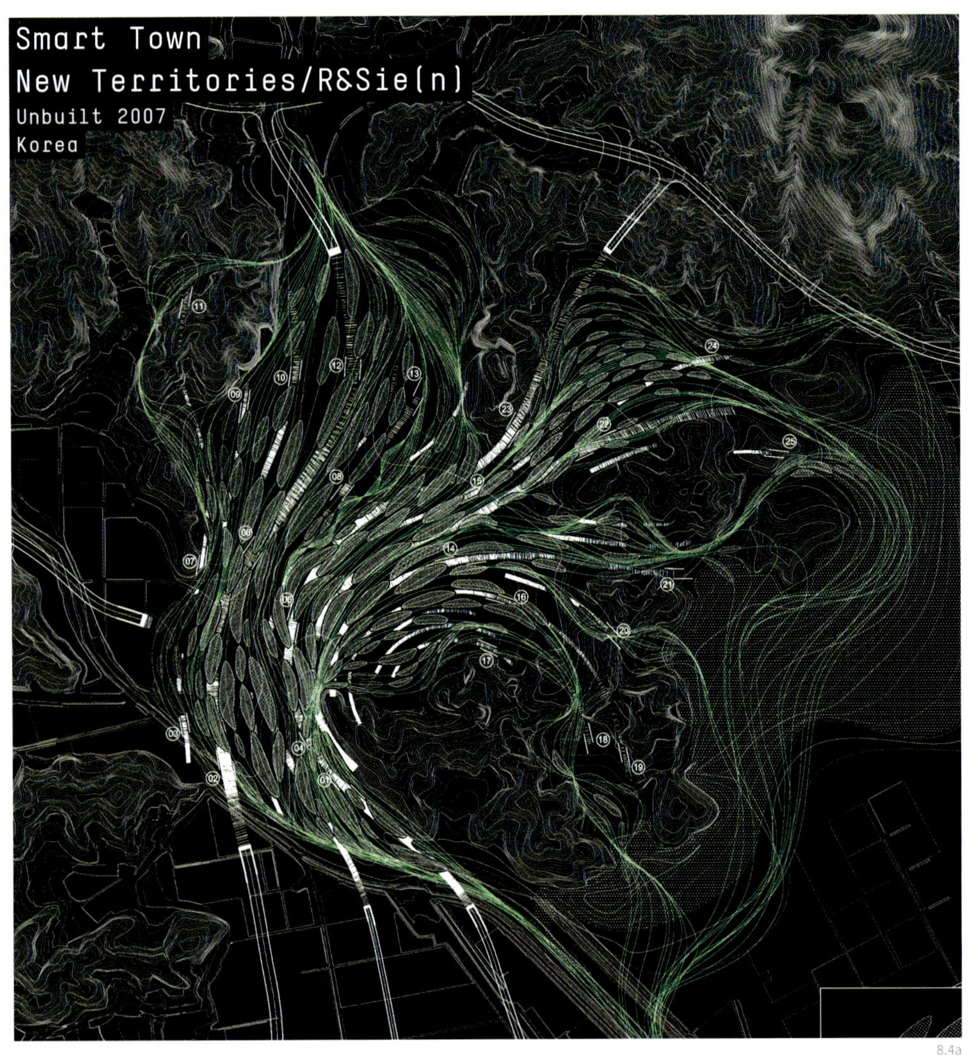

8.4a

Smart Town, a masterplan for an administrative town in Korea, is algorithmically generated according to the shifting relationships of geographic, programmatic and environmental parameters that control its evolution. The urban morphologies of the town are produced through the interaction of three automatic scripts: a Flow script that is a generator of urban grids and determines the relationship to the site, the organizational substrate of the whole, and the distances between buildings; a ZXY scaling script that involves processes of urban densification determining, with the flow script, the combination, programmatic distribution, position, and size of buildings; and a Nerves script that manages the indoor-outdoor interface through the development and robotic assembly of the façade. Influenced by the feature's of the site's natural geography and environment, a new inhabitable topography emerges from the interaction between flows and the characteristics of the terrain determining the overall profile of the city. Rather than operating as a static abstract form laid upon the site, the initial organizational grid of Smart Town is drawn by mobile particles and trajectories flowing through the site that follow, respond to, and preserve its morphological properties such that the dominant features of its existing natural topography remain as "green zones" within the city. In addition to determining the city's organization and its distribution of green space and urban agriculture, these trajectories also locate the infrastructural network, which includes a subterranean vehicular system buried five meters below the new grade level and a smart network for bicycles and pedestrians above. The different administrative, commercial, residential and cultural/recreational programmatic requirements of the masterplan are then embedded and distributed along these mobile vectors as a programmatic necklace by the ZXY script that automatically incrementally shapes these into spaces of varying amplitude—continuous urban forms mimetic of the morphology of the region—according to topographical, volumetric, and relational parameters and in response to local pressures on the site. The final script determines the external skin of the buildings—a weave of vertical topographic contours that define the perimeter structural framework of the undulating volumes and green glazed infill panels with their own variable micro-topography—constructed and assembled by a swarm of mobile robots.

8.4b

8.4c

8.4d

8.4e

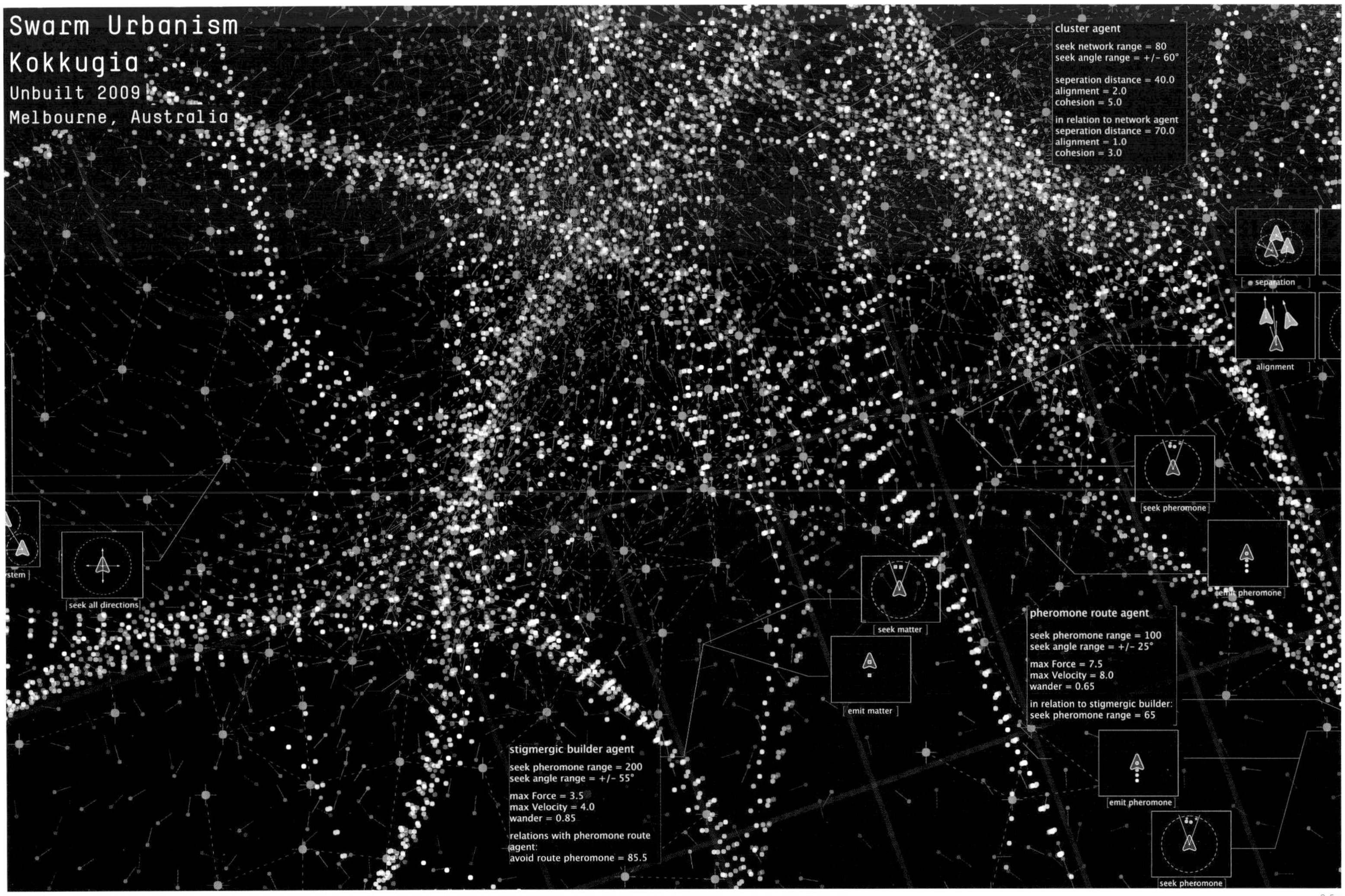

Swarm Urbanism

Kokkugia

Unbuilt 2009

Melbourne, Australia

8.5a

This speculative proposal posits an urban design methodology based on the emergent capacities of swarm intelligence in rethinking the redevelopment of the Melbourne Docklands. Swarm systems involve the local interaction of autonomous agents, which give rise to emergent behavior and the self-organization of structures. An application of swarm logic to urbanism enables a shift from notions of the master plan to that of the master algorithm as an urban design tool. This shift changes the conception of urban design from a sequential set of decisions at reducing scales, to a simultaneous process in which a set of micro or local decisions interact to generate a complex urban system. Rather than designing an urban plan that meets a set of criteria, urban imperatives are parametrically programmed into a set of agents, which are able to self-organize. This conception of urbanism generates systems that are flexible to respond to the constantly changing political, economic, and social pressures of urban development. The decentralized structure of multi-agent systems changes the nature of hierarchy in urbanism. Hierarchies of scale and intensity are of course imperative to urbanism, however, the swarm logic developed for the Melbourne flattens hierarchy within the design process. All elements of the urban fabric are conceived of as possessing agency, enabling them to interact without a sequential design hierarchy. Rather, the hierarchy of intensities at a macro scale become an emergent outcome of a self-organizing operation. Agents within this system are not generic, instead there is an ecology of agent systems that interact, each set of agents programmed with their own desires and information. In this first category agents operate to self-organize program through a process of stigmergic growth similar to the logic of termite colonies in aggregating matter to form termite mounds. The second category of agents work in a similar manner to the processes that govern the self-organization of slime mold cells into minimal path systems or the collective organization of ants to create bridges. These agents are primarily used to generate infrastructural and circulatory networks. Consequently this project isn't an attempt to map the motion of swarming agents in creating an urban plan, but instead to create a system capable of generating a collective intelligence in self-organizing urban structures.

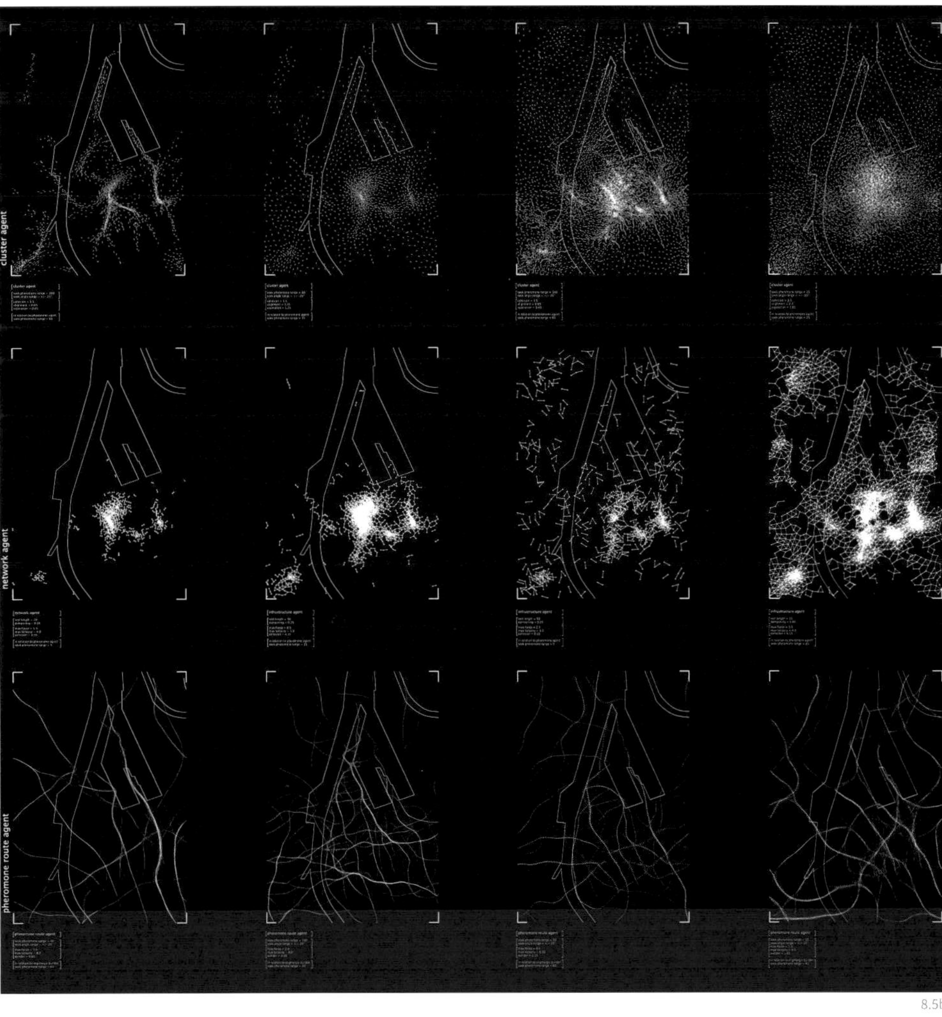

8.5b

The Rise
CITA
Built 2012
Paris, France

8.6a

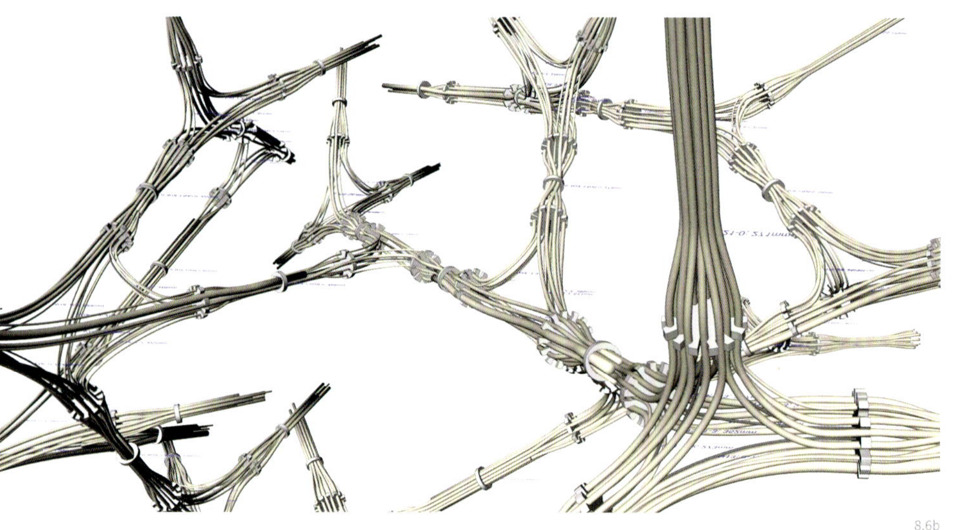

8.6b

"The Rise" is a research-based installation by the Center for Information Technology and Architecture for the EDF Foundation's exhibition: *ALIVE: Designing with Living Systems*. The work is guided by the concept of a growing architecture, able to sense and dynamically adapt to its environment while responding to its own material performance and behavioral constraints. The approach hybridizes material experimentation and prototyping with generative computational strategies modeled on living vegetative systems to simulate the complex arborescent growth patterns of variably sized bundles of rattan core as these multiply, bend, branch, and recombine into a distributed, networked assembly. The project draws from an investigation of leaf venation systems and the relationship of the hormone auxin—the mechanism for plant differentiation during formation—to cellular growth patterns and the emergence of plant geometry. Akin to the geotropism and phototropism of plants, the installation therefore grows in response to its environment, thickening or extending its bundled branches according to variations of light, the self-weight of its structure, and the spatial parameters of its surroundings. Parametric growth algorithms are used to create a self-propagating structure where "shoots" can accrete, bifurcate (branch), climb, and converge (graft) to increase the structure's overall strength and stability. The interwoven branching structure consists of 5, 10, and 19 mm thicknesses of rattan core wood harvested from Malaysia that are bundled using plastic nodes that are CNC machined to hold and organize the individual wooden members. The woody material is soft and comprised almost entirely of continuous, tightly packed hollow fibers that lack internal cellular bracing, which accounts for its extreme flexibility in bending yet requires a reliance on other plants for structure, making it a preferred material for the weaving of furniture and baskets. In The Rise, these characteristics are exploited to enable a more dynamic, woven geometry, while using bundling, redundant triangulation, and grafting to ensure its self-support.

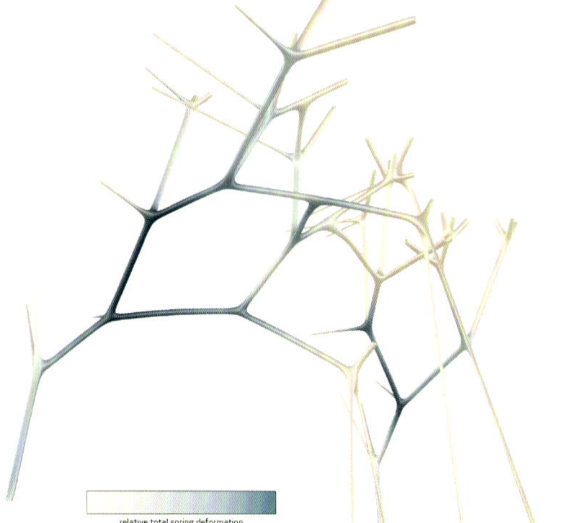

8.6c

8.6d

Composite Wing
Kokkugia + Roland Snooks
Built 2014
Melbourne, Australia

Installed as part of *The Future Is Here* exhibition at the RMIT Design Hub in Melbourne, Composite Wing is a composite fiber installation that compresses surface, structure, and ornament into one intricate and irreducible assemblage, amalgamating and extending three strands of intertwined research in algorithmic design, robotic fabrication, and composite fiber materials. The project consists of two large, doubly curved, translucent fiberglass surfaces that fill and float within the space—one suspended from the wall and the other mounted on the floor—each laced with an intricate, curvilinear pattern that appears to dance across its surface. This inlaid structural network, fabricated from foam and silicon, operates as a series of continuous beams whose pattern is generated using a multi-agent algorithm based on the self-organizing logic and emergent behaviors of swarm intelligence. As a reference to their mode of derivation, these beams are therefore described as "agentBodies," and provide not only the formal organization and ornamental surface design for the project, but also the necessary structural depth for the molded and layered 3-mm-thick fiberglass to be self-supporting. There are two scales of these agentBodies in the project—large foam bodies that are milled and small silicon bodies that are robotically extruded, both of which are painted and hand-finished before being laminated into the fiberglass surface. Akin to the intricate structural pattern of a dragonfly's wing that enables its expansive wingspan, the surface of Composite Wing gains its strength through the location of these beams in addition to the fine-scale surface articulation that together allow the 65 m² surface to remain extremely thin while spanning and cantilevering considerable distances.

8.7a

8.7b

8.7c

8.7d

Subdivided Columns
Michael Hansmeyer

Built 2010

Orleans, France and Gwangju, South Korea

8.8a

This project involves the algorithmic, generative design of a column order based on subdivision processes, exploring how subdivision can define and embellish this column order with an elaborate system of ornament. An abstracted Doric column is used as an input form, which conveys significant topographical and topological information about the form to be generated, including data about the proportions of the column's shaft, capital, and base, and its fluting and entasis. The input form is tagged to allow the subdivision process to distinguish between individual components. This allows a heterogeneous application of the process, with distinct local parameter settings that enable endless permutations of the columns as the parameters are adjusted. The single subdivision process generates the form at all scales, from the overall elements and their proportions and curvatures, to local surface formations, down to the columns' micro-structures. Information is integrated at all scales without repetition. The result is a series of columns exhibiting highly specific local conditions as well as overall coherence and continuity, whereby the complexity of the form contrasts with the simplicity of its generative process. The final 2.7-meter-high columns were fabricated as a layered model using CNC-milled 1 mm ABS sheets, where the six million faces of the intricate 3D model are serially intersected with planes representing the sheets, which are then hollowed out to reduce the weight of the whole.

8.8b

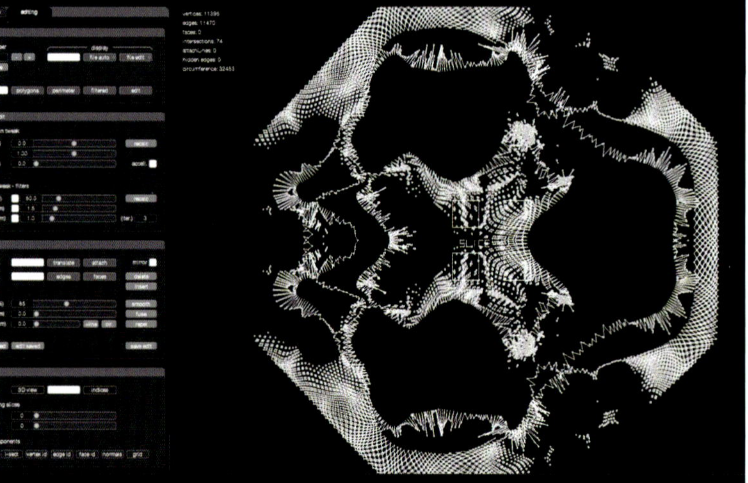

8.8c

8.8d

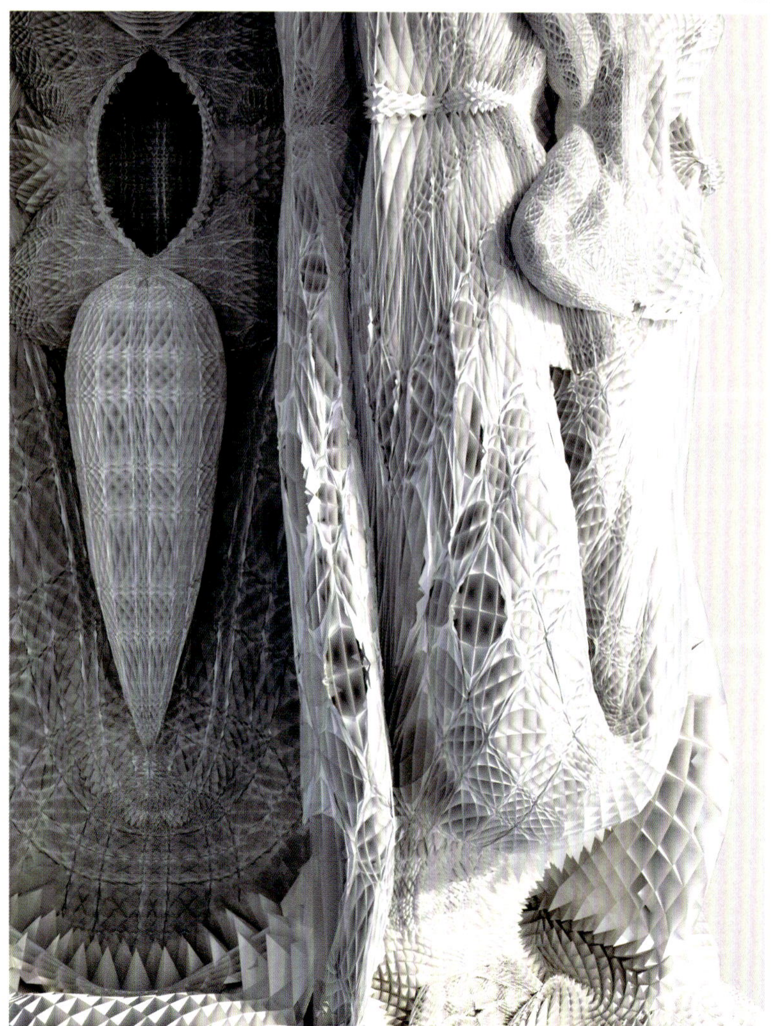

8.8e

Digital Grotesque I and II
Michael Hansmeyer / Benjamin Dillenburger
Built 2013 and 2017
Orleans and Paris, France

8.9a

8.9b

The Digital Grotesque project, rather than being developed using traditional compositional design methods, uses algorithms that define procedures to generate forms that appear both synthetic and organic. Although the algorithms are deterministic as they do not incorporate randomness, the results are not necessarily foreseeable. The combination of computational design and high-resolution additive manufacturing lead to a nonstandardized, highly differentiated, and spatially complex architecture that is defined at the scale of millimeters where every detail of the architecture is generated through customized algorithms, without any manual intervention. Digital Grotesque II, a full-scale, 3.2-meter-high, 3D-printed sandstone grotto that premiered at the Centre Pompidou's *Imprimer le monde* exhibition thus amplifies the generative potential of these tools by expanding their capacity for agency, whereby the computer can learn to generate architectural structures that evoke interest, curiosity, and an emotional response. The project attempts to identify geometric properties of architectural form that can be measured and correlated with human perception and desirable emotions. These include the capacity to experience changes in a form's appearance or visibility through a shift in the position or perspective of the viewer, the degree of geometric information that cannot be simplified through symmetry groups, and the form's depth-complexity identified as the measure of topological alternation between solid and void. Instead of explicitly programming a set of predefined rules to reach these design criteria, the computer learns to calibrate the design with the goal of evoking stimulation and the interest of the beholder. The computer is thus trained by using design variations that have been evaluated online by hundreds of volunteers where abstract geometric properties are paired with statistical data measuring viewer preference, as quantified through the number of views, viewing duration, sharing, etc., such that it constructs a model of the relation between abstract geometric properties and human perception without any architectural precedents and without direct control of the form that is generated. The resulting architecture is at once disorientating, intriguing, and evocative without being prescriptive, exposing the potential agency of computation and a new form of human-machine interaction in the design process.

8.9c

8.9d

8.9e

8.9f

Aegis Hyposurface

dECOi + hyposurface team

Built 2003

Cambridge, United States

8.10a

8.10b

8.10c

8.10d

8.10e

Aegis Hyposurface is a tessellated, pneumatically controlled, interactive display surface that can potentially erupt into an infinite number of undulating surface topographies or patterned events as it is parametrically programmed to respond to a range of data forms or sensory inputs. The movements of this terrain-like metallic surface can be autoplastic (determinate) or alloplastic (indeterminate) , that is, either mathematically predefined to generate dynamic choreographed patterns and fluid sequences or programmed based on interactive rules to be responsive to external stimuli such as sound, movement or temperature and thus operate with more unpredictable forms of live data. Goulthorpe refers to this as a "translation surface ... a synaesthetic transfer device, a surface-effect as [a] cross-wiring of the senses." As a physical analog to, and extension of, the pixelated computer screen, the potential of the Hyposurface resides in the ways in which its tangible yet highly mediated surface landscape can be reconfigured by the real-time algorithmic information driving its protean morphology. Hidden behind the triangulated, facetted surface is a gridded bed of pneumatic actuator cylinders—a framework of horizontal pistons driven by compressed air that are controlled by digital signals. These pistons rapidly move in and out according to programmed sequences that can vary the speed, amplitude, and direction of movement. The linear force that these pistons produce is then transferred to, and used to, temporarily displace the adjacent facets of the surface. An interior rubber membrane that conjoins the pistons with the vertices of the tessellated matrix ensures the continuity and flexibility of the surface's topography, while its triangulated metal pixels that reflect light and color, geometricize, and thus articulate, its architectonic folds. Initially developed for the 2002 Venice Biennale and later installed at the CeBIT Technology Fair in Germany (2003) and the Ars Electronica in Austria (2004), the Hyposurface prototype has evolved through multiple incarnations, each iteration advancing its role as new dynamic form of tangible media and interactive architecture.

Hylozoic Ground
Philip Beesley
Built 2010, 2016
Venice, Italy

Hylozoic Ground transformed the Canadian Pavilion of the 2010 Venice Biennale into a living artificial forest—an intricate lattice of transparent acrylic meshwork links, covered with a network of interactive mechanical fronds, petals, filters, and whiskers. To animate this complex suspended landscape of lily canopies, anemone weeds, hylozoic burrs, cricket clusters, clamping needles, breathing pore columns and other interwoven kinetic devices, tens of thousands of lightweight digitally fabricated, interconnected components were fitted with microprocessors and proximity sensors that react to the presence of humans and their bodily movements. Functioning like a giant lung that breathes in and out around its occupants, this artificial rainforest-like environment envelopes its inhabitants within a responsive biomimetic web of continuously moving contiguous elements whose precise geometric forms and carefully interlocked assemblies are seemingly countered by the animate affective nature of the whole. Akin to the microscopic complexity of the biomorphology that it emulates, each synthetic botanical specimen is a compound assembly made up of numerous elements whose geometry and machinic laser-cut contours, in combination with their repetition, variation, and diversification, allow them to aggregate into larger wholes—interlinked lattices that architecturalize the fibrous celluloid structure of plants and their flowering symmetrical blossoms. Arrays of touch sensors and shape-memory alloy (SMA) actuators, a type of nonmotorized kinetic mechanism embedded and interwoven within these assemblies, create waves of empathic motion in response to the ambulatory and gestural movements of the living, luring visitors into the eerie, shimmering depths of this mythical landscape, a fragile animated forest of light.

8.11a

8.11b

8.11c

8.11d

HygroScope Project
Achim Menges + Steffen Reichert ICD

Built 2012
Paris, France

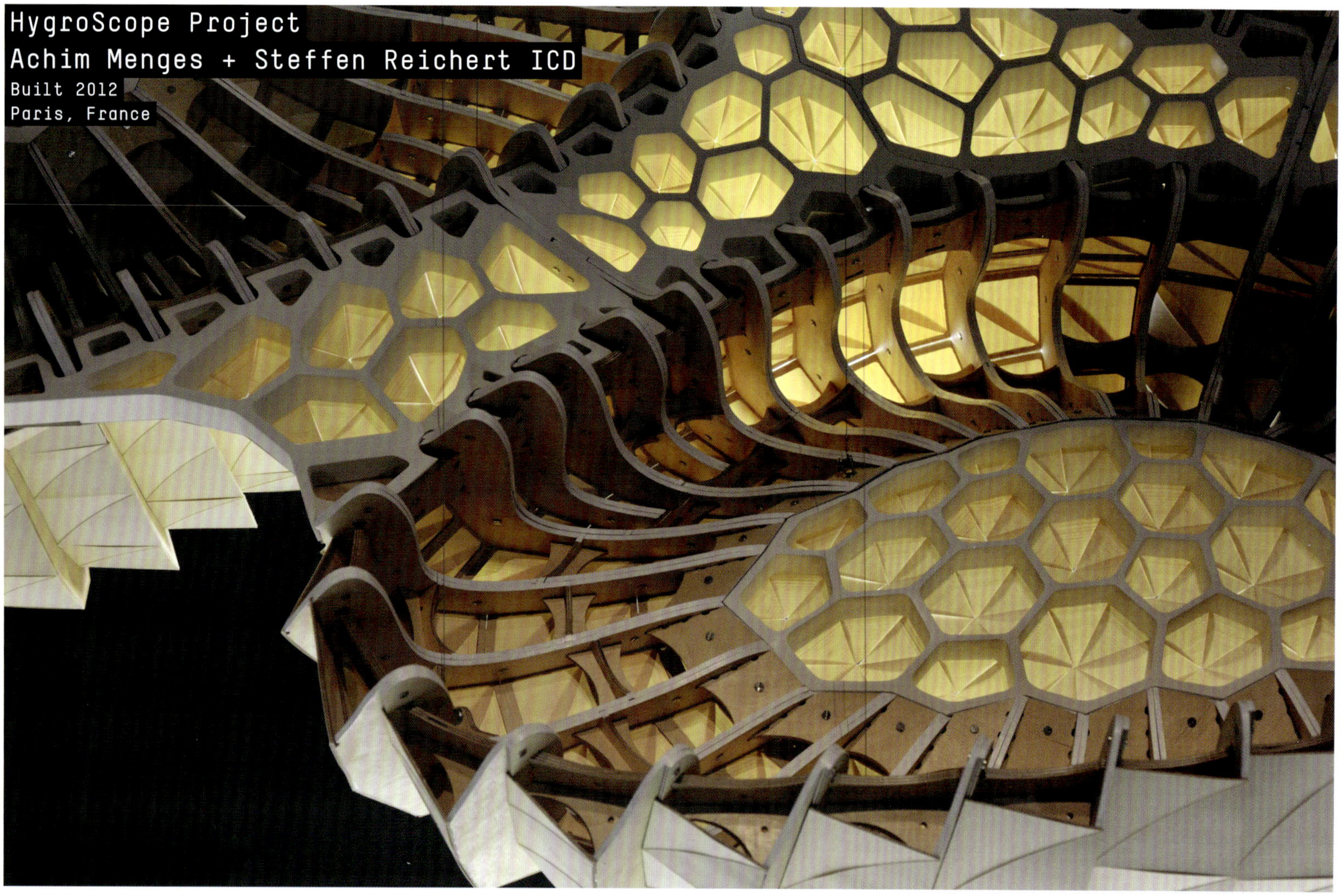

8.12a

HygroScope explores a novel mode of responsive architecture based on the combination of material inherent behavior and computational morphogenesis. Climate-responsiveness in architecture is typically conceived as a technical function enabled by myriad mechanical and electronic sensing, actuating, and regulating devices. In contrast to this superimposition of high-tech equipment on inert material, biological natural systems follow a fundamentally different, no-tech strategy where the responsive capacity is quite literally ingrained in the material itself. This project employs similar design strategies of physically programming a material system that neither requires any kind of mechanical or electronic control, nor the supply of external energy whereby material computes form in feedback with the environment. In HygroScope, the dimensional instability of wood in relation to moisture content is thus employed to construct a climate responsive architectural morphology. Suspended within a humidity-controlled glass case the model opens and closes in response to climate changes with no need for any technical equipment or energy. Within the case the climate corresponds to an accelerated database of the relative humidity in Paris. In this way, the case functions less as a separation from the interior space of the Centre Pompidou, arguably one of the most stable climate zones in the world, but rather provides a virtual connection to the outside, showing the subtle variations in humidity levels that we hardly ever consciously perceive through the system's silent movement. These cyclic changes are interspersed with spontaneous climate events triggered by threshold transitions within a second data set of visitor vapor emission. These fluctuations in relative humidity trigger the silent changes of material-innate movement in the structure. The resultant autonomous, passive actuation of the surface provides for a unique convergence of environmental and spatial experience. The perception of the delicate locally varied and ever-changing environmental dynamics is intensified through the subtle and silent movement of the meteorosensitive architectural morphology. The changing surface literally embodies the capacity to sense, actuate, and react, all within the material itself where the material structure itself is the machine.

8.12b

8.12c

8.12d

Oculus
DO|SU
Built 2016
Los Angeles, United States

Oculus is one of a series of innovative architectural projects that uses thermobimetal to explore the physical potential of material to be responsive and to operate as a self-shading and self-ventilating device. The responsive oculus—an automatic-operating aperture—can be triggered by the flame of a candle or other heat source. The eight identical pieces mimic the flickering of the flame and take advantage of the natural properties of thermobimetal, a smart sheet metal made of two alloys of metal laminated together. The layers have different coefficients of expansion and automatically curl when the temperature rises. Each thermobimetal piece is carefully designed to be a universal and repetitive geometry that ingeniously straddles two openings for the highest amount of efficiency in manufacturing. One single piece, when rotationally installed, can make a continuous field of oculi of unlimited size. The surface will open and close as the temperature changes controlling the passage of air, temperature, light, and view without the use of energy. The most developed application of the single oculus for architecture is a product by DOSU Studio Architecture called Tracheolis. The oculi are designed to conform to irregular openings parametrically and perform as valves to control the flow of heated or cooled air in a 3D-printed concrete block system. Mimicking the tracheoli of grasshoppers, the temperature of a building is intended to be modulated through the outer wall by these individual valve controls for highest efficacy. The product proposes the replacement of a standard concrete block system with one that is lighter weight, easy to fabricate using 3D printing technology, and with added performance capabilities such as releasing smoke during fires and other life-saving situations.

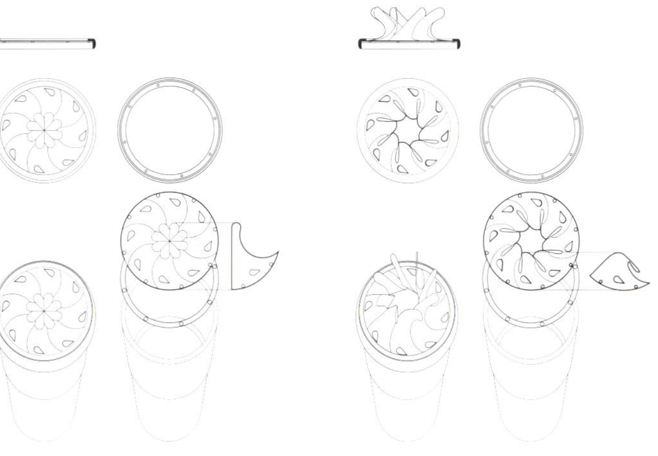

8.13a

8.13b

8.13c

8.13d

8.13e

White Noise White Light

Höweler+Yoon

Built 2004

Athens, Greece

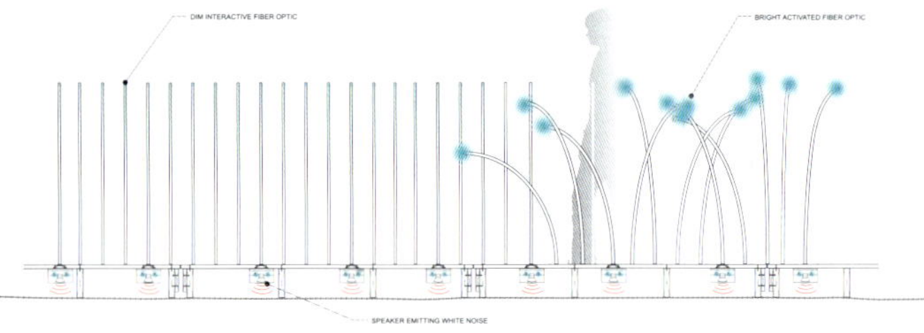

8.14a

White Noise White Light was one of nine interactive urban installations commissioned and installed for the Athens 2004 Olympics. Part of the programmed Listen to Athens route, the project inserted a luminous, interactive, sonorous landscape within an urban public plaza to create a choreographed field in flux. The installation consists of four hundred vertically oriented, semi-flexible, fiber-optic strands that are arranged in a grid and “grow” out of a raised wooden platform. These translucent strands, whose flexibility enables them to bend, sway, and oscillate as a tall grass field might in response to the directional forces of the bodies that traverse it, collectively operate as a responsive infrastructural field that is activated by the movement of pedestrians as they occupy the site. Custom-designed electronic modules contain passive infrared (PIR) sensors that are capable of registering the proximity of visitors. When triggered by the sensor, each electronic module delivers a degree of white noise and white light, emitting light through the fiber-optic stalks and sound through a small hidden speaker mounted to the underside of the raised deck. The light and sound increase as visitors approach and decrease as visitors move away. The trajectory of each visitor’s passage through the field thereby actuates a sonic and visible wake. Fleeting programmatic choreographies are thus transcoded through electronic circuitry that signals physical systems to materialize and amplify the transient movements inhabiting the work. Within the field, flickering white lights signal the presence of others, and white noise is emitted that muffles and mutes the sounds of the surrounding city. As the territory of stalks is inhabited over time, the movement of visitors transforms the static field into an unpredictable synthesis of space, light, and sound.

8.14b

8.14c

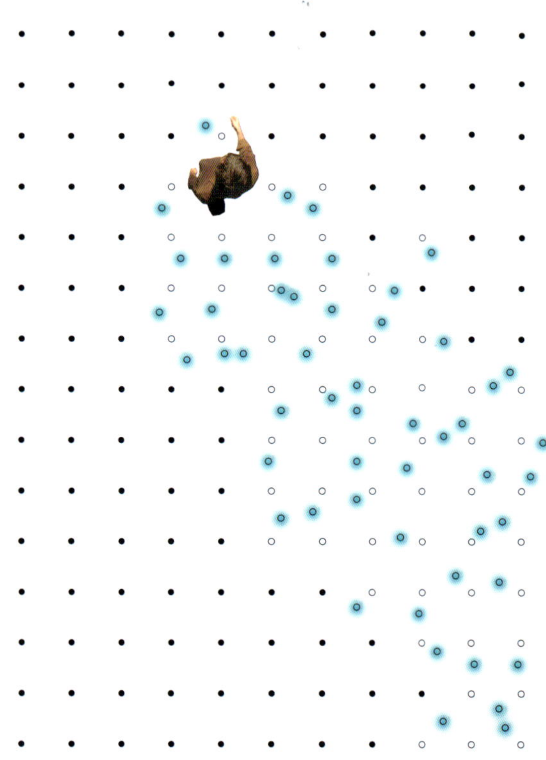

8.14d

8.14e

8.14f

Windscreen
Höweler + Yoon
Built 2011
Cambridge, United Kingdom

8.15a

8.15b

8.15c

8.15d

Windscreen is an environmentally responsive, kinetic screen system designed as part of a series of temporary installations developed for a festival celebrating the 150th anniversary of the founding of the Massachusetts Institute of Technology. Located along the southern façade of Green Building 54, the project is constituted by a pixelated array of wind-powered micro-turbines that directly transcode wind velocity into an elusive flickering field of light. These small-scale turbines, each consisting of three digitally fabricated, plastic components folded to catch the wind, are vertically stacked and woven into a diagonally braced, tensioned-cable lattice network to minimize the disruption of the system's structural support. As the wind flows invisibly across the screen, it causes each of the turbines to spin, which then activates and directly powers the vertically oriented tubular light embedded at the center of each rotating element. As the wind increases its speed and shifts direction, its effects are immediately registered and indexed in the rotational velocity of the turbines and thus the changing intensity of lights distributed across the screen's surface. The generation and consumption of energy harvested from the wind is thus simultaneously translated into legible information and immersive affect, exposing, through the subtle balance of movement and light, the potential untapped energy of the wind and the productive transformation of this endlessly renewable resource from one material matrix into another.

Lightswarm
FutureForms

Built 2014

San Francisco, United States

Lightswarm is an interactive light installation consisting of a vertically-arranged pixelated field of illuminated fins located behind the south facing façade of the Yerba Buena Center for the Arts in San Francisco. This swarm of glowing modules, which pulse and vary in luminous intensity and color, are designed to be activated by the sonorous landscape of the city. The acoustic vibrations of the vicinity's ambient sounds, from vehicles and nearby cyclists to the muffled conversations of those walking by, are captured by a series of networked "sound sensing spiders" distributed across, and affixed to the façade. The real-time acoustic data collected by these sensors is then transcoded (using Arduino hardware with Grasshopper and Firefly software) into a set of physical responses that enable the visualization of the urban soundscape. Like a school of teaming fish in perpetual motion, swarms of light are propelled across the façade whose wavelike motions are augmented by the apparent rotation and shifting directionality of the fins—each a perforated translucent shell, laser-cut out of recyclable PET plastic and synthetic paper, that encloses a 3D printed component encasing the microcontroller and addressable LED module. To amplify the perceived movement of the swarm and the intensity of light as it cascades across the field, each fin is rotated about its center horizontal axis, using its local geometry and rotational mobility to simultaneously track and underscore the directionality of the swarm's movement. Rather than generating a one-to-one response between acoustic data and LED light and color values, the system is designed using swarm algorithms to provide greater continuity to the whole. The algorithm is used to compare sensor data and determine the location of inputs of greatest value in order to set these as shifting attractor points for the virtual movement of the swarm. As these points change location over time they trigger continuously emerging and dynamic fluid behaviors that are rendered evident by the changing luminosity and color of the swarm.

8.16a

8.16b

8.16c

8.16d

Urban Syncopation
Scaleshift/Beites & Co./X-Topia
Built 2016
Toronto, Canada

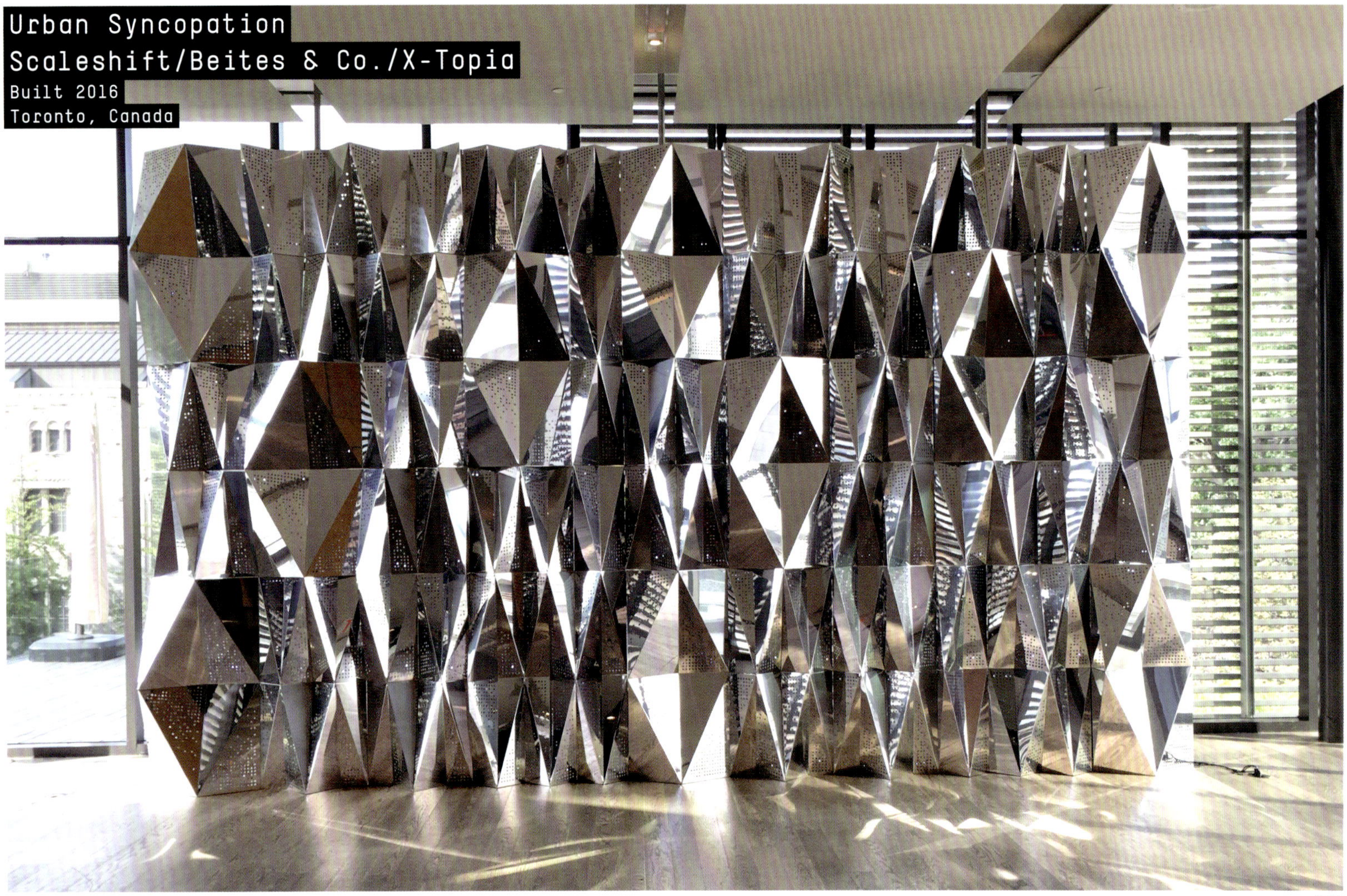

8.17a

8.17b

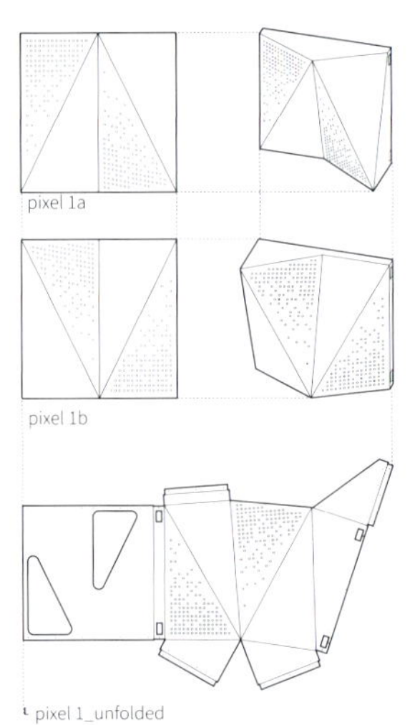

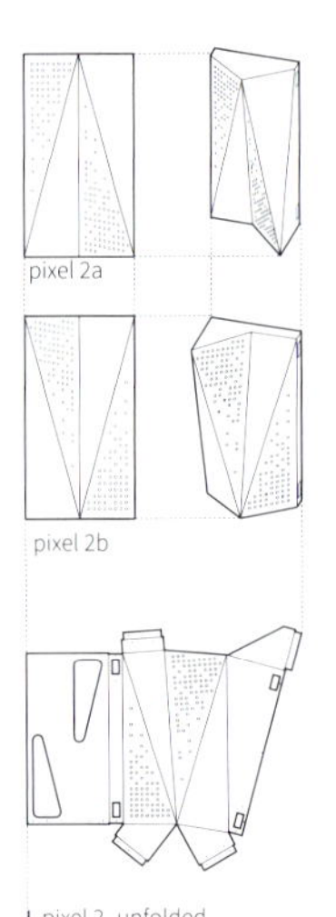

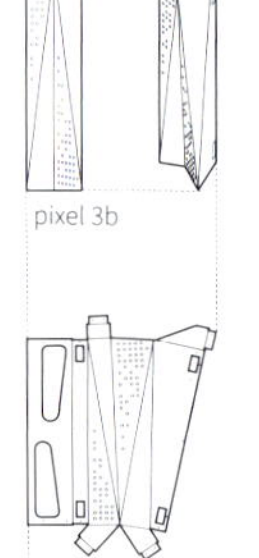

8.17c

Urban Syncopation is an undulating metal wall system and audio-reactive light installation—a performative screen that temporarily inhabits the city and functions as a responsive, dynamic urban interface. As in the encryption of data that underlies the invisible orgware of the city's systems, the patterned, faceted surface of this installation acts as an infrastructural device and living thickened topography that collects, transcodes, and re-transmits, in a rhythmic syncopated fashion, the collective heartbeat of the city as this is interwoven with the reflected movements of its immediate environs. The work is a repository of urban information that renders visible the unseen traces of the city's occupation while simultaneously weaving them into a new architectural and spatial network. The patterned surface of Urban Syncopation is defined through a series of faceted, mirrored, and perforated "pixels" that are rhythmically arrayed according to rules that modulate their width, depth, and triangulated surface topography. These variations in the pattern, perceived as lateral compressions and expansions of the folded undulating surface, emphasize the tracking and directionality of the way in which the information is redeployed across the thickened skin as it captures and spatializes temporal and aural inputs. The pattern is an interdependent, repetitive system generated through operations of folding, scaling, stacking, and weaving so that multiple elements are integrated into a new visual, spatial, and tectonic configuration. Each pixel is constructed out of a CNC-cut, perforated, scored, and folded aluminum composite surface. The rhythmic series of faceted pixels, which passively fragment and reflect surrounding motion, are organized into six horizontal strata, each of which receives data from a different remote downtown site and that collectively refer to the layered streets that constitute the downtown fabric of Toronto. Sound sensors located along commercial east-west urban corridors and along with those situated within the immediate environment of the piece, are employed to track urban activity levels throughout the day and night and transcode this data into a rhythmic series of pulsing lights that undulate and move laterally across and within each of the strata. This layering of passive and active systems productively recircuits the movements of collective urban life while weaving them into a single syncopated surface.

8.17d

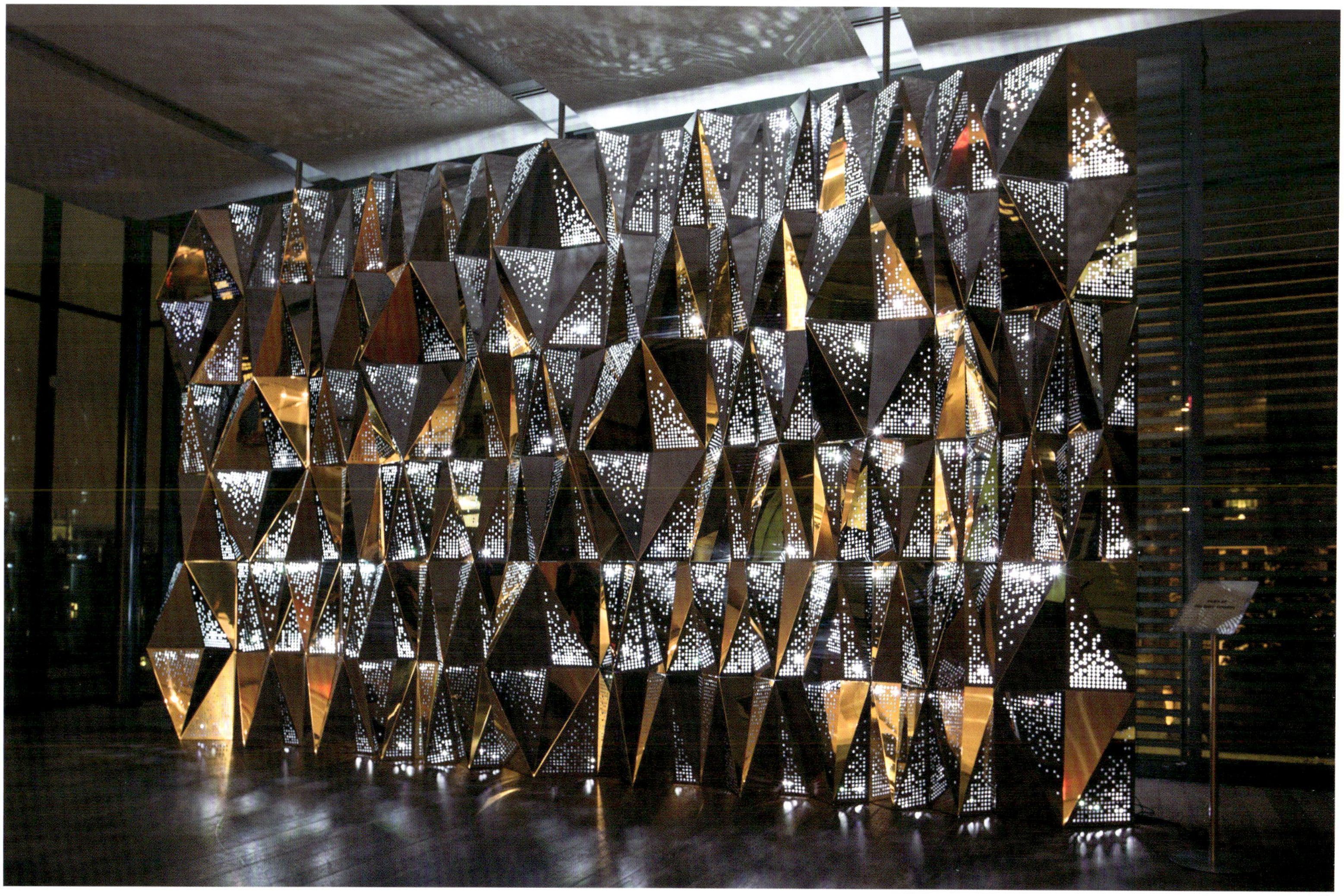

8.17e

8.17f

8.17g

8.17h

8.17i

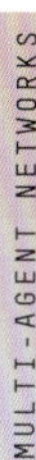

Ostenda Illuminata
Networked Public Space

Built 2020
Charlottesville, United States

8.18a

Ostenda illuminata is an interactive prototype for urban public place-making that seeks to advance data literacy through digitally mediated public spaces. It uses urban sensing to gather environmental information and respond in real time through patterned illumination while making data and analytics publicly available through online networks. The ground of the project, defined by a series of circular geometries, consists of solid islands of varying diameters and thicknesses that establish a multifunctional aggregate topography that serves as a shell to host sensors, network nodes, and power sources that connect to an artificial plant species above. The collective system consists of three different island sizes designed for human-scaled occupation with integrated public seating elements. The islands are populated with an ecology of six distinct species, and their surfaces are perforated with openings that function as illuminated earth holes accessing the technology embedded below. "Moss" organized as connected patches of small responsive light elements create a surface that illuminates when approached. "Shrubs," consisting of a field of variable vertical elements, respond to noise through the intensity of their illumination, and the largest "tree-like" elements, with a vertical trunk and canopy, collect sound data over the day and calculate aggregated noise pollution that is communicated through bright red light when mean thresholds are surpassed. To inform community members of environmental changes of collective interest, all data are stored in a timeseries database and rendered publicly accessible through web-based real-time data visualization. Data collection and environmental sensing are meant to reveal environmental conditions that vary over time and to address public health concerns that are less identifiable through direct human sensing. The project thus operates as a technologically enhanced "species" that consists of multiple ecologies and multi-agent components defining its typological architectures, responsive technologies, and codes, as well as forms of stakeholder engagement. The concept of ecology is applied to conceptualize interactions between different project components and the emergent behavior it produces. It can thus be compared with a living system that consists of architectural, technological, and digital components as well as human-related interactions and reactions that are embedded in an environment and connected through the Internet.

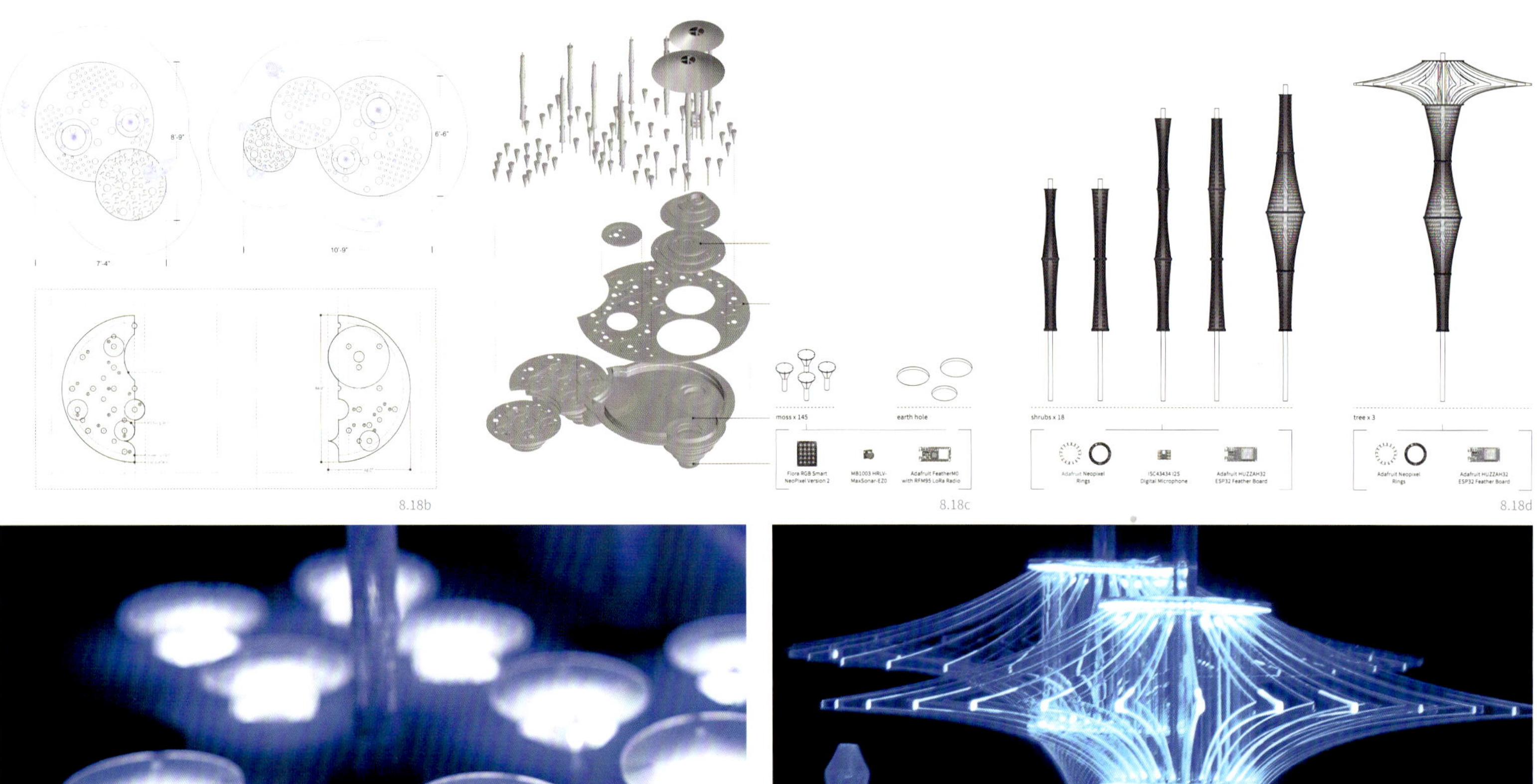

8.18b 8.18c 8.18d

8.18e

8.18f

8.18g

8.18h

Ada

Jenny Sabin Studio with Microsoft Research

Built 2019

Seattle, United States

8.19a

8.19b

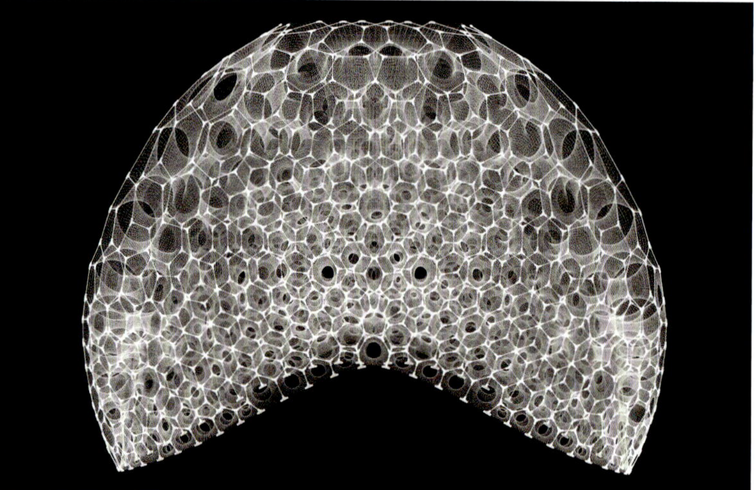

8.19c

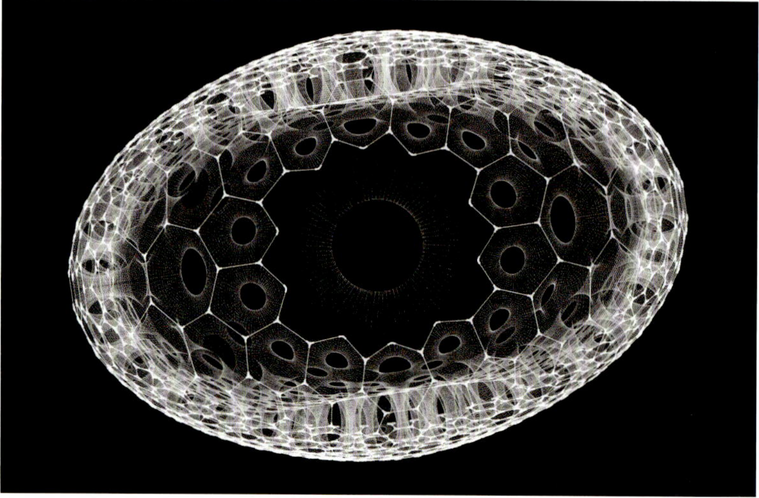

8.19d

8.19e

8.19f

Named after the polymath, mathematician, first computer programmer, and early innovator of the computer age, Ada Lovelace, this collaborative project with Microsoft Research embodies performance, material innovation, human-centered adaptive architecture and emerging technologies, including artificial intelligence. Ada is human-driven with the capacity to reveal hidden expressions and emotion in the built environment by blending technology and bio-steered concepts. The first architectural pavilion to incorporate AI, Ada knits light with data, immersing visitors in a responsive and interactive glow of photo-luminescence. Ada is a cyber physical architecture that is adaptive, personal, data-driven and informed by individual and collective participation. It is a project that celebrates AI, an architecture that is "happy to see you" and "smiles back at you."

The pavilion is a lightweight digitally knitted structure of responsive and data-driven tubular and cellular components employing textiles and photo-luminescent fibers to absorb, collect, and emit light. An external rigid experimental shell structure assembled from a compressive network of 895 unique 3D-printed nodes and fiber glass rods holds Ada's form in continuous tension. Ada is driven by individual and collective sentiment data collected and housed within the Microsoft Research Building 99. A network of sensors and cameras located throughout building offer multiple opportunities for visitors and participants to engage, interact with, and drive the project. The data includes facial patterns, voice tones, and sound that are processed by AI algorithms and correlated with sentiment. Three scales of responsive and gradated lighting including a network of addressable LEDs, a custom fiber optic central tensegrity cone, and five external PAR lights respond in real time to continuous streams of data. Specific sentiment data are correlated with colors, spatial zones within the project, and responsive materials. Suspended from three points and hovering above the ground, Ada is a socially and environmentally responsive interactive structure that offers spaces for curiosity and wonder, individual and collective exchange, and rigorous research experimentation.

8.19g

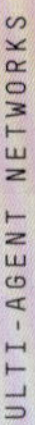

Generative Logic Physics Simulations

Architects, designers, and engineers such as Antonio Gaudi, Frei Otto, and Heinz Isler have used physical models to simulate the behavior of structures under force. Many of these simulations can be performed using digital abstractions of the physical forces such as gravity, bending, and collisions that operate on geometric entities such as vertices and line segments. Applying physical forces to digital geometry is the basis of particle systems.

Modeling with physical forces requires a high level of abstraction to both increase the simulation speed and make the logic relatively simple. Most design simulations involve interactions of very few forces with a small number of elements. More forces and elements results in a more accurate simulation, but it may take much more time.

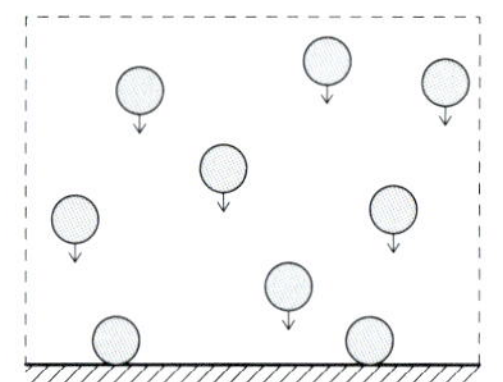

Gravity: The most basic force in many simulations is gravity, or a uniform force in a singular direction.

Collision Detection of Spheres: If the distance between any two spheres is less than or equal to the sum of their radii, they are colliding.

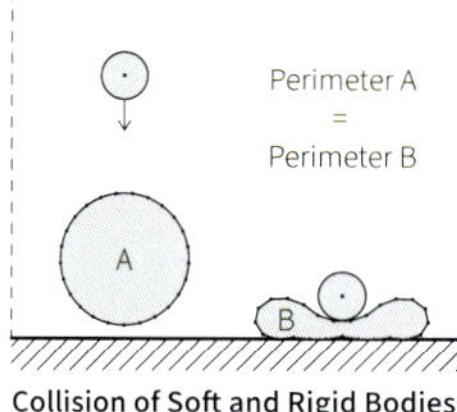

Collision of Soft and Rigid Bodies: A body can be subdivided into smaller reactive components that respond to collisions.

Length Constraints: The distance between objects can be kept fixed or changed to simulate stiffness, repulsion, or attraction.

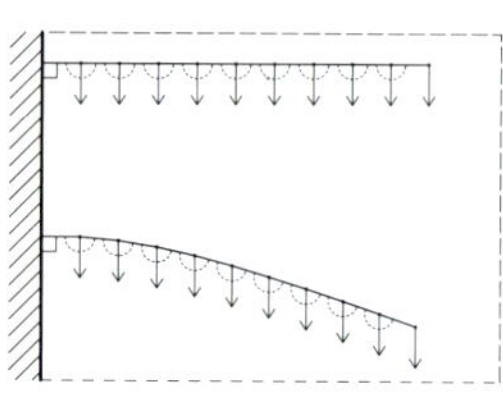

Bending Resistance: In addition to keeping the length of a segment fixed, the angle between segments can be used to simulate bending.

Soft Body Pile

The simulation of objects piling on each other can be accomplished with gravity, collision, bending, and an area constraint. The area of each body wants to stay the same as does the total perimeter. As the bodies fall and stack on each other, they fold and press into more horizontal forms.

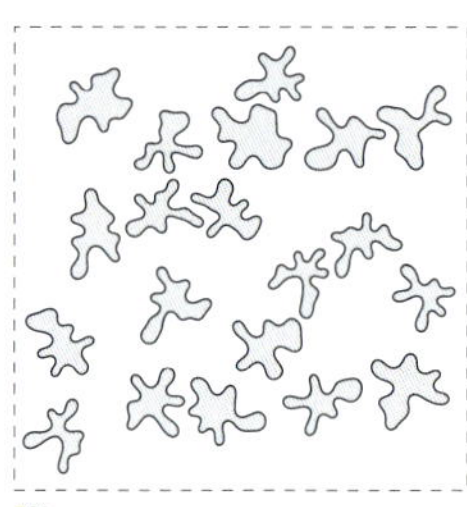

5%

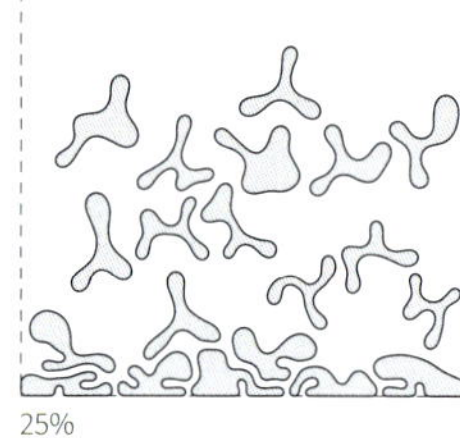

25%

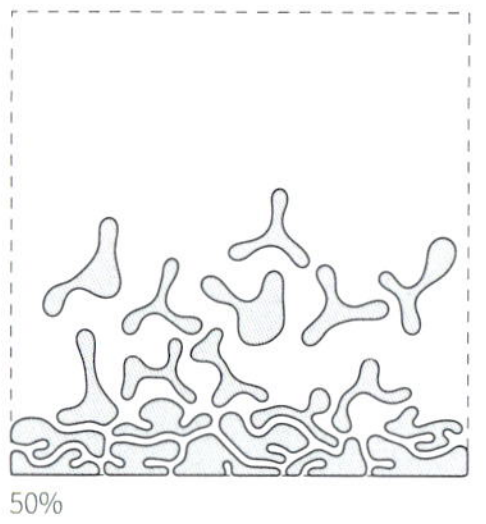

50%

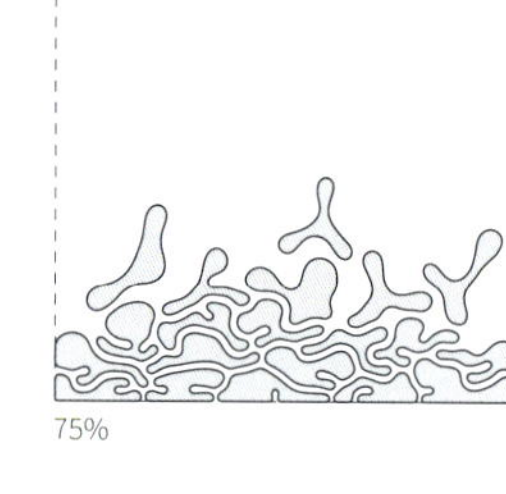

75%

100%

Growing Boundary

This simulation starts with a simple circle. The circle is subdivided into hundreds of small nodes that are prevented from getting too close together. The distance between the nodes is increased while keeping a bending stiffness to the perimeter curve. As the curve grows, it begins to bump against the outside boundary forcing the nodes to fill up the center.

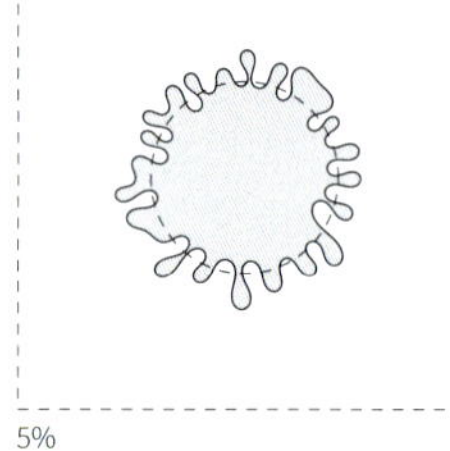

5%

25%

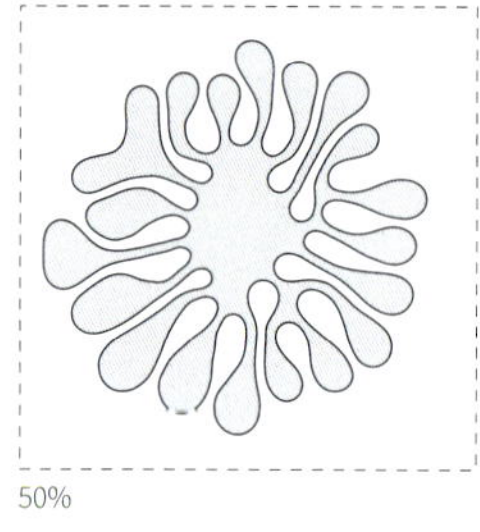

50%

75%

100%

Generative Process Stranded Sears Tower

The Stranded Sears Tower project could have used a physics engine to simulate the unbundling of the Sears Tower along the Chicago River. This process is divided into three generations. First the primary form's nine square towers are peeled off from each other. Next, the structural grid of each bundled tower is used to create even smaller strands that peel away and begin to align with the river and city streets. Finally, the ends of some of these bundles are frayed into even smaller strands.

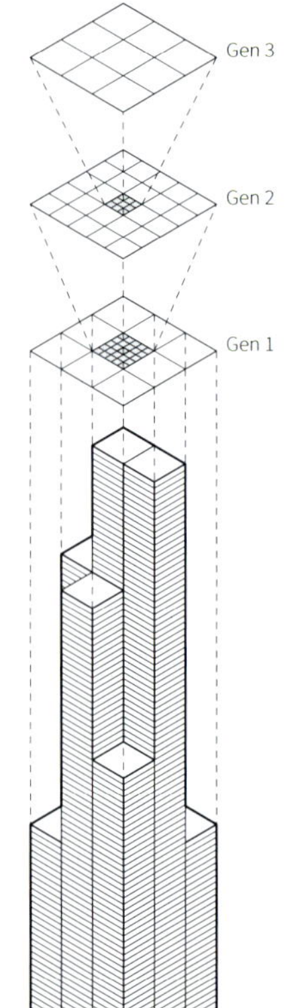

1. The Sears Tower is composed of nine bundled squares, each composed of a 5 x 5 structural grid, each with three façade subdivisions.

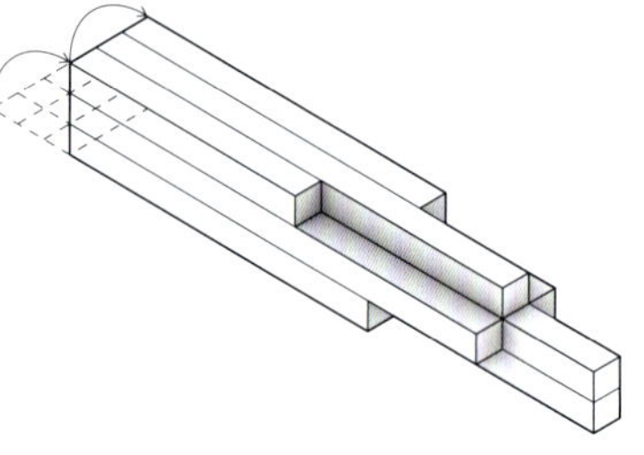

2. The form of the tower is rotated on the landscape.

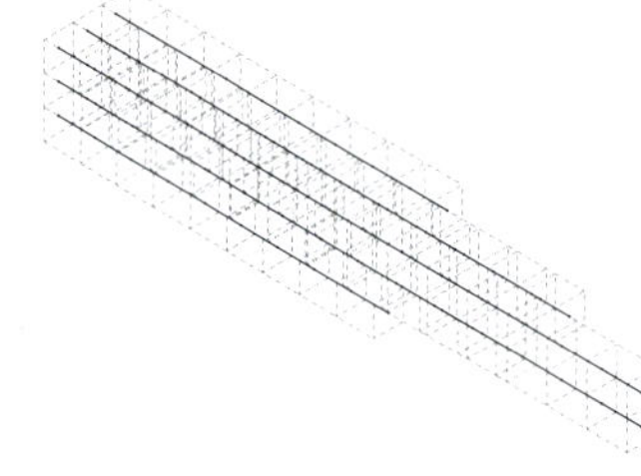

3. The central spine of each bundled tower is extracted, subdivided, and gravity, bending, and collision forces are applied.

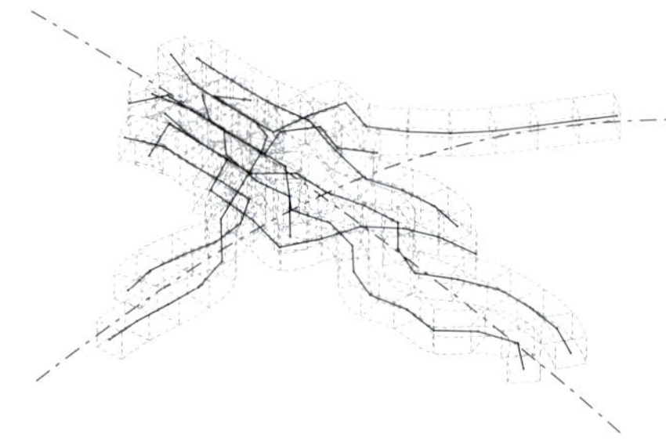

4. Site curves are used as guides during the simulation to draw the bundles along the river and city streets.

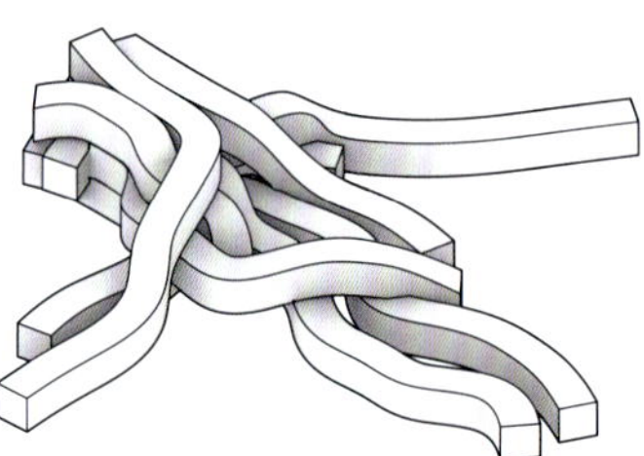

5. The result of the 9 bundles after the first simulation generation (Gen 1).

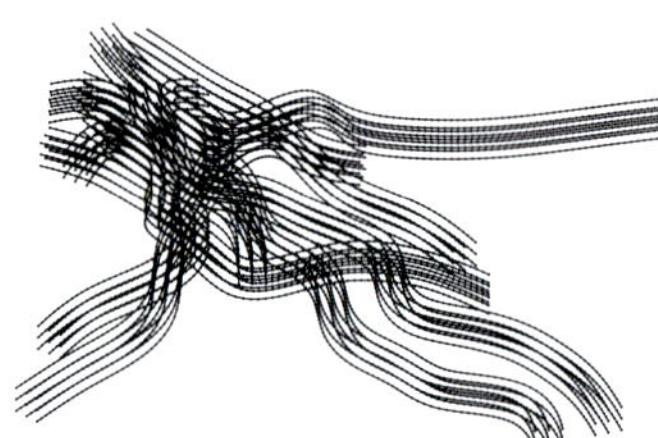

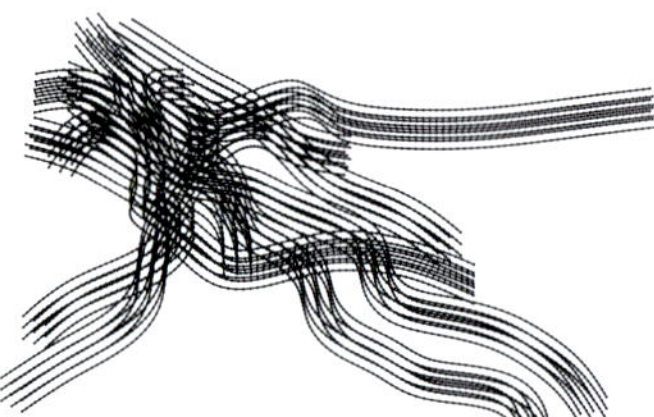

6. For the second generation of the unbundling of the tower, each of the original nine bundles are further subdivided into twenty-five more central spines (reduced here to nine for visual clarity).

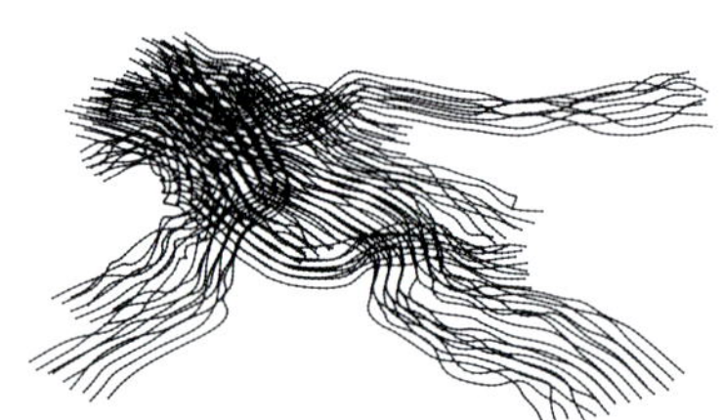

7. The same gravity, bending, and collision forces are applied again to these new spines, and the simulation is run.

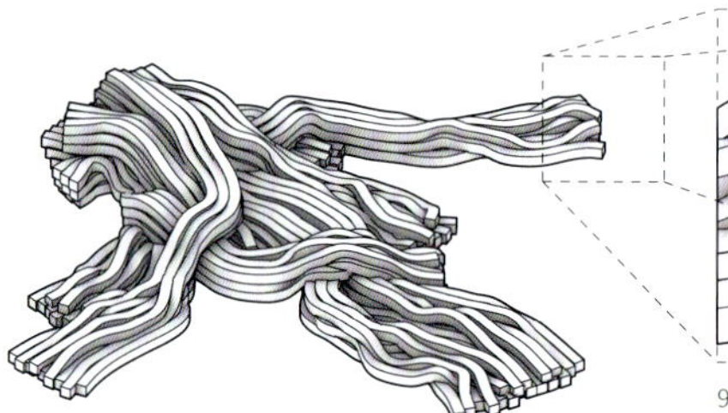

8. The result of the second simulation generation (Gen 2).

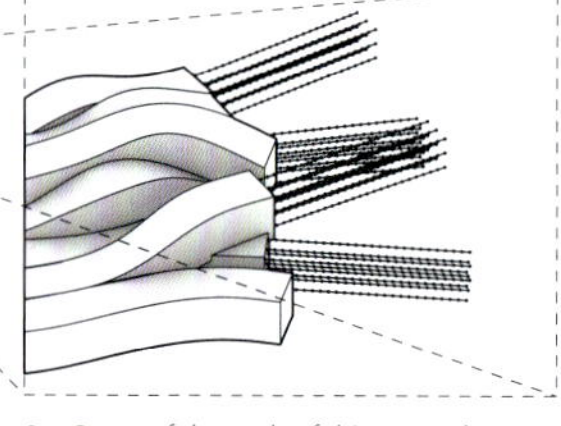

9. Some of the ends of this second generation of bundles is further unbundled into loose ends. Again, central spines are extracted and gravity, bending, and collision forces are applied.

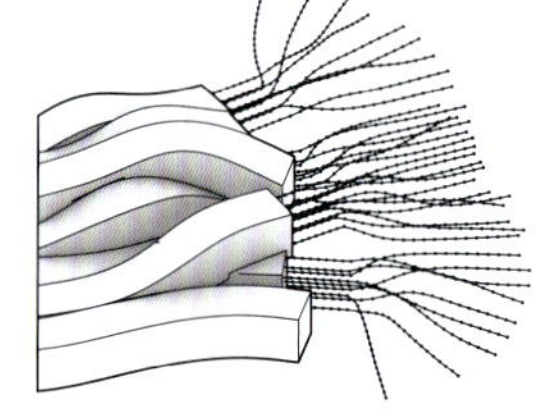

10. The central spines are simulated while their ends are anchored to the second generation bundles.

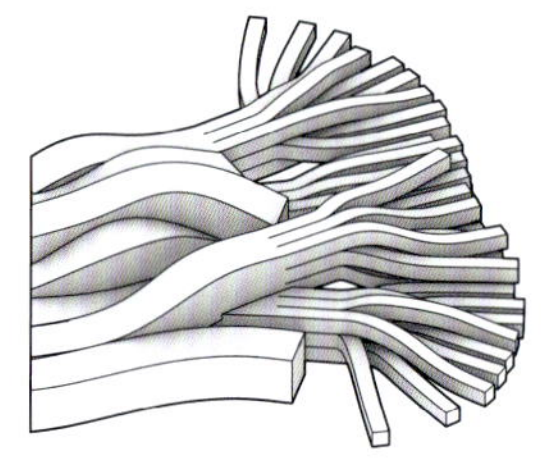

11. The result of the third simulation generation (Gen 3).

Generative Logic
Flocks, Swarms, and Crowds

Particle systems can be extended by giving each particle certain behaviors such as alignment, cohesion, and separation. These behaviors are the foundation of emergent behaviors among collective living systems in the form of flocks, swarms, herds, and crowds. These behaviors are often subconsciously performed as we move through space and are essential in the programming of semi-autonomous robots like drones.

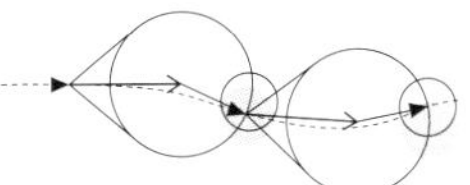

Wandering: The wander behavior introduces a semi-random movement to the agent. At each time step, the agent's direction and velocity is randomly changed within a limited range.

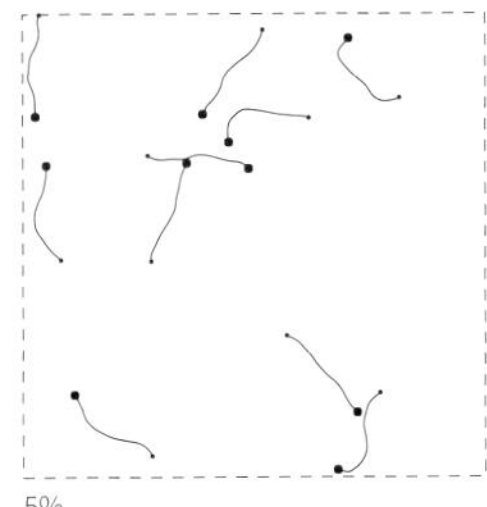
5%

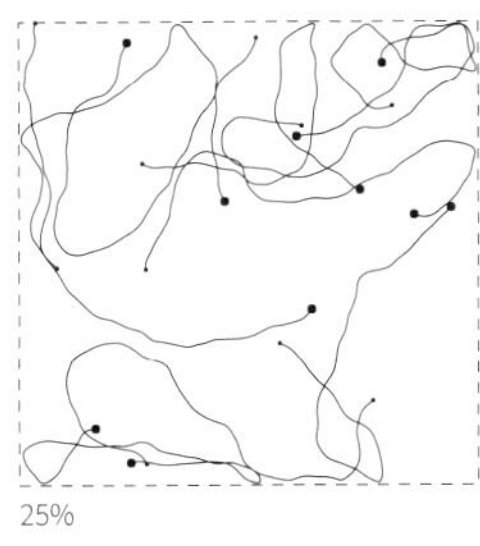
25%

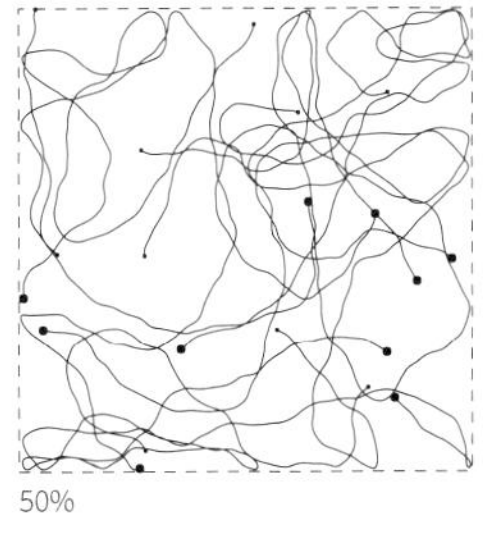
50%

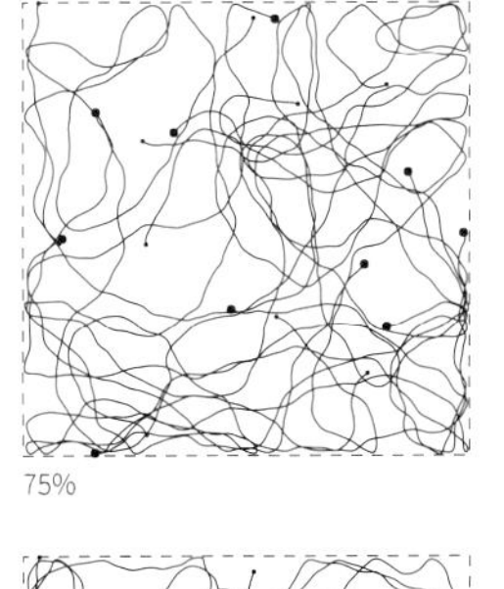
75%

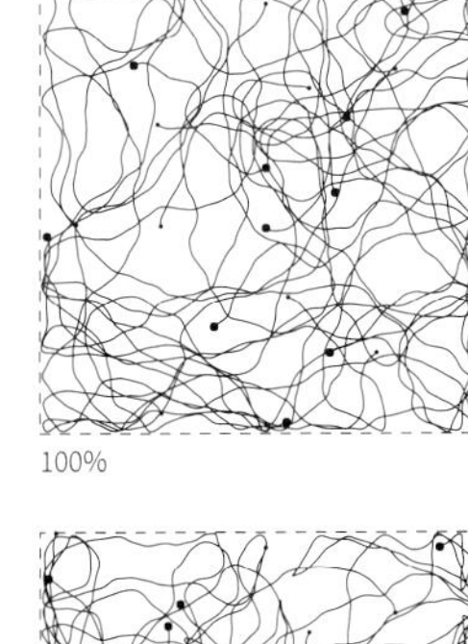
100%

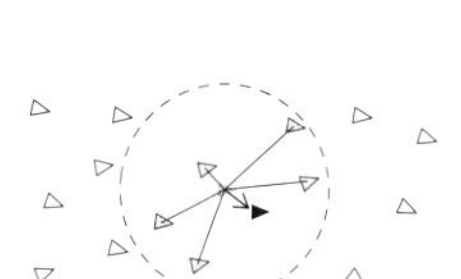

Separating: At each time step, the distance between an agent and its close neighbors is calculated. The agent changes its vector inversely proportional to the distance to each neighbor.

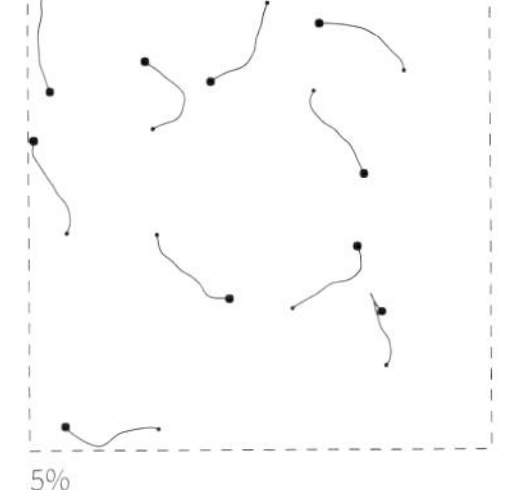
5%

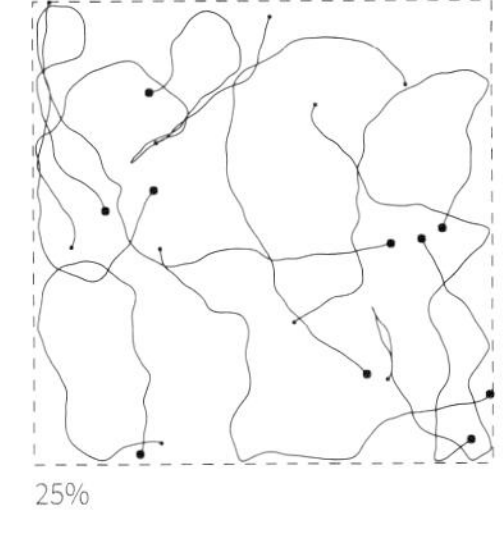
25%

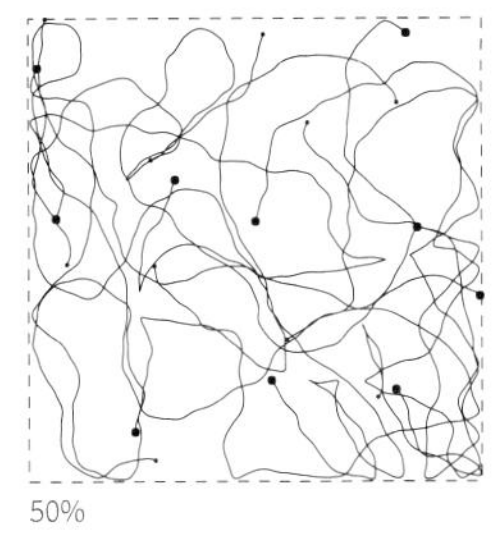
50%

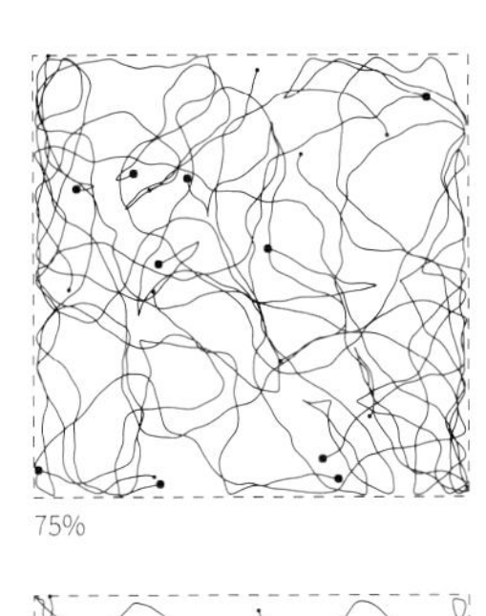
75%

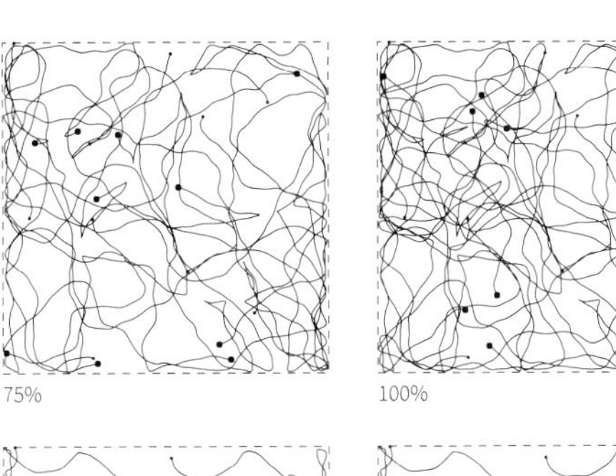
100%

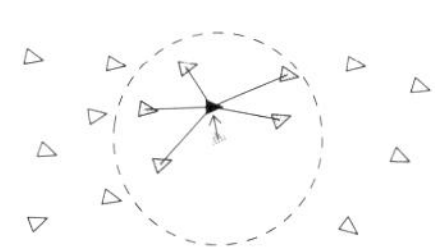

Cohering: At each time step, the centroid of each agent's neighbors is calculated and the agent moves towards this center.

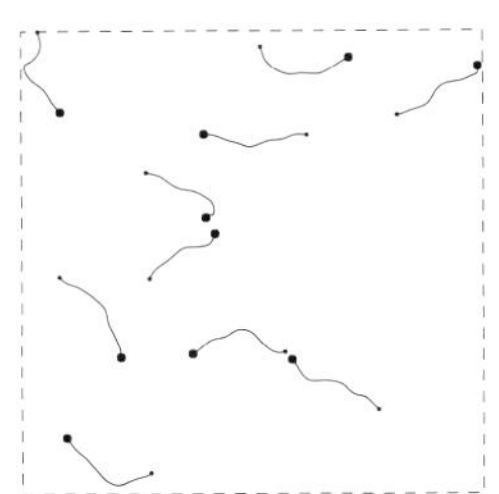
5%

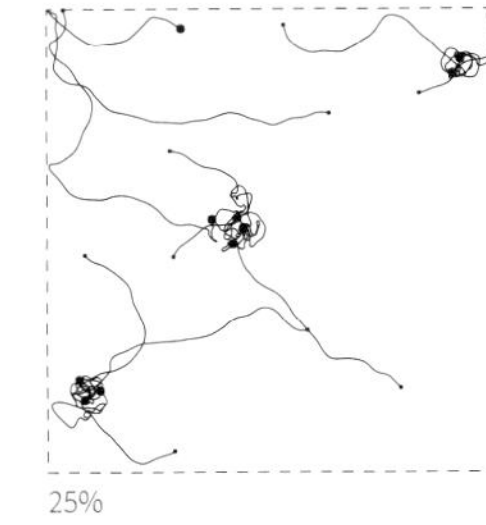
25%

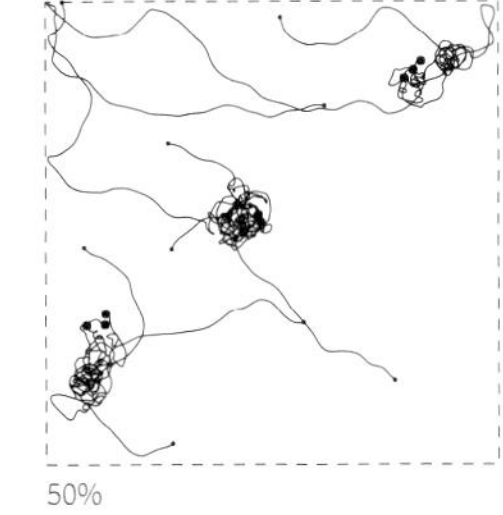
50%

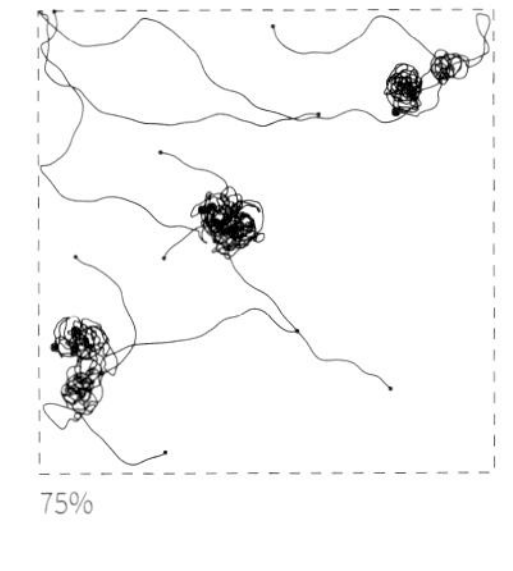
75%

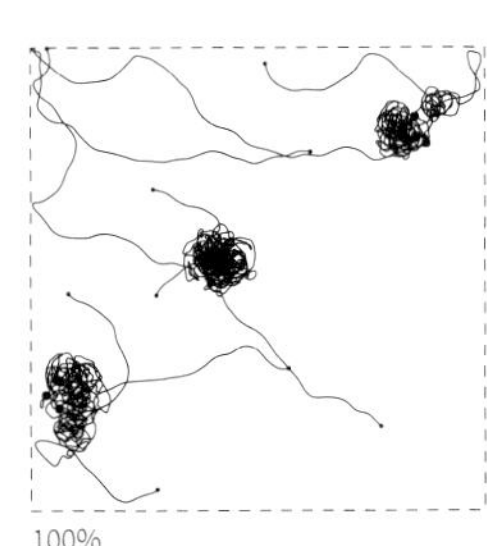
100%

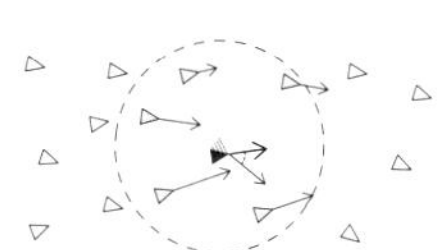

Aligning: At each time step, the agent adjusts its heading (vector direction and magnitude) to the average of its neighbors.

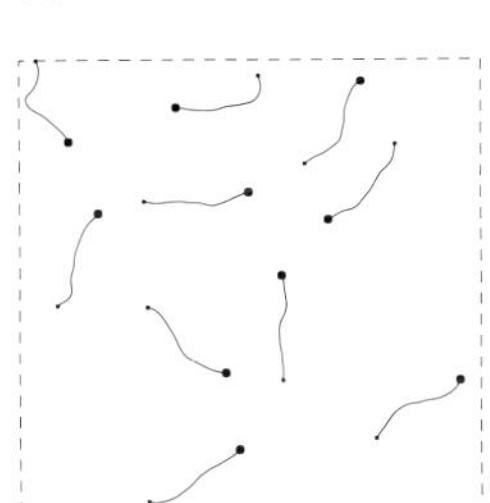
5%

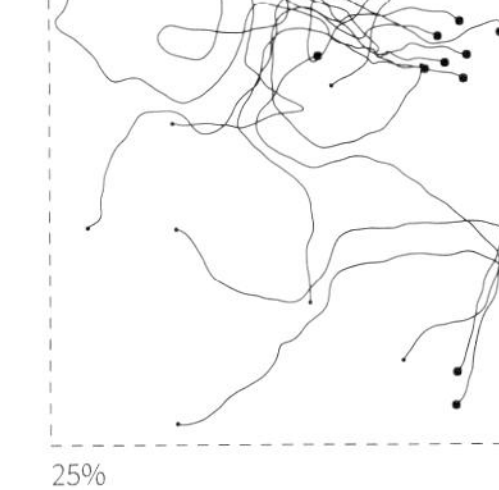
25%

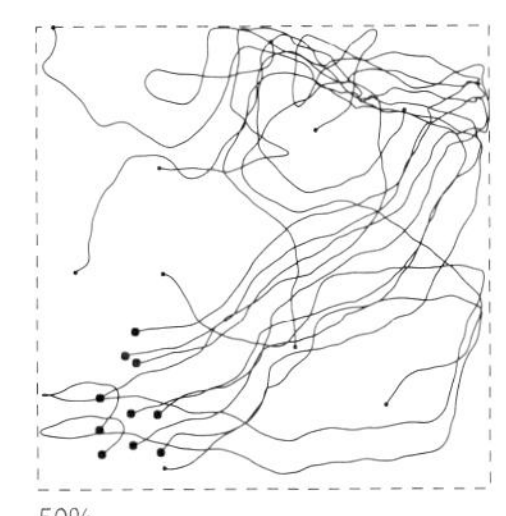
50%

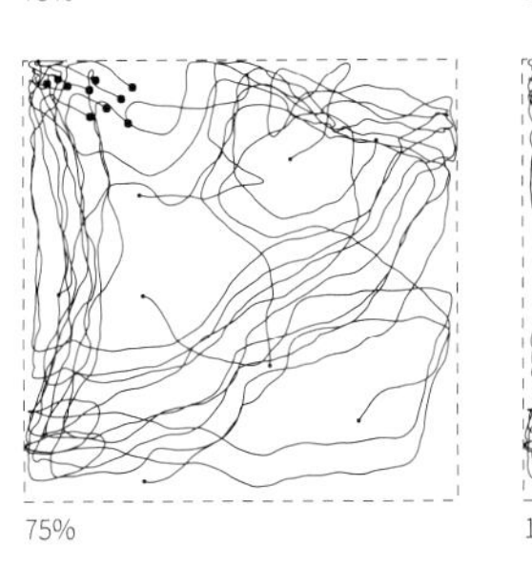
75%

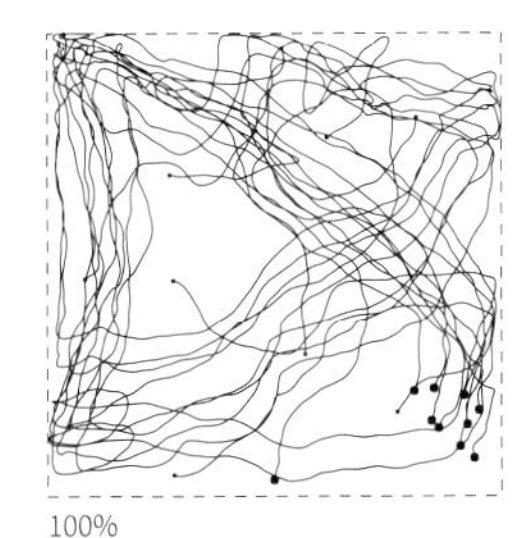
100%

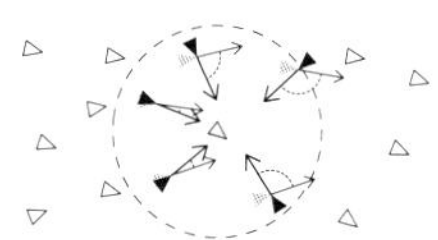

Seeking: If the prey is within the agent's neighborhood, the agent adjusts its heading and velocity towards the prey.

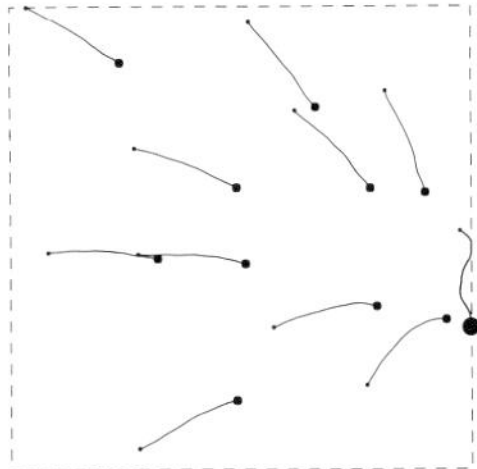
5%

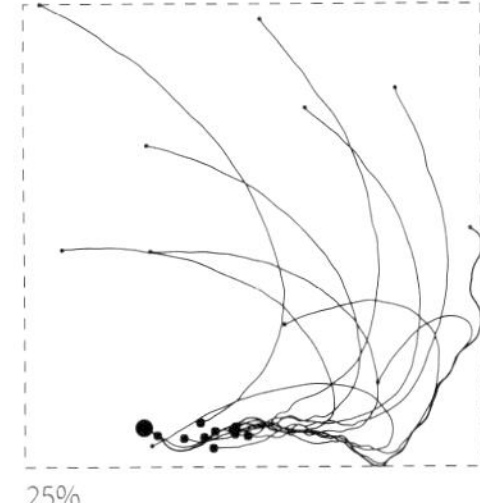
25%

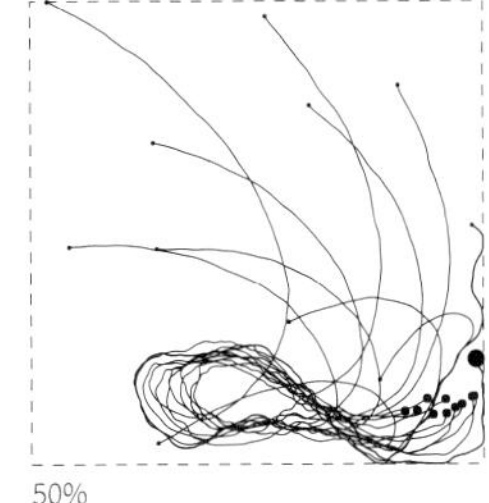
50%

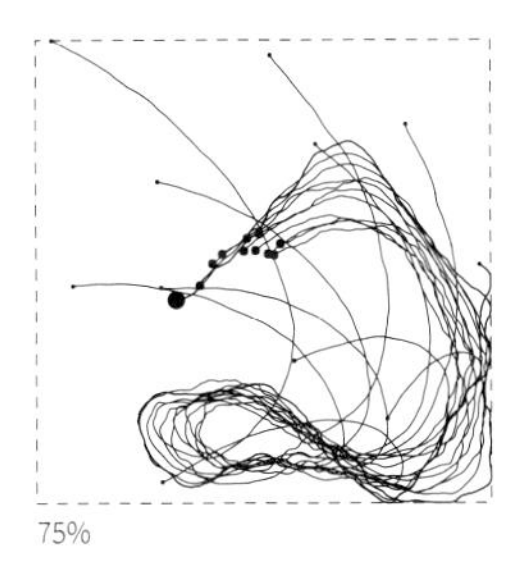
75%

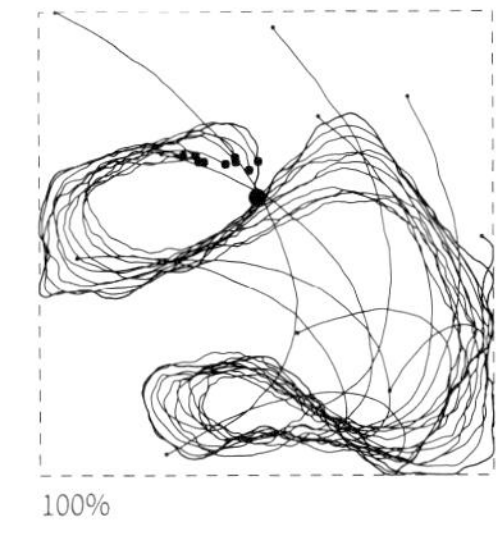
100%

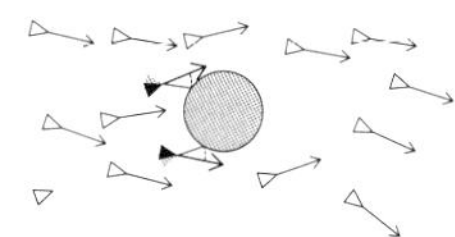

Avoiding: At each time step, the agent looks ahead by a certain distance. If this point ahead intersects an object or boundary condition, the agent steers away from it.

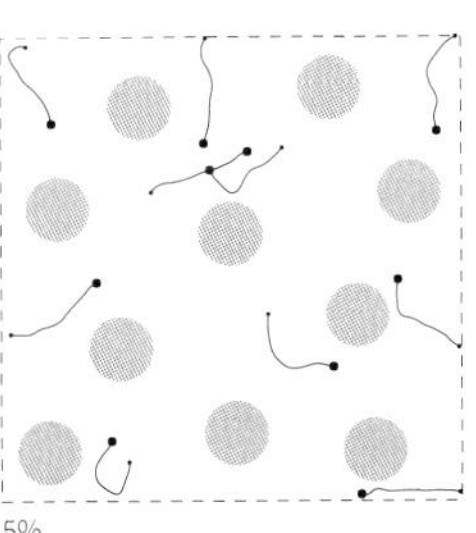
5%

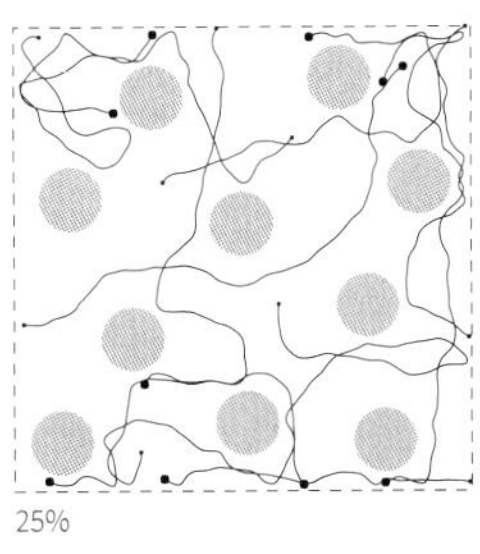
25%

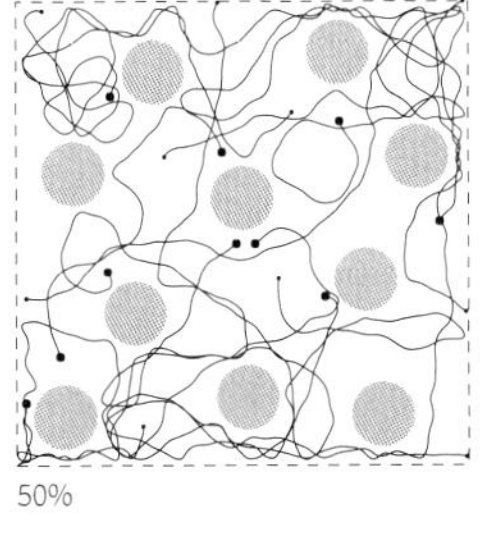
50%

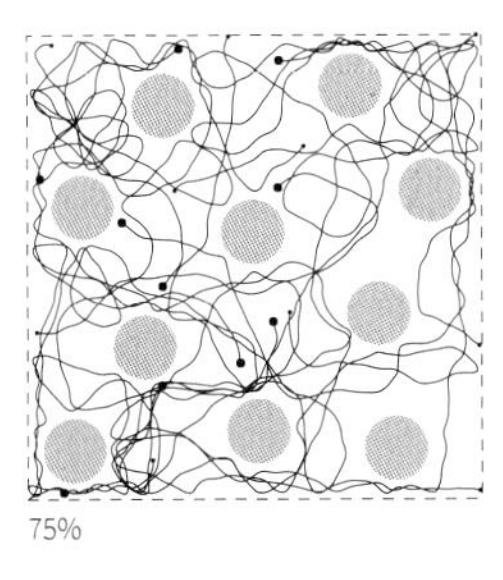
75%

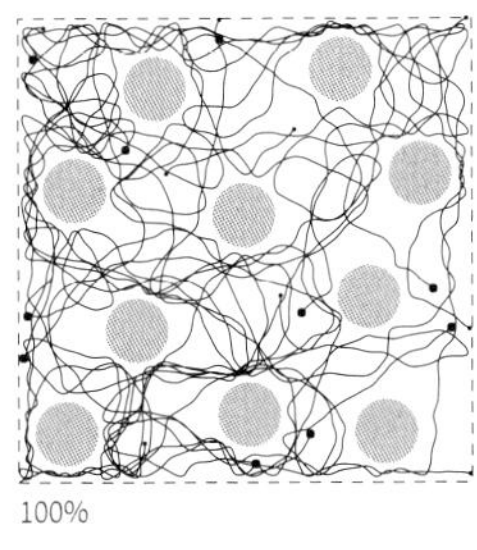
100%

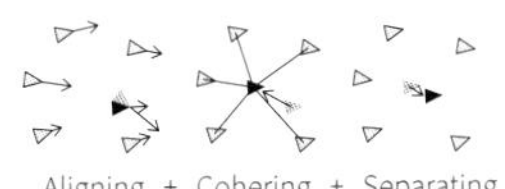

Behavior Priority: When multiple behaviors are combined, their priority can be adjusted depending on the context. Typically alignment is calculated first, followed by cohesion, and then separation.

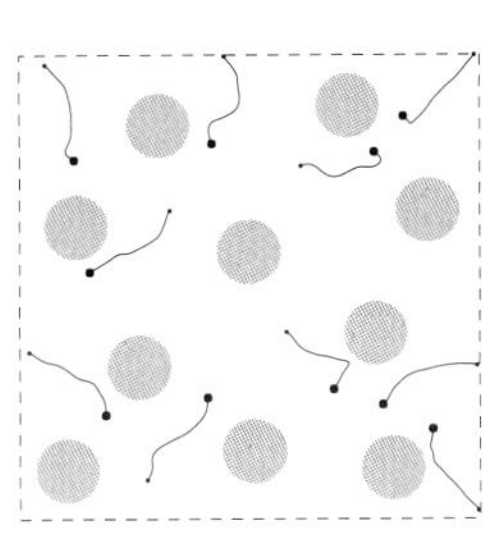
5%

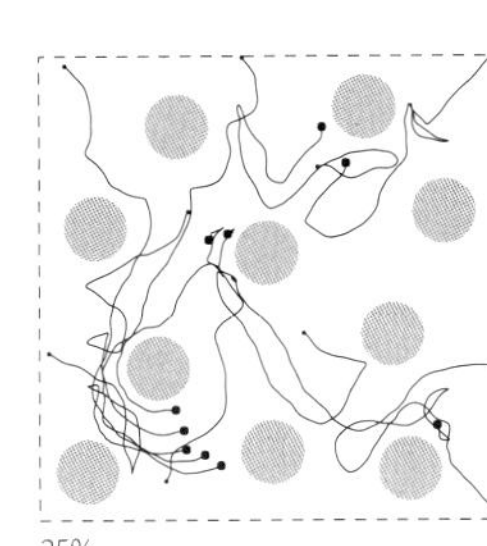
25%

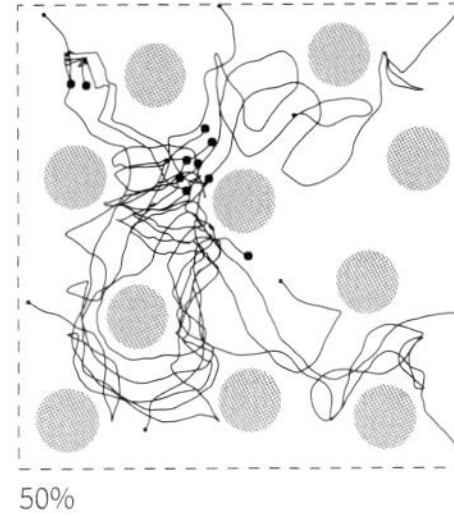
50%

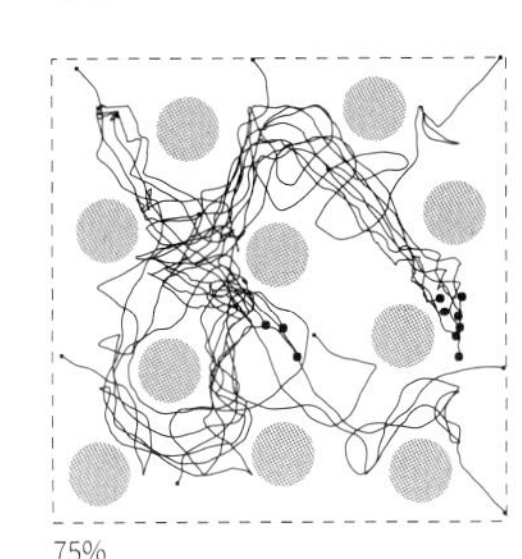
75%

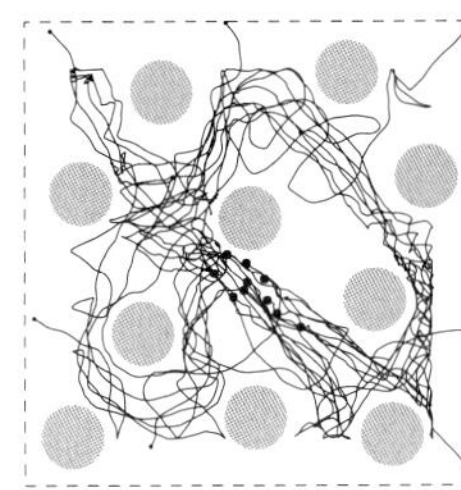
100%

Generative Logic Physical Computing

Physical computing is a field that blends computer science and electrical engineering with art and design. It focuses on the design and fabrication of interactive systems that can sense physical phenomena, process interactions, and respond with physical output devices. By integrating software and hardware, physical computing allows for the creation of interactive systems, ranging from simple smart home devices to high-performance, interactive architecture.

Inputs

Light: Visible Light

Sound: Audible Sound

Movement and Orientation: Motion, Electromagnetic, Proximity, Touch

Atmosphere: Temperature, Humidity, Air Pressure

Communication and Geolocation Networks: GPS, Radio Spectrum

Input Devices

Sensors are diverse and specialized tools designed to detect and measurea myriad of phenomena, ranging from temperature and light to magnetic fields and radio waves.

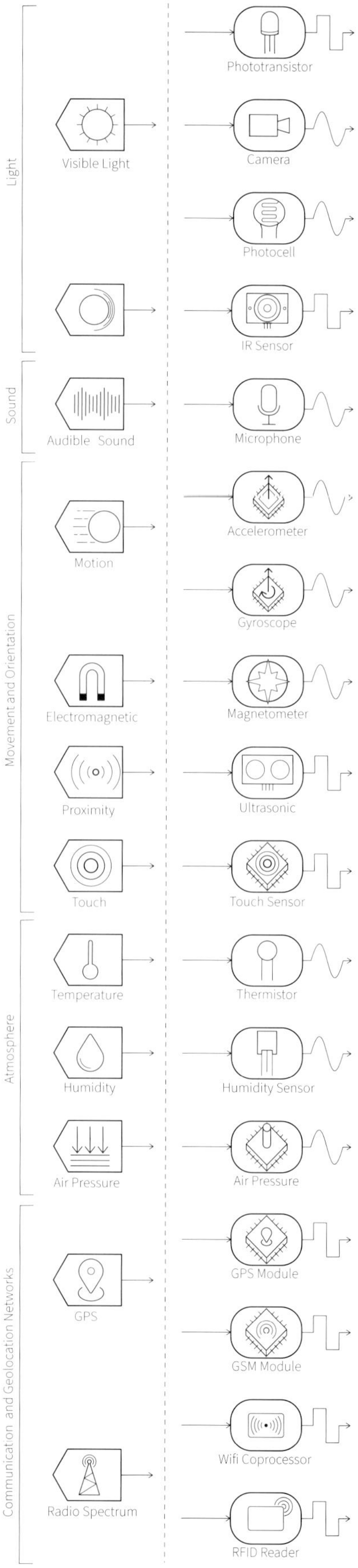

Phototransistor, Camera, Photocell, IR Sensor, Microphone, Accelerometer, Gyroscope, Magnetometer, Ultrasonic, Touch Sensor, Thermistor, Humidity Sensor, Air Pressure, GPS Module, GSM Module, Wifi Coprocessor, RFID Reader

Essential Data Types, Processing Logics, and Hardware Devices

Data Types

Booleans are either true (1) or false (0) values. They are the most basic data type and are essential to understanding the various forms of logic processing.

Numeric Types come in several forms:

Integers: Any positive or negative whole numbers

Floating Point: Any positive or negative rational numbers

Complex: The sum of any real and imaginary number

Strings are sequences of characters and are used to store any combination of letters, numbers, puncuation marks, symbols, and blank spaces.

Arrays are used to store combinations of other data types. Arrays are also known as sequences, lists, and vectors. Arrays usually store a sequence of similar types, but don't have to. Arrays can have multiple dimensions and can be nested inside of other arrays. Common examples of arrays include:

Color Array
There are many digital color models each with their own advantages and disadvantages. In the examples below, the HEX color of #f5f542 is shown in each color model array:

RGB (red, green, blue) with a range of 0–255).
RGB (245, 245, 66)

CMYK (cyan, magenta, yellow, black) with a range of 0–100.
CMYK (0, 0, 73, 4)

HSL (hue, saturation, lightness) with ranges of (0 - 360, 0–100, 0–100).
HSL (60, 90, 61)

HSV (hue, saturation, value) with ranges of (0 - 360, 0 - 100, 0 - 100).
HSV (60, 73, 96)

Coordinate Array
Common coordinate arrays include two and three dimensional arrays:
XY Point = (0.5, 0.5)
XYZ Point = (0.5, 0.5, 0.5)

Point Arrays are an example of a nested array as the top level array stores a list of points and each item in that list is itself another list of coordinates:
a = (3, 65, 43)
b = (49, 26, 32)
c = (14, 80, 81)
pts = (a,b,c)

String Arrays are used to store a list of strings such as names, passwords, or other alphanumeric data:
names = (Andrew, Ila, Bob)

Logic Processors

Boolean Operations use a type of algebra that operates with only true and false values as input and output.

Boolean AND: Return true only if both inputs are true.

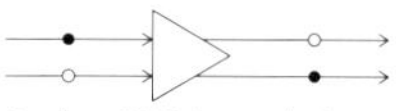

Boolean NOT: Invert the input. If input is true, output is false. If input is false, output is true.

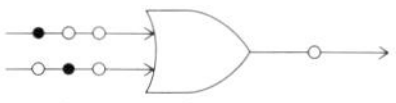

Boolean OR: If either or both inputs are true, the output is also true.

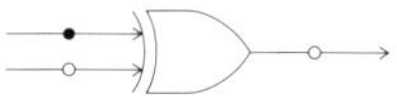

Boolean XOR: If one but not both inputs are true, the output is also true.

Boolean NAND: If one or both inputs are false, the output is true.

Comparisons Operations compare numeric data types and output true and false values.

A, B, ==
Equality: Return true if A is equal to B

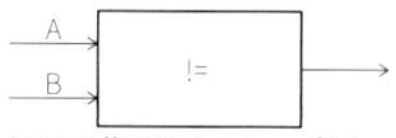

A, B, !=
Inequality: Return true if A is not equal to B

A, B, >, >=
Greater Than or Equal: Return true if A is greater than or equal to B

A, B, <, <=
Less Than or Equal: Return true if A is less than or equal to B

Control Flow Operations are often broken down into two categories: conditional and looping operators. Conditional operators determine if a certain statement should be executed while looping operators iterate until a certain condition has been met.

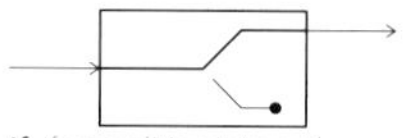

If: If a condition is true, the statment is executed. Nothing happens if it is false.

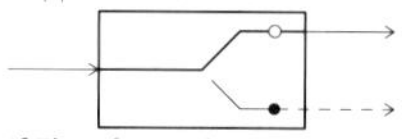

If Else: If a condition is true, the statment is executed. If false, something else happens.

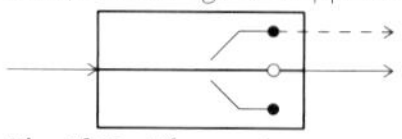

Else If: Test if several conditions are true.

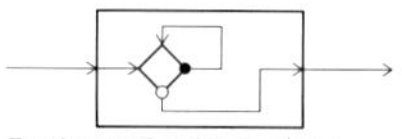

For Loop: Continue a loop until it reaches the last item or count.

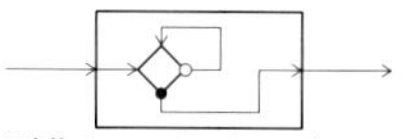

While Loop: Continue a loop while a condition is true.

Microcontroller

A microcontroller is a small hardware device that integrates a processing unit with onboard memory along with various input/output ports and pins to connect to external sensors, actuators, and other networking devices. An open-source Arduino Uno is shown below.

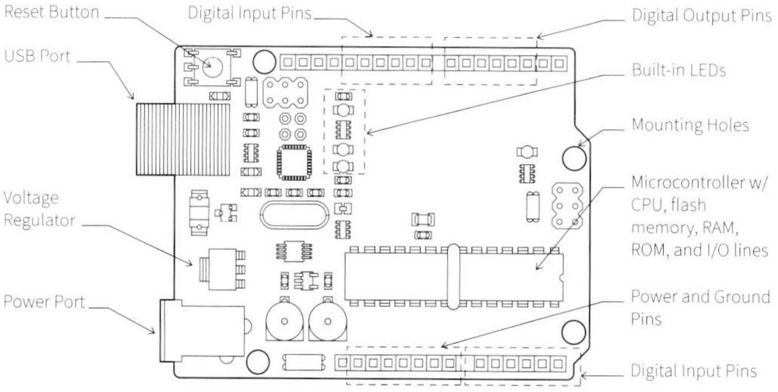

Reset Button
Digital Input Pins
Digital Output Pins
USB Port
Built-in LEDs
Mounting Holes
Microcontroller w/ CPU, flash memory, RAM, ROM, and I/O lines
Voltage Regulator
Power Port
Power and Ground Pins
Digital Input Pins

Output Devices

Numerous output devices can be used to produce light, sound, motion, and further communications with external networks.

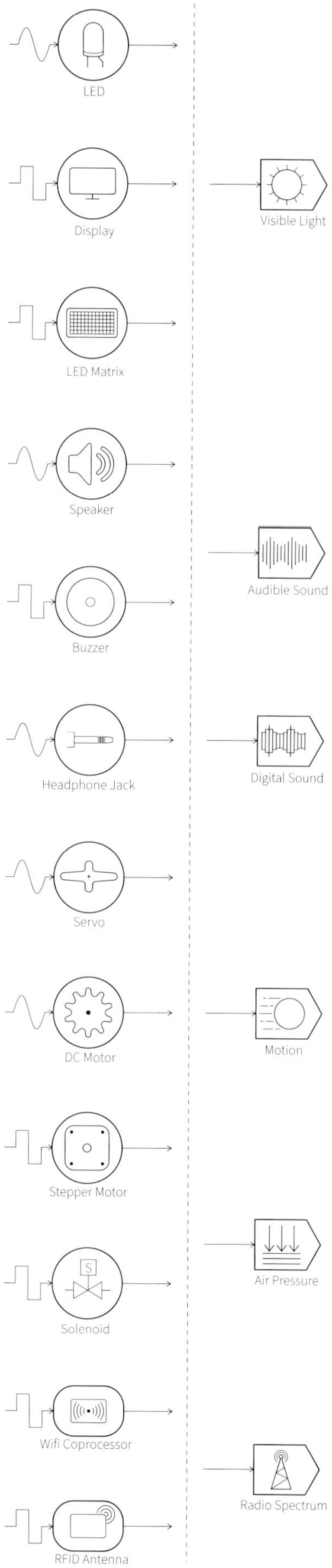

LED, Display, LED Matrix, Speaker, Buzzer, Headphone Jack, Servo, DC Motor, Stepper Motor, Solenoid, Wifi Coprocessor, RFID Antenna

Outputs

Visible Light, Audible Sound, Digital Sound, Motion, Air Pressure, Radio Spectrum

Generative Process
White Noise White Light

White Noise White Light is a field of autonomous agents that sense local movement and transform it into light and sound. Although each agent is only aware of itself and movement in its local environment, the installation reveals larger emergent patterns such as a gust of wind or the ghost trail of a person's movemnt.

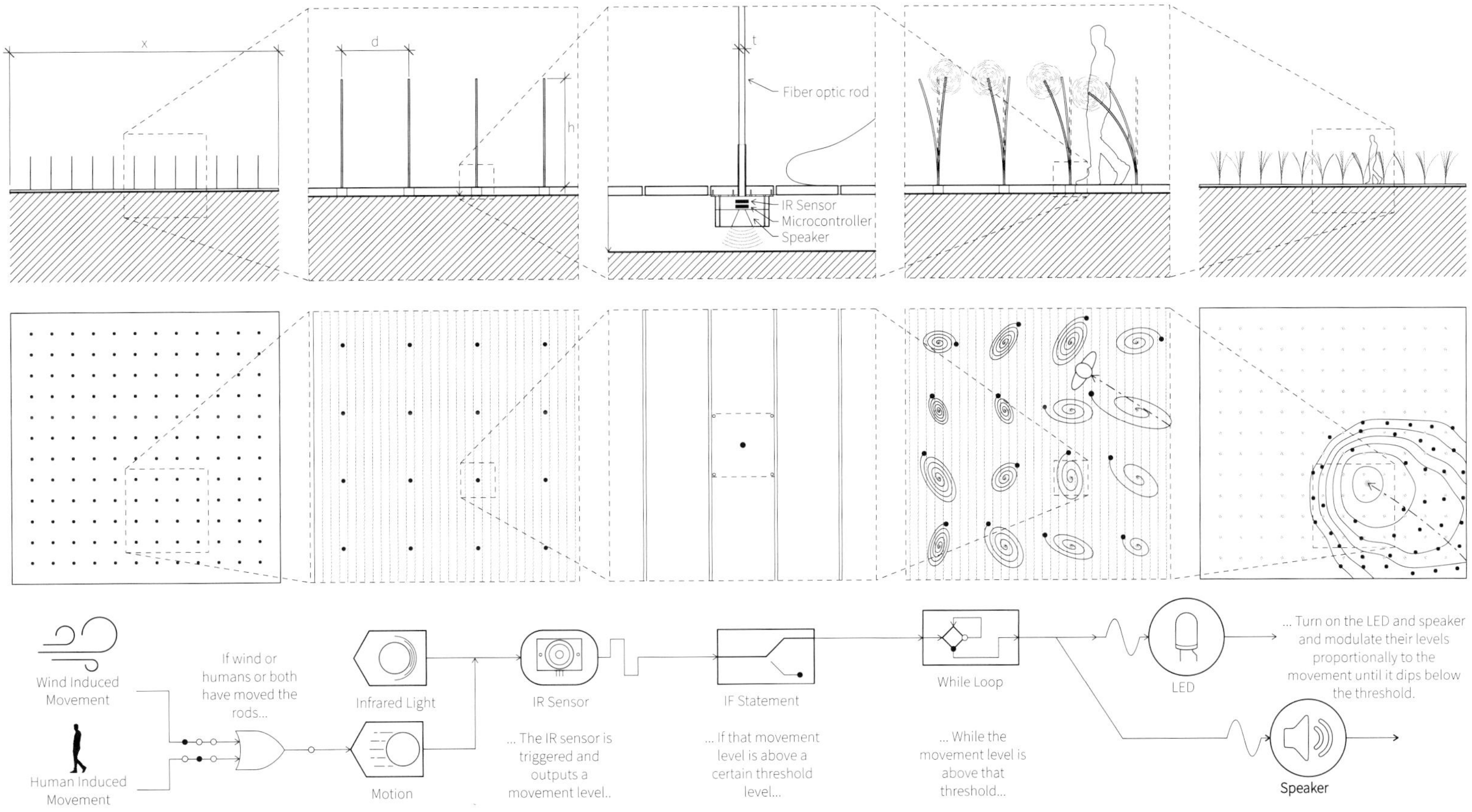

White Noise White Light can be activated by either passive or active forces or both simultaneously. As the wind blows or human visitors pass through the installation, the flexible rods move. This movement is detected via infrared light using an IR sensor. The sensor works by transmitting infrared light towards an object, in this case the bottom of the flexible rod. The sensor also has a infrared received that measures the reflected light off the object. If there is a change in the reflected light, the object has moved. If the amount of movement has reached a certain theshold, the installation code triggers two outputs: white light projected along the fiber optic rod and white noise projected out of a speaker. As the movement dissipates, there is a propotional decrease in the light and audio volume levels. When the movement falls below the specified threshold, the light and audio turn off completely.

Generative Matrix

x = 15.2 m
d = 0.75 m
h = 1.2 m
t = 10 mm
Wind Speed = 0 km/hr
Humans = 1

Single Human Path

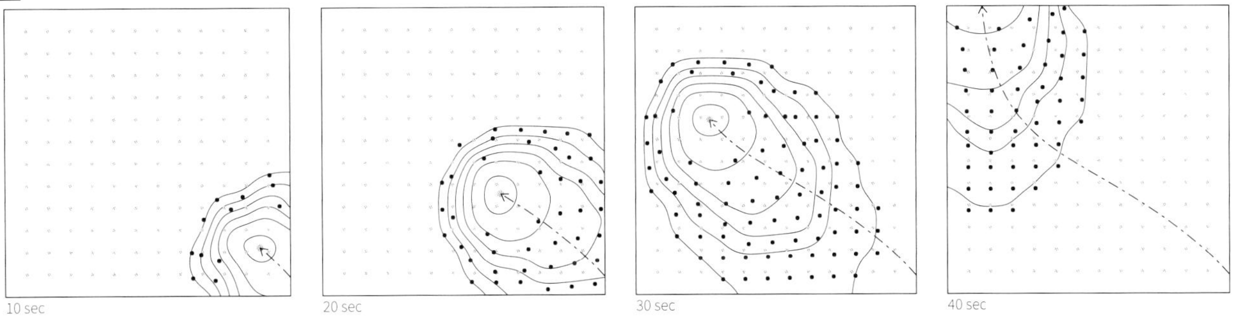

10 sec | 20 sec | 30 sec | 40 sec

x = 15.2 m
d = 0.75 m
h = 1.2 m
t = 10 mm
Wind Speed = 0 km/hr
Humans = 3

Multiple Human Paths

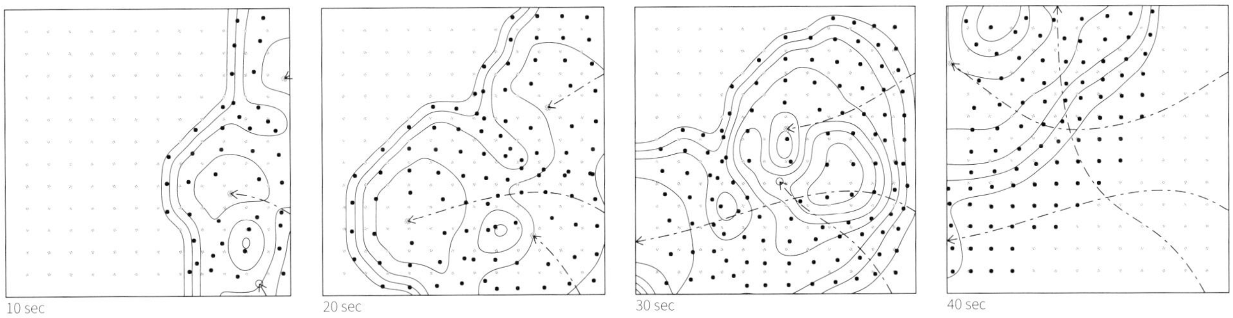

10 sec | 20 sec | 30 sec | 40 sec

x = 15.2 m
d = 0.75 m
h = 1.2 m
t = 10 mm
Wind Speed = 20 km/hr
Humans = 0

Wind Activated Field

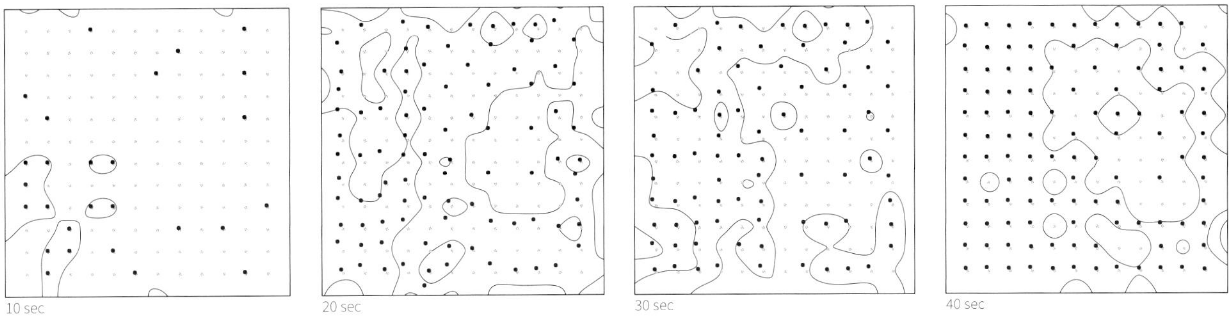

10 sec | 20 sec | 30 sec | 40 sec

Project Credits

STACKED AGGREGATES

Encoded Stereometry • Courtesy of Gramazio Kohler Research, ETH Zurich [frontispiece, 7, 14, 15], Courtesy of NADAAA [1, 3, 8], Courtesy of Gramazio Kohler Architects © Ralph Feiner [4, 5], Courtesy of SHoP Architects [6], Courtesy of Archi Union [2, 9, 10], Courtesy of Matter Design [11], Courtesy of Höweler + Yoon Architecture [12, 13] ● **Church of Christ the Worker** • Designer: Eladio Dieste • Photos: © CPCN, Getty Foundation / Javier Villasuso [1.1a-b, 1.1d, 1.1f], © Lomobaires, Flickr [1.1c], © Gonzalo Viramonte [1.1e] ● **Casa la Roca** • Designer: Office dA • Project Team: Nader Tehrani, Monica Ponce De Leon, Natalia Maric-coordinator, Vorapochana Ansvananda, Jeffrey Asanza, Gene Miao, Kazuyo Oda, Apisek Wongvasu, Patricia Szu-ping Chen, Thamarit Suchart, Diego Toledo, Rusty Walker • Drawings: Courtesy of NADAAA [1.2e] • Photos: Courtesy of NADAAA [1.2a-d] ● **Gantenbien Winery** • Designer: Gramazio & Kohler + ETH DFAB Group • Consultants: Bearth & Deplazes Architekten • Drawings: Gramazio & Kohler + ETH DFAB Group [1.3d-f] • Photos: Courtesy of Gramazio Kohler Architects © Ralph Feiner [1.3a, 1.3c, 1.3g], © Ila Berman [1.3b] ● **290 Mulberry St.** • Designer: SHoP Architects • Photos: Courtesy of SHoP Architects [1.4b], photographer: Amy Barkow [1.4a, 1.4c-d] ● **Structural Oscillations** • Designer: Gramazio & Kohler + ETH DFAB Group • Project Team: Fabio Gramazio, Matthias Kohler, Michael Knauss, Ralph Bärtschi, Tobias Bonwetsch, Nadine Jerchau, Michael Lyrenmann, Gregor Bieri, Michael Bühler, Hannes Oswald, Lukas Pauer • Consultants: Reto Geiser • Drawings: Courtesy of Gramazio Kohler Research, ETH Zurich [1.5c] • Photos: Courtesy of Gramazio Kohler Research, ETH Zurich [1.5d], photographer: Alessandra Bello [1.5a-b] ● **Sequential Wall 2** • Designer: Gramazio & Kohler + ETH DFAB Group • Project Team: Silvan Oesterle, Ralph Bärtschi, Mike Lyrenmann, (students: Michael Bühler, David Dalsass, Simon Filler, Milena Isler, Roman Kallweit, Morten Krog, Ellen Leuenberger, Jonas Nauwelaertz de Agé, Jonathan Roider, Steffen Samberger, Chantal Thomet, Rafael Venetz, Nik Werenfels) • Consultants: Häring Timber Engineering, Isoflock • Photos: Courtesy of Gramazio Kohler Research, ETH Zurich [1.6a-c] ● **The Stacked Pavilion** • Designer: Gramazio & Kohler + ETH DFAB Group • Project Team: Fabio Gramazio, Matthias Kohler, Roman Kallweit, Michael Knauß (project lead), Ralph Bärtschi, Michael Lyrenmann, Valentin Brenner, Tom Dowdall, Raphaël Dunant, Phillip Hegnauer, Andreas Jäger, Matthias Krucker, Roger Lienert, Roberto Schumacher, Andreas Schuster, Stefan Vetsch, Franz von Wietersheim • Consultants: Basler & Hofmann - Ingenieure und Planer AG Zürich, Franca Comalini • Photos: Courtesy of Gramazio Kohler Research, ETH Zurich, photographer: Roman Keller [1.7a-c] ● **Mantra Hookah Den** • Designer: Office dA • Project Team: Monica Ponce de Leon, Nader Tehrani, Zack Hinchliffe, Duks Koschitz, Christine Mueller, Carlos Arnaiz, Chat Chuenrudeemol, Andrew Cruse, Elisa Silva, Tim Clark, Kristine Synnes, Hamad Al- Sultan, Achille Rossini, Albert Garcia, Jeff Asanza, Hansy Luz Better, Elise Shelley, Tali Buchler, Richard Lee, Chris Eidt • Consultants: Alexander Coogan Architect Inc. • Drawings: Courtesy of NADAAA [1.8a] • Photos: Courtesy of NADAAA [1.8b-c] ● **Olzweg** • Designer: New-Territories / R&Sie(n) • Consultants: Pierre Huyghe, Stephan Henrich • Images: Courtesy of New-Territories / R&Sie(n) [1.9a-f] ● **Max Planck Institute** • Designer: Gramazio Kohler Architects • Project Team: Fabio Gramazio, Matthias Kohler, Sarah Schneider, Pandjaitan Poltak, Henning Proske • Consultants: Strauss Elektroakustik GmbH • Photos: © Thomas Ott, www.o2t.de [1.10a-c] ● **Chi-She Gallery** • Designer: Archi-Union Architects, Inc. • Project Team: Philip F. Yuan, Alex Han, Xiangping Kong, Tianrui Zhu, Qinrong Liu, Yuchen Hu, Liming Zhang, Wen Zhang • Consultants: Rui Wang, Junchao Shen, Xiaofeng Zhang, Jin Wang, Fab-Union • Drawings: Courtesy of Archi Union, Phillip Yuan [1.11b] • Photos: Courtesy of Archi Union, Phillip Yuan, photographer: Bian Lin [1.11a], photographer: Su Shengliang [1.11c], photographer: Yucheng Hu [1.11d] ● **Flight Assembled Architecture** • Designer: Gramazio & Kohler and Raffaello D'Andrea with ETH Zurich • Photos: Courtesy of Gramazio Kohler Research, ETH Zurich [1.12a-c] ● **Helix** • Designer: Matter Design • Consultants: Matthew Johnson of Simpson Gumpertz & Heger • Photos: Courtesy of Matter Design, photographer: Brandon Clifford [1.13a-e] ● **Round Room** • Designer: Matter Design • Consultants: Quarra Stone • Drawings: Courtesy of Matter Design [1.14d] • Photos: Courtesy of Matter Design, photographer: Brandon Clifford [1.14a-c, 1.14e-f] ● **Sean Collier Memorial** • Designer: Höweler + Yoon Architecture • Project Team: J. Meejin Yoon, Eric Höweler, Yoonhee Choe, Paul Cattaneo • Consultants: Knippers, Helbig, Ochsendorf, DeJong, and Block Consulting • Drawings: Courtesy of Höweler + Yoon Architecture [1.15a, 1.15e, 1.15h-i] • Photos: Courtesy of Höweler + Yoon Architecture [1.15f-g], photographer: John Horner [1.15b], photographer: Iwan Baan [1.15d], © Iwan Baan [1.15c] ● **Rock Print** • Designer: Gramazio Kohler Research, ETH Zurich, and Self-Assembly Lab, MIT • Project Team: Fabio Gramazio, Matthias Kohler, Skylar Tibbits, Andreas Thoma, Petrus Aejmelaeus-Lindström, Volker Helm, Sara Falcone, Jared Laucks, Lina Kara'in, Michael Lyrenmann, Carrie McKnelly, George Varnavides, Stephane de Weck, Jan Willmann • Consultants: Walt + Galmarini AG, Hans J. Herrmann and Falk K. Wittel (Institute for Building Materials, ETH Zurich), Heinrich Jaeger and Kieran Murphy (Chicago University) • Drawings: Courtesy of Gramazio Kohler Research, ETH Zurich [1.16i-j] • Photos: Courtesy of Gramazio Kohler Research, ETH Zurich [1.16a-h]

MODULAR ASSEMBLAGES

Part-to-Whole Relations and Genetic Families • Courtesy of Gramazio Kohler Research, ETH Zurich [frontispiece, 5, 6], Courtesy of MVRDV [1], Courtesy of Variable Projects [2], Courtesy of SHoP Architects [3, 4], Courtesy of FOA [7], Courtesy of MOS Architects [8], Courtesy of Jose Sanchez and Alisa Andrasek [9], Courtesy of Rael San Fratello [10, 11, 12], Courtesy of Gilles Retsin Architecture [13, 14, 16], Courtesy of Gilles Retsin Architecture © NAARO [15] ● **Berlin University** • Designer: Candilis-Josic-Woods • Drawings: Candilis, Josic and Woods & Candilis, Georges & Josic, Alexis & Woods, Shadrach. Free University Berlin. n.d. https://jstor.org/stable/community.10801005 [2.1b] • Photos: © Svenwerk, Flickr [2.1a], Candilis, Josic and Woods & Candilis, Georges & Josic, Alexis & Woods, Shadrach. (1963). Free University Berlin. https://jstor.org/stable/community.10801383 ● **Delft Housing Study** • Designer: MVRDV • Drawings: Courtesy of MVRDV [2.2a, 2.2c-e] • Photos: Courtesy of MVRDV [2.2b] ● **Porter House** • Designer: SHoP Architects • Drawings: Courtesy of SHoP Architects [2.3a, 2.3c-e] • Photos: Courtesy of SHoP Architects, photographer: Seong Kwon [2.3b, 2.3f] ● **Modular Variations (I and II)** • Designer: Variable Projects • Drawings: Courtesy of Variable Projects [2.4b, 2.4e-g] • Photos: Courtesy of Variable Projects [2.4a, 2.4c-d] ● **Resolution Wall** • Designer: Gramazio Kohler Research, ETH Zurich • Project Team: Tobias Bonwetsch, Ralph Baertschi, Daniel Kobel, Michael Lyrenmann, (students: Marcia Akermann, Gregor Bieri, Stefan Bischof, Eliza Boganski, Philip Bräm, Frank-Olivier Cottier, Andreas Kast, Irene Lo Iacono) • Consultants: Ytong • Drawings: Courtesy of Gramazio Kohler Research, ETH Zurich [2.5a-b] • Photos: Courtesy of Gramazio Kohler Research, ETH Zurich [2.5c] ● **Federation Square** • Designer: LAB Architecture Studio + Bates Smart Architects • Photos: © Bates Smart Architects [2.6a], photo 21212233 / Federation Square Melbourne © plumtrees | dreamstime.com [2.6b], photo 19521247 / Federation Square Melbourne © Mariusz Pruxaczyk | dreamstime.com [2.6c] ● **Ravensbourne College** • Designer: Foreign Office Architects • Project Team: Alejandro Zaero-Polo and Farshid Moussavi with Cristina Parreno, Maider Llaguno, Penny Sperbund, Azizah Sulor, Mio Sato, Emory Smith, John McLean, Daniel Spreier, Sukyeong Kim, Nankuei Lyn, Carmen Sagredo, and Changho Yeo • Drawings: © Foreign Office Architects [2.7b] • Photos: © Morley Von Sternberg and Foreign Office Architects [2.7a, 2.7c-d] ● **Ivy aka Coathooks** • Designer: MOS Architects • Drawings: Courtesy of MOS Architects [2.8a-c] • Photos: Courtesy of MOS Architects [2.8d-e] ● **Shenzhen Variations** • Designer: MOS Architects • Images: Courtesy of MOS Architects [2.9b] • Photos: Courtesy of MOS Architects [2.9a, 2.9c] ● **Bloom the Game** • Designer: Alisa Andrasek and Jose Sanchez • Drawings/Images: Courtesy of Alisa Andrasek and Jose Sanchez [2.10b, 2.10d, 2.10f] • Photos: Courtesy of Alisa Andrasek and Jose Sanchez, photographer: Jose Sanchez [2.10a, 2.10c, 2.10e] ● **Polyomino and Wireflies** • Designer: Plethora Project • Project Team: Jose Sanchez, (students: Yuchen Cai, Yanping Chen, Setareh Ordoobadi, Can Jiang, Dimitra Agelopoulou, Iro Karantaki, Vassia Diamanti) • Drawings/Images: Courtesy of Jose Sanchez [2.11a-f, 2.11j-k] • Photos: Courtesy of Jose Sanchez [1], Courtesy of Jose Sanchez [2.11g-i] ● **Polybrick** • Designer: Sabin Lab with Dr. Christopher J. Hernandez and Dr. Dan Luo • Drawings/Images: Courtesy of Jenny E. Sabin [2.12a] • Photos: Courtesy of Jenny E. Sabin [2.12b-c] ● **Seat Slug** • Designer: Emerging Objects / Rael San Fratello • Project Team: Ronald Rael, Virginia San Fratello, Emily Licht, Nick Buccelli, Kent Wilson • Drawings: Courtesy of Rael San Fratello [2.13c-d] • Photos: Courtesy of Rael San Fratello [2.13a-b] ● **Bloom** • Designer: Emerging Objects / Rael San Fratello• Project Team: Ronald Rael, Virginia San Fratello, Kent Wilson, Alex Schofield, Sofia Anastassiou, Yina Dong, Dr. Stephan Adams, Alex Niemeyer, Ari Oppenhiemer, Reem Makkawi, Steven Huang • Drawings: Courtesy of Rael San Fratello [2.14d] • Photos: Courtesy of Rael San Fratello, photographer: Matthew Millman [2.14a-c, 2.14e-f] ● **Thinness Pavilion** • Designer: APTUM Architecture with CEMEX • Project Team: Julie Larson and Roger Hubeli (students: Sean Morgan, Ethan Schafer) • Consultants: Sinead MacNamara • Drawings: Courtesy of APTUM Architecture / CEMEX [2.15e-g] • Photos: Courtesy of APTUM Architecture / CEMEX [2.15b-c, 2.15h], © F.M. Campos (AerialShotz) [2.15a, 2.15d] ● **Diamonds House** • Designer: Gilles Retsin Architecture • Drawings/

Images: Courtesy of Gilles Retsin Architecture [2.16a-e] ● **Tallinn Architecture Biennale** • Designer: Gilles Retsin Architecture • Drawings: Courtesy of Gilles Retsin Architecture [2.17d] • Photos: Courtesy of Gilles Retsin © NAARO [2.17a-c, 2.17e-f] ● **Royal Academy of Arts** • Designer: Gilles Retsin Architecture • Drawings: Courtesy of Gilles Retsin Architecture [2.18b-d, 2.18f] • Photos: Courtesy of Gilles Retsin © NAARO [2.18a, 2.18e, 2.18g-h] ● **House Block** • Designer: Automated Architecture (AUAR) • Drawings/Images: Courtesy of AUAR [2.19b] • Photos: Courtesy of AUAR, photographer: James Harris [2.19a, 2.19c-f]

PIXELATED FIELDS

Digital Territories to Voxelized Space • © Alexey Fedorenko [frontispiece], Courtesy of Herzog & de Meuron [1], © Aholm, Dreamstime [2], © Ila Berman [3], Courtesy of RUR [4, 5], Courtesy of and © Junya. Ishigami + Associates [6], Courtesy of MVRDV [7–10], Courtesy of EZCT [11–12] ● **Amsterdam Orphanage** • Designer: Aldo van Eyck • Photos: © CCA Mellon Lectures [3.1a], © Aerophoto-Schiphol Courtesy of Aerostock Photo [3.1b] ● **Nakagin Capsule Hotel** • Designer: Kisho Kurokawa • Drawings: Kurokawa, Kisho. Nakagin Capsule Tower. 1971. https://jstor.org/stable/community. 16513041. [3.2b], Kurokawa, Kisho. Nakagin Capsule Tower. 1971. https://jstor.org/stable/community. 16513042. [3.2c] • Photos: © Noritaka Minami [3.2a, 3.2d], © Nathan Willock-VIEW, Alamy Stock Photo [3.2e] ● **Memorial to the Murdered Jews of Europe** • Designer: Eisenman Architects • Drawing: Courtesy of Eisenman Architects [3.3a] • Photos: © Ila Berman [3.3b-e], © Eisenman Architects [3.3f] ● **Torre Agbar** • Designer: Ateliers Jean Nouvel • Local Architect: Fermin Vazquez - b720 • Drawings: Nouvel, Jean. Torre Agbar. 2002. https://jstor.org/stable/community.10818381 [3.4d] • Photos: © Ila Berman [3.4a, 3.4g], Courtesy of Ateliers Jean Nouvel © Philippe Ruault [3.4b-c], photo 158577205 © DiegoFiore | Dreamstime [3.4e], © DanTanman [3.4f] ● **Kanagawa Institute of Technology Workshop** • Designer: Junya.Ishigami + Associates • Drawings/Images: Courtesy of © Junya.Ishigami + Associates [3.5e-f] • Photos: Courtesy of and © Junya. Ishigami + Associates [3.5a], © Iwan Baan [3.5b-d] ● **O-14 Tower** • Designer: Reiser + Umemoto (RUR) • Project Team: Jesse Reiser, Nanako Umemoto (Principals), Mitsuhisa Matsunaga, Kutan Ayata, Jason Scroggin, Cooper Mack, Michael Overby, Roland Snooks, Michael Young, Tina Tung, Raha Talebi, Yan Wai Chu • Consultants: Ysrael A. Seinuk, PC, Erga Progress • Drawings: Courtesy of RUR [3.6b-d, 3.6g] • Photos: Courtesy of RUR [3.6a, h], photographer: Torsten Seidel [3.6e], photographer: Nelson Garrido [3.6f] ● **Shenzhen Bao'an International Airport** • Designer: Reiser + Umemoto (RUR) •8 Images: Courtesy of RUR [3.7a-f] ● **Computational Chair Design** • Designer: EZCT Architecture & Design Research • Project Team: EZCT / Philippe Morel, Jelle Feringa, and Félix Agid, with Hatem Hamda, Marc Schoenauer, and François Jouve • Drawings/Images: Courtesy of and © EZCT Architecture & Design Research [3.8b, 3.8d], Courtesy of EZCT Architecture © Centre Pompidou [3.8c] • Photos: Courtesy of and ©EZCT Architecture & Design Research, photographer: Ilse Leenders [3.8a, 3.8e-g] ● **Rødovre Skyvillage** • Designer: MVRDV + ADEPT • Drawings/Images: Courtesy of MVRDV [3.9a-c] ● **PoroCity** • Designer: MVRDV + the Why Factory • Photos: Courtesy of MVRDV, photographer: Frans Parthesius [3.10a-d] ● **King Toronto** • Designer: Bjarke Ingels Group (BIG) • Project Team: Bjarke Ingels, Thomas Christoffersen, Ryan Harvey, Lorenz Krisai, Andrea Zalewski • Local Architect: Diamond Schmitt Architects • Consultants: BA Group, BIG Ideas, ERA Architects, Gladki Planning Consultants, Gunn, Greenberg Consultants, Reinbold Engineers, Nemetz and Associates, Read Jones Christoffersen Ltd, Public Work • Images: Courtesy of BIG and Hayes Davidson [3.11d] • Photos: Courtesy of BIG and Hayes Davidson [3.11a-c] ● **Serpentine Gallery Pavilion** • Designer: BIG-Bjarke Ingels Group • Project Team: Bjarke Ingels, Thomas Christoffersen, Maria Sole Bravo, Aaron Powers, Alice Cladet, Claire Thomas, Daniel Sundlin, Jakob Lange, KaiUwe Bergmann, Kristian Hindsberg, Kristoffer Negendahl, Lorenz Krisai, Maria Holst, Maxwell Moriyama, Rune Hansen, Tianze Li, Tore Banke, Wells Barber • Photo: Courtesy of BIG, photographer: Iwan Baan [3.12a-d]

CELLULAR CLUSTERS

Generative Organicism and Polyhedral Patterning • Courtesy of Matsys [frontispiece, 5–8], Courtesy of IwamotoScott Architecture LLP[1], ©Radstyle, Dreamstime[2], ©PIXXart Photography iStock photo 157632313 [3], Courtesy of Chris Bosse, PTW ARUP CCDI [4], Courtesy of Office NADAA [9–12], Courtesy of Aranda\Lasch [13, 14] ● Montreal Biosphere: Expo '67 Geodesic Dome •Designer: Buckminster Fuller• Photos: © carterdayne, Stock Photos [4.1a], © Vladone, Stock Photos [4.1b] ● **The Eden Project: The Biomes** • Designer: Grimshaw Architects • Photos: © Fgcanada, dreamstime [4.2a], © Alexandra King, dreamstime [4.2b], ©Radstyle, dreamstime [4.2c] ● **Sagrada Familia Church Ceiling, Clerestory and Rose Windows** • Designers: Antoni Gaudi (original) + Mark Burry (1993-present) • Project Team: Mark Burry, Jane Burry • Images: Courtesy of Mark Burry: Nave, transept, and apse clerestory original design by Antoni Gaudi, digital interpretation Mark Burry, rendered image Grant Dunlop (1993–96) [4.3c], Passion Façade Rose Window by Mark Burry interpreting sketch designs by Jordi Bonet I Gari, Ididre Puig I Boada from the 1960s and Jordi Bonet I Armengol, renderings: Mark Burry [4.3e, 4.3f]• Photos: © Ila Berman [4.3a, 4.3b], Courtesy of Mark Burry, photographer: Rupert Truma [4.3f] ● **Beijing National Aquatics Center / The Water Cube** • Designer: PTW Architects, Arup, CCDI • Photos: © Chris Bosse, PTW ARUP CCDI [4.4a-b, 4.4g-h], ©tsvibrav iStock photo 503916241 [4.4c], Courtesy of Chris Bosse, PTW ARUP CCDI [4.4d-f] ● **1774 / Fauteuil Chair** • Designer: Aranda/Lasch • Drawings/Images: Courtesy of Aranda/Lasch [4.5c-h] • Photos: Courtesy of Aranda/Lasch [4.5a-b] ● **Quasitable** • Designer: Aranda/Lasch • Drawing: Courtesy of Aranda/Lasch [4.5c] • Photos: Courtesy of Aranda/Lasch [4.6a-b, 4.6d] ● **PS1 Grotto** • Designer: Aranda/Lasch • Drawings/ Images: Courtesy of Aranda/Lasch [4.7a-e] ● **PS1 Loop** • Designer: Höweler + Yoon Architecture (HYA) • Project Team: Eric Höweler, J. Meejin Yoon • Drawings/Images: Courtesy of HYA [4.8a-c] ● **Voromuro** • Designer: Office dA • Project Team: Nader Tehrani, Brandon Clifford, Monica Ponce de Leon, Arthur Chang, Remon Alberts, Catie Newell, Jumanah Jamal, Aishah Al Sager, Janghwan Cheon, Richard Lee, Aude-Line Duliere, Jiyoung Park • Consultants: C.W. Keller & Associates, Shawn Keller, David Anderson, Simpson Gumpertz & Heger: Matthew H. Johnson • Drawings: Courtesy of NADAAA [4.9b-c] • Photos: Courtesy of NADAAA, photographer: John Horner [4.9a, 4.9d] ● **Nature Boardwalk** • Designer: Studio Gang • Consultants: Atomic Props, Christopher B. Burke Engineering, Cosgrove Construction, Inc., Fox River Components, Magnusson Klemenic Associates, Pepper Construction, RLD Company, Shaw Environmental & Infrastructure, Inc., Shaw Sustainable Design Solutions of Illinois, Shelton Lam and Deck, Sunrise Fiberglass, WRD Environmental • Drawing: Courtesy of Studio Gang [4.10b] • Photos: © Hedrich Blessing, photographer: Steve Hall [4.10a], © Ronald Leon Hale [4.10c], © Mary Warren [4.10d], photo 10780 modlar.com [4.10e] ● **Voussoir Cloud** • Designer: IwamotoScott Architecture LLP • Project Team: Lisa Iwamoto, Craig Scott, Stephanie Lin, Manuel Diaz, John Kim, Alan Lu, Tiany Mok, Chris Chalmers, John Kim, (SCIArc Student Installation Team:Joanne Angeles, Oliver Liao, Liona Avery, Mathew Cavender, Jimmy Chan, Tim Francis, Channah Levy, Marisol Mejia, Zarmine Nigohossian, Davis, O'Reagan, Nicholas Paradowski, Brett Phillips, Justin Rice, Sarah Strauch, Ali Sykes, Judson Terry, Yohei Uchino, Vincent Wu • Consultants: Andrew Kudless, Buro Happold (LA), Lenderink Technologies, Advanced Laser • Drawings: Courtesy of IwamotoScott Architecture LLP [4.11b, 4.11d] • Photos: Courtesy of IwamotoScott Architecture LLP [4.11a, 4.11c, 4.11e-f] ● **Chrysalis III** • Designer: Matsys • Project Team: Andrew Kudless, Jason Vereschak, Emily Kirwan • Drawings: Courtesy of Matsys [4.12b-c] • Photos: Courtesy of Matsys [4.12a, 4.12d-f] ● **Strand Screen** • Designer: Matsys • Project Team: Andrew Kudless, Clayton Muhleman, Sitou Akolly, Marianna Munguia-Chang, Mengjie (Tina) Shen, Xiaoxue (Amy) Guo, Sam Villasenor, Armughan Faruqi, Taylor Metcalf, Anh Vu • Image: Courtesy of Matsys [4.13a] • Photos: Courtesy of Matsys [4.13b-e] ● **2011 ICD/ITKE Pavilion** • Designer: ICD / ITKE Stuttgart • Project Team: Achim Menges, Jan Knippers (leads), Oliver David Krieg, Boyan Mihaylov, Peter Brachat, Benjamin Busch, Solmaz Fahimian, Christin Gegenheimer, Nicola Haberbosch, Elias Kästle, Oliver David Krieg, Yong Sung Kwon, Boyan, Mihaylov, Hongmei Zhai, Markus Gabler (project management), Riccardo La Magna (structural design), Steffen Reichert (detailing), Tobias Schwinn (project management), Frédéric, Waimer (structural design), support: KUKA Roboter GmbH • Drawings: Courtesy of and © ICD/ITKE University of Stuttgart [4.14b, 4.14f] • Photos: Courtesy of and © ICD/ITKE University of Stuttgart [4.14a, 4.14c-e, 4.14g-h] ● **Media TIC** • Designer: Cloud 9 / Enric Ruiz Geli • Project Team: Enric Ruiz Geli, Javier P. Contonente, Max Zinnecker, Daniel Cosi, Patricio Levy, Veronica Mansilla, Rubén Alonso, Beatriz Mínguez, Cristina Guadalupe, André Macedo, Hale YoungBlood, Felix Fassbinder, Maé Durant, Marta Yebra, Marta Puértolas • Consultants: BOMA, G3, PGI, CAST, 22@, Jaume de Oleza, Mario Serrano, Marta Casas • Photos: © Ila Berman [4.15a-f] ● **KAPSARC** • Designer: Zaha Hadid Architects • Project Team: Zaha Hadid, Patrick Schumacher, Lars Teichmann, Charles Walker, DaeWha Kang • Consultants: Arup, Woods Bagot, GROSS.MAX, OVI • Photos: Courtesy of Zaha Hadid Architects © Hufton + Crow photographer [4.16a, 4.1.6d], Courtesy of and © Zaha Hadid Architects KAPSARC [4.16b-c] ● **Little Island** • Designer: Heatherwick Studio • Project Team: Paul Westwood, Neil Hubbard, Sofia Amodio, Simona Auteri, Jordan Bailiff, Einar Blixhavn, Mark Burrows, Mat Cash, Darragh Casey, Jorge

Xavier, Méndez-Cáceres, John Cruwys, Antoine van Erp, Alex Flood, Michal Gryko, Hayley Henry, Ben Holmes, Ben Jacobs, Stepan Martinovsky, Simon Ng, Wojtek Nowak, Hannah Parker, Giovanni Parodi, Luke Plumbley, Jeff Powers, Enrique Pujana, Akari Takebayashi, Ondrej Tichy, Ahira Sanjeet, Charles Wu, Meera Yadave • Drawings/ Images: Courtesy of Heatherwick Studio [4.17c-e] • Photos: Courtesy of Heatherwick Studio [4.17a-b], Courtesy of Heatherwick Studio © Timothy Schenck photographer [4.17f] ● **The Tide** • Designer: Diller Scofidio + Renfro • Project Team: Benjamin Gilmartin, Elizabeth Diller, Charles Renfro, Ricardo Scofidio, Anthony Saby, Bryce Suite, Ning Hiransaroj, Alex Knezo, John Newman, Swarnabh Ghosh, Erioseto Hendranata • Consultants: Neiheiser Argyros, GROSS.MAX, AKT II, Arup, AECOM, David Bonnett Associates, Gardiner and Theobold, NLP Planners, Stace, WSP, Cimolai, Urban Street Design, Mace, Maylim • Photos: Courtesy of Diller Scofidio + Renfro, photographer: Ben Luxmoore [4.18a, 4.18c], photographer: Luke Hayes [4.18b]

SERIAL ITERATIONS

Continuous Differentiation and the Micro-Interval • Courtesy of Matsys [frontispiece, 12, 13, 14], © Ila Berman [1, 4], Balla, Giacomo, 1871-1958. Swifts: Paths of Movement. n.d. Oil on canvas, 38x47.' https://jstor.org/stable/community.13576361© • 2007 Artists Rights Society (ARS), New York / SIAE, Rome [2], Edgerton, Harold, 1903–1990. Densmore Shute Bends the Shaft. 1938. Gelatin silver print, sheet: 16 x 20 in.; 40.64 x 50.8 cm; image: 14 x 14¾ in.; 35.56 x 37.465 cm. Smith College Museum of Art, Northampton, MA; Gift of Lynn Hecht Schafran, class of 1962. https://jstor.org/stable/community.15670427. [3], © Foreign Office Architects, source: Foreign Office Architects & Moussavi, Farshid & Zaera Polo, Alejandro. Yokohama International Port Terminal. 2002. https://jstor.org/stable/community.10798066. [5], © Anton Grassi [6], Courtesy of dECOi Architects [7], © John Horner [8], © Nash Baker, www.nash-baker.com [9], Courtesy of Designtoproduction [10, 11], Courtesy of Matsys [13, 14] Courtesy of DBT ETHZ photographer: Sofia Michopoulou [15], © Elliot Ross [16], Courtesy of Rael San Fratello [17], Courtesy of The Living [18] ● **Waterloo International Terminal** • Designer: Grimshaw Architects • Drawings: Ariane Mates [5.1b, 5.1e, 5.1f], Courtesy of Grimshaw Architects [5.1c-d] • Photos: Courtesy of Grimshaw Architects [5.1a, 5.1g] ● **Ricola Storage** • Designer: Herzog & de Meuron • Project Team: Jacques Herzog, Pierre de Meuron • Consultants: R. Schmidlin, Elektro Burger, A. Schmidlin, G. Kämpf AG • Photos: © Ila Berman [5.2a-c] ● **Signal Box** • Designer: Herzog & de Meuron • Project Team: Jacques Herzog, Pierre de Meuron, Harry Gugger, Philipe Fürstenberger • Consultants: ARGE, Herzog & de Meuron, Proplaning AG, Silzer Energieconsulting AG, Selmoni AG, Balduin Weisser AG, Tecton AG, Pratteln, Switzerland • Photos: © Nelson Garrido, NGPHOTO.com.pt [5.3a], © Ila Berman [5.3b-d] ● **Lafayette 148 Global Headquarters in China** • Designer: Studio for Architecture • Project Team: Mehrdad Hadighi, Tsz Yan Ng, Christopher Romano, Adesh Michael Singh, Michael O'Hara, Jose Chang, Maciej Kaczynski, and David Nardozzi, The Shantou Building Consortium • Photos: Courtesy of Studio for Architecture, photographer: But Sou Lai [5.4a-f] ● **Inventioneering Architecture** • Designer: Designtoproduction and Instant Architects • Project Team: (DesigntoProduction) Christoph Schindler, Markus Braach, Fabian Scheurer, (Instant Architects) Dirk Hebel, Jörg Stollmann • Consultants: Bach Heiden, Franz Roman Bach, Hansueli Dumelin • Drawing: Courtesy of Designtoproduction [5.5a] • Photos: Courtesy of Designtoproduction [5.5b-c] ● **Henderson Wave Bridge** • Designer: IJP Corporation + Adams Kara Taylor (AKT) Engineers • Local Architect/ Engineer: RSP Architects Planners & Engineers • Photos: © Kok Leng Yeo photographer CC-BY-2.0 wikimedia commons [5.7a], © Wee Sen Goh photographer creative commons [5.7 b, c] ● **Rip Curl Canyon** • Designer: Ball-Nogues Studio • Project Team: Benjamin Ball, Gaston Nogues • Consultants: Arup Los Angeles: Bruce Danziger • Drawings: Javier Rodriquez [5.7e] • Photos: Courtesy of Ball-Nogues, photographer: © Nash Baker [5.7a, 5.7b-d, 5.7f] ● **FLUX Armature** • Designer: Andrew Kudless, Kory Bieg, Andre Caradec, Ila Berman CCA mLAB • Project Team: Marc Fornes, Jessica Gibson, Andy Payne, Melissa Spooner, Andy Payne, Laurice der Bedrossian, Yoon Choi, Stephanie Close, Loi Dinh, David Garcia, Jessica Gibson, John Hobart-Culleton, Charlotte Hofstetter, Madaline Honig, Wayne Lin, Sandra Lopez, Mariko Low, Jen Melendez, Michelle Mucker, Andrew Peters, Jason Rhein, Ocean Rogoff, Angela Todorova, Dianne de la Torre, Michael Victoria, Olesya Yefimov, Olutobi Adamolekun, Lynn Bayer, Ripon DeLeon, Anthony Diaz, Alexa Getting, Jessica Gibson, Noah Greer, Benjamin Harth, Madeline Honig, Elizabeth Jackson, Pouya Khakpour, Anna Leach, Ryan Lee, Charles Ma, David Manzanares Garcia, Ariane Mates, Andy Payne, Harsha Pelimuhandiram, Michael Perkins, Javier Rodriguez, Ricardo Ruiz, Melissa Spooner, Jessica Stuenkel, Vladimir Vlad, Duncan Young • Consultants: Ryan Buyssens, Jo Slota, Chris Chalmers, Andrew Sparks • Drawings: Courtesy of CCA mLAB [5.8a] • Photos: Courtesy of CCA mLAB [5.8b], © Kory Bieg [5.8c-f] ● **Centennial Chromagraph** • Designer: Variable Projects / Adam Marcus • Drawings: Courtesy of Variable Projects [5.9b-c, 5.9e] • Photos: Courtesy of Variable Projects [5.9a, 5.9d] ● **Aqua Tower** • Designer: Studio Gang • Consultants: Horvath Reich Cdc, Loewenberg Architects • Magnusson Klemencic Associates, McHugh Construction • Drawings: Courtesy of Studio Gang [5.10c] • Photos: Courtesy of Studio Gang © Hall + Merrick, photographer: Steve Hall [5.10a-b, 5.10e], © Butler V. Adams photographer [5.10d] ● **Zero/Fold Screen** • Designer: Andrew Kudless, Matsys • Project Team: Andrew Kudless, Jason S. Johnson, students of University of Calgary • Drawings: Courtesy of Matsys [5.11a] • Photos: Courtesy of Matsys [5.11b-c] ● **Foxtel Screens** • Designer: Andrew Kudless, Matsys with Studio Workshop • Photos: Courtesy of Matsys [5.12a-c] ● **Roka Bar Wall** • Designer: Andrew Kudless, Matsys with Arcanum Architecture and S/U/M • Photos: Courtesy of Matsys [5.13a-b] ● **Foxtel Walls** • Designer: Andrew Kudless, Matsys with Studio Workshop • Photos: Courtesy of Matsys [5.14a-c] ● **One Main** • Designer: dECOi Architects • Project Team: Mark Goulthorpe, Raphael Crespin, Gabriel Blue Cira, Matt Trimble, Priyanka Shah, Kaustuv de Biswas (MIT), Alex Scott (Oxford University) • Consultants: Gensler Associates, Tricore, CWKeller • Drawings: Courtesy of dECOi Architects [5.15e-g] • Photos: © Anton Grassl [5.15a-c], Courtesy of dECOi Architects [5.15d] ● **Embodied Computation Lab Façade** • Designer: The Living • Project Team: David Benjamin, John Locke, Danil Nagy, Ray Wang, Jim Stoddart, Lorenzo Villaggi, Damon Lau, Dale Zhao • Architect of Record: NK Architects • Consultants: BuroHappold Engineering, Epic Construction, Axel Kilian, Forrest Meggers • Drawings: Courtesy of The Living [5.16c] • Photos: Courtesy of The Living © Michael Moran and Pablo Marvel [5.16b], Courtesy of The Living [5.16a, 5.16d-f] ● **Ashen Cabin** • Designer: HANNAH Design Office LLC • Project Team: Leslie Lok, Sasa Zivkovic, Christopher Battaglia, Jeremy Bilotti, Elie Boutros, Reuben Chen, Justin Hazelwood, Mitchie Qiao, Alexandre Mecattaf, Ethan Davis, Russell Southard, Dax Simitch Warke, Ramses Gonzales, Wangda Zhu, Byungchan Ahn, Alexander Terry, Xiaoxue Ma, Alexandre Mecattaf, Freddo Daneshvaran, Ramses Gonzalez, Jiaying Wei, Jiayi Xing, Xiaohang Yan, Sarah Elizabeth Bujnowski, Eleanor Jane Krause, Todd Petrie, Isabel Lucia Branas Jarque, Kun Bi, Brian Havener, Lingzhe Lu • Consultants: Peter Smallidge (Cornell Arnot Teaching and Research Forest) • Photos: Courtesy of Leslie Lok/Sasa Zivkovic [5.17f], photographer: Andy Chen [5.17a-e] ● **Strand Table** • Designer: Matsys • Project Team: Andrew Kudless • Consultants: Emerging Objects, Ania Burlinka • Photos: Courtesy of Matsys [5.18a-f] ● **Concrete Choreography** • Designer: MAS DFAB in Architecture and Digital Fabrication, ETH Zurich (DBT ETHZ) • Project Team: Benjamin Dillenburger, Ana Anton, Patrick Bedarf, Angela Yoo, students: Antonio Barney, Aya Shaker Ali, Chaoyu Du, Eleni Skevaki, Jonas Van den Bulcke, Keerthana Udaykumar, Nicolas Feihl, Nik Eftekhar Olivo, Noor Khader, Rahul Girish, Sofia Michopoulou, Ying-Shiuan Chen, Yoana Taseva, Yuta Akizuki, Wenqian Yang • Consultants and Partners: Origen Foundation: Giovanni Netzer, Irene Gazzillo, Guido Luzio, Flavia Kistler, Research: Robert J. Flatt, Lex Reiter, Timothy Wangler, Technical Support: Michael Lyrenmann, Philippe Fleischmann, Andreas Reusser, Heinz Richner • Drawings/Images: Courtesy of DBT ETHZ [15.9b, 15.9e] • Photos: Courtesy of DBT ETHZ, photographer: Benjamin Hofer [15.9a, 15.9d], photographer: Axel Crettenand [15.9c, 15.9f], photographer: Keerthana Udaykumar [15.9g], photographer: Sofia Michopoulou [15.9h, 15.9i, 15.9j, 15.9k] ● **Terra Performa** • Designer: IAAC Advanced Architecture Group • Project Team: Sameera Chukkappali, Iason Giraud, Abdullah Ibrahim, Raaghav Chentur Naagendran, Lidia Ratoi, Lili Tayefi,Tanuj Thomas, (research advisors: Areti Markopoulou, Angelos Chronis, Sofoklis Giannakopoulos, Manja Van De Warp, Mathilde Marengo, Grégoire Durrens, Djordje Stanojevic, Rodrigo Aguirre, Kunaljit Singh Chadha, Ji Won Jun, Ángel Muñoz, Wilfredo Carazas Aedo, Josep Perelló, Pierre-Elie Herve, Jean-Baptiste Izard, Jonathan Minchin) • Consultants: Pylos Extruder, Tecnalia CoGiro Cable Robot • Drawings: Courtesy of IAAC [5.20b, 5.20f-h] • Photos: Courtesy of IAAC [5.20a, 5.20c-d, 5.20i-k], © Ila Berman [5.20e] ● **Casa Covida and MUD Frontier** • Designer: Emerging Objects • Project Team: (Casa Covida) Ronald Rael, Virginia San Fratello, Mattias Rael, Sandy Curth, Logman Arja, Danny Defelici, Joshua Tafoya (Mud Frontier) Ronald Rael, Virginia San Fratello, Mattias Rael, Sandy Curth, Logman Arja, Danny Defelici, Christine Rael, Zane Defelici, Dennis Vandergriff • Photos: Courtesy of Rael San Fratello [5.21c-h], photographer: Elliot Ross [5.21a-b]

WOVEN MESHES

Stranded Systems, Rhizomes and Meshworks • © ARUPSPORT [frontispiece], Courtesy of RUR [1], Courtesy of Toyo Ito & Associates, Architects [2, 3, 6, 7, 10, 11], © Iwan Baan [4], © ARUP [5], Courtesy of theverymany [8, 9], Courtesy of ICD/ITKE University of Stuttgart [12], Courtesy of Jenny E. Sabin [13], © Luke Hayes [14] ● **Gatti Wool Factory** • Designer: Pier Luigi Nervi • Drawing: Nervi, Pier Luigi. Rome: Gatti Wool Factory Plan. 1953. https://jstor.org/stable/community.13912155. [6.1c] • Photos: Source: Antoine Baudin, Photographie et Architecture Moderne: La Collection Alberto Sartoris © PPUR (Press Polytechniques et Universitaires Romandes) [6.1a-b, 6.1d] ● **Continua Series** • Designer: Erwin Hauer • Drawing: © Erwin Hauer [6.2c] • Photos: © Erwin Hauer [6.2a-b, 6.2d-e] ● **30 Saint Mary Axe–Swiss Re** • Designer: Foster + Partners • Project Team: Grant Brooker, Neil Vandersteen, Robert Harrison, Ben Dobbin, Gamma Basra, Narinder Sagoo, Michael Gentz • Consultants: Arup • Drawings: Courtesy of Foster + Partners [6.3b] • Photos: Courtesy of Foster + Partners, photographer: Nigel Young [6.3a, 6.3c-d] ● **Sendai Mediatheque** • Designer: Toyo Ito & Associates, Architects • Consultants: Mutsuro Sasaki • Drawings: Courtesy of Toyo Ito & Associates, Architects [6.4a-b] • Photos: Courtesy of Toyo Ito & Associates, Architects [6.4c-e] ● **Serpentine Gallery Pavilion** • Designer: Toyo Ito & Associates, Architects and Balmond Studio • Project Team: Toyo Ito, Takeo Higashi, Hiromi Hosoya, Takayuki Miyoshi • Consultants: Arup: Cecil Balmond, Daniel Bosia, Charles Walker • Drawings: Courtesy of Toyo Ito & Associates [6.5e, 6.5g], Andrew Kudless [6.5f] • Photos: © MFT26F, Alamy [6.5a], Courtesy of Toyo Ito & Associates, Architects [6.5b-c, 6.5h], © Serpentine Galleries [6.5d] ● **Beijing National Stadium** • Designer: Herzog + de Meuron • Project Team: Jacques Herzog, Pierre de Meuron, Stefan Marbach, Linxi Dong, Mia Hägg, Tobias Winkelmann, Thomas Polster, Peter Karl Becher, Alexander Berger, Felix Beyreuther, Marcos Carreno, Xudong Chen, Simon Chessex, Massimo Corradi, Yichun He, Volker Helm, Claudia von Hessert, Yong Huang, Kasia Jackowska, Uta Kamps, Hiroshi Kikuchi, Martin Krapp, Hemans Lai, Emily Liang, Kenan Liu, Donald Mak, Carolina Mojto, Christoph Röttinger, Roland Rossmaier, Luciano Rotoli, Mehrdad Safa, Roman Sokalski, Heeri Song, Christoph Weber, Thomasine Wolfensberger, Pim van Wylick, Camillo Zanardini, Xiaolei Zhang • Consultants: Ove Arup & Partners, China Architectural Design & Research Group • Drawings: © Arup [6.6d] • Photos: © Iwan Baan [6.6a-c, 6.6e] ● **Tokyo Airspace** • Designer: Faulders Studio with Proces2 (façade) and Hajime Masubuchi/Studio M (building) • Project Team: Patrick Flynn, Jessica Kmetovic, Tomohiko Sakai, Agnessa Torodova-Dowell, Sean Ahlquist • Consultants: Hiroki Kume, Yamamoto Tech Co., Ltd., TONY Co., Ltd. • Photos: Courtesy of Hajime Masubuchi and Thom Faulders [6.7a-c] ● **DAW/Double Agent White** • Designer: theverymany • Project Team: Marc Fornes • Photos: Courtesy of THEVERYMANY, photographer: Guillaume Blanc [6.8a-c] ● **Taichung Theater** • Designer: Toyo Ito & Associates, Architects and Kuramochi + Oguma • Taichung Theater is built by the Taichung City Government, The People's Republic of China • Drawings/Images: Courtesy of Toyo Ito & Associates, Architects [6.9a, 16.9c-e, 6.9g], © Kuramachi + Oguma [6.9b] • Photos: © Lucas Doolan [6.9f, 6.9h-i] ● **nonLin/Lin Pavilion** • Designer: theverymany • Project Team: Marc Fornes, Jon Becker, Peter Nguyen, Jeff Quantz, Claudia Corcilius • Consultants: Plastik Banana, Shawn Komlos, Chris Hone, Alan Hurst • Drawing: Courtesy of theverymany [6.10b] • Photos: Courtesy of theverymany, photographer: Francoise Lauginie [6.10a, 6.10c-e] ● **Fiberous Tower** • Designer: Kokkugia • Images: Courtesy of Kokkugia [6.11a-c] ● **Polymorph: Digital Ceramics** • Designer: Jenny Sabin Studio • Project Team: Jenny E. Sabin, Martin Miller, Jillian Blackwell, Jin Tack Lim, Liangjie Wu, Lynda Brody • Drawings: Courtesy of Jenny Sabin Studio [6.12a-b] • Photos: Courtesy of Jenny E. Sabin [6.12c-e] ● **2012 ICD/ITKE Pavilion** • Designer: ICD Institute for Computational Design and Construction and ITKE Institute of Building Structures and Structural Design • Project Team: Achim Menges (lead ICD), Jan Knippers (lead ITKE), Jakob Weigele, Manuel Schloz, Sarah Haase, Markus Mittner, Josephine Ross, Manuel Schloz, Jonas Unger, Simone Vielhuber, Franziska Weidemann, Jakob Weigele, Natthida Wiwatwicha, Michael Preisack, Michael Tondera, Riccardo La Magna, Steffen Reichert, Tobias Schwinn, Frédéric Waimer, Oliver Betz, James Nebelsick, Markus Milwich • Drawings: Courtesy of ICD Institute for Computational Design and Construction and ITKE Institute of Building Structures and Structural Design [6.13a, 6.13b, 6.13c] • Photos: Courtesy of ICD/ITKE University of Stuttgart [6.13d-g] ● **2013–2014 ICD/ITKE Pavilion** • Designer: ICD Institute for Computational Design and Construction and the ITKE Institute of Building Structures and Structural Design • Project Team: Achim Menges (lead ICD), Jan Knippers (lead ITKE), Moritz Dörstelmann, Vassilios Kirtzakis, Stefana Parascho, Marshall Prado, Tobias Schwinn, Leyla Yunis, Ondrej Kyjánek, Desislava Angelova, Hans-Christian Bäcker, Maximilian Fichter, Eugen Grass, Michael Herrick, Nam Hoang, Alejandro Jaramillo, Norbert Jundt, Taichi Kuma, Ondrej Kyjánek, Sophia Leistner, Luca Menghini, Claire Milnes, Martin Nautrup, Gergana Rusenova, Petar Trassiev , Sascha Vallon, Shiyu Wie and Leyla Yunis, Hassan Abbasi, Yassmin Al-Khasawneh, Yuliya Baranovskaya, Marta Besalu, Giulio Brugnaro, Elena Chiridnik, Eva Espuny, Matthias Helmreich, Julian Höll, Shim Karmin, Georgi Kazlachev, Sebastian Kröner, Vangel Kukov, David Leon, Amanda Moore,Paul Poinet, Emily Scoones, Djordje Stanojevic, Andrei Stoiculescu, Kenryo Takahashi, Maria Yablonina, Michael Preisack, Michael Tondera, Oliver Betz, James Nebelsick, Gerald Buck, Michael Münster, Valentin Grau, Anne Buhl, Markus Maisch, Matthias Loose, Irene Viola Baumann, Carina Meiser, Thomas van de Kamp, Tomy dos Santos Rolo, Tilo Baumbach, Thomas Stehle, Rolf Bauer, Michael Reichersdörfer, Markus Milwich • Drawings: Courtesy of ICD/ITKE University of Stuttgart [6.14f-g] • Photos: Courtesy of ICD/ITKE University of Stuttgart [6.14a-e] ● **Cloud Pergola–Croatian National Pavilion** • Designer: Alisa Andrasek • Project Team: Alisa Andrasek, Madalin Gheorghe, Bruno Juricic • Consultants: Arup London, Ai Build •Drawings: Courtesy of Alisa Andrasek [6.15c, 6.15e] • Photos: © Luke Hayes [6.15a-b], © Ila Berman [6.15d] ● **Flotsam/Jetsam** • Designer: SHoP Architects • Consultants: Branch Technology, Thornton Tomasetti, Oak Ridge National Laboratory, Dassault Systèmes • Photos: Courtesy of SHoP Architects, video still image: Spirit of Space [6.16a], Courtesy of SHoP Architects, photographer: Robin Hill [6.16b-c] ● **Aguahoja** • Designer: Neri Oxman and The Mediated Matter Group MIT • Photos: Courtesy of Neri Oxman and The Mediated Matter Group MIT [6.17a-f] ● **Silk Pavilions I and II** • Designer: Neri Oxman and The Mediated Matter Group MIT • Photos: Courtesy of Neri Oxman and The Mediated Matter Group MIT [6.18a-g]

EMERGENT SURFACES

The Computations of Matter • Courtesy of Matsys [frontispiece, 5, 7–9], Antoni Gaudi Hanging Chain Model [1], • Otto, Frei. Institute for Lightweight Structures. 1966–1967. https://jstor.org/stable/community.16515508. [2], © Ball-Nogues Studio [3, 4], Centro Social de las Hermanas Hospitalarias, Madrid, by Miguel Fisac, Courtesy of The Miguel Fisac Foundation, © Javier Azurmendi [6], Courtesy of ETH Zurich, Block Research Group [10–12, 14], Courtesy of Sean Ahlquist [13] ● **La Sagrada Familia/ Church at Colònia Güell** • Designer: Antoni Gaudi • Photos: © Ila Berman [7.1a-e] ● **Los Manantiales Restaurant** • Designer: Felix Candela • Drawings: source: ArchDaily, AD Classics: Los Manantiales/Felix Candela, https://www.archdaily.com/496202/ad-classics-los-manantiales-felix-candela [7.2a-b] • Photos: www.rkett.com, Archdaily [7.2c-e] ● **Olympiapark 1972** • Designer: Frei Otto • Photos: © Pxel, Alamy Stock Photos [7.3a], © Christian Schittich, Alamy Stock Photos [7.3b] ● **The Basento Viaduct** • Designer: Sergio Musmeci • Drawing: source: Shell-supported footbridges, 2020 [7.4c] • Photos: © Arturo Tedeschi [7.4a-b, 7.4d-e] ● **CADenary Software** • Designer: Axel Kilian • Project Team: Axel Kilian, Dan Chak, Megan Galbraith • Consultants: Ben Fry, Casey Reas, Simon Greenworld • Images: Courtesy of Axel Kilian [7.5a-f] ● **PS1 Afterparty + MOScat** • Designer: MOS Architects • Project Team: Michael Meredith, Hilary Sample, Matthew Allen, Heather Bizon, Michael Faciejew, Jose Miguel Ahedo Fernandez, Darby Foreman, Steven Gertner, Jerome Haferd, Maciej Kaczynski, Yair Keshet, Jason Kim, Taekyoung Lee, Ryan Ludwig, William Macfarlane, Patrick McGowen, Miriam Peterson, Zachary Snyder • Consultants: Nathaniel Stanton, Erik Verboon, Buro-Happold, Eric Hines, Le Messurier Consultants • Images: Courtesy of MOS Architects [7.6b-c] • Photos: Courtesy of MOS Architects, photographer: Florian Holzherr [7.6a, 7.6d] ● **Maximillian's Schell** • Designer: Ball-Nogues Studio • Project Team: Benjamin Ball, Gaston Nogues • Consultants: David Bott, Hardy Wronske, Dieter Srobel, James Lumb, Materials & Applications • Drawing: Courtesy of Ball-Nogues Studio [7.7c] • Photos: Courtesy of Ball-Nogues Studio, photographer: Neil Cochran [7.7a], photographer: Benny Chan [7.7b], photographer: Oliver Hess [7.7d] ● **Unseen Current / Venice Project** • Designer: Ball-Nogues Studio • Project Team: Benjamin Ball, Gaston Nogues, Ben Dean, Mark Bowman, Michael Ferrante, Christopher Bartek, Lindsay Grote, Jack Donoghue, Kasia Mielniczuk, Pei San Ng, Marine Manigault, Martina Dolejs, Cady Chintis, John Wolters, Ryan Johnson, Dana Andersen, Melodi, Zarakol, Sarah Forbes, Bryant Pitak, Kathryn McRay, Christina Halatsis, Vince Rivera, Kate Cain, Mariga Medic • Consultants: Sparce Studio • Drawing: Courtesy of Ball-Nogues Studio [7.8b] • Photos: Courtesy of Ball-Nogues Studio, photographer: Michelle Litvin [7.8a], photographer: Benjamin Ball [7.8c-d] ● **Sensory PLAYSCAPE** • Designer: Sean Ahlquist / Material Architectures • Project Team: Sean Ahlquist, Costanza Colombi, Dale Ulrich,

Leah Ketcheson, Oliver Popadich, Shahida Sharmin, Adam Wang, Erin Almony, Erika Goodman, Sile O'Modhrain, David Chesney, Taylor Boes, Evan Buetsch, Karen Duan, Patty Hazle, Yu-Jen Lin, Henry Peters, Jason Chao-Chung Yang, Evan Cann • Consultants: Mark Burke, Julian Lienhard, Onna Solomon, Peter von Buelow, Mary Burke, Joshua Plavnick, Tabitha Wisecup • Drawing: Courtesy of Sean Ahlquist [7.9c] • Photos: Courtesy of Sean Ahlquist [7.9a-b, 7.9d] ● **Mobius Rib-Knit Textile Hybrid** • Designer: Sean Ahlquist (Material Architectures) • Project Team: Sean Ahlquist, Pandush Gaqi, Yi Yuan, Karen Duan • Consultants: Julian Lienhard, Jane Scott • Drawings: Courtesy of Sean Ahlquist [7.10a, 7.10d-e] • Photos: Courtesy of Sean Ahlquist [7.10b-c, 7.10f-g] ● **Shellstar** • Designer: Matsys w/ Riyad Joucka • Project Team: Andrew Kudless, Riyad Joucka, Ricci Wong, Wong Sifu, Geoff Wong, Wilton Ip, Justin ling, April Lau, Eric Lo, John Thurtle, Garkay Wong, Felice Chap, Kenneth Cheung, Godwin Cheung, Quentin Yiu, Rena Li, Garesa Hao En, Cheryl Ceclia Lui, Huang Xinliu • Consultants: Topcon HK • Drawings: Courtesy of Matsys + Ryad Joucka [7.11b] • Photos: Courtesy of Matsys + Ryad Joucka, photographer: Dennis Lo [7.11a, 7.11c-d] ● **La Voute de LeFevre** • Designer: Matter Design • Project Team: Brandon Clifford, Wes McGee, Jake Haggmark, Maciej Kaczynsk, Aaron Willette, Edgar Ascaño, Kristy Balliet, Katherine Bennette, Beth Blostein, Jenna Bolino, Chris Carbone, Tim Cousino, Anthony Gagliardi, Brian Koehler, Darwin Menjivar, Paul Miller, Tony Nguyen, Bart Overly, Aaron Powers, Steve Sarver, Katy Viccellio, Sean Zielinski • Drawings: Courtesy of Matter Design [7.12a] • Photos: Courtesy of Matter Design, photographer: Brandon Clifford [7.12b-h] ● **P_Wall Series** • Designer: Andrew Kudless, Matsys • Project Team: Andrew Kudless, Ivan Vukcevich, Ryan Palider, Zak Snider, Austin Poe, Camie Vacha, Cassie Matthys, Christopher Friend, Nicholas Cesare, Anthony Rodriguez, Mark Wendell, Joel Burke, Brandon Hendrick, Chung-tzu Yeh, Doug Stechschultze, Gene Shevchenko, Kyu Chun, Nick Munoz, and Sabrina Sierawski, Ronnie Parsons • Drawings: Courtesy of Matsys [7.13b-c] • Photos: Courtesy of Matsys [7.13a, 7.13d] ● **Heap** • Designer: Rhett Russo • Project Team: Rhett Russo, Foekje Fleur van Duin, Aniek Meeldijk • Drawings/Images: Courtesy of Rhett Russo [7.14d, 7.14f] • Photos: Courtesy of Rhett Russo, photographer: Nathan Sayers [7.14a-c, 7.14e, 7.14g-i] ● **Soft Cast** • Designer: Minimaforms • Project Team: Theodore Spyropoulos, Stephen Spyropoulos, Apostolos Despotidis, Manuel Jimenez Garcia, Mustafa El Sayad, Sophia Tang, Chien Shou Pai, Georgia Tsoli, Akber Khan • Images: Courtesy of Minimaforms [7.15a, 7.15d] • Photos: Courtesy of Minimaforms [7.15b-c, 7.15e] ● **KnitCandela (Mexico)** • Designer: ETH Zurich, Block Research Group (BRG) and Zaha Hadid Architects Computation and Design Group (ZHCODE), Architecture Extrapolated (R-Ex) • Project Team: Philippe Block, Mariana Popescu, Matthias Rippmann, Tom Van Mele, Alessandro Dell'Endice, Cristian Calvo Barentin, Nora Ravanidou, Andrew Liew, Tom Van Mele, Filippo Nassetti, David Reeves, Marko Margeta, Shajay Bhooshan, Patrik Schumacher, Lex Reiter, Robert Flatt, Alicia Nahmad Vazquez, Horacio Bibiano Vargas, Jose Manuel Diaz Sanchez, Asunción Zúñiga, Agustín Lozano Álvarez, Migue Juárez Antonio, Filiberto Juárez Antonio, Daniel Piña, Daniel Celin, Carlos Axel Pérez Cano, José Luis Naranjo Olivares, Everardo Hernández, Ramiro Tena, Jose Alfredo Rodriguez, Carlos Eduardo Juarez, Delia Peregrina Rizo, Jillian Nishi, Margaratia Valova, Daria Zolotareva, Paz Bodelon, Elena Castaldi, Manon Janssens, Woody Yao, Leo Bieling, Federico Borello, Henry David Louth • Photos: Courtesy of ETH Zurich, Block Research Group, photographer: Philippe Block [7.16a], photographer: Mariana Popescu [7.16b-c], photographer: Juan Pablo Allegre [7.16d-f] ● **Freeform Tile Vault** • Designer: ETH Zurich, Block Research Group (BRG) • Project Team: Philippe Block, Oscar Andrés Mazuera Sanmiguel, Tom Van Mele, Marcel Aubert, Lindsay Howe, Luka Piskorec, Dominik Werne, Thomas Jaggi, Patrick Morf, Eleni Chatzi, Mohammad Miah, ETH Zurich, D-BAUG • Drawing: Courtesy of ETH Zurich, Block Research Group (BRG) [7.17b] • Photos: Courtesy of ETH Zurich, Block Research Group, photographer: Klemen-Breitfuss [7.17a, 7.17c-d] ● **Catalan Vault Droneport Project** • Designer: ETH Zurich, Block Research Group (BRG), Norman Foster Foundation, Red Line - EPFL, ODB Engineering • Project Team: Philippe Block, Tom Van Mele, Tomás Méndez Echenagucia, Hannes Hofmann, John Ochsendorf, Matthew DeJong, Giorgia Giardina, Lord Norman Foster, Jonathan Ledgard • Consultants: CReA, MIT, Foster + Partners, Universidad Politécnica de Madrid, Lafarge Holcim Research Centre • Image: © The Norman Foster Foundation [7.18b] • Photos: © The Norman Foster Foundation, photographer: Nigel Young [7.18a, 7.18c] ● **Armadillo Vault** • Designer: ETH Zurich, Block Research Group (BRG), ODB Engineering, Escobedo Group • Project Team: Philippe Block, Tom Van Mele, Matthias Rippmann, Edyta Augustynowicz, Cristián Calvo Barentin, Tomás Méndez Echenagucia, Mariana Popescu, Andrew Liew, Anna Maragkoudaki, Ursula Frick, Matthew DeJong, John Ochsendorf, Philippe Block, Anjali Mehrotra, David Escobedo, Matthew Escobedo, Salvador Crisanto, John Curry, Francisco Tovar Yebra, Joyce I-Chin Chen, Adam Bath, Hector Betancourt, Luis Rivera, Antonio Rivera, Carlos Rivera, Carlos Zuniga Rivera, Samuel Rivera, Jairo Rivera, Humberto Rivera, Jesus Rosales, Dario Rivera • Drawings: Courtesy of ETH Zurich, Block Research Group (BRG), ODB Engineering, Escobedo Group [7.19a, 7.19f] • Photos: Courtesy of ETH Zurich, Block Research Group, photographer: Iwan Baan [7.19b-e] ● **Isoropia** • Designer: CITA (Centre for Information Technology and Architecture) • Project Team: Mette Ramsgaard Thomsen, Martin Tamke, Yuliya Sinke Baranovskaya, Vasiliki Fragkia, Rune Noël Meedom Meldgaard Bjørnson-Langen, Sebastian Gatz • Consultants: str.ucture, Alurays, AFF - A. Ferreira & Filhos, DSM Dyneema •Drawing: Courtesy of and © CITA [7.20d] • Photos: Courtesy of and © CITA [7.20a-c] ● **NEST HiLo Roof** • Designer: ETH Zurich, Block Research Group (BRG), Architecture and Building Systems Group, ROK Architects, supermanoeuvre, Bollinger + Grohmann Ingenieure • Consultants: Institute of Structural Concrete–RWTH Aachen, Mathematical and Physical Geodesy–ETH Zurich, Automatic Control Laboratory–ETH Zürich, Jakob, Bruno Lehmann, Blumer Lehmann, Dafotech, Bieri, Marti Construction SA, Bürgin Creations • Photos: Courtesy of ETH Zurich, Block Research Group, photographer: Juney Lee [7.21a], photographer: Nadia Iljazov [7.21b], photographer: Michael Lyrenmann [7.21c], photographer: Stefan Liniger [7.21d] ● **Confluence Vault** • Designer: Matsys, Lake Flato Architects, Rialto Studio, Architectural Engineers Collaborative • Project Team: Andrew Kudless, Bob Harris, Tenna Florian, Sunnie Díaz, Jordan Tsai • Consultants: Architectural Engineering Collaborative, Kreysler & Associates, CNG Engineering, Rialto Studio, Mazzetti, SpawGlass, Ball-Nogues Studio • Drawings: Courtesy of Matsys [7.22c] • Photos: Courtesy of Matsys [7.22a-b, 7.22d-e]

MULTI-AGENT NETWORKS

Collective Behaviors and the Intelligence of Populations • Courtesy of Kokkugia [frontispiece, 3], Courtesy of Aranda/Lasch [1], Courtesy of Alisa Andrasek [2], Courtesy of New Territories - R&Sie(n) [4], Courtesy of Thomas Grabner [5], Courtesy of Höweler + Yoon Architecture [6, 9], Courtesy of ICD University of Stuttgart [7], Courtesy of DOSU Studio Architecture [8], Courtesy of FutureForms [10], Courtesy of Ila Berman, Scaleshift, Photographer: Cris Ponce [11] ● **Stranded Sears Tower** • Designer: Greg Lynn FORM • Drawing: Courtesy of Greg Lynn FORM [8.1b] • Photos: Courtesy of Greg Lynn FORM [8.1a] ● **Port Authority Triple Bridge Gateway** • Designer: Greg Lynn FORM • Drawing/Images: Courtesy of Greg Lynn FORM [8.2a-c] ● **I've Heard About** • Designer: New-Territories/R&Sie(n) with Benoît Durandin, Stephan Henrich • Project Team: François Roche, Stéphanie Lavaux, Jean Navarro, Benoît Durandin, Stephan Henrich • Consultants: Berokh Khoshnevis, Francois Roustang, Julien Blevarque, Chris Delaporte, Christophe Berdaguer, Marie Pejus, Mathieu Lehanneur, Laurent Genefort, CNRS Grenoble, Laboratoire de Spectrometrie, M/M, Gilles Schaeffer, Michel Boulcourt, Alexandra Midal, Matthieu Kavyrchine, Sebastien Szczyrk, Alexandre Merlet, Ufacto, David Toppani, One Star Press, Christian Hubert Delisle, Thibaut Boyer • Drawings/Images: Courtesy of New Territories/R&Sie(n) [8.3a-g] ● **Smart Town** • Designer: New-Territories/R&Sie(n) • Project Team: François Roche, Stéphanie Lavaux, Jean Navarro, Benoît Durandin, Stephan Henrich, Petra Jenning, Florian von Hayek, Alain Marder-Greco, Eglantine Bigot-Doll • Drawings/Images: Courtesy of New-Territories/R&Sie(n) [8.4a-e] ● **Swarm Urbanism** • Designer: Kokkugia • Project Team: Roland Snooks, Robert Stuart-Smith • Drawings/Images: Courtesy of Kokkugia [8.5a-b] ● **The Rise** • Designer: Centre for Information Technology and Architecture (CITA) • Project Team: Mette Ramsgard Thomsen, Martin Tamke, Dave Stasiuk, Hollie Gibbons, Shirin Zaghi • Drawings/Images: Courtesy of CITA [8.6b-c] • Photos: Courtesy of CITA [8.6a, 8.6d] ● **Composite Wing** • Designer: Studio Roland Snooks • Project Team: Roland Snooks, Cam Newnham, Drew Busmire, Amaury Thomas, Pei She Lee • Consultants: Bollinger + Grohmann Engineers • Photos: Courtesy of Roland Snooks [8.7a-d] ● **Subdivided Columns** • Designer: Michael Hansmeyer • Project Team: Michael Hansmeyer, Manuela Koller, Thomas Raoseta, Edyta Augustinowicz • Drawings/Images: Courtesy of Michael Hansmeyer [8.8b-e] • Photos: Courtesy of Michael Hansmeyer [8.8a] ● **Grotto (Digital Grotesque II)** • Designer: Michael Hansmeyer, Benjamin Dillenburger • Project Team: Michael Hansmeyer, Benjamin Dillenburger, Michael Thomas, Philippe Steiner, Allegra Stucki, Florentin Duelli • Jan Francisco Anduaga, Katharina Wepler, Lorenz Brunnner, Nicolas Harter, Dominik Keller, Max Spett, Alexander Canario, Matthias Leschok, Alvaro Lopez • Photos: Courtesy of Hansmeyer/Dillenburger [8.9a], photographer: Demetris Shammas [8.9b], photographer:

Fabrice DallAnese [8.9c], photographer: Jann Erhard [8.9d], photographer: Michael Hansmeyer [8.9e], photographer: Hyunchul Kwon [8.9f] ● **Aegis Hyposurface** • Designer: dECOi & MIT • Photos: Courtesy of dECOi & MIT [8.12a-e] ● **Hylozoic Ground** • Designer: Philip Beesley Architect Inc. • Project Team: Hayley Isaacs, Eric Bury, Federica Pianta, Adam Schwartzentruber, Jonathan Tyrrell, Carlos Carrillo, Andrew Kmiecik, Katherine Kovalcik, Manuel Kretzer, Carlo Luigi Pasini, Tommy Paxton-Beesley, Siobhan Sweeny, Andreea Toca, Rob Gorbet, Rachel Armstrong • Photos: Courtesy of Philip Beesley Architect Inc [8.11a-d] ● **HygroScope Project** • Designer: Achim Menges • Project Team: Achim Menges, Steffen Reichert, Boyan Mihaylov, Nicola Burggraf, Tobias Schwinn with Claudio Fabrizio Calandri, Nicola Haberbosch, Oliver Krieg, Marielle Neuser, Viktoriya Nikolova, Paul Schmidt, Thomas Auer, Daniel Pianka • Photos: Courtesy of ICD University of Stuttgart [8.12a-d] ● **Oculus** • Designer: DOSU Studio Architecture • Project Team: Doris Sung, Stephanie Truong, Michelle East, Esther Ho, Adelfrid Ramirez • Drawings: Courtesy of DOSU Studio Architecture [8.13a] • Photos: Courtesy of DOSU Studio Architecture [8.13b-e] ● **White Noise/White Light** • Designer: Höweler + Yoon Architecture • Project Team: Eric Höweler, J. Meejin Yoon • Drawings: Courtesy of Höweler + Yoon Architecture [8.14a-b, 8.14d] • Photos: Courtesy of Höweler + Yoon Architecture [8.14c, 8.14e-f] ● **Windscreen** • Designer: Höweler + Yoon Architecture • Project Team: Eric Höweler, J. Meejin Yoon • Photos: Courtesy of Höweler + Yoon Architecture [8.15a-d] ● **Lightswarm** • Designer: FutureForms • Project Team: Jason Kelly Johnson, Nataly Gattegno, Ji Ahn, Fernando Amenedo, Nainoa Cravalho, Ripon DeLeon, Jeff Maeshiro, Katarina Richter • Photos: Courtesy of FutureForms [8.16a, 8.16d], photographer: Peter Prato [8.16b-c] ● **Urban Syncopation** • Designer: Scaleshift, Beites & Co, X-Topia • Project Team: Ila Berman, Mona El-Khafif, Steven Beites, Marcella Del Signore • Drawings: Courtesy of Scaleshift [8.17c] • Photos: Courtesy of Scaleshift, photographer: Steven Beites [8.17a-b], Courtesy of Scaleshift, photographer: Cris Ponce 8.17d-i] ● **Ostenda Illuminata** • Designer: Networked Public Space • Project Team: Mona El Khafif, Andrew Mondschein, Zihao Zhang, Eric Field, Karan Matta, Gabe Andrade, David Eddy, Darcy Engle, Lucas Ames, Abigail Cox, Luis Felipe Rosado Murillo, Meng Huang, Ehsan Baharlou, Philip Speranza • Drawings: Courtesy of Networked Public Space [8.18b-d] • Photos: Courtesy of Networked Public Space, photographer: Tom Daly [8.18a, 8.18e-h] ● **ADA** • Designer: Jenny Sabin Studio with Microsoft Research • Project Team: Jenny Sabin Studio Team: Jenny E. Sabin (lead), Dillon Pranger, John Hilla, Jeremy Bilotti, William Qian, Arup Design Engineering: Clayton Binkley, Judy Guo, Microsoft Research Ada Core: Eric Horvitz, Shabnam Erfani, Asta Roseway, Wende Copfer, Jonathan Lester, Daniel McDuff, Mira Lane • Consultants: Fabrication and Manufacturing: GoProto, Dazian, Avatar Knit, Fabric Images, Accufab • Drawings: Courtesy of and © Jenny Sabin Studio [8.19c, 8.19d] Photos: Jake Knapp for Microsoft [8.19a-b, 8.19e, 8.19g], John Brecher for Microsoft [8.19f]

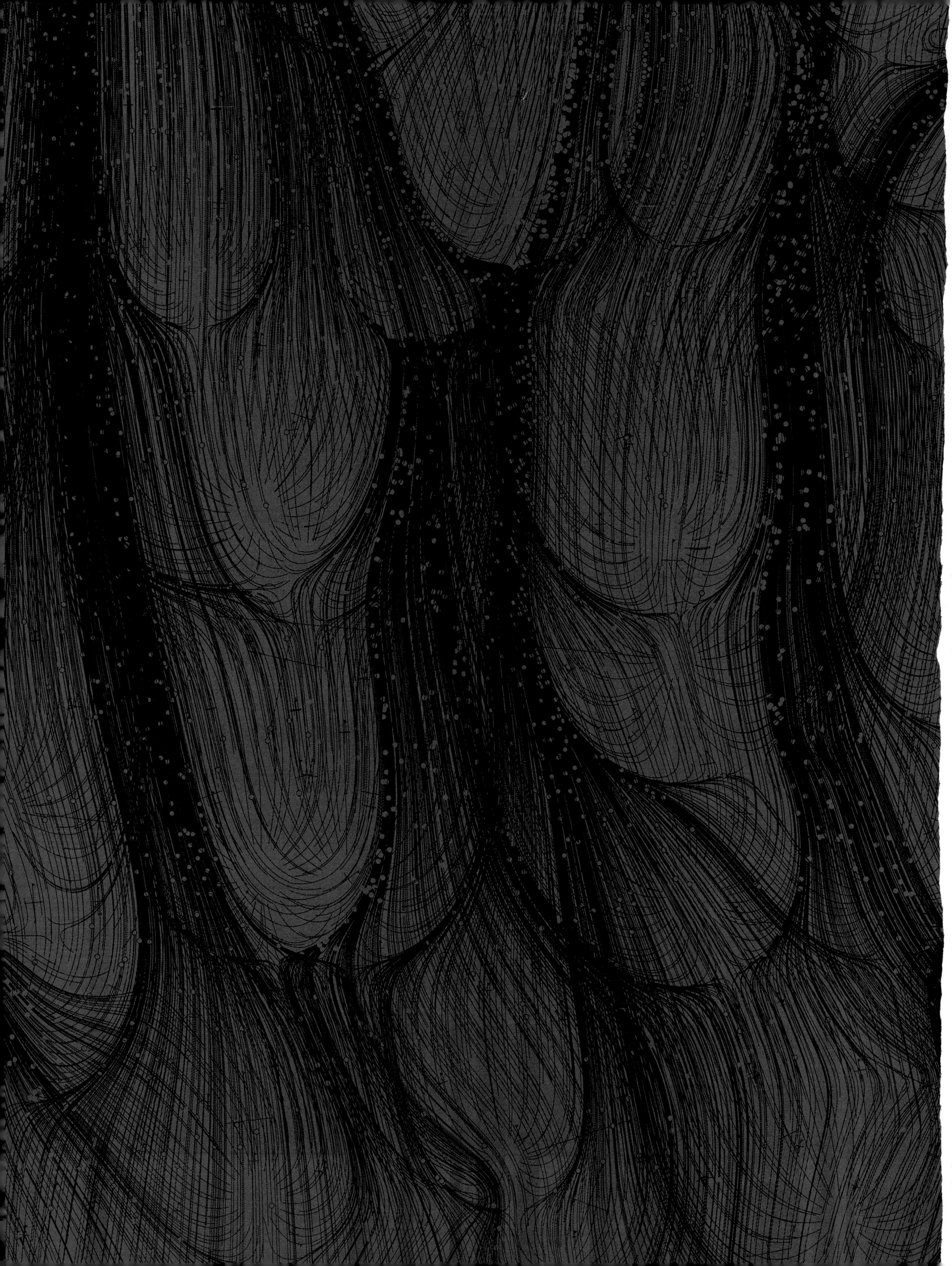